FAMILY POLITICS

FAMILY POLITICS
DOMESTIC LIFE, DEVASTATION AND SURVIVAL
1900–1950

PAUL GINSBORG

YALE UNIVERSITY PRESS
NEW HAVEN AND LONDON

For information about this and other Yale University Press publications, please contact:

U.S. Office: sales.press@yale.edu   www.yalebooks.com
Europe Office: sales@yaleup.co.uk   www.yalebooks.co.uk

Typeset in Minion Pro by IDSUK (DataConnection) Ltd
Printed in Great Britain by TJ International Ltd, Padstow, Cornwall

Library of Congress Cataloging-in-Publication Data

Ginsborg, Paul.
  Family politics : domestic life, devastation and survival, 1900-1950 / Paul Ginsborg.
    pages cm
  Includes bibliographical references and index.
  ISBN 978-0-300-11211-5 (cloth)
1. World politics—1900-1945.   2 World politics—1945-1955.   3. Families—
History—20th century.   4. Families—Political aspects—History—20th
century.   5. Revolutions—History—20th century.   6. Revolutions—
Social aspects—History—20th century.   7. Dictatorship—History—20th
century.   8. Social change—History—20th century.   9. Europe—Politics
and government—20th century.   10. Turkey--Politics and government—
1918-1960.   I. Title.
  D445.G516 2014
  909.82`1—dc23

                                                              2014022289

A catalogue record for this book is available from the British Library.

10 9 8 7 6 5 4 3 2 1

Contents

Illustrations

Figures

Foreword

This book employs an innovative approach to the great events and regimes of the first half of the twentieth century, viewing them primarily through the lens of family life. Surprisingly enough, in the vast majority of studies of the century families are perennially off-stage. They seem to be taken for granted or are 'hidden from history', to use the famous phrase that Sheila Rowbotham coined in 1973 with regard to women. When I remarked upon this fact to my friend and colleague Elisa Chuliá, who teaches family sociology in Madrid, she put her hands close to her face and crossed them so that her fingers formed a lattice-work in front of her eyes. 'The family is so important to Spaniards', she said, 'that we cannot see it.' This defect, as we shall see, is not only Spanish.[1]

In trying to redress this historical imbalance I have dedicated considerable space not just to family *policies* – in broad terms, what states do for, or to, families – but also to family *politics*, which implies a wider consideration of the place of families in the social and political life of a nation-state. This broad approach suggests that families are not simply on the receiving end of political power but are themselves actors in the historical process. Families are subjects as well as objects, even in conditions as unfavourable as those of the dictatorial regimes described in this book. Nor should they be considered in isolation or relegated to an Indian reserve of family history. An examination of continuous but often conflictual relations – between the family and the state, but also between individuals and families, and between families and civil society – suggests a theoretical framework for inserting family history into a wider and deeper general history.[2]

The book's underlying structure is primarily comparative. The histories of families in five nation-states are taken into consideration, all of them during a period of dramatic transition: Russia, in its revolutionary passage from Empire to Soviet Union; Turkey, in the transition from the decadent Ottoman Empire to a modern Republic; Italy, from hesitant Liberalism to rampant Fascism; Spain, before, during and after the cataclysm of the Civil War; and Germany, from the failure of the Weimar Republic to the National Socialist state. These five countries have not been chosen at random: all of them witnessed, after a long period of social and political turmoil, and in some cases of revolution, the development in the 1920s and 1930s of dictatorial regimes, of differing capacities and strength. The Nazi and Soviet regimes, the most powerful, are also the most often compared. I have tried to take a broader approach in terms both of content – with families as my central focus – and also of the nations examined, which include not only Russia, Germany, Italy and Spain, but also Atatürk's Republic of Turkey (1923). All these regimes attempted to mould and manipulate family life, occasionally in benign ways but more often at the price of untold numbers of families destroyed and hearts broken. Yet the story I have to tell is not only one of family devastation but also one of survival.

Within this broad comparative framework, I employ various methodologies. The first is biographical. In each chapter I have chosen to concentrate upon a specific individual and his or her family history. These are mostly figures who had something strikingly original to say about the family or whose own families are of particular interest. Thus for Russia I have chosen Aleksandra Kollontai, the only woman commissar in Lenin's revolutionary government; for Turkey the nationalist writer Halide Edib; for Italy the Futurist Filippo Tommaso Marinetti, who once described the family as a Bedouin tent; for Spain the courageous and outspoken feminist Margarita Nelken; and for Germany Joseph Goebbels, who erected his own family into a Nazi archetype. Behind these figures lie the stories of others: in the first place, those of the great dictators themselves – Mussolini, Franco, Atatürk, Hitler and Stalin; in the second, those of other noteworthy figures, such as Inessa Armand and Antonio Gramsci, who reflected upon the family.

In addition I reconstruct the stories of ordinary families faced with great danger and adversity – those, for instance, who found themselves on the wrong side of the lines in the Spanish Civil War, those who attempted to continue to live as Jews in Germany in the 1930s, and those who, though loyal to the regime, saw their lives and families destroyed by Stalin.

Another fundamental method of comparison is social history. For each country I try to describe and compare the family life and conditions of major sections of the population, above all peasants and workers. Here classic themes of family history come to the fore – family structures and size, marriage patterns, religious beliefs, everyday life. And here too I am helped in my reconstruction by some extraordinary testimonies, such as those contained in the school notebooks (*quaderni*) of Tuscan sharecropper children in the school of San Gersolè in the 1930s, with their minute descriptions of family lives.

Gender difference is to the fore in all these families, whether they are extended or nuclear, large or small. One of the most interesting comparative themes is that of patriarchy, fiercely under attack in some parts of this complex story, strongly reasserted in others. Mustafa Kemal, for instance, liberates Turkish women from many traditional restrictions, but simultaneously reasserts the power of patriarchy in a modern form. By contrast, the Soviet Union sides very clearly with women against men in more than one area of family life, offering a really distinctive view of gender relations. The book is full of feminists of one sort or another, most of whom are defeated and dispersed.

I concentrate on the policies of the great dictatorships and their need for obedient, traditional and functional families, but I also examine radical alternatives to family life – communes, collectives and sharing communities, from working-class Berlin to revolutionary Barcelona. The first half of the twentieth century is not only a period of exceptional violence but also one of revolutionary dreams – of Spanish anarchists' advocacy of the abolition of money; of Konstantin Melnikov's undulating apartment blocks, whose movement, when accompanied by soothing music, put tired workers to sleep; of 'free love' in its various connotations.

Of particular importance to my comparative endeavour are the fields of family law and political theory. Radical changes in the law are very prominent in some national experiences, such as those of revolutionary Russia and Kemalist Turkey, but very marginal in others, such as those of Fascist Italy. Political theory's treatment of the family in this period is fragmentary but occasionally very interesting, from Gökalp's Turkish reflections on the role of the family in the clash between culture and civilisation, to Giovanni Gentile's irritable dismissal of Hegel's 'triad' of family, civil society and state, to Antonio Gramsci's vision of the family as an 'organ of moral life'. As this book grew so too did my profound scepticism about a general interpretative framework that employs 'totalitarianism' as its guiding concept.

Giambattista Salinari and I have produced as an accompaniment to this volume a comparative statistical essay dedicated to demographic and economic themes.[3] We concentrate especially on three connected issues: first, the long historical process which has come to be known as the demographic transition – that is, from high levels of mortality and birth rates to low levels of both; secondly, the very widespread destruction of human life occasioned by the unprecedented sequence of world wars, civil wars and famine; and thirdly, what can be called 'the challenge of eugenics' facing all the political regimes under consideration.

A last point of method. I have tried to keep visual representations of the family very much to the fore. The book is illustrated with photographs for each chapter, but also examines and compares depictions of the family by major artists of the first half of the twentieth century – Arshile Gorky, Pablo Picasso, Mario Sironi, Max Beckmann and others. The most striking, and anguished, portrayal of the family undoubtedly comes from Mario Sironi in his paintings of 1927–34, very much in contrast to official expressions of the Fascist family. Of great fascination, too, is Rudolf Arnheim's suggestion of the existence of a 'family group' in Picasso's *Guernica*.

I am very aware that there are many areas which I have merely touched upon, such as the depiction of families in the cinema of these decades, and that everywhere a great deal of research, mapping and theoretical reflection remains to be undertaken. It is also true that I have chosen to write a book primarily about families and dictatorships. In a second moment I would love to write another, about families and democracies after 1945. My endeavour here can perhaps best be described as preliminary: to ensure, by means of a comparison which spans five nation-states and employs many different methodologies, that family life, in all its richness and complexity, assumes its proper place in the convulsive history of the first half of the twentieth century.

Acknowledgements

My greatest debt is to my wife, Ayşe Saraçgil, to whom I have dedicated this book. She was my instructor and inspiration for chapter 2, and without her the Turkish part of my story would never have been told. She has also been a constant intellectual comrade, suggesting, supporting and criticising. When writing a book this long about the family, one needs to ask many favours of one's own family and to plead forgiveness, especially for the isolation essential to such an enterprise. My family may not fit exactly the canons of convention (which family does these days?), but it is a loving entity and everyone who forms part of it has been deeply generous and patient with me. As for friends, I have to thank Susan James and Quentin Skinner for their constant support and for the passion they expressed for this project from its very beginning. John Barber was endlessly generous, as he always is, sharing not only his great knowledge of the Soviet Union with me but also his Grantchester house with my family. John Dunn has always pushed me gently onwards and has never ceased asking me questions to which I have difficulty in replying. Anna Di Biagio has not only shared the same teaching room in our Florentine department over the last twenty years, but has given me the benefit of her deep knowledge of the Soviet family. Jürgen Kocka, Peter Wagner and Dieter Gosewinkel kindly invited me to be part of that precious intellectual experience which went by the name of CiSoNet, the European Civil Society Network.[1] Patrick Joyce much encouraged me in the latter stages of the book, as did John Keane. Michele Battini brought me not only his constant friendship but also many stimuli from the realm of political theory.

In the making of the book I was extremely fortunate to have the support of a team of colleagues, friends and researchers: Chiara Stefani, who was not only in charge of picture research but can justly be called the coordinator of the whole enterprise; Eva Balz, whose researches in Berlin and constant critical intelligence were invaluable to me; and Elisa Chuliá, whose great enthusiasm and generosity, as well as deep knowledge of Spanish family matters, dissolved many of my doubts. My thanks also to Bruna Bocchini and Maria Casalini for their expert help on specific points, to Christoph Kreutzmueller for his reading and criticism of the German chapter, and to Paul Corner and Marco Palla for doing the same with the chapter dedicated to Fascism. The librarians of the Biblioteca Nazionale in Florence, the European University Institute at San Domenico di Fiesole, the Cambridge University Library and the British Library have been unfailingly helpful and cooperative.

At Yale University Press Robert Baldock has been extremely patient as well as perceptive and wise. Laura Davey has been an exceptional copy-editor. My literary agent, Caroline Dawnay, has given me a lot of encouragement and very sound advice. I must also thank my Italian publisher, Ernesto Franco, of Giulio Einaudi Editore. I am sure that many errors remain in the book, perhaps unavoidably in a work of such wide scope. The responsibility for them remains entirely my own.

CHAPTER 1

Revolutionising family life: Russia, 1917–1927

I. BEFORE THE REVOLUTION

1. A nonconformist

Aleksandra Kollontai was born in St Petersburg in March 1872. Her mother was a formidable woman from a rich merchant family whose second husband was an aristocratic army colonel, Mikhail Alekseyevich Domontovich. Aleksandra was his daughter and she was born even before her mother's divorce had been formalised. Both her parents were liberals. Her father, who came from an old Ukrainian landowning family, more than once incurred the Tsar's wrath for advocating constitutional ideas, but he was eventually promoted to general and taught in the capital's elite cavalry school. 'Shura', as Aleksandra was called at home, was brought up for most of her childhood in a handsome St Petersburg town house; summers were spent on her maternal grandparents' estate at Kuusa in Finland. Family life for her was comfortable and stimulating, though her mother was strict and domineering, in constant conflict with her daughter. An English nanny, Miss Hodgson, provided Shura with some of the emotional warmth that her mother was incapable of giving. Kollontai wrote in her autobiographical notes, 'There was order in everything: to tidy my toys up by myself, to lay my underwear on a little chair at night, to wash neatly, to study my lessons on time, to treat the servants with respect.'[1] It was from this unlikely background that there emerged the most famous female figure of the Russian revolution, the only woman commissar in Lenin's revolutionary government of 1917, the theorist of new and freer sexual relations, and the passionate advocate of the need to abolish the bourgeois family and replace it with a higher form of communal living.

What clues are there in her own family of origin and in the years of her childhood to suggest that she would become so notable a figure and hold such extraordinary views? Her relationship with her father provides one line of enquiry. He was the person she most adored in her large family, a handsome and scholarly figure, but she had great difficulty in getting him to pay her any attention. After all, she was only a little girl. Once, she recalled, she crept into his study and, standing on tiptoe, kissed him on the forehead; 'Father looked up surprised as if he had never seen me before. Then he smiled.'[2] It could be suggested that Kollontai was 'standing on tiptoe' for much of the rest of her life, trying to show herself worthy of so formidable a male alter ego.

A second clue concerns the pre-eminent role in her life, even at this early stage, of figures who are not blood relations. One is Miss Hodgson, her nanny. Another, of even greater significance, is Zoya Shadurskaya, a childhood friend who was to remain by Kollontai's side throughout her life.[3] In future years Kollontai's own 'family' was often to consist of just two other persons – Misha, her only child, and Zoya, her greatest female friend. The three of them lived together in 1901, after Aleksandra's father had died. They did so again, both when Kollontai was a commissar and during the terrible days of the Civil War.

A final clue lies in the dreaming and restlessness that marked her character from her early years. Towards the end of her life she wrote, 'This childlike ability to dream helped me all my life; I not only saw what was real but I could easily imagine how it would be if life were changed.'[4] This constant imagining accompanied a strong desire for romantic self-realisation and public recognition.[5]

In her youth Kollontai came to feel that the security of her family life impeded her own development. Her favourite novel of this period was Turgenev's wonderfully romantic *On the Eve*, first published in 1860. Yelena Nikolayevna, the heroine of the book, lives a tranquil existence with her parents in a dacha in the heart of the Russian countryside. She is courted, beautiful and intelligent but she is not at peace. As she confides to her diary, 'Oh if someone would say to me: "There, that's what you must do!" Being good – isn't much; doing good . . . yes that's the great thing in life. But how is one to do good? Oh, if I could but learn to control myself!'[6] Yelena falls passionately in love with a young and earnest Bulgarian nationalist who is visiting one of her friends but is anxious only to return to fight for his country's independence from the Ottomans. They flee together to Venice, he twenty-six years old and she just twenty. In the lagoon city he dies of consumption. In the last phrases of the book Turgenev leaves his readers in uncertainty regarding the fate of his heroine: some suggested that she had been seen in Herzegovina with the army that was then being formed; others had even described how she was dressed, in black from head to foot. In any case, Yelena's traces were lost forever, without hope of return.[7]

Kollontai was as impatient with family life as was Turgenev's Yelena, but she had no intention of following her man to foreign shores, or of becoming a martyr to the cause, whatever that cause turned out to be.[8] Her rebellion took time to come to the boil. In 1893, at the age of twenty-one, she married – against the wishes of her parents, especially of her mother – a cheerful and pragmatic young engineer called Vladimir Kollontai, a distant cousin. 'Two paupers' was how her mother scathingly described the couple, and she refused to put on a new dress for the wedding. A year after the marriage Shura gave birth to a son, Mikhail, always to be called 'Misha'. Although she often deserted him, Kollontai was devoted to him throughout her life – 'modest, wise, dear Misha', as she once called him.[9] But even while she was breast-feeding she was impatient to return to her books, writings and political discussions. She felt the impelling need to assert her own autonomy, not just from her family of origin but also from the family that she had just created. This pulling of women in opposing directions simultaneously – outwards towards the public sphere and inwards towards domestic life – was a problem with which she grappled all her life. It was to remain an unresolved element of her family politics. She wrote in her autobiography, 'Although I personally raised my child with great care, motherhood was never the kernel of my existence. A child was not able to draw the bonds of my marriage tighter. I still loved my husband, but the contented life of a housewife and spouse became for me a "cage".'[10]

In August 1898 came her first great flight. She left Russia for Switzerland, where she was to study at Zurich University under the supervision of a Marxist economist called Professor Herkner. This was unusual but not unheard of. In the last decades of the nineteenth century, well-to-do Russian women, denied access to universities at home, had begun in small numbers to educate themselves abroad. But for Kollontai the departure was a profound rift. She left the four-year-old Misha with his grandmother, in the mansion at Kuusa. And she left, definitively, her husband Vladimir Kollontai, to whom she wrote while journeying to Zurich. On the train she sobbed with grief and guilt – she missed 'Misha's soft little hands', she had behaved badly towards her husband, she wanted to go home. But she stayed in Zurich for over a year, and when she came back she had to try to rebuild the relationship with her son.

On the train from St Petersburg to Zurich she had also written another letter – to her dear friend Zoya. In it she explained that she intended to dedicate her life to the working class and to the rights of women.

How had she come to that choice of 'doing good', not just 'being good', to return to the distinction drawn by Yelena in On the Eve? With regard to the working class, Kollontai herself recounts an episode. It was one of those traumatic and iconic moments which many Bolsheviks used post hoc to explain their conversion to the cause. Yet it is of great significance in this context because of its emphasis on family life, or lack of it. In 1896 she had accompanied her husband Vladimir to Narva, where she visited the vast Kronholm textile works, which employed 12,000 men and women. Aleksandra asked to see the workers' housing. She found conditions to be appalling. 'Home life' was a row of cots in a large foul-smelling room. Married and unmarried workers were mixed promiscuously, without any privacy at all. Children milled around between the cots, some playing, some crying. Kollontai noticed a small boy, the age of her own son, who was lying very still. He was dead, but nobody had noticed or done anything about it.[11]

From the turn of the century onwards, right up to the outbreak of revolution in Russia in 1917, Kollontai was to dedicate herself to the workers' cause. These were the decades during which the march of European history and Marxism as a theory of history most closely coincided. The industrial proletariat was self-evidently the class of the future. Its terrible exploitation was all too evident but so too was its ability to organise itself in increasing numbers in trade unions and political parties. Marxism reflected this growing power, gave it a 'scientific' basis and granted it great historical dignity. Was not Communism, as the young Marx had written, the 'solution to the riddle of history' and the proletariat the universal class which with its own liberation would emancipate the whole of humanity?[12] Kollontai imbibed these ideas, in Zurich and afterwards, and was never to waver from them for the rest of her long life.

She was also convinced, unlike her 'revisionist' professor in Zurich, of the necessity of revolution to bring the working class to power. Her baptism by fire came in 1905, with the first Russian revolution. She took part in the march to the Winter Palace on Bloody Sunday (9 January 1905), when hundreds of peaceful workers who wished to hand in a petition to the Tsar were shot down in cold blood. In the weeks that followed, Kollontai spoke often at illegal factory meetings in St Petersburg. According to the historian Richard Stites, witnesses recall the stunning effect she had, both in 1905 and 1917, 'her musical and impassioned voice and her immaculate grooming enhancing rather than weakening the impression she made'.[13]

The revolution of 1905 failed. Three years later Kollontai was forced to leave Russia, once again leaving her son behind. Misha was dispatched to boarding school, sometimes visiting his mother during the vacations.

In Europe Kollontai became a well-known and respected member of the Russian Marxist left, closer to the Mensheviks than to Lenin's Bolsheviks. She also increasingly concentrated in her speeches and writings upon the question of women's rights – the second great theme of her political life, as she had announced in her letter to Zoya from the Zurich train. She travelled tirelessly throughout Germany and other European countries, speaking on women's emancipation and the situation in Russia. Her command of many languages made her an excellent ambassador. She also wrote a great deal, though she was never a theoretician and did not have the profundity of a figure such as Rosa Luxemburg.

In one respect, however, Aleksandra Kollontai was highly original. She alone, among all the leading European Marxists of that time, recognised sexuality as a crucial revolutionary theme. Following a long Russian radical tradition dating back at least to Herzen, she raised awkward but vital questions about sex and love, about how women and men could share a natural eroticism in the context of everyday life in a new society.[14] In the face of widespread scorn within her movement, from both male and female comrades, she pursued these themes until it was no longer permitted to her to do so. And from her reflections on sexuality there also came an argument concerning the transformation of families and even their complete superseding.

The line of reasoning that she developed – though with a certain vagueness and never to any great depth – in various writings between 1908 and 1914 took

fig. 1 Aleksandra Kollontai in 1909.

as its starting point the oppression of women.[15] In her article 'The new woman' (1913) she stressed that women needed to find autonomy and independence from men, and that work would be a crucial element in their liberation. But differently from many Marxist feminists of the time she insisted that part of this new autonomy would reside in the sphere of sex. In this context, Kollontai introduced an expression, 'the winged Eros', that was destined to become both internationally famous and widely misunderstood as an invitation to unbridled promiscuity.[16] For her, free and joyous sexual relations – for this was the core of the 'winged Eros' for both women and men – could flourish only in certain social conditions, not in others.

Kollontai made a list of conditions inimical to her project. Bourgeois marriage was the first. Following both Marx and Engels, as well as August Bebel, Kollontai saw bourgeois marriage as the reducing of women to the property of men. Wives became 'mere shadows' of their husbands and were inevitably confined to the domestic sphere. To these well-known arguments Kollontai added others, connected to the 'egoism' of contemporary life. In modern, urban solitude women and men reached out to each other and clung together as a couple, but in the end women always paid for this bonding, since it stunted their individuality. Prostitution, the inevitable accompaniment to bourgeois marriage, offered only further oppression for women: 'it suffocates love in human hearts; from it Eros flies in fear of soiling its golden wings'.[17]

Unusually and highly significantly, romantic love was also dismissed by Kollontai as a possible basis for fulfilment. Kollontai was certainly a romantic but of a rather peculiar sort, because for her the usual relationship between private and public which characterised Romanticism was reversed. She was a high romantic in the *public* sphere, believing as she did in the extraordinary transformative powers of socialist revolution. But in the *private* sphere she rejected romantic love as being a pernicious basis on which to build new, intimate relations. For her, romantic love was the height of possessiveness and from it there derived the need for lovers to devour each other:

> Contemporary lovers with all their respect for freedom are not satisfied by the knowledge of the physical faithfulness alone of the person they love. To be rid of the eternally present threat of loneliness we 'launch an attack' on the emotions of the person we love with a cruelty and lack of delicacy that will not be understood by future generations. We demand to know every secret of this person's being.[18]

Her preferred model for intimate relations in the new society was one in which men and women were equals, each defined as friend and comrade, neither possessive nor dominant, both able to show passion and consideration towards their partner. From these premises 'winged Eros' could take substance and form, could 'weave his delicate strands of every kind of emotion [. . .] emerge from the shadows and [. . .] demand his rightful place'.[19]

These may well seem generic formulae. Yet Kollontai inserted them into a radically different and collectivist context. In her imagining of the future it is not the individual couple that is strong but the collective. Traditional roles are reversed. It is the collective that demands first loyalty and offers stability and identity to the individual; the intimate relationship between two adults takes second place. Men and women are carried forward by their collective endeavour, by being part of a shared project, by the rich network of social relations which the new collectivity creates, but they do not necessarily stay together for always. Women are free and independent, able to live their lives to the full:

> But when the wave of passion sweeps over her, she does not renounce the brilliant smile of life, she does not hypocritically wrap herself up in a faded cloak of female virtue. No, she holds out her hand to her chosen one and goes away for several weeks to drink from the cup of love's joy, however deep it is, and to satisfy herself. When the cup is empty she throws it away without regret and bitterness. And again to work.[20]

Furthermore, the preferred form of cohabitation for men, women and children is not for Kollontai the private home but the commune. It was Nikolay Chernyshevsky's famous novel *What is to be Done?* (1863), with its story of a precocious and radical commune, that heavily influenced Kollontai and others. Narrow, limited family life could be overcome. To live together in a group, to share income and food, to work collectively for the new socialist state, was her ideal, though it was never one that she personally practised in her own lifetime.[21]

What did all this mean for the family? I shall come back to this central point in detail a little later on. Suffice it to say here that the family was clearly demoted and risked being discarded as the cardinal form of social organisation. Kollontai herself imagined that after the revolution it would disappear. Henceforth children would be looked after and educated in a collective fashion; in the new communes men and women workers would be freer, more fulfilled and better protected by the new socialist state. Kollontai treated the family as a *residue*, the site of *meshchanstvo*, 'petty bourgeois backwardness', a term which, as Elizabeth Waters has written, 'encapsulated all that was politically, culturally and socially unacceptable in the old way of life'.[22] Nowhere, according to the Marxist revolutionaries, was *meshchanstvo* more present than in the vast expanses of the Russian countryside, with all the prejudices and superstitions of rural family life.

At the outbreak of the First World War Kollontai and Misha, who was with her for the summer of 1914 and was now twenty, were both arrested in Germany and accused of being German spies. They were soon released but the next few years were very difficult for both of them.[23] Kollontai was horrified at the German Social Democrats' decision to back the war. She moved much closer to Lenin and spent the following years speaking out incessantly against imperialist war. She even toured the United States for an exhausting four months, recording in her diary on 10 December 1915, 'On the train between Indianapolis and Louisville. I speak almost daily. I have been in America 62 days and I have spoken at meetings 53 times. Sometimes it seems to me that I will simply be unable to speak. I want to implore – let go of me.'[24]

By 1917 Kollontai was forty-four years old. Like Lenin, who was by then forty-six, she thought she was too old to see the revolution in her lifetime.[25] When the electrifying news of the events of February of that year reached her, she was in Oslo and he in Zurich. Riding on a tram, Kollontai glimpsed the morning headlines of someone else's newspaper: 'REVOLUTION IN RUSSIA'.

2. Peasant families

In the first half of the nineteenth century, Prince Nikolay Gagarin, a magnate and government office-holder, owned approximately 27,000 serfs distributed over various estates in central European Russia. One of these was the estate of Mishino, consisting of four villages and some 1,500 inhabitants in 1858, located in the province of Ryazan some 170 kilometres south-east of Moscow. The layout of villages in Ryazan province was linear in form, with peasant dwellings standing close together on the banks of a lake or stream, or along a road. Arable land surrounded and spread out from the village. At Mishino the principal product was rye.

Thanks to Peter Czap Jr's exceptionally detailed demographic study of this estate, it is possible to gain a clear insight into the structures of traditional peasant family life in the Russia of that time.[26] Let me begin with the 'dvor'. This term had two principal and complementary usages. It described the peasant's household in material terms – the dwelling, barns, threshing floor, animals, etc. And it also referred to the group of individuals who lived and worked there, who were principally but not exclusively blood relations. Thus the family as a group and the household as a physical space were both 'dvor'.[27]

Traditional European Russian peasant families were unusually large domestic groups. The *dvor* invariably boasted a complex structure, with more

fig. 2 A Russian peasant family, 1892.

than one conjugal family unit housed under its roof. The members of these large multiple-family households were connected to each other by kinship patterns of infinite variety. At Mishino the mean average size of households between 1814 and 1858 was nine persons. Each was headed by a patriarch (*bolshak*). Thus the *dvor* of Dmitry Fedorov, a widower aged fifty-three, was made up of two kinship groups. The first was that of his son, aged twenty-three, who was also already widowed, his daughter of fifteen and his granddaughter of just three; the second was that of his younger brother and his wife, aged thirty-seven and thirty, and their three children of tender age.

The life cycle of individuals in these families was very precarious. Men had an average life expectancy of no more than thirty-one years, women of thirty-three. Marriage was precocious and so was childbirth. Peasant women expected to become mothers aged eighteen to twenty, grandmothers at thirty-eight to forty. The normal run of their lives was fraught with danger and disaster – illnesses, accidents, the death of farm animals, recruitment to the army (which until the reforms of 1874 took peasant sons away for twenty-five years) and the perennial threat of famine. To face these dangers each family needed as many children, especially male children, as possible: 'One son is not a son, two sons equal half a son, three sons equal one son.'[28]

Centrifugal tendencies, present in any large domestic group, were certainly also to be found here – disputes between brothers, the domineering of mothers-in-law over daughters-in-law, and the rivalry of one conjugal family unit with another. But what is striking is the number of these households that held together over time, both peasants and landowner insisting on family unity for reasons of productivity and of social stability. On the estate of Mishino in this period, family fission – the splitting up of households – was rare. Czap concludes, 'what we find is a family system of "perennial households", households for which one can determine no beginning or end in a continuous sequence of generations'.[29]

Much changed in the decades after the Emancipation Decrees of 1861, which formally put an end to serfdom. Peasants were freer to move around, though still obliged to pay redemption payments, as they were known, to landowners. The development of industry, especially in the Central Industrial Region, enabled many young male peasants to earn wages for the first time, even if not for the whole year.[30] The period of recruitment to the army was reduced. Education increased as the battle against illiteracy spread to the countryside. Sons came to challenge fathers; family division, the *razdel*, became much more frequent. The net result was that the structure of rural households in European Russia assumed an aspect that was less complex and more nuclear.[31]

Greater individualism thus began to penetrate some parts of rural Russia, but right up to the revolution of 1917 deprivation and tradition weighed heavily upon peasant families. The sanitary and hygienic conditions of their homes were appalling.[32] It was not surprising that the Russian Empire had the highest infant mortality rate in the whole of Europe. In the Russian countryside at the turn of the century more than 25 per cent of infants died within the first year of birth, while another 20 per cent did not reach adulthood. Doctors sent by the local authorities to the estates in the 1890s were shocked by mothers' neglect of infants during the summer months, but they often had little option.[33]

Women were habitually treated with great brutality. Submissiveness, fertility and the 'endurance of a horse' were the qualities to be sought in a young wife. According to one proverb, 'The more you beat the old woman the tastier the soup will be.'[34] Small wonder then that the prospect of marriage was greeted by young girls with anything but joy. Pushkin noted that traditional Russian marriage songs were as sad as funeral laments. Thirteen was the lawful minimum age for females to marry under Russian Orthodox canon law, fifteen for boys. Arranged marriages were the order of the day and it was here that the patriarch's wife (*bolshukha*) found her place and power within the patriarchal system.

Partible male inheritance governed the customs of property devolution, sons usually inheriting from fathers in equal amounts. The wife of the deceased patriarch was entitled to one-seventh of his property. Patriarchs exercised nearly as much arbitrary power over the male elements of the *dvor* as over the women. They could refuse sons a passport to leave the village, use violence on them and, until the reforms of 1874, threaten them with enforced recruitment. From more than one point of view, then, the attractions of family fission were evident. As opportunities increased, sons and their young wives tried to take advantage of them – to flee from the site of their oppression and set up smaller, nuclear families of their own.[35]

Intimately linked with patriarchal power were the influence and codes of the Orthodox Church. The religiosity and superstition of Russian peasant society created exactly the sort of popular culture which the Bolsheviks, wedded as they were to scientific explanation, to rationalism and modernity, abhorred. Bread was never to be cut but always broken, nor had it ever to be found upside down on the table. The evil eye had to be warded off in innumerable ways. In order to stop spirits from stealing babies in cradles, women left scissors and a spindle in a bag on top of an old twig broom on the floor. Magic was everywhere and each family had always to watch its step and take precautionary measures.

Orthodox Christianity overlaid but did not replace these customary practices. The 'elaborate misogynist ideology'[36] of the peasant world was supported firmly by the Church. Many of its key texts, from the sermons of St John Chrysostom, St Basil the Great, Ephrem of Syria, and so on, warned against the wickedness of women, who, from the Garden of Eden onwards, had become the 'evil tools of the Devil'. Women were inferior but also impure. They were dangerous because of their natural sexual insatiability – a theme which, as we shall see, crossed religious and national borders and flourished wherever patriarchal systems were most entrenched. Under the stipulations of Russian Orthodoxy, women were not allowed into the main body of the church during services and were kept segregated from men; nor were they allowed to take communion if they were menstruating. There none the less existed a tense and complex relationship between this evident misogyny and the ubiquitous presence of the icons of the 'Mother of God' – on the 'sacred shelf' in each *dvor*, as protectors of individual households and entire villages and even saviours of the nation. In the invocation and celebration of the miracle-performing capacities of the icons of the Virgin Mary, superstition and Christianity joined hands. The Marian cult was all-pervasive, and peasant women, excluded and castigated by the Church, were its greatest supporters.[37] The weakness of the parish system and the strength of the *dvor* also led to the peasants' religion being a family cult.[38] The priest had to present himself at the *dvor* to celebrate the various rites demanded by tradition and in his absence the male head of the *dvor*, the *bolshak*, could lead prayers before the family icons.

Church statistics for 1900 show very high levels of regular confession and communion – 87 per cent for men and 91 per cent for women.[39] Right up to the revolution of 1917, the Church controlled and supervised the major rites of passage in peasant life. Its courts exercised considerable jurisdictional powers on a daily basis. But the earlier revolution of 1905–7, which had a major rural component to it, shattered the Church's complacency and showed just how much deprivation, resentment and anger existed in the villages of the Empire.

One final peasant institution, of great significance for my story, must be introduced here – the land commune (*obshchina* or *mir*).[40] Communes were widespread all over European Russia but not in the Ukraine, and their habitual form was the so-called 'redistributional' commune. This was a commune which united the peasant households of a certain locality, periodically redistributing the land that the peasants owned collectively. A peasant's dwelling and vegetable garden were his own and considered permanent, hereditary household property. Arable fields, however, belonged to the commune. Strips of land were allocated to each household, usually on the basis of a family's size or effective labour force. Thus the plough-land of each *dvor* consisted of an assortment of strips scattered among the commune's fields.[41]

The land commune was thus a self-governing association of peasants. Naturally, some members of the community did more governing than others. Decisions were reached at the general meeting of the *mir*, but only household heads had the right to vote. Meetings were lengthy occasions, based on customary law and rendered rowdy by the constant consumption of vodka. The commune exercised responsibility not only for land but also for local taxes, the maintenance of roads and bridges, the upkeep of local schools and churches, as well as for the peasants' redemption payments. The communes, with their relative autonomy and self-government, and their social practice of broadly egalitarian land distribution, attracted the attention of radicals and revolutionaries, who thought they might serve as the nuclei for agrarian socialism in Russia.[42] But the strongest characteristics of the *mir* were those of a traditional, inward-looking community, dominated by the richer male heads of household. Amongst the families that composed it, gender and generational hierarchies reigned supreme.[43] So, too, did suspicion and rejection of the outsider. The communes exercised fierce collective control over the habits and customs of the peasants themselves, especially over women. They left the running of each complex domestic aggregation (*dvor*) to its male head, but they were ready to intervene if he was not up to the task. Thus Kollontai's idea of a commune was light years away from the *mir*. But she would have answered – and so would Karl Marx before her – that the question was not what the *mir* was but what it might *become*.[44]

After the revolution of 1905 the Stolypin reforms attempted, with some success, to create a new class of small landowners in the Russian countryside. Yet the broadly egalitarian practices of the redistributional communes still represented a formidable force by the time of the 1917 revolution.

Before leaving peasant families I must say something, however inadequate, about conditions in Russian Central Asia. This huge and inhospitable expanse of territory, measuring some 1.5 million square miles, had a population of only ten million people in 1897. It was made up of infinite steppe land, either grassy or arid, deserts, high plateaux and mountains. Its population belonged broadly to two types – the nomadic-pastoral peoples of the steppes and the sedentary populations which clustered around the oases and fertile river valleys. There were few cities, but some of great antiquity and distinction, such as Bukhara, Tashkent and Samarkand. In ethnic terms Turkic predominated, subdivided amongst Uzbeks, Kazakhs, Kirghiz and Turkmen. The other two principal ethnic groups were Iranians and Slavs. Islam was the predominant religion. Codified Muslim law (*shariat*) was upheld by local canonical courts staffed by qualified clergy (*ullama*), but was accompanied, modified or even defied in many zones by local customary law (*adat*). In general, Central Asia presented an extremely complex mixture of religious and tribal tribunals, usages and laws. The whole vast area had become part of the Russian Empire only in the second half of the nineteenth century and after bitter resistance. The last Turkmen lands succumbed in the 1880s and the Empire's southern border with China and Afghanistan, in the high Pamir mountains, was fixed only in 1895.[45]

Little is known of family life at this time in these vast and generally unvisited lands of Russian Central Asia. Concentrating only on the sedentary-agricultural areas, there emerges the picture of an even more ferocious and unyielding patriarchy than that which I have described for European Russia. Women were 'hidden', both in dress and in terms of their confinement to domestic space. When they emerged from their homes they followed behind their husbands at several paces' distance. In customary law and many peasant sayings, women were considered scarcely superior to animals. A father could dispose of a daughter as he saw fit: 'A girl is a sack of nuts; she can be bought and sold.' And so she was, often for a high bride price (*qalin*) if she was attractive and healthy. According to the *shariat*, a girl could be married off at nine, a boy at twelve. A husband usually treated his wife with brute force. Furthermore, the existence of polygamy, practised above all in the more prosperous peasant and merchant families, placed women in odious competition in the same household and at the mercy of the changing sexual desires of the patriarch.[46]

Of course, this general picture is far from universal. So vast an area with so many different cultures could never have boasted a single model of family life.

Especially in the large cities of the southern river basins, women lived the most secluded of lives, in households built upon rigid gender division of space and without external windows. From the time of the Russian conquest of their territory, Uzbek women had taken to wearing a total veil that deeply impressed all visitors – including the Communist women reformers of the 1920s. It was formed by a heavy cotton robe (*paranji*) which covered the whole body and which held in place a formidable face and upper-body screen of woven horse-hair, called a *chachvon*. But this form of veiling was anything but universal, even among the Uzbeks. Turkmen women wore a *yashmak*, a lighter face covering which left eyes, nose and forehead uncovered. Kazakh and Kirghiz women rarely veiled.[47] Nor was the Islam of Central Asia of one, unchanging voice. The most important group of reformers of the time, those in the *jadīd* tradition, concentrated on educational innovation aimed at producing a modernising Muslim society, able to hold its own with the Christian West. They argued against veiling of any sort and in favour of new family relations based on the end of polygamy and a more active role for women in the public sphere. Their teachings were to have considerable influence both in Russian Central Asia and amongst the reformers of the late Ottoman Empire.[48]

In the early summer of 1917 a packed train left from Saratov and headed towards Samarkand, a journey that usually took six days. On board was a twelve-year-old boy, Jascha Golowanjuk, who for four years had attended the music conservatory in Saratov and was now going back to his family. His Danish foster-father, who had married into the Russian aristocracy, was at the time the manager of the Russo-Asiatic Bank in Samarkand. One morning in Saratov, the boy, carrying his violin and on his way to the conservatory, had been swept up by the revolutionary crowds: 'It was', he wrote later, 'the moment that marked the end of my childhood.' Outside the conservatory one of his friends was killed by a stray bullet. Traumatised but uninjured, Golowanjuk was put on a train and began his long journey back to his parents. He spent most of the time gazing out of the window at the interminable steppes.

At one of the later stations a rich Kirghiz got on with his two wives. He had massive silver rings on his fingers and a gold chain round his waist, and his wives had silver rings through their noses. One of them, obviously the favourite, had a little piece of silver hanging from her nose-ring, and it bobbed about in front of her lovely mouth. When she wanted to eat she put the silver ornament into her nostril very elegantly so that she could enjoy without interference the crusts of bread and cheese that her husband deigned to throw her when he had finished his meal, in much the same way as we should throw bits of bread to a monkey in a cage. These two beauties squatted in the corridor, and if they got in the way they were kicked and cursed by their fellow-travellers while their natural protector sat quite unmoved, chewing away at his piece of goat cheese.[49]

3. Workers' families

The industrial proletariat upon whom the Russian Marxists – Kollontai included – pinned their hopes for revolution constituted a tiny minority of the Russian population in 1917. Even when Stalin began his great modernisation drive in 1929, out of a total population of some 157 million, 85.4 per cent of the active population still worked in agriculture, only 7.5 per cent in industry and 7.1 per cent in the tertiary sector.[50]

To talk of 'workers' families' in European Russia at the end of the nineteenth century and the beginning of the twentieth is something of a contradiction in terms. The conditions of workers – both male and female – in most industrial zones were prohibitive to the raising of a family. The squalor of the living quarters which had so shocked Kollontai at the Kronholm textile works in 1896 was repeated to a greater or lesser extent wherever a factory or mill was in operation. If workers kept their families with them, they did so in often desperately inhospitable and unhygienic conditions. In the bast-matting industry, workers usually slept on the floor under their hand-powered looms and their children entered the workforce from the age of five. Statistics for the Vladimir province of 1907 comparing infant mortality among workers and peasants showed that one-fourth of peasant children and two-thirds of workers' children died in their first year. Family life in these conditions was next to impossible.[51]

In fact Russian male workers in these decades sought a solution by separating family life from work and themselves from their families. Worker-peasants, as they were accurately labelled, married young, left their wives and children in their village of origin, and emigrated for many months at a time to the nearby city. Thanks to village contacts and extended kinship networks, they soon found a job and somewhere to sleep. They never altogether severed their ties to the countryside, however. They would try to return on feast days and for other important moments in the life of the family. Yet while their earnings sustained the village home in a dignified way, these 'male breadwinners' managed to spend very little time with their wives and children and some gradually lost touch altogether. In his memoirs, P. Timofeyev, a St Petersburg worker of the time, interrogated his work companions about their home lives. Eleven out of eighteen were married and all their wives lived in villages. But one man had lived in the city for five years without ever seeing his wife or children, while another had been visited by his wife just once, before which they had not seen each other for four years.[52] These were the worst cases, but severely depleted family life of this sort was commonplace all across industrialising Russia.

The life of male workers in Russian cities was one of very long hours, very low wages, high risk of accident, and rough male companionship. Semyon Kanachikov has left us a vivid description of his first weeks as an apprentice at the Gustav List engineering works in Moscow:

> We rented the apartment communally, as an *artel* [a work crew or associa-tion] of about fifteen men [. . .] I was put in a tiny, dark, windowless corner room; it was dirty and stuffy, with many bedbugs and fleas, and the strong stench of 'humanity'. The room contained two cots. One belonged to Korovin, my countryman and guardian; the other I shared with Korovin's son Vanka, who was also an apprentice and worked in the factory's pattern shop. Our food and the woman who prepared it were also paid for communally [. . .] All fifteen men ate from a common bowl with wooden spoons [. . .] After the soup came either buckwheat kasha with lard or fried potatoes. Everyone was hungry as a wolf; they ate quickly, greedily.[53]

The artel of men workers, though offering protection and solidarity, was a poor substitute for a family. Come payday or a public holiday, the dominant form of male bonding and practically the only form of entertainment was to get drunk on beer. Kanachikov recalled that in the Smolensk factory neigh-bourhood, 'Twice a month on the Saturday paydays, our *artel* indulged in wild carousing.' Everyone would return home late at night or on Sunday morning, 'sombre, cross, often bruised.'[54]

By no means all workers were men. By 1901 26.8 per cent of those in factory employment in the Russian Empire were women, rising by 1914 to some 31.7 per cent, or some 663,000 workers.[55] As in western Europe many of these were seasonal workers in rural industries, especially textile mills. Peasant girls lived in dormitories, worked long hours for a few months and returned to their villages when there was no more work for them to do.

Many others, however, began to make a life for themselves in the cities. Theirs was an extremely harsh and often dangerous existence. Women worked in the garment and tobacco industries, as cooks and domestic servants, as laundresses and washerwomen. Many finished up as prostitutes. In St Petersburg on the eve of the 1905 revolution there were an estimated 30,000–50,000 prostitutes in a city with a population of more than 1.5 million.[56]

Slowly, the separate worlds of men and women workers met. In the face of every difficulty, a minority began to establish more settled patterns of home life, especially in St Petersburg.[57] Sons succeeded fathers in the same shop or factory and the new generation began to leave the countryside behind them. They encountered formidable obstacles in doing so – the cost of housing in working-class quarters, which rose rapidly after 1905, the absence of running water in apartments, the impossibility of keeping clothing, children and adults clean, and the lack of public transport to take them to work. The workplaces of female factory hands – tobacco and textile factories – were often on the opposite side of the city to the machine and metalworking plants of their men. If workers had to commute, they did so by foot, beginning at five in the morning. If they had children, family organisation became even more difficult. A male worker at the Prokhorov factory in Moscow remembered how he took his baby child each day to the factory gates: 'My wife would come out, take the baby and go home with him, and I'd go to work. We'd do that everyday, whatever the weather.'[58]

In order to have a family and ensure its survival, many women gave up factory work – if they could afford to do so – and concentrated on childcare and house-work. Statistics showed that infant mortality rates were much lower when a wife was no longer a factory worker. To make ends meet, the couple would often take in boarders, and this created new problems of every sort. Spatial ones, because workers' living quarters were already cramped enough without having to sublet a room by the bed or even by the corner to single workers or other families. Emotional ones, because living in such asphyxiating proximity gave rise to quar-rels of every sort. And physical ones, because the wife was transformed into a *khozyayka*, a landlady. She had to look after the running of the entire apartment, cook for the boarders, bring in the wood and water, as well as care for her children and husband. A *khozyayka* was notoriously pale and worn out by her labours.

In these dark, malodorous apartment blocks, each room a testimony to personal tragedy – a drunken husband, the death of a beloved child, the exhaustion and illness of a mother – working-class families were perforce nuclear in structure, even though in both Moscow and its provinces, given the numerous presence of boarders and artels, households remained very large.[59] Some couples kept just one child in the city with them, sending any others back to the countryside to be with their grandparents. Illegal abortion, with all its inherent risks, was widely practised by working-class women. Men suffered too, but their horizons were less housebound than their women's and they found it easier to escape – in drinking bouts and male camaraderie. When the socialist movement began to put down roots, the gap between men and women often widened. Female militants existed but they were few and far between. Women were far more illiterate than men. As Barbara Engel has written, 'A woman migrant from the village might live for decades in the city and remain unable to decipher a street sign, or read an advertisement, or scratch her name on a piece of paper.'[60] They were left behind, at home, by socialism and it frightened them terribly – if a husband was arrested the whole family could perish or be dispersed within a few months.

In her pre-war pamphlet *Sexual Relations and the Class Struggle*, Kollontai showed herself convinced that in the search for 'healthier' relations between the sexes it was necessary to look not to the bourgeois quarters of a great city but 'at the huddled dwellings of the working class'. There, 'amidst the horror and squalor of capitalism, amidst tears and curses, the springs of life are welling up'.[61] This was the comment not of a stupid or ignorant woman, but of one convinced that the future liberation of humanity could be achieved only by the 'progressive and revolutionary class'. In the hovels of St Petersburg, however, the welling up of 'springs of life' could barely be discerned. Men and women were divided by grinding poverty, by impossible hours of work and by constant exhaustion and ill-health. Kollontai dreamed of a 'radical re-education in our psyche',[62] of an end to women's submission and suffering, of healthy relations between male and female comrades, living communally and working together for a new society. But there was little evidence of the potential for all this in the family lives and social realities I have just described. Nor was a single *political* revolution, even the most famous of the twentieth century, ever likely to make so gargantuan a transformative leap.

4. The First World War

The rural and urban realities of family life were turned completely upside down by the outbreak of the First World War. As in all other parts of Europe, the war, with its massive mobilisations of young men – some fifteen million in the Russian case, 80 per cent of whom were from peasant families – cast its long and doom-laden shadow over what had been the very harsh but mainly peaceful daily life of the population. It exacted a price in terms of human suffering that could not even have been conceived of at the beginning of the war. An estimated 1,660,000 Russian citizens were killed, died in hospitals or disappeared without trace. Some historians put the figure still higher. It can be compared with the 767,000 men lost by the British Empire as a whole, the more than 600,000 Italians, the 1,383,000 French and the 1,686,000 Germans, these last suffering very heavily from waging war on two fronts. The modern world had never witnessed such appalling loss of life, deriving not from natural disaster but from collective human choice, if such it can be called. 'Half the seed of Europe, one by one', to use Wilfred Owen's haunting words, was wiped out.[63] This terrible cataclysm was to shape each of the national stories here recounted (with the exception of Spain, which wisely declared its neutrality), though not, as we shall see, in the same way.

The Russian peasants went to fight for 'Christ and Holy Russia', but without the enthusiasm and 'hurrah-patriotism' which accompanied mobilisations in the West. After some initial success, all the weaknesses of the Russian army's organisation, especially of its supply lines, came to the fore. Shortages of food, boots, overcoats and above all arms sapped morale very fast. In 1915 soldiers wrote home with increasing bitterness:

> It is very bad now. We haven't received bread for two weeks, only rusks; that's what we are expected to fight on. There is a shortage of rusks too and no snuff at all. [. . .]
>
> I am at my post all the time – frozen, soaked and, on top of all that, hungry as a dog. Some days I have nothing to eat but bread. What a waste of energy and health! [. . .]
>
> They feed us very badly. We walk barefoot or in rope-soled shoes. It's incredible that soldiers of the Russian army are in rope-soled shoes![64]

By August 1915, up to 30 per cent of the Russians at the front were without arms and ammunition. Often the soldiers were sent 'over the top' armed only with a bayonet fixed to an empty rifle. Casualties were massive and the second line of Reservists had to be called up, many of whom were family men. There were drunken protests and riots at the recruiting stations. Alexey Brusilov, one of the most brilliant of the Russian frontline generals, described in tragic terms the quality and motivation of the reinforcements he had received:

> Time after time I asked my men in the trenches why we were at war; the inevitable senseless answer was that a certain Archduke and his wife had been murdered and that consequently the Austrians had tried to humiliate the Serbians. Practically no one knew who these Serbians were; they were equally doubtful as to what a Slav was [. . .] They had never heard of the ambitions of Germany; they did not even know that such a country existed.[65]

From this time onwards, the army, in Brusilov's opinion, became 'a sort of badly trained militia'.[66] In June 1915 the Germans broke through decisively and their offensive was only halted in September by the Russian mud. During their headlong retreat from Galicia about a million Russian soldiers surrendered. At the same time hundreds of thousands of families fled eastwards before the advancing armies.[67]

Throughout 1916 the letters from the front reflect two connected themes: first, the conscripts, or rather the minority of them who were literate, write continuously of how tired they are of the war and how much they wish to be reunited with their families; and secondly, they explicitly blame the officers, generals and politicians for the seemingly endless tragedy that has enveloped them. In the peasant mind, the war came ever more to be seen as a punishment from God – not for their own sins, but for those of the ruling class. Here, as on other fronts, the protracted fighting and constant presence of death exercised a traumatic and often brutalising effect on both men and officers. Plundering, robbery and rape were commonplace, as were punitive expeditions against the Jews.

The overall effect of this catastrophic sequence of events upon families and family life has never been systematically charted. Obviously, not all families fared in the same way. In the extended families of the *dvor*, the absence – even the death – of one or more sons could be absorbed with difficulty, but for an urban nuclear family the departure of the husband and father to the front was a major disaster. The Moscow and Petrograd court lists for 1915 register a marked rise in the detention of homeless girls, ten out of every hundred of whom were prostitutes. Gennady Bordyugov writes, 'Mothers often quietly obeyed their "fallen" daughters for they were materially dependent upon them.'[68]

Of course, geography mattered a great deal. Rural families in the south- and north-west of the Empire were those most at risk. All too easily, as they fled before invading armies, families could fragment and disappear. I will deal below with the terrible plight of abandoned and homeless children, the *besprizornyye*, who by 1921–2 numbered somewhere between four and seven million. In Russia the imperial war gave way almost immediately to civil war, with consequences that far exceeded those in other belligerent countries, the Ottoman Empire included. Jay Winter has noted convincingly the way in which in western Europe, in spite of the millions of dead and crippled, conditions were created which acted not to weaken but rather to strengthen family ties and the institution of marriage.[69] The same cannot be said of the East.

By the winter of 1916–17 the Russian armies were ready for rebellion. The head of the Petrograd military censorship commission wrote in November of the growing discontent 'arising from the internal political situation of the country'. A few months later, in February 1917, the overthrow of autocracy was seen by peasant soldiers as the long-awaited opportunity to free themselves from the hated war: 'Now we have all come to life.'[70] Eight months later the Bolsheviks were in power.

5. Traditions and passions

Before examining the specific areas in which the Bolsheviks tried to change family life and relations in the period 1917–20, I must say something about the

Marxist tradition from which they came. The entire way in which Marxism developed as an intellectual and political endeavour militated against its exploring the terrain of family life in depth. Marx himself paid scant attention to the role of families in history. In his famous youthful critique of Hegel's *Philosophy of Right* he chose to concentrate his fire only on that part of Hegel's work which deals with the state, leaving aside completely the preceding sections on the family and civil society.[71] This early neglect was never remedied. Marx ascribed families to the superstructure of any given society, rather than to its economic base, with the result that families were not considered a natural site for politics or accorded any autonomous historical agency. Instead, according to Marx, they reflected in their forms and culture the dominant economic and social relations of the time. When these latter changed, so too would families.[72] As a consequence, on the rare occasions when families appear in Marx's reflections, they do so not as agents but as social entities which reflect other, more important realities.

This subordinate, even forgotten place in Marxist theory meant that Marxist revolutionaries, including the Bolsheviks, were pretty vague about what family life might look like after the revolution. Would families and private households be abolished, and, if they were, what would replace them? Was there to be any domestic property after the revolution or did the 'abolition of private property' entail the end of all possessions and inheritance? In a Communist society, what was to be the relationship between parents and children? These were hardly secondary questions, but they never received adequate answers. Indeed, they were rarely discussed at all.

The Communist Manifesto (1848) did little to help matters. In it, Marx and Engels launched an excoriating attack upon the 'bourgeois family', lamented with considerable justification that capitalism rendered proletarian family life all but impossible, but wrote almost nothing about the family-to-be. There is an aside to the effect that they intended to 'replace home education by social', but no elaboration upon the theme.[73] In his 'Principles of Communism', written in October 1847, Engels went a little further. Communist society would advocate 'the education (*Erziehung*) of all children, as soon as they are old enough to do without the first maternal care, in national institutions and at the expense of the nation'. The use of the term 'Erziehung' was significant, implying as it did not only formal education but any training of children, including that normally given by parents.[74] When, according to Engels, communal education was linked to the abolition of private property, then the twin foundations of hitherto existing marriage – the dependence of the wife upon the husband and that of children upon their parents – would disappear.[75]

These suggestions announced the death knell of the family, but in the long London years, right up to Marx's death in 1883, neither he nor Engels ever returned to the question. It was only when Engels came across the copious notes that Marx had left on the work of the American anthropologist Lewis Henry Morgan that he was inspired to return to the theme. The outcome, however – *The Origins of the Family, Private Property and the State* (1884) – was primarily a work of history and anthropology, not politics.[76] It aimed to demonstrate, with Morgan's help, how in the distant past communal social relations had predominated, involving greater sexual freedom and allowing women a much more authoritative role. It was only with the ancient Greeks and the introduction of private property that women became clearly subjugated to men. Morgan's theses, supplemented by those of the Austrian anthropologist Johann Bachofen, appealed greatly to Engels for at least two reasons: they demonstrated, first, that the family was not immutable in history, but rather proceeded through a whole series of stages, exactly as Marx had outlined with regard to economic relations,[77] and, secondly, that it was far from historical truth to state that women had always been subjugated to men. The matriarchal societies studied by Bachofen 'proved' the opposite. Engels ended on a rousing note: the new 'higher plane of society [. . .] will be a revival, in superior form, of the liberty, equality and fraternity of the ancient *gentes*'.[78] This sounded impressive, but it was hardly a serious attempt to answer the thorny questions concerning the organisation of private life in a post-revolutionary society.

Marx and Engels, then, left a very uncomfortable legacy, for it combined extremism with considerable vagueness. As the working-class parties of Marxist inspiration increased their influence all across Europe at the end of the nineteenth century, it became clear that there was no consensus amongst industrial workers over the 'abolition of the family', or on future relations between family life, private households and public space. At the time, the most widely read text on this subject was August Bebel's *Woman under Socialism* (1879), which offered a compromise on the spiky questions raised above: 'Domestic life', Bebel wrote, 'will be limited to the strictly necessary, while great space will be reserved for the needs of sociality.'[79] What this meant was that family life and private domestic space were to be maintained, but in view of the parlous conditions of working-class households as much time as possible would be spent outside the home, in the structures and palaces of a rapidly expanding working-class civil society. The great 'Houses of the People', constructed in Germany and Holland and Belgium, with their theatres and public baths, their night classes and dance halls, gymnasia and libraries, are testimony to a very serious attempt to dissolve family deprivation and ignorance into collective spaces and activities, without thereby abolishing the family itself. Victor Horta, the architect of the famous and beautiful Maison du Peuple in Brussels (1899), wrote in his memoirs, 'The theme was interesting: to construct a palace that was not a palace but a real "house", whose air and light would constitute the luxury so long denied to the workers in their hovels.'[80]

As for the Bolsheviks, it would be fair to say that before the revolution of 1917 they had neither the breadth of mind nor the freedom of action to address such themes. Theirs was a tiny clandestine party, without the liberty or material resources of its counterparts in western Europe. In any case, its male leaders, Lenin in the first place, had no interest in the question of the family at all. There were more important things to debate and analyse – the form of the party, the development of capitalism in Russia, and so on.

The emancipation of women, on the other hand, had more solid bases in their traditions, though very oriented to industrial production. Women had to be freed from domestic slavery and have the possibility of becoming workers, enjoying equal rights and pay alongside their male companions. The great agent of women's socialisation for Marx and Engels was thus to be the factory, not the family. In his major work on the development of capitalism in Russia, written at the end of the nineteenth century, Lenin followed the same line. The 'patriarchal isolation' of women, he wrote, would be fatally undermined by drawing them into production: 'large-scale machine industry stimulates their development and increases their independence'. As a result the 'narrow circle of domestic, family relations' would be destroyed, but quite what was to take its place was never made clear.[81]

Another, crucial aspect of women's (and men's) liberation, that of sexuality and love, was totally ignored. Kollontai's themes, of natural love and of ideal relations between the sexes, were regarded with embarrassment and derision, especially as the canonical texts of Marxism had nothing to offer on the subject. Male Russian revolutionaries took love and life much as they found them. Accustomed to long years in exile, to imprisonment and to Siberia, they acquired as a group no special sensibility to interpersonal relations and still less to family life. Male comradeship and service to the cause predominated in their lives.

Lenin himself was married to Nadezhda (Nadia) Krupskaya. Theirs was a union of comrades, based on affection rather than passion, and on her total devotion – and submission – to him. They had no children. It has often been said that the revolution was Lenin's only child, and this is certainly true. But it has also to be said that Lenin had one carefully hidden, passionate relationship in his life – that with his lover, Inessa Armand. Inessa was in some ways more extraordinary than Kollontai. The French-born daughter of an opera singer, she married into the wealthy Armand family, which had settled in Moscow province and owned several wool-weaving and dyeing factories. In 1893, the same year that Aleksandra Domontovich married Vladimir Kollontai, Inès (Inessa) Stéphane, then aged nineteen, married Alexander Armand, with whom she rapidly had four children. But this young mother nurtured a deep romantic and intellectual attraction not for her husband but for his younger brother, Vladimir. They went to live together and Inessa had a fifth child, Andrey, by him. In 1909, Vladimir died tragically of consumption.

Inessa Armand and Aleksandra Kollontai shared the same deep-founded restlessness and the same absolute dedication to the Marxist cause. In Inessa's case, more than in Aleksandra's, a terrible tension developed in her life – between her love for her children and the febrile political activity that led her far away from them, into Europe and more than once into harsh prison conditions. But she would renounce neither her family nor her politics. Just before the outbreak of the Great War she was holidaying with four of her children at the Adriatic town of Lovran, still part of the Austro-Hungarian Empire. It was one of those fleeting, sunlit moments of family life which she and her children were to remember for the rest of their lives. Then suddenly Austria and Russia were at war. Armand had to move fast to get her children, now enemy aliens, on to a boat at Genoa and back to Russia. Once it was done she returned to the

fig. 3 Inessa Armand in 1910 with her five children.

house in Lovran to clear up: 'I went back with a sore heart,' she wrote to them; 'it was so empty and I was sad to see the bare table in the dining room and not to hear your happy voices and your laughter. I was sad to look at the things you left behind, sad to enter your rooms now so empty.'[82] She was not to see her children again for nearly three years, though she wrote to them with constancy and passion. Throughout this time, her estranged husband Alexander, without doubt the silent hero of this unconventional family tale, continued to look after all the children and send her money regularly.[83]

Almost certainly, Lenin and Armand became lovers in 1911, at a Bolshevik summer school at Longjumeau in France. The 'almost certainly' is de rigueur, for the precise contours of their relationship have never been established. The Communist authorities subsequently did their best to bury the whole story and many letters have been censored or destroyed. Lenin himself insisted, in June 1914, that as a precautionary measure Inessa bring him all the letters he had written to her. Their relationship flared and subsided by turn. Inessa loved Lenin above all for his great political intelligence and charisma. But she also found his hectoring tones and authoritarianism unbearable, and would then be forced to take her distance from him. At the end of 1913 Lenin decided that their relationship must end, probably to protect Krupskaya from the consequences of his passion. Armand wrote to him from Paris, in one of the very few intimate letters that has survived, 'Even here I could cope without your kisses if only I could see you. To talk with you sometimes would be such a joy for me – and this would not cause pain to anyone. Why deprive me of that? You asked me if I was angry with you for "carrying through" our separation. No, for I don't think that it was for your own sake that you did it.'[84]

In 1914 a sharp exchange took place between Armand and Lenin concerning a pamphlet she was trying to write on love and the family. Armand was an ardent feminist who had contributed much while in exile to the preparation of Rabotnitsa, a radical periodical devoted to women's issues. The draft of her pamphlet has been lost. What has survived instead are Lenin's comments, which are revealing. With his usual surgical technique, he honed in on the call for 'free love' which Armand had made in the pamphlet. He judged this as totally inappropriate and quite unclear, and proceeded to make a list of ten possible ways in which the phrase could be interpreted. He finished in brutal style: 'What matters is not what you subjectively "want to understand" by it; what matters is the objective logic of class relations in matters of love.'[85]

This obtuse phrase, so soaked in dogma, certainly has less meaning than Armand's 'free love'. It encapsulates Lenin's resistance to any serious consideration of connections between sexual relations, families and socialist revolution. An eminent biographer of Lenin, Louis Fischer, has pointed rightly to the way

Lenin's political radicalism cohabited with his personal conservatism.[86] In his personal life, which he believed to be entirely separate from his public one, he behaved like a respectable, if not impeccable, Victorian (Victorians, it should perhaps be added, were not usually impeccable). Even if it was for honourable reasons – the desire to protect Krupskaya – that he was anxious to hide away his one great passion, he was certainly too much inclined to bully the women – and men – closest to him. Lenin had many comrades but almost no friends. These were not promising bases on which to build the New Socialist Order, as both Armand and Kollontai, comrades and rivals, were to discover.

II. DURING THE REVOLUTION

1. Kollontai as commissar

We left Kollontai sitting on an Oslo tram in February 1917, staring at the headlines of someone else's newspaper. She quickly returned to Russia and in the months that followed threw herself into the extraordinary events of the revolution. From April to October 1917 she consistently backed Lenin's line on the need to pass immediately from bourgeois to proletarian revolution, from the initial revolution of February, which had seen the deposition of the Tsar, to a second revolution organised and led by the Bolsheviks. 'Theory, my friend, is grey', Lenin had proclaimed on his arrival at Petrograd (quoting Goethe's *Faust*), 'but green is the tree of life.' The chance had to be taken, whatever the consequences. On 10 October 1917, when Lenin urged the immediate seizure of power at the Central Committee of the Bolshevik party, Kollontai was by his side. A month later, on 13 November, she was appointed Commissar of Public Welfare – the only woman in Lenin's Council of People's Commissars. Inessa Armand, by contrast, spent most of 1917 in Moscow. In August she chose to return to the family estate in Pushkino, to be with her son Andrey, now thirteen, who was suffering from suspected tuberculosis. She was to remain there during the crucial months of the October revolution.

Kollontai's activity as Commissar for Public Welfare, which lasted only a few months, was characterised by the wealth of her ambition and the poverty of her resources. The Commissariat, which had previously been called the Ministry for State Charity, was responsible for foundling and old people's homes, orphanages and hospitals, as well as welfare programmes for hundreds of thousands of war-disabled soldiers. Its responsibility for the manufacture and sale of playing cards and tobacco gave it some much-needed but absolutely inadequate income. The many emergencies of revolution and civil war made demands which were impossible to meet.[87]

Kollontai did her best. In January 1918 she founded a Central Office for Maternity and Infant Welfare. Its purpose was to reduce Russia's terrible rates of infant mortality by introducing hygienic and scientific care for mother and child, both before and after birth. Working mothers were to be given adequate maternity leave for the first time. Here at last, proclaimed Kollontai, there had dawned the 'radiant epoch where the working class can build, with its own hands, forms of child care that will not deprive a child of its mother or a mother of her child'.[88]

Within her Commissariat, Kollontai, aware of her own administrative inexperience, formed an auxiliary council composed of doctors, jurists and experts of various sorts. Each day a constant flow of people sought her help for their individual problems. By the end of the day she would return exhausted to the little flat she shared with her son Misha and her loyal friend Zoya. Louise Bryant, a sympathetic and acute American witness to the revolution, noted at a later date,

[Madame Kollontai] is so carried away by her enthusiasm that she is unmindful of how easily wings are broken in this age of steel. But if her inspiration, which aims to lift women to the skies, lifts them only from their knees to their feet, there will be nothing to regret. Civilisation, in its snail-like progress, is only stirred to move its occasional inch by the burning desire of those who will to move it a mile.[89]

Her impetuousness also led her to make mistakes. In mid-January 1918 she tried to requisition the wealthy Aleksandr Nevsky monastery in Petrograd in order to transform it into a home for war invalids. The need was acute, but the regular and lay clergy mobilised violently against her. When Kollontai called in sailors to take over the monastery, fighting broke out and a priest was killed. Lenin was furious, for Kollontai had not consulted him and he did not want the new regime to face religious war on top of everything else.[90] In fact, the distance between Lenin and Kollontai was now to grow rapidly. When the Brest-Litovsk treaty with Germany, which made very large territorial concessions in return for peace, was ratified on 18 March 1918, Kollontai announced her resignation as commissar.

Power may have proved all too ephemeral for her, but her anomalous and attractive figure nevertheless continued to attract many comments and much attention. John Reed underlined her oratorical powers but also her femininity and humanity.[91] Louise Bryant noted that she was 'slim and pretty and vivacious'.[92] Jacques Sadoul, who had arrived as an attaché to the French military mission in 1917, was one of many men who felt a deep sexual attraction to her.[93]

Kollontai had no time for the likes of Sadoul. She had fallen in love with Pavel Dybenko, a sailor of modest peasant origins, one of the leaders of agitation in the Baltic navy and the newly appointed Commissar for Naval Affairs. It was Dybenko's sailors whom Kollontai had called on to occupy the Aleksandr Nevsky monastery. For Kollontai, Dybenko was the very embodiment of proletarian virility. She was forty-five years old and he twenty-eight. She lived out with him her idea of 'winged Eros', sexual comradeship and shared service to the cause. Later she wrote, 'Our meetings always overflowed with joy, our partings were full of torment, emotion, broken hearts. Just this strength of feeling, the ability to live fully, passionately, strongly, drew me powerfully to Pavel.'[94]

In the photograph of Lenin's Council of People's Commissars of 1918 we can discern Kollontai's diminutive figure seated at Lenin's left, and next to the council's female stenographer. The bearded Dybenko towers up behind her, as if to protect her in that fierce assembly of male revolutionaries. In reality, it was she who protected him. Dybenko was arrested in March 1918 for allegedly having abandoned his command on the front line against the Germans.

fig. 4 Council of People's Commissars, early 1918. Kollontai is seated at Lenin's left, Dybenko stands behind her.

Kollontai secured his bail and he was later acquitted of all charges, though for a time expelled from the party. Furthermore, when Dybenko asked Kollontai to marry him, she accepted, in the face of all her principles and the heated opposition of Misha and Zoya.[95]

Kollontai was never again to rise so high in Lenin's party, and she and Dybenko were gradually marginalised. Yet to the end of her days she remembered these first few months of revolution as the dream time of her life – 'months of the real romanticism of Revolution', as she wrote in her autobiography.[96] She and Trotsky (and even Lenin sometimes) were convinced that their revolution would share the fate of the Paris Commune of 1871, which had been crushed after only seventy-one days in a terrible bloodbath. Hers was a testimony for the future: 'The feeling that helped us was that all we produced, even if it was no more than a decree, would come to be a historical example and help others move ahead.'[97]

2. Family laws and family lives: the Code of 1918

In her work on the history of family law, Mary Ann Glendon has referred to the interaction between 'two moving systems': on the one hand, the laws affecting the family, and on the other, actual family life.[98] Theirs is a complex and fascinating relationship to which I shall return often during the course of this work. Sometimes governments legislate in a way that is far in advance of families' social and cultural conditions, with all sorts of surprising and even tragic results. Sometimes the law instead lags behind the realities of family life, blocking trends that are already manifest in society. Both tendencies are present in this book. In the case of the Russian Communists, as in that of the Turkish nationalists of Mustafa Kemal, new family legislation ran way beyond customary practice, especially in the countryside.

Family law regulates, or tries to regulate, many different aspects of family life: relations between men and women and between parents and children, marriage and divorce, abortion, inheritance, alimony, adoption, and so on. In the Bolshevik case it is necessary to add another aspect, specific to their political ambition – the reorganisation of families' daily life, with much greater emphasis placed on the public and collective spheres at the expense of the familial and domestic. As we have seen, there was no clear consensus among the Bolsheviks about 'abolishing' the family. However, all agreed, Lenin included, that Communism's life blood beat primarily in the public sphere, not the private one.

Like all Family Codes, the Bolshevik one of September 1918, taken together with the piecemeal measures that preceded and followed it, had as its targets certain aspects of family life rather than others. In particular, it introduced really radical changes in marriage and divorce, in women's and children's rights, in the laws of inheritance and in those governing abortion. It is worth examining each in turn.

The Orthodox Church's centuries-old control over marriage procedures and rules was abolished.[99] All authority over these matters passed to the local courts of the new state. Civil marriage was thus introduced for the first time in December 1917, and it was under the new provisions that Kollontai married Dybenko. It is not true, as some commentators have written, that civil marriage took the place of religious marriage. The two continued to exist side by side, but all legal authority concerning such matters was thenceforth exercised by the state, not the Church. Divorce proceedings were likewise revolutionised. Article 81 of the Code stated simply, 'The mutual consent of the husband and wife or the desire of either of them to obtain a divorce shall be considered a ground for divorce.'[100] If the couple were in agreement, the procedure was a simple bureaucratic one. If they were not, the case had to be heard in public before a local judge (Article 93), but even here no serious impediment to the dissolution of the marriage was introduced.

In the second place, women's equality with men was vigorously proclaimed, both within marriage and outside it. This was not an absolutely symmetrical equality: the age of marriage was sixteen for females and eighteen for males. The parties to marriage could, however, choose either the husband's or the wife's name, or else use a joint surname. Men and women were to enjoy equal property rights and either could be head of household. Parental authority was to be exercised jointly (Article 150). If an unmarried mother could correctly identify the father of her child, 'the court shall deem him to be the father and at the same time compel him to share in the expenses connected with the gestation, delivery, and maintenance of the child.'[101] The question of alimony, as we shall see, was to become the object of heated discussion in 1926.

As for children's rights, no discrimination was thenceforth to distinguish 'legitimate' from 'illegitimate' children. Parents had the right to decide 'on the upbringing and instruction of their children', but they could not contract employment for a child aged sixteen to eighteen without his or her consent (Article 157).[102] Adoption was forbidden, on the grounds that orphans would be better off in state orphanages than in individual families. The architects of the Code feared that adopted children in rural families would continue to be ruthlessly exploited.

The third area of radical change – the first two being marriage provisions and individual rights – concerned inheritance. Here the new Code was terse, even lapidary, in its pronouncement. Article 160 reads, 'Children have no right to the property of their parents, or parents to the property of their children.'[103] Behind this extraordinary statement, which abolished at a stroke all the ancient inheritance customs of imperial Russia and undermined the whole basis of rural patriarchal property, lay the hard kernel of Bolshevik ideology. Communism could be constructed only in a property-less society.

This was, however, easier said than done. In the Family Code – and the decree of 27 April 1918 that preceded it – an important exception to the 'abolition of property' was already being made. Article 129 stated that small properties not exceeding 10,000 rubles in value, consisting of 'a house, furniture, working implements for agricultural or trade purposes', could pass to the surviving spouse and relatives of the deceased.[104] Priority was given to them over any creditors' claims on the estate. Aleksandr Goikhbarg, a young jurist who was the principal architect of the Code, and who was later to be liquidated in Stalin's Purges, explained the reasoning behind this provision: 'While we were abolishing the private right of inheritance, it was impossible not to take into account the existence of individual families and the fact that free education and maintenance of children has not yet been thoroughly accomplished and that the social insurance of all persons incapable of work has not yet been secured.'[105]

Two other important reforms must be mentioned here. The first was that abortion was legalised on 18 November 1920. The decree of that date noted that while in the past clandestine abortions had led to up to 30 per cent of women being infected in the course of the operation, and up to 4 per cent of deaths, thenceforth abortions were 'to be performed freely and without any charge in Soviet hospitals'.[106]

The other reform concerned the legal position of homosexuals. There was little in the Russian tradition to compare with the increased policing of sex between men which was to be found in France, Britain and Germany in the second half of the nineteenth century. Sodomy was condemned by law in tsarist Russia but little interest was shown in enforcing the law in this area, and cases of 'lesbian love' were simply ignored. With the introduction of the new Soviet Criminal Code in 1922, sodomy between consenting adults was decriminalised. Here again, as in other parts of early Soviet legislation on the private sphere, the prevailing attitudes appear to be more permissive than repressive, although it is hard to find any evidence for the enthusiastic acceptance of departures from heterosexual norms. The comparison with some western countries is revealing: in Germany the crime of 'unnatural vice' carried a maximum sentence of five years, while in Britain 'buggery' could result in life imprisonment.[107]

Overall, the new Soviet legislation on family and private life was deeply radical. The degree of equality afforded to women, for instance, was far in

advance of that offered by western European codes of the same date. In France
and Italy it was not until 1975 that women and men enjoyed broadly equal
rights in the family and that male headship of the family was abolished. The
same sort of story can be told for children's rights. In the area closest to
Kollontai's heart, however – that of building *alternatives* to the family, of
creating communal living arrangements, a collectivist ethos and liberated
sexual relations – the jurists remained silent. Their doing so reflected both
majority thinking within the Bolshevik party and a deeper uncertainty as to
how to treat such themes.

Aleksandr Goikhbarg defended the Code from its critics by underscoring
that it represented transitional legislation in transitional times – history would
in any case soon sweep away the last vestiges of the old family and all its backwardness, and the law would become increasingly unnecessary.[108] History, as
we shall soon see, behaved in quite a different manner.

Many commentators have defined the Code as more liberal than socialist,
but 'liberal' is not really the right adjective. Classic liberalism, with only a few
exceptions, such as John Stuart Mill's famous *The Subjection of Women* (1869),
was not principally concerned with the rights of women and children. Neither
would any liberal, even Mill, have gone along with Article 160 of the Code,
abolishing inheritance.[109] The Code *is* confusing because it is a hybrid, on the
one hand astonishing in its promotion of individuals and their rights, on the
other ready to ascribe wide-ranging responsibilities and powers to the new
Bolshevik state, though the latter was not yet developed enough to become a
modern Leviathan.[110]

3. The Civil War, 1918–1920

The Family Code of 1918 was to be a crucial legal and cultural element in the
long-term formation of families in the Soviet Union. But in the short term
Russia was devoured by a conflict which exceeded even the First World War in
its horror and loss of life. The vast and terrible scale of the Civil War, with its
multiple actors, locations and atrocities, makes it very difficult to encompass
and recount. If we concentrate for a moment on the Bolsheviks then we see
that the events of the war highlighted the two *anima* of that political movement: on the one hand, the aspiration to revolutionary social transformation,
and on the other, the creation of a ruthless and highly centralised party and
war machine. These two aspects of the new regime explain both its appeal and
its survival. Indeed, they were intimately intertwined.[111]

Lenin had proclaimed, all too blithely, that the 'imperial war' would be
replaced by 'civil war', and that the rule of the propertied classes would swiftly

succumb to the dictatorship of the proletariat. No such thing happened. The combatants in the protracted war were not only Reds and Whites (the latter the armies loyal to the Tsar), but also contingents of foreign armies, Greens (independent peasant movements), Blacks (Nestor Makhno's anarchists) and nationalist movements. Many of these last – in Finland and Poland, Bessarabia, Estonia, Latvia and Lithuania – successfully broke away from the new state (at least until the Second World War). Others were less fortunate.

All these forces clashed with great violence, expecting no quarter and giving none. In some regions of European Russia, every provincial town had its piles of mutilated bodies, their hands and feet cut off, their eyes gouged out. As Catherine Merridale has written, 'Anyone who was able to do so wrote desperately to Moscow. "Do you know what is happening in the countryside?" a former comrade asked Lenin's friend and aide Vladimir Bonch-Bruevich in 1918. "Where is our honour?" wrote an ex-Bolshevik, despairing at the slaughter around him. "Where is our love of freedom?"'[112] Terror was commonplace on all sides, as was the shooting of prisoners of war and the massacre of civilians. One of the few eyewitness accounts, that of Nikolay Borodin, describes the fate of a group of Red prisoners of war, one in five of whom had been selected for execution. They were shot in front of a crowd of civilian onlookers: 'When their turn came, each condemned man quickly undressed, as soldiers do, and having put their folded clothes aside walked in their worn-out dirty underwear to their last resting place [. . .] Some crossed themselves with the orthodox cross, then all quickly disappeared into the grave.'[113]

At first it seemed as if the Bolsheviks would impose their authority with ease, but by the autumn of 1918, a year after the revolution, the situation had become desperate. Insufficient grain was reaching the urban markets, and with food severely rationed the city populations were beginning to die of cold and starvation. Meanwhile, the number and strength of anti-Bolshevik forces were becoming ever greater. In the face of these impelling circumstances, Lenin introduced a number of draconian measures, which went under the general heading of 'War Communism'. Centralisation and control from above were their keynotes. Requisitioning squads were sent from the cities to the country-side, with instructions to root out the 'hoarders' of grain and treat them with the utmost severity. The tax burden on the villages increased dramatically. At the same time, Lenin attempted to turn the poor peasantry against the rich. In May 1918 Committees of Poor Peasants (*kombedy*) were formed, ostensibly to lead the 'second stage' of socialist agrarian revolution but in reality to confis-cate provisions from the richer peasantry. But the *tempi* of peasant revolution could not be accelerated in this way, or the complex mechanisms that underlay their social solidarity so easily undermined.[114] By December of the same year the experiment had ended in ignominious failure.

In the end the Bolsheviks won the war, principally because they never lost control of the Russian heartlands, which contained the majority of the population, the industries necessary for the war effort, and the stores of old army and navy equipment. Their opponents, by contrast, had their strongholds only in the peripheries. The forcible enrolment of many tsarist officers also favoured the Bolshevik cause, as did the vast territorial expanses into which they could retreat in times of military adversity.[115] But the costs of the war were cataclysmic. Deaths in the fighting armies were estimated at 800,000, perhaps as many as 100,000 were killed behind the lines in the White and Red Terror, while an estimated two million died from cholera, typhus and typhoid in the period 1919–20 only. Worst of all was the famine that gripped the grain-producing regions of the south in 1921–2. In the spring of 1921 a terrible drought occurred in the Volga region, the southern Ukraine, the Crimea and the northern part of the Caucasus,[116] resulting in an estimated four million deaths. Adverse agricultural conditions were undoubtedly made much worse by the Bolshevik policy of indiscriminate requisitioning of seed stores, confiscation of farm animals and surrender of horses and carts to the army. In many areas grain could not be sown, in others it withered away. In his book on the Civil War, Ewan Mawdsley estimates a total death toll of around eight million, though he adds wisely that 'any attempt to count the Civil War dead makes depressing work, and does not even result in a reliable figure'.[117] Four to five times those killed in the First World War died in the Civil War.

What did all this mean for Russian families? Answering this question is rendered very difficult by the almost total absence of social, let alone family, history of the regions most affected. Matters are not helped by the positioning off-stage of the Civil War in many standard accounts of the period, especially those sympathetic to the Bolsheviks. It is as if the war was a separate episode, inevitable but necessary, which the Bolsheviks did well to win, and that was that.[118] In reality, the war not only killed but traumatised large sections of the rural population in the regions where it was fought. It also transformed demographic structures. The great Ukrainian famine, for instance, killed off nearly all children under the age of three. From one day to another slightly older children could find themselves orphans – quite possibly they were already without elder brothers and fathers, lost in the world war. If yours was a Jewish family trapped in the killer regions, especially those of the Cossacks, then the possibilities of an imminent pogrom were high. The front lines changed position with great rapidity and family groups frequently found themselves in the wrong place at the wrong time. The level of violence was extraordinarily high, with torture and arbitrary shootings everywhere to be found. One Bolshevik document of June 1921 from Tambov region, late on in the Civil War, gives us some idea of the menacing connections made between combatants and kin groups:

> The family in whose house a bandit is hiding is to be arrested and *exiled from the province*, and *the oldest working member of such a family is to be shot on the spot without trial* [. . .]
>
> If the family of a bandit succeeds in fleeing, *its property is to be distributed to the peasants who remain loyal to Soviet power, and the abandoned houses are to be burned* [all italics original].[119]

Later on in this work, I intend to look in some detail at the fate of families in another civil war, that of Spain between 1936 and 1939. A preliminary comparison of the two reveals, as is to be expected, points of contact and of separation. Numerically, the difference is very dramatic, the war in Spain costing 'only' half a million deaths – an enormity by most standards but not by those of the Russian Armageddon. The two cases also differ markedly in the nature of their victors. The Spanish Civil War sees the triumph of conservative forces with the Church very much at their forefront, while in Russia it is the usurper of the social order, the Communist Party, which emerges victorious – very much against the odds, especially as it had no equivalent of the International Brigades to help it along the way. This diverse outcome is in part explained if we compare the two *holy* wars – the Spanish and the Russian. The crusading discourse of the Spanish Church proves to be a far more potent mobiliser than anything the Orthodox Church could offer, in spite of high levels of religiosity being a stable part of the Russian rural tradition. The two civil wars were fought with the ferocity tragically characteristic of all civil wars. Neither of the two victors, or the many vanquished, distinguished themselves in terms of human rights, though we need to know much more, in comparative terms, about the extent to which women and children were spared. In Spain, as we shall see, the Church was reluctant to protest in any way the practices, including torture and rape, of Franco's army (especially his Moroccan troops). In Russia the Bolsheviks behaved with the same savagery as their opponents, with little regard for possible rules of conduct which might distinguish them from their enemies. Lastly and rather surprisingly, the two forces which most proclaimed radical social change – the Russian Communists and the Spanish anarchists – differed in their attitudes to family life. Whereas the Russian experience was rich with debate and innovation, the Spanish one was more mundane and limited.

4. Communism and the family

The innovative quality of the Russian debate on the family emerges very clearly in one of the most famous of all radical pamphlets on the subject – Kollontai's *Communism and the Family*, which grew out of a long speech she delivered at the First All-Russian Congress of Worker and Peasant Women, held in Moscow in November 1918, not long after the Family Code had become law.[120] The congress was an extraordinary event, organised by women such as Inessa Armand, Vera Golubeva and Kollontai herself. They had to face much scepticism from most of the male elite of the party – now called the Russian Communist Party (Bolsheviks) – which was opposed to women organising separately from their male comrades. In the event over 1,100 delegates turned up, far more than the organisers had thought possible in a time of civil war. Only 10 per cent of delegates were peasant women. As Beatrice Farnsworth has written, 'For many of the kerchiefed women in worn out boots, quilted or sheepskin jackets, and men's army greatcoats who gathered in the great columned hall of the House of Unions, the Moscow Congress of 1918, at which Lenin himself appeared, was the first – and greatest – political event of their lives.'[121]

Kollontai began her pamphlet by celebrating that part of the new Family Code of which she most approved – the introduction of divorce: 'Henceforth a working woman will not have to petition for months or even for years to secure the right to live separately from a husband who beats her and makes her life a misery with his drunkenness and violent behaviour.' Many working women, said Kollontai, had welcomed the measure, but there were others, totally reliant on their husbands, who were too frightened to divorce. The solution was to put more trust in the community and the state: 'a woman must accustom herself to seek and find support in the collective and in society, and not from the individual man'. She was always to be against alimony.[122]

Kollontai then went on to examine the different forms that the family had taken over the centuries, in order to show that no single domestic form was fixed once and for all, and that customs and habits could change over time. Once again she announced the imminent withering away of the family. In the conditions of revolutionary Russia '*the family is ceasing to be necessary either to its members or to the nation as a whole*' (her italics).[123] Of its former functions only two remained: women's housework and the upbringing of children. Both these responsibilities would now be assumed by the state. For the first, 'the working woman will not have to slave over the washtub any longer, or ruin her eyes in darning her stockings'. She would simply take her washing to 'central laundries' and 'special clothes-mending centres'. Liberated from housework, she would be able to 'devote her evenings to reading, attending meetings and concerts'. As for the rearing of children, that would also be the responsibility of the state: 'Here too, the workers' state will come to replace the family; society will gradually take upon itself all the tasks that before the revolution fell to individual parents.'[124]

If that last phrase sounded rather ominous, Kollontai was quick to deny the many rumours, circulated by the Orthodox Church and other opponents of the new regime, that the Communists intended to deprive mothers of their children and take them into state care: 'Working mothers have no need to be alarmed; communist society is not intending to take children away from their parents or to tear the baby from the breast of its mother, and neither is it planning to take violent measures to destroy the family. No such thing!'[125] The conclusion of the pamphlet, however, made a dramatic plea for the triumph of collective values over private ones, and of the 'great proletarian family' over the individual one. It was anything but reassuring for those who believed in the virtues of the nuclear family:

> The woman who takes up the struggle for the liberation of the working class must learn to understand that there is no more room for the old proprietary attitude which says: 'These are my children. I owe them all my maternal solicitude and affection; those are your children, they are no concern of mine and I don't care if they go hungry and cold – I have no time for other children' [. . .] The worker-mother must learn not to differentiate between yours and mine; she must remember that there are only our children, the children of Russia's communist workers.[126]

Kollontai ended the pamphlet with a revolutionary cry; not the French revolutionary cry of 'liberty, equality and fraternity', but rather one of 'equality, liberty and the comradely love of the new marriage'. On these bases women and men, workers and peasants, would stand together for the 'rebuilding of human society'.[127]

Communism and the Family lends itself to a number of comments. The first concerns the very strong *contraposition* that Kollontai establishes between individual families and collective forms of being together. It is as if she is telling us that we have to choose in draconian fashion between one and the other, rather than to seek possible connections between them. As a close corollary to this, Kollontai's vision allows almost no space for privacy. The Bolsheviks, indeed, never theorised privacy in any way. Life was to be lived to the full in the public sphere and in collective space. There was little or no space for 'family time' – in and for the family. Instead Kollontai stressed what she had called in 1914 the 'large family-society'.[128] But the use of such a phrase begged more questions than it answered and risked reducing to a mere hyphen the many complex strands of family-society relations.

Her vision of society was rather a peculiar one. Though she was one of the most libertarian of the Bolsheviks, her society was barely pluralist in political terms, and in that sense was not 'civil' at all. Rather it was holistic and hyperactive. For Kollontai, as for the other Bolshevik-Communists, the factory was *the* privileged site of society – the workplace of the future and the collective organiser par excellence. *Communism and the Family* is written very much with proletarian women in mind. There is no echo in it of peasant women's strong attachment to, and influence upon, domestic space.

Another striking, even disconcerting, element of the pamphlet is the *symmetry* that it accords to the two tasks still to be undertaken in order to supersede the family – the caring for children on a communal basis and the abolition of individual housework. It was as if the two transformations belonged to the same analytical framework, linked essentially by the responses which a scientific and progressive organisation of society could offer. But this was to underestimate drastically at a psychological level, and in a strangely superficial manner, the importance of parenthood, and of motherhood in particular. The fundamental question of the bonding between children and parents and the existence of family love, such as Kollontai herself bore for Misha throughout her life, was not treated in any depth at all.

Lastly, it is worth noting with admiration how doggedly Kollontai continued to insist that emotional and sexual relations between women and men, not just economic relations, were at the heart of liberation – both female and male. To raise the cry not only of liberty and equality but also of 'the comradely love of the new marriage' was an extraordinary thing to do at any time, let alone at the height of Russia's Civil War.

5. Imagining liberation

In March 1919 the Russian Communist Party (Bolsheviks) held its Eighth Party Congress. It also prepared the draft of a new party programme to replace the outdated one of 1903. Kollontai saw this as an excellent occasion to introduce new ideas regarding women's liberation and the future of families. Lenin was not at all of the same opinion. He felt this was not the time to raise questions about families, and he had his own view of what constituted liberation for women, a view that in part coincided with Kollontai's but to a great extent did not. Without doubt, his relationship with Inessa Armand, also an ardent feminist, prompted him to think, and occasionally to write, about these matters.

In a pamphlet of July 1919 Lenin expressed himself clearly.[129] For him the Russian woman, in spite of advances enshrined in the Family Code, continued to be a *'domestic slave'* (all italics are his). He went on, in the supercharged style so typical of his polemical works, *'Petty housework* crushes, strangles, stultifies and degrades her, chains her to the kitchen and the nursery, and she wastes her labour on barbarously unproductive, petty, nerve-wracking, stultifying and crushing drudgery.' For Lenin, and this was crucial, 'The real *emancipation of women*, real communism, will begin only where and when an all-out struggle begins [. . .] against this petty housekeeping, or rather when its *wholesale transformation* into a large-scale socialist economy begins.'[130] Here Lenin clearly derives women's emancipation from a dual economic process: first, the creation of public, collective services, and secondly, the consequent liberating of women to enable them to become full-time workers alongside their male comrades. Everywhere, he continues, *'shoots of communism'* are springing up: 'Public catering establishments, nurseries, kindergartens – here we have examples of these shoots, here we have the simple, everyday means, involving nothing pompous, grandiloquent or ceremonial which can *really emancipate women*.'[131] As in Kollontai's pamphlet, both housework and childcare are pinpointed. But there is in Lenin no discussion of a different concept of family life, or any reference to the creation of communes.

Above all, he had no patience with Kollontai's insistence that the rethinking of human relationships – including their sexual aspects – was an integral part of revolutionary praxis. In a famous conversation with Clara Zetkin in the Kremlin in 1920 he gave vent to his feelings on the matter. It is a testimony that must be treated with caution, in that Zetkin only published it four years later, with all the risks of distortion that distance entails. Even so, the passion and nuances of the conversation give it an air of authenticity. Lenin denounced with vehemence the excessive concentration upon sexual matters prevalent amongst the youth of both Germany – where Clara Zetkin was a prominent Communist leader – and Russia. 'I am an old man,' he said. 'I may be a morose ascetic [but] I do not like it.' He continued,

No doubt you have heard about the famous theory that in communist society satisfying sexual desire and the craving for love is as simple and trivial as 'drinking a glass of water'. A section of our youth has gone absolutely mad over this 'glass-of-water theory' [. . .] To be sure thirst has to be quenched. But would a normal person normally lie down in the gutter and drink from a puddle? Or even from a glass whose edge has been greased by many lips [. . .] Young people are particularly in need of joy and strength. Healthy sports, such as gymnastics, swimming, hiking, physical exercises of every description and

a wide range of intellectual interests is what they need [. . .] Promiscuity in
sexual matters is bourgeois. It is a sign of degeneration. The proletariat is a
rising class. It does not need an intoxicant to stupefy or stimulate it.[132]

Although there is no evidence that Kollontai ever used the 'glass of water'
analogy, the attack upon her ideas is evident. What is striking is the way in
which Lenin has grotesquely distorted them, using images such as the 'puddle'
and the glass 'greased by many lips'. Kollontai never advocated promiscuity
and indeed was much more open and honest about her sex life than Lenin was
about his. Her idea of 'the comradely love of the new marriage' was certainly
utopian, but it was greatly superior to Lenin's ad hoc approach and recommendation of 'gymnastics, swimming and hiking' as the solution. The uninten-
tional sexual innuendo of his reference to the proletariat as 'a rising class', not
in need of stimulants, is perhaps best left without comment.

The contest between Kollontai and Lenin was a very uneven one. At the
party congress Kollontai managed to get through a motion calling for the party
to fight for equal rights for women. In her autobiography she claimed this as a
great victory, but she had wanted more and her imagining of liberation, as we
have seen, went far beyond equal rights. Louise Bryant wrote, 'As for Lenin, he
has crushed her with his usual unruffled frankness.'[133]

It would be wrong to present this battle over the future of family politics as
being exclusive to these two protagonists. Other voices were raised in these
bitter and radical years. Very few of them followed Kollontai on to what was
the most original and attractive terrain of her thought – that of a new
'comradely love' and 'sexual morality'. Many more agreed with her drastic and
ill-thought-through positions on family and parental love. Thus, in a work of
1920, Aleksandr Goikhbarg, the principal author of the Family Code, encouraged parents to reject 'their narrow and irrational love for their children'.[134]
Nikolay Bukharin and Yevgeny Preobrazhensky were even more brutal in their
very well known *ABC of Communism*, published at the height of the Civil War.
Rarely have the relationships between individuals, families and society been so
slanted in favour of the last:

The individual can only live and thrive owing to the existence of society. The
child, therefore, belongs to the society in which it lives [. . .] From this point
of view, the parents' claim to bring up their own children, and thereby to
impress upon the children's psychology their own limitations, must not
merely be rejected, but must be absolutely laughed out of court [. . .] Of one
hundred mothers, we shall perhaps find one or two who are competent
educators. The future belongs to social education.[135]

At the end of the day, however, the higher echelons of the party were not inter-ested in the 'withering away' of the family, and were even less interested in recasting personal life.[136] There were far more important things to be done, the most essential of which was to survive, and win, the Civil War. After that came economic reconstruction and the laying of the economic bases for socialism. The family, as always in Marxism, could wait.

6. Avant-garde art and family life: the missing connection

In January 1918 the great Russian poet Aleksandr Blok declared, 'Let's begin again from scratch: let's act in a way so that our deceitful, squalid, boring and horrible lives will now become just, clean, beautiful and joyful.'[137] With the revolution came the hopes of the artists and intellectuals of the major cities that profound transformations would take place not just in politics and economics, but in the nature of daily life. Such ambitions were to remain unfulfilled. The Communists, as we have just seen, had little sensibility to questions of family life and the domestic sphere, and offered no encourage-ment to the artistic vanguards to treat of these themes in their work.

Vladimir Mayakovsky, soon to become known as the principal poet of the revolution, wrote,

> Communism it's not only on the land,
> in the mill, in the sweat of your toil.
> It's at home, at table, in family life and daily round.[138]

It was not true. The themes of family life and the 'daily round' never emerged fully into the open. Perhaps only in the arena of children's books, with the beau-tiful, laconic works of Vladimir Lebedev, did the avant-garde and the family come into contact.[139] In 1919–20, Lazar Markovich Lissitzky, better known as El Lissitzky, Kazimir Malevich and others formed the famous group called UNOVIS, an acronym for 'Affirmers of New Forms in Art'. They were eager to sustain the propaganda offensive of the regime, and their adherence to collec-tivist ideas was fanatical in tone. But the themes that the party leadership dictated – such as 'The workbenches of the depots and factories are waiting for you. Let us move production forward'[140] – had everything to do with production and little with domestic life, gender equality, or intimacy. Nor did the Proletkult Movement offer much more. Its historian, Lynn Mally, notes that the only family that really mattered to it was 'the surrogate family of the working-class', based on 'the conviviality of the shop floor and the comradeship of male workers' organi-sations'. Women and children were minor, almost missing, themes.[141]

Lenin himself had a quite narrowly instrumental view of art's function, concentrating on the need for its massive pedagogical presence in public life. Taking his point of departure from Tommaso Campanella's utopian *City of the Sun*, he noted that 'the walls of his ideal city are covered with frescoes which, serving youth as a graphic lesson in natural science and history, arouse civic feelings and in a word participate in the business of raising and educating the new generation [. . .] I have called what I am thinking of monumental propaganda.'[142] In harmony with these indications, in 1919 Vladimir Tatlin designed his *Monument to the Third International*, a leaning spiral tower constructed in steel, a symbol of dynamism, velocity and progress, very much in keeping with the aesthetic concerns, though not the politics, of the Italian Futurists.[143] Models of the monument proved extremely popular and were pulled through the streets on the occasion of public holidays and celebrations.

On such occasions the needs of the artistic avant-garde and those of the party coincided, but it was not always so, by any means. The most original artists moved rapidly from figurative to abstract art, to an aesthetics that privileged form rather than content, to the abandonment of decorative and descriptive features, to a masterly and disquieting use of photography. After Lenin's

fig. 5 A simplified version of Tatlin's *Monument to the Third International* (1919)
displayed in the streets of Moscow, 1927.

death, there was a national competition for the construction of a monument in his honour, as reported by *Art News* in April 1924:

> Malevich, who like all other Bolshevik artists has been working to express the greatness of Lenin in a model for his monument, proudly exhibited a huge pedestal composed of a mass of agricultural and industrial tools and machinery. On top of the pile was the 'figure' of Lenin – a simple cube without insignia. 'But where's Lenin?' the artist was asked. With an injured air he pointed to the cube. Anybody could see that if they had a soul, he added. But the judges without hesitation turned down the work of art. There must be a real figure of Lenin, they reasoned, if the single-minded peasant is to be inspired.[144]

I will return to the 'single-minded peasant' in a moment.

7. Inessa and the Zhenotdel

In only one sphere, that of women's work, could Kollontai and others who thought like her find some degree of satisfaction. After months of neglect, the male party leadership finally agreed in August 1919 to set up a separate section of the party for work among women, the Zhenotdel. At its head the party chose Inessa Armand, who had Lenin's ear and was more of an orthodox Bolshevik than Kollontai. As Barbara Clements has written, 'Inessa and Kollontai were never friends. They had been rivals before the revolution and they were temperamentally different: Kollontai expansive and emotional, Inessa aloof and a bit ascetic.'[145] In any case, Kollontai became seriously ill in November of that year, suffering a heart attack at the age of forty-seven, and was unable to return to work for many months.[146]

Inessa's Zhenotdel had many formidable tasks before it. Its primary one was to mobilise Russian women for the war effort. The Civil War was at its height, and women were needed to take the place of men in factories, to care for the wounded on the various fronts, and if necessary to fight. Inessa wanted to introduce, as best she could in such terrible circumstances, the underlying theme of women's liberation, not just of women's service and sacrifice. She wanted women to be protected from work which involved hazards to their health, to undertake vocational training to upgrade their skills, to become 'delegates' in their factories and attend courses and meetings several times a month. In the spring of 1920, the Zhenotdel launched its own monthly newspaper, *Kommunistka*.

The new organisation's greatest problem was the lack of women willing to dedicate time to it. The central office in Moscow was woefully understaffed, and in the provinces even those women sympathetic to the Communists were often too exhausted and malnourished to take on extra work. To meet the needs of the organisation she was so proud to direct, Inessa Armand worked up to sixteen hours a day. When in February 1920 a friend visited her in her apartment, she was shocked at what she found: 'The room was terribly cold, it was unheated, everything was neglected. Everywhere one could see only dust.' Inessa's clothing was old, her voice was hoarse and she 'coughed and shook from the cold'. She was destroying herself.[147]

At the end of the summer, Lenin heard that she had pneumonia. He advised her to go immediately to a sanatorium at Kislovodsk, in the Caucasus, and telegraphed to the local authorities to take care of her. Armand accepted, also because her sixteen-year-old son Andrey was again ill. The sanatorium was anything but luxurious, there were White troops in the hills above it, and the weather was not warm, but Inessa slept incessantly. She also began a little diary which revealed the great conflicts and loves of her life, and showed that she still felt unworthy of the classical model of motherhood:

> The only warm feelings I have left are for the children and V. I. [Lenin]. In all other respects it's as if my heart has died; as if, having given up all my passion to V. I. and the work, I have exhausted all sources of love and compassion toward people to whom previously I was so richly open. I have no one apart from V. I. and my children. I have no relations with other people, except in my work. And people feel this deadness in me [. . .] Some patients here are very worried. They are afraid of attacks [from the Whites]. I'm worried only for Andrushka, my little son. In this respect I am weak – not like a Roman matron who could easily sacrifice her children in the interests of the Republic. I could not. I am terribly worried about my children.[148]

Lenin, preoccupied for Inessa's safety, incessantly telegraphed the local Communists, who decided to evacuate her, her son and a few other patients. It was against her will and the journey turned into a nightmare. There were enemy troops all around, the train made little progress, and the towns it passed through were indescribably filthy and disease-ridden. The little party stayed four nights in its railway carriage. Typically, however, Inessa decided to make a foray into one of the towns to find a little food for one of the seriously ill members of the group. She found some food but contracted cholera. It was not long before she began to suffer from convulsions, vomiting and diarrhoea. She was taken to a local hospital where saline injections at first gave her a little relief. But she was too weak to fight the disease and succumbed to it on 24 September 1920. She had tried to send Andrey away from the hospital lest he contract the disease, but he had stayed with her.

When her coffin finally returned to Moscow's Kazan Station, Lenin was waiting to meet it. He was overcome by grief and by guilt. At Inessa's funeral he could hardly stand. The testimonies of the eyewitnesses come from many years later, but there is every reason to believe them. Angelica Balabanoff remembered, 'Not only his face but his whole body expressed so much sorrow that I dared not greet him, not even with the slightest gesture [. . .] He seemed to have shrunk [. . .] His eyes seemed drowned in tears held back with effort.'[149]

Lenin and the generous-hearted Nadezhda Krupskaya became the unofficial guardians of Inessa's youngest three children – Inna, who was twenty-two, and who shared her mother's political passion, Varvara (Varva), aged nineteen, who was about to become an art student, and the sixteen-year-old Andrey. They were often at the Kremlin. In February 1921, Lenin and Krupskaya paid a surprise late-night visit to the hostel where Varvara was living while studying at the Higher Art-Technical Institute. A debate broke out, the students siding with the avant-garde and Lenin, unsurprisingly, defending realism in art.[150]

III. After the revolution

The Civil War slowly drew to a close at the end of 1920. By that date Moscow had lost half its population, Petrograd two-thirds. People had streamed back to the countryside, placing themselves at the mercy of their relatives, hoping to find in the rural areas the means of sustenance that were totally lacking in the cities. They were greeted in many regions by epidemics which took an estimated two million lives, of which Inessa Armand's was but one. What Alan Ball has rightly called 'the twentieth century's relentless opening sequence' – warfare, epidemics and famine – constrained and determined in a very tragic way the possibilities of Soviet family politics.[151]

In the years 1921–6, two political processes were under way. The first was the consequence of that terrible succession of events outlined above – a macroscopic gap between what Soviet family reformers wanted to do and what they actually could do. In no other chapter of this book will that gap, between ambition and possibility, between law and social reality, appear so wide. The second process has less to do with material conditions than with ideology: with or without such terrible conditions, Kollontai and her ideas were destined to be rejected by the Communist Party. Peace had finally come to the new Soviet Union. Now was the time, wrote Kollontai for 'winged Eros' to take to the air. Yet for her the reality of these years was quite another – one of emargination, frustration and defeat.

1. Towards party dictatorship

None of the experiments to create a new form of democracy based on workers' councils (the Soviets) survived the Civil War.[152] The draconian conditions of the time and Bolshevik determination to win at any cost meant that control and command soon replaced self-government from below. One-man management took the place of factory councils and committees. The trade unions were emarginated. Communist cadres, answerable only to the party hierarchy, came to replace at every level the embryonic structures of Soviet democracy. Political pluralism and opposition parties disappeared. Nor can this swift degenerative process be ascribed solely to the emergencies and material necessities of the time. Democracy was never a *sine qua non* of Bolshevik ideology, the central political pillar that was to sustain socialist revolution. It was more of an optional extra, the adoption of which could be first suspended in the name of the war, and then endlessly postponed in the years after 1921.

Towards the end of 1920 Kollontai became one of the principal spokespersons of the Workers' Opposition, a minority trend within the party which in the spring of 1921 was to fight a losing battle against the Communist leadership at the Tenth Party Congress. In her pamphlet *The Workers' Opposition*, published in 1921, she argued for the reintroduction of democracy and freedom of criticism, a central role for the trade unions as the autonomous expression of workers' 'self-activity', and the weeding out from the party of the bureaucratic elements which had taken ever greater control of it.[153]

Kollontai's pamphlet had its faults and blind spots. Instead of identifying Bolshevik leaders and their ideology as those really responsible for democratic decline, she adopted a narrowly class approach, calling for the expulsion from the party of all 'non-proletarian elements' – technicians, administrators, managers, etc. It was a convenient way of creating an 'other', the petty bourgeois elements that needed to be eliminated from the party, but it was not a good way to identify where the core of the problem lay. Nor did she appeal for political pluralism – that is, the creation of political parties other than the Communist one. Kollontai remained an old Bolshevik, faithful to her party and its actions till the end of her days.

The Workers' Opposition none the less contains many passages of great political courage and far-sightedness. Its author did not hesitate to attack all the party leaders for their patronising and limited vision of the role of the trade unions, writing, 'The trouble is that Lenin, Trotsky, Bukharin and others see the functions of the trade unions not as control over production or as the taking over of industries, but merely as a school for bringing up the masses.' For them, continued Kollontai, the workers were simply to learn from vanguard comrades, the exemplary 'Peters and Johns' (Pëtr and Ivan), but without ever 'touching with their own hands the rudder of control, for "it is too early yet". They have "not yet learned enough".[154]

In her pamphlet the desire to place power in the hands of working people, to trust in their creativity and self-organisation, is everywhere apparent. Here is one such passage, on the unlikely theme of bird preservation societies:

> Every independent attempt, every new thought that passes through the censorship of our centre, is considered as 'heresy' [...] What would happen if some of the members of the Russian Communist Party – those, for instance, who are fond of birds – decided to form a society for the preservation of birds? The idea itself seems useful. It does not in any way undermine any 'state project'. But it only seems this way. All of a sudden there would appear some bureaucratic institution which would claim the right to manage the undertaking. That particular institution would immediately 'incorporate' the society into the Soviet machine, deadening thereby the direct initiative.[155]

There remains an enigma in Kollontai's thought which it is worth airing here. Nowhere in her pamphlet is there any reference to families or private life, themes on which (as we have seen) she had spent so much energy and passion. They simply found no place in *The Workers' Opposition*. It was as if there were two different worlds which could not be connected – the first political and the second domestic, the one concerned with democracy, the other with everyday life. There seemed also to be no connection between the workers' 'creativity' in the factories and what went on at home. This was obviously not the impression that Kollontai wanted to give, but she took no steps to avoid it in her pamphlet.[156]

There also seemed to be two different states in play. The first one, belonging to the world of hard politics and brilliantly described by Kollontai, had the repellent physiognomy of the early bureaucratic and authoritarian Soviet state. But was this the same state whose intervention Kollontai was so constantly invoking for the private sphere, the all-embracing welfare state which was going to look after children while mothers worked, and if need be substitute itself for the family? And if it was, then what guarantees or rights were individuals and families to have against such a juggernaut if it turned out to be less than benign? On all this Kollontai was silent.

2. Family life in the cities

The introduction of the New Economic Policy (NEP) in these same months marked a slow return to some semblance of normality after the horrors of the years 1914–21. Though there was a drastic housing shortage, there were clear signs that urban families were beginning to make lives of their own. A comparison of the national censuses of 1897 and 1926 for the city of Moscow shows a dramatic shift in the number and composition of households in the city. Whereas in 1897 there were fewer than 88,000 households with an average of more than eight persons each, by 1926 the number of households had increased more than five times, to 482,000, but with an average membership of just 3.5. The elimination of complex bourgeois and noble households, with their retainers and servants, obviously helps to explain this transformation. But it was also true that the practice described earlier – that of taking in boarders and thus swelling numbers in a single, confined household space – had become less of a necessity. The trend was quite clear – towards small nuclear family units.[157]

This was not at all what radical family reformers had hoped would happen. For families to be 'proletarian' signified ideally making collective arrangements at home as at work. Yet during the NEP period the Soviet state apparatuses gave very little encouragement to the urban population to form domestic communes or to move in a collectivist direction. There were a few 'Workers' Communes' in Moscow in the early 1920s, covering one or more apartment buildings, managed by elected committees and offering communal services such as bakeries, food stores and laundries.[158] But these urban experiments were never espoused by the leadership, nor did they become a subject of the Soviet propaganda machine.

Stolovyye – communal dining halls – did flourish in the terrible conditions of 1918–20 and at the end of that period nearly a million Muscovites were being fed in this way. The queues were long and the food very poor.[159] As soon as they could families fled from these halls and returned to making their own meals at home. From 1923 onwards communal eating enjoyed a modest revival thanks to the formation of a company called Public Catering, supported by the Commissariats of Labour and Health. By 1927 it was running 678 canteens, not a high number for so vast a country. In Moscow, workers finishing their soup discovered the following message glazed on their bowls: 'Public catering is the path to the new way of life.'[160] In reality, there were scant signs of the 'new way of life'.

In another area, that of the growth of literacy, progress was considerable, with classrooms and communal reading rooms in every quarter. Women in particular benefited. Between the two censuses of 1897 and 1926 the national female literacy rate rose from 16.6 per cent to 45.7 per cent. By 1925, 74 per cent of urban women could read and write.[161]

Urban women, then, appeared more emancipated than ever before – they were literate, enjoyed equal rights with men, could divorce when they wanted to and had more control over their own destinies. But they were not free, for the terribly harsh realities of trying to make a socialist and egalitarian revolution in a backward country told against them. Furthermore, enlightened Bolshevik legislation often worked against the very persons it was designed to protect and help.

The first and greatest problem remained that of work. During the NEP years there was not enough work to go round for both men and women. The managers who now ran Soviet factories and workplaces gave priority to men – because they were men, because they were often war veterans, and because they were more skilled. But they also cost less. Various aspects of Soviet labour legislation – paid maternity leave, the ban on night work for women, and work restrictions for pregnant women and nursing mothers – made women more costly to employ. The number of crèches which the regime had been able to institute corresponded to less than 1 per cent of those needed. Women in no way competed with men on an equal footing in the world of work.

This meant that the families of city dwellers were characterised by a pattern of single, nearly always male, breadwinners upon whom women and children were dependent. Thus in the most fundamental sphere – that of economic self-sufficiency – women remained highly vulnerable. Furthermore, Bolshevik family legislation on marriage and divorce, designed to protect women from violent husbands and to liberate them from unhappy unions, could be used in quite a different way by the other sex. Men slipped in and out of marriage with embarrassing ease, often acting irresponsibly in terms of the families they had created. By 1925–6 the urban parts of the USSR had far higher divorce rates than those of western Europe.[162] We have no way of telling how many of these divorces were instigated by men and how many by women, but many social and political commentators of the time commented upon the plight of single, unemployed mothers who were unmarried or divorced or widowed.

Very often the only way out for these women was prostitution. At the Sixth National Trade Union Congress in November 1924 delegates voted to repeal the ban on night work for women and allow them to take work that was potentially damaging to their health. As a woman delegate from Rostov-on-Don explained, 'It is better if the professional organisations offer the woman worker less protection so that she can have the chance to earn a crust of bread and not be forced to sell herself on the boulevard.'[163]

3. Homeless children

Linked to prostitution but going far beyond it was the greatest single human tragedy of these years: the very widespread presence of homeless and abandoned children, known as *besprizornyye*. It is impossible to quantify accurately the phenomenon accurately. At the height of the wave, in 1921–2, the *besprizornyye* numbered somewhere between four and seven million. Their presence in the streets and markets of the cities, in and around railway stations, on trains and in any sort of derelict building or shelter was the cause of much anguished comment by both Russians and foreigners.[164] Wendy Goldman cites the case of one organiser for the Commission for the Betterment of Children's Lives, who in March 1921 travelled south from Moscow into a famine-stricken area. He wrote in his report,

> Our train arrived at night and stopped not far from Samara. For some reason we could not go any farther. It was one or two in the morning. It was quiet and there was frost on the beets. Our train slept, all was silent, but suddenly I could make out a thin, weak, remote wailing. I listened – the wailing grew strong and then fell again. I went out onto the platform. In the moonlight, at a great distance, lay some kind of gray rags. As I looked I could see them turning, and from the bosom of these rags came a weak, lingering wail: 'Kh-le-b-tsa, Kh-le-b-tsa'. One could scarcely distinguish the separate voices, but due to their faintness, they all merged in a weak, drawn-out wail. They were children, perhaps three, maybe four thousand, and at my disposal I had ten pounds of bread.[165]

The causes of the phenomenon were cumulative, one layer of deprivation and suffering being added to another. First, as we have seen, the absence and frequent death of men who left for the trenches in 1914 left women struggling to hold families together as best they could; then the retreat eastwards before the Germans brought a stream of refugees in its wake – over three million of them just from four provinces in Belorussia; afterwards the horrors of civil war meant the destruction of family homes and families themselves by marauding soldiers from both sides; then came the terrible epidemics of cholera, typhus and scarlet fever; finally, and worst of all, the famine in the Volga basin in 1921. By the late summer of 1921, legions of children from that region, having lost their parents or been abandoned, bedraggled and lice-infected, tottering from exhaustion and hunger, began to appear on the streets of Moscow.[166]

From the very many life histories cited by the historian of the *besprizornyye*, Alan Ball, let me select just one, an account dictated to the authorities by an orphan boy from the city of Grodno. It illustrates very well how families coped with successive layers of disaster, only finally to succumb:

> His family numbered among the millions pouring from western districts to the interior during World War I, in this case to a village in Cheliabinsk

province. Here the boy quit school and found work with local peasants in order to help support the family, his father having died in 1914. For six years they managed in this fashion, until famine arrived to eliminate the village's food and drive them in desperation to [the city of] Cheliabinsk. Five people in a starving multitude, they were swept into a cold, typhus-ridden barracks that soon claimed the boy's mother and sister. Three days later his other sister died, leaving him alone with an ailing brother. 'There were many like us.'[167]

The homeless children were usually organised in gangs, mostly of boys. Single children, especially girls, stood little chance of survival. 'Ailing brothers', such as the one described above, often defended in heart-rending ways by elder brothers or sisters, also stood little chance. The gangs typically numbered under a dozen members, though a few were much larger. They selected and defended a space – garbage tip, shed, barrel or market stall – in which to huddle together and survive the night. Moscow and other cities, beginning to recover from the Civil War, were full of building sites. Asphalt or tar cauldrons, heated and used during the day, retained their warmth well into the morning hours and were a favourite site for the *besprizornyye*. Begging, stealing and prostitution were their most common activities. Begging was the least lucrative, but in the period of greatest destitution was all that many children were capable of. Stealing was rewarding but carried high risks. Prostitution, both of boys and girls, could take a child out of a gang and into the warmth of a brothel but inflicted indelible harm upon already traumatised children.

A newspaper illustration of the time shows one little homeless boy lighting up his cigarette from that of another. One boy is inside a tar cauldron, the other outside. Many citizens found the abandoned children repulsive and feared their attacks. Even so, a good number of individuals, factories, military units and trade unions did what they could, and they are estimated to have maintained some 200,000 children, of whom more than half were supported by the trade unions.[168] But primary responsibility rested with the state, which proved dramatically unequal to the task.

In the months after October 1917, as we have seen, there had been great hopes that children's homes would prove to be an environment culturally and materially superior to that of families. Projects abounded and pedagogic debate flourished. Soon, though, the harshness of reality constrained all discussion. The state did not have the resources or the organisational capacity to cope with successive waves of emergency. Moscow children evacuated during the Civil War, for instance, were sent to abandoned manor houses in the countryside, many of which proved quite unfit for human habitation. The number of children in homes (*detdoma*) grew steadily but was always

fig. 6 Illustration from the newspaper *Izvestiya*, 17 February 1926. The caption reads, 'Remember the *besprizornyye*! Assistance to the *besprizornyye* is the obligation of every Soviet citizen.'

insufficient – 125,000 in 1919, 400,000 in 1920, 540,000 in 1921.[169] Conditions in many of them were appalling: there was no oil or electricity and the rooms were freezing in winter. It was useless to think of rehabilitation and education in these circumstances.[170]

State apparatuses were rapidly overwhelmed by the effects of the Volga famine. There were nowhere near enough homes to meet the needs of the moment and the prevailing atmosphere was one of chaos and desperation. The government opened the Volga basin and the Crimea to foreign relief organisations. According to Soviet figures, by July 1922 some 3.6 million children were being fed by foreign aid organisations in these regions, the American Relief Administration (ARA) being responsible for over 80 per cent of aid.

In the following years the situation slowly eased and the numbers of homeless children declined radically. Some had died and others grown up, while better organisation of children's homes allowed them to be trained and to re-enter Soviet life. It has to be said, in partial defence of the Soviet regime, that so great had been the calamity that even a modern European welfare state would have had difficulty coping. The tragedy of the *besprizornyye* revealed a third version of the revolutionary state – not the bureaucratic monolith suffocating the initiatives of civil society, nor the benign welfare institution of Kollontai's dreams, offering an alternative to family life, but

fig. 7 Homeless brother and sister encountered by the American Red Cross during the Civil War. The little girl implores the volunteers, 'Please, help my brother!'

rather an under-resourced and chaotic administration that never accorded high enough priority to the problems of human suffering and the wholesale destruction of family life.

4. Trotsky and the family

In the early years of the NEP, the most interesting reflections on the family, brief as they were, came from Leon Trotsky. In July 1923 he published in *Pravda* a series of articles on everyday life.[171] In one of the best-known, 'Not by politics alone', Trotsky noted that whereas in the pre-revolutionary period 'everything was ruled by politics in the direct and narrow sense of that word', after the revolution the main emphasis was shifting to the needs of culture and economic reconstruction.[172] Within this context, Trotsky's fertile gaze also fell upon family questions. 'From the old family to the new' was published on 13 July and it was followed the next day by 'Family and ceremony'. Other articles included one on 'Habit and custom' and another dedicated to 'Vodka, the Church and the cinema'.

Trotsky's arguments were fascinating. His starting point was that the family, contrary to conventional Marxist thinking, could not simply be considered as one of the institutions of an obsolescent superstructure, destined to change or indeed to disappear as a result of revolutionary change in the economic and political spheres. Rather the family had a primacy, and indeed an obduracy, of its own. Trotsky asserted provocatively that 'the easiest problem was that of assuming power'. Domestic life, by contrast, had proved much more resistant to reorganisation. 'Some great process' was under way in the evolution of proletarian families, of which 'we are witnessing now the first chaotic stages'. To govern it had become the most difficult of Communist tasks, but also the most important. On gender relations, for instance, Trotsky wrote, 'it is quite obvious that unless there is actual equality of husband and wife in the family, in a normal sense as well as in the conditions of life, we cannot speak seriously of their equality in social work or even in politics'.[173] Thus in a causal sequence of social change, family relations were not the mere *product* of other, more important, economic and political processes. Rather, they were the *foundations* upon which further structural transformations could be built.

This inversion was a considerable theoretical intuition. Sadly, it was not one that Trotsky, who was pulled in many different directions and who distributed his volcanic energies and intellect over many distinct areas, ever followed up. When we look at what he actually proposed in these articles, we find a rather conventional approach. The 'new family' was to be based on two premises: rising standards of culture and education in the working class; and improved material conditions, as organised by the state. The key struggles were 'the public education of children and the releasing of the family from the burden of the kitchen and the laundry'. This was standard Leninist stuff. He did add, and this took him a little closer to Kollontai, that the 'more enterprising and progressive families' could group themselves into 'collective housekeeping units'. But Trotsky himself, like Kollontai, preferred not to live in a commune. In fact, he lived in the Kremlin. He, his wife and his children occupied four small rooms in the Kavalersky building. Opposite them were Lenin and Krupskaya, with whom they shared a dining room and bathroom.[174] Lenin, when he had a moment, stopped to play with Trotsky's children in the corridor. Inessa Armand's children – Inna, Varva and Andrey – although much older, must occasionally have been there too.

The last thing to note about Trotsky's articles on the family and everyday life is how little emerges from them of any idea of an autonomous civil society. Quite the opposite is true. Although he genuinely believed in artistic dissent and working-class creativity, he believed even more strongly in the discipline and, if need be, the coercion of the party. Freedom from the Church, certainly, but submission to the party; outside which, as Trostky was famously to say, there could be no salvation.

5. Peasant families and the revolution

In a paradoxical way, during the 1920s the revolution achieved considerable success in the rural areas of the country – precisely where the Bolsheviks judged their great enemy, the cloying traditionalism of families, to be most pervasive. This unlikely story has its roots in the fact that the great majority of peasants, whose point of reference continued to be the *mir*, or peasant commune, made their own revolution in 1917, and then held on to significant elements of local power in the following decade. In 1917 they expropriated the landowners' arable estates, took over the forests of the Tsar and of the state, and forced the 'splitters', whose enclosed farms derived from the Stolypin reform, back under communal control. They then carried through a general land redistribution in the time-honoured tradition. In some areas all the land was pooled and then divided *equally* in relation to the size of each *dvor* – a 'Black Revolution', to use the terminology of Russian peasant millenarianism. In others, peasant holdings remained untouched and only non-peasant land was divided up, priority being given to landless families. The net result was that by 1919 a great levelling down had taken place amongst the Russian peasantry. The number of extended families who farmed more than twenty-five *desyatiny* (67.5 acres or 35 hectares) had decreased by 90 per cent. At the other end of the scale, many landless families received arable plots for the first time. Overall, the number of households that farmed less than two *desyatiny* (5.4 acres or 2.18 hectares) increased by more than 60 per cent. During the 1920s inequality in landholding began to grow again, but in overall terms the land settlement that emerged from the revolution was a remarkable result.[175]

A very pronounced rate of household partitioning accompanied this levelling down. The men who returned from the war – 'mature, aggressive, marriageable', to use the words of Theodor Shanin[176] – wanted to start families of their own, independent of the authority of fathers and uncles. Youth challenged age. The old patriarchal households, based on extended kinship ties and large numbers of relatives living under the same roof, began to break up under the dual assault of land redistribution and household partition.

By the mid-1920s the Soviet countryside had recovered from the terrible events of the preceding years, though no family would easily forget its menfolk who had died fighting in the wars, or the women and children killed by disease and famine. This remained a very primitive society – three-quarters of spring sowing and the same proportion of the grain harvest were still executed by hand.

But it was also a society of greater freedoms than in the past, the communes enjoying a considerable measure of autonomy and self-government.

Of course, divisions existed. The interests of individuals, the control of families and the stipulations of a communal society were in constant tension. The Land Code of 1922 itself reflected and reproduced these tensions. While according new rights to women and to the younger generations, it also made frequent reference to the responsibilities of the household as a whole rather than to those of the individual. It also has to be said that women rarely used their new democratic prerogatives in the 1920s. Male hostility to their presence remained strong and rural correspondents reported that the heavy tobacco smoking of the men and their rowdy and bawdy behaviour often drove women away.[177]

Throughout the 1920s Communist authorities and peasant families eyed each other with suspicion. With rural dwellers constituting more than 80 per cent of the population, the Russian Communists could not afford to be as scathing about the peasantry as Marx had once been. But they were impatient with the fact that, even in a bumper year such as 1926, insufficient grain was coming into the state granaries. State planning still seemed to be at the mercy of peasant producers.

The Communists also wanted to reform daily life (*byt*), and to make Soviet culture and political institutions count for far more in the rural areas. As Farnsworth has written, 'from the outset, Bolshevik culture was didactic, moralistic and atheistic'.[178] The party wished not only to combat religion and superstition but also to castigate wife-beating, drunkenness, lying, thieving and even swearing. This was a pretty stiff agenda. Both the Zhenotdel, with its special responsibilities for women, and other parts of the party found the reform of daily life very tough going.

In Tula, about one hundred miles south of Moscow, a Bolshevik woman organiser by the name of N. S. Kokoreva had tried in the summer of 1918 to get peasant women to accept the idea of public nurseries. She received the following revealing reply: ' "Soviet power is our power. The land has been given to the peasant, his greatest joy". A deep bow. "Thanks for caring for us mothers and children. Equal rights for us are also fine. But we won't give our child to a kindergarten or nursery." '[179]

More than two years later the Zhenotdel comrades in Tula managed to organise a delegate conference of peasant women. Kollontai attended. The first business of the conference was supposed to have been the approval of women delegates to preside over the meeting. The organisers made a crucial mistake, however, choosing one young woman who, although she came from Tula, had been educated in Moscow and who, in Kollontai's words, 'came to the platform with bobbed hair, in a short dress, with a cigarette in her lips'. There was uproar in the hall and the conference continued only with difficulty. On her return to Moscow Kollontai issued instructions urging organisers to be more sensitive to local customs and traditions.[180]

It would be a mistake to overemphasise the notion that peasant families and the Communist state faced each other in stark hostility and incomprehension – a face-off that was to lead inevitably to Stalinist catastrophe at the end of the decade. The NEP period was notable for the extension of individual rights in the countryside, especially those of women and of younger men, for the spread of rural literacy and of rural cooperatives, and for the return of modest prosperity. Orlando Figes, certainly no Bolshevik sympathiser, wrote at the end of his study on the Volga countryside, 'Once the famine crisis had been overcome and the economy restored to peaceful conditions, the Russian peasantry enjoyed a period of unparalleled freedom and well-being during the 1920s.'[181] The state tried hard at this time not to accept rural families as static entities but to influence by means of its laws their inner dynamics, with special emphasis placed on women and youth. The NEP period was an interlude between two great rural calamities, both to a great extent man-made. With a different leadership it might have been something more.

6. The 1925–6 debate on the Family Code

In the mid-1920s a very extended and rather extraordinary discussion took place at all levels of Soviet society. Its subject was what was happening to the family, and how the original provisions of the Family Code of 1918 now needed to be modified. The 1918 Code, approved on the eve of the Civil War, had not been the object of lengthy debate. Its successor, although considerably less significant, was the focus for a great controversy, all the more surprising for taking place in a one-party state. Some 6,000 village meetings and an unspecified number of urban ones were held to discuss the draft version of the new Code. Neither were these meetings mere rituals, designed to cover in a populist way decisions already taken elsewhere. They were genuine discussions, as we shall see in a moment, extending from the lowest levels of society right up to the highest echelons of the Soviet state. This was possible only because family issues occupied a strange no man's land in Soviet politics. A great power struggle was going on in the Kremlin, but the unstable lines of factional division which characterised 1925 and 1926 were not reflected in the debate on the Family Code.[182] Leaders, cadres and citizens expressed their opinions in relative freedom and without fear of reprisal. Everyone, for obvious reasons, considered him- or herself to be an expert on the family. It would be too much to claim that the Soviet regime made good, even for a fleeting moment, on its frequently proffered promise of participatory democracy. But it can be said that a huge public sphere was permitted the space to debate the family for many months.

The main preoccupation of the new Code, as of so much Soviet legislation, was the position of women and the need to protect them. This was made clear by the People's Commissar for Justice, Dmitry Kursky, when he first introduced the draft Code to the VTsIK, or All-Union Central Executive Committee, on 17 October 1925. VTsIK was the closest thing that the Soviet Union got to a parliament, though it exercised very limited powers.[183]

Kursky noted in his introduction the fundamental ways in which the Family Code of 1918 had broken with bourgeois conceptions of marriage and the family. It had deprived church marriages of any legal significance, granted civil recognition only to state-registered marriages, and rejected the traditional vision of the family as a property-owning unit, in which men enjoyed privileges and rights 'at the woman's expense'. For Kursky, the sum of these measures had constituted a 'fundamental revolution'. In the ensuing years, however, new problems had arisen in Soviet society. In particular, the number of non-registered marriages, as well as of divorces, had increased greatly, bringing in their wake the problem of abandoned and destitute women, whose plight was augmented, especially in the cities, by the lack of work opportunities. The old Family Code had envisaged quite inadequate support for women and children in the event of marriage break-up, especially if the marriage was a *de facto* one. In 1926 the Soviet legislators wanted to institute effective alimony payments and at the same time to abolish the distinction between registered and *de facto* marriages. All women in relationships – and out of them – were to enjoy equal rights, including the right to alimony. Kursky was categorical on this point:

> We intend to make the material consequences of *de facto* marriage the same as those of registered marriages. That is the fundamental standpoint of our new project [. . .] As regards the rights of women and children the most essential point is the so-called question of alimony [. . .] A destitute spouse who is unable to work has a right to support.[184]

Kursky and others who had drafted the new Family Code, such as Yakov Brandenburgsky, the dean of the Law Faculty at Moscow University, expected their draft to go through the VTsIK without much difficulty. Instead they ran into a barrage of criticism – from fellow intellectuals and party leaders, but also from working-class and peasant delegates to the All-Union Central Executive Committee, both men and women. P. A. Krassikov, a member of the

Supreme Court, underlined, as did many others, that the provisions of the draft Code effectively denied any meaning to marriage. From that moment onwards it would be enough to send a postcard to the registry office if either partner wanted a divorce.[185] He also referred to what was to become a very common theme: male heads of peasant households feared that alimony payments, involving only one member of the extended family, might be made the economic responsibility of all, thus grievously damaging the economic interests of the *dvor* as a whole.[186] Women delegates, on the other hand, underlined that the primary problem was the frequency with which men were abandoning their wives, often to remarry or cohabit with a younger woman. An older peasant delegate from Siberia, Shupurova, insisted, 'A comrade takes two wives, gives each of them a baby, so he must pay both of them. It is nobody else's fault: if you like tobogganing you must like pulling your sledge uphill.'[187]

Over the next year the draft Code was to be the object of intense discussion not just in the upper echelons of the Soviet state, but in both town and countryside, as well as in the party press.[188] Many feared that in the absence of any real insistence on marriage there would be a mass return, especially in the countryside, to church weddings, even though they enjoyed no legal value. One commentator, writing in the youth organisation's journal *Komsomolskaya Pravda*, lamented the inadequacies of Communist ritual with regard to the family. He described a 'red' christening in a working-class district:

> In an underheated, grey hall sat the women weavers, munching sunflower seeds. The men smoked *makhorka* and spat the leaves out onto the floor. On the platform there was a table covered with red calico at which sat a dozen people, ill-at-ease. Various speeches were made and the baby was presented with two volumes of the works of V. I. Lenin.[189]

The debate on the Family Code in 1925 and 1926 was marked by two fundamental dividing lines. The first was between countryside and town. The peasant voices that have come down to us were not unanimous, but there was a heavy bias against the recognition of *de facto* marriage, against divorce and alimony, all of which were held to threaten the stability and harmony of rural life. The other great divider was that between men and women. Amidst much ribald laughter and sniggering during the sessions of the VTsIK (dutifully reported in the stenographer's minutes), male delegates consistently suggested that women were cunning and greedy creatures, ready to use the courts in order to have themselves supported by their former lovers.

Not for the first time, though sadly for the last, one woman's voice rose above the debate to take an entirely original line. After the defeat of the

Workers' Opposition at the Tenth Party Congress in 1921 and her own effective disgrace, Aleksandra Kollontai had spent much of the following years outside Russia. She had been appointed as Soviet representative to Norway in the autumn of 1922 and ambassador the year after. She had always loved Scandinavia, its landscapes reminding her of the childhood summers spent on her maternal grandparents' estate at Kuusa in Finland. Kollontai remained in Oslo until December 1925, but then asked to return to Moscow, where she soon found herself embroiled in the Family Code debate. By this time she was fifty-four years old and not in the best of health.

Kollontai's proposal was to create a progressive General Insurance Fund, which would take the place of alimony and guarantee both women and children in the event of unemployment, illness or destitution. She insisted that it was degrading for women to be reliant on men for their upkeep; in any case alimony was difficult to collect on a regular basis. The entire adult working population should instead contribute to the General Insurance Fund on a graduated scale, the lowest contribution being two rubles a year. With sixty million adult contributors, the fund could rely initially on a capital of at least 120 million rubles. Now that the Soviet economy was recovering fast, Kollontai was convinced that within a few years the state would finally be able to help systematically those most in need – both women and children.[190]

Her proposal found very little support. Brandenburgsky thought it a good idea but unfeasible in the immediate future. Trotsky took her plan seriously but denied its basic premise. It was not the state but men who should be made responsible for abandoned women. Men were stronger than women, as a gender and in economic terms. For Trotsky alimony was fair and just.[191] On a very different front, Sofia Smidovich, who had been head of the Zhenotdel (as had Kollontai herself in 1920–2), argued that Kollontai's insistence on the strong and autonomous 'new woman', no longer reliant on men, would merely increase promiscuity, divorce and women's own unhappiness. Love and fulfilment were rather to be found in stable marriage, and in the long cycle of pregnancy, birth and child-rearing. Her own family was a loving and tightly knit unit.[192]

Once again, Kollontai found herself practically alone and the subject of derision. But her General Insurance Fund was not as utopian as her opponents made out. Unlikely though it may seem, more than one point connected it directly with the proposals of William Beveridge's famous National Insurance Plan for Great Britain in 1942.

In October 1926, after all the local discussions had taken place, the VTsIK was convened for a final discussion of the Code. Kursky reported on the widespread consultations that had taken place. He did not hide the peasants' continuing alarm at the proposals, but he carefully dissected the different parts of peasant opinion, which was far from unanimous. Not everyone in the countryside was in favour of defending at all costs the patriarchal *dvor* with its complex family composition and shared responsibilities. At the village meetings, up to 40 per cent of those present opposed compulsory registration of marriages.[193] As for the towns and cities, they voted overwhelmingly, especially in workers' districts, for the extension of legal protection to non-registered marital relations.

In its final form the 1926 Family Code was a compromise, made all the more necessary by the depth of the discussion that had preceded it. The key point, on which Kursky had insisted from the very beginning, became law – women in *de facto* marriages, or in their aftermath, were to enjoy the same rights as those who had registered their marriages. Article 12 of the Code, in response to the many criticisms that marriage was being denied any meaning, tried to define carefully the constituent elements of *de facto* marriage: cohabitation, proof of a common household, and statements made to third persons 'tending to prove the existence of marital relations', particularly with regard to 'the presence or absence of mutual material support, joint raising of children, and the like'.[194]

Women's rights were reaffirmed throughout the Code. The marriage age for girls was raised to eighteen (Article 5), all decisions regarding children were to be taken by both parents jointly (Article 38), the manner in which a household was run was to be 'determined by the mutual agreement of the two contracting parties' (Article 9). As regards the division of property in the event of marriage failure, the Code allayed many peasant fears. Neither land nor livestock were to be used as part of settlements in the countryside, which were rather to take the form of money or household products.[195] Men in the cities, on the other hand, were to surrender half of all family goods acquired since marriage, whether the latter was registered or *de facto*. Either spouse was liable for alimony, depending on his or her economic conditions, but the duration of payment was in any case not to exceed one year.

If we compare the 1926 Code with that of 1918, a number of salient features stand out. The fierce denunciation of inheritance in the earlier Code (Article 160: 'Children have no right to the property of their parents, or parents to the property of their children') had weakened considerably. The amount of property that could be inherited was significantly increased. The Code also stressed the rights and duties of relatives: not just parents and children, brothers and sisters, as in 1918, but also grandparents and grandchildren, stepparents and stepchildren. As a result of the many crises of Soviet society, the nets of familial responsibility were being cast ever wider. It was as if the legislators recognised that the state was weak in what it *could* do, even if not in what it *wanted* to do. Families were going to be around for some time yet; within them, the sense of duty needed to be strengthened. Article 26 established that the mutual rights of children and parents were to be based primarily on consanguinity. It was blood that mattered when defining family, not the collective ideals of unrelated individuals.

Some expert commentators in the West interpreted the 1926 Code as another step towards the dissolution of marriage and family, and a further radicalisation of Soviet family politics: divorce procedures had been further simplified, *de facto* marriage recognised, and women's freedom of choice underlined.[196] Elements of the Code justified this view, but its overall spirit was otherwise. The Code was a compromise between different parts of Soviet society and opinion and as such a classic document of the NEP period. Brandenburgsky was probably nearest the mark when he wrote that the Code was in many ways not radical at all, that it tried to encourage marital stability and responsibility, that it reaffirmed blood relations, and that it had been promulgated out of a sense of concern for the vulnerability of mother and child.[197]

7. The 'surrogate proletariat': the *hujum* in Soviet Central Asia, 1927

The most radical and ambitious of all the Russian Communists' attempts to transform family life came not with the Code of 1926, but in that part of the Soviet Union where they were least equipped and least likely to achieve success. The vast expanses of Soviet Central Asia, as we have seen, were populated by a large number of different ethnic groups, subjugated to Russian control only in the previous fifty years. The Russian minority in the region numbered only a few hundred thousand, concentrated in the major cities. Soviet rule was viewed with good reason by the local populations, overwhelmingly rural and of Muslim belief, as the continuation of a repressive and very recent colonial past. Even with the creation in the 1920s of the new and 'autonomous' Soviet republics of Uzbekistan, Turkmenistan and Tajikistan, directed by indigenous political elites, the concentration of power in Moscow was evident to all. So too was the 'integral' nature of the Soviet project, its desire to transform both centre and far-flung periphery, private as well as public life. Such overarching political ambition was bound to meet with resistance of every sort. The distances – ethnic, cultural, linguistic and religious – between rulers and ruled could hardly have been greater.

On 8 May 1927, International Woman's Day, the Communist ruling elites launched a major 'hujum' (offensive) aimed at tackling family life, gender relations and religious beliefs. In the absence of any industrial proletariat upon which to base revolutionary transformation in these regions, the Communists theorised the presence of a 'surrogate proletariat' – the downtrodden and heavily veiled women of Muslim families. So great was their exploitation in the patriarchal system that they would rise up against their male oppressors, throw off their veils, and join the ranks of women citizens of the Soviet Union, enjoying equal rights and opportunities. The *hujum* had different focuses in different parts of Soviet Central Asia, but everywhere it was concerned with women's liberation and family reform. In Uzbekistan, the attack was against the heavy and total veiling described earlier in this chapter; elsewhere the Communist offensive concentrated on such issues as polygamy, blood feuds and bride abductions. The tone is well captured by a speech made by the Zhenotdel activist Serafima Lyubimova at a Women's Congress in Moscow in October 1927:

> The *hujum* – the attack against old ways of life – has begun with the casting off of the *paranji*. At the Congress's exhibition hall many of you have seen a *paranji*. This attire is not a simple dress like the ones we all wear and then change for another. It is a way of dressing connected to centuries-old statutes and institutions [. . .] To throw off the *paranji* means to break [completely] with the old way of life. It means quarrelling with mullahs, quarrelling with all kinds of old-style people in the family and neighbourhood, it means standing in defiance of all that is old.[198]

In the summer of 1927, during the course of carefully staged and dramatic mass meetings, thousands of Uzbek women cast off the *chachvon*, the heavy woven horsehair cover for head and shoulders, as well as the body-length cotton *paranji*. Frequently, both garments were then burnt in public. The *hujum* was conceived as a swift and overwhelming offensive, a sort of Winter Palace attack upon patriarchy, to be completed in time for the tenth anniversary of the Bolshevik revolution in October 1927. Communist activists counted upon Muslim women's natural solidarity and sociability, developed through generations of seclusion, as the motor force of a cultural revolution.

There were certainly elements of the local populations on the side of the *hujum*. High-ranking Central Asian Communists welcomed the offensive not only for ideological reasons but also for geo-political ones. Atatürk's Turkey, as we shall see in the next chapter, had made family reform and women's emancipation – though *not* compulsory unveiling – essential building blocks in construction of the new nation-state. For these local Communist leaders there was a real danger that the Soviet Union could lose its vanguard role in the

whole region, with 'bourgeois' nationalism, rather than Soviet internationalism, taking the lead on issues of everyday life. Reforming clergy in the *jadīd*
tradition also supported unveiling, arguing that there was nothing in the
shariat that imposed the wearing of the *chachvon*, and that there were even
elements in the Koran that supported its abolition. A significant minority of
Muslim women in the cities, especially on the social margins, embraced the
offensive and sought support from party organisations. A handful of them
joined the Zhenotdel, and one or two, such as the prominent women's activist
Tojikhon Shadieyva, became veritable icons of liberation, their family stories
being recounted in popular books and films.[199]

Yet all these were as nothing by comparison with the vast Muslim and
patriarchal backlash against the *hujum*. The 'surrogate proletariat' was no
proletariat at all. Female solidarity proved evanescent and all too vulnerable in
the face of clerical mobilisation and patriarchal violence. Women's primary
loyalties were to their own families. Within these patriarchy ruled supreme,
but in the context of a complex hierarchy of powers. Senior female figures –
the mother of the male head of the family and his first wife – very often played
significant directive roles in relation to the younger women of the household.
They were also the depositories of long-standing religious traditions. In these
conditions, it is not surprising that many of the women who unveiled did so
hesitatingly. According to one story, the wife of a leading local Communist
publicly unveiled on a theatre stage, but with her daughter waiting in the
wings, ready to reclothe her mother in the *paranji* for the journey home.[200]
Women who unveiled were often subject to ridicule and abuse in their neighbourhoods, unveiling being linked with loose sexual morals. 'Prostitute' was
the most common epithet of abuse, used by women as well as men. The most
reactionary parts of the Muslim clergy fanned the flames of revolt. A Soviet
source reported their speeches as follows:

> The prophet Muhammad commanded [us] to veil women; it follows that the
> unveiling of women violates the principle of religion. Woman is a debauched
> creature. God gave nine-tenths of all lusts to the woman, and only one part in
> ten to the man. The veil of women's lust is the paranji. The unveiling of
> women entails the debauchery of the entire world. Cursed be the days of our
> life! Cursed be those who are the first to proceed with the unveiling of
> women, and who give an evil example.[201]

With propaganda like this, women activists were greatly at risk, and so too
were younger women who dared to defy their elders, whether male or female.
Many of them – both local women and Russian Zhenotdel activists – were

assaulted and raped, while others were stoned and murdered. Male kinship gangs hunted down female relatives who had dared to unveil. The number of women killed is unknown, but it certainly ran into thousands.

This terrible story cannot be summarised merely as the battle between the followers of a reactionary clergy and the supporters of an enlightened state. At its centre was another discourse, which rapidly became the dominant one in 1927–9 – that of popular and local resistance to an invasive and intolerant external power. The patriarchal system was presented as the bedrock for violent and heroic male opposition to Soviet rule, and the great majority of women, whether out of conviction or fear, went along with this representation of what was happening. Thus the veil, instead of being a symbol of oppression, became one of resistance. The degree to which this resistance was successful can be seen in figure 8, in which Uzbek women, rigorously complete with *paranji* and *chachvon*, are photographed attending a Soviet school in Tashkent in 1929.

Was the *hujum* of 1927 the first act of the Stalinist era or the last of the New Economic Policy? There are many indicators in favour of the first proposition. In their actions in central southern Asia from 1927 onwards, the Soviet Communists showed little inclination for gradualism or compromise – both

fig. 8 Uzbek women in a Soviet school, Tashkent, 1929.

characteristics of the NEP. The internal documents of the time reveal them as impatient, anxious in the name of women's liberation and family reform to wage outright war against Muslim religion and customs. Even the more progressive *jadīd* wing of the clergy by 1927 came to be considered a dangerous rival to Soviet power. Religious schools were shut down, the assets of religious institutions confiscated and many mosques closed or turned into Soviet clubs, offices and even anti-religious centres.[202] It is hard not to recognise the justice of the Soviet case against the odious patriarchal system of central southern Asia, just as it is hard not to be outraged by the way in which they pursued their cause. Neither could ends in any way justify means, here or elsewhere in the Stalinist system.

CONCLUSION

The early Soviet, pre-Stalinist attempt to revolutionise family life must rank as one of the most fascinating cases of relations between states and families in the twentieth century. It is enough to read the 1918 Family Code, with its extraordinary emphases on the equality of women, the demotion of marriage and the abolition of inheritance, or Trotsky's articles on the 'new family' in 1923, with their acknowledgement that the 'easiest' problem in the Russian revolution had been that of assuming power, or extracts from the great debate of 1925–6 on the new Family Code, to realise the significance of the Russian case. Furthermore, Russian family politics boasted the striking figure of Aleksandra Kollontai. Briefly occupying a key role at the highest level of the new Soviet state, she fought tenaciously – and lost overwhelmingly – the battle for her radical ideas.

The single most important theme to be isolated from this history is that of the contesting of patriarchy. In the mixed bag that constituted pre-revolutionary Marxist writing on the family, the need for gender equality emerges with considerable force. Both Engels in his *The Origins of the Family* and Bebel in *Woman under Socialism*, the two works most widely read in the Social Democratic movement before 1917, insisted on equal rights and work opportunities for men and women. Even Lenin, so much the traditional Victorian, had no doubts on certain issues: women were no longer to be 'domestic slaves', crushed by housework and family obligations. They were to emerge as full and equal members of society. The echoes of these attitudes were to be heard all over Asia and eastern Europe throughout the twentieth century. Göran Therborn is right to suggest that, perhaps surprisingly, 'the dismantling of patriarchy might be seen as Communism's lasting legacy'.[203]

Yet the Russian case is full of blindness and failure. One strong and somewhat consolatory explanation for the failure has always been the backwardness of the huge empire in which the first Communist revolution took place. The material and cultural conditions of the Russian countryside – never mind those of Soviet Central Asia – heavily constrained the forces of change and made their progress painful and slow. This was as true for family life as it was for other areas. Shupurova, the Siberian peasant delegate to the VTsIK, insisted in October 1925, 'We women are not yet fully educated; we are still in the dark, we were enslaved for centuries. All we know is priests' gossip.'[204]

Economic and cultural backwardness is not by itself, however, a sufficient explanation for the light and shade of the Russian Communist case. There was also the Civil War. For many peasants the first years of the new regime were far worse than anything they had suffered under tsarist rule. Natural and man-made disaster intertwined, with responsibility for the cataclysm by no means only to be attributed to counter-revolutionaries. Even after the Civil War ended, urban and Communist Russia was to be haunted throughout the 1920s by the *besprizornyye*, the homeless and abandoned children, whose ragged and desperate presence in the streets lasted until the mid-1920s.

In the realm of family policy, too, to objective conditions must be added subjective responsibilities. It is enough to read Lenin's comments on Armand's draft pamphlet on love and the family, or to follow Kollontai's losing battle for women's rights at the Tenth Congress, or to register the suspicion and hostility towards the Zhenotdel, to understand that 'backwardness' lay not just in the material and cultural conditions of the Russian villages but within the heads of male party cadres. Theirs was a one-party state, and to a great extent a single-gender one as well. Within it family reform was always relegated to a secondary sphere. The destruction of all political democracy and the closure of a free press, both negative hallmarks of the great Bolshevik experiment, were to weigh heavily on prospects for emancipation, both within the family as well as outside it.

Kollontai must also bear some part of the subjective responsibility for the failure of Russian experimentalism. In her famous pamphlet *Communism and the Family* she offered a vision of the Communist future which took little account of individual parenthood or family love, and aroused more fear than support. Rather than trying to theorise the possible connections between families and civil society, she preferred to collapse the two into a single 'family-society', as she called it.

She did so because she shared with the other Bolsheviks a particular view of society as an all-embracing, hyperactive sphere which broke down the barriers of traditional family life and sucked individuals into activism. Civil society, in her conception of it, was full of sharing and association, but it was not necessarily pluralist or democratic, and it tended to serve closely the Communist state. Walter Benjamin visited Moscow in late 1926 and early 1927. He spoke no Russian and stayed less than two months. His diary and letters of that time are none the less of great interest, for he commented acutely on the way in which the public realm had invaded the private one.[205] 'The tensions of public life', he wrote, '– which for the most part are of a theological sort – are so great that they block off all private life to an unimaginable degree.'[206] Benjamin had put his finger on a fundamental characteristic of the great tyrant regimes of the twentieth century – their collapsing of the private into the public, their lack of respect for privacy and home life, and their bending of the associations of civil society to serve the state and its ideology. Public life in Moscow in January 1927 was 'theological' for Benjamin in the sense of being endlessly dedicated to debate on how best to serve Communism and the state that embodied it. The possibilities of a plural and dissenting civil society were correspondingly diminished, as was the space for the 'innocent' pursuit of daily and family life. *Byt* was to be replaced by *bytiye*, the patterns of mundane everyday life by activities that were transcendental and supercharged, both emotionally and spiritually. Individuals lived their 'interiority' in anxious relation to these public expectations, wondering constantly if they were up to the mark.[207]

The most radical forms of these anxieties still lay in the future. Communism in the NEP period was a relatively free society – that is, in relation to what was to come. Benjamin returned to Berlin and found it a 'dead city' in comparison to Moscow. What he missed was the shared poverty, the sense of purpose and of collectivity; Orwell was to feel something similar on his return to London from Barcelona in the summer of 1937. Here is Benjamin:

> [In Berlin] the people on the street seem desperately isolated, each one at a great distance from the next, all alone in the midst of the broad stretch of street. Furthermore: as I was travelling from the Zoo railway station toward the Grunewald, the neighbourhood I had to cross struck me as scrubbed and polished, excessively clean, excessively comfortable. What is true of the image of the city and its inhabitants is also applicable to its mentality: the new perspective one gains on this is the most indisputable consequence of a stay in Russia.[208]

Germany was soon to discover its own sense of community, 'scrubbed and polished' for those who belonged to it, lethal to those who did not, Benjamin included. But before reaching the German case, I must look to Asia Minor and the Mediterranean, in order to add three more very different cases to my notebook on family politics.

CHAPTER 2

The nest and the nation: family politics in the transition from Ottoman Empire to Turkish Republic, 1908–1938

I. FAMILIES IN OTTOMAN SOCIETY

1. Halide Edib

Halide Edib, Turkey's most famous early twentieth-century female author and patriot, was born in 1883, some eleven years after Aleksandra Kollontai. She too came from an upper-class background, for her father, Edib Bey, was a high functionary at the court of Sultan Abdülhamit II. She too lived a childhood of considerable comfort, in a large, old, wooden house in Beşiktaş, at that time a little-developed residential quarter of Istanbul. From the garden she could see the blue water of the Sea of Marmara, and near at hand, at Yıldız, the 'majestic white buildings' of the summer residence of the Sultan. The child Halide slept in the large room where she had been born. Her bed and that of her grandmother were 'Turkish beds', as she called them in her memoirs, laid out every evening on the carpet and then gathered up and put away in the morning. The room looked out to the garden:

> Three large windows open over the long, narrow divan, covered with the traditional clean white cloth of all Turkish divans. There is a red carpet on the floor and the curtains are white. Purple wisteria is in bloom, sunlight patches fall on the white cover under the windows [...] the little girl is faint with colour and beauty and the smell of it all.[1]

This idyllic environment contrasted strongly with the emotional disturbance and constant flux in her family. Whereas Aleksandra Kollontai's family of origin was a very stable one, marked by the rigid household routines and disciplines of her mother – a family, in other words, to revolt against – Halide

Edib's was splintered and evanescent. Her mother died of consumption when she was very young, one of Halide's few memories of her being when she cut her little daughter's fingernails so low that it hurt. She then 'quietly fades out from the background of her [daughter's] life'.[2] As for her father, Halide, like the young Shura, did everything she could to attract a father both busy and distracted. But in Edib's case her father quickly married again and his daughter was forced to leave her grandmother's beloved wisteria-covered house to go and live with her father's new wife and her family. Worse was to come. Her father decided to take a second wife, an act entirely within the precepts of Islamic law (which allows men to take up to four wives simultaneously), but one that was considered in increasingly negative terms by members of the Ottoman modernising elite at the end of the nineteenth century. Halide Edib writes movingly of the deleterious effects of polygamy[3] upon herself and her family:

> The nature and consequences of the suffering of a wife, who in the same house shares a husband lawfully with a second and equal partner, differs both in kind and in degree from that of the woman who shares him with a temporary mistress. In the former case, it must also be borne in mind, the suffering extends to two very often considerable groups of people – children, servants and relations – two whole groups whose interests are from the very nature of the case more or less antagonistic, and who are living in a destructive atmosphere of mutual distrust and a struggle for supremacy.
>
> On my own childhood, polygamy and its results produced a very ugly and distressing impression. The constant tension in our home made every simple family ceremony seem like a physical pain, and the consciousness of it hardly ever left me.
>
> The rooms of the wives were opposite each other, and my father visited them by turn.[4]

Little surprise, then, that Edib would come to reject the model of what she called 'father's incompatible family',[5] even though she continued to love certain members of it very much. What she hankered after – and in this she was very different from Kollontai – was a 'normal' family: a man and a woman living together with their children. This was, she thought, the model that best suited human beings. It was also the one best suited not to the decaying patriarchy of a great empire, but to the construction of a new nation-state, based upon the equal rights of women and men.

Halide Edib grew up as an intellectually precocious child, physically delicate and, by her own account, inclined to laziness. But like many people with a tendency to laziness, she was to spend her life in furious activity, constantly placing herself in situations that required considerable physical and psychological endurance. Her father, a traditionalist with regard to his employment at court and his own sexual practice, admired much about the English-speaking world and held liberal ideas in relation to the education of his daughter.[6] She was sent by him to the American College for Girls in Istanbul, from which she graduated in 1901. One of her teachers, Hester Donaldson Jenkins, recalled in 1910 that Halide was one of only two Turkish women she knew 'who care to read philosophy or can understand higher mathematics'.[7]

From childhood onwards, Halide Edib was deeply aware not only of gender injustice but of gender difference. In a light-hearted way she recalled the different reactions of her grandmother and grandfather to the onset of minor ailments. If her grandmother suffered from stomach pains she had mint leaves and lemon peel boiled together in a little water, which she then drank; if she had a headache she used rose leaves steeped in vinegar. Faced with the same ailments, her grandfather in the first case ate raw onions, crushing them with his fist because he believed that a knife spoiled their juice; in the second, he applied peeled potatoes to his forehead, tying them round his head with a white cloth. But there were also other, general gender differences which Halide found much more sinister during her childhood and youth. One was the behaviour of boys. For her, boys were 'emphatically not children'. She recalled, at a distance of thirty years, the dreadful howl of a yellow dog whose hindquarters had been crushed by a falling wall. It tried to escape with its fore paws, 'struggling in agony, and looking with that wonderful dumb appeal in its almost human eyes'. The boys present at the scene laughed and threw stones at the dog.[8]

Aleksandra Kollontai, though living through all the horrors of war, revolution and civil war, seemed none the less to possess an unlimited, peculiarly Marxist, faith in the capacity of the human race to improve itself. Halide Edib did not. On the contrary, the incident involving the dog 'was a symbolic and ominous revelation for me of the ugly instinct which stains the human species'.[9] Time and again, so she writes, she longed to be anything except a human being. Mankind – her emphasis was firmly on the 'man' – seemed incapable of living in peace. If only history would refuse to record martial glories, and art to immortalise them, she argued, then 'there might be some semblance of peace and relative human happiness in the world'.[10] But as she wrote these words in 1925 she must have known that her own actions contradicted them, for in 1921 she had volunteered to take up arms in Mustafa Kemal's Anatolian army of liberation.

fig. 9 A young Halide Edib at the beginning of the twentieth century, at the time of her
marriage.

Halide Edib was never a religious person, in the sense of belonging to a
congregation and regularly supporting the institutions and preachers of religion. She recounts in her memoirs her first and only visit to Sinan's great
Süleymaniye mosque, on its hill overlooking the whole of Istanbul:

> I quietly sneaked away and knelt before a preacher's pulpit. A pale man with
> eyes of liquid flame was speaking, condemning every human being to eternal
> fire, since his standard for a good Moslem was such that it was quite imprac-
> ticable to get to heaven [. . .]. His arms in their long loose black sleeves had a

prophetic gesture; his voice had a troubling tone, something so burning, so coloured lending itself to the wonderful rhythm and beauty of the verses of the Koran which he read and interpreted. It was really sublime nonsense, rendered in most artistic gestures and tones.[11]

On the other hand, Edib was neither an atheist nor anti-Islamic. She appealed regularly to Allah, even if she did not pray to him, and after she became well known in 1908 she continued, in the words of her former American teacher, to be 'moderate, sane and unselfish, never leaving off her veil, nor behaving otherwise than as becomes a modest Turkish lady'.[12]

At the end of 1901, having graduated from the American College just six months earlier, Halide Edib, aged eighteen, petite and with very striking features, chose to marry a man more than twenty years older than herself. Salih Zeki Bey was a talented mathematician and philosopher who harboured soaring intellectual ambitions. Had Halide read George Eliot's *Middlemarch* before she got married, she might have thought twice about the risks she was going to encounter. Salih Zeki was a latter-day Turkish Mr Casaubon, setting himself impossible goals and then harnessing all those closest to him in the attempt to realise them. His new wife threw herself happily into the undertaking:

I belonged to the new house and its master and gave the best I had to create a happy home and to help him in his great work. He had begun at this time his colossal work in Turkish – the 'Mathematical Dictionary' – and I prepared for him from different English authorities the lives of the great English mathematicians and philosophers.

Her abnegation was total: 'No little Circassian slave bought from the slave-market at the lowest price could have entered our common life in such an obedient spirit as I did.'[13]

They had two sons together, Ali Ayetullah and Hasan Hikmet, but theirs was not a happy union. He treated her with heavy condescension, regarding her as a wayward little student. She was nothing of the sort, and fought back. They quarrelled for entire nights. At the age of twenty-three she began translating Shakespeare into popular Turkish:

There is a wild harmony in the Anglo-Saxon diction of Shakespere [*sic*] the parallel of which I thought I could find in the simple but forcible Turkish of popular usage, the words and expressions of which belong more to Turkish than to Arabic or Persian sources [. . .] Salih Zeki Bey used to go over my version scratching out with a red pencil here and putting in Arabic words and the usual orthodox terms of high literary Turkish there [...] When I began the sonnets, however, even his mathematical accuracy and correctness in expression felt that there was some intangible lyrical vein which one could not always convey in strictest orthodox phraseology.[14]

After nine years of marriage, Halide Edib was forced to face the fact that her husband was having a very public affair with a teacher, and that he was considering taking her as a second wife. Halide was outraged by the prospect: 'A believer in monogamy, in the inviolability of name and home, I felt it to be my duty to retire from what I had believed would be my home to the end of my life.'[15] She took their little boys to Yanina for two months, near to her father's house. On her return, she found that Salih Zeki Bey had indeed married again, 'but to my great surprise he added that polygamy was necessary in some cases, and he asked me to continue as his first wife.'[16] She refused indignantly, and after a long and painful struggle he agreed to a divorce.

Halide Edib was shattered. She developed a serious chest infection, constant fevers and headaches, and was confined to bed for three months. Her iron will saw her through: 'I meant to conquer all physical ills, and I meant to make a home for my sons equal to the one they had had to leave, and to surround them with a happy and normal home atmosphere.'[17] As she lay in bed in the summer of 1910, once again at her grandmother's house, she listened to the evening sounds of her great city, 'the sellers of yogurt, kadayıf, the chanting of beggars, the footsteps of workers who pass down to Kum-Kapı, and at last the call of the childish voices and the patter of small feet scampering in the dusk in those large, lonely streets.'[18]

Eleven years later, in June 1921, serving as a nurse in a field hospital on the Anatolian front, Halide Edib was informed that her former husband had died in an asylum for the mentally ill. Her epitaph to him was a generous one: ' "Halidé", he would call from his bed before turning in, "thou wilt never free thy mind from mine." And it was true.'[19]

2. 1908

In 1908 Halide Edib was eyewitness to, and then participant in, one of the key moments of modern Turkish history – the constitutional revolution. The Sultan Abdülhamit II – 'with the imposing nose and shifty eyes', as she remembered him[20] – had acceded to the throne in 1876. At first he had promised to uphold the first-ever Ottoman Constitution. It provided for a bicameral parliament, with the Senate nominated by the Sultan and the House of Deputies elected by restricted male suffrage. It also established a wide range of civil liberties, including equality before the law regardless of religious belief. In less than a year, however, the Sultan went back on his constitutional promise. Using the war against Russia as a pretext, he took all power upon himself and for the next three decades ruled by means of an autocratic police state, famous for its system of spies. He also surrounded himself with conservative and reactionary Muslim clerics, and embraced 'pan-Islamism' as the regime's ideological base. His long reign was not without interest, especially in terms of its modernising features, to which I shall return; but the first timid steps towards democracy had been halted and the political opposition driven underground and abroad.[21] Midhat Paşa, the liberal architect of the Constitution and the Sultan's grand vizier in 1876, was strangled on the Sultan's orders in May 1883, in the Saudi dungeons of Al-Taif. The Young Ottoman movement, in many ways the most interesting and plural of the reform movements at the end of the Ottoman era, was definitively crushed.[22]

In 1908, after a thirty-year interval, a new opposition, rather different from the preceding one, forced Sultan Abdülhamit II to readopt the 1876 Constitution. The Young Turks were a wide-ranging conspiratorial movement, consisting for the most part of captains and majors in the army and minor bureaucrats in the Ottoman state administration. With few exceptions, they were all in their twenties and thirties. Their organisation was named the Committee of Union and Progress and one of its most important centres was a group of officers based in Salonica and serving in the Third Army, among whom were Enver, İsmail Hakkı and Mustafa Kemal.[23] They were soon to imprint upon the movement an intense Turkish nationalism, and to shift their loyalty away from the Sultan towards a 'Turkified' central state and nation. It was when various army units took to the hills in Macedonia and the troops sent to crush them joined the rebellion that Abdülhamit II hastily took up the 1876 Constitution again.

Suddenly, in July 1908, Istanbul became the site of extraordinary demonstrations, unprecedented in the history of the Empire. Old and young, poor and rich, Muslim and non-Muslim, intermingled in spontaneous rejoicing. The testimony of all the European newspapers of those days bears out the account of that moment of intense public joy and unexpected social and gender intermingling that Halide Edib has left us in her memoirs:

The papers might have been printed on gold-leaf, so high were the prices paid for them. People were embracing each other in the streets in mad rejoicing. Hussein Jahid [a family friend] smilingly added, 'I had to wash my face well in the evening, for hundreds who did not know me from Adam, hundreds whom

I have never seen, kissed me as I walked down the road of the Sublime Porte; the ugly side of the revolution, vengeance and murder, will not stain ours'.

The next day I went down to see Istamboul [*sic*]. The scene on the bridge caught me at once. There was a sea of men and women all cockaded in red and white, flowing like a vast human tide from one side to the other. The tradition of centuries seemed to have lost its effect. There was no such thing as sex or personal feeling. Men and women in a common wave of enthusiasm moved on, radiating something extraordinary, laughing, weeping in such intense emotion.[24]

Just as Aleksandra Kollontai first became well known at the time of the 1905 revolution in Russia, so Halide Edib, a young mother of two little boys and the daughter of one of the Sultan's secretaries, emerged to prominence as a most unusual reforming female voice in an overwhelmingly patriarchal society.

She rapidly became a well-known journalist and received many letters asking her opinion on social and political issues: 'Some of the letters', she wrote, 'were about family problems and secrets; no Catholic priest could have

fig. 10 Public demonstration in Istanbul, 1908.

received fuller and more candid confessions than I did during those months. I carefully burned them with professional discretion.' She also received visits from women of different social classes who came to ask advice about their personal problems. Edib wrote afterwards, 'It was through these visits that I first became aware of the tragic problems of the old social order [. . .] The surface of the political revolution was of passing interest, but the undercurrents of life, which started in the social depths of Turkey, drew me irresistibly into its whirlpool.'[25]

The 'surface of the political revolution' proved to be a treacherous one. At the end of March 1909, counter-revolutionary forces in the Turkish army and society, tacitly supported by the old Sultan and egged on by senior clerics and certain Sufi leaders, staged a coup in Istanbul. Many deputies and other supporters of the Young Turks and the Committee of Union and Progress were lynched and killed. Halide Edib's life was very much in danger and she was forced to flee with her two children to Alexandria in Egypt. The counter-revolution was quelled thanks to the intervention of the Third Army, which marched on Istanbul, but it was to be many months before Halide Edib returned. The events of 1908–9 served to show how fierce was the reaction to change within the Empire, how restricted was the progressive elite to which Halide Edib belonged, and how much that elite was beholden for further progress to dynamic, though not necessarily democratic, elements in the army.

3. Istanbul families at the turn of the century

In 1914 the total population of the dwindling Ottoman Empire – if we adopt the census figures of that year – was some twenty-six million.[26] This bald demographic figure hid two opposing tendencies. The first was the *increase* in population in the Turkish heartlands of the Empire, especially Anatolia, consequent upon both internal immigration and the diminution of disease – especially bubonic plague, typhoid and cholera – in the period after 1880. The second was the forced *decrease* in the overall imperial population after defeat in the Balkan Wars of 1912–13. The loss of the Balkans was a very grave blow, for it deprived the Empire of all but a fraction of its most populated provinces, which in the 1850s had accounted for nearly half the total Ottoman population.[27] The flow of Muslim refugees from the new Balkan states to Istanbul and then to Anatolia – perhaps as many as 400,000 persons – was the tragic human evidence of the end of the Empire's influence in Europe.[28]

As in the Russian case, so in the Ottoman, the horrors of the first two decades of the twentieth century threatened in unprecedented fashion the stability and indeed the very survival of countless families. Three great wars – first that of the

Balkans, then the First World War and finally the War of Independence – led to huge losses of life, the forcible migrations of millions of people, and atrocities of all kinds. The Turks were to be victims of great injustices but also perpetrators of them.

Historical research on Ottoman families is very much less developed than that on Russian ones. The rural areas of the Empire, which constituted perhaps as much as 85 per cent of the population, remain to a great extent uncharted territory. The same is not true for the cities, for thanks to some path-breaking work on Istanbul it is possible to reconstruct in some detail family life in that great capital city at the turn of the century.[29] Working from the censuses of 1885, 1907 and 1927, Alan Duben and Cem Behar have established a total city population of some 874,000 in 1885, over a million in 1907, but less than 700,000 by 1927. This last figure reflects the calamities of the war years and the abandonment of the city by many of its non-Muslim families. Traditionally, the non-Muslim communities – mainly Greek, Armenian and Jewish – had constituted between a third and a half of the city's total population.[30]

Little evidence regarding the family life of the Istanbul popular classes has come down to us. We do know that income differentials between families were very much more contained than in London or St Petersburg in the same period. The average daily wage of an Istanbul labourer in 1913 was 14.1 *kuruş*, or around 350 *kuruş* a month; the average monthly salary paid to officials in the Foreign Ministry was only 1,177 *kuruş*, barely three times more.[31]

Duben and Behar have focused their attention upon the city's Muslim population, and their research has produced more than one surprise. The mean average household size in 1907 was only 4.2 persons, much lower than in other major pre-industrial Muslim cities. Lower too was the total fertility rate, already only 3.9 in the last quarter of the nineteenth century. The structure of families was overwhelmingly nuclear, two parents and two children, as can be seen not only from the statistics but from many of the family photographs of the time. At most the widowed mother of the male head of household (or more rarely that of his spouse) joined the central family group. Extended families were fewer in Istanbul than in the rest of Turkey, forming just 31 per cent of all Istanbul households in 1907.[32]

Before the end of the Ottoman Empire, then, a transition to modern family forms in Istanbul had already reached a surprisingly advanced stage. This impression of the city's exceptionality is confirmed by two other, co-related elements: the widespread use of contraceptive techniques; and the significant increase in the marriage age of women, which rose from twenty to twenty-three years old in the period 1900–30. The city had mainly neolocal residency patterns (that is, the setting up of autonomous households on marriage) rather than patrilocal ones. And it was characterised, as we have seen, by nuclear families rather than extended ones. All this suggests that Istanbul was much more a cosmopolitan Mediterranean port than a traditional Muslim capital, more Beirut than Cairo.[33] It also suggests, without wishing to exaggerate or to draw rigid causal connections, that in Istanbul at the beginning of the twentieth century family structures and patterns provided some of the necessary pre-conditions for the birth of a civil society.

4. The traditional bases of Ottoman patriarchy

The Muslim middle- and upper-class families of Istanbul – those about whom we have most information – were thus an extraordinary mixture of the old and the new. To bring their transitional status into sharp relief, it is worth sketching briefly what they were leaving behind: the traditional order, rules and precepts of Ottoman elite families.

Over the centuries, ethnic traditions, imperial power and Islamic codes of conduct had together created a particular version of Islamic patriarchy. Male heads of family, with the collaboration of the senior women, controlled the movements, the sexuality and the life patterns of all female and male members of their households. In arranging marriages, the head of family exercised a power of constraint (*cebr*) over all his children. There was no minimum age for marriage according to Islamic law. Marriage itself was a private contract without any of the institutional and sacramental character of its western and Christian counterpart. Among the few requirements for marriage was the presence of two witnesses. The *mehr*, the marriage gift or payment which devolved from the groom's family to the bride, was not a validating proof of marriage, but was considered an essential element in proceedings. It took many forms and was the result of intense negotiations, the details of which were inserted in the marriage contract. From the sixteenth century onwards, religious judges (*kadı*) ruled on the validity of these contracts.[34]

Though Islamic marriage law contained some elements which protected a wife's condition – she was accorded legal status in the marriage contract and her property was kept separate from that of her husband – by and large male heads of households exercised great and arbitrary power over their wives. It was they who dictated the terms of married life. Husbands could take as many as four wives, provided they could maintain them, and an unlimited number of concubines, if they were wealthy enough. The difference between concubine and wife was that while the first was a piece of property, a commodity to be bought and sold, the second enjoyed some juridical status and protection. Even so, the post-classic[35] definition of marriage in Islamic law – 'a contract by which a man acquires the right legitimately to enjoy a woman' – was not exactly consolatory.[36] A husband was entitled to use physical violence to 'correct' his wife's conduct but was not to indulge in 'brutality'. For her part, a wife could seek redress before a *kadı* only if the physical signs of a beating were still visible upon her body.

The making and conduct of marriage was thus almost entirely in male hands, and its termination even more so. In the hanefite school of Islamic law, the one followed by the Sunni Muslims of the Ottoman Empire, there were almost no grounds on which a woman could seek divorce before a religious court. A man, on the other hand, had many avenues open to him. One of the most frequent was that of repudiation: a husband simply announced that he no longer wished to live with his wife. Repudiation took many forms. The more emphatic its formulation – for instance, if the husband declared, 'I repudiate you as much as there are fish in the sea, or hairs on your head, or men upon the earth' – the more irrevocable it was. Sometimes men even entrusted to one wife the task of announcing the repudiation of another. All this was allowed by the religious courts. The repudiated wife had no recourse to law except in very exceptional circumstances.[37]

Yet Ottoman patriarchy did not just rest on unbridled male power, but was diffused in a more complex and fascinating way. In the household there existed a second, female power hierarchy, at the peak of which stood the eldest woman, either the mother or the first wife of the patriarch, provided she had kept his sympathy over time. This leading female figure exercised considerable authority over the overall shape of domestic life. The Ottoman elite household, like the Russian peasant one, thus had two binary divisions of power at work within it: male–female and older–younger. And in no area of family life did the senior male and female figures exercise greater weight than in the choice of marriage partners for their children, often at a very tender age.[38]

The traditional Ottoman version of the relationship between private and public was reflected in the spatial organisation of households. Women and children lived their lives in the harem, the untouchable and inviolable part of the house, whose purity was guaranteed by men and elders. Women's presence in external space was to be kept as brief as possible, for the outside world was potentially polluting. When they went out, women were to be veiled and accompanied by an older woman or relative. Wives were to follow behind their husbands at a respectable distance. Young children from 'old Turkish households', such as that of Halide Edib, had to be accompanied by their *lala*, their manservant and protector. Halide's *lala* was called Ali and bought her little coloured sweets in the street, a purchase strictly forbidden by her father.[39]

Adult males, by contrast, lived mainly in the part of the house called the 'selamlık', which was situated in proximity to the outside world, thus enabling the head of the family to receive friends and visitors and to conduct his affairs without violating the exclusivity of the harem, in which the women of the household lived unveiled. Men, too, were expected to spend limited time in public space, mostly for work or religious purposes.

In these family constructions, male control was exercised above all over women's bodies and their sexuality. Women were considered incapable by nature of preserving the purity of their own bodies and potentially dangerous for the ordering of the *ümmet* (the community of believers) on account of their capacity to undermine the self-control of men. In the preachings of the Russian Orthodox Church and in the Şeriat we find remarkably similar diatribes against the licentiousness of women. In the Turco-Islamic world women's sexuality was strongly associated with 'fitne', a word which alludes to chaos, disorder, even civil war. The Muslim conception of sexuality was not as sin but as positive energy, a vital necessity and a gift of God, but one which had to be reined in by the social regulation of women's bodies.[40]

Men's sexuality, by contrast, enjoyed a great deal of freedom and variety, provided it was lived within the confines of the household, broadly inter-preted.[41] Polygamy was praised for its advantages in guaranteeing reproduc-tion and avoiding prostitution. Concubinage was also a common feature, further catering to male libidinousness. At the end of the nineteenth century Istanbul still boasted an active slave market. Slaves could be bought both for use as domestic servants and for sexual purposes. Young Circassian girls, often blond and of considerable beauty, were most sought after. Sometimes they had been sold by their families into slavery, or else had been kidnapped by slave merchants. Once in an Istanbul harem they were taught to sing and dance and were initiated into other arts and practices appropriate to their role. After many years of loyal service to master and household, they could hope to obtain their freedom; alternatively they might be given away as a gift to another household and harem.[42]

5. Cultural transformations and Istanbul families

By the beginning of the twentieth century many of these traditional elements of the Turco-Islamic family were subject to considerable tension and change. The attraction of the West and the resistance of the East made Istanbul a unique cultural battleground in which the destinies of the family became a central issue.[43] As so often happens, conflicting cultural tendencies produced fascinating combinations, mixtures and compromises. No European influence was stronger than the French. Indeed, the two dominant schools of cultural taste in Istanbul at this time were described as 'alaturka' and 'alafranga'.

Let me look first at emotions and generations. One of the potentially most disruptive influences in Istanbul in the last decades of the nineteenth century was French romantic thought, and in particular the category of *amour passion*, so memorably explored and dissected by the literary tradition which passed from Rousseau to Stendhal and Flaubert.[44] Love had always existed in Ottoman society – it is enough to think of the extraordinary passion of Süleyman the Magnificent for his ex-concubine and then wife Hürrem Sultan[45] – but it was only at the end of the nineteenth century, with the widespread diffusion of French literature at an elite level, that love played a crucial role in breaking up the time-honoured Ottoman practice of arranged marriages. Previously, it was a widely held precept that love or affection (*muhabbet*), if it came at all, 'comes after the wedding'. Parents' interests, not children's hearts, determined the choice of partners. By the turn of the century love matches were disrupting these patterns severely. Halide Edib married for love, and so did many of her contemporaries. Naturally, there was no sudden and total transformation of practice. The patriarchal family of origin still exerted great pressure on the younger generation and played a crucial financial role, as in negotiations over the *mehr*. But the mould of arranged marriages had been broken, and the great imbalance between the generations had been partially redressed.

In 1872 Namık Kemal, a pioneer journalist and a major figure in the Young Ottoman movement, wrote a famous article entitled 'Aile' (Family):

> Until when will fathers go on wanting their sons to be exactly as they were? For how long will they consider it a mortal humiliation if, for example, the son of an imam [mosque preacher] chooses to become a doctor? How can we go on thinking that we are giving our sons a good education if we refuse in the meantime to recognise their rights and inclinations?[46]

Not by chance was the movement to which he belonged called the *Young* Ottomans, just as its successor took the name of the *Young* Turks.

Nowhere was the distance from a traditional model more marked than on the question of polygamy. Although all foreign travellers concentrated on the phenomenon in their accounts, the statistics for Istanbul strongly suggest that it had long been on the wane in that city. The 1885 census showed only 2.5 per cent of married Muslims having more than one wife, and by 1907 the percentage had dropped to 2.16. Polygamy, as all modern commentators agreed, was an expensive business and risked destroying the serenity of a household. Halide Edib's father had discovered this to his cost. Those who were polygamous came almost exclusively from the upper classes, and even then had on average only two wives.[47]

Other, more subtle changes were also taking place within the home. Forms of address between family members gradually shifted. In the traditional Ottoman family, the wife (or wives) addressed her husband by title – usually 'bey' (mister) or 'efendi' (sir) – rather than by name; she would also use the formal 'siz' ('vous'). Her husband, on the other hand, precisely to mark the difference between them, would use the informal 'sen' ('tu') and the generic term 'hanım' (wife). These usages began to give way in the new century to more egalitarian forms of address. At the same time the Muslims of Istanbul began to use the word 'familya' rather than the age-old Arabic word for family 'aile'.[48]

Of equal symbolic importance were changes in eating habits. Families of all classes were used to dining crouched around a large tray (sini), raised perhaps a foot above the floor. Hands or spoons were used rather than knives or forks. Naturally, there was a gendered and generational etiquette which accompanied this communal eating, but its shared nature was evident. Eating in the alafranga style, by contrast, implied a new separateness and individualism. Single plates took the place of the sini, knives and forks replaced hands and spoons, and above all the family moved from crouching on the floor to sitting on separate chairs around a table.[49]

At the same time many traditional patterns of gender behaviour went unchanged. The younger generation of men certainly contested their fathers, who were held responsible for the Empire's inexorable decline, and the absence of strong father figures in the Turkish novels of the time has been remarked upon.[50] But the 'new' Ottoman men, while seeking their own liberation, were far from seeking it for the other sex. Asymmetrical power relations within the family were still very much the order of the day. An independent and outspoken female figure such as Halide Edib was the exception rather than the rule. Edib's teacher Hester Donaldson Jenkins, who spent ten years in Istanbul at the beginning of the twentieth century, has left us this revealing cameo, both of the author and of her subject, which is the passivity and patience of middle-class Istanbul Muslim women:

> The amusements of a Turkish lady we should consider rather mild. She is seldom intellectual [. . .] nor have lectures, clubs, concerts, and reading circles been opened to her under the old regime. She is not athletic even in her youth, so she plays no tennis or golf [. . .] She plays no games, such as bridge, whist or dominoes, although Turkish men are fond of games of chance. She does not become absorbed in fancy work, her hands do not require her to be occupied. What then does she do?

For the most part she *sits*. The Turkish verb *to sit* is constantly used where we should say *stay* or *live* or *visit* [. . .] All Oriental women occupy an enormous proportion of their time in sitting. And when they sit it is not in the restless way that we have, but with the hands idly folded in the lap, in the perfect repose of a sleeping cat, often for hours without even conversation. They often sit cross-legged on the low divans, or on cushions on the floor [. . .]

Turkish women love to go out of doors and sit. On a Friday afternoon one may see all the open fields and hill-sides, and even the sides of the roads, in Scutari or some other half-country suburb, bright with the *charshafs* and parasols of sitting women. Perhaps a husband brings his wives out, perhaps a group of women is escorted by a servant, perhaps a mother has brought her children to the *maidan* – there they are, hundreds on the greensward.[51]

6. Sociality and civil society

This evocative reference to sitting out brings me to Istanbul families in their social context. Traditionally, community life in the Muslim quarters of Istanbul was founded on the *mahalle* – a grouping around a mosque of ten or fifteen streets at most, sometimes with a focal point in a small piazza (*meydan*). From the notebooks of the imam of the Kasab İlyas *mahalle*, which consisted of twelve streets and 150 residences, it has been possible to reconstruct in detail one such quarter for the year 1885. The *mahalle*, which formed part of the historic centre of the city and skirted the Sea of Marmara, boasted two mosques, a *tekke* (dervish lodge), three public fountains, five market gardens, a *hamam* (public bath), two bakeries, thirty-seven other shops and a police station.[52] These small communities were marked by their inter-class nature – a large *konak* (wooden urban mansion) would stand next to much more modest dwellings.

Much of the social life of the families that constituted the *mahalle* centred around the mosque – its calendar of prayers and observances, its instructions and festivals. Another crucial religious and social institution was the *tekke*, the dervish or Sufi brotherhood or lodge. Exclusively male in membership, such confraternities provided a series of intense and personal religious experiences that could combine with the mosques' activities or transcend them. Their members gathered for communal prayer (*zikr*) and to perform specific devotional practices. Those of the Mevlevi brotherhood, for example, famously whirled around in circles seeking mystical visions. Others chanted. The lodges were widely diffused – perhaps as many as three hundred in late Ottoman Istanbul, divided into twenty different brotherhoods.

Two other institutions, not religious but secular, characterised social life: the public bath (*hamam*) and the coffee house. Both were rigorously separated on gender lines. While the coffee house was a place of male sociability, the *hamam* served in the first place to fulfil hygienic functions as laid down by religious precept. There was a *hamam* for women and one for men, and sometimes the same public bath was open on some days of the week to one gender and on other days to the other. The female *hamam* was a unique location for socialising and for discussing prospective marriage alliances.

The unabashed nudity of the baths both attracted and embarrassed western women visitors, accustomed as they were to the much more tightly buttoned social habits of Europe, especially of north-west Europe. Lady Montagu's description of the women's *hamam*, written with early eighteenth-century detail and eroticism, remains unparalleled.[53]

Coffee houses were the public male space par excellence. In the early seventeenth century, Murat IV, 'the bloodthirsty', had gone around the streets of Istanbul at night, cutting off the heads of coffee drinkers, the drink then being regarded as both potent and subversive.[54] Three centuries later, cleared of any whiff of Janissary conspiracy, coffee-house society was in full swing. Men drank and smoked, listened to music, played cards and backgammon, told stories and discussed the events of the day. The odd spy of the Sultan was almost certainly in attendance.

Abdülhamit II was certainly no liberal – Perry Anderson has memorably called him the 'King Bomba of the Bosphorous'[55] – but he was a moderniser in his own way. His innovations – increased primary schooling for both sexes, no longer based solely on the Koran, the development of urban transport and the construction of railways, the greater centralisation of the state apparatus – were hardly designed to promote political and civil liberties. But as often happens in such circumstances, society became freer even if its civil and political practices could not be. This was particularly true for women. They began to go out more frequently, in their carriages or simply covered with a veil. Some of them even used the new public transport facilities, which had special sections reserved for women. Conservative Ottoman thinking of the time considered these innovations a dangerous blurring of the barriers, not only between male and female but also between internal and external spaces. And they were right. Istanbul families, especially those of the elites, were on the move – in terms of their structures (ever more nuclear and less polygamous), their gender relations and their presence in the outside world.

The potential of the city and of its elite families in particular was thus considerable, once the carapace of the Sultan's police state was removed.

The extraordinary demonstrations of 1908 were the clear manifestation of these political possibilities. Furthermore, the deep structures of Istanbul families were not inimical to change. The heterogeneity of the Istanbul population and the habitual mixing of the upper ranks of non-Muslim society with the dominant Muslim elite allowed for a greater penetration of the new ideas.

Unlike Arab and Kurdish families, or indeed Turkic ones in parts of Anatolia, Ottoman Istanbul families were *exogamous*, not *endogamous*.[56] In the Arab world, the traditions of the endogamous 'community' family, characterised by frequent marriages between first cousins, the cohabitation of married sons with their parents and equal inheritance between brothers, have had considerable influence upon social and political formation. No family could be stronger but at the same time more 'closed' than one in which the marriage partners of the next generation are chosen from within its midst.[57] Late Ottoman urban families were not of this type. While caution must be exercised in the attempt to derive political forms from family structures, we can certainly say that Istanbul Muslim families at this time did not present the structural features of *over-powerful* families or clans. Their overall culture, in other words, was not one which inclined towards the exercise of family or clan power at the expense of the state. State and family were not caught in a vicious circle in which the first was inextricably dependent upon the second.[58]

Why then, it may be fair to ask, did Istanbul families not fulfil all their cultural potential in this crucial period of transition? Why were they not the powerhouse on which a lasting public sphere was stably constructed? Why did 1908 remain an isolated date in the Turkish historical calendar, rather than being the founding-point of a new political and cultural tradition?

The answer to such questions is a complex one. At one level, it has to do with long-term trends within the Empire's history: no tradition of self-governing towns or other semi-autonomous institutions had ever been allowed to develop. Coffee houses were no substitute for independent urban associations or societies.[59] At another level, employment was all-important: Istanbul was the dying capital of a great empire, and very many Istanbul families remained dependent for their livelihood upon the Sultan's bureaucracy. The economic system was still governed by rigid corporative rules and the enormous interests on the Ottoman debt did not allow for investment in public works. For all the elite's new-found western habits, its loyalty was built upon centuries of obedience, and was in part reinforced by Abdülhamit II's self-legitimating and self-celebratory practices.[60] Even after 1909 the loyalty of the city to its ruling house was still firmly intact. Not by chance, as we shall see, did Mustafa Kemal begin his fight for modern Turkey from Ankara, which was little more than a swollen Anatolian village, rather than from the shifting and unreliable political sands of the imperial capital.

Nor did Istanbul in these decades give birth to a working-class movement of any significance. The contrast with St Petersburg is striking. Many of the features of Russian proletarian life that underlay the formation of self-governing Soviets in 1905 and 1917 – mass employment in large factories, the significant presence of women workers, intolerable conditions for family life in run-down worker neighbourhoods – were completely absent in Istanbul. The latter was a city of artisans and shopkeepers, not industrial workers. By itself this fact explains nothing, for the class bases of Parisian radicalism in the nineteenth century were overwhelmingly artisan, whatever Marx had to say on the matter. But the Muslim artisan classes of Istanbul were in a sense 'held' by other traditions – by that of the Islamic *ümmet*, and by neighbourhoods which mixed rich and poor. The popular classes were integrated into their *mahalle*, surveyed by the state, and organised into corporations and patron–client networks of great density and tradition.

A final level of explanation is perhaps the most potent of all. It has to do with non-Muslim Istanbul families, heretofore absent from our account, but always a significant minority of the city's population. Organised in separate communities according to their religion, Greeks, Armenians and Jews had for centuries lived side by side with the Muslim majority, rarely intermarrying with them but co-existing in a mainly cordial fashion.[61] Each community (*millet*) was organised hierarchically, its leading male members, often rich and powerful merchants, being accountable directly to the Palace. From the reforms of 1839 (Tanzimat) onwards, such communities began gradually to enjoy equal civil rights, though not political ones, with the Muslim population.[62] By the end of the century there were at the highest levels of Ottoman society a significant number of non-Muslims, both intellectuals and high-ranking members of the Sultan's administration, who enjoyed particular respect for their knowledge of European culture. They often knew more than one European language and were the natural intermediaries for relations with a constantly expanding European capitalism. It was they who sent their sons abroad to study, and they in turn became motors of cultural modernisation in the Empire.

The Young Ottoman movement was laced with the younger generations of these minority families. The first Ottoman novel, *Akabi's Story* (1851), recounted an impossible love affair between two Armenian youths, one Catholic and one Gregorian. It was written in Ottoman Turkish using Armenian script by Yovsep Vardanean, an Ottoman Armenian statesman and journalist. The Ottoman theatre was created, performed and managed almost enitirely by Armenians and Jews.[63] The pluralism, cultural collaboration and youthful political enthusiasm of the Young Ottoman movement, for all its many limitations and contradictions, boded well for the civic wealth of the city. So too, after the decades of repression (1877–1908), did the collaboration between different ethnic and religious groups – Turks and Armenians in particular – which was responsible for the tax revolts and mobilisations prior to and during the revolution of 1908, both in Istanbul and elsewhere.[64]

It was not to be. Rampant nationalism triumphed rapidly over the possibilities of mutual co-existence and collaboration. The Balkan Wars of 1912–13 were a watershed, with the forcible expulsion of Muslims from the new Balkan nation-states and their influx into Istanbul and other Turkish cities. The possibilities of collaborative urban family politics all but disappeared. The new political objective propagated by the Young Turks was 'Turkism', by which the Turkish-speaking Muslim population would constitute the nation, to the exclusion of all those who did not fit into such a scheme. As ethnic Turks emerged as a majority of the Empire's population for the first time in its history, Greek, Armenian and Jewish minorities in Istanbul came to be regarded with growing hostility. Nationalism, overlaid by religion, became the dominant form of self-identification, throughout the Balkans and the Middle East. The Great Powers, with their differing agendas for the partition of what remained of the Empire, and with their own religious and ethnic preferences, fanned the flames. The First World War dramatically reinforced these trends. By 1919 the level of inter-group tension in Istanbul was so great that Halide Edib wrote in her memoirs,

> The feeling of hatred between the different races [. . .] had gone so deep that the Turkish children and the Christian children could not pass each other's quarters without being stoned or beaten. Sometimes they fought singly, and sometimes in packs [. . .] Allah knows how closely the miniature warfare resembled the World War. The bigger and more brutal type of boys of both sides enjoyed it immensely, like their prototypes.[65]

7. Kemal, Enver and the Young Turks

As a boy, Mustafa Kemal, who was later to take the name of Atatürk, the Father of the Turks, was neither particularly big nor brutal. He was, though, the only surviving male child in a family which had lost its father figure at a relatively early age. Ali Rıza, Mustafa's father, had died aged forty-seven, when his son was seven years old. He was generally considered a failure in the family – a customs official who drank too much and had dabbled rather unsuccessfully in the timber trade. Mustafa thus became at an early age the most important male in his family, used to getting his own way and dominating all those around him. His sister Makbule was later to recount that he was too proud as a child to play leapfrog, as he would not bend down to allow other children to vault over him. Whatever the truth of the tale, it gives the measure of the boy – and then the man.[66]

He and Halide Edib had very different family origins – she the daughter of a numerous, complicated, high-ranking family at the heart of the Empire, he the only surviving son of a lower-middle-class family of limited economic resources resident in a provincial centre – Salonica. Family and gender separated them radically and only Turkish nationalism brought them together – for a time. At Ankara at the beginning of the War of Independence, Mustafa Kemal set himself to study the history of Islam, and discussed it with Halide. For her, the hero of the story was Ali, the fourth Caliph, the 'Lion of Allah' and the son-in-law of the Prophet: 'Ali', she told Mustafa Kemal, 'is the least successful Islamic hero. Every adversary takes advantage of his nobility of heart [. . .] He finally dies unsuccessful but undaunted, always morally clean, manly and humane.' Kemal's reaction was brutally concise: ' "Ali was a fool", he used to say.'[67]

Mustafa Kemal's education began at the civil service preparatory school in Salonica, but after a brief period he insisted on transferring to the city's military school instead. He wrote later, 'It was when I entered the military preparatory school and put on its uniform that a feeling of strength came to me, as if I had become master of my own identity.'[68] At about this time his mother remarried, much to the fury of her son, who refused to return to the family home and went to lodge with an aunt.

His military education was to last thirteen years, first at Salonica and then from 1899 onwards at the elite War College of Istanbul. He loved being part of the army – the rigour of its discipline, its male camaraderie, even its primitive stews of beans, mutton and rice – and regarded it throughout his life as his true family. In the language of the time he became a 'school trained' (*mektepli*) officer, a group which up and down the Empire formed the most important nuclei of the Young Turks, and which was successfully to challenge the hegemony of the older, 'regiment trained' (*alaylı*) officers. By the time of the 1908 revolution, Kemal was a staff officer in Salonica, one of the chief centres of revolt. But he was still relatively junior and little more than a rank-and-file member of the Committee of Union and Progress, the secretive organisation of the Young Turks which was to rule the Empire, almost without interruption, until the disastrous end of the First World War. Mustafa Kemal's time was still to come, first at Gallipoli in 1915 and then above all in the fight for Turkish independence after 1919.[69]

The revolution of 1908 had unleashed many positive forces in Ottoman society. One of them was the flowering of a free press: in the years after the revolution some 722 newspapers and journals were published in Turkish, 70 in Greek, 67 in Armenian, 49 in French and 42 in both Turkish and French.[70] Another fundamental innovation was the election of a parliament with more than merely token powers. Yet the formidable and contrasting forces of modern nationalisms, Islamic conservatism and imperial nostalgia never lurked far below the surface.

The Young Turks' Committee of Union and Progress (henceforth CUP) tried to steer an uneasy path between these countervailing tendencies. They were not sufficiently sure of themselves to abolish the sultanate, though they finally deposed Abdülhamit in 1909 and replaced him with his feeble brother. Nor did they want direct responsibility for government, preferring instead to indicate the older generations of soldiers and bureaucrats for ministerial posts. Behind this facade of deference to seniority and to the Sultan, however, the CUP's semi-clandestine central committee of forty persons held the reins of power.

fig. 11 An Ottoman family reading newspapers. The newspapers are *Hürriyet*, *İttifak*, *Karagöz* and *Tanin*, all published from 1908.

The CUP leaders were more pragmatists than ideologues, more soldiers than statesmen, and their limitations as a new ruling class were not long in coming to the fore. They operated politically at two levels. Superficially, and in their early years of power, they proclaimed a civic and plural nationalism, open to any citizen of the Ottoman state, regardless of ethnic origin or religious creed. In reality, though far from unanimous, they were working towards a modern state dominated by ethnic Turks and professing the Islamic faith.[71] They were anything but Islamic fundamentalists: the state was to take the lead and religion was to follow, knowing, or eventually learning, its place. In this respect they rather admired the French Third Republic's elaboration of Church–state relations.[72]

Though the CUP boasted a collective leadership, three men came to dominate it and to bear principal responsibility for what was to come: Enver, Cemal and Talât. Enver and Cemal were both 'school trained' officers, Enver having been two years ahead of Mustafa Kemal at military high school, while Talât had been a functionary in the post office system. Of the three, Enver was the most dangerous and flamboyant.[73] After the disaster of the Balkan Wars of 1912–13, the CUP staged a coup which involved the assassination of the Minister of War and the direct assumption of power. The liberties and spaces opened by the 1908 revolution were henceforth to be severely restricted. Enver became the Turkish hero of the day when he led the army to retake Edirne, the only European provincial centre left to the Ottomans. He wrote to his wife at the time, 'Our anger is strengthening: revenge, revenge, revenge.'[74]

8. The invention of the Turkish family

The last figure I would like to consider in this little album of Young Turks is the least known outside Turkey but the most interesting for the arguments of this book. Ziya Gökalp is recognised as the most original and influential of Turkish political thinkers of the twentieth century. Like so many of the Young Turk leadership, he was born in the provinces, to a modest family of civil servants in the city of Diyarbakır in south-east Anatolia. This was a Kurdish area and his political opponents were later to accuse him of being more Kurd than Turk, an accusation he treated with derision, for he was always to base national identity on culture rather than ethnicity. Gökalp was a shy, fat and swarthy man, much liked – even loved – by those around him. He was a sort of spiritual guide to the CUP, an inspiration, a *mürşid*, as he was called in Turkish.[75] In 1909, on becoming a member of the central committee of the CUP, he moved to Salonica, where he met Mustafa Kemal, and in 1912 to Istanbul. He directed the party's youth department and founded the chair in sociology at the

University of Istanbul, but he never held any major position of political responsibility.

Influenced by Henri-Louis Bergson, Ferdinand Tönnies and above all Émile Durkheim, Gökalp never wrote a major treatise of political theory, instead adopting the dominant form of the short essay. Often popularising and didactic in tone, these essays were frequently published in obscure journals between 1911 and his death in 1924 at the age of forty-nine. Gökalp's reflections take as their starting point a fundamental and, in his hands, fecund distinction between civilisation (*medeniyet*) and culture (*hars*).[76] Civilisation was international while culture was national. Civilisation expressed shared scientific knowledge and institutions common to more than one nation. France, Germany and Britain, though different from one another, all belonged to a single (and all-conquering) western civilisation. Culture, on the other hand, was peculiar to each single national formation and took its identity from that nation's uses, customs, traditions and sentiments. Thus Turkish culture was as distinct from Greek as Greek was from Italian. Furthermore, culture and civilisation were to be distinguished on gender grounds. *Hars* (culture) was essentially male, corresponding to the deepest level of national identity, while *medeniyet* (civilisation) was female. The two had to interrelate but it was *hars* which dominated, taking from *medeniyet* that which it needed to establish its modern national identity. The complex intertwining between cultures and civilisations was for Gökalp the key to historical understanding and explanation.[77]

When he examined the Turkish case in this light, Gökalp had few doubts about what had gone wrong. In the cosmopolitan, eastern and doomed civilisation of which the Ottoman Empire had formed such a distinguished part, the Turkish *hars* had never had a chance to emerge – to rescue from oblivion its folklore and traditions, to place on a firm historical footing its deepest values. This had been the fundamental reason for defeat in the Balkans: 'The traditionalist nation [that is, one firmly founded upon its traditions] lives in the freedom of history, the formalist in the bondage of geography. During the Balkan wars, the Bulgarians were inspired by their fiery traditions; we were inspired by our cold rules. The result was the victory of history over geography.'[78] The task now awaiting the Turks was to discover, fortify and develop their culture, beyond the 'cold rules' which had dominated the Empire. It was also to enter fully into western civilisation, while always adapting that civilisation to Turkish needs and traditions.

For no institution was this journey more necessary than for the family. In the last six productive years of his life, between 1917 and 1923, Gökalp dedicated a number of key articles to the theme of the family.[79] Unlike Kollontai, whose model for social and domestic life was projected far into the future, Gökalp, good nationalist that he was, looked backwards not forwards: 'in order to anticipate the future course of the family among the Turks, we have to go back to its origins'.[80] In a splendid and highly original 'invention of tradition', his studies returned to the pre-Islamic Turkish past. There he identified an original Turkish family, surprisingly based on a broad equality between the sexes. Once again his principal dichotomy, as for culture and civilisation, was a gendered one. In the ancient Turkish past, magic – in the form of shamanism – was represented by women and *töre* – customary law – by men. As these two systems had an equal value amongst the ancient Turks, so men and women were broadly equal. It was only later, in the Abbasi period, 'when the ascetic conceptions of the Iranian and Greek Orthodox religions penetrated through to the Muslims',[81] that magic was condemned as false and consequently women's inferior status became commonplace throughout the Muslim world. Polygamy, according to Gökalp, had not been any part of indigenous Turkish culture.

Gökalp went so far as to proclaim that 'democracy and feminism were the two bases of ancient Turkish life'. His account is both naive and powerful, a striking contrast to rigid Ottoman patriarchy:

The ancient Turkish women were all amazons and they, as well as Turkish men, were noted for their horsemanship, skill in the use of arms and feats of heroism. Women could become rulers, fortress commanders, governors and ambassadors in their own right. Among ordinary families the house belonged jointly to husband and wife and the right of guardianship over children lay with the mother as much as with the father. A man always respected his wife and would have her ride in the cart while he would walk behind.[82]

Furthermore, in the ancient world of magic, where sacred power resided with women, shamans even had to compensate for being men, pretend to belong to the other sex, and undergo symbolic sex changes: '[They] had to disguise themselves as women. They would wear women's clothes, let their hair grow, refine their voices, shave their mustaches [*sic*] and beards, and even get pregnant and bear children.'[83] This hardly fitted the traditional picture of Turkish masculinity – in Gökalp's time or in ours.

It was highly significant that Gökalp, the principal theoretician of the new 'national' Turkish family, took this semi-mythical, 'democratic' and 'feminist' past as his starting point.

His debt to Durkheim, in this area as in others, is quite considerable. Durkheim had always been fascinated by the historical evolution of the family, kinship and marriage. He had intended to publish a volume on the sociology of the family but did not succeeded in doing so before his premature death in 1917 – in no small part caused by the earlier death of his only son, André, who was mortally wounded fighting against the Turks on the Bulgarian front. In his family studies, which are almost as fragmentary as those of his Turkish acolyte, Durkheim traced out an evolutionary scheme, beginning with the broad expanses of the amorphous, endogamous clan and culminating in the narrow confines of the contemporary conjugal family. In a famous lecture first delivered in 1892 but published only posthumously in 1921, Durkheim identified a number of key characteristics of the modern 'famille conjugale'.[84] First, the family had assumed its *nuclear* form in which only parents and children now lived together. Extended kinship was fading in significance and marriage had become the determining act of union. Secondly, individuals were becoming increasingly autonomous within this modern family structure, and needed strong extra-familial ties – such as professional associations – to check their growing individualism. And thirdly, the state was increasingly intervening to control, sustain and regulate family life.

We cannot be sure if Gökalp read this lecture on its publication in 1921. Unlike many of his contemporaries he never visited Paris, nor did he maintain a correspondence with Durkheim. But he would certainly have recognised the characteristics singled out by Durkheim and embraced their implications. For Gökalp, Turkish culture needed a modern family form, neither excessively western nor eastern, but distinctly more the first than the second. Gökalp referred to it as the national or 'millî' family, and sometimes very evocatively as the 'yuva', or nest. As we have seen, the idea of a small nest-like family corresponded in part to developments within Istanbul households, as extended families gave way to nuclear ones and neolocal residency patterns became the order of the day. Extended kinship loyalties, however, still remained of greater importance in Turkish urban centres than in the great cities of western Europe. For Gökalp, the new Turkish family was to become the powerhouse of the nation. In 1913 he had lamented the fact that the 'Turkish soul' had not yet found its ideal breeding ground; the *ümmet* (the Islamic community) was too large and the traditional family too self-enclosed. Now it had found its ideal family form.[85]

Within this general framework, there remained the question of what Gökalp called 'family morality'. What was to go on inside families? What were to be their innermost values and practices? And how were they to connect to the outside world? Men and women were certainly to be more *equal* – Gökalp's 'democracy' and 'feminism' carried this signifier more than any other – but there were still to be distinct gender roles and duties. The new, national family was to be bound by western civilisation but infused with Turkish culture:

'Turkish womanhood certainly will better itself by benefiting from the progress of modern civilisation. But the Turkish woman will not be a copy-cat of French or of English or of German womanhood.' Gökalp was particularly worried about the effects of romantic love upon Turkish women. Untamed by social morality it would lead, in his opinion, to 'sexual immorality or even amorality'. A family's honour was still to depend greatly upon the chastity and restraint of its women. Individuals, both women and men, were not to be allowed too free a rein. They were to be firmly integrated into a corporatist and homogeneous society, the Muslim religion serving as a sort of social cement.

At the end of his life Gökalp told his followers, 'I am of the Turkish race, of Muslim religion, of western civilisation.' In his *Principles of Turkism* he compared favourably the nascent Turkish national culture to its German equivalent. Whereas German *Kultur* had aspired to world conquest through its 'military and economic forces', Turkish culture 'was not chauvinistic or fanatical at all [. . .] We shall build our own culture for our own taste and enjoyment.'[86] Tragically, as we shall now see, nothing could have been further from the truth during and after the cataclysmic years of the Great War.

II. WORLD WAR, GENOCIDE AND NATIONALISM

1. The affirmation of Mustafa Kemal

In late October 1914 the Ottoman Empire entered the First World War on the side of the Central Powers.[87] By this time little remained of the democratic and constitutional impetus of the 1908 revolution, or of the fraternal reconciliation between different religious and ethnic groups that had marked its first manifestations. In 1913 a tightly knit CUP triumvirate seized power by means of a *coup d'état*: Enver became Minister of War, Talât took over the Ministry of the Interior and Cemal was in charge of the navy. The history of the next five years was marked by almost unmitigated disaster, culminating in the Allied occupation of Istanbul in 1919.

There are two moments in these war years upon which I want to concentrate. They occurred almost simultaneously. The first is revealing of the character and ideas of the founder of the Turkish nation; the second is a terrible act of mass killing, ordered by the Ottoman government, but whose very existence is still today fiercely denied by official Turkish history. The first concerns Mustafa Kemal's role in the Turkish defence of the Dardanelles (Gallipoli) in the spring of 1915. An Allied expeditionary force, composed of British, French and Anzac (Australian and New Zealand Army Corps) troops, had landed on 25 April, aiming to break through to Istanbul itself. Their line of advance was blocked by scrub-covered hills, deep ravines and above all by the under-equipped but highly determined Turkish Fifth Army. This force was commanded by the German Liman von Sanders, for at the beginning of the war a restricted number of high-ranking German officers had assumed key posts in the Ottoman army. Mustafa Kemal's command was of the Nineteenth Division, which was called in at the outset to try to halt the Allied advance. Kemal recounted later that when his Fifty-Seventh Regiment reached the battlefield he greeted it with the memorable words, later to be imprinted upon the memory of successive generations of Turkish schoolchildren, 'I do not order you to attack. I order you to die. By the time we are dead other units and commanders will have come up to take our place.' The regiment was almost entirely wiped out.[88]

Kemal's division stubbornly held on against heavy odds and eventually it was the Allied forces who were forced to withdraw, abandoning the Arıburnu-Anafartalar beachhead on 19–20 December. The casualties had been immense on both sides. Mustafa Kemal had written to his French friend Corinne Lütfü on 20 July 1915,

> Our life here is truly hellish. Fortunately, my soldiers are very brave and tougher than the enemy. What is more, their private beliefs make it easier to carry out orders which send them to their death. They see only two super-natural outcomes: victory for the faith or martyrdom. Do you know what the second means? It is to go straight to heaven. There, the virgins of paradise, God's most beautiful women, will meet them and will satisfy their desires for all eternity. What great happiness![89]

There is no evidence that Kemal shared these beliefs or was seeking his ideal female company in paradise; his ambitions were far more terrestrial. He had rapidly emerged as the outstanding front-line commander in one sector of the front, but he was still under the command of a German marshal and regarded with suspicion by many of his fellow officers and by the CUP leadership. Enver, whose relations with Mustafa Kemal were always tense and characterised by mutual suspicion, is reported to have said of him (on his promotion to brigadier general), 'You can be sure that when he is made *Paşa*, he will want to become Sultan, and that if he became Sultan, he would want to be God.'[90] After Gallipoli, Kemal was sent in the spring of 1916 to the crucial south-eastern front, where the Russians had made considerable incursions into eastern Anatolia. During this campaign Mustafa Kemal kept a diary. It is of considerable interest because although his remarks are glacial in their detachment, he also makes a number of social annotations which are not at all those of the average 'school trained' officer of the Ottoman army:

> 22 November [1916]. For eight or nine hours, until after 9 p.m., I chatted with my chief of staff on abolishing the veiling of women and improving our social life. 1. Educating capable mothers, knowledgeable about life. 2. Giving freedom to women. 3. Leading a common life with women will have a good effect on men's morals, thoughts and feelings. There is an inborn tendency towards the attraction of mutual affection.[91]

These were unusual remarks, to be further developed, as we shall see, in the family history of the new Turkish Republic.

2. Armenian genocide, 1915–1916

More or less at the same time that Kemal was leading the defence of the Dardanelles – the spring of 1915 – many regions in Anatolia were witnessing the murderous ethnic cleansing of their Armenian populations. This brings me to the second moment in the war years that I want to analyse in some detail, its occurrence being of the greatest overall significance not just for Turkish history but for the history of family politics in the twentieth century.

The Armenians were historically one of the most important 'elements', as they were called then, or minorities, as we would call them now, composing the Ottoman population. At the beginning of the century, they accounted for perhaps some two million out of a total population of the Empire of over twenty million. But unlike the Greeks, the Bulgarians, the Serbs or the Albanians, they were not the majority population in any of the lands in which they lived. They boasted an active intellectual class and some of the most important merchant families of Istanbul and Izmir. The great majority of them, however – an estimated 70 per cent – were peasants, living either in Cilicia, which borders the eastern Mediterranean coast, or in the eastern provinces of Anatolia, dominated by Turkmen and Kurdish tribes. The Armenians were Christians, the majority belonging to the Armenian Apostolic Church (Gregorian), with Catholic and Protestant minorities.

There was nothing inevitable about the Armenian genocide. It is worth remembering, as the historian Feroz Ahmad asks us to, that after the 1908 revolution relations between the various religious-ethnic communities 'were still based on mutual respect and trust forged by a common hostility to the Hamidian autocracy'.[92] But it is also true that by the beginning of the Great

War the CUP was deeply suspicious of the frequent contacts being made between Russia, an official enemy, and the Ottoman Armenians.

The poisoned chalice of nineteenth-century nationalism – so liberating, even sublime, at one level, so dangerously exclusive at another – wreaked havoc with all the checks and balances that had been established over a long period of time within the Ottoman Empire. The Ottoman system of government had been asymmetrical, heavily weighted in favour of the majority Turkish and Islamic population of the Empire. It had never hesitated to use the tool of exemplary repression when faced with rebellion, often deporting or massacring the populations of entire villages. But it had never allowed nor sought the systematic murder of the civilian population of any one of its minority 'elements'.

By the beginning of the twentieth century this military and territorial control was crumbling, and the *fin-de-siècle* ethno-nationalisms were its gravediggers. In the west of the Empire it had become dangerous indeed to be a Muslim, inhabiting not just the frontier zone between Islam and Christianity but also contested national territory. In the last Balkan Wars of 1912–13 an estimated 62 per cent of Muslims disappeared from the lands conquered by Greece, Serbia and Bulgaria (27 per cent dead, 35 per cent refugees). The British made great play of the 'Bulgarian atrocities' committed by the Turks, but rarely if ever mentioned the fate of the long-established Islamic communities in the Balkans.[93]

The frontier zone of religious, ethnic and territorial division lay not only in the west, in the Balkans, however, but also even more tragically in the east, in Anatolia and the Caucasus. Here the balance of power between contending forces was very different. Turks, Armenians and Kurds pressed upon the same territory. After the Turkish defeat in the Russian-Ottoman war of 1877–8, a massive influx of Circassian and Turkish refugees into eastern Anatolia upset all previous equilibria. Land-hungry Turkish agricultural families now coveted Armenian land. At the same time, Armenian nationalism, emboldened by vague promises of Russian support, grew in strength. Nationalist groups were formed, bombs were thrown. In 1894 some Armenian communities in the east refused to pay taxes both to the Ottoman authorities and to local Kurdish chiefs. They were massacred. Abdülhamit II, no lover of the Armenians, enrolled Kurdish tribesmen in irregular units and sent them to re-establish order. Between 60,000 and 150,000 Armenians died.

This was the curtain raiser for the extermination of the Armenians, but it was not yet genocide. To make that transition, two further elements were needed: one was the exceptional military and political conditions created by the First World War, in which enormous death tolls – though not yet of civilian populations – had rapidly become the norm; the other was a Turco-Ottoman leadership intent on the survival of their state at any cost, indifferent to any discourse, however rudimentary, on human rights, deaf to any distinctions between combatants and unarmed civilian populations, and absolutely impenitent about undertaking mass murder of men, women and children on an unprecedented scale.

The Russians' defeat of Enver's expeditionary force in the Caucasus in December 1914 lit the touch-paper for genocide. The Turks suffered terrible losses in the Caucasus, and when retreating identified the Armenian villagers as their principal internal enemy, all too ready to ease the passage of Russian armies into Anatolia. Their loyalty could not be relied upon; they had to be cleared away and fast. Ethnic cleansing and deportation on an enormous scale was undertaken mainly in the spring and summer of 1915, in the same weeks that, on another front, Mustafa Kemal was defending the Dardanelles. The two events must be taken together as the founding elements of the Turkish Republic.

At the beginning of the war, the CUP triumvirate had created the 'special organisation' bands, commanded by the murderous Bahaettin Şakir and recruited from three principal sources: Kurdish tribesmen, released convicts and Turkish refugees from the Caucasus and the Balkans. It was they who were to carry out the extermination of the Armenians, alongside the gendarmes of the Ministry of the Interior. The historical evidence clearly demonstrates the direct responsibility of the CUP leadership. On 7 November 1915 the German ambassador Metternich described the Minister of the Interior, Talât, as 'the soul of the Armenian persecution.'[94] Talât came from a very modest family of Bulgarian converts to Islam and his mother had been a layer-out of corpses. He peppered the provincial administration with telegrams concerning the details of the killings. In the various echelons of the Ottoman state there were a few officials who refused to comply. The governor of Ankara, Mazhar Bey, was one of them. He gave evidence to the effect that 'Atif Bey came [. . .] and gave me a verbal order to massacre and liquidate the Armenians. I said, no, Atif Bey, I am a governor, not a criminal; I can't do it. I shall leave this chair; you come here, sit here and do it.'[95] But such men were few and far between.

The extermination took a very specific form, one that differed in many respects from the other two principal examples of mass killings examined in this book – the Shoah and Stalin's various waves of Terror in the 1930s. In the Armenian case very many of the menfolk were killed immediately, in the vicinity of their home villages. Women and children were then deported and made long, forced marches under appalling conditions from their villages of origin, southwards towards the deserts of what is today northern Syria and Iraq. It is highly significant, and a further terrible condemnation, that Armenians were deported not only from the eastern provinces near to the war zone, but from all over Turkey and from Mediterranean Cilicia in particular, hundreds of kilometres from the front. The Cilician deportees were treated better, but the overall death rate from exposure, starvation and thirst was very high. During these long marches, the Turkish and Kurdish 'special organisation' bands regularly raped, kidnapped and killed Armenian women, as well as forcibly stealing children and young girls. Many of those who made it to the desert camps were subjected to a further series of attacks in 1916. Taken together, these events constitute the Armenian genocide. Although the overall numbers will never be known with certainty, most genocide scholars concur that between 700,000 and 900,000 Armenian Ottomans died, some 50 per cent of the pre-war population.[96]

The form the genocide took – deportations and forced marches – was a highly convenient one for those who perpetrated the crime. What was happening could be masked as simply the transference of the Armenians to another location rather than their liquidation. Deaths were covered up as much as possible. Talât sent a telegram from his ministry in July 1915 ordering that all corpses left on the roads were to be buried, not thrown into streams, rivers or lakes. The belongings of the dead left on the road were to be burned immediately.[97]

Those who suffered the deportations were subjected not just to untold physical deprivation but to extraordinarily cruel psychological choices, principally related to the dismemberment of family groups. Parents, especially mothers, had to make a number of impossible decisions as they travelled along the deportation routes. Were their own lives worth more than those of their children? Should one leave a weaker and younger child behind in order to give more of a chance to the older ones? When were the elderly, one's own parents, to be left by the wayside?

Thanks to some careful oral history of the 1990s involving survivors of the genocide, the details of these terrible family dismemberments have come to the fore.[98] Most of these survivors had been very young at the time of the extermination and so their testimonies were subject to the vagaries of distant memory. They also tell us how it was to be children in this calamity, not mothers or fathers. They are none the less immensely valuable, for they bring home to us the horrific nature of the choices families faced. A survivor originally from Çanakkale, a city in the far west of Turkey, recounted the destiny of her family on the deportation route. Unusually, her father was still part of the family group. The donkey on which she and her eight-year-old brother were riding died of starvation and so they were both forced to walk. Her brother complained increasingly, finally declaring,

' "Leave me here. I can't go on". He said that his legs were bleeding from rubbing against each other. But how can a mother leave a child? My father said, "Leave him. We will be left behind, too. We will all be left. Armenian woman, leave him". Now my parents were arguing. Finally they left him, sat him down, and left some food with him. But no water. We walked on, but my mother kept looking back to the child and kept crying. But my father kept saying, "Walk woman. We will each stay behind one by one. We must. This is our fate." '

This survivor said that she remembers this event as clearly as if 'it's across from me now'. Her mother's eyes, she said, continued to be 'behind her', looking back at her abandoned child.[99]

Another terrible dilemma was the following: would one's child have a greater chance of survival if given or sold en route to a Turkish or Kurdish family? One of the singular aspects of the Armenian genocide was its relatively muted racial element. The Armenians were the 'other', the internal enemy that merited deportation. But they were not regarded as *racially* inferior, and their children were accepted, indeed sought, by some Turkish families that needed their labour or simply had no children of their own. One testimony among many of this type is that of a young woman called Aghvani from the Anatolian town of Sivas. In 1915 she was twenty years old, married and the mother of two small children. A month before the deportation, local Armenian political leaders were imprisoned and many were hanged; Aghvani's own husband was shot in these days. During the forced march to Der-Zor, now in eastern Syria, she lost first her mother, who was shot by the guards, and then her mother-in-law, who died from exhaustion. Finally, she lost both her children, though she could not bring herself, when interviewed, to describe how. By the time she reached Der-Zor her family had been destroyed and she had lost any will to live:

Exhausted, she lay down naked on the bank of the Euphrates river, ready to die. But as she lay there two elderly Turks came upon her: '[One of the Turks] took his stick and poked me with it. You know, even when you're dead, you still don't want to die. So I turned when he poked me. When I moved he said, "Tabour, take this girl home. She is a sweet one. Bring her up, and when your son returns from the army, give her to him [. . .]." I was lying down, dead. I got up but I could not walk [. . .] Also, I was all naked. And I was embarrassed.'

One of the men took Aghvani home. While his wife bathed her, he went out and bought clothes. She lay in bed for three weeks, and after that she went to live with a servant and his wife [. . .] She survived because someone cared for her. These themes reverberate throughout our interviews, with susbstantial variations.[100]

Often in survivor accounts we find details of the transition, more or less traumatic, between a Christian family of origin that has been lost in deportation and a new Muslim one that welcomes or at least provides for an abandoned child. But these are the family stories of *survivors*. For each of them there must be hundreds of others, unwritten and unrecounted, of the forcible extinction of whole family groups, destroyed by starvation, separation, shootings and rape along the deportation roads.

The Armenian painter Arshile Gorky, born Vosdanik Adoian, has left us an unforgettable image of the destruction by genocide of pivotal family relationships. His testimony is in two parts and is a masterpiece of understatement. The first is a photograph of himself and his mother taken in Van in 1912, when he was eight years old, three years before the hurricane of deportation hit the Armenian people. He stands and she sits. They are both very solemn and he holds a bunch of flowers in his right hand. The photograph was sent to his father, who had emigrated to the United States in 1908 in order to avoid conscription in the Turkish army. The second is the famous painting *The Artist and his Mother* (of which there are two versions), based on the photograph of 1912 (see plate 2). A number of things have changed. His mother's long dress is no longer patterned but rather resembles a white shroud. Arshile seems to have a withered arm and both he and his mother have hands that are only white blobs. The painting is a protest against the destruction of individuals; above all it is Gorky's way of mourning his mother, who died from malnutrition not in the first years of the genocide but in March 1919, aged only thirty-nine. Gorky, then aged fifteen, and his sister Vartoosh, aged thirteen, somehow survived, reached first Istanbul and then New York, where they rejoined their father after a separation of twelve years. Gorky went on to become a renowned New York painter but committed suicide in 1948.[101]

3. Responsibilities

The Entente Powers were swift to denounce what was taking place. On 24 May 1915, in a famous formulation, they declared that 'in the light of these crimes, which Turkey has perpetrated against humanity and civilisation', they would hold personally responsible members of the Ottoman government and their

fig. 12 Arshile Gorky (Vosdanik Adoian) and his mother Shushanik der Madosian, Van city, 1912.

subordinates who had been involved in the massacre.[102] They did not keep their word. Although the post-war Ottoman government began trials in 1918 these soon petered out. Faced with a resurgent Turkey in 1921, the victors in the First World War preferred to let the question of genocide slip and make their peace with the new Republic. Just as the Central Powers' interference had done so much to foment hatreds before the war, so their indifference to genocide after it contributed greatly to letting the new Turkish Republic off the hook. The Republic came into being without ever having had to face the facts or make public amends for them. It was allowed free rein to deny that the genocide had ever taken place and even to make reference to it was a crime against the fatherland.

How do the protagonists of this chapter – Mustafa Kemal, Enver, Gökalp, Halide Edib – fare in relation to the Armenian genocide? As Perry Anderson has written, Mustafa Kemal had the 'moral luck' to be on another front at the time of the genocide. His hands were therefore clean with regard to what had taken place and no great stain blotted out his prospects for future national leadership. But in the spring of 1916 he had been transferred to the front around Diyarbakır, in south-east Anatolia, an area which had been heavily involved in the ethnic cleansing of its Armenian population less than a year earlier and from which the Kurds had been deported.[103] He must have known what had happened, even if he had had no part in its organisation. Later on, he was at very great pains to separate officially the new Republic from its CUP past. The fact remains that it was the Republic that in 1926 granted pensions, properties and lands seized from the Armenians to the families of Talât, Enver, Şakir and Cemal. Mustafa Kemal's regime, to quote Anderson again, 'was packed from top to bottom with participants in the murders of 1915–1916'.[104]

Enver was one of those most heavily responsible. At the beginning of November 1918 he and seven others of the incriminated CUP leadership boarded a German torpedo boat which whisked them away to safety. But the Armenian revolutionary party, the Daşnak, vowed to assassinate them all. One by one they fell, beginning with Talât, who was shot down in March 1921 outside his home in Berlin (where he had disgracefully been granted asylum). Enver did not wait for a bullet. True to his adventurist soul, he joined the Muslim bands (basmacı) who were fighting the Bolsheviks in Tajikistan. There he died – some suggest at the hands of an Armenian Chekist – in August 1922.[105]

As for Gökalp, the gentle but austere theorist of the new Turkish family that was to be based upon 'feminism' and 'democracy', he was arrested and imprisoned in early 1919, after the Allies had entered Istanbul. Together with other leading figures of the CUP who had not fled abroad, Gökalp was accused by a Turkish military tribunal of having contributed to the anti-Armenian agitations which had led to the massacres. According to the testimony of Hakkı Süha, Gökalp denied any crimes against humanity, insisting rather that the Armenians had been killed in a war against the Turks, whom they had stabbed in the back. He admitted without hesitation that he had approved of the deportations. He was sentenced to exile in Malta in the summer of 1919 but was later able to rejoin Mustafa Kemal's Turkish resistance in Ankara.[106]

Even though she occupies a lesser place in Turkish history than the other three, the case of Halide Edib is perhaps the most significant, as well as the saddest. She had not hesitated before the war to condemn all attacks upon minorities, Armenians included. Her own feelings of repulsion in the face of male violence run like a silver thread through all her writings. Yet her fervent Turkish nationalism and her belief that the Turkish heartlands of the Empire should not be given away to foreign powers meant that she was unable to disassociate herself from the official line on what had happened and incapable of recognising that the nature and scale of the Armenian deportations put them upon a different plane from all the other terrible events that had taken place from 1911 onwards. In September 1919 the King–Crane Commission came to Istanbul to hear evidence before going on to the Paris peace conference.[107] Edib was there to translate for the Thracian and eastern Anatolian Turks:

> Things went smoothly till one member of the Commission mentioned the word 'massacre'. This immediately set Suleiman Narif Bey [the leader of the eastern Anatolians] on the high horse. He poured forth an eloquent and just view of the case – how the massacre was two-sided, and if they would condemn the Turks they must also condemn the Armenians.[108]

In the following decades, the Turkish republicans stubbornly continued to deny the very existence of the genocide, and to do everything they could to cancel its memory and remove it from the history books.

4. 'Magnificent national madness': the making of the new Republic, 1919–1922

In the post-war settlement no space was foreseen or provided for an independent Turkish state. Although different victorious powers naturally had different agendas, the old Anatolian heartlands of the Ottoman Empire were to be split up, either to become parts of new or old states, or to be placed under Protectorates, as in the case of Palestine. On 16 May 1919 the Greeks occupied Izmir (Smyrna), using great violence against the majority Muslim population of the city. They then pushed onwards into Anatolia. They had the blessings of the British, who felt strongly that Turkish Muslims should be 'punished' for wartime atrocities.

The Greek invasion, together with the Allied occupation of Istanbul, were
the triggers of Turkish nationalism. Halide Edib wrote that after the Greek
'atrocities on the sea front', 'nothing mattered to me from that moment to the
time of the extraordinary [Turkish] march to Smyrna in 1922. I suddenly
ceased to exist as an individual: I worked, wrote and lived as a unit of that
magnificent national madness.'[109] On 6 June 1919 she made a famous speech
in front of 200,000 people in Sultan Ahmet Square in Istanbul. She asked the
massive crowd to swear with her that they would not rest until 'the proclamation of the rights of the peoples'. The plural 'peoples' was sincerely meant, but
the rights to which Halide Edib referred were self-evidently Turkish ones. As
she spoke, Allied aeroplanes flew low over the square, close to its famous
minarets, in an obvious act of intimidation.

Mustafa Kemal set up headquarters in Ankara and asked all patriots to join
him there in the fight for independence. His summons confronted Halide Edib
with a very difficult choice between maternal love and national duty. Although
the risks were high, she very much wanted to join Mustafa Kemal in Ankara,
but she also had two young sons in Istanbul to whom she felt deeply attached:
'I, who for years had grandfather's boiling nature and could have kissed my
children continually and carried them in a pouch attached to my body like a
kangaroo'. Her dilemma was similar to that of Inessa Armand (Kollontai seems
never to have hesitated), and was resolved in the same terms: she arranged for
her sons to be accepted as boarders at Robert College in Istanbul. In March
1920, the last night before her departure, she called her elder son Ali Ayetullah,
now fourteen, to her side:

> Every one retired and he sat squatting against the hard sofa, his dark little
> hand supporting his face, and watching me with all the life that was in him.
> 'Come and hold me while I write', I said. And I really wondered at the
> strength of the little boy as he held me tight and I tried to write. The most
> important letter was written to Mr. Charles Crane, telling him that I was
> going to Anatolia, and that whether I escaped alive or not the struggle would
> be hard and long. Would he take the boys to America and educate them and
> protect them?[110]

Crane replied in the affirmative and Halide Edib left Istanbul for a long and
adventurous journey, avoiding British and Greek troops, to reach Ankara. She
took with her her new companion, the distinguished surgeon Adıvar (Adnan),
who was a leading CUP figure in the National Assembly in Istanbul. He had
decided to stay in the city and allow himself to be arrested, but Edib would
have none of it. She was ready to carry him away by force if need be: 'This was

not the time for thinking and acting like characters in a medieval epic poem. The atmosphere was not romantic but entirely brutal.[111]

The shift of focus from Istanbul to Ankara, from the cosmopolitan seaboard capital to the small, landlocked town surrounded by 'the Anatolian wastes, with their ruthless silence and desolation',[112] was to have profound consequences for the formation of the Turkish nation. Istanbul was marginalised as never before. Its families, once a great pot-pourri of races and religions, able to give expression to a plural, if not civil, society, became overwhelmingly Turkish. The period 1911–20 saw a whole series of negative occurrences for them: the men were forced to depart for the front, inflation gripped the city during the war years and real wages plummeted.[113] It was if the stuffing had been knocked out of the city, an impression confirmed by the humiliation of Allied occupation.[114] Its inhabitants could still fill Sultan Ahmet Square, but the city was henceforth unable to play a leading role, either in resistance to the Allies or in the forging of the new nation.

On the other hand, Ankara and the Anatolian rural population afforded no convincing substitute. Halide Edib was at pains to point out the positive qualities of the Anatolian peasants, their great patience and stoicism – 'the inexhaustible patience which belongs only to Anatolians'. One might say she romanticised them, following a long European intellectual tradition, to be cruelly disabused time and again. By and large, peasants were not willing to fight spontaneously for national causes, nor did their culture correspond to the romantic representation of it. The Turkish peasantry of Anatolia was no exception. It was willing enough to defend its own villages and families against Greek occupation, and to occupy ex-Armenian land after the forcible deportation of its rightful owners. But its deep-rooted culture – Islamic and local – was a far cry from the secular, westernising ideology of the nationalist elite.

The fight for Turkish nationhood was thus constructed on fragile class bases, without deep basins of support in either city or countryside. As a result, the role of the military, already very present in the CUP experience, was to be further accentuated under Kemalism. All this boded ill for the possibilities of democracy and for the growth of a republican civil society.

Once in Ankara, Halide Edib was able to study Mustafa Kemal at close quarters. She did not much like what she saw. She paid constant tribute to the intelligence and obdurate, overarching ambition that had made him the ideal leader of the national cause. But she also felt that he had many blind spots: 'his mind is two-sided, like a lighthouse lantern. Sometimes it flashes and shows you what it wants you to see with almost blinding clearness; sometimes it wanders and gets itself lost in the dark.'[115] What she really objected to was his cynicism. There was almost no one of whom he did not speak badly or who escaped his suspicion:

> Occasionally his eyes flashed, then again went cold and pale; the lines of his face deepened, his eyebrows stood out and altogether he looked extremely dangerous [. . .] pity, affection, sacrifice were to him useless weaknesses. Intelligence and self-interest were what mattered in the intricate scheme of human life [. . .] I can still see him standing in the middle of the room talking every one to exhaustion, while he remains as fresh as the moment he began. And I can remember saying to myself: 'What an outstanding man! Is he just some elemental force in a catastrophic form? Is there anything human about him at all? And how can this cyclone ever come to rest when the nation has reached its goal?'[116]

She recognised that it would not and that Kemal, even at this early stage, 'was shrewd enough to see that the more old landmarks he destroyed the easier it would be to get people to look to his new ones'.[117]

During these critical months of the War of Independence, Halide Edib worked in the press office at Mustafa Kemal's headquarters in Ankara. As the military situation worsened and the Greek army came ever closer to Ankara, she first went to work as a nurse in a field hospital and then volunteered to become a simple soldier in the liberation army. This was a very unusual gesture – there were no women soldiers in the Turkish army. Kemal welcomed warmly the initiative she had taken. She was quickly accorded the rank of corporal (the officer ranks were reserved for trained men) and rose to the rank of sergeant-major by the end of the war.[118] Though often at the front, she refused to shoot, asking to be excused when one Turkish artillery colonel ordered her to take a pot shot at the enemy from one of his cannons: 'My exaltation never went so far.'[119] She continued to be profoundly non-violent, even though such a belief flew in the face of all the choices she had made. In her memoirs she called this her 'lonely philosophy of life'.[120]

While in Ankara in 1920 and 1921, Halide Edib came into contact with both Turkish and Russian Communists. Soviet Russia and Kemal's new Turkey, though rivals in central southern Asia, had many interests in common. The Bolsheviks were to supply the Kemalists with more than 45,000 rifles, 300 machine-guns and nearly 100 field guns during the War of Independence. The Communists whom Halide Edib met were of varying quality. With one of them, a Turkish Bolshevik called Vakass, who resembled 'a poor preacher in the mosque corners or in the open places during Ramazan', she had an extended conversation about Bolshevik family policy. Vakass explained with fervour that as long as children were brought up in the old bourgeois environment there was no hope of changing the world. The family as a unit had to be broken. Though he was uncertain about the future of marriage, he had no doubt that children were to be 'state owned', trained in state institutions to construct the new order.[121]

It is fascinating to pick up these simplified and distorted echoes of the Russian debate which were carried on the wind of the Bolshevik propaganda machine and thus reached Halide Edib's receptive ears. Commenting upon the figure of Vakass she wrote, 'I believe that there are men all over Asia preaching in this way.'[122] She had considerable sympathy for the gender-equality arguments of the Bolshevik feminists, but none at all for their ideas about gradually replacing family life with new collective forms of living. Edib wanted a stronger family, not a weaker one; monogamy, not 'free love'; parents who educated their children, not those who devolved the task to the state. In all this she was close to Gökalp, and she embraced his image of the Turkish family as a 'nest'; it existed to give protective space to its members and at the same time to serve as the kernel of the new nation.

The battle of Sakarya, fought in August of 1921 and lasting twenty-one days, sealed the fate of Anatolia. Some 90,000 Turkish troops faced 100,000 much better armed Greeks and forced them to retreat. Mustafa Kemal had declared that the enemy would be 'throttled in the inner sanctuary of the fatherland'. A year after the battle of Sakarya he kept his word and delivered the killer blow to the Greek armies at Dumlupınar. The Greeks fell back towards the Mediterranean, adopting a scorched earth policy and committing numerous atrocities as they retreated. The Turks replied in kind. Once they reached Izmir the fanatical Nurettin Paşa was made military commander of the city. The Greek Archbishop Chrysostom was lynched by a crowd of Muslims outside Nurettin's residence and on his instigation. Fire consumed the Armenian and Greek quarters of the city, which were mercilessly looted. Tens of thousands fled to the waterfront, saved from death only by a large fleet of Allied warships and transports, which took on board some 213,000 people – a majority of the city's inhabitants.[123]

Halide Edib had been witness to the after-effects of the Greek atrocities, though not to the Turkish ones, on which she remained silent. The nation was made, but at what cost? Towards the end of her memoirs, which take us only as far as 1922, Edib describes her feelings of total hopelessness:

The nameless whispering in my brain succeeded in making me realise that the supreme instinct of mankind was to kill – and only that. It made me see clearly that those who lacked the instinct to kill did not belong to the human species. They were forced to be strangers to mankind [. . .] I was stricken with an uncontrollable loathing for everything in human likeness: the beast with the disturbing eyes and the treacherous hands that walked on earth only to destroy its kind and to exterminate itself.[124]

At last, in October 1922, she came back to her beloved city, to her sister's house, to the room where two years earlier she had taken her last view of her boy squatting on the floor: 'Good and evil take turns, this was the good – I put my arms around Mahmoure Abla's neck and we wept and we laughed just as we used to do as children.'[125] Meanwhile, her sons had returned from the United States and she was reunited with them some days later.

III. Mustafa Kemal's revolution from above

1. The new Turkish Republic

The new Turkish state that came into being at the end of the War of Independence bore a heavily military stamp, deriving both from the history of its formation and from the character and experience of its leadership. The army was always to be a 'state within a state' in the Turkish Republic, ready to intervene in civilian affairs when the occasion arose. Looking at the chosen group of great dictators of the first half of the twentieth century, it becomes immediately apparent that Mustafa Kemal is not a Mussolini. Or perhaps it would be better to say that Mussolini is no Mustafa Kemal, a man of steel, extraordinarily determined and ruthless. The closest comparison is without doubt with Francisco Franco, another 'Generalissimo' who triumphed in a war of unbelievable ferocity. But Franco was the champion of organised religion, whereas Mustafa Kemal was its whip. And if Franco sought to resuscitate the greatness of Spain by evoking its formidable imperial tradition, Atatürk, the 'Father of the Turks' as he renamed himself, turned his back contemptuously on the Ottoman past. The Republic was intended to mark the end of Ottoman history and the beginning of a Turkish national identity.

In November 1922, Vahdettin, the last Ottoman Sultan, fled the capital with his young son aboard a British army ambulance. He later settled in San Remo, where he was joined by his three wives and his sister. The sultanate was abolished but the caliphate lived on – a religious institution with a great popular following that could not be liquidated overnight. Vahdettin's cousin, Abdülmecit, was appointed Caliph in his place. This interim arrangement lasted for less than two years. In October 1923 the Republic was declared; Mustafa Kemal, its president, was just forty-two years old. In March 1924 the caliphate was abolished and it was Abdülmecit's turn to be escorted from Istanbul and on to the Orient Express.[126] On the day the Republican Assembly abolished the caliphate it also did away with the Ministry of Canon Law and pious foundations, and established a single system of public, secular education.

The new Republic boasted a liberal constitution, promulgated in 1924. It was based on representative government, political plurality and freedom of expression and belief. In reality, Turkey was rapidly to become a one-party state, with the ruling Republican People's Party, founded in 1924, dominating the public administration. There were regular elections every four years, but the slate of candidates was drawn up by the national party chairman, who happened to be prime minister as well. The official ideology of the new regime, Kemalism, had little time for parliamentary procedures or the separation of powers, being constructed in the image of a brilliant and thoughtful general bent on radical reform.

The Republic was based on a single ethno-nationalism, that of the Turks, and reflected the terrible decade of ethnic cleansing which had preceded its formation. The massive 'exchange of populations' with the Greeks in 1923, part of the peace settlement, further destroyed any lingering idea of a multicultural nation.[127] There remained the problem of the Kurds. They were fellow Muslims, had fought alongside the Turks in the war, and their 'special organisation' bands had played a significant and lurid part, as we have seen, in the Armenian genocide. But it was also true that in 1915–16 the Kurds could already be considered not only murderers but victims. The year after the deportation of the Armenians, signs of a nascent Kurdish nationalism provided the pretext for vast numbers of them to be forcibly deported and resettled. The CUP leadership believed it possible to absorb the Kurds culturally, linguistically and politically in the new Turkish nation only by removing them from their own culture and traditions and dispersing them amongst the Turkish-speaking population.[128]

In return for their support during the War of Independence Kemal promised the Kurds respect for their language and traditions, as well as forms of autonomy in the areas in which they constituted a majority. 'There are Turks and Kurds,' he said in 1920; 'the nation is not one element [. . .] All the Muslim elements which make up this entity are citizens.'[129] But once the war was won, Kurdish was banned from courts and schools, Turkish officials governed in Kurdish areas, and a wholesale policy of Turkification was initiated. The abolition of the caliphate further alienated the Kurds, for they saw it as the destruction of the unifying symbol of Islam. In early 1925 they rose in revolt under a tribal religious leader, Şeyh Said. Needless to say, the revolt was brutally suppressed.

The year 1925 was destined to become another of those key negative moments by which this story has been punctuated, to be placed alongside

Sultan Abdülhamit II's abolition of the Constitution in 1877 and the CUP leadership's seizure of absolute power in 1913. In March 1925, in the wake of the Kurdish revolt, the Law on the Maintenance of Order was passed,[130] establishing special courts by which all opposition in the country was silenced. In particular, the new regime banned the only organised national political opposition, the Progressive Republican Party (Terakkiperver Cumhuriyet Fırkası). Halide Edib and her husband Adnan (Adıvar), who had both been part of the leadership of the party, were sent into exile, living in Europe and the United States from 1926 onwards.

Halide Edib spent her time in exile lecturing frequently on the political and intellectual history of the Near East, as well as on contemporary Turkish literature. She also continued to publish novels. She remained a fervent Turkish nationalist, but always attempted to temper her defence of her country with an underlying pacifism. She was heavily influenced by Gandhi's teaching, and in January 1935 went to India to give a series of talks. On 19 January Gandhi chaired one of her lectures in Delhi, of which *The Hindustan Times* reported, 'She spoke with a quaint Persian accent, but her English is lucid and forceful, and her voice is admirably clear, because she is used to addressing mass meetings of thousands of people.'[131] Gandhi ended the meeting by expressing graciously the hope that Halide's 'coming in our midst [may] result in binding Hindus and Muslims in an indissoluble bond'.[132]

Halide Edib and her husband were able to return to Turkey only in 1939, a year after the death of Mustafa Kemal.

In October 1927 Kemal made a thirty-six-hour speech before the Congress of the Republican People's Party. It was later to be referred to simply as the *Nutuk*, 'The Speech', becoming a tome of some six hundred pages, translated into many languages. As the founding document of the nation it is deeply disappointing, consisting mainly of interminable denunciations of those whom he had purged in 1925–6, many of whom were his former colleagues and friends from the heroic years of the Anatolian struggle. All are depicted as hesitant, incompetent and either real or potential traitors. For the historian of the twentieth century it is impossible not to draw a comparison with the documents of the Stalinist Purges of the 1930s – the same deep suspiciousness, the same sudden flipping of an individual's reputation from hero to traitor, the same portrayal of the dictator as the personification of history.

2. The revolution in daily life: religion, language, dress and gender

If there were nothing more to Mustafa Kemal than the battleground and the interminable accusatory *Nutuk*, he would be boring indeed, a mere bit player among the dictators of his time. But his ambitions extended far beyond mere military and political dominion. Like so many of the last Ottomans, Kemal longed for the new that came from afar. He was relatively indifferent to Gökalp's formula of the necessary *balance* in the coming national revolution between western civilisation and Turkish culture, of the need for the second to modify and contain the first. Instead he embraced western modernity with a fierce and often uncritical passion. He wrote in 1924, 'Surviving in the world of modern civilisation depends upon changing ourselves. This is the sole law of any progress in the social, economic and scientific spheres of life.'[133] The Turks had miraculously come through the cataclysmic years from 1911 to 1921 to make their own national revolution. But for Kemal that revolution stood no chance of surviving unless it moved rapidly with the spirit of the times; and that spirit came not from Anatolia but from Paris and London, and even, as we shall see, from Bern – of all places.

Mustafa Kemal proposed that the national revolution should be accompanied by nothing less than a revolution in everyday life. This separated him starkly not only from all the leaders of the new Balkan nationalist regimes, most of whom were just happy to survive, but also from the rest of the Islamic world. The new Turkish state was the first to propose a fundamental shift in the relationship between the state and religion. The revolution in everyday life began here. The Şeriat courts were deprived of their jurisdiction, every religious school (*medrese*) and dervish convent (*tarikat*) was closed down, and public shrines and tombs – the focus for many popular cults – were boarded up. Kemal declared war against obscurantism of every sort. In the *Nutuk* of 1927 he warned that there were not only external enemies but also internal ones, prime among which were the old clerical strata, the purveyors of superstitions and unfounded prejudices. Henceforth, imams and other preachers, such as the *hoca*, were to be allowed to wear clerical garb only while performing their religious duties. State 'directorates' took over the ownership of mosques, the appointment of imams and the administration of pious foundations (*vakıf*). Religion was to be organised, if not conducted, by the state.[134]

The reaction to such a frontal assault was long-lasting, particularly among the rural populations,[135] and was to continue up to and beyond Mustafa Kemal's death in November 1938. The new Turkey was split: in the cities, very many of the middle classes embraced with enthusiasm Kemalism's secular revolution. In the country, on the other hand, most of the peasantry were fundamentally hostile. The task ahead was well summarised in 1933 by Nusret Kemal, writing in *Ülkü*, the journal of the Halk Evleri (the People's Houses), the cultural organisation of the ruling Republican People's Party: 'We have between fourteen and seventeen million "citizens" of whom over 90% are alien to civilisation. Scattered over a territory of almost 800,000 square kilometres are some 40,000 villages. The devoted citizens prepared to bring some sort of enlightenment to them do not themselves number more than 40,000.'[136]

Yet it would be a mistake to draw these battle lines – urban/rural, secular/religious – too sharply. The regular practice of private and public worship was never forbidden in modern Turkey. On the contrary, Islam was a defining, if rarely elaborated, element of Turkish nationality.[137] Mustafa Kemal was shrewd enough to understand this and to remember that the defence of Islam had been fundamental in mobilising the Anatolian peasants during the War of Independence. Gökalp's teaching on the necessary balance between civilisation and culture may have been put to one side, but his famous nationalist self-definition – 'I am of the Turkish race, of Muslim religion, of western civilisation' – was of undeniable efficacy.[138]

A second element of Kemal's proposed transformation of everyday life concerned time. He had a profound impatience with the *longueurs* of the Ottomans, particularly as expressed in the old, slow-moving civil bureaucracy. The Republic was to embrace modern time, abandon the old Islamic calendar and adopt the western one. The clock, not the sun, was to guide the making of the nation. In a famous speech of 1933, Kemal explained how the Turks were in tune with the twentieth century:

> The criterion of time as we see it should be thought of not according to the lax mentality of the past centuries, but according to our century's notion of speed and movement [. . .] The Turkish nation is industrious. The Turkish nation is intelligent. [This is] because the Turkish nation has known how to overcome difficulties through unity and togetherness. And positive science is the torch that the Turkish nation holds high as it marches along the path of progress and civilisation.[139]

Another deeply radical innovation regarded language. Ottoman Turkish, using a variant of Arabic script, had been the written language of the court and the educated elites. Kemal abandoned it, instead introducing the Latin alphabet for Turkish and initiating a wholesale reform of the national language. All Arabic and Persian words and grammatical features were to be eliminated from Turkish. Begun in 1928, the reform was to continue for years.[140] From 1930 onwards all imams and other clerics were instructed to recite prayers only in Turkish.

Like all those concerned with social engineering on a mass scale, Kemal looked to future generations to realise his dream. It was they, not their parents, who held the key to national transformation. As early as 1923, primary

fig. 13 A classroom of the 'Schools of the nation' (*Millet mektepleri*), established on 24 November 1928. They were obligatory for all citizens aged between sixteen and forty as a means of learning the new Latin alphabet.

education, lasting for five years, was rendered free and obligatory for children of both sexes. Every morning, from the 1920s through to the 1960s, at the beginning of the day's lessons primary school children had to chant in chorus the following words: 'I'm Turkish, I'm hardworking and I'm just / My duty is to protect smaller children and respect all adults / My guiding light is to love the fatherland and the nation more than myself.'[141] A national curriculum came into being; new technical schools, lycées and universities welcomed the younger generation. The nation was on the move. The history it chose to recount to itself, as was true of so many nineteenth- and twentieth-century nationalisms, was one of ancient supremacies and modern heroism.

This educational transformation was accompanied by a more symbolic one, that of appearance. The so-called 'Hat Revolution' of 1925 forbade the wearing of the fez – symbol of the Ottoman past – in favour of 'modern' western head-ware. It also encouraged the wearing of western clothes, such as suits and raincoats. To our eyes this reform now has something of the farcical, almost Chaplinesque, about it. Kemal had himself photographed in a large variety of headgear – floppy hats with sloping rims, Panama hats, bowler hats, and so on. Sometimes he looked ill at ease, as did those around him. At other times, as in the case of the photograph of him in a top hat (see overleaf), all his intelligence and ruthlessness is brought sharply into relief. This breaking of rigid dress codes had an underlying importance: to challenge the fixedness of the past, in appearance as in politics and religion.

fig. 14 Mustafa Kemal wearing a top hat, late 1920s.

On the critical question of veiling, however – the most symbolically significant dress code of them all – Mustafa Kemal proceeded with great caution. Here any reform would touch one of the most sensitive areas of everyday life – the traditional reserve and reticence of Turkish women, whose faces were not to be seen by the other sex, excepting close relatives and friends, and by whose chastity the honour of a family was defined. Obligatory unveiling would have been a step too far. Kemal tried instead to proceed by persuasion, and his cajoling was first of all addressed to his own sex. If men could be convinced, the battle would be more than half won. As early as 1923 he addressed a male audience in the following enlightened, even revolutionary, terms:

During my journey, I have noted that our female companions take great care to cover their faces and their eyes [. . .] My friends, this is evidence only of our own pride and egoism. It is the consequence of our obsession with honour. Dear friends, our women are, like ourselves, intelligent and thoughtful persons. If we suggest to them the sacred morality [of the nation], if we explain to them national customs, if we illuminate their minds with purity, we will no longer have need to pay such excessive attention [to the question of the veil]. Let us leave them free to show their faces to the universe. Let us allow them to look at the world with attention. Such an occurrence should not frighten us.[142]

In the cities, women – especially younger women from middle-class republican families – followed this lead and abandoned the veil. In the countryside they did not, and looked with suspicion upon those who did. But nowhere in the new Turkish Republic did the hostility to anti-veiling take the terribly violent form of the reaction to the Communist *hujum* of 1927 in Soviet Central Asia.[143] Kemal was far too shrewd to imagine for a moment that the unveiled women of Anatolia could somehow be mobilised as a 'surrogate proletariat' on the side of the secular Republic. Veiling was far too delicate a terrain for blundering 'offensives'.

Within what framework, then, did the 'Father of the Turks' view gender relations in the new Republic? An oxymoronic reply would be 'emancipatory paternalism'. He never had any doubts about the supremacy of the male gender. Men were to lead and females to follow. Nor did he doubt that women played the crucial role in the creation of the family 'nest', both as mothers and as wives. But he felt passionately that women belonged to the public sphere, to the nation, not just to the family.

Two stereotypes of the 'new woman' emerged in Kemalist ideology and both were to become central to nationalist iconography. One was the generous, solid and powerful figure of the Anatolian peasant woman. The second, to whom Kemal dedicated a great deal of attention, was the emancipated and educated woman of the cities, who turned her back on the frivolities of life, and trained herself to serve the nation. She was to be a teacher or a nurse, a doctor or even an engineer. She was to have the vote, at local elections from 1930 and at national ones from 1934 – not that that meant anything much in a one-party state.

In terms of gender relations, Kemal's Turkey thus occupied an interesting middle position amongst the great authoritarian regimes of the first half of the century. Atatürk certainly showed more interest and conviction with regard to the emancipation and education of women than did either Mussolini or Hitler.

Baş örtüsü nasıl bağlanır?

Baş örtüsünü güzel bağlamak nasil mümkündür?
Soldan itibaren sıra ile resimleri takip ederseniz kuçücük bir-
krep saten parçasıyle zarif bir kadın kaşının nasıl süslendiğini
göruürsünüz.
Avrupalı kadınlar bizim sokaklarda türk hanimlarının başlarında
gördükleri baş örtülerini suvarelerde kullanmaktadirlar!

fig. 15 'How can you create beautiful headwear? With a little piece of satin you can
become very fashionable.' Hints for covering the hair without reference to the veil from
the magazine *Haftalık Mecmua*, 1928.

But he did not pursue the collectivist and egalitarian solutions which characterised much of early Soviet society and ideology. The presuppositions of
his 'emancipatory paternalism' were quite other: that men were to lead and
command as befitted their gender, but that a crucial part of their leadership
was to consist in emancipating and educating their women. The family, as
I shall now try to show, was to become *more* solid, not less. Within it, male
supremacy and the gendered division of labour went unquestioned, but they
were to be tempered by women's rights and education. The republican family
was to be constructed as a nuclear and monogamous unit, a secure 'nest',
which would serve as the primary cell in the life of the new nation.

3. Family politics: the Civil Code of 1926

Atatürk's adoption in 1926 of the Swiss Civil Code, first promulgated in its
home country in 1912, must rank as one of the most remarkable elements in

his attempt to revolutionise daily life. It is always mentioned in histories of Turkey but has been little studied. No act could have constituted a more dramatic embracing of western values and procedures. A significant part of the Code concerns key elements of family law – marriage, divorce, inheritance, intra-familial rights and duties, etc. – and is thus of central importance to the themes of this book. It is also worth comparing and contrasting the Code with the two Bolshevik Family Codes of 1918 and 1926.

I must begin, though, by taking a step backwards. Islamic family law was not codified at all, but rather the result of a constantly evolving process of interpretation of the sources of Islamic revelation. This evolving process, which depended to a great extent on the ability and prestige of the jurists concerned, was known as 'fıkıh' (Islamic jurisprudence). Its sources were often plural, involving elements of mysticism, local factors and links with state action. Western observers judged it to be 'random', but this was to miss the point, namely, that it was based on a different theory of knowledge from that of western law.[144]

Codification, the freezing of law into fixed norms, was anathema to *fıkıh*. When the Tanzimat reformers began to put Ottoman law on to a 'rational' western basis, the *ulema*, the doctors of law, and the *kadı*, the religious magistrates, lost not only status and power. They also lost, as Şerif Mardin has eloquently put it, 'their world of ideation'.[145] The plural sources of their jurisprudence and its mobile nature, based on *phronesis* or ethical know-how, were mortally threatened. The realms of commercial and penal law were the first to succumb. Family law was the last, on account of the fact that the family was considered an inviolable sanctuary, to be regulated by the Şeriat.

Even here change eventually became inevitable. The CUP was strongly in favour of regulation but was constantly blocked by the strong clerical presence in early twentieth-century Ottoman parliaments. The war years, with their terrible social disruptions, marked the crucial turning point. In 1915 an imperial decree allowed wives to petition for the legal dissolution of their marriages four years after their husbands' disappearance or presumed death in war. Two years later, a major reform was passed. The new Law of the Family (Hukuk-u Aile Kararnamesi) of 1917 constituted a first attempt to codify the realms of marriage and divorce. It obliged couples to register their marriage with the civil authorities and to make public their biographical details before the wedding ceremony took place. It also raised the age of first marriage to eighteen for men and seventeen for women, attempting in this way to limit forced or arranged marriages. The law made it possible for both parties to have recourse to the law if they wished to seek divorce, though the grounds for divorce were not rendered equal for both genders. As for polygamy, no specific article abolished it, but a wife was henceforth allowed to insert a clause in the marriage contract forbidding her husband to take further wives. No effective sanctions were prescribed, however, in the case that he chose to ignore the clause.

Overall, the law of 1917 can be judged a first, timid step to expand the rights of women within marriage. It aroused great fury and opposition in the clerical world. One of the leading *ulema* of the time, Sadreddin Efendi, defended polygamy with force, pointing out that 'In the Koran and the Islamic tradition it is quite clear that to contract a second marriage a man has no need of the approval of his first wife. To consider this a point of departure has absolutely no justification in Muslim jurisdiction. Thus the clause in question is an unacceptable interpretation.'[146] In any case the law of 1917 had a short life. With the end of the war and the disgracing of the CUP triumvirate, it was abrogated in 1919.

The Kemalist Republic had, therefore, to begin all over again. At first it seemed oriented to reproducing a version of the 1917 law, and in that way to placate the *ulema*. In March 1924, however, Mustafa Kemal intervened, making it clear that in this as in so many other areas he was not interested in compromise:

> The important point is to free our legal attitudes, our Codes and our legal organisations from principles dominating our lives that are incompatible with the necessities of the age [. . .] The direction to be followed in civil law and family law should be nothing but that of Western civilisation. Following the road of half measures and attachment to age-old beliefs is the gravest obstacle to the awakening of nations.[147]

A new Minister of Justice, Mahmut Esat, was appointed and the Civil Code was finally promulgated in February 1926. In its preamble Mahmut Esat made clear that the creative tension between *medeniyet* and *hars*, civilisation and culture, so beloved of Gökalp, had been brutally resolved: 'We must never forget that the Turkish nation has decided to accept modern civilisation and its living principles without any condition or reservation [. . .] the Turkish nation [must] adjust its steps to the requirements of contemporary civilisation at all costs.'[148]

The new Civil Code turned its back entirely on the Şeriat and the centuries-old methodology of the *fıkıh*. Not only was family law to be codified, in itself a revolution, but it was to be codified on Swiss lines! The symbolic significance of this choice was very great indeed.

Why did Turkey choose Switzerland? The answer to this question is as yet far from clear. The Swiss Code of 1912 was certainly one of the most recent to have been promulgated in the Europe of that time; it was simply written, with a limited number of articles; and it spoke to a nation that contained within its frontiers linguistic and religious minorities. Furthermore, the Treaty of Lausanne of 1923, which effectively granted international recognition to the Turkish Republic, contained a specific request for Turkey to promulgate a Civil Code that could be applied to all its inhabitants, including what little was left of the Greek and Armenian communities. It may be that from Lausanne itself came the idea of adopting the Swiss Code.

There was probably another motive, however, more directly related to specific content. Switzerland had an outstanding tradition of local democracy, based on adult male suffrage, but it was one of the countries in which the request for parity between men and women, in both the private and the public sphere, proceeded with most difficulty. The Swiss view of women's emancipation, in other words, was as paternalistic as that of Mustafa Kemal. At a federal level Swiss women gained the vote only in 1971, later than anywhere else in Europe. The two countries thus expressed the same gendered political closures, though in different ways. Turkey granted the vote to women early on (1934), but in a male-dominated one-party state women's suffrage was little more than tokenism. Switzerland, perhaps more honestly, simply considered men politically superior to women and accordingly denied women the vote for much of the century.

The details of the Turco-Swiss Code (there were limited variants from one to the other) are of historical significance in two different respects.[149] In the first place they mark a radical departure from previous Ottoman and Islamic practices, women finally acquiring formal rights, especially in the making, conducting and ending of marriage; in the second they reveal, alongside these advances, how the Code ensured continuing male dominion not just in the public sphere but in the domestic one as well.

Marriage was henceforth to be a public affair, duly registered with and by the state. Chapter 3 (Articles 97 to 111) laid down the procedures. The most important were prior publication of the spouses' biographical details (to prevent bigamy or the like) and the issuing of a marriage certificate. Religious ceremonies had no legal validity, and could take place only after the civil rites were concluded (Article 110). Men were to be at least eighteen years old and women seventeen, though exceptions were allowed in special circumstances. Polygamy was not mentioned (it was after all a Swiss Code) but was abolished by default. Article 151 stipulated that husband and wife swore to be faithful to each other.

The list of grounds for divorce, in all their bald and repetitive equality, is very impressive, especially if we remember what had gone before in terms of the arbitrary repudiation of wives:

> Article 129: Either spouse may request a divorce on the grounds of adultery committed by the other [. . .]
>
> Article 130: Either spouse may request a divorce on the grounds of an attempt on his or her life or maltreatment by the other [. . .]
>
> Article 132: Either spouse may request a divorce on the grounds of malicious abandonment by the other (with the intention of not discharging his or her duties) [. . .]
>
> Article 143: Either spouse may request a divorce if the deterioration in conjugal well-being is such that marital life has become intolerable [. . .][150]

In many other areas, too, the legal status of women improved drastically. Inheritance was one of them. Islamic practice had been to grant a daughter only half the share of a son. Under the Code of 1926 all children inherited equally, regardless of sex. Under Article 144 the concept of alimony was introduced for the first time, to be paid for a year to the 'innocent spouse who has fallen into destitution' and to be proportionate to the income of the other partner (almost invariably the husband). Within marriage, if a husband neglected his economic duties to his family, a judge could order third parties to pay all income directly to the wife (Article 163).

On the other hand, and this was the Code's second defining feature, male dominance was clearly reaffirmed – not arbitrary or without recourse, not violent or polygamous, not a power that trampled all other family members underfoot, but rather a new paternalism in which men had certain responsibilities and women others. This direction emerges unequivocally from the section of the Code which treats of 'The general effects of marriage' (Articles 151–69). The husband is 'the head of the conjugal union. He chooses the marital abode and provides adequately for the maintenance of his wife and children' (Article 152). The wife is to bear the husband's name and owes her spouse, 'in so far as her capacities allow, assistance and advice towards the attainment of common prosperity'. She runs the household (Article 153), but the husband represents the family in the outside world (Article 154). Husband and wife together have responsibility for 'the current needs of the household'. However, 'the husband may revoke, in whole or in part, the powers of the wife in the event of her abuse of the right to represent the conjugal union or her incapacity to exercise it' (Article 156). No parallel clause exists for comparable male incompetence. Finally (though the list could be much longer), Article 159 establishes the conditions under which a woman could take employment outside the home. She could do so only with the express or tacit consent of her husband. If he refused she could appeal to the courts, but she would have to demonstrate that her decision was dictated not by her own interests but by the interests and needs of her family.[151]

Overall, the new Turkish Code aimed to increase the degree of stability of the family as an institution. Within it, the genders were to have clearly delineated but not identical rights and duties, the male head of the household being clearly in command. Women were to serve their families but above all to serve the nation as mothers. The family as an institution was further reinforced by the Family Names Law of 1934. Everyone was henceforth to choose a second name and wives were to adopt the names of their husbands. Thus Halide Edib became Halide Edib Adıvar, the last name being that which her (second) husband took in 1934.

A comparison, however brief, of the Russian Codes of 1918 and 1926 with the Turkish one of 1926 is revealing. All three were profoundly secular, intent on demoting religious marriage and destroying the power of religious courts. All three made it clear that the state had the right and the duty to intervene in family life and regulate its everyday relations.

There is nothing in the Turkish experience, however, to match the massive discussion both in town and in the countryside of the Russian Code of 1926. No semblance of democratic participation ever marked Atatürk's revolution from above. At most there was dissent and discussion in the Great National Assembly, summarily curtailed in 1925–6. Furthermore, far greater attention was paid in the two Russian Codes to genuine gender equality. The emancipation that the Soviet legislators had in mind was far more robust and less paternalist than in the Turkish case.[152]

Yet on at least one level – that of the strengthening of family bonds and identity – the real distinction to be made is between the early Bolshevik Code of 1918 and the two later ones – Turkish and Russian – of 1926. The 1918 Code is revolutionary with regard to inheritance, which it sought to abolish. And under Goikhbarg's influence, and more indirectly Kollontai's, it emphasised the *transitory* nature of the family, its eventual if not imminent dissolution in the name of a higher way of life – the collective and statist one. By contrast, both the Turkish and Russian Codes of 1926 – even if the Russian one controversially recognised *de facto* marriage – were primarily concerned with protecting the stability of family bonds and the effective functioning of families.

4. Family life in town and country after Kemal's reforms

In the major cities, Kemal's radical reform of family law both coincided with and reinforced the general lines of development of Turkish families. As I tried to show in the first part of this chapter, the trend towards nuclear family forms and new, less unequal relations between the genders had already been manifest in late Ottoman Istanbul. Women of the urban middle classes had begun to emerge from the harem, the inner sanctuary of the household, and to reach outwards, towards external, public space. These trends were greatly reinforced during the first decade of the new Republic. As Duben and Behar have noted, 'there is little doubt that the women of Istanbul in the 1930s had made considerable progress as compared to their Ottoman sisters'.[153]

Such progress could be measured in innumerable ways: women had a far greater say in the choice of a marriage partner, they were marrying three or four years later than their counterparts had done at the end of the nineteenth century, they could now petition for divorce on the same grounds as their husbands, and they were participating in ever greater numbers in the labour force. They were also much better educated. By 1929–30 approximately 75 per cent of all girls in Istanbul aged seven to eleven were attending primary school, almost the same percentage as for boys. This was an extraordinary transformation, considering that in Turkey as a whole in these years 80 per cent of boys and 87 per cent of girls were still illiterate. Between 1920 and 1938, women constituted 10 per cent of university graduates.

Furthermore, the secular Republic greatly stimulated the trend for urban men and women to feel freer, socially if not politically. They could celebrate in modest ways what Michel de Certeau has called the 'modern art of every-day expression'. Many time-honoured and religiously based restraints were placed on one side. Husbands and wives began to socialise as couples and to go out together in the evening, eating in restaurants on the shores of the Bosphorus, visiting dance halls and going to receptions. The regime looked on benignly. There was a strong sense of beginning again, after the horrors of the previous decade, both in Ankara and in Istanbul.[154]

In the countryside there was a very different story to tell. As early as 1924 the republican legislators had promulgated a vast and comprehensive new 'Village Law' (Köy Kanunu). It laid down a set of thirty-seven standards for all villages, covering every aspect of their lives. Village water was to be kept clean, every house was to have a covered privy, and a wall was to separate families' own sleeping quarters from those where their animals were stabled. Every four years all adult peasants were to elect a village *muhtar* (leader) and a village council. The *muhtar* was to represent the interests of the village, but he was above all to be an administrative official beholden to the instructions of central government. The Village Law, together with the Civil Code and educational reform, were intended to lay down new bases for village life – secular, hygienic and scientific, with far fewer disparities between men and women. Individuals and families were to be inserted into a collective, though not collectivist, project of nation-making.[155]

All this was easier said than done. While in the cities Kemalist law and the general evolution of families found many points of convergence, in the countryside the new regime's innovations were often met with hostility and incredulity. Let me take the case of civil and religious marriages. Although the stipulations of the Civil Code were bolstered by Article 237 of the Penal Code – which foresaw prison sentences of up to two years for imams or others who celebrated religious marriage without a prior civil ceremony – the whole idea of registered civil marriage was largely ignored in the countryside.[156] The lack of available historical sources for the countryside in the 1930s and 1940s makes it very difficult to gauge peasant reaction. In 1949–50 the anthropologist Paul Stirling went to study two villages on the central Anatolian plateau, Sakaltutan and Elbaşı (in the province of Kayseri). He found – even at that late date – a great gulf separating republican legislation and peasant practice. For the villagers, the only marriage that had any meaning was one based on a religious ceremony, to be performed by the local imam or anyone of sufficient learning to know the required formulae. Civil marriage was held to have no meaning or significance. For the villagers, 'registration is not a rite within their system, but a meaningless piece of bureaucratic mumbo jumbo'.[157] The marriage rites which *did* matter hardly conformed to the culture and precepts of the Turco-Swiss Code, their proceedings underlining above all the disparity between the sexes, the mourning of the bride on leaving her family of origin, and her imminent submission to her new family:

> Four of the visiting *yenge* [women chosen to play a leading role in the marriage ceremony], and one woman of the girl's side, also called *yenge*, take the bride into an inner room or cave where, solemnly lamenting and weeping, they dress her for her new husband. From this moment until she is alone with him, she is not allowed to speak, but weeps constantly [. . .] Numerous rites at the threshold of the new house are reported from all parts of Turkey. In Sakaltutan, the bride entered her new home under the legs of the mother-in-law, who was held up for the purpose.[158]

The Civil Code thus expressed a vision of family relations that was in strong contrast to the culture and habitual practice of Anatolian peasant life. But the meta-category of 'Anatolia', so powerful and omnipresent, must be at least partially broken down. The impression that results is of considerable diversity across agricultural regions but in general of a peasantry hostile to change, deeply attached to religious practices and to conventional patriarchal gender relations.

In the villages of the steppe, residence was mainly patrilocal, with the male head of household continuing to exercise a potentially despotic power over the whole extended family. Relations between fathers and sons were strict and formal. Sons were not to speak in public unless invited to do so by their fathers. They were never to answer back. Nor were they permitted to smoke

fig. 16 A wedding in Anatolia. The bride leaves her home followed by the *yenge*.

in their fathers' presence. Under no circumstances did fathers and sons refer to sexual matters in each other's presence. From the age of about eight sons had to take responsibility for farm animals and at twelve they learned how to handle a plough. Inheritance was delayed until the death of the paterfamilias.[159]

Men and women still lived rigidly separated lives. The main room of the houses in the villages studied by Stirling was called the 'ev'. It was the domain of women and children, and had at its centre a beehive-shaped oven called the 'tandır'. 'Round the oven, when guests call or women have time to sit, are spread mats and rugs and cushions.'[160] No man was ever allowed to enter the *ev* unless he was a member of the family or a very close relative. Even a first cousin might hesitate to call, unless he had special business, in which case he would first knock and call out to give warning.

Men, by contrast, farmed in male household groups, and returned to the *ev* only to eat and sleep. Some of the larger dwellings had another room which was called the 'guest room', the site of male sociality. There the men of the household would sit in the evenings, brew coffee and tea if they could afford it, and welcome neighbours and guests. These rooms had a built-in divan, which ran right along the walls. A few, older women occasionally penetrated this male enclave. What was very striking was that men seemed to spend as much time as possible away from their own house and family. It was almost as if an undeclared war existed between the sexes. Stirling noted, 'I have seen men standing out in a snowstorm under a sheltered wall rather than to go join their wives in the house.'[161]

In a famous account of village life, once again from central Anatolia, written in the early 1950s by a young village school teacher of peasant stock, the limited impact of the Kemalist revolution after two decades of power is even more strongly evident.[162] The villages described by Mahmut Makal (born in 1931) were even poorer than those studied by Stirling. The literacy programme, which should have guaranteed five years' primary education to the village children, was a shambles. The dominant culture was that of the *hoca* (preacher in the mosque) and of Islamic teaching. There were village dervishes, even though the *tarikat*, the dervish convent, had long since been abolished. Magic, as in the case of the Russian peasantry, was everywhere.[163]

Overall, the picture that emerges is of an austere and traditional peasantry, physically and culturally isolated from the rest of Turkey, trying to make a living in a region only marginally suitable for agriculture, and dependent for survival on slight and unpredictable rainfalls. Of course, conditions varied greatly in so vast a region. The barrenness of the central Anatolian plateau, with its 'ruthless silence and desolation',[164] was in stark contrast to the fertile valleys nearer the coasts and to the lush if restricted plains to be found, for example, around Adana. Certain common characteristics none the less stand out. This was a smallholding peasantry, not a landless one. In 1907 holdings of 4.5 hectares and less constituted 81 per cent of all Anatolian cultivated land.[165] Partly as a result, the Turkish peasantry lacked the strong collectivist traditions of its Russian counterpart. Neither did it have a long tradition of unrest or rebellion. It was, rather, a peasantry of long-suffering and patience, condemned to high mortality rates, not only among infants, and with a diffused rather than intense religiosity.

The great majority were small proprietors, and it was difficult for an Anatolian family to enrich itself during the normal cycle of rural life. The hazards were too many and the opportunities too few. The richest man in Elbaşı had become so by occupying considerable tracts of land forcibly abandoned by the inhabitants of a nearby village of Greek Orthodox Christians. This had been in 1923, and the Greek Christians had been unwilling participants in the so-called 'exchange of populations' of that year.[166]

In general, Turkish villages had always worn a poorer and less animated aspect than those of their Christian neighbours. Back in 1904 an acute American observer, Lucy Garnett, had noted the simple honesty and sobriety of the Turkish peasants, their abstemiousness – in which they contrasted so strikingly with their Russian counterparts – and 'their passive contentment and dignified resignation'. But she also noted that unlike the Greek or Armenian peasant the Turkish one had 'no weekly dance, no frequently recurring village feast, and but little music to vary the uniformity of life'. Nor did Turkish rural women sit out as Christian women did, spinning, knitting and sewing at the doors of their dwellings.[167]

The decade of war had lacerated these peasant families as no previous period had done. Here, too, as in the cities, the peace brought by Kemalism was welcomed with open arms. But the peasantry eyed the new regime with suspicion – in spite of its oft-declared and oft-celebrated Anatolian origins. Mustafa Kemal, for his part, was a shrewd enough dictator not to launch an open assault on peasant custom and practice. As with regard to the wider question of veiling, he preferred to adopt a long-term view, hoping that time and education would work their customary magic. He was absolutely not prepared to pass from a 'war of position' to one of frontal assault. Not for him the terrible war waged by Stalin against the Russian peasantry in the course of the first Five-Year Plan. In contrast to Stalin, Kemal had an acute sense of limit. He was aware that Anatolian families had contributed in no small part to the War of Independence. He also knew that they were what the demographers call a 'natural fertility population', having no recourse to contraception and with a family culture oriented to having many children, preferably of the male sex. Atatürk needed those boys for his army and for the defence of a national territory which had been acquired at so high a cost.

5. 'It seems marriage was not meant for me'

I will end this chapter by looking at the role of family in Kemal's own life, and to make a first comparison, under this profile, with the other great dictators of the first half of the century.[168] Reading about the families of origin of this tyrants' cohort, the historian springs readily to a first conclusion: a highly unsatisfactory father figure and a devoted mother are the necessary, if not sufficient, familial conditions for forming a dictatorial personality, one ready to affirm in violent fashion his own individuality and masculinity. Stalin hated his father, who beat him and his mother regularly. Franco's father was unloving and absent, Hitler's uninterested and authoritarian. Kemal's own experience fits these patterns very well. His father, as we have seen, was judged by his family to have been a failure, given to drink and dying young, whereas his mother, Zübeyde, was a very strong figure from whom Kemal never fully emancipated himself. He had a double image of her. On the one hand, he idealised her. When the Italian sculptor Pietro Canonica came to Ankara to execute a number of busts of Mustafa Kemal in 1926, Kemal told him, 'She was my best friend [. . .] Losing her, I lost everything.'[169] On the other, Zübeyde was an authoritarian influence in his life, pushing him as a child towards the religious schooling he did not want, opposing his military career, and never fully satisfied with her son's choices, especially of women.

Unloving and absent fathers and over-protective, anxious and interfering mothers thus seem to constitute the family substrata from which dictators are regularly made. So, too, is the syndrome of a boy left as the only surviving male in the family at an early age. However, any neat psychological symmetry is in part broken by the case of Mussolini. His mother, selfless, very Catholic and devoted to her family, certainly fits the bill, but his father, Alessandro, while not hesitating to use the belt on his recalcitrant son, was also appreciated by Benito for his political views and for the education he had given him.[170]

All the dictators insisted on their subjects leading proper and ordered lives. They all stressed the importance of the family's stability and its centrality as an institution in their various 'New Orders'. As we shall see, however, only one of them, Francisco Franco, could conceivably be described as a 'good family man', and could present himself to his subjects with some sincerity as a model of devotion and fidelity. Profoundly Catholic, Franco was married for fifty-two years to María del Carmen Polo, from 1923 to 1975.[171]

Mustafa Kemal, by contrast, had no time for home life, nor did he want to create a family of his own. His spare time at the end of the day was invariably spent with his military drinking companions; once in their cups male virility was a favourite topic of conversation. Kemal, who was strikingly good-looking in his youth, fair-haired and blue-eyed, could boast an infinite number of casual conquests. According to one anecdote, in reply to the question 'What do you appreciate most about women?' he replied, 'Their availability'. But this was not the whole man. As we have seen, alongside his own appetites he expressed a genuine and passionate interest in women's emancipation. He wanted very much, within the tight paternal boundaries he had established, to free them from superstition, enclosure and ignorance.

In November 1914, when his bosom companion Fuat got married, Kemal sent him a congratulatory and highly revealing letter about marriage:

> Life is short, and most men see in marriage the most reasonable means of crowning it with happiness. Those who do not observe this rule are few and exceptional. These exceptions do not prove the general rule. These unfortunates are rather the victims of circumstances which do not permit the observance of this pleasant rule, perhaps because they are afraid of marriage.[172]

He was obviously talking about himself. But Kemal *did* marry, just once. At the end of the War of Independence, in September 1922, he met the twenty-four-year-old daughter of a rich Turkish merchant, in whose mansion he was staying in the recently reconquered Izmir. Lâtife had been studying law in France but had returned to Turkey after the battle of Sakarya. She was not especially pretty but she impressed Kemal with her European manners and learning, with her easy and direct ways. She was also a dynamic sort of person and a very good organiser. Mustafa referred to her jokingly as 'the lady commander of the headquarters'. A few months later, at the end of January 1923, they were married in Izmir. The wedding was kept a secret, and Kemal, rather typically, did not bother to ask Lâtife's father for her hand. The bride wore a headscarf but her face was not veiled.

There was no honeymoon and the couple went straightaway to live in Kemal's villa at Çankaya, in the hills south-east of Ankara. It was far smaller than Lâtife's father's house and a long way from the Mediterranean. On their first night there, Lâtife had to dine alone because her husband wanted to be with his male friends until three thirty in the morning. Over the next two years she felt thoroughly neglected and increasingly resentful. Nor did their union lead to her becoming pregnant. In August 1925, so the story goes, Kemal returned late one night and before turning in stopped to chat with the sentries.

From the balcony an infuriated Lâtife shouted, 'Kemal, come in at once. Aren't you satisfied with your friends in the neighbourhood? Do you have to make friends of your sentries too?' So public a reprimand in front of ordinary soldiers was too much for him. The next day he wrote to her that they should have a period apart and suggested that she return to her father's mansion. He then instructed his ADC to accompany her forthwith to Izmir. A few days later, on 11 August 1925, he informed the government that he had divorced his wife. 'It seems marriage was not meant for me,' he ruefully told Pietro Canonica in 1926.

In the story of this unhappy marriage we see again the extent to which Kemal's only real family, the object of his unceasing devotion, was the army and the men who composed it. Even the title-deeds of his villa at Çankaya were transferred, on his instructions, to the Turkish army, the villa becoming known as the Army Mansion. Kemal, like Hitler, did not have any children, perhaps because he was not able to. The emotional barrenness of his private life – an internal Anatolia – was broken only by his decision to adopt a number of children, of whom all but one were female. They ranged from the very young to women in their teenage years. Their future was, as one of them put it, 'shaped by Mustafa Kemal with his own hands'.[173]

His favourite was Afet, who was a fair-haired elementary school teacher aged eighteen when he first met her in October 1925. He had just divorced Lâtife. There seems little doubt that Afet became his mistress as well as his adopted daughter; she was certainly his constant companion in his latter years. Unlike Lâtife, everyone agreed she knew how to handle Mustafa Kemal, making herself available when he wanted her but never making demands upon him, or attempting to rein him in. In his personal life he had no desire for, or patience with, emancipated women, least of all an emancipated woman as his wife. A woman who had the ambiguous, more subordinate status of adopted daughter/mistress suited him much better. Afet was his willing amanuensis, very often present at dinner, taking copious notes of his table talk. She went on to become a professor at the University of Ankara after Atatürk's death in 1938.

There is a magnificent photograph of 1927 which shows the wife of a high-ranking functionary kissing Mustafa Kemal's hand as he enters the palace of Dolmabahçe. It is the same hand that Halide Edib analysed with such sensitivity and ferocity in her memoirs:

In that light his hand was the only part of him which I could see distinctly, and it is that part of him which is physically most characteristic of the whole man. It is a narrow and faultlessly shaped hand, with very slender fingers and a skin which nothing darkens or wrinkles. Although it is not effeminate, one would not expect it to be a man's hand [. . .] It seemed to me that the merciless hunting of the human tiger in Turkey had its answer in this hand. It differed from the large broad hand of the fighting Turk in its highly strung nervous tension, its readiness to spring and grip its oppressor by the throat.[174]

All the great dictators of the first half of the twentieth century were reliant upon their propaganda machines to present imaginary versions of their families, whether those of origin or those of procreation. They all insisted on their own exceptionalism. These were great men, working in their studies late into the night, inventors of invincible military strategies, guardians of their nations' destinies, father figures more than fathers. For them, the private persona was

fig. 17 Mustafa Kemal is greeted by the wife of a senior functionary, Istanbul, 1927.

merged with, and subsumed into, the public one. It was from the daily experience of their exalted role, which unceasingly fed their narcissism, that they drew their strength.

Mustafa Kemal made explicit reference to his paternal role in the title he chose for himself. He was not to be a 'Duce' or a 'Führer', or even a 'Generalissimo'. Having no children of his own, he sought compensation in becoming the 'Father of all the Turks'. In 1934, as we have seen, a law was passed making it obligatory for everyone to choose a surname, as in the West. In November of the same year a special law attributed to Mustafa Kemal the surname of Atatürk, literally 'Father Turk'. A month later another law forbade the use of the name Atatürk, or any variant of it, by anyone else.[175] There was work for Pietro Canonica and many other sculptors of the time. Atatürk's statue was to dominate every town and village square throughout the land. There he was, the Father of the Nation, staring indomitably and severely into the beyond.

The real Mustafa Kemal, for all his icy determination, was much more fragile. He drank himself to death. When his secretary Hasan Rıza Soyak pleaded with him to drink less, he replied,

I've got to drink: my mind keeps on working hard and fast to the point of suffering. I have to slow it down and rest it at times. When I was at the War College and then at the Staff College, my mates in the dormitory usually had to wake me up in the morning. At night my mind would get fixed on a problem, and, as I thought about it, I was unable to sleep. I would spend the whole night tossing and turning in my bed, until finally I dozed off exhausted just before dawn. Then, naturally, I couldn't bear the sound of the reveille. It's the same now. When I don't drink, I can't sleep, and the distress stupefies me.[176]

CONCLUSION

There were many negative strands in the great Ottoman tradition of government – the ruthless suppression of revolt and dissent, the farming-out of tax collecting and the consequent over-taxation of the peasantry, the smothering of any autonomous urban associationism, the lack of competent administrative institutions in the many conquered territories of the Empire . . . the list is a very long one. But there is one element of Ottoman despotism which stands out with extraordinary poignancy in the light of what happened in the first two decades of the twentieth century: its firm belief in the virtues of the peaceful cohabitation of different races and religious beliefs. Not that all were equal; far from it. The Turkish-Islamic population was always both the majority and the most privileged. But the fact remains that in many fields the regime permitted the minorities freedoms and provided for their protection. To take just one example: the Ottomans permitted any subject – and after 1867 any foreigner who conformed to Ottoman laws – to hold land. At the end of the nineteenth century we find Albanian and Arab, Circassian and Armenian, Druze, Slavic, Turkish and Jewish peasant cultivators. Tax collectors, too, could belong to any ethnic or religious group.[177] In Istanbul the presence and constant flux of an extraordinarily heterogeneous population fascinated many foreign visitors.

Not that all was a bed of roses. There was little intermarrying and relations were often no more than 'cordial' – the adjective cautiously chosen by the great Turkish historical sociologist Şerif Mardin. Often, too, there were violent tensions between different quarters of Ottoman cities. In Izmir the older houses of the Armenians were designed for defence as much as for living, 'having often on the ground floor no windows overlooking the street, and the great double gateways are faced with iron and defended inside with heavy bars'.[178] Only later, unaware of what was to come, did the Armenians construct houses which boasted spacious entrances and marble steps, leading down freely to the street. But it is worth reiterating that in Istanbul the non-Muslim communities – mainly Greek, Armenian and Jewish – constituted traditionally between a quarter and a third of the city's total population. The extraordinary cohabitation of different populations in the capital city was one of the great Ottoman achievements.

It was the Young Ottomans, more than any other political or cultural movement, at least until the civil society movements of the 1990s, who most celebrated this diversity and intermingling. Their cultural renaissance marked out the middle decades of the nineteenth century. They were not democrats or revolutionaries and the majority Muslim component was firmly convinced of the superiority of its religion and culture. But they had understood the riches that pluralism and tolerance had to offer.

Halide Edib, in spite of what she called her 'national madness', was in many ways their heir. From exile in 1935 she published a novel written in English called *The Clown and his Daughter*. Underlying the whole story, set in late nineteenth-century Istanbul, is the theme of mixing and diversity, as well as the peaceful confronting of different beliefs and origins. In some senses the world she describes is a dreamworld, but in others it corresponds to historical reality, a reality which the Turkish nationalist movement, of which Halide herself was such a signal member, did so much to destroy. Or we can take the autobiography of a teacher and civil servant, Mahir İz, who described himself as a 'religious conservative' but who served the Republic faithfully for many decades.[179] His work laments the passing of an age of plural networks, Islamic and otherwise, which enriched his education and his view of the world. As Mardin comments, '[His] is the loss of the combinations and permutations that were accessible to what we may describe as the agents of a late Ottoman Islamic "civil society".'[180]

The possibilities of civil society were further enhanced by the form and culture of middle-class Islamic families in the late nineteenth and early twentieth centuries. These were families on the move, open to new influences from the West, ready to experiment, to mix ancient religious customs and modern *mores*, much more curious about the use of public space than had previously been the case – for men, above all, but also for women. The revolution of 1908 appeared as the apotheosis of these tendencies – the sudden and intense fraternisation in the face of a new world, and against the old one, which seemed dead on its feet.

This precious strand in Ottoman history found no protector in the Young Turks. Their political education was positivist rather than liberal, nationalist rather than internationalist, supremacist rather than respectful of difference. It is true that they came to power in a rapidly changing situation by which they were heavily constrained, caught up as they were in the dismemberment of the Empire, the wildfire spread of Balkan nationalism and the onset of world war. But they embraced and supported many of the worst ideas and aspects of the period and very few of the positive, countervailing ones. The new, timid life of parliament and the flowering of a free press merited much more attention and support than they received. The real agenda of the CUP, a revived and exclusive Turkish nation-state, led them in world-war conditions directly to the Armenian genocide. Louise Bryant, the widow of John Reed, met the fugitive Enver Paşa in Moscow after the revolution. For all his great charm nothing could hide his 'very obvious opportunism'. His utter refusal to reflect on the nature and dimensions of the Armenian massacres was startling to her: 'He said he could never understand why Americans were so sentimental about Armenians. "Do they imagine that Armenians never kill Turks? That is indeed irony."'[181]

Mustafa Kemal was different, but not because he cared more about the Armenians. The important counter-factual question 'Would he have behaved any differently from Talât, Enver and Cemal had he held power in the spring of 1915?' does not evoke any comforting answers. But once in power he promoted a revolution in daily life – in family customs, in language, in dress, in education and in culture – which was extraordinarily vital and interesting, even if confined principally to the cities and to seaboard Turkey.

Having said this – and it is a lot to say by comparison with other regimes of the same type – it is essential to underline the political limits of his revolution. Kemal was also a Young Turk, and continuities between the CUP regime and his were inevitable. On the key question of pluralism and difference, Kemal was little better than his predecessors. The case of the Kurds is a telling one. In post-genocide Anatolia, the Kurds constituted around a quarter of the population. They had not hesitated, both in the name of Muslim brotherhood and in self-interest, to play a significant part in the murder gangs that undertook the mass killings of the Armenians. Kemal had made it clear that 'bonded Muslim elements', not just Turks, would constitute the citizens of the new Republic. The reality was quite different. From 1916 onwards, as we have seen, regions which historically had been characterised by a strong Kurdish presence became the starting points for mass deportations. Kurdish areas were taken over by Turkish officials, Kurdish place names changed and the Kurdish language banned from courts and schools. The fierce Kurdish uprising of February 1925 against the ending of the caliphate, led by the tribal religious leader Şeyh Said, was put down with great ruthlessness. It led directly to the highly repressive and widely used Law on the Maintenance of Order of March 1925.

A similar story, as ruthless if not as murderous, can be told for the destinies of the associations of a very fragile civil society. Even within the relatively safe confines of the Turkish nationalist movement, no space was granted to autonomous organisation. One of the most important associations to pay attention to family themes, the Türk Ocakları (the Turkish Hearth movement), which had tried to introduce nationalist, positivist and secular ideas throughout the country, was closed down in 1931. At that time it had 30,000 members and 267 branches – not many in relation to the vastness of the country but highly significant for the new Republic. Another organisation took its place in 1932, this time tightly controlled by the provincial branches of the Kemalist party. The Halk Evleri (the People's Homes) in the towns and cities and the Halk Odaları (the People's Rooms) in the larger villages were to become official meeting places for party-organised initiatives, aimed at the diffusion of nationalist culture.[182]

As for democracy, there was little space for it in the Republic, either as concept or as practice. Kemal did use the term quite frequently and was concerned that formal democratic rituals were to be adhered to: 'Our form of government', he wrote in 1922, 'is entirely democratic government. And in our language this government is called "People's Government".[183] What he meant, though, was a regime in which the ruling party made all the decisions on behalf of a people tacitly deemed to be politically immature. Elections took the form of carefully staged and managed plebiscites. The population was to be organised in corporative structures designed to dissipate social tensions and the possibility of conflict. Presiding benignly but severely over the whole structure stood the Father of the Nation, the charismatic political and military hero par excellence. These were patterns of authoritarian government which the twentieth century was to make its own.

By contrast, the family politics of the regime were many times more spacious and original. The comparison with the Russian experience is a fascinating one. Whereas Kollontai and many of the Bolsheviks considered the western, 'bourgeois' family to be in an advanced state of decomposition, Kemal on the contrary considered it to be a positive model, waiting to be transplanted into Turkey. This was the basic reasoning behind the decision to adopt the Swiss Civil Code in 1926. And if that particular Code continued to reserve a whole series of prerogatives to the male head of the family, so much the better. No one in the new Turkey, for obvious reasons, wanted to call into question the dominance of father figures.

The Turco-Swiss Code was not just about the dominance of fathers, however. For a state with an overwhelming majority of Muslim subjects, the Code of 1926 – when combined with other parts of Kemal's social and cultural legislation – opened up extraordinary vistas for both women and children. Within the family, wives had more rights than ever before, including the crucial negative one of initiating divorce proceedings that was granted to their husbands. Outside the family, women could aspire to be educated and to serve the nation in responsible jobs requiring professional skills. They could walk freely in Turkish society, at least in its urban part, unveiled, holding their heads high. As for children, they were to be as disciplined and obedient as in the past, but they were not to be forced into marriage at totally inappropriate ages.

There can be little doubt that the Bolshevik experience of family politics was, in a number of significant respects, more advanced than the Kemalist one. Never under Kemalism was there anything remotely to compare with the widespread popular discussion, in both town and country, of the 1926 Soviet Code. In gender terms, too, the Russians were a long way ahead, even the more moderate of them. If Mustafa Kemal had happened to be a Russian Communist rather than a Turkish nationalist, he would have been horrified by Kollontai, who was far more radical than the domesticated Halide Edib, about whom he was anyway suspicious. He would have been particularly shocked by Kollontai's desire for open, public debate on male and female sexuality. For Kemal, sex was to be talked about only in primitive terms, with fellow officers and male friends, at the end of long evening drinking sessions. But leaving sex aside, he would have found it pretty hard to digest even Lenin's version of women's emancipation. Lenin, it may be remembered, had denounced women's 'domestic slavery' – their subjection to 'petty housekeeping' and their confinement to the kitchen and the nursery. In his view, emancipation would occur only when the family kitchen and female housework could be abandoned in favour of numerous, massive public and collective services – nurseries, laundries, canteens and schools. These would permit women to become full-time workers, alongside and equal to men.[184] They would also supplant families as the chief providers of services, making the family much less important in daily life.

This was not at all what Kemal had in mind. His revolution in everyday life aimed to make the Turkish republican family more solid, not less. It was to be constructed as a nuclear and monogamous unit, in which women and men had rights and duties, a secure 'nest' which would serve as the primary cell in the life of the new nation. The Bolshevik idea of dissolving all previous relations, including family ones, into a hyper-collectivist society-state was not much to Kemal's taste. He shared with Gökalp the view that in the Turkish revolution 'there is no "you" or "I" – only "we" ', but he had no intention of pushing such an affirmation to extremes. Family, society and state were to remain three separate entities in the new Turkey – connected rather than dissolved into one another. Families were to be strengthened following the western nuclear model, society was to be corporative, and the state – especially the military – was to wield power with traditional ruthlessness.

CHAPTER 3

Fascism and the family

I. MARINETTI, GRAMSCI AND ITALIAN FAMILIES

1. A Futurist

Filippo Tommaso Marinetti, the founder of Italian Futurism and the principal author of its first manifestos, had a family upbringing that brought him into close contact with the world of Islam and the decaying Ottoman Empire. In 1873 his father and mother had left the provincial life of Voghera, a small town in Piedmont, to seek their fortune in Alexandria in Egypt. They were encouraged to do so by the opening of the Suez Canal in 1869. Marinetti's father was a commercial lawyer, tireless and punctilious, nicknamed 'Felfel' (pepper) by the locals, with clients at the court of the khedive İsmail Paşa. He soon became a wealthy man. Marinetti's mother was, in the words of her adoring second son, 'an entire poem of utter delicacy and musicality of tenderness and affectionate tears.'[1]

Marinetti described his own birth in the following dramatic fashion: 'On 22 April 1876 with the prior annunciation of the scirocco wind the Hamsin and its searing fifty days of desert-laden bleeding burns he was born of a Milanese mother and Vogherese father in a house by the sea in Alexandria in Egypt.'[2] Marinetti, as is immediately evident, believed neither in punctuation nor in self-effacement. More than fifty years later he returned to Egypt and commented on 'the enduring amalgam of odours colours tastes and stenches which defend themselves heroically against European modernity [...] My nose and eyes will never again be full of that sea of beautiful green crystal of extreme saltiness into which my father brutally threw my little body at a tender age to teach me to despise all lifebelts.'[3]

Alexandria was the embodiment of Ottoman tolerance and commercial pluralism. Visiting the city for the first time in 1894 an Italian Catholic priest noted its 'extraordinarily thriving commerce', 'a constant flow of peoples of every nationality, each with different customs and strange and resplendent clothes. Just to walk through its streets is to witness a remarkable mixture of features and races that it is quite impossible to imagine.'[4] In 1888 the young Marinetti, aged twelve, was sent by his parents to the recently opened school of the French Jesuits. Its playground – a misnomer if ever there was one – was the site of running battles between boys of different nationalities, a foretaste in miniature of what would happen in the Great War. It was the time of the Italo-French trade war and the adolescent Marinetti, violently pro-nationalist and anti-papal, was in the thick of the fights. Halide Edib would have recognised his type: a boy but not a child.[5] Back in the school refectory he was required to read aloud from some pages from a biography of Pius IX, redolent with anti-Italian sentiment. He threw the book in a soup tureen, his first 'Futurist' act.[6]

In 1894, when his now wealthy parents moved back to Milan after twenty years in Egypt, Marinetti was sent to the Sorbonne to take his *baccalauréat* in arts and philosophy. Seventeen years old, with no one to control him, money in his pocket and an unbridled self-confidence, he made the most of being in Paris. The only thing that disturbed him was that everyone called him 'l'Egyptien', while he preferred to call himself, justly in the long run, 'Poète italien'. At his lodgings in a large international *pension* situated in the Latin Quarter, he tried to study for his exams. But his books, so he wrote, were 'appalled at the prospect of being mixed up in the lovers' entanglements further down the heaving corridor'.[7] They may have been appalled but he was not. Given his dynamic energy, irreverence and love of life, his close attention to appearance and immaculate dress sense, he was always going to be a highly successful seducer of women.

In his final exams Marinetti was asked – at eight o'clock in the morning in the great hall of the Sorbonne – to write an essay on the thought of John Stuart Mill. It is difficult to imagine two figures further apart, the one austere, meticulous and profound, who in his private life had chosen to turn his back on his own sexuality, the other vibrant, riotous and superficial, endlessly seeking satisfaction for his desires. But Marinetti would have considered the comparison futile: for him Mill was a 'passatista', one who was lodged firmly in the nineteenth century, while he, Marinetti, was a 'futurista', able to interpret and give expression to the new century.

He scraped through his *baccalauréat* and returned to Milan, which was to remain his city until the triumphs of Fascism bore him away to Rome. His father had rented an immense, luxurious flat in the centre of Milan, decorated in the oriental style, with furnishings and carpets brought back from Alexandria. This flat became the site of Marinetti's inspiration, the place where, in his own words, he stoked the fires of his own imagination. Everywhere around him the city was changing: new railway lines and stations connected Milan to Lombardy, Switzerland and beyond, factories were springing up on the city's peripheries, workers were demonstrating and being arrested and repressed. For Marinetti all this amounted to 'the febrile insomnia' of the new century. He increasingly aspired to give voice and visual images to the new era, to shock and shake the old world in the name of the new.[8]

At the turn of the century, his family was hit by a series of tragedies. His beloved elder brother Leone died in 1897 at the age of only twenty-three, his sweet and patient mother Amalia, heartbroken, followed him in 1902, his father Enrico in 1907. Marinetti was suddenly alone. For more than a decade he had been an active figure in the Milanese literary world, but it was only after his father's death that he made the great leap to international fame. In February 1909 the Parisian *Le Figaro* published on its front page the first Futurist manifesto. Marinetti had secured this coup by floating the idea of his marriage to the daughter of one of the newspaper's principal shareholders, the Egyptian Mohamed el Rachi, who had known Marinetti's father in Alexandria.

The eleven points of the manifesto made for iconoclastic and compulsive reading. If before the birth of Futurism literature had celebrated 'anxious immobility, ecstasy and slumber', it was now time for 'aggressive movement, feverish insomnia, marching at the double, death leaps, slaps and punches'. These violent, nervous impulses and images were to underlie much of Fascism's later self-portrayal. According to Marinetti, they went hand in hand with a new kind of beauty (*bellezza*), that of speed, an eternal, omnipresent *velocità*, whether of the motor car or the machine gun. War, in a famous dictum, was to be 'the only hygiene of the world'. Men were patriots and heroes, women subordinate beings. The Futurists denounced all 'moralism, feminism, and opportunistic or utilitarian cowardice'. They also wished to destroy all the repositories of past culture – museums, libraries and academies. Their task was rather to give voice and form to 'the great masses agitated by work, by pleasure or by insurrection'. Their poets were to sing of 'the multicoloured and polyphonic tides of revolution in the capital cities of the modern world'.[9]

Marinetti's manifesto, then, celebrated male virility, velocity and violence. Women were poor creatures, their sentimentality often impeding men's forward march. Family life was not an object of analysis – yet.

Over the next few years the Futurist movement grew considerably, attracting some of the most capable artists of the era – Umberto Boccioni, Carlo Carrà, Giacomo Balla and others. Without their talents, it is doubtful whether Marinetti, for all his extraordinarily innovative and musical way with words, would have made the mark he did.[10] In 1912 the Futurists staged an exhibition in Paris which took the city by storm. Boccioni, probably the greatest talent of the group, wrote home, 'The whole battle has been waged around my *Stati d'animo* [. . .] The French are amazed that from a small provincial city such as Milan there has emerged a word which leaves them flabbergasted, they who are accustomed to the most absurd of novelties.'[11] In their own 'Manifesto tecnico' of 1910 the Futurist painters explained that what they sought to capture was not a '*moment frozen* from the course of universal dynamism' but rather '*dynamic sensation* made eternal as such.'[12]

There followed a period of feverish activity, as Futurism put down roots both in Italy and elsewhere. Marinetti visited Russia in 1914, giving lectures in various cities and discussing art and politics with the Russian Futurists.[13] On the outbreak of the First World War, Marinetti, Boccioni and others immediately volunteered for the front. Boccioni, in a revealing pre-war letter to Vico Bauer, had written, 'I feel a furious rage within me, the need to overturn everything and to shake everything violently, to violate and assault, to cut and wound myself, to bleed.' Once at the front, in the autumn of 1915, he wrote again: 'a veritable tempest of grenades and shrapnel has rained upon us without pause. How beautiful it all is!'[14] He was killed on 17 August 1916, not by German fire but by falling from his horse.

Marinetti, on the other hand, whose courage was never in doubt, had been declared unfit for the front because of his proneness to riotous behaviour ('dedito alla rissa') and his 'criminal' record: his 1909 novel, *Mafurka*, had been judged obscene. In August 1916, instead of being in the trenches, he was to be found at the seaside town of Viareggio, eyeing up the women and writing a little semi-ironic 'Guide to being a perfect seducer', summarised in twenty-two points. Number 4, reiterating innumerable other patriarchal views on the danger of women's eternal insatiability, states, 'All adulterous women lie when they tell their lovers that they hardly ever give themselves to their husbands. The war proves that women need daily copulation.' Number 12 affirms, 'As the war aims to increase national territory, the woman's sexual organs become imperialist, expansionist, colonial. The problem is that since there are no more good territories left, the female sex organ conquers deserts, marshes, hospitals, mummies, corpses, old medals and becomes numismatic.' Number 18: 'A good seducer must undress and dress again with the maximum speed. He must never be seen wearing only his shirt.' Number 22: 'The brain is an unsuitable and unnecessary motor for the chassis of the woman, whose natural motor is the uterus.'[15] In April 1917 he confided to his diaries, 'I cannot live more than one day without a woman! I am always a man of violent and rapid coitus. Then comes sleep and detachment.'[16]

At the end of the war, Marinetti's manifest contempt for women found a larger canvas on which to vent itself – that of the family. His comments, which are principally to be found in the collection of articles *Democrazia futurista: Dinamismo politico* (1919), are of the greatest interest.[17] They express in a particularly vivid form the scepticism about the future of the family that is common to much of the social and artistic European avant-garde at the beginning of the new century. Marinetti was the last type of man whom Kollontai hoped to meet along her emancipationist road, but they had the same view of the restrictive and hypocritical qualities of the bourgeois family and of the need to sweep it away. Given the date of his book and his previous contacts with the Russian avant-garde, it seems possible that Marinetti knew of Kollontai's writings and perhaps even of Soviet legislation on the subject.

His vivid critique has as its starting point the family as a negative institution which brings out the worst in its members, fosters the wrong values, crushes all individual initiative and destroys youthful endeavour:

> The family as it is constituted today by means of marriage and without divorce is absurd, harmful and prehistoric. Nearly always a prison. Often a Bedouin tent with its lurid mixture of frail old people, women, children, pigs, donkeys, camels, chickens and excrement. The family dining room is the twice-daily dumping ground for bile, ill humour, prejudice and gossip. In this grotesque compression of nerves and souls, any personal élan, any youthful initiative, any practical and effective decision-making are corroded and squeezed out systematically by continuous boredom and vain irritability [. . .] [All family members] suffer, are depressed, have nervous breakdowns, become cretins, in the name of a fearful divinity that we must overturn: feeling [*sentimento*].[18]

Not that Marinetti was against all feeling. Rather he distinguished between the negative, privatising feeling for family and the glorious sentiment of patriotism, to which all else was to be subjugated. Thus Marinetti, like Mustafa Kemal, put the nation first, but their views of the family's role in nation-building contrasted stridently. For Kemal, a properly constituted family – on western, not Ottoman, lines – was the kernel of the nationalist state, the necessary basis for national well-being and future survival. For Marinetti, the family had rather to be curbed, trained and if necessary dissolved. As for the eternal dilemma of conflicting loyalties to family and to state, Mustafa Kemal believed in the necessary reconciliation of the two, under the aegis of a militarist state, while Marinetti claimed that he wanted to consign family 'loyalties' to the dustbin:

The idea of the fatherland is not for us an ideal extension of family sentiment. Rather, family feeling is an inferior emotion, almost an animal-like instinct, founded on the fear of wild beasts roaming in liberty and of nights brimming over with ambushes and adventures [. . .] Father, mother, grandmother, aunt and children, after various stupid skirmishes, always end up plotting together against divine danger and doomed heroism. The steaming soup tureen is the thurible of this temple of monotony [. . .] The idea of the fatherland is generous, heroic, dynamic, *futurista*, while the idea of the family is narrow, fearful, static, conservative, *passatista*.[19]

What did Marinetti want to put in the place of the family emotions he so despised? His ideas bore some resemblance to Kollontai's but, hardly surprisingly, differed radically with regard to gender relations. He shared the idea of collective care for children, but insisted that the two sexes were to be separated at an early age. Otherwise, the hardy, necessary training for boys would be undermined by the weaker female presence. As the American scholar Barbara Spackman has wickedly written, the concern that underlay this position ran counter to the commonplace that 'boys will be boys': 'given half a chance', she writes, 'boys will be girls'.[20] Marinetti insisted that throughout their lives nothing was to compromise the virile forward march of Italian men. Women were to serve the needs of the race. They could love men and become pregnant by them, they could get divorced, they could even vote, but men were not to be weighed down by them or by family sentiment. Ideally, Marinetti's world was to be populated, in his own words, by 'ardent males and inseminated females':[21]

We want a woman to love a man and to give herself to him for as long as she wants to; then, not bound by contract, nor by moralistic tribunals, she gives birth to a creature which society must educate physically and intellectually to acquire a high conception of Italian liberty [. . .] That atmosphere of whining and holding on to skirt hems and morbid kisses which characterises early childhood will be completely abolished. At last there will be no more of that mixing up of boys and girls which in infancy produces a damaging feminisation of males.[22]

The family, then, was for Marinetti the site of stifling restrictions, cowardice that flew in the face of the nation and feminisation that undermined the self-respecting male. It was to be replaced by a national community in which women and men were free to do as they chose, and in which collective education of children was to be accompanied by the rigid separation of the sexes.

One other element needs to be added. Italy was to be 'de-Vaticanised', and the sooner the better. The Church's overbearing presence in Italian society blocked all attempts at reform: 'It is impossible', wrote Marinetti in *Democrazia futurista*, 'to touch the principle of the family and the juridical conception of marriage as long as the power of priests remains.' It was frustrated priests who reprimanded men for their sexual adventures, who encouraged women to remain stoically in failed marriages and who urged both sexes to earn their place in the afterlife. There was only one way of tackling the long-lasting and insidious influence of the clergy: to make a great bonfire of their black cassocks and melt down all church bells, using the metal to weld rails on which new high-speed trains could flash by.[23]

2. Marinetti and Mussolini

More than once Benito Mussolini was to recognise that without Futurism there would have been no Fascism. This was undoubtedly true, but it was also the case that the founders of the two movements were very different from one another. Both were ardent nationalists, both had fought with courage in the First World War (Marinetti had eventually gone to the front), and after it both declared themselves revolutionaries. But Mussolini was a politician to his fingertips, while Marinetti was an artist, an 'Italian poet' as he described himself. Although he published a political manifesto for a Futurist party in February 1918 he was never going to be able to compete with Mussolini on that terrain. In fact, Mussolini was to gobble him up with great ease.

The two men also came from very different family backgrounds. Marinetti had been accustomed from infancy to the wealthy, upper-bourgeois lifestyle of his parents' spacious home in Alexandria, with its view over the Mediterranean, its rich furnishings and servants at the family's beck and call. All this could not have been further away from Mussolini's modest rural upbringing in Predappio, in the central Italian region of Romagna. His family lived in two rooms, the children's bedroom serving as the kitchen. Mussolini's father was a blacksmith, sometimes drunk and violent, a man who did not hesitate to use corporal punishment on his two male children. In spite of this, Mussolini admired him greatly. In the wretched gallery of twentieth-century dictators' fathers, Arnaldo Mussolini emerges as the best of a bad bunch. He was a man who filled his modest home with books and who took a long-standing interest in radical, international socialist politics at a regional level. Mussolini's mother could not have been more different. She was a primary school teacher and devout Catholic, the lynchpin of the family.[24]

In 1893, at the age of ten, as 'a child with an impulsive character, prone to get into fights',[25] Mussolini was sent away to the Salesian priests' school at Faenza. This was a far worse experience than Marinetti's brush with the French Jesuits. The children were divided according to family income and at mealtimes Mussolini was in the third and last group. He was punished and isolated repeatedly. He told Emil Ludwig at a later date, 'I could perhaps have forgotten the ants in the bread that was distributed to the third class. But that we children were divided into classes – that still makes my blood boil! [...] Such unmerited and unbearable humiliations turn a man into a revolutionary.'[26]

Following in his father's footsteps, Mussolini duly became a socialist revolutionary and rose to the highest ranks of the young Italian Socialist Party. But when the Great War broke out, he abandoned international pacifism in favour of a militant and interventionist nationalism. His positions clashed violently with those of the Italian Socialists and he was expelled from the party. He founded his own nationalist newspaper, *Il Popolo d'Italia*, and from then onwards conceived his role as that of the saviour of Italy in the face of the Socialist menace. He was interested not only in counter-revolution, however, but also in formulating a radical new vision of the country's politics. This was where he and Marinetti came to overlap.

In Italy, the war's aftermath was characterised by great social unrest, during the famous 'two red years' (*biennio rosso*) of 1919–20. The echoes of the Russian revolution rebounded throughout the Italian peninsula and the Italian Socialist movement went from strength to strength. But other actors also rapidly came to the fore, those officers and NCOs who had fought in the trenches and had no intention of letting Italy follow the Bolshevik example. The mass violence of the northern trenches was transferred to the politics of the time.[27]

At the end of 1918 Marinetti met Mussolini in the latter's office in Milan. At that time Marinetti was by far the more famous of the two, renowned throughout the world as the founder of Futurism, whereas Mussolini was a little-known renegade Italian socialist. Marinetti's description of him in his diary is ironic but also shows acute awareness of the other's force of character: 'I feel the reactionary growing in him, his violent and agitated temperament full of Napoleonic authoritarianism and growing aristocratic contempt for the masses. He comes from the people but no longer loves them [...] [While we talked] his enormous eyes glanced continuously at my costly raincoat.'[28]

Throughout 1919 Marinetti and Mussolini met frequently. In the spring they planned a violent counter-demonstration in Milan, which sowed terror amongst the women and men of the Socialist movement. On 15 April 1919 a general strike had been proclaimed in Milan. About a thousand ex-officers and shock troops (*arditi*), armed with revolvers, waited in Piazza Duomo for their opponents to arrive. Here is Marinetti's version of events:

> At last their demonstration arrives with their women in the lead red flags and the portrait of Lenin held high. They advance at a stiff pace swift and fearless and halt behind the line of the Carabinieri. We on one side of them and they on the other [. . .] Officers decorated in the war, fearless and indifferent in the face of the sss sss sss of pistol bullets, fire in the air and then directly at the long column which is immediately gripped by wild panic. Our enemies, 2,000 in all, throw themselves on the ground against the steps of the Loggia dei Mercanti. No longer do their cries of 'Down with Italy! Long live Lenin!' rend the air.[29]

A month earlier, in March 1919, in Piazza San Sepolcro in Milan, Mussolini had founded his 'Fasci italiani di combattimento' (Italian fighting groups), the first nucleus of what was to become the PNF, the National Fascist Party, a model that was to be imitated all over Europe.[30] There were hardly more than a hundred people there, including Marinetti, who was highly sceptical of the movement's potential. In the autumn of the same year, the first Fascist congress was held in Florence. Marinetti continued to poke fun at Mussolini's weird dress sense and political incompetence: 'he was wearing a black and white check beret utterly ridiculous and much too small for his enormous cranium'.[31] But Mussolini knew what he was doing far better than Marinetti. In November 1919 the Socialists had become the largest single party in the Italian parliament and had also taken electoral control of many major city councils. In 1920 Mussolini's movement began to assume mass proportions, as Fascism offered itself as the violent defender of those centres of power and social classes which had most to fear from the forward march of socialism.[32]

Marinetti continued to stress the need to remove both the Pope and the King from Italian shores. For him the Futurists were 'practical anarchists' and their credo was one of individualism and inequality. At a certain point the two men took different paths. Marinetti, not without bitterness, moved away from politics, in which he had invested considerably in these years. Mussolini on the other hand went from triumph to triumph, his strong-arm tactics effectively destroying the workers' movement in both town and countryside and his increasingly explicit right-wing politics earning him considerable support. In 1922 his so-called March on Rome brought him the prize he wanted – the role of prime minister. Henceforth the Fascist 'revolution' would be organised from above.[33]

3. Beny, Marinetti and the family revisited

As for Marinetti, these years were far from unhappy, for if politics offered him little his love life took an unexpected and passionate turn. At the end of 1918 he met a beautiful young girl with large dark eyes and an oval face. Her name was Benedetta Cappa, her family belonged to the Piedmontese bourgeoisie, and when she met Marinetti in Rome she was twenty-one and he was forty-two. She was intelligent, creative and determined, and was to play an active part in the Futurist movement, both as a writer and as a painter. Marinetti fell hopelessly in love with her, and she with him. Flying in the face of everything he had written about the family, he declared Beny (as he called her – she called him Marinetti) to be the person that not only he but all his forebears had long awaited: 'You are, dear Beny, the final point of arrival and repository for all those different blood flows which have prepared the chemical mixture of my actual being [. . .] The most remote of my ancestors now gaze at you through the crystal of my personality they admire you and they love you.'[34]

Marinetti took Benedetta everywhere – to the meetings of the Futurist painters, to the movement's noisy printing presses, to political assemblies. His love for her did not prevent him from making love constantly with other women, but Benedetta seems to have treated his behaviour with detachment, convinced that it was of little importance. In January 1920 she confided her theory to him: men in love need to *empty* themselves inside their loved ones but can also do the same with other women without changing their feelings; women on the other hand, *receive* the seed of their beloved but cannot receive that of others without changing and muddying their emotions. Marinetti commented in his diary: 'She is extremely intelligent. I have physical and spiritual difficulty in separating myself from her.'[35] In May of the same year the couple went out into the Roman countryside. There, during a memorable afternoon more romantic than Futurist, they made love in the long grass:

> [Beny] asked me not to look. She took her distance from me. Then she came back, running through the grass, utterly beautiful, with her great luminous eyes, her hair free and outlined in the wind, an agile aeroplane in the deep blue sky of this transparent afternoon [. . .] We had flattened some eight square metres of grass – I think – Beny said – that never again will we enjoy so large a bed.[36]

In 1923, on a suitably semi-clandestine occasion, Marinetti and Benedetta married. The great derider of that institution which 'discourages and suffocates the development of children, truncates the youth and virility of the father and renders effeminate the adolescent' quietly accepted the civil ceremony.[37] The married couple, who seem to have moved effortlessly from romantic to conjugal love, were to have three daughters, Vittoria (Victory, 1927), Ala (Wing, 1928) and Luce (Light, 1932). It was ironic that Marinetti, so much a boys' man, should have had only daughters. Many years later the eldest of them, Vittoria, remembered their father as being of 'profound goodness and innate courtesy', always ready to encourage and be with his children during their long holidays on the island of Capri. She described her parents as 'two very strong and parallel personalities, who crossed over, with affection and tenderness, into each other's territories'. Certainly, continued Vittoria, her father had had many lovers, but 'all of his women whom I have known, years later, remembered him with admiration and affection'.[38] The second daughter, Ala, confirmed these family memories, insisting on the 'normality' of their family. In Rome, the girls were sent for their education to the French nuns at the Collegio del Sacro Cuore at Trinità dei Monti, where they remained from early morning until six in the afternoon. Ala remembered her father as 'extremely affectionate and permissive, like all fathers who are no longer young'. The girls were forbidden to associate with the 'artistic bohemians' who flocked to their house. They had separate living quarters with an entire room painted for them by Giacomo Balla, another devoted Futurist and family man. One or two ceremonies in the Cappa–Marinetti household harked back to more iconoclastic times: Marinetti, for instance, always posed in front of Boccioni's painting *Dinamismo di un footballer* when formally presenting his newborn daughters to the world.[39]

How can we explain his metamorphosis into an archetypical family figure? Some of his erstwhile admirers make light of his contradictions, and he himself sometimes argued that to ignore his own theories was the height of Futurism.[40] But this was all too easy a way out. Though Marinetti avoided ever again writing about the family, it is relatively easy to identify a number of explanations for his behaviour. One was the aging process, which, working its subtle changes upon him as upon others, caused him to surrender silently to the very enemy which he had previously denounced – family sentiment. Another was his young wife, who clearly had a family agenda of her own, one which Marinetti came to share. Their Roman house was full of penniless artists and poets, while they themselves were Fascist Italy's most famous avant-garde couple, but the family they brought up was an entirely conventional one. In the domestic sphere 'arte' and 'vita' were not joined by a meaningful hyphen, as in the Futurist canon, but firmly separate.

Another reason was the trajectory of the Fascist regime itself. In 1919 Mussolini and Marinetti seemed briefly to be following the same revolutionary

fig. 18 Filippo Tommaso Marinetti with his wife Beny and their three daughters Vittoria,
Ala and Luce.

direction, but Mussolini's long-term agenda was one of taking power through compromise with the old regime, not destroying it at its roots. Marinetti at first, as we have seen, took the opposite view, but he was too much a lover of the limelight ever to stay away from the new regime for long. In 1929 he even became a member of the Regia Accademia d'Italia, exactly the type of institution which the first Futurist manifesto had sworn to destroy at all costs. He dutifully swore allegiance to the King and collected his lucrative stipend. The regime had become respectable and Marinetti with it.

There is a final point. Both in the Fascist regime (as we shall see) and in Futurism there is a fundamental gap between rhetoric and reality, much more so than in the other dictatorial regimes under examination in this book. At best this gap took the form of exaggeration, at worst of bald dissimulation. Mussolini was a master practitioner of the art, but so too was Marinetti. The famous 'Poète italien' could denounce the family as a Bedouin tent and family feeling as an inferior, almost animal-like instinct, and he could deride the domestic dining room as a daily dumping ground for bile, ill humour and prejudice, but in reality he celebrated his own family as a loving and conventional structure, with an aging, benevolent and increasingly jealous patriarch at its head and a powerful and dedicated woman at its helm.

4. Worker families in Italy in the 1920s

The demonstrators who flocked to the major squares of the northern Italian cities in May 1919, convinced that the Italian revolution would soon take its place alongside the Russian one, but who were to be met instead by the truncheons and pistol fire of Marinetti, Mussolini and their friends were for the most part workers employed in the factories of the 'industrial triangle' of Turin, Milan and Genoa.

Italy's social structure was far more advanced than those of the Soviet Union and Turkey and its territory far less ungovernable. By 1931 46.8 per cent of Italy's adult population was occupied in agriculture, compared with the Soviet Union's 85.4 per cent (figures for 1929). At the same time average per capita income in Italy was twice that of the Soviet Union, while life expectancy was 53.8 years for men and 56 for women, compared with the Soviet Union's paltry 34 years for men and 40 for women. Total fertility rates were still very high in the Soviet Union (5.7 children per woman in 1930), but so too, as we have seen, was infant mortality: in 1930 nearly 200 children out of every 1,000 died during the first year of life. Italian total fertility was much lower, 3.38 children per woman in 1930 – a statistic which, as we shall see, was to preoccupy Mussolini greatly and shape part of his family policy – while infant mortality in Italy in 1930 was half that of the Soviet Union. Finally, of Italy's forty-four million inhabitants in 1931 40 per cent lived in urban conglomerates of more than 5,000 inhabitants, compared with only 14 per cent in the USSR.[41]

Let me concentrate briefly upon working-class families in the cities of Turin and Milan in the first decades of the twentieth century. In the working-class quarters on the peripheries of the northern Italian cities – such as Borgo San Paolo, on the western outskirts of Turin, and Sesto San Giovanni, a booming industrial town immediately to the north of Milan – a very particular relationship between family and collectivity had developed by 1920. The men and women who populated these new peripheries had mostly begun to emigrate from the surrounding countryside at the turn of the century. Many were single male workers but there were also a great many young couples who decided to bring up their children in the new urban environment rather than leave them with grandparents back in their villages. Families were nuclear in structure, numerically below the national average of 4.3 members, usually with one or two children.[42] Kinship networks in workers' districts extended well beyond the individual family, as did loyalties to those who came from the same village (*compaesani*). The age of marriage was later than in the Russian case, men becoming husbands at between twenty-six and thirty years of age, and women wives at between twenty-three and twenty-seven.[43] Families were thus much more present than in the working-class districts of St Petersburg or Moscow.

They were usually characterised by a rigid separation of gender roles and networks. Men occupied their own world, both at work and during their few hours of free time, most often spent in cafés or taverns; women, especially after marriage and childbirth, created strong neighbourhood networks and extended female kinship patterns. Fathers saw little of their children, except on Sundays.[44]

Housing took a number of forms – dormitories for temporary workers and girls in from the countryside, *pensioni* offering rooms with multiple beds, rented flats in tenement blocks for more stable working-class families. The tenement blocks had long connecting balconies on each floor, looking inwards on to a communal courtyard where the children were often at play. Here, every morning, 'all the alarm clocks would go off at almost the same time'.[45] In these courtyards and neighbourhoods, far from the centres of the great cities of Milan and Turin, a strong sense of community flourished: 'In San Paolo everyone knew everyone else [. . .] We used to sit outside our doors, on chairs and stools, chatting away'.[46] Material exchanges were commonplace – a wardrobe constructed for one family in return for a pair of shoes for another.[47] The courtyards were certainly supportive and communal, but they were also marked by the very reduced dimensions of workers' dwellings and severe overcrowding. Constant conflict between families at a micro-level was the order of the day. Spatial constraints were not helped by the fact that many families maintained rural habits and customs: chicken coops were everywhere. One testimony from Sesto San Giovanni records that 'the neighbours from downstairs kept their rabbits in boxes behind the wall of our bedroom'.[48] There were few luxuries: working-class families ate little meat and a good deal of minestrone and polenta.

Work was often less constant and characterising than were the courtyards of family life, with high turnover rates as young single workers came and went. Strong distinctions existed between small and large factories, between unskilled labourers and highly skilled metalworkers, between men and women. Both boys and girls went to work at an early age, between ten and twelve years old. Women, employed for the most part in tailoring shops or textile factories, would continue to work until they married, after which, in addition to running the household and rearing the family, they would take on extra domestic labour such as washing and sewing. A minority of women found long-term industrial jobs, such as at the Magneti Marelli works of Sesto San Giovanni, which by 1938 employed 7,000 workers.[49] The firm had started production by making magnetos, expanding in the interwar years to produce numerous electric parts for cars, aeroplanes and trains, as well as radios and military equipment. The women who worked there were proud of their jobs and relative privileges.

The ambition of most male youths, having served an apprenticeship under the watchful eye of a relative or *compaesano*, was to enter the metalworking

fig. 19 Women and children in a typical tenement block with connecting internal balconies, Turin, 1910–20.

factories as skilled operatives. FIAT, founded in 1899, had 5,000 workers before the Great War and 17,000 by the advent of Fascism. The hours of work were long, usually ten or more; the eight-hour day was introduced by law only in 1921.

A shared political culture contributed to, and overlaid, solidarities at home and at work. The years 1919–20 saw the working class of Turin in particular at the forefront of socialist agitation. Class-consciousness in the city reached its height with the demonstrations in opposition to the First World War, the factory-council movement of 1919–20, the Piedmontese general strike of April 1920 and the nationwide occupation of the factories in September 1920. One worker from Turin remembered his mother, a convinced Catholic, going every Sunday to eat in one of the 'social canteens' set up inside the occupied factories – testimony to the continuation of that very long tradition which insists on the social virtues of communal eating.[50] At the workplace and in the cafés men talked socialist politics as a matter of course: 'On a Sunday they played cards in the taverns [. . .] At the end of the day, when it was time to settle the debts, 6–8 lire were left over [. . .] and with the agreement of all the money went off to *Avanti!* [the socialist newspaper].'[51] These were communities of strong opinions, loyalties and solidarities, but also, as always happens, of many controls and limitations, imposed above all on the younger generation.

As for the comparison between the conditions and culture of families in major Italian and Russian cities at this time, it is true that worker-peasant families (that is, urban families that maintained very strong links with the countryside) were the norm in both cases. There were, however, fundamental differences. Although life was hard in the Italian workers' districts and Fascist statistics were to speak of 'severe overcrowding' in Milanese workers' quarters, Italian families were not afflicted by that abject and life-numbing poverty, constant exhaustion, disease and death which so characterises the Russian story. The artel of Semyon Kanachikov and his experience as an apprentice at the Gustav List engineering works in Moscow find no easy Italian equivalents.[52] Families are more present in the Italian experience, more able to shield those who had just arrived from the countryside, more successful in creating some semblance of 'normal' family life. Climate certainly made a difference, with the possibility of living out of doors for many hours each day in the spring, summer and autumn, and for children to play in the open.

Furthermore, Italian worker–employer relations, although characterised by the same ruthlesness and exploitation as their Russian equivalents, had none the less to be framed within the confines of a liberal state. For much of its early history the Russian working class had to organise clandestinely, its militants pursued by the agents of the state-owned factories and by the police of an autocratic state. Italian workers, on the other hand, although frequently harassed, enjoyed the legal freedom to create associations of their own, first as mutual aid societies and then as trade unions. The powerful Chambers of Work (Camere del Lavoro), which offered the possibility of solidarities between different categories and trades, resisted the Fascist menace for some time.

Strangely enough, all this probably made the Italian working classes less revolutionary than their Russian equivalents. Lenin's proletariat truly gave the impression of having nothing to lose but its chains, whereas Italian workers never seemed quite to embrace spontaneously the role ascribed to them.

5. Gramsci: the family as an 'organ of moral life'

The Italian Socialist and Communist movement assumed significant proportions and theoretical importance in at least three different periods in the twentieth century – 1919–20, 1943–8 and 1968–73 – but in none of them did it have much to say about the family. Antonio Gramsci constitutes a partial exception. A leading figure in the Italian Communist Party until his arrest in 1926 and subsequent imprisonment, Gramsci's *Prison Notebooks* marked him out as one of the foremost twentieth-century theoreticians of Communism.[53]

Gramsci's was an exemplary story of struggle against adversity. From an early age he suffered from the affliction of being hunchbacked, and was constantly in poor physical and often mental health throughout his life. In 1923 he wrote that since the age of ten he had always felt himself to be 'an intruder within my own family'; a child so weak as to be a burden upon even his closest relatives. To hide such feelings as an adult, he often withdrew 'behind a mask of hardness or an ironic smile'.[54]

Gramsci was born in 1891 in Ales, in Sardinia. His family, at least to begin with, lived well enough, as his father, Francesco, was a local civil servant who enjoyed a steady income. But in 1898, when Antonio was seven, Francesco was suddenly arrested. He had supported an alternative candidate at the local elections, and as an act of revenge the dominant local political faction denounced him to the authorities for embezzlement. The sums concerned were very small, but he was sentenced to five years' imprisonment. Such major trauma left permanent damage. Antonio had not been told what had really happened and learned the truth in the cruellest of ways – from the other children of the village. Relations between him and his father, who even at the best of times does not appear to have been the most supportive of parents, were thenceforth always to be very tense. Her husband disgraced and in prison, Antonio's mother suddenly found herself without an income and having to care for seven children. She coped extraordinarily well. In his prison letters her son pays moving tribute to her efforts, explaining to his Catholic mother how it was that, by his way of looking at things, she was already in Paradise:

> You can't imagine how many things I remember in which you appear always as a force for the good and as a mother full of tenderness towards us. If you think about it, all the questions concerning the soul and the immortality of the soul, hell and paradise are at the end of the day a way of looking at this simple fact: that every one of our actions is transmitted to others according to its value, of good or evil, and is handed down from father to son, from one generation to another, in a perpetual movement. As all the memories we have of you are of your goodness and will power, and as you have dedicated all your strength to bringing us up, this means that you are already in the only real paradise that exists for a mother, that is to say in the hearts of her own children. Do you see now what I have written to you? And don't think that I want to offend your religious opinions, even if I suspect that actually you're more in agreement with me than at first appears.[55]

Gramsci was always to stress the strength of virtuous family-based education, emotion and action. He felt these qualities to be particularly evident in working-class and peasant families: in the face of constant insecurity, of uncertainty as to whether one would be able to clothe one's children or provide a roof for aging grandparents, these families none the less managed to transmit a profound sense of love and sacrifice. Morality, he explained, consisted of connecting minimal actions to a maximum aim, of creating what he called – with evident Catholic overtones – an 'infinite rosary' of benign everyday initiatives. When his mother, in spite of having a hundred things to do in the course of a single day, found the time to sit down with him to teach him that 'uccello' (bird) was written with two 'c's, she was taking just such an initiative. The family was thus the primary theatre for instruction and for the transmission of love.[56]

Like nearly all the protagonists of this book, Gramsci wrote very little on the family – less than Marinetti, much less than Kollontai. But by assembling numerous fragments it is possible to identify his very particular position. The most significant single piece he dedicated to the subject was a newspaper article of 9 February 1918 entitled simply 'La famiglia', written while he was still a Socialist and three years before the founding of the Italian Communist Party in 1921.[57]

Gramsci begins by acknowledging that the Socialists had often been viewed as the greatest enemies of the family. In his opinion nothing was further from the truth. The family was an institution to be preserved and cherished, a vital element of 'morality, training in humanity [preparazione umana] and civil education'. The present ordering of society, however, based as it was on the 'inhuman solution' of private property and the division of society into classes, prevented the great majority of families from performing these precious functions. Only bourgeois children lived in security, free from want, and received a proper education; other children suffered from ill health, were illiterate and were forced into work at an early age. Socialists believed that such gross inequities had to be removed so that all children could be 'looked after in their physiological and moral development'. The solution, therefore, was to abolish private property but at the same time to strengthen the family: 'Only the abolition of private property and its conversion into collective property can ensure that the family will be able to fulfil its destiny: that of being an organ of moral life.'[58]

Gramsci thus accepted one central part of Marxist doctrine on the family – the abolition of private property – but denied the other, which foresaw the family's functions being gradually transferred to the socialist state. For Gramsci there had to be necessary limits to collective life and collective power. He warned against 'state worship' and insisted that under a socialist regime children's education was not to be entrusted to state institutions, which operated 'impersonally, mechanically and bureaucratically'. Rather it was the family, freed from its preoccupations over subsistence, that could take its rightful place as the great educator, the bearer of the 'torch of civilisation from one generation to another'.[59]

All this was hardly Socialist orthodoxy. In his classic work Woman under Socialism (1879) the German Social Democrat August Bebel, as we have seen, had advocated limiting domestic life to the 'strictly necessary'. He described the private sphere primarily in negative terms, stressing the oppression of women in the home and the need for family life to be replaced in large measure by collective society. Here was a real difference: for Gramsci the 'great educator' was virtuous family relations, for Bebel it was working-class civil society.[60]

The most striking comparison, however, is with Gramsci's contemporaries, especially the Bolsheviks. The years 1918–20 saw the publication of some of the most important reflections on the future of the family. Gramsci wrote the article I have just analysed in February 1918, Kollontai *Communism and the Family* in the winter of 1918–19, Lenin *A Great Beginning* in July 1919, and Bukharin and Preobrazhensky *The ABC of Communism* in 1920. Nor should Marinetti's *Democrazia futurista* (1919) be forgotten. The extraordinary political ferment of the post-war years had finally pushed debates on the future of the family into intellectual visibility.

None of the authors just cited remotely shared Gramsci's view of the family as an 'organ of moral life'. Kollontai, it may be remembered, wrote that in revolutionary Russia the family was 'ceasing to be necessary either to its members or to the nation as a whole'. Lenin took a line close to that of Bebel: the 'petty housekeeping' of family life reduced women to 'domestic slaves'; they were better off in the factory. Bukharin and Preobrazhensky went even further in a direction diametrically opposite to Gramsci's rosary of everyday actions: in their opinion, out of a hundred mothers only one or two were capable of being good teachers. The future lay with socialised education.[61] As for Marinetti, the only unashamedly patriarchal figure in this group, the family was the site of unnecessary sentiment, stifling restrictions and feminisation, all of which undermined the self-respecting male. Much better for family nurture to give way to rigidly gender-distinct state instruction.[62]

Why is Gramsci so different? The question may be answered on two different levels: with reference to the psychological sphere and with reference to the culture of the region in which he was brought up. As a child his deformity made him feel, as we have seen, an outsider within his own family. Far from wanting less family life, he wanted more, to be treated as a fully fledged member of his family, to be properly supported by his father for his education, to have a 'normal' family, not one disrupted by dislocation or sudden impoverishment. In this he was closer to Halide Edib and her aspirations to bourgeois family life than he was to the radical views of Kollontai, let alone Marinetti.

Secondly, rural Sardinia at the end of the nineteenth century was a very Catholic place, and Catholicism was a very family-based religion. Gramsci was strongly anti-clerical, constantly denouncing the Church for its hypocrisies and superficiality, but he never contested the Church's emphasis on the centrality of family life. Indeed, Catholic metaphors, such as the 'infinite rosary' of everyday life, were an intrinsic part of his political vocabulary. In a polemical article of April 1917, suitably entitled 'Seriousness', the framework of Gramsci's argument comes into focus. It is not a question of abolishing the family, or of giving good riddance to Catholicism, but rather one of taking them both seriously. His appeal is a highly gendered one – to Socialist fathers to counteract the 'Catholic vanities' of their wives:

> Holy Week has begun. The passion of Christ lives on in the catarrh-laden dirges of old parish priests, in the tobacco-reeking church devotees, in the 'passion' of children and adolescents who are forced by their families to fulfil what are supposedly religious duties. We've seen these children in the street, dressed all in white, holding palm leaves in their little hands, a living testimony to the vanity of their mothers [. . .] It should not be difficult for mothers and fathers to reach an agreement on the spiritual education of their children, based on the widest degree of liberty of conscience [. . .] The danger is that children do not receive a true religious education, that they become accustomed to hollow ostentation, to little Easter dresses, to palm leaves and hypocrisies [. . .] Fathers, instead of sinking deeper into their armchairs, should be out and about, actively protecting them.[63]

In May of 1922, Gramsci left Turin for Moscow, where he was due to represent Italy on the executive committee of the Comintern, the Communist International. He was ill when he arrived, however, utterly exhausted from his long years of militancy and the series of defeats which the Turin working-class movement had suffered. Grigorij Zinoviev, the president of the International, decided that he should be nursed back to health at the Serebrany Bor (Silver Forest) sanatorium on the outskirts of Moscow. He had been showing alarming symptoms – convulsive trembling and 'ferocious-looking' tics. Many of those who looked after him and came to visit confessed afterwards that they had been scared stiff. 'They knew I was Sardinian, and thought I might have been on the point of knifing someone!' In the sanatorium he met a fellow patient, Eugenia Schucht, who was some years older than him. She came from an anti-tsarist family which had taken the path of exile, lived in many European cities, including Rome, and returned to Russia after the revolution. Eugenia Schucht spoke very good Italian. She was often visited by her younger sister Julca, twenty-six years old, tall and striking, with sad eyes and shoulder-length hair. Julca was fascinated by the young, malformed Italian who had such force of intellect and an inner strength which seemed to cancel out his many physical weaknesses. Gramsci fell overwhelmingly in love with her, for she seemed to be an ethereal angel – a messenger bearing the greetings of the Russian revolution. He wrote to her on 10 January 1923,

My very dear comrade,

The world is wide and terrible: perhaps we will meet again in Peking or Lhasa, in New York or Sydney [. . .] Up to now I believed that I was completely arid and dried up, but I have discovered a small spring (really, really small . . .) of melancholy and of moonlight, with a light blue surround.

A cordial handshake,

Gramsci.[64]

In December of the same year he finished a letter to her with the Russian words 'Dorogaya, milaya, lyubimaya Julca' (Dear, sweet, beloved Julca). Another time, he asked himself (and Julca) whether 'it is really possible to love a collectivity [the working class] when one has not been deeply loved oneself by individual human creatures.'[65]

Fleeting references in their correspondence suggest that they argued fiercely over the nature and qualities of the Russian revolution. Some of the debate concerned the roles of the family and of the state. In a letter of October 1924 Gramsci poked fun at Julca's obvious sympathy for collective nursing and her belief in the superiority of the Russian model:

When you described to me the scene [in the maternity clinic] of all those crying babies in a large trolley being distributed to the mothers who must then feed them, the scene was so clear before my eyes that I thought of provoking you by suggesting that they perhaps give the mothers a different baby each time, given that Soviet discipline is so absolutely perfect as to give a faultless training to all hospital nurses.[66]

Julca was duly furious, though perhaps Kollontai might have approved of the idea. She had after all written in *Communism and the Family*, 'The worker-mother must learn not to differentiate between yours and mine; she must remember that there are only our children, the children of Russia's communist workers.'[67]

In the period 1922–6, before Gramsci's arrest, the two lovers spent little time together – principally the first halcyon months when Gramsci was in the clinic and in Moscow, and then again in 1925, in Moscow and in Rome, where Julca worked briefly in the Soviet embassy. Too many impediments stood in their way: Gramsci always put political obligations first; graver still, their relationship was gradually undermined by Julca's fragile mental health and deep uncertainties. Few of her letters have survived, but Gramsci's contain repeated requests for her to join him – to no avail.

These years were marked by one political defeat after another. In 1924 Gramsci reflected bitterly on the inadequacies of the Italian working class, 'which in general judged everything for the better and loved songs and fanfares more than sacrifices'.[68] On 8 November 1926 he was arrested, and eighteen months later, in May–June 1928, he was put on trial in Rome before the Fascist Special Tribunal for the Defence of the State. On 2 June the Fascist state prosecutor uttered the infamous phrase, 'We must prevent this brain from functioning for twenty years'; Gramsci duly received a sentence of twenty years, four months and five days.[69] Yet in spite of his very poor health and the deprivations of prison life, his brain continued to function as never before. His extraordinary *Prison Notebooks* were to become the fundamental text of European Communism in the post-war period. In them Gramsci's thought developed in many directions, though sadly the family was not one of them. All we have are occasional references which suggest – differently from many other areas – a substantial continuity between his earlier reflections and his prison writings. In one brief note he returns to the theme of the dangers of an over-powerful state abrogating all education to itself.[70]

From their fleeting and fragile love affair, Julca Schucht and Antonio Gramsci had two sons, Delio (Delka) and Giuliano (Julik). In his prison letters, we find Gramsci trying very hard to keep his deeply dislocated family in some way connected. He wrote to his children regularly from prison, telling them of his own childhood in the Sardinian countryside and of the many animals he

fig. 20 Julca Schucht, Giuliano and Delio Gramsci

had taken care of. There is one letter in particular of February 1932 which merits being reproduced at length. In it Gramsci explains to his children how a family of hedgehogs collects apples. The family he describes in loving detail seems, at a subconscious level, to express all his longing for a 'normal' family of his own, endowed with everyday activities and sharing a common strategy:

One evening in autumn, when it was already night but with a splendid moon, I went with another boy, my friend, to set up station in a field full of fruit trees, and of apple trees in particular. We hid ourselves in a ditch, against the wind. At a certain moment there they were, two big hedgehogs and three little ones. In single file they headed towards the apples, wandering through the long grass before setting to work. Using their little faces and legs, they rolled the fallen apples which the wind had blown from the trees and collected them in a little clearing. But it soon became clear that there were not enough for their needs. And so the largest hedgehog, sniffing the air and looking around him, chose a branch of an apple tree that was bent under the weight of its fruit and climbed up on to it, with his wife behind. There they sat on the laden branch and began to swing rhythmically back and forth. Their movements communicated themselves to the branch, which in turn began to swing from side to side, propelled by shaking that became ever more forceful. Many more apples fell to the ground. The hedgehogs collected these, too, into the little clearing. Then all of them, large and small, rolled over with their spikes erect and draped themselves over the apples, which in this way they successfully skewered. The little hedgehogs managed only one or two, but the father and the mother managed to spike seven or eight each.[71]

In his prison years Gramsci was cared for not by Julca, who never left Russia again, but another of the Schucht sisters Tatiana (Tania), who loved him devotedly and served him selflessly. Antonio was deeply grateful to her, and held her in the greatest affection, but his heart belonged to Julca.

From 1933 onwards, in response to growing international pressure and his own deteriorating health, Gramsci was transferred to clinics in first Formia and then Rome. He was also granted provisional freedom, but by 1936 his condition had become desperate. In the last months of his life, he 'seemed to be thinking only of Julca and his distant sons'.[72] Delio was twelve years old when Gramsci wrote to him on 2 December 1936:

Dear Delio
[. . .] thank you for embracing Mummy so hard for me: I think you ought to do so every day, every morning. I'm always thinking of you; so I'll imagine

you doing it every morning, and say to myself, 'Julca and my two boys are thinking of me now, this very instant.' You're the elder brother, but you should tell Julik about this too; so every day you will have 'five minutes with Daddy'. What do you think of the idea?[73]

Gramsci died on 27 April 1937, aged forty-six. He had been formally released from prison six days earlier.

6. Peasant families

The Sardinia of Gramsci's childhood was just one of many different Italian rural environments, and his political reflections while in prison returned constantly to the need to 'link the countryside to the city', as he put it, to give common objectives to peasants and workers. This was easier said than done. In the harsh reality of the aftermath of the First World War, with so many peasant families mourning those lost in what appeared to have been a pointless war, many sections of the Italian rural population did organise and protest, demanding social justice and land redistribution. Theirs was a rural protest movement larger than that of any other part of Europe except Russia.[74] Even so, different aspirations and regional experiences outweighed possible elements of unity. Age-old relations of deference, the general dominance of conservative Catholic culture, the very isolation of many villages, and above all deep ideological divisions and poor leadership meant that city and countryside did not meet.

In the pages that follow, I have chosen to concentrate on just one rural experience, that of the sharecropping families of Tuscany. They are of great interest on account of their relative prosperity and security on the land. In an ideal world, other experiences, in particular those of the landless labourers of Puglia and of the peasant Leagues of the Po, would merit equal attention.[75]

In rural Tuscany sharecropping had, over the centuries, been the dominant rural contract. Put simply, it was the system by which the landowner provided the farm and the peasant family the labour, the expenses and the crop being shared between the two. Sharecropping families lived not in villages or agro-towns, but in farmhouses directly on their land. Their contracts were annual, but in practice were usually renewed for many years without difficulty. The landlord was not a distant figure, on the other side of an unbridgeable class divide, but rather took an active interest in the running of his farms. The relationship between him and the sharecropper was a direct and paternalistic one, based, as Carlo Pazzagli has written, on the profound subjection of the peasant to his landlord, but also on the landlord's care and protection of his sharecroppers.[76]

Over time the Tuscan *mezzadri* (sharecroppers) came to be considered a privileged caste, to be contrasted with the minority of peasants in the same region – the *pigionali* – casual labourers enjoying no security on the land. A considerable indigenous literature grew up in praise of sharecropping; even as late as the Second World War foreign visitors gave glowing accounts of what they saw. Doubtless the reality, seen from the peasant side, was not all that idyllic. Marriages in the family could not take place without the landlord's consent, nor could the sharecroppers work off the estate without his permission. Peasant debt accrued to him from year to year. Security on the land was also not as great as myth and landlord literature would have us believe. Even so, these were privileged peasants by early twentieth-century European standards – much closer to the southern German peasantry than to the southern Italian one.

Sharecropper households were unusually complex formations, housing more than one married couple and more than two generations under the same roof. A comparison with the extended families of the *dvor* in European Russia springs immediately to mind. In both cases, household numbers frequently reached double figures. The male head of the family, the *capoccia*, the Tuscan equivalent of the Russian *bolshak*, ruled over his large household in patriarchal and authoritarian fashion. Yet his was not the sole authority. The *massaia*, usually his wife, also exercised considerable power, as in Russia, especially over the other women

fig. 21 Grape harvest in Tuscany, 1914.

of the family and her daughters-in-law. The sharecropping family thus presented a united and much admired face to the outside world, but it was one based on notable gender and generational tensions, spanning many decades.

The religiosity of these families was much remarked upon. At Easter, in preparation for the priest's visit and blessing of the farmhouse, every household item was cleaned and polished. Here too the comparison with Russia is a fascinating one. There can be no doubt that Tuscan women felt more part of the Church than their Russian Orthodox counterparts, for Catholicism was infinitely more welcoming to them. But the two peasantries – and their women-folk in particular – linked hands in their often autonomous re-elaborations of models proposed to them by the Church hierarchies. For no figure was this truer than that of the Virgin Mary. In the course of the nineteenth century Tuscan peasant families developed their Marian cult, worshipping her more than previously as the embodiment of maternal love. Shrines to the Madonnas of Milk, of Birth, of Blood and of Fevers became ever more frequent in the Tuscan countryside. At the same time the Madonna came to be considered as the special protector of farm animals such as oxen, sheep and chickens.[77]

Given this diffused religiosity in the Tuscan countryside, it is hardly surprising to find a strong Catholic component in the rural protests that occurred after the Great War. Bitterness and anger made themselves felt even in this deeply pacified, family-oriented countryside. Catholic and Socialist organisations vied with each other to give voice to sharecropper grievances. In July 1920 the Tuscan socialist sharecroppers' federation imposed a 'Red Pact' upon the landowners, which effectively won for the peasants security of tenure, an end to indebtedness and a greater voice in the running of their farms. As was true throughout Italy, their triumph was short-lived; blackshirt squads soon set about restoring 'normality' to the countryside.

In the middle of the 1930s, at San Gersolè in the commune of Impruneta, just a few miles from the gates of Florence, a strict and enterprising elementary school teacher, Maria Maltoni, a supporter of the Fascist regime, ordered her pupils to fill their notebooks with diaries of their own lives and those of their families.[78] They responded with spontaneity and autonomy, describing religious processions and Fascist ritual, wandering friars and agricultural work, animals and insects. These notebooks, so vivid and immediate in their observations and their language, written in a dialect resembling Dante's Italian, enable us to view sharecropping families through the eyes of their children, an extraordinary and perhaps unique historical privilege.

In his path-breaking work on the Tuscan peasant 'aristocracy', Giovanni Contini has focused on the very long story of just one sharecropping family, the Caroti.[79] As one of his sources he used the San Gersolè school diary of the ten-year-old Fernanda Caroti. I will follow in his (and her) footsteps, concentrating on certain themes: religiosity, family love, violence and cruelty, death.

In the 1930s the Caroti family, numbering some ten members living under the same roof, was firmly established on a prosperous farm in the commune of Impruneta, not far from the villa of the aristocratic Corsini family, the proprietors of all the land there around. The Caroti *podere* (family farm) was particularly handsome to behold, with its seven hundred ancient olive trees which produced an excellent oil, its peach and pear trees, its grain fields and vineyards. The family employed casual labourers at peak moments in the agricultural year and produced sulphur candle wicks for sale at the Florentine market.

The Caroti declared themselves to be Fascist and some of them even attended the local party meetings, but theirs was above all a deeply religious domestic culture. Fernanda's grandmother, Assunta, a particularly dominant figure in these years, was always quoting religious mottoes and proverbs, reciting rosaries, recounting miraculous appearances of angels and of the Madonna. She told her granddaughter of the occasion in 1919 when the Madonna was sighted at midnight at nearby Montorsoli, amidst bramble bushes at the bottom of a ravine. She and her friends rushed to have a look for themselves. They found a crowd of people praying: a sixty-year-old carter, famous locally for his bad language and anti-clericalism, was on his knees begging the Madonna to make herself visible. She did not, but Fernanda wrote that her grandmother 'was satisfied just the same for all the spectacle she had witnessed'.[80]

Inside the home, relations between adults and children were authoritarian but vivacious, with habitual recourse to the use of physical force. Fernanda wrote of her sister Renza being beaten by their father for some minor misdemeanour. Renza, amidst floods of tears, told her father that she hoped his bad back 'would never get better' and got more lashes for her impudence. Often the two sisters would take their revenge on the animals and birds that were so much part of their lives. Sent by their father on a hot June day of 1938 to scare off the sparrows from a wheat field, they managed to take one of the birds prisoner. 'I said to her: if you had been good and less badly behaved, I'd have let you live but instead you must pay for your bad behaviour, and so I banged her head on a nail and she died.'[81]

In spite of the relative prosperity of this part of the countryside, death and disease were ever present. The Caroti daughters were taken to all the funerals in their locality, and according to Fernanda were terrorised by the scenes of mourning. Once Fernanda was in the fields working alongside her father. They chatted about death:

'If you were to die there'd be one little protesting rascal less' [. . .]
'But I don't want to diiiieee! I'm too young to die.'

'Don't you believe it – there are lots and lots of children who die young'
[. . .]

And my father went on roaring with laughter, but I was all upset because
I wanted to die old.[82]

Such rough humour and the habitual physical violence used on children did
not mean that their parents lacked deep affection for them. Fernanda reported,
'When I was ill the last time he [her father] was always popping into the
bedroom to ask how I was.'[83]

The overall picture that emerges from the diaries produced for Maria
Maltoni and from other sources is of large sharecropping families with
complex and articulated inner lives, with a real sense of domestic space and
with formal hierarchies mediated by much informal banter. Yet neither their
size and self-sufficiency nor their isolation in individual farmhouses led them
to be excessively inward-looking. Rather a rich network of exchanges, social
rituals and mutual aid linked one farmhouse to another. No practice better
epitomised these frequent contacts between families than the *veglia*. On winter
evenings, usually from the beginning of November onwards, families would
gather in the farmhouse stables to play cards and games, to knit and to mend,
to listen to, and tell, stories. These gatherings were not closed but rather
involved frequent hospitality and a complex system of visiting.[84] Thus Tuscan
sharecropping families, to use a modern analytical category, were rich in social
capital; not so much as to boast a self-governing organ such as the Russian *mir*,
but sufficient to constitute a real peasant community, with all its passions and
controls, its generosities and prejudices.

These peasants families were thus connected to each other, but they
remained separate from the world. The peasants of Impruneta studied by
Contini may have lived only a few kilometres from Florence but they were
light years away from it in cultural terms, inhabiting a world of their own where
roads were still dirt tracks or mule paths, and where news from the great city
was brought by wandering friars and nuns who were received warmly by the
Caroti family if less so by others.[85] It was a world that the Fascist regime wanted
to break into and mould in its own image.

II. FASCIST FAMILIES

1. The regime's view of families: models, images, discourses

Robert Paxton has written convincingly of Fascist policy's being a combination
of febrile activism and shapelessness.[86] If this is true in general terms, it is

even more applicable to the area of family politics. Like the other regimes examined in this book, Fascism never put family life at the centre of its politics. Nor did it ever really decide the exact contours of the family discourse that it wanted to propagate. This uncertainty began at the top and is at least in part explained by the poverty of Mussolini's own intimate and domestic relations. Beginning with the Duce's own family, I want to examine different views of, and discourses on, the family, from the Catholic family to the Roman one, from Giovanni Gentile's high, metaphysical approach to more prosaic models based on specific social classes or historical experience, from Mario Sironi's great paintings of the early 1930s to the question of the type of gender relations and the sort of patriarchy that were supposed to characterise Fascist family life.

2. Inside Mussolini's family

In January 1910, at the height of his radical socialist phase, Mussolini set up household with Rachele Guidi, a barely literate peasant girl from the same social background and region as himself. They were to have five children together, three before Mussolini came to power and two afterwards. In December 1925, responding to Vatican pressure and in consideration of his own long-term political interests, he married Rachele in church.[87] The relationship between Benito and his wife was an unequal and mainly unhappy one. He was very much her intellectual superior, and made her suffer greatly through his disinterest, his indifference to their children and, above all, a long series of lovers. As his career developed he seemed mainly intent on leaving her behind, first in Forlì when he was in Milan, and then in Milan when he was in Rome. Only in 1929 did Rachele and her children finally move to the Villa Torlonia in Rome. There she continued to live simply, keeping chickens and even pigs in the grounds of the villa, but also creating her own network of informers and making friends and enemies amongst the Fascist elite – creating her 'clan from Romagna', as it came to be known. Mussolini lived in a separate wing of the same villa, where he lunched alone and received his lovers.[88] His last mistress, Claretta Petacci, recorded his ruminations on love and sex:

I have never loved a woman. I have had many women, but always as the fancy took me [. . .] At the beginning I loved my wife, but more than anything it was a sexual attraction: she had a rounded, beautiful figure and a large bosom. I liked her a lot and took her often [. . .] The second was S. [Margherita Sarfatti]. Yes, perhaps for two years I loved her and it was not only physical attraction: there was also a spiritual attraction, we talked a lot, about many things [. . .] I can't even remember the other women; they used to come and see me, as many as five of them, one after the other, in a single day; one in the morning, one at midday, another in the afternoon, one in the evening and one at night. It was an endless stream, a procession. Cesira [Mussolini's faithful chambermaid] entered into the spirit of it – she commented on them and sometimes even imitated them.[89]

Doubtless Mussolini exaggerated the number of his conquests to impress Claretta, but his priapism and emotional coldness were hardly likely to make him think deeply about family life, either his own or that of the nation.

Divorce was out of the question in an Italy in which the Fascist state had just made its peace with the Catholic Church, and in any case Rachele and Benito, in spite of their endless violent rows, were, as is often the case, perversely tied to each other. The comparison with Marinetti is not a favourable one. For all his misogynist statements and glaring contradictions, Marinetti was able to love Benedetta Cappa in a constant and passionate way, and the same can be said of his love for his daughters, and theirs for him. Mussolini, on the other hand, seemed to love no one. He had his children regularly followed by the secret police to keep tabs on what they were up to, but rarely saw them.[90]

The Duce was by all accounts closest to his first daughter, Edda. When she married the handsome and intelligent Galeazzo Ciano in April 1930, Fascist Italy was at last able to celebrate the rites of passage of a 'first family', up to that point kept firmly in the shadows. Edda and her husband lived a brilliant, modish and expensive life, further enhanced when Ciano became Minister of Foreign Affairs in 1936. During the 1930s they became close friends of Joseph Goebbels and his wife Magda.

At the end of the war tragedy and retribution rent the family apart. Ciano was convicted of conspiring against the Duce and was shot in early 1944. Edda did everything she could to save him and never forgave her father for not intervening. Her mother, on the other hand, who had always hated Ciano for his smooth and condescending ways, openly worked for his execution. Edda fled to Switzerland, where the authorities interned her briefly in the mental asylum of Malévoz. There she was analysed by the distinguished Freudian psychiatrist André Repond, who wrote a long report on her and on the Mussolini family.[91] It is an interesting document, though one that obviously reflects Edda's version of events. Repond registered that the Mussolini family had appeared to enjoy 'some periods of harmony', but in general was marked by its 'roughness' and was even marred by 'hereditary defects'. Rachele was described as very impulsive and jealous; Benito as an opinionated primary school teacher who could not bear to be contradicted. Together they staged violent, physical rows in front

fig. 22 Mussolini with his family, 1929. From the left, Mussolini's wife Rachele holding Anna Maria, Benito holding Romano, Edda, Bruno and Vittorio.

of their children which left permanent mental damage. Edda revealed to Repond in the course of her analysis that she was totally frigid, a state that had had traumatic consequences for the early part of her marriage with Ciano: 'She has always expressed a profound disgust for all things sexual, a suffering reinforced by her parents open display of all the miseries of married life.'[92]

The picture that emerges is a chilling one. For Mussolini his own family was clearly an embarrassment, even a humiliation, and the Fascist press was instructed not to write about it. But sometimes even family could come in useful. When his son Bruno, who had enrolled in the air force, died in an aviation accident in 1941, Mussolini published a sixty-page pamphlet entitled 'Conversing with Bruno' (*Parlo con Bruno*), something he had singularly failed to do when his son was alive.[93] It presents a totally invented version of family life, loving and regimented.

3. Beyond Hegel: the state and family as 'one'

In a famous speech of June 1925, Mussolini asserted the 'ferocious totalitarian will' of his regime. Of all the great dictatorships of the first half of the twentieth century, it was Fascism that made the earliest and most systematic use of totalitarianism as a political concept. In a celebrated aphorism of October of the same year, the Duce made crystal clear what he had in mind: 'Everything in the state, nothing outside the state, nothing against the state.'[94] The entry 'Fascismo' written for the new *Enciclopedia italiana* in 1932 by Mussolini himself and the leading philosopher of his regime, Giovanni Gentile, took as its starting point this rudimentary intellectual scaffolding:

> Anti-individualistic, the Fascist conception of power is *for* the state; and it is for the individual only in so far as his interests coincide with those of the state [. . .] Liberalism denied the power of the state in the interests of the particular individual; Fascism reaffirms the state as the true reality of the individual [. . .] For the Fascist, everything is in the state, and nothing which is human or spiritual exists, even less has value, outside the state. In this sense Fascism is totalitarian.[95]

Nothing could have been clearer and at the same time more evasive. Of particular interest to us, the fate of the family under Fascism was not mentioned at all. Nor did the modern family have a separate entry in the new *Enciclopedia*. It appeared rather as an appendage.

This omission received an intellectually fascinating, but only marginally influential, remedy in a paper on the state delivered by Giovanni Gentile at a conference on Hegel in Berlin in October 1931.[96] In his great work *Elements of the Philosophy of Right* of 1822, Hegel had argued for the need to *distinguish* between the three principal spheres of human activity – the family, civil society and the state. For Hegel, the task of the philosopher was to analyse the intricate dialectical relationship between these spheres, a process which for him culminated in the triumph of the state, in which the 'universal' and the 'particular' were reconciled.[97] Gentile wanted to go further. Rather than maintaining family, civil society and the state as separate analytical spheres, and tracing the connections and distinctions between them, Gentile argued instead for the need to collapse them into one. Hegel's famous triad was dismissed summarily as 'irksome, illusory and arbitrary'.[98] Family and state, as 'spiritually lived', could only be *one*, without any real distinction between them. Gentile's formulation of this relation was as radical in its way as that of Kollontai:

> The state, known in as much as it is spiritually lived, is a form of self-awareness which cannot be compared with the family because *the state cannot realise itself unless it absorbs the family and annuls it* [my italics]. Only

in this way can it silence within man's conscience every discordant voice deriving from divergent laws; only in this way can it unify spiritual interests which would otherwise appear to conflict with one another.[99]

As for civil society, it too could not exist outside and separate from the state, for by itself it could express only an atomistic self-interest bereft of any ethicality: 'There is no civil society which is not also state.'[100]

In his Berlin paper Gentile did not mean to imply that family and civil society should in a physical and empirical sense disappear. Unlike the more radical Bolsheviks, he had no specific plans for reducing families' domesticity, or for dissolving them into society. Rather he wanted individuals, but also families, to express value systems and a spirituality that reflected Italy's national mission. In this order of things there could be no autonomy for the family sphere.

Thus the perennial tension between family loyalty and obedience to the state, immortalised in Sophocles' *Antigone*, was cancelled at a stroke.[101] Gentile's formulation was a long way from Gramsci's faith in the working-class family as an 'organ of moral life', 'the torch bearer of civilisation from one generation to another'; it was far from the Catholic Church's view of the sanctity of the Christian family, as we shall see in a moment; and it was fundamentally an ahistorical position, as it took no account of the strength of family life in the development of Italian society.

4. The Catholic family

Catholicism offered the dominant model of family life in Italy, a cultural imprinting that went back many centuries and one that the Fascists could neither ignore nor totally embrace. In its very long history the Church had developed, though not in linear fashion, a theology of social life which put the family at the very heart of Christian activity.[102] This primacy of family is asserted in at least two key elements of Catholic doctrine. The first is that of marriage. Catholic marriage is not a simple agreement between two human beings of different sexes, but a sacrament, a holy pact between the two betrothed and God. As such it is indissoluble. The family which derives from this pact is endowed with a transcendental quality – it was, to use Rosmini's celebrated phrase, 'a little church enclosed within domestic walls'.[103] Secondly, to protect this 'little church' and accord it its rightful place, the Church developed the theory of 'anteriority': the family was a 'natural' social formation that *preceded* both temporally and in importance civil society and the state. Leo XIII, in his famous encyclical *Rerum Novarum* (1891), made this quite explicit.

The family, he wrote, was 'a domestic society, small but real, anterior to any civil society'.[104]

As for the role of the state, the same encyclical contains stern words of warning: 'It is a great and pernicious error to think that the state can interfere as it likes in the sanctuary of the family'.[105] Christian parents, not the state, were to have full control over the education of their children. Only if they were unable to fulfil their mission, for material or other reasons, did the state then have the duty to help them. These were not encouraging positions for a Fascist regime which harboured 'totalitarian' ambitions, let alone for Gentile's idea of spiritually subsuming the family into the state.

Furthermore, the Church had all-encompassing, 'totalitarian' ideas of its own. From the last decades of the nineteenth century onwards it launched a great campaign to reassert what it called the 'social kingdom of Christ'.[106] In this mediaeval hierocratic model, the Church once again became both *spiritual* and *temporal* ruler, with the 'social kingdom of Christ' as the modern equivalent of the mediaeval communities of believers, piously gathered around their great Gothic cathedrals. In 1924 Cardinal Laurenti summarised dramatically what was entailed: the kingdom would be realised 'when all states are Christian, that is to say truly Christian, belonging to the one and only Church of Christ; when all laws, schools, marriage, law courts and armies are exclusively Christian'. A year later, in 1925, Pius XI enshrined this doctrine in his encyclical *Quas Primas*.[107]

Consequent upon this 'integralist' strategy was the Church's view of civil society. The 'civility' of civil society was not measured in any way by its autonomy or pluralism, but by the degree to which it was integrated holistically into the life of the Church and service to God. In June 1940, in an allocution to newly-weds, Pius XII offered the following definition:

> Society is not formed of a conglomerate of individuals, sporadic beings who appear one moment and disappear the next. Rather it arises from the economic sharing and moral solidarities of families which, by passing on from generation to generation the precious inheritance of the same ideal, the same civilisation, the same religion, ensure the cohesion and continuity of social ties.[108]

Rather confusingly, Pius XI (1922–39) and Pius XII (1939–58), the two popes of the Fascist years, generally used the term 'civil society' to describe not society, or parts of it, but rather the state. In this they were following in a long doctrinal tradition. Society thus acquired three habitual adjectives: 'civil' society was the state, which needed to be watched with the eye of a hawk;

'perfect' society was the Church, which alone could assure the spiritual well-being of Christian families; and 'modern' society was the series of execrable errors which had produced the French revolution and, worse still, Liberalism and Communism.[109]

As for relations *within* the family, it was again Leo XIII who spelt out most clearly the drastic Catholic gender hierarchy, this time in his encyclical *Arcanum Divinae Sapientiae* (1880): 'The husband is prince of the family, the head [*capo*] of his wife, who is in any case flesh of his flesh and bone of his bones, subject and obedient to her husband, not as slave but as companion.' Woman was part of the body of the man, just as their children were 'an extension of his personality'.[110]

In *Casti Connubii*, Pius XI's famous encyclical on the family of 31 December 1930, this gender hierarchy was restated, primarily with regard to Catholic women. The Church ascribed to them a 'sublime vocation', that of being wife and mother. Through their dedication to home and family, expressed always with modesty and humility, women could aspire to 'sanctity'. Taking paid work outside the home, on the other hand, meant putting their families at risk; and claiming emancipation and equality was tantamount to perdition:

> This false liberty and unnatural equality with man come to damage the woman herself; since if the woman descends from the truly regal throne within the home to which she has been raised by the Gospel, she will soon fall back into her former slavery (if not in appearance then certainly in reality) and will become again, as in pagan times, the mere object of the man.[111]

Catholic fathers and husbands received far less attention in *Casti Connubii* (and elsewhere) than their spouses. Within the family, their authority went unquestioned, but they were exhorted to be companions not tyrants. They were also to be pious and never forgetful of the sacrament which tied their actions to the teachings of God the Father; furthermore they were to be constantly present in the family and concerned with their children's education. Outside the family, as well as within it, they were to strive to realise the 'social kingdom of Christ'.

Many criticisms can be made of the vision of the family as it emerges from *Casti Connubii* and other Church documents of the time. The Catholic historian Cecilia Dau Novelli has pointed to the number of admonitions and vetoes the Church enunciated for women, without ever really understanding 'the female *animus*, its relationship with the body and with nature'.[112] The spectacle of single men pontificating on young married women's habits and behaviour was never likely to be an illuminating one. Nor was an overall strategy which inserted Catholic families in a crusade against the modern world.

Opportunities were also lost with regard to overall values. In the first section of *Casti Connubii*, dedicated to the values of Christian marriage, Pius XI limited himself to reaffirming the three elements identified by St Augustine as constituting the essence and purpose of Christian marriage: 'proles', 'fides' and 'sacramentum'. Together they constituted the 'chastity' of the married couple, the 'casti connubii'. According to at least one account, Pius XI would have liked to have found room for the concept 'love' as a primary element of Christian marriage, but was dissuaded by his Jesuit counsellor, Father Franz Xavier Hürth, who found the term 'ambiguous'.[113]

For all its limitations (and perhaps because of some of them), this was a mighty family model, the most formidable we shall encounter in this book, and one which plays a central role in the history of both the Italian and Spanish dictatorships. The Italian Fascists could take some comfort in its convergence with a number of their own ideas. Both Church and regime sought prolific families and were utterly opposed to feminism, homosexuality and abortion. Both identified the French Revolution and its attendant individualism as the founding evil of the modern world. Both preferred rural to urban society and feared the corruption of the great cities. They were, however, profoundly divided over many issues and in competition with each other with regard to Italian society. Mussolini aspired to total control over society as a prelude to imperial expansion and Mediterranean war; families were supposedly to serve the state. But the Church's own programme of temporal and spiritual control was no less absolute. Families were to serve God the Father through the Church and to work to realise the 'social kingdom of Christ' upon earth.

In spite of these radical divergences and conflicts of interest, Fascism and Catholicism, as we shall see, were to travel a long and opportunistic road together.

5. Romans and others

In general terms, the Fascists boasted no more fundamental a reference point or more fecund a source of images and ideas than Roman civilisation.[114] It was easy for the Fascist to make a long list of Roman virtues corresponding to his or her own daydreams: exceptional courage and natural aggression; rigid discipline and self-control; effective organisation of a powerful state; grandiose architecture. On the eve of his March on Rome in 1922, Mussolini stated that the Roman example was *not* to be viewed with 'nostalgic contemplation of the past', as the bourgeois Romantics had done, but as 'hard preparation for the future'.[115]

Yet the Roman family, one of the lynchpins of this civilisation, was rarely used as a model in Fascist propaganda. There were many reasons for this. One was that the draconian powers accorded to the male head of household in the Roman system were a long way away from the more muted version of patriarchy proposed by the Fascists. Another was that the Roman cult of the ancestors had no easy equivalent in Catholic Italy. Indeed, public opinion was easily frightened by the pagan elements of Roman family religiosity. Every time Roman culture and that of Catholicism came into conflict, the regime was to opt for the second.

Three other models – from the Fascist point of view, one negative and two positive – are worth mentioning. They are based not on history or religion, but on social class. The first, negative model was that of the execrable 'bourgeois' family. Some of the Fascist regime's most high-blown rhetoric was reserved for denouncing families that were urban, prosperous, hedonistic, egoistic and of limited fertility. These families were breeding grounds of female emancipation and homoeroticism, of pacifism and the absence of national spirit. Luigi Chiarini wrote in *Critica fascista* in August 1933,

> The bourgeois family is founded on absolute individualism; it is diffident towards the state and towards any form of hierarchy. As a result it is generally anarchic, with all the consequences that we have come to recognise. Its ideals are privacy and reservedness. Everything has to be private – school, governess, house and car. The interests of the bourgeois family and those of the collectivity are on a collision course.[116]

The two positive models emerged as the history of the regime unfolded, one explicit, the other much less so. The first was the hard-working, independent peasant family, like the sharecropping one described above. This rural archetype seemed to offer the regime a number of guarantees – high fertility, a complex and numerous family structure rather than a miserably restricted nuclear one, a clear gender hierarchy and a deep attachment to the soil. This family type was the object of much propaganda, though organising and mobilising it in real terms was much more difficult.[117]

The second was the urban petty bourgeois family from which Fascism drew its core support. The demarcation line between bourgeois and petty bourgeois, clear enough in Fascist rhetoric, was less so in social reality. But it is possible to identify very strong pockets of active support for the regime amongst the salaried employees of the state, both local and national, those

fig. 23 Mino Maccari, 'Cocktail', illustration from *Il selvaggio*, 1931.

working as clerks in banks, insurance and other services, as well as shop-keepers and other self-employed.[118] Numbers of state employees rose under Fascism from some 400,000 before the Great War to 1.14 million in 1941. New Fascist residential quarters, such as Flaminio in Rome, catered specifically to them. The fertility rates of these families could not compare with those of sharecroppers, but their members were easily pulled into different Fascist organisations, and were a constant presence at the regime's parades and cele-brations. These 'famiglie fascistissime' sometimes had themselves photo-graphed in poses that broke with traditional family portraits. In one, the father is holding a long truncheon, a *manganello*, as a reminder of the movement's 'heroic' early days, while one of the two children is wearing a woollen beret embroidered with one of the more demented of Fascist slogans: 'Me ne frego' (I don't give a damn).

6. Gender, sexuality and patriarchy

The regime's discourse on male virility, as Barbara Spackman has pointed out, did not necessarily constitute a single rhetoric.[119] It is possible to discern two main strands with regard to the family. On the one hand there was that which

fig. 24 A Fascist family waiting to greet the train on which Mussolini is travelling on his way to Switzerland, 1923.

derived strongly from early Futurist writing, and from Marinetti in particular, according to which, as we have seen, men were above all sexual marauders, possessing and despising women at the same time. They were not fathers and husbands, but rather soldiers and adventurers. They were naturally adulterous, as was the Duce himself, boasting of their prowess in the sexual field as in the martial one. Conquest was all. The pantomime of such attitudes was often to be seen in Fascist parades, where overweight Fascist leaders and officials, often men of urban petty bourgeois origin, were immortalised by the newsreels of the regimes with feathers on their helmets, goose-stepping or running down the street out of breath.[120]

A second strand of the discourse was quite opposite. As Mussolini developed his population policies, which we will examine in detail in a moment, so the sexuality of the marauding, Futurist male had to be reined in and redirected. Virility was now to be defined in strictly family terms. The principal family task of the Fascist 'new man' was to impregnate his wife as often as possible, so that the nation's armies, repopulated by Fascist male children, could hold their own on a world scale. Naturally, the two strands of the discourse on male sexual virility – the one celebrating orgasm without responsibility, the other orgasm with strictly pro-natalist intentions – were not incompatible. Fascist men, provided they were married, could still hope to have the best of both worlds. But if they were not married, they were punished by a heavy tax on celibacy.

A much greater difficulty arose with regard to virility expressed in martial terms. If men were to be summoned frequently to war, what role could they hope to play at home? This was a question which assailed all the great dictators, and they found different ways of responding to it. Both Hitler and Atatürk had stentorian answers: men were raised by the state in order to die for it; only secondarily were they husbands and fathers. While the words employed by Fascist rhetorical discourse were similar, the reality was not. Deep-rooted Italian family culture was not noted for its bellicosity, and Catholicism, as we have just seen, preached the primacy of the family, *not* of the state. It also clearly preferred the wholeness of the family to the lacerations of war. These great cultural and familial differences were highly insidious for the regime, undermining some of its most cherished beliefs and postures.[121]

As for women, the Futurist-Fascist view of men as sexual hunters and marauders found its counterpart in the myth of female insatiability. 'The war proves that women need daily copulation,' wrote Marinetti in 1916, giving voice to a timeless, transnational gender stereotype. In general, the first Fascists had an extraordinarily belittling and reductive view of the female sex, one from which they never really freed themselves.[122] Women were hysterical, they could not be replied upon, they had no place in the political sphere. Their pretensions to emancipation and to extra-domestic work were defeminising: women had to serve men. It was with incomparable sarcasm that Carlo Emilio Gadda observed, 'For everything then was male and Martial: even broads and wet nurses, and the tits of your wet nurse and the ovary and the fallopian tubes and the vagina and the vulva.'[123]

This one-dimensional woman was, however, as insufficient for the requirements of the regime as was the male marauder. Women had to serve the nation, not only their men. The primary means of doing this was to remain firmly at home, having children. Suddenly their status changed: the 'new

Italian woman' was a precious activist in the reproductive sphere, bearing as many children as possible. She was to be a family creature: ever pregnant, ever present. Maternity was to be defined not as it had been in the women's movement before and after the Great War – as a precious choice, belonging to the woman herself – but rather as a national duty. Peasant women, given their sturdiness and reproductive capacities, had a specially important role to play. What counted, to quote Gadda again, was 'the virile vulva of the Italian woman'.[124]

There was one other aspect of the regime's attitude to women, upon which Victoria de Grazia has placed much emphasis.[125] Fascism offered a highly conventional and traditional family model, in some aspects close to the Catholic one. But the regime was also the bearer of a modernist discourse, the champion of mass mobilisation, transformation and progress. Strong tensions existed between these two elements. Young women from the popular classes and the petty bourgeoisie were often to be mobilised – for gymnastic displays and mass celebrations of one type or another. Newsreels, cinema and the radio laid the foundations of a new mass culture. At another level, the elite women of the regime, from Edda Ciano downwards, were an expression of an international consumer culture, however much Mussolini rhetorically denounced the bourgeois family and its egoistical values.

If we place the 'new man' alongside the 'new woman', what sort of specifically Fascist patriarchy emerges?[126] Pro-natalism is certainly a central element. Amongst the great dictatorships, the Fascists were the first in the field, highly explicit about what they wanted to do, though far from the most successful. Another element regards men. Homoeroticism and celibacy were respectively severely punished and heavily taxed by the regime, but 'conforming' males had a pretty easy time in relation to those in the other regimes.[127] Despite all the rhetoric, the Fascist male was not, like his counterparts in Germany and Turkey, brought up by the state in order to die for it. Italian family life, with maternal care and indulgence at its centre, certainly did not constitute an effective preparation for such a destiny. Finally, and most importantly, the Fascist regime throughout its history had an extraordinarily restrictive attitude towards women. The really illuminating comparison here is with Atatürk's new regime in Turkey, and it is worth going back for a moment to the 'new' Turkish woman. Two stereotypes had emerged in Kemalist ideology and both were to become central to nationalist iconography. One was the solid and powerful figure of the Anatolian peasant woman, and here we can find a clear equivalence with Italian sharecropping women. The second, to whom Kemal dedicated a great deal of attention, was the emancipated and educated woman of the cities, who was to train herself to serve the nation (see plate 1). She was to be a high school teacher or a nurse, a doctor or even an engineer. By 1940 Italy could boast a small percentage of women with university degrees, but they formed little or no part of the ruling class of the regime.

7. Mario Sironi: family and alienation

By way of a conclusion to this section dedicated to images, discourses and representations of the Italian family, I want to examine briefly the contribution of Fascism's greatest painter, Mario Sironi. To do so I must recapitulate for a moment. As we have seen, the Russian artistic avant-garde, in keeping with the priorities and requests of the Communist Party, had privileged economic themes over family ones, production over reproduction.[128] No modernist representations of the family ever emerged in Russia before artistic endeavour succumbed to Stalinist repression and conformism. In Italy, the development of the avant-garde took a very different political direction. Although there were initial sympathies and links between the Futurist painters and the idea of socialist revolution, by the end of the *biennio rosso* Futurism's heart beat firmly for Fascism. In November 1922, shortly after the March on Rome, a group of artists including Marinetti, Carrà and Sironi signed a statement which applauded Mussolini's coming to power: 'At long last', they wrote, 'that mediocre mentality which for so many years has suffocated the principal quality of the Italian race – the excellence of its artistic spirit – has been dismantled.'[129]

At this time Sironi was thirty-seven years old. The son of a civil engineer, he had been a volunteer during the Great War, like Marinetti and Boccioni. Afterwards, he painted a series of extraordinary 'Urban landscapes' which portrayed deserted peripheries, factory chimneys, walls and warehouses, animated only by solitary lorries or trams (see plate 3). Taciturn and depressive in character, Sironi had married Matilde Fabbrini in 1919. Their marriage was to be a very difficult one. For many years the couple were penniless, but Sironi's friendship with Margherita Sarfatti, the Duce's mistress, brought him a deservedly pre-eminent place in the Novecento group of artists.[130]

One of Mussolini's many political and cultural insights was to allow a considerable degree of artistic freedom in his regime. In this, as we shall see, he distanced himself strikingly from both Hitler and Stalin. In 1926–7 there was a lively discussion in the pages of *Critica fascista* as to whether there could be such a thing as Fascist art, and if so what were to be its characteristics. At the end of the debate, which saw the participation of many leading artists, Giuseppe Bottai, later to become Minister of Education, summarised the results. There were to be no rigid instructions on the part of the regime, and no imprisoning of artistic creativity. It was simply better to avoid certain elements and characteristics. Fascist art was not to be 'fragmentary, syncopated, psychoanalytical, over-intimate or crepuscular'. Above all, it had the task of connecting to the 'great native Italian artistic tradition'.[131]

Between 1927 and 1933 Mario Sironi produced a series of paintings explicitly dedicated to the theme of the family. They are far from immediately attractive and in no way conventional, but are of unrivalled power and honesty. (See, for example, *La famiglia*, 1932, plate 4.) A convinced Fascist, Sironi was in no way prepared to adopt a simple or propagandist view of the family. Instead, he presented it as a human group scarred by alienation and separation. In these pictures the male figure is alone, always on the left-hand side of the canvas, part of the family but not part of it. Often he gazes with longing and despair at the mother and child on the other side. They, by contrast, are closely linked, even so far as to seem part of a single body. The mother's gaze is nearly always directed towards her child but never towards the male figure. The family group is depicted not in a contemporary urban landscape, but as part of an archaic, primitive humanity.[132] The background is one of barren and jagged rocks, of dead trees and ancient temples. Often the man is carrying a primitive work tool; his arms and legs are deliberately depicted as over-large and ugly, seared with red veins. The mother and child suffer from no such (Picasso-like) elephantiasis, more closely resembling Renaissance figures – the Madonna and child of a Masaccio or a Bellini.[133]

The relationship between these pictures and Sironi's own family situation seems to have been substantial. By the end of the 1920s, he and his wife had become ever more estranged, Sironi dedicating much of his time to working for the regime. In 1930 the couple separated, hardly more than a year after the birth of their second daughter Rossana, who was later to commit suicide aged nineteen. Sironi, who was very attached to her, never forgave himself for his role in her unhappiness.[134]

His family pictures go beyond his own family tragedy, however. They seem quintessentially modern in their depiction of male separateness, alienation, longing and absorption in work. Hardly surprisingly, they were not at all popular with leading Fascists, who had quite different ideas of how the Fascist male and Fascist family should be represented. Roberto Farinacci, who was part of the faction closest to the Nazis, denounced these ugly, big-footed (*piedoni*) pictures, with their gross distortion of the male form.[135] Margherita Sarfatti defended Sironi as best she could, and he continued to work tirelessly for the regime, as an illustrator for *Il Popolo d'Italia* and principal architect of the campaign for mural painting, inaugurated in Milan in 1934.[136]

III. THE REGIME IN ACTION

1. Population politics

On 26 May 1927 Mussolini made one of his most important socio-political statements, which has come to be known as the Ascension Day speech. In it he traced the lines of what was to be a demographic and welfare revolution, transforming Italian families, multiplying the Italian population, and preparing the nation for war. The speech was posited on the totalitarian capacity of the Fascist state and the omniscience of its leader: 'Let no one deceive themselves into believing that I do not know what is happening in this country, right down to its last village. Perhaps I will know about it a little late in the day, but in the end I will know'.[137]

The speech concerns the rise and fall of nations, viewed from a crude perspective of demographic Darwinism. According to Mussolini, all nations and empires begin to feel the deadly grasp of decadence when they witness a decline in the number of births. In the competition between nations that had opened up during and after the Great War, Italy was not well placed:

> Let us speak clearly: what are forty million Italians when faced with ninety million Germans and two hundred million Slavs? And if we turn our attention to the West: what are forty million Italians when faced with forty million French plus ninety million inhabitants of their colonies; or forty-six million English plus four hundred and fifty million others who inhabit their colonies? [. . .] Gentlemen, if our population diminishes, our destiny is that of a colony, not of an empire. It is well nigh time to state these facts; if not, we will go on living in a regime of false illusions and lies which can only bring in their wake atrocious delusions. [138]

The target that Mussolini set for Italy was a population of sixty million by 1950, to be obtained by reducing mortality rates, especially infant mortality, and by greatly accelerating the birth rate. The main obstacles to this plan were identified as families in the major industrial cities of the north: between 1925 and 1926, Milan had increased its population by just twenty-two inhabitants! Its performance, continued Mussolini, was to be contrasted with the southern region of Basilicata, which boasted the highest birth rates in the country: 'It wins my sincere applause because it has demonstrated its virility and its strength. It is clear that Basilicata is not yet sufficiently infected by all the pernicious currents of contemporary civilisation'.[139] The Fascist state was to assume full responsibility in this field, as in others. If it did not, then the national collective would fragment into a conglomeration of nuclear families; at that point 'a mere hundred Normans would be sufficient to conquer the whole of Puglia.'[140]

A year later Mussolini returned to these themes in his preface to the Italian edition of a book by the German Richard Korherr, *Regresso delle nascite: morte dei popoli*, which also boasted a second preface by Oswald Spengler.[141] Korherr argued for a spiritual transformation of the West, guided by a charismatic political leader and a strong Church and founded on traditional, prolific families. Women's emancipation was to be stopped in its tracks, all contraception was to be banned, and the state was to assist mothers and children. The Catholic Korherr was later to become a functionary in the SS.[142] Mussolini's contribution largely duplicated the contents of his Ascension Day speech, but he introduced a new, racist element: 'the entire white race, the race of the West, risks being submerged by races of other colours, who are multiplying at rates which are quite unknown to us'.[143]

Mussolini's speech has to be placed in its proper international context, for he was far from alone in preaching the dangers of population decline. Many factors pushed nations, both democratic and otherwise, towards active demographic policies: the appalling casualties in the Great War; continuing very high levels of infant mortality; the rapid decline in fertility in major urban centres; and in the Italian case massive emigration – between 1909 and 1913 Italy lost nearly one million of its inhabitants.

Reactions to the demographic crisis varied from country to country. In 1918 the British parliament approved the Maternal and Child Welfare Act. Between 1919 and 1924, the French parliament approved a new law against abortion, banned publicity for contraceptives, created Mothers' Day and paid child subsidies for poor families. All over Europe there was new interest in national statistics, accompanied by the growth of a 'technical class' of doctors, social workers, nurses and the like, ready to intervene in family life, in terms not only of protection but also of regulation.[144]

There was thus widespread interest not just in *increasing* national populations but also in *ameliorating* them. A profound international division developed over the nature of eugenics, the science of population or race improvement. On the one hand, France, Italy and other Catholic nations limited themselves to 'positive' eugenics, that is to say the gradual improvement of their populations through the provision of better social, dietary and hygienic conditions. Intervention such as this was consonant with the Church's long-standing teaching, reaffirmed in *Casti Connubii*, that any tampering with reproduction was a sin. On the other hand, some predominantly Protestant nations, such as Germany and Sweden, also embraced, though to different degrees, 'negative' eugenics. This latter was very much more sinister. It involved the state regulation of 'undesirable elements', the hunting down not only of disease but also of defects (medical, social or racial), and, if necessary, the enforcement of compulsory sterilisation.[145]

In 1927–8 Mussolini's population politics were racist and warmongering, but they did not yet extend to 'negative' eugenics.

2. The battle for births

A great question mark hung over Fascist population politics: how on earth were they to be implemented? It is as well to begin by separating out the different instruments used not just by Mussolini but by the other great dictators in their pro-natal campaigns. There were three major groupings. The first was the creation of special agencies or programmes, most often dedicated to combating infant mortality and to improving conditions for maternity, but also concerned, as was the case in Italy, with limiting and controlling internal and external migration. The second consisted of a wide variety of piecemeal economic incentives and rewards: family allowances, special provisions for large families, marriage loans, tax deductions, prizes for hyper-productive mothers, and so on. The third involved the prohibition and punishment of all those practices that impeded procreation: contraception, abortion and celibacy, but also women's work outside the home. Each of the dictatorial regimes under consideration in this book employed a different combination of these instruments.

2.1 ONMI: illusion and reality

In Italy, ONMI, the Opera Nazionale per la Maternità e l'Infanzia, was a state agency founded in 1925 but radically reorganised and centralised by Mussolini in 1927, after his Ascension Day speech.[146] The 'commissars' or presidents who directed the agency from 1926 to 1943 were all men. The principal tasks of the organisation, which was heralded as the regime's most important instrument of social policy, were to reduce radically the level of infant mortality, which stood at 105.5 first-year deaths per 1,000 births in 1930, and to guarantee 'rational and scientific' conditions for maternity and early infant education. In its first years the organisation was involved in a myriad of tasks. It distributed powdered milk, arranged for assistance to single mothers, and from 1933 onwards ran 'Mother and Child's Day', introduced by the regime and scheduled, not by chance, for Christmas Eve of every year. In time, ONMI came to concentrate its efforts more on qualified professional aid to mothers and children. Paediatric and obstetric clinics were set up and psychiatric counselling was made available, along with crèches and 'offices of social assistance'. The idea was to create in every Italian commune a so-called Centre of Assistance for Maternity and Infancy.

All this sounded wonderful, and admirers of the regime were escorted around model centres by uniformed staff.[147] In reality, the agency was a gigantic bluff, deeply deficient at many levels. The first was financial. Its original funding was a derisory eight million lire per year, rising to 150 million by 1941. A large part of this funding, however, went to the maintenance of single mothers, whose welfare had been entrusted to the agency by a law of May 1927. In 1933 their subsidy was reduced to a third of its previous level, but the strain upon the agency's modest finances remained very great.

As a result, the bulk of the work carried out at a local level was done on a voluntary basis. Local activities were directed by so-called 'Comitati di patronato', committees whose members were most often politicians, priests, nuns, and the wives of the wealthy bourgeois whom Mussolini continued roundly to denounce. Catholic charitable institutions, often of antique foundation, looked with suspicion at the new state structures, which often existed only on paper. Nothing could have been further from Mussolini's dynamic but imaginary 'totalitarian' welfare state. Furthermore, given the lack of funding, the agency had very soon to abandon its original aim of giving welfare attention to all mothers and children, and instead to concentrate on only the most needy cases, and not all of them. The figures from even a major city such as Florence are desultory.[148]

Another fundamental flaw in the agency's activities was geographical imbalance. Somehow the majority of the funds found their way to the northern cities and not to the southern countryside, where infant mortality was highest. Statistics for 1943 show that by that time there were 80 Centres of Assistance in the north of the country, 43 in the centre, 31 on the southern mainland and just 7 for Sicily and Sardinia combined. A total of 161 centres for a population of nearly forty-four million was hardly a 'totalitarian' result.[149] This state of affairs was denounced from within ONMI itself. In October 1937, Angelo Buffa wrote in the organisation's journal, Maternità ed infanzia, that ONMI's 'activity is deficient precisely where it is recognised to be most necessary and most interesting, that is to say in the agricultural centres'. Here obstetric and paediatric assistance 'are in almost all cases insufficient and defective. They leave unresolved the basic causes of death during childbirth and of neo-natal infections. The same is true for premature births and for insufficient growth in newborn babies.'[150]

The failures of ONMI emerge clearly from the statistics – even the regime's statistics – for infant mortality rates. These are measured by the annual number of deaths of infants in their first year per 1,000 births. As Ipsen shows, Italian infant mortality declined between 1928 and 1934, but the overall graph for the period 1930–40, the decade of maximum investment in ONMI, reveals very little difference between the beginning and the end. The results were particularly poor in southern regions, precisely those which Mussolini had applauded for their 'virility' in 1927 but which he had then abandoned to their fate. In 1934 Italy registered its best overall result: 99 first-year deaths per 1,000 births. This is to be compared with Holland's 40 in the same year, 57 in England and Wales, 72 in France, 99 in Germany, 109 in Spain and 170 in Russia. Southern Italy, however, still hovered between 120 and 160 infant deaths per 1,000 births. No demographic revolution could be built on such a foundation.[151]

2.2 City and countryside, colonisation at home, concentration camps abroad

If we turn from improvement to movement – that is, to the uprooting and physical relocation of individuals and families – we can easily discern the same gap between grandiose propaganda announcements and extremely modest results. By 1927 a multifaceted policy emerged with regard to population movements. First, on the home front, the Italian population was to be firmly rooted on the land and severely discouraged from emigrating spontaneously towards the cities. Secondly, select parts of the rural population were to be moved from one region to another, to colonise and reclaim parts of the national territory. Thirdly, as Italy built her Empire, so settler families would be transferred to the freshly conquered terrain. Special state agencies were to administer all three parts of the policy.

On the first point, Mussolini never ceased to denounce the dangers of urbanisation, both in demographic and in moral terms. Healthy, prolific families tilled the soil; near-sterile ones lived and worked in industrial cities. In his Ascension Day speech he proclaimed himself 'rural'. No heavy industrial plants were to be built around Rome; only the healthy industries of agriculture and fishing would ever be allowed. Various measures were announced to discourage internal immigration. The most draconian was that of 1939, which trapped the would-be immigrant in a catch-22 situation: in order to change residence to a city of more than 25,000 inhabitants the immigrant had to show evidence of having a job in his or her new place of abode, but getting such a job was dependent on having the new residence certificate. The law was repealed only in 1961.

In the event, Fascist legislation proved quite powerless to stop constant internal migration towards the towns and cities for the greater part of the

Fascist decades.[152] In the year 1937 alone, registered changes of residence numbered one and a half million people, an enormous figure. There were many different situations and motivations behind these statistics. One was that of individuals and young families abandoning hill and mountain villages along the whole length of the Apennines and heading for urban environments, the fall in the price of agricultural goods in the years after the Great Depression being one of the strongest factors in their decision to go. Fascism appeared impotent, even acquiescent, in the face of these massive autonomous population movements, unplanned and undesired.

Organised internal colonisation such as the reclamation of the Pontine Marshes, the second element of the regime's strategy, was very limited by comparison. Gaetano Salvemini noted that not a single distinguished foreign visitor to Rome ever escaped the obligatory visit to the 'Agro Pontino' in the company of some high-ranking Fascist official. Indeed, the photograph of Mussolini digging away with a spade, naked to the waist, was perhaps the most famous of his many 'virile' images. Considerable sums of money were invested in the Pontine Marshes – far more than in ONMI – but the overall results in terms of family resettlement were modest. Under the aegis of the newly created Commissariat for Internal Migrations and Colonisation (Commissariato per le migrazioni interne e la colonizzazione), prolific peasant families from the Veneto and Emilia-Romagna were moved to land reclamation areas. The Pontine Marshes project was the largest of these, yet between 1930 and 1938 no more than 10,000 families were settled there, a very small percentage of the total Italian families of the time.[153]

Finally, the regime promoted, as did all the colonial powers, settler colonisation by citizens of the home country. Italy's colonial territories were of limited extent and possibilities, and important distinctions must be made between them. The Agency for the Colonisation of Libya (Ente per la colonizzazione della Libia), founded in 1935, organised Italian settlement in Libya, but it was always on a modest scale. Between 1938 and 1940, Tripolitania witnessed an influx of an average 1,700 families per year. The figures for the Cyrenaica region were even lower, totalling 1,649 settler families in all by 1941. As for the newly proclaimed Italian Oriental Africa, only a few hundred Italian families were transferred there before the Second World War.[154]

In all these cases the human rights of native families were ruthlessly violated, their ways of life ignored and their territories occupied. In the case of Cyrenaica, the Italians were the authors of crimes which bear a distinct resemblance, though on a smaller scale, to the genocide of the Armenians.[155] This time it was not Islamic Turks and Kurds perpetrating the massacres but

Christian Italians. Their victims were the Bedouin Muslim rural population of the region, numbering around 200,000 at the time of the Italian invasion of 1911. The Bedouins of Cyrenaica were a population primarily of shepherds and animal breeders: sheep, goats, cows and camels. They were an independent and semi-nomadic people, whose homelands were cultivated mainly with barley. From these they migrated with their animals in search of pasture, returning at different seasons of the year. Divided into many tribes, they lived in moveable tents. The great social anthropologist Edward Evan Evans-Pritchard wrote of the difficulty in 'discerning a *naja*, a Bedouin encampment, because the tents are erected in hollows and on the banks of the wadys [dried up river beds] and their tributaries, protected from the rain, from the wind and from inopportune visitors. On the upland plains they are hidden in the forests.'[156] The region was one of great natural beauty, with the Mediterranean to the north and the desert to the south, a land of striking contrasts between mountain and plain, forest and steppe, stable encampments and nomadism, the grazing of goats and cows and that of sheep and camels. It was, as Evans-Pritchard wrote, 'a land considered rich by the Bedouins, poor by the Europeans'.[157]

fig. 25 Italian settlers arrive in Libya, November 1938.

The resistance to Italian occupation and expropriation was led by 'Umar al-Mukhtar. It had the strong backing of the traditionalist Muslim confraternity of the Senussi, whom the Bedouins recognised as their spiritual leaders and whose monasteries were spread throughout the region. In 1929 'Umar al-Mukhtar listed the eminently reasonable demands of the Bedouin resistance: a Libyan national government with a Muslim president, a Constituent Assembly, a representative and freely elected National Council, Arabic as the official language and respect for Muslim custom.[158]

The Fascists were represented by Pietro Badoglio, who was at that time the governor of Libya. In 1928 he offered an amnesty to the rebels; anyone who refused would know no peace 'either for himself, or his family, or his animals, or his heirs'.[159] In the face of continued resistance, Badoglio decided to 'empty out' the whole of Bedouin territory and herd the population into concentration camps on the shores of the Mediterranean. He wrote to General Rodolfo Graziani on 20 June 1930, 'I am not attempting to hide the gravity and extent of these measures, which imply the total ruin of the so-called "subjugated" native population. But by now the path has been clearly marked out and we must follow it to its end, even if that means that the whole population of Cyrenaica must perish.'[160]

Graziani carried out his instructions in the most ruthless fashion. Although there is considerable controversy over numbers, as in the Armenian case, it is safe to say that over 100,000 men, women and children were subjected to forced marches and held in concentration camps. In the camps the Bedouins were deprived not only of their freedom but of almost all their animals. Deaths from disease and malnutrition, and from the shooting or hanging of those who tried to escape, were probably as high as 50,000. The men who survived were set to work as labourers on the construction of roads for the new settler families. All Senussi property was confiscated and the monasteries and their personnel suppressed. In 1931 Graziani began the construction of a 300-kilometre-long barbed-wire fence on the Egyptian border, thus depriving the resistance of its last support line. In September of the same year 'Umar al-Mukhtar was captured and five days later hanged in front of the deportees of the concentration camp of Soluch.[161]

In the area of population movements, then, Mussolini's much-vaunted policies were a farce, but also a tragedy. Preaching anti-urbanism, he presided helplessly over the most significant population movement towards the cities prior to Italy's famous 'economic miracle' of 1958–63. Boasting all over Europe of the Pontine Marshes and similar experiments, he actually managed to resettle only a few thousand families. And proclaiming in 1936 that the Italians had the right to Empire because 'they are a virile people in the strict sense of the term, and as such have the desire and the pride to propagate their race upon the face of the earth',[162] he encouraged his lieutenants in Africa to wipe out thousands of entirely innocent families.

2.3 Incentives and prohibitions

Returning to the less horrific environment of Fascist domestic policy, I want to look at economic incentives and rewards, as well as prohibitions and punishments. Both present a very patchy picture, confirming the impression of a regime that had no firm grasp on what it was doing. One of the 'positive' measures was the law of June 1928 which offered tax breaks to numerically large families. State employees qualified if they had seven or more children, private employees if they had ten or more. These were not modest demands to make upon women's reproductive capacities, in return for modest economic rewards.

Family loans were introduced quite late in the day, in June 1937. Ten years after Mussolini's Ascension Day speech, the failures of the regime's population politics were too evident to ignore. New policies had to be tried, of which family loans were the most significant. These were a system of state rewards for marrying and having children, the Italian initiative being based largely on the 'marriage' loans introduced by the Nazi regime in June 1933.[163] The difference in name between the two schemes ('family' in the Italian case, 'marriage' in the German) does not appear to have had any real significance. In many respects, the Italian scheme was a pale imitation of the German one. The number of Italian loans was greatly inferior to the German – 157,989, compared with 817,060 for the period 1938–40. So too was their funding: the German scheme was administered directly by the Ministry of Finances, which pumped considerable resources into the initiative. In both schemes the interest on the loan was reduced on the birth of every child, and was cancelled after the birth of the fourth. There were some differences in the objectives of the two countries. The German loans were dependent on the woman giving up paid work outside the home; all applicants were also subjected to a rigorous examination from the racial and social point of view. The Italians did not insist on women giving up paid work and were generally less discriminating, although from 1938 onwards they too excluded Jews. They also placed an emphasis on youth (couples had to be under twenty-six years of age), in the hope that early marriage would encourage fecundity. In terms of results, the German scheme undoubtedly contributed significantly to the rise in marriage and fertility rates during the 1930s, even if many German couples ceased to have children much earlier than the regime would have wished. The Italian scheme came too late, and was too meagre to make much difference. Birth rates were 23.5 per 1,000 inhabitants in 1940; in 1926 they had been 27.7. Marriage rates were 7.1 in 1940; in 1926 they had been 7.5.[164]

If we turn now to the category of prohibition and punishment, two measures stand out. The first is the tax on celibacy. Introduced at the beginning of 1927, the tax was levied on all unmarried men (excepting priests, monks, soldiers and the gravely handicapped) between the ages of twenty-five and sixty-five. Celibacy was punished to different degrees in relation to age group: men between twenty-five and thirty-five years of age paid 35 lire per year; those between thirty-five and fifty (those considered most 'irresponsible') 50 lire; and those between fifty and sixty-five a mere 25 lire. These sums were increased considerably in 1934 and again in 1936, and to these flat rates must be added further payments in relation to income. The tax was thus economically progressive – richer single men paid more – as well as age specific. It was, of course, deeply discriminatory in relation to gay men of whatever age or income.[165] Initially, funds from the tax were directed towards welfare spending, especially the omnivorous ONMI, but after 1936 they were redirected towards imperial expansion in north-east Africa. Although lucrative, the tax was a resounding failure with respect to its proclaimed objectives. Not only did marriage rates decline instead of increasing, as we have seen, but the average age of marriage for men actually increased during the Fascist period.[166]

If the tax on celibacy targeted single men, the campaign on abortion was aimed at all fertile women. Abortion had already been illegal in Liberal Italy, but under Fascism it was punished much more severely as a crime against the community and the state, as well as – and here eugenics comes back into play – against the interests of the race ('contro la razza'). A number of show trials against abortionists helped to discourage women from seeking illegal terminations. In the world of work, however, the regime made provision for only rudimentary health and safety measures inside factories and workshops. Given the nature of their work, in which they were often bent over in one position for many hours of the day, women workers suffered from illnesses of the female reproductive organs, leading to thousands of so-called 'spontaneous' abortions.[167]

This leads us naturally to the last of Fascism's prohibitive policies – the attempt to limit or forbid women's work outside the home, and to confine them to their caring and reproductive roles within the family. This was always going to be a gargantuan task because the female presence in the workforce was significant: in 1936 one third of all industrial workers were women. Once again, Fascist legislation appears half-hearted. In May 1923 and December 1926 the regime excluded women from competing for posts as headmistresses or teachers in certain categories of secondary schools. From March 1928 onwards male heads of families were given preference both for recruitment and for promotion within the state administration. In March 1934 the number of women employed by the state was limited to 5 per cent in managerial roles and 20 per cent in jobs with lesser responsibility. Similar provisions followed for banks and insurance companies. Finally, in September 1938, in what appeared to be the most draconian measure of all, medium and large firms were compelled to respect a female employment quota of 10 per cent, while in firms employing fewer than ten workers there were supposed to be no women at all.

Some of this legislation, especially in relation to jobs in the public administration, was effective to a degree, but for the most part it was sheer bombast at work again. The 1938 law, for example, contained a long list of exceptions with regard to jobs considered 'particularly suited to women'. Employers had no intention of substituting men for women if that meant, as it did, higher labour costs. In any case, firms were granted three years to comply. By that time (1941) Italy was at war and the demand for female labour had become acute.[168]

Whichever way the historian looks, the poverty of the regime's population politics is clear to see. The Fascist state boasted of its panoptic qualities, and through its secret police it certainly kept a firm control over anti-Fascist dissent. But its capacity to shift social realities and carry through demographic and welfare reform was desultory. In June 1929 a Fascist deputy, Gaetano Zingali, professor of economics and statistics at Catania University, made reference in parliament to the great Fascist campaign which aimed at 'the quantitative increase and the qualitative amelioration of the population'. Progress was to be measured with respect to the 'famous demographic quintet': birth, marriage and death rates, and external and internal population movements. All of them, claimed Zingali, 'have been reviewed and disciplined by the Duce in so harmonic and unequivocal a way [that] the statistical data has itself become dynamic'.[169] In reality, the statistics tell no such story, even ten years later. Birth, marriage and infant mortality rates had stagnated. Organised internal colonisation, whether in the Pontine Marshes, Sardinia or elsewhere, had been modest in extent, perhaps involving 15,000 families at most. As for settlers in Libya (and later in East Africa), all one can say is that the Italian Fascists killed and destroyed a great many more families than they ever managed to settle. The fact that these were Bedouins who lived in tents made it easy to downgrade them as human beings. Not by chance in 1919 had one of Marinetti's resounding negative metaphors for family life been a Bedouin tent, 'with its lurid mixture of frail old people, women, children, pigs, donkeys, camels, chickens and excrement'.[170] Families like these did not count.

3. Pushing in and pulling out

The extensive historiography of Fascism, in so much as it has dealt with families, has tended to assume that family politics and population policies are one and the same, that the one is encapsulated in the other. This is not the case. There are many other aspects which complicate and enrich the patterns of relations between Italian families and the regime. Some of them are as make-believe and mediocre as those described above. But others had considerable, long-term effects upon families. Put simply, the regime was notably unsuccessful in pushing into families – convincing them to alter the number of children they had, changing the country's social structure, altering long-standing beliefs, habits and customs or even, as we shall see in a moment, introducing new family law. One reason why all this was so was that there was no leading Fascist intellectual or politician who thought deeply about the family. Ferdinando Loffredo, a minor Catholic and Fascist figure, wrote an interesting treatise in 1938 (a bit late in the day!) entitled *Politica della famiglia*, but he was the first to lament that Fascism had 'no organic theory of the family'.[171]

On the other hand, the regime was undoubtedly effective, above all in the cities, in pulling out family members, young and old, male and female, to join their mass organisations and activities. It was also effective in making productive compromises with traditional forces in Italian society and the state, of which the Catholic Church was certainly the most important. And it was very able in the field of propaganda and mass culture, following the example of the Futurists and making its own many of the new phenomena of Italian society of the 1930s.

3.1 Family law

This is a crucial area in which the Fascist regime, once again, was grossly deficient. Quite how deficient emerges clearly from comparison with the Russian and Turkish cases. Both the Russian Family Code of 1918 and the Turkish adoption of the Swiss Civil Code in 1926 represented fundamental breaks with traditional practices and principles in the area of family law. Both regimes, in their different ways, introduced really radical change in many areas of family law – women's rights, especially with regard to marriage and divorce, but also inheritance, alimony, abortion, and so on. They both tried to offer an organic view of the relations between family, society and the state, in keeping with their vision of society as a whole. It is worth returning for a moment to Mary Ann Glendon's idea of two moving systems, on the one hand family law, on the other hand family life. In both Russia and Turkey the law ran far beyond the realities of family life, especially in rural areas. In time, however, the two 'moving systems' came closer to each other, as the new family law made its influence felt – in the daily experience, educational processes and gender relations of family life.[172]

This was not so in Italy, and it is important to try to understand why. A first distinction to be made is that between the Fascist Civil and Penal Codes. The reform of the Civil Code, which habitually contains and defines family law, proceeded in the Italian case with excruciating slowness. The new Civil Code was finally promulgated in 1942, just in time for the regime to fall the following year. Behind this twenty-year delay lay a long-running battle within the reform commission set up by parliament. One side, headed by the two presidents of the commission (Vittorio Scialoja until his death in 1933 and then Mariano D'Amelio) argued in favour of a limited, technical adjustment of the Liberal Code dating back to 1865. They saw no reason for an explicitly Fascist concept of civil law, especially as there was no agreed vision of the 'Fascist' family. Their opponents favoured a highly politicised code but were divided over what that entailed. The result was paralysis.[173]

The same cannot be said for the Penal Code. Here the able and determined Alfredo Rocco, Minister of Justice between 1925 and 1932, carved out a space for his own nationalist and Fascist ideas and ensured that a new Code was ready by 1930. Rocco's Penal Code turned its back on previous Liberal legislation, which had aimed at least in part at protecting individual rights, favouring instead a framework which accentuated the authoritarian and repressive nature of state power. The new Code, as Mario Sbriccoli has written, was 'dense, ample, articulated, obsessed by "the enemy of the state", ever preoccupied with being sufficiently vigilant and severe'.[174]

The family occupied little space in the new Penal Code. It was described in virile terms by Rocco as the 'primordial cell of the state's potency', its vital organ of reproduction. As such it had to be protected from those who threatened its functioning – parents who educated their children in subversive, non-Fascist ways, men who expressed 'unnatural' sexual tendencies, and all those who conspired against family morality. Rocco had a two-layered vision of the exercise of power with regard to the family. Internally, the family was a social unit bound together by the authority of its male head, with little or no space for individual rights. Externally, the family was not an independent agent but one tied strictly to its duties to the state. Thus individuals were bound to families, and families to the state.

This was a clear enunciation of a specifically Fascist view of the family. It had many points in common with that of Giovanni Gentile, examined above, only that Gentile's position was more radical in its insistence that family and state, as 'spiritually lived', could only be *one*. Rocco did not go that far, but he went far enough to stir up Catholic sensibilities regarding the 'natural' and necessarily autonomous space of Christian families.

Here we reach the nub of the matter. If in the Italian case there is no Civil Code before 1942 and very little family law in general, one major underlying explanation must be sought in the peculiar nature of the relations between Church and state. Whereas in the Russian and Turkish cases the regimes were intent on striking blows against the power of religion to regulate family life, the Fascist regime was actually marching backwards, making major concessions to the Church in return for its support. I will examine below the detailed history of the Lateran Pacts of 1929 and the specific provisions regarding marriage and schooling. Suffice it to say that compromise with the Church and paralysis over the Civil Code combined to snuff out any autonomous elaboration of Fascist family politics.[175]

Without a new Civil Code, the laws governing the conduct of Italian families under Fascism dated back to the 'Liberal' Pisanelli Code of 1865, which was itself in no small part a re-elaboration of the Napoleonic Code of 1804. Thus, far from introducing dynamism into this delicate field, the Fascist regime was reduced to being exquisitely 'passatista', to use Marinetti's scornful expression. It was able to be so because the Code of 1865 was far from ill suited to its purposes. In particular, it offered a robust, if antiquated, version of male dominion. Article 131 recognised the reciprocal duties of the married couple, but the husband chose the family's place of abode and 'managed' his wife's property. In the case of adultery, the two sexes were treated differently: whereas the husband had the right to request a separation on the mere grounds of the wife's adultery, the wife had a similar right only if her husband kept a concubine in their house, or was well known to do so elsewhere, or created 'intolerable and insulting circumstances for his wife'.

When the new Civil Code was finally introduced in 1942 (its first volume had been published in 1940), it did little to introduce a new ethos. The asymmetrical treatment of the two genders was reinforced, but the really sinister innovations concerned race rather than gender. In the 'Dichiarazione sulla razza', voted by the Fascist Grand Council in October 1938 and the law of 17 November of the same year (no. 1728), Italians had been forbidden by law to contract marriage 'with those belonging to the Hamitic, semitic or any other non-Aryan race'. State employees were forbidden to marry 'foreign women of whatever race'. These provisions were incorporated into the new Civil Code of 1942. The long hand of the racist state had arrived in Italy, liquidating once and for all the idea of shared citizens' rights.

3.2 Reconciliation

Nearly ten years before the 'Dichiarazione sulla razza', Fascism had achieved what was undoubtedly its greatest victory and one that altered its status in the eyes of very many Italian families: it put an end to the bitter dispute between Church and state that had characterised the culminating phase of the Risorgimento. After 1870, the fiercely anti-modern and anti-nationalist Church of Pius IX was left in tatters. It had been deprived of its territorial possessions and its temporal power, the land and buildings of its lay orders had been confiscated and sold off, its model of family life, which took as its starting point sacramental marriage, no longer enjoyed any legal recognition, and priests could no longer teach religious education in schools.

From very early on in the history of Fascism, as we have seen, Mussolini had turned his back on Marinetti's furious, if transient, anti-clericalism and had sought both in his private life (his church marriage to Rachele in December 1925) and in his public one to prepare the ground for a reconciliation between Church and state. He remained, as Renzo De Felice has written, 'anti-clerical to the depths of his soul',[176] but was pushed onwards by the inestimable advantage that would accrue to his regime, both nationally and internationally, if he managed to pull off the coup of reconciliation. The Church, too, had everything to gain from a Concordat. It was little concerned with the fact that it was making peace with a regime which had destroyed Italian democracy. Indeed, it theorised an 'accidentalist' approach to different political regimes, whereby it chose not to distinguish between them but to judge them in terms of their benevolence, or lack of it, towards the great project of the 'social kingdom of Christ'. Such attitudes, though perhaps advantageous in the short term, were to serve very poorly the overall reputation of the Church in the European cauldron of the 1930s and 1940s.

The negotiations between Church and state were never going to be easy. Mussolini expressed explicitly 'totalitarian' ambitions; Pius XI rebutted calmly that the social kingdom of Christ was itself a 'Catholic totalitarianism'.[177] The scene was thus set for lengthy deliberations. Alfredo Rocco referred to parliament that Pius XI had observed, as only a Pope could, that 'when one is pronouncing a soliloquy one can say what one likes, but when there is a dialogue one does indeed need to listen to the other side'.[178]

Within the Fascist ranks hostile voices made themselves heard. The most authoritative was undoubtedly Giovanni Gentile, at that time president of the Fascist Institute of Culture. In an article which appeared in the *Corriere della Sera* on 30 September 1927 Gentile denounced a possible legal pact with the Church as an 'ugly and unpresentable utopia'. In his opinion a *de facto* conciliation already existed, and that was more than sufficient. It was made up of innumerable 'courtesies' that the regime had bestowed upon the Church, such as the introduction of religious teaching in primary schools, an innovation 'that until a short time ago had seemed impossible'. Gentile was highly apprehensive of the undermining of state control – both in schools and in the 'spiritual lives' of families.[179]

Negotiations went ahead all the same. From the point of view of the family, the most contested areas were those concerning matrimony and schooling. Because of the importance that the Church accorded to the concept of marriage as a sacrament, Pius XI proved extremely insistent on the state's acceptance of the Catholic construction of family relations. On 20 January 1929, as negotiations reached their climax, Mussolini wrote a dramatic letter on the subject to King Victor Emmanuel III:

> I cannot hide from Your Majesty that the most serious obstacle to overcome in the Concordat is the clause concerning marriage. Here the state has been forced to step back significantly and almost to become extraneous to the fundamental sphere which deals with the formation and development of the family. Viewed from the other side, it seems as if His Holiness considers the question to be all-absorbing and prejudicial, so much so that the rest of the Concordat depends upon its resolution.[180]

Traces of this papal insistence and corresponding Fascist ductility are clearly visible in the final version of Article 34 of the Concordat, that which deals with marriage. It opens as follows: 'The Italian state, wishing to restore to the institution of marriage, which forms the basis of the family, the dignity which is in keeping with the Catholic traditions of its people, accords civil status [effetti civili] to the sacrament of marriage as regulated by canon law.'[181] What this meant was that for the first time in united Italy religious matrimony enjoyed the same status as civil marriage, both being recognised as valid by the state. But religious matrimony was a sacrament governed by canon law, which placed it beyond the jurisdiction of the Fascist state. Alfredo Rocco, amongst others, was well aware of the enormity of this concession. He tried to insist that during the religious ceremony itself the priest was to be obliged to read aloud articles of the Civil Code (of 1865!) regarding the rights and duties of the newly-weds in relation to the state. The proposal came to be incorporated in Article 34, but with a crucial modification: instead of the Civil Code being read *during* the religious ceremony, it was to be read immediately *afterwards*. Thus the altar was replaced by the sacristy, in a symbolic act which left little doubt about the relegation of the state.[182] Furthermore, at the end of Article 34, when dealing with the separation of a couple, the Concordat reads as follows: 'the Holy See consents that these cases are to be dealt with by the civil judiciary'. The verb 'consent' enshrined the precedence of Church over state, not that of state over family, as both Rocco and Gentile, in their different ways, would have liked.

On 11 February 1929 the Lateran Pacts were signed, Cardinal Pietro Gasparri representing the Holy See and Benito Mussolini the Italian state. The pacts consisted of three separate elements: the Treaty, the financial Convention and the Concordat. The first put an end to the 'Roman question', founded the Vatican City state and recognised the Catholic religion as the official religion of the Italian state. The second resolved all outstanding financial questions between Church and state, and compensated the Church for the damages it had suffered. The third, the Concordat, regulated in forty-five articles the conditions governing religion and the Catholic Church in Italy, granting to the Church a position of pre-eminence and particular privilege in fields such as the family and religious education.

Two days later, the Pope declared Mussolini to be 'a man whom Providence has placed in our path'.[183] The church bells pealed out all over Italy. In the world at large Catholics rejoiced and governments took stock of Mussolini's achievement. His international reputation and that of his regime were enhanced as never before, and never after.

The harmony of February 1929 was soon to be replaced, however, by the discord of May. Both sides had wanted to reach agreement, almost at any cost, but they had different agendas. The sparking point in May was provided by the question of schooling.[184] Here, so Mussolini told parliament on 13 May, the state was intransigent: 'Ours must be the task of education. The new generations must be given a religious education befitting our beliefs, but we need to integrate this education into a greater whole, we need to give to these young people a sense of virility, of potency, of conquest.' To which the Pope replied on 16 May,

> It is not for us to say whether, in order to carry through the state's work in the educational field, it is necessary, convenient or opportune for it to breed conquerors, to accustom its pupils to conquest [. . .] Unless, that is, the intention was to underline (and perhaps this really was the intention) the need to educate the younger generations to the conquest of truth and virtue, in which case we would be in perfect agreement.

The liberal economist Ernesto Rossi, who was imprisoned for many years under Fascism, commented at a later date on this sharp exchange of views,

'Walking alongside the "man sent by Providence", the Pope began to smell unpleasant whiffs of inflammable sulphur.'[185]

3.3 Mass organisations and family life

In the 1930s Mussolini's attempts to build consent through the mass organisations of his regime proved highly successful. Fascism pulled individuals, both children and adults, male and female (though much more the first than the second), out of family life, inculcating them with nationalist and military values and encouraging them to identify their peer groups and free time with the organised activities of the regime.

If we compare Fascism's achievements in this field with those of the other two cases so far examined, it is immediately apparent that the Turkish regime had far fewer and far smaller mass organisations than its counterparts in the Soviet Union and Italy. For Mustafa Kemal the traditional instruments of the state – the army, the law and the school – had to suffice in the transformation of a heretofore primitive society. By contrast, both Bolsheviks and Fascists believed strongly in the creation of new mass organisations under the control of the regime. Italian civil society, frail in many parts of the country, lost all its elements of autonomy, pluralism and dissent, and became little more than a series of assembly points for the regime's parades and activities. The Russian Communist insistence on *bytiye*, activities that were supercharged both emotionally and spiritually, as opposed to *byt*, the repetitive and mundane patterns of everyday domestic life, thus found a close correspondence in Italy. The 'secular religion' of Fascism ('la religione laica'), to which the historian Emilio Gentile has made frequent reference, was widespread, even if we cannot be sure of its precise contours.[186] Perhaps it is possible to suggest the image of a central core of Fascist belief and organisation, represented above all by the party, being flanked by a much wider panoply of organisations with varying degrees of commitment and conviction amongst their participants.

In the first ten minutes of Ettore Scola's film *Una giornata particolare* (1977) there is a memorable portrait of the members of a Roman lower middle-class family being woken up by the mother and wife (played by Sofia Loren), grabbing breakfast, pulling on their Fascist uniforms and rushing off, along with thousands of similar families, to celebrate Adolf Hitler's visit to the Italian capital.[187] They have been sucked into the regime's mobilisation of society. It is seven o'clock on the morning of Friday 6 May 1938. The family consists of father, mother and six children, all living in a cramped little flat of three bedrooms, a kitchen and a bathroom. The mother, Antonietta Tiberi, is described in the film's script as a 'woman of great patience, no longer young and of faded beauty, sacrificed on the altar of her family; she is an "exemplary wife and mother", that is to say the constant servant to her husband and children'. All the children leave for the celebration, even little Littorio, dressed up in the uniform of a 'Figlio della Lupa' (see figure 25), who is carried on his father's shoulders. At the end of the day, in which much more happens to Antonietta than to her family, husband and children return exhausted. With a slap on her bottom her husband announces, 'A day like this needs celebrating in the proper way ... and if our seventh child comes along, we'll call him Adolf.' Antonietta elbows him aside: 'I don't feel like it, not this evening.'[188]

There were a great many Fascist mass organisations, both inside and outside the party. Having already considered ONMI, I now want to concentrate briefly on two other organisations that were of particular importance for families and everyday life: the ONB (Opera Nazionale Balilla), dedicated to the organisation of youth, and the OND (Opera Nazionale Dopolavoro), responsible for the organisation of leisure time.

Let me begin with children. The ONB took its name from a Genoese boy nicknamed 'Balilla', who according to local legend had initiated his city's insurrection against the occupying Austrians in 1746. It was founded in 1926 and grew rapidly. It was divided into three basic age groups – the Balilla proper, for boys aged between eight and thirteen, the Avanguardisti, for those between fourteen and eighteen, and from 1933 onwards the Figli della Lupa, for children aged between six and eight . At first an exclusively male organisation, in 1929 it took over the ailing Fascist Party's girls' section. The Piccole Italiane became the equivalent of the Balilla and the Giovani Italiane that of the Avanguardisti.

In formal terms the ONB was a non-profit organisation (*ente morale*) with the task of providing 'assistance and moral and physical education for Italian youth'. It aimed to take over where school left off, enveloping Italian children in an uninterrupted sequence of activities, first scholastic and then recreational. Giovanni Gentile, responsible for the major Fascist reform of the Italian schooling system, wrote in 1923 that the individual child belonged to the family but also to the state. Indeed school, in his view, was the 'natural continuation of the family'. The ONB was conceived as the natural continuation of school, thus creating a seamless web in which the Italian child was to be enmeshed.[189]

This was the theory. In reality the greater part of ONB activities were dedicated to gymnastic and sporting displays, aimed at providing a spectacular backdrop to the regime's parades and celebrations. The Avanguardisti received military training of a rudimentary nature – often they were lent rifles to hold in parades and to give back at the end of the day. The Giovani Italiane were given instruction in hygiene and domestic economy, as befitted their future role as 'exemplary' mothers and wives. They also took part in gymnastic displays, much to the Vatican's fury, but were instructed by the Fascist authorities to maintain a 'natural feminine reserve'. The dominant values for all sections of the ONB were those of discipline and obedience, the eighth commandment of the organisation stating reassuringly, 'Mussolini is always right.' In 1937 the Balilla was given a new name, the Gioventù Italiana del Littorio, and inscription was made obligatory.

This last measure was impossible to enforce, but the numbers of children and youths involved in the second half of the 1930s were very considerable. The 1937 statistics refer to a total of more than six million members, of which the great majority, both male and female, were from eight to thirteen years old – 2,478,768 Balilla and 2,130,530 Piccole Italiane.[190] The comparison with Nazi organisations is instructive: the Jungvolk was for those aged between ten and fourteen and the Hitlerjugend for those between fourteen and eighteen, while the regime made no special provision for children of younger age. The Figli della Lupa, by contrast, welcomed children from the age of six upwards. These differences in membership account in no small part for the fact that the military preparation of German male youths was far superior to that of their Italian counterparts, their oath of loyalty being of blood-curdling quality: 'Live faithfully, fight bravely, die laughing.'[191]

There can be little doubt that the successive waves of youth organisation, directed at both genders and different age groups, made a considerable impact upon the everyday life of Italian families. In the ongoing battle between family time and time accorded to the regime, the ONB, under its thuggish but dynamic leader Renato Ricci, made a multifaceted attempt to draw the younger generations closer to itself. In June 1935 the regime instituted the 'Fascist Saturday': at one o'clock every Saturday employees in both the private and the public sector were to stop working, as the afternoon was to be dedicated to party-organised activities – educational, recreational and paramilitary. Special attention was to be paid to youth, the third Saturday of every month being specifically dedicated to youth activities. The regime's decision to create the Figli della Lupa for six- to eight-year-olds was another step in the same direction, signalling as it did the regime's interest in an age group usually reserved for family care or for play groups organised by nuns.

It was also true that the ONB offered a sociality outside the home or the school that was often alluring, especially to girls accustomed to close familial control. Each age group had its own uniform, which families had to purchase and mothers to iron. As always in Italy, clothes were the object of close attention. An editorial in the suitably named magazine *Mammina* complained that

fig. 26 A group of Giovani Italiane in uniform, with a baby wearing a Fascist hat, 1930s.

the skirts of the Piccole Italiane contained too many pleats, which made them hard to iron.[192] Much of the ONB's activity was tedious – gymnastic displays involving a lot of waiting around, parades regularly punctuated by bombastic speeches – but it was a good way to get out, even liberating in its own regimented way. The modernist temple of the ONB was the Foro Mussolini in Rome, a huge sporting complex complete with playing fields and swimming pools, dormitories and meeting rooms, as well as a new Advanced School for Physical Training. Ricci wanted to erect a bronze statue symbolising Fascism there, eighty-six metres high with two lifts, one in each leg, and a panoramic balcony on its head. Only the head, one foot and a knee were ever cast.[193]

The ONB was not all gymnastic displays and outsized statues. For the older children there were also camps in the mountains, where outdoor life, fervent nationalism and religious values happily combined. A sermon at Mass in one of these Avanguardisti camps was reported as follows: 'Every person in the camp lifts his thoughts and soul towards God so that He may illuminate in glory and fortify in the sun the heroic youth of Mussolini and of Fascist Italy. Fidelity to their forefathers' beliefs and to their superb, self-imposed discipline will enable them to construct their future and that of the world.'[194]

The organisation was also principally responsible for one of the most socially spectacular of the regime's activities – its seaside 'colonie'. At first Ricci conceived of these as holidays targeting poor and unhealthy children, tuberculosis and typhoid being the major killers. The pilot scheme involved 50,000 'boys enrolled in the ONB who were poor and thin', but only 4,000 girls in the same condition.[195] The scheme was a resounding success, not least in propaganda terms at an international level. By 1939 the *colonie* had become a mass phenomenon, with more than 800,000 children (at least according to the regime's statistics) enjoying a month's holiday at the seaside. The Istituto Luce's newsreels of thousands of little Italians, marching along the beach in the morning to pay homage to the national flag and then rushing into the water for their first dip of the day, became one of the regime's most famous and ingratiating images.[196]

In the Fascist case, therefore, it is possible to suggest that the inherent tension between the regime and families over the organisation of children's 'spare' time never reached boiling point, not at least until the last years of the war. This was not the case, as we shall see, for Nazism or Stalinism. Fascism managed to project a predominantly welfare-oriented, even homely view of its activities in this key area, targeted for the most part at primary school children, who were likely to be more sweet than military. In June 1930, when the Roman sections of the Giovani Italiane (fourteen- to eighteen-year-olds) assembled in one of the capital's theatres, the girls' mothers decided to come along as well. The then secretary of the Fascist Party, Augusto Turati, was highly embarrassed. He asked pardon for not having invited the mothers and reassured them that although their daughters were wearing uniforms they were not real uniforms but only charming sportswear, with 'truly nothing militaristic or squadristic about it'.[197] This was fine at one level, that of calming the apprehension of families, especially mothers, but it was not at another, the forging of the new character of the Italian nation. Mussolini wrote about this in 1938, when he declared his desire for the rapid transformation of Italians who were 'easy-going, disordered, amusing, given to playing the mandolin' into citizen-soldiers of a nation which was 'regimented, solid, silent and powerful'. ONB fitted this bill only in small part, as the disastrous years of 1940–3 were to show.[198]

Running parallel with the ONB was the Opera Nazionale Dopolavoro (OND), founded in 1925. Its brief was that of adult leisure-time activities, especially those of male workers and clerks after they had clocked off at the end of the working day (thus the name 'dopolavoro'). Like the ONB, the organisation was to reach vast proportions by the end of the 1930s, with some four million members. Workers outnumbered clerks by more than two to one.

fig. 27 Three young girls giving the Fascist salute at the entrance arch to a seaside *colonia* in Marina di Pietrasanta, Tuscany, 1930s. The words of Mussolini inscribed on the arch proclaim, 'You are life's dawn, the fatherland's hope, above all the army of tomorrow.'

The OND offered a great range of activities, on the one hand long-standing pursuits such as playing bowls, belonging to a choral society or taking part in traditional dancing, and on the other the activities of modern mass culture – sporting competitions, listening to the radio at the local headquarters, organising day trips out of the cities or watching film and theatre performances. The Fascists had forcibly taken over – that is, when they had not burned down – the hundreds of buildings which had previously housed the associations of the Italian working-class movement, and in the 1930s they constructed many more. The *dopolavoro* facilities for railway workers, for instance, with their showers and canteens, meeting rooms and billiard tables, boasted 274 branches and 134,000 members by the end of the 1930s. With its full-time salaried staff of 700 and more than 100,000 volunteers, mainly from the lower middle classes, the OND, like the ONB, was well equipped to permeate Italian society.[199]

Of course it too had failings and limits. The organisation was very weak in the rural south, as was Fascism as a whole. In 1934 the local Fascist secretary in the province of Matera in Basilicata, the region Mussolini had thanked in 1927 for having contributed most to the Italian birth rate, reported that 'nothing, absolutely nothing, had been done to give local people a tangible sign of the fascist era'.[200] There had been the brief apparition of one of the OND's much-vaunted touring theatre companies, the so-called Thespian Cars (there were also the Lyrical Cars founded in 1930 for operatic performances). The Cars made a great impression with their scores of actors and special effects – starry nights, rainfall, waves, and so on.[201] By 1933–4 the OND was spending over a fifth of its annual budget on the Thespian and Lyrical Cars, and by 1936, according to the regime's statistics, they were reaching about a million spectators a year, a very high number by any standards. But performances were concentrated in the cities and towns. They came and went, and were a poor substitute for a stable network of circles and clubs.

It was also true that the OND did not, by and large, attract women or families. It was far more natural for men to stay on at the club after work, to play cards or billiards, listen to the radio, or else take part in some rowdy discussion concerning the events of the day. Women, if they were not women workers, were at home, closely tied into kinship and neighbourhood networks. They were far more likely to be involved with the parish and with Catholic Action than with the OND.

There was, however, one spectacular exception to this general picture, a moment when the mainly separate social networks of husbands and wives came together for a very particular family outing. In 1932 the regime instituted the so-called 'popular trains' (*treni popolari*), with the aim of giving families the possibility of visiting, often for the first time in their lives, the Mediterranean, or one or other of Italy's maritime cities. The trains had only third-class carriages with wooden seats, their passengers enjoying a 70 per cent discount on the normal price of the ticket. The descriptions that have come down to us communicate the exceptionality of these expeditions, so different from the routines of working-class and petty bourgeois family life. The journeys conveyed an innate sense of liberty rather than of regimentation. The trains left at midnight on Saturday from the great stations of the centre-north, and had to be back twenty-four hours later so that employees could be punctually at work on Monday morning. The favourite destinations were San Remo on one side of the peninsula and Riccione on the other, as well as Venice, Naples and Bari.

In spite of a rather sweet-toothed approach, the journalist Gian Franco Venè has left us a vivid and convincing description of the preparations for these outings, which is revealing not just of the micro-rituals of family life in Italy in the 1930s but also of its inherent gender division of labour:

[On Saturday afternoon] the children were kept in bed, with the daylight shut out by the curtains, faithful to their promise to keep their eyes firmly shut ('otherwise, we're not going'). While mothers ironed the clothes for the journey and attended to many other tasks, fathers sat at the kitchen table, carefully laying out the tickets for the journey as if they were precious documents, reading the regulations point by point and driving their wives to distraction with their constant remonstrations: 'Don't forget the coffee thermos' [. . .] The bread rolls with omelette fillings, wrapped up in transparent greaseproof paper, were laid out on the table next to the bottles of fizzy water. To get out of the house a few minutes before midnight, with the few necessary items of luggage for the journey, was an undertaking which seemed to deny the laws of nature. Before getting on the tram to the station, the children, severely overexcited because they had finally fully woken up, complained that they needed a lavatory desperately. They were reprimanded in no uncertain terms, as their mothers, before shutting the door of the house, had made them swear that they would not need a lavatory: 'Listen carefully, on the train there's no possibility of going, you've been warned' [. . .] The novelty of the journey, the changing landscape, the confusion of day with night, the long distances involved, even the inevitable exhaustion, all signified a memorable holiday for a people who had no notion of what holidays were.[202]

The *treni popolari* lasted for eight years, being cancelled definitively in the first week of September 1939. Even with the 70 per cent reduction in the standard price of tickets, many working-class families could not afford such expeditions. The trains remained in popular memory, as Venè writes, as 'an adventure halfway between the licit and the permissive',[203] a strange and original invention of the regime.

3.4 Propaganda and mass culture

Nowhere was the regime more able than in the realm of propaganda. As we have seen, Mussolini and other major Fascist figures were experts in the art of invention, exaggeration and bald-faced lying. In the 1930s, that 'low dishonest decade' as Auden famously called it, such talents served them very well.[204] In 1933 Joseph Goebbels, the new Nazi Minister for Propaganda, visited Italy to explain the ways in which his ministry intended to intervene in mass culture. Galeazzo Ciano, Edda Mussolini's husband, became Minister for Press and Propaganda in the critical years of 1934–6, and in May 1937 the Ministry for Popular Culture was founded. Throughout the second half of the 1930s Nazis and Fascists vied with each other in their manipulative control of the complex societies they had come to dominate.

Fascist propaganda took much from Futurism's dynamism and violent sense of purpose, as well as its explosive symbiosis of words and images. In its first decade, the regime placed the emphasis on a new nationalist sense of purpose – the reclamation of the Pontine Marshes ('bonifica' was a key Fascist word, applicable in many contexts), the construction of 'new cities', as well as modern residential and administrative suburbs, the 'battle for grain', and the supposed colonisation of the great estates of the southern countryside. In the second decade, imperial themes came to dominate: conquest and subjugation, Italy's defiant stand against the League of Nations, and the necessary living space for the Italian race. In the last years, and with fading success, anti-semitism and the semi-militarisation of society in the face of war took priority.[205]

Dominating all these campaigns was the figure of the Duce himself. Mussolini's was the first personality cult of the West, using both traditional and modern instruments of communication – newspapers and weeklies of every sort, but also the unforgettable images and bombastic commentary of the newsreels of the Istituto Luce, taken under public control in 1925. As audiences grew in the 1930s – by 1942 there were 2,876 cinemas in Italy – it was obligatory for every feature film to be preceded by a Fascist newsreel.[206] Of increasing importance, too, was the radio. In Mario Biazzi's extraordinary picture *Ascoltazione del discorso del Duce* (Listening to a Talk by the Duce, *c.* 1939), painted for the Premio Cremona (a painting competition organised by leading

Fascist, Roberto Farinacci the bombastic opponent of Mario Sironi's modernism), an extended family of Cremonese landless labourers – ten in all, depicted more as troglodytes than humans, shorn of any possessions, bare-footed and dressed only in black or brown frocks – listens to a radio talk by the Duce (plate 5). Yet there is no radio; simply, in the top right-hand corner of the picture, Mussolini's enormous stern and wise face.[207] By 1939 the number of radio licences in Italy had reached one million, though the corresponding figure in Great Britain was nine million and in Germany thirteen million.

The cult of the Duce was primarily public, but it entered cleverly into homes and the private sphere. If we return for a moment to Scola's film *Una giornata particolare*, with its innate sensibility of the intimate sphere, we find the mother-figure, Antonietta, proudly displaying her own album of Mussolini photographs. The captions are written out badly in her childish handwriting: 'Pomezia, August 1937, 16th year of the regime. Mussolini: "War befits a man as maternity does a woman." '[208] Often the simplest instruments of everyday life bore the imprint of the regime. Primary school notebooks, for instance, boasted dynamic designs on their covers, full of colour and movement, often dedicated to an elementary and highly effective aestheticisation of war.[209]

The 1930s was a decade in which mass culture developed many new forms. The old, mainly male pastimes – playing cards or bowls, going fishing with friends, frequenting the *osteria* – gave way, at least in the cities, to more gender-mixed and extensive leisure pursuits – dancing, sport, the cinema, popular music. Considerable tensions came to the fore: between tradition and modernity, repression and permissiveness, one generation and the next. Fascism itself was caught up in these tides of change. On the one hand it took pride in distinguishing itself from the Church's unyielding traditionalism and phobic pre-occupation with sexual matters. Was the regime not the very epitome of modernity, with its celebration of fitness and speed, machines and aviation, gymnastics and competitive sport?[210] The list of sporting triumphs of the 1930s was a long one – at the Olympics, on the football field (with Italy world champions in both 1934 and 1938) and in the boxing ring (Primo Carnera briefly became world heavyweight champion in 1935).[211] But beneath this shining, modern surface lay a view of the family which was heavily subordinate to traditional Catholicism and in no sense an autonomous elaboration by the regime. Individual rights fared no better. Mussolini, Gentile and other leading Fascists repeatedly asserted their 'anti-individualistic' conception of power: the individual had few or no rights and existed only in so far as his or her interests coincided with those of the state. So authoritarian a view clashed stridently with the individualism, freedom and consumerism which dominated modern cultural trends of the 1930s and American mass culture in particular. Fascism, it could be said, was a two-layered phenomenon: deliciously modern on the surface, highly traditional and repressive underneath.

How families reacted to this mixture depended, of course, on the infinite number of variables which went to make up each individual family culture. As a broad generalisation, it is possible to say that the tension between modernity and tradition found its most vivid expression in a constant conflict between generations, above all in the cities. Traditionally minded parents were Fascism's best friends in terms of control and discipline, but often its worst enemies with respect to the regime's violent ambitions.

The running battles within families often concerned the imposition and violation of limits and boundaries. Daughters were the prime target. How long a skirt should be, whether to wear a skirt or shorts for athletics, what time to be home, smoking and make-up, were all objects of contention. So too were hairstyles. American films totally dominated the Italian market in the 1930s – hardly the culture of 'totalitariansim' – and their stars became the object of adoration and imitation. Jean Harlow, with her platinum blond hair and exuberant sexuality, was perhaps the best known and most admired.[212]

If we return briefly to the areas of the country that we examined in the first part of this chapter – the working-class neighbourhoods of the industrial cities of the north and the countryside near Florence cultivated by sharecropping families – we can see how much the regime managed to change and how much it left untouched. In the peripheries of the northern cities the tight-knit communities of workers and their families, deprived of their civil and political liberties, began to fall apart. Fascism entered these quarters armed with truncheons but also with more subtle weapons for winning over the majority of the population. In particular, young male workers were seduced by the new possibilities of mobility and leisure-time consumption, by the sporting achievements of the regime, by membership of the Fascist trade unions and by the chance to thumb their noses at their doctrinaire and defeated fathers. Under Fascism there was a growing tendency for women to give up working after marriage and maternity. As for their families, welfare provisions were never as extensive as the authorities made out, though the beginnings of social insurance schemes and leisure-time activities certainly softened the contours of the regime. The workers who had been caught up in the epic moments of 1919–20 were reduced to symbolic gestures of defiance – wearing red braces on May Day or scribbling graffiti in the toilets of the great FIAT works of Lingotto and Mirafiori in Turin. But many of them were still ready to contest Mussolini when he opened FIAT Mirafiori in 1939.[213] Those with hot heads and a lot of courage (both old and young) slipped away to fight in the Spanish Civil War.

Amongst the sharecropping families of Tuscany, the influence of the regime was much less felt. There were no shortage of new institutions designed to control agricultural production and population, but the agricultural calendar, with its recurrent seasonal obligations, imposed its own priorities and logic. There was little chance or desire to be caught up in the regime's mass organisations and mobilisations. On the contrary: families viewed with considerable hostility the Fascist 'battle for grain', with its enforced consignments to state granaries. And the Fascist Sharecroppers' Charter of 1935 remained a dead letter, like so much else in the regime.

For the rest, life went on as usual. In Fernanda Caroti's diary from San Gersolè, Fascism receives only occasional and marginal reference – the new songs of the regime sung by the children, the school visit to the new Casa del Fascio, the painting of an approximate 'fascio' on the crupper of a calf which had won a prize and was being taken into the city.[214] The Caroti were one of those families that were very traditional, profoundly Catholic, sympathetic to the regime but not at all in synchrony with its violent propaganda.

We catch a glimpse of the old meeting the new on the road to Florence in May 1939. Fernanda and her friends have gone to visit relatives at Pozzolatico, a tiny huddle of houses a few kilometres from the Tuscan capital. For the sharecropping girls it is a major expedition. On the way they meet three girls, 'all with tinted hair, if you got close to them you could smell the perfume, but it was more of a stink than anything else, seeing how much they'd sprayed on; and they gave themselves such airs and graces'. Fernanda is adamant in her disdain, but her friend Bianca comments, 'Even the poorest girl in Florence dresses up more than we do.'[215] In this little story, rejection of, and longing for, the attributes of modernity seem to go hand in hand. It serves also to remind us of the enduring remoteness of Italian rural life, even at the gates of Florence in the late 1930s.

4. Apotheosis and disaster

4.1 The Giornata della Fede

The regime reached the height of consent and support amongst the Italian populace in the years 1935–6. The invasion of Ethiopia in October 1935 was an act in flagrant contradiction of the rules of the League of Nations, of which Italy was a founding member. It was followed by the ineffectual sanctions imposed by the League, which allowed Mussolini to present to Italian public opinion the image of Italy as the victim of an international plot.

The ensuing indignation in Italy was very widespread and in part spontaneous. In the realm of family politics it led to one of the regime's most interesting and symbolically charged initiatives – the Giornata della Fede (Wedding Ring Day) of 18 December 1935. From early that morning long queues of women formed at the Vittoriano, the monument to Italy's first king and site of the tomb of the Unknown Warrior in Rome. They were there to offer their gold wedding rings to be melted down to raise funds for the war effort, receiving in return a simple ring of base metal. Dressed all in black, hundreds of mothers and widows of those who had died in the Great War had assembled on the white marble steps of the Vittoriano, to underscore the links between their sacrifices and the new imperial adventure. The choirs of the OND and the band of the Carabinieri took up flanking positions. Queen Elena of Savoy was the first to offer her own wedding ring and that of her husband. In the afternoon of the same day Rachele Mussolini and her daughter Edda appeared, almost unheralded, to donate their marriage rings and receive the adulation of the Roman crowds. All over the country similar events took place. Mussolini himself was in the Pontine Marshes, laying the first stone for the new town of Pontinia. In many branches of the OND, silver and gold sporting and hunting trophies were willingly donated. The percentage of Italian women who actually wore the regime's metallic rings was never made known, but it was clear that the initiative had made a deep impact, not only in Italy. The German ambassador to Rome, Ulrich von Hassell, wrote to Berlin that day,

Some weeks ago Mussolini told me that the world has no idea of the magnitude of the sacrifices he is able to ask of his own people. Today he has given a powerful demonstration of this grand claim [. . .] Whichever way you look at it, the Giornata della Fede (where 'fede' means not just wedding ring but also conviction, fidelity, faith!) shows that Mussolini holds his people in the palm of his hand.[216]

The Giornata is of considerable interest, not just for its extraordinary success and theatrical presentation but because it highlights some of the most delicate issues of Fascist family politics. The first of these was the tug of war over marriage between regime and Church. The negotiations at the time of the Concordat had already revealed how contested an area this was. It might therefore have been suspected that the melting down of women's wedding rings, the most precious symbol of the sacramental nature of Catholic marriage, would have aroused furious objections from within the Church. Nothing of the sort happened. Instead, a great wave of enthusiasm for both the regime and the war swept through *all* ranks of the Church. In December 1935, in the crowded cathedral of Campobasso, Monsignor Alberto Romita explained, with an extraordinary sleight of hand, how precious was the wedding ring and how

fig. 28 The Giornata della Fede (Wedding Ring Day), Rome, 18 December 1935. A woman consigns her gold wedding ring to the bronze brazier in front of the Vittoriano.

much, therefore, God would appreciate its sacrifice: 'Only persons educated in the Catholic faith [. . .] consider marriage to be a divine institution; we have no desire for, or knowledge of, divorce, a concept realised by northern and Protestant peoples. And it is precisely for these reasons that your sacrifice is so appreciated by God and by the Fatherland.'[217]

How is the fervent support of the clergy for the Ethiopian expedition to be explained? In the documents of the time, a number of linked themes predominate: conversion of the native population to the Catholic faith, the fight against slavery, Italy's civilising mission. But what makes the clergy's behaviour even more astonishing is that the Vatican itself had severe doubts about supporting the war. At first Pius XI made these doubts public. On 27 August 1935, speaking at an international congress of two thousand nurses from more than twenty countries, he condemned the Ethiopian invasion as an 'unjust war'. Later on, he chose silence as the best policy. But the Vatican's efforts to calm the waters seem to have been swept away by a tide of religious nationalism which left Mussolini surprised and grateful. Of the very few discordant voices, one from within the Vatican was that of Monsignor Domenico Tardini, a close adviser of the Pope. In the notes Tardini prepared for the Pope on 1 December 1935 he expressed all his anguish at Fascism's successful seduction of the Italian clergy by imperial war:

> And the clergy? They are the greatest disaster. The clergy should be calm, disciplined and obedient to the requests of the fatherland; so much is clear. But instead on this occasion they are tumultuous, beside themselves with excitement, warmongers. If only the bishops were to keep their heads, but far from it. They are more verbose, more excited, more . . . unbalanced than all the others. They offer up all sorts of objects of pure gold or silver: rings, chains, crucifixes, watches, sterling gold coins. And they talk of civilisation, of religion, of our mission in Africa [. . .] Meanwhile Italy is getting ready to use heavy artillery and machine guns on thousands and thousands of Ethiopians, guilty only of wanting to defend their homes.[218]

The second theme in family politics highlighted by the Ethiopian invasion (the first being the regime's successful appropriation of the wedding ring, the most precious symbol of Catholic family life, and the clergy's fervid support for such an appropriation) is the definition of the relationship between state and family in times of war. The bellicose enthusiasm of much of the urban population encouraged Mussolini to reassert the primacy of the state over the family. Gentile's rendering of 1931 – that family and state, as 'spiritually lived', could only be one – acquired new force. Mussolini himself, in a speech of 7 March 1936, thanked Italian women for having made of 'each and every Italian family a fortress in which to resist the sanctions of the League of Nations'.[219] The recalcitrant Italian family had at last been militarised, at least on a metaphorical level.

The invasion of Ethiopia, and the more or less simultaneous Italian Fascist support for Francisco Franco, were, however, misleading preambles. They were only very partial mobilisations of the population which left the vast majority of Italians as enthusiastic spectators, consumers of propaganda, but not soldiers. The war was a fiction. At the cinema, families could view it from afar, on the Istituto Luce's newsreels before the main feature film. Less than five years later, when the war became total, and total the regime's collapse, the underlying contradiction between the aggressive state and a mainly peace-loving and impoverished population became very clear.

In 1935, while the clergy were busy blessing rings, the young anti-Fascist writer and painter Carlo Levi was exiled to the village of 'Gagliano' in the deep south. There the peasants described to him their attitude to the state: 'There are hailstorms, landslides, droughts, malaria, and . . . the State. These are inescapable evils; such there always have been and there always will be. They make us kill off our goats, they carry away our furniture, and now they're going to send us to the wars. Such is life!'[220] Such observations seem to ring far truer than the German ambassador's enthusiastic view, based on narrow Roman experience, that Mussolini had his people in the palm of his hand. On the contrary: Italian families, especially in rural areas, were by and large sceptical with regards to the state and loath to be regimented, especially after the horrors of the Great War. Time and again, the regime's pretensions to totalitarianism, spiritual or otherwise, would founder on family interests and strategies.

4.2 'La guerra è bella . . .'

On 22 December 1935, just four days after the Giornata della Fede, the Italian air force responded to a series of peremptory telegrams from Mussolini by intensifying its indiscriminate use of toxic gas on the Ethiopian population. This was only one of the atrocities committed by Fascist troops. Another was the massacre in Addis Ababa in February 1937. After two young Eritreans had tried to assassinate Marshal Rodolfo Graziani a terrible reprisal took place in the Ethiopian capital, with mass shootings, homes set alight indiscriminately and native families burned to death. The estimates of the dead vary widely from 1,400 to 6,000 in the capital city alone. These were human-rights crimes for which no one was ever called to account. Outside the capital, the Coptic Christian monastery of Debre Libanos, dating back to the thirteenth century, was suspected of having harboured the young Eritreans. On 21 May 1937, the monks, some 297 in all, were shot dead on Graziani's orders. Five days later, not yet satisfied, he ordered the 129 young deacons of the monastery to be shot as well.[221]

Ethiopia was also the occasion for the reappearance of Marinetti the soldier. Aged fifty-nine, fatter than before but still in good physical shape, he volunteered for the war and received the rank of captain directly from Mussolini. He came under fire in the first battle of Tembien and commemorated his experiences in his long, grotesque *Poema africano della divisione '28 ottobre'.*[222] Earlier, in the newspaper *La Stampa*, he had sung the praises of war, which remained for him the 'only hygiene of the world':

War is beautiful because thanks to gas masks, terror-inducing megaphones, flame-throwers, and small tanks man's dominion over the subject is proven. War is beautiful because it ushers in the dreamt-of metallization of the human body. War is beautiful because it enriches a meadow in bloom by adding the fiery orchids of machine-guns. War is beautiful because it combines rifle-fire, barrages of bullets, lulls in the firing, and the scents and smells of putrescence into a symphony. War is beautiful because it creates fresh architectures such as those of the large tank, geometrical flying formations, spirals of smoke rising from burning villages, and much else besides.[223]

The conquest of Ethiopia marked a further stage in the development of Italian racism in Africa. In 1936 many Fascist military personnel, such as Marshal Graziani, who had organised the earlier concentration and extermination of Bedouin families in Cyrenaica, were the same as five years earlier. Much else had changed. At an international level, Hitler's coming to power and the first pieces of Nazi legislation against the Jews exercised a profound influence upon Italian policy. From now on, pseudo-scientific theories of the hierarchy of races occupied the forefront of Fascist discussion and legislation. The Fascist minister Giuseppe Bottai offered a succinct formulation of rampant Italian racism. It was only natural, he wrote, that the Duce, having first concentrated upon the *quantitative* aspects of the population question, should next pass to *qualitative* issues. With the declaration of Empire, 'the Italian race has been brought into contact with other races and must therefore be defended against dangerous contaminations of blood'.[224]

At its outset the Ethiopian campaign had been marked by rather different attitudes, easily recognisable in the catalogue of Fascist and Futurist masculinities. The indigenous black female population was there to be taken, the natural prey of war. The popular Roman song 'Faccetta nera' (1935) was much criticised by the regime's ideologues for its playful tone and strong hints of mixed-race copulation. The men at the front sent thousands of postcard pictures of naked black women home to brothers and male friends. Soon much more rigid racist attitudes were imposed, as the regime tried once again to rein in and redirect Fascist male sexuality.

In the context of family politics in Italian East Africa, two issues in particular – the 'madamato' and the fate of the so-called half-breed (*meticcio*) children and adults – need to be examined. The *madamato* was the custom by which an Italian colonial male in East Africa would take an indigenous woman as concubine and domestic servant during his period of service in the colony. The practice had become widespread in the older Italian colonies, especially Eritrea. The quality of these relations varied greatly, but sometimes bonds of affection were formed and children recognised. The practice of *madamato* also coincided, though not in all respects, with Coptic Christian traditions which allowed for the possibility of marriage for a fixed period of time.

After the conquest of Ethiopia such practices were severely forbidden. The Fascist racist legislation of 1937 imposed prison sentences of between one and five years for white males who were found to be 'biologically guilty'. The Minister for the Colonies, Alessandro Lessona, wrote to Graziani: 'once it was said that the Italian colonies were a good place for bachelors. Now in the Fascist era they will be for married couples.'[225] This proved to be yet another unsubstantiated Fascist projection. In reality, the Italian population in East Africa was dominated by single, male workers. The regime catered to their sexual needs by offering the services of rotating state brothels, employing only white women. When these proved insufficient, native women were provided instead.

The sordidness of these solutions is worth reflecting upon. Turning its back on any possibility of affective relations between Italian men and African women, or even the creation of a colonial patriarchy, the regime had only prostitution to offer as an alternative, and 'mixed-race' prostitution at that. Even in the regime's own terms, this was a spectacular failure, and was crowned by the regime's incapacity to create stable farming families. By the end of 1940 the Fascists had settled on the land fewer than five hundred Italians, and of these only two hundred had brought their wives with them.[226]

The second issue, that of mixed-blood adults and offspring, was another human disaster. Gradually but persistently the discrimination and persecution of the Empire's mixed-blood inhabitants increased. From 1938 onwards all marriages between them and members of the 'dominant race' were prohibited. Law no. 822 of 1940 prohibited Italian parents from recognising or even maintaining their 'meticcio' children, who from then on were classed indiscriminately as colonial subjects. They were at great risk of being rejected by both Italian and indigenous communities, and the orphanages of the Catholic missionaries were full of such abandoned children.

4.3 Anti-semitism

What was happening in the Empire and developments in Italy now took the same sinister direction, the persecution and expulsion of Jews from the civil life of the nation mirroring the racially segregated world of Italian Oriental Africa. The alien 'other' had been identified, both at home and abroad. Italian Jews were a tiny percentage of the population as a whole, some 0.1 per cent, and numbered not more than 47,000 in 1938.[227] But they were a significant presence in the country, especially in its cultural and professional life. They had gained civil and political rights during the Risorgimento, and had served the new nation faithfully in its early decades and during the First World War.

The year 1938 was one of disaster and tragedy for European Jewry. On 21 January Rumania introduced anti-semitic legislation; on 5 March Hungary announced it would do the same. The Germans occupied Austria on 12 March, bringing with them the certainty of further persecution for Vienna's large Jewish population. The night of 9–10 November was *Kristallnacht* in Germany and Austria. As shop windows were smashed and synagogues burned, Jews were beaten and killed in the streets, and 25,000 were deported to the camps.

It is in this context that we must place Italian racist declarations and laws. In July 1938, a document entitled 'Il fascismo e i problemi di razza' was published. It came to be known as the 'Manifesto degli scienziati razzisti' and was eventually signed by 1,800 Italian intellectuals and scientists. It was an evil hotchpotch. Article 3 stated that the 'concept of race is purely biological'. Article 7 said that it was time for the 'Italians to proclaim themselves frankly racist'. They were not to mix their blood with that of the semitic and Hamite races; the idea of a common Mediterranean race was to be rejected absolutely. Article 9 stated baldly that the Jews did not belong to the Italian race. They were the only population 'which has never been assimilated in Italy because it is composed of racial elements which are not European'.[228]

A few weeks later, on 5 August 1938, the fortnightly magazine *La difesa della razza* was launched. Its infamous first cover showed a sword descending to separate the Jewish man (with suitable nose) and negroid woman (with suitable lips) from the noble (Roman) Italian.

On 1–2 September 1938 the first wave of anti-semitic legislation was passed. Amongst other measures, all Jewish children were to be expelled from state schools and universities, as were Jewish teachers. All foreign Jews who had sought refuge in Italy after 1918 were ordered to leave the country. Further measures followed between 7 and 10 November: the legal definition of 'belonging to the Jewish race' was finalised, while marriage between 'Aryan Italians' and other races was forbidden. Jewish state employees were sacked and property rights limited. Between 1938 and 1942 the general conditions of Italian Jews steadily declined.

All this came as a profound shock to Italian Jewish families. In spite of their centuries-old persecution by the Church, Italian Jews had felt themselves to be safer in Italy than in many other parts of Europe and were profoundly assimilated. Vittorio Foa, who was to be arrested at the age of twenty-five for anti-Fascist activities and condemned to fifteen years' imprisonment, recalled in his splendid memoirs that at the time he considered the anti-semitic campaign to be 'a betrayal of the tradition of tolerance, liberty and equality which had marked out the Italian nation in the Risorgimento'.[229] Although his grandfather had been the chief rabbi of Turin, Foa's own family of origin was far

fig. 29 The cover of the first issue of *La difesa della razza*, published on 5 August 1938.

from deeply religious. The family was celebrated through religion, not religion through the family: 'at home there certainly was a Jewish religiosity, but it had an entirely family quality; its attention to ritual did not presuppose individual faith but only a profound sense of family unity'.[230] When the racial laws were enforced in 1938, Foa's brother and sister, urged on by him from prison,

emigrated to the United States. His parents, despite all his entreaties, stayed
behind to be close to him. They all survived the war.

The 1938 laws were the beginning of a process which I cannot analyse in
detail here, but which would reach its climax in October 1943, when the Jews
of the Roman Ghetto were rounded up by the SS and deported to extermination camps. As Michele Sarfatti has written, 'During the twenty years of
Fascism, the Jews had to witness first the limitation and then the cancellation
of their equality as a group with other citizens, followed by the gradual elimination of other rights – to state education, to work, to be Italian residents, in
the end to existence itself.'[231] Some 7,700–7,900 Italian Jews were killed in one
way or another during the years of world conflict.

4.4 The war

With the outbreak of the Second World War in September 1939, and Italy's
entry into it in 1940, all the pretence and lies, propaganda and invention which
had sustained the Fascist regime came crashing down. Despite the oceanic
crowds which greeted Mussolini's declaration of war, the great majority of
Italian families did not desire it, and their menfolk had no wish to take up
arms. The military camps of the Avanguardisti, with their ancient rifles, were
of little use for what was to come. The army was woefully unprepared and
Mussolini was no Mustafa Kemal. By early 1943 the Italian armed forces had
suffered one disaster after another, the major cities had been bombarded, and
the long wave of pro-Fascist public opinion, so strong in the mid-1930s, had
ebbed away. On 10 July 1943 the Allies invaded Sicily. In a memorable short
story, Leonardo Sciascia described the reactions of the Italian soldiers and
inhabitants of one Sicilian village:

Meanwhile the soldiers didn't know what to do. To guard against all eventu-
alities, they went round in search of civilian clothes. They knocked hesitantly
at the doors, asking timidly if there was anything available. They were happy
to settle for a pair of trousers or a shirt; given how hot it was, they had no
need of jackets. The women pulled out old and new clothes from chests and
wardrobes, for in the forefront of their minds were their own sons and
husbands and brothers, and they hoped that, wherever they might be, they
would be treated with corresponding compassion. But it was easy enough, all
the same, to sniff out those who had just abandoned military uniform,
because of the unmistakable sickly-sweet smell of naphthalene which
emanated from their new attire.[232]

The news of the Allied invasion was brought by a travelling salesman who had slipped out of Licata at dawn:

> He had managed to get back home by walking for some of the way and hitching a lift on an army lorry for the rest. Stupefied, even hallucinated, he described what he had seen – an armada of boats filling the sea for as far as the eye could see. 'That cuckold! How did he think he could possibly win?' Of those who listened to his tale, almost all smiled with approval; only a fanatic or two, for there were still some around, pretended not to have understood at whom the insult was directed.[233]

Initially, Filippo Tommaso Marinetti had greeted the war with enthusiasm, as an occasion for the rediscovery of his subversive youth. He promoted the republication of his infamous *Come si seducono le donne*,[234] only to discover that Fascism's 'new man' had by now little in common with the irreverent eroticism of the first wave of Futurism. Alessandro Pavolini, the Minister for Popular Culture, ordered the immediate confiscation of all copies of the booklet, much to Marinetti's fury.[235]

Undaunted, Marinetti volunteered at the age of sixty-six to go to the Russian front and was accorded the rank of lieutenant colonel. There is an old and out-of-focus photograph of him, serious and rather shrunken, at Verona railway station in July 1942, waiting to leave for the front. He is surrounded by his three beautiful daughters, but he looks more like their grandfather than their father. Benedetta is sitting down, impeccably turned out in a polka-dot dress. With them is Benedetta's brother, Alberto Cappa, the beloved uncle of the three girls and the person who had first introduced Marinetti to Benedetta.

Alberto, nicknamed 'Alto' because he was so tall, was a sweet man, a scholar and liberal anti-Fascist, who none the less felt in 1942 that he had to fight for his country. He volunteered with the Alpine regiment from Cuneo and, like so many other of its members, did not survive the Russian campaign. Marinetti did, but there was little in his behaviour and writing which corresponded to his elation at the time of the African war of six years earlier. One of his companions, the doctor and Futurist Emilio Buccafusca, recounted that 'this time it was I who did all the talking [...] He listened and seemed to be suffering from inner distress [...] He simultaneously followed what I was saying and gazed out at the oak trees and sunflowers of the Russian countryside, where prisoners-of-war captured by the Germans were working in the fields.' In November, as the ice and snow took hold, Marinetti fell ill and returned home.[236]

fig. 30 Marinetti at Verona station, waiting to leave for the Russian front, 1942.

Benedetta, too, threw her energies and intellect into the war effort. In April 1942, three months before Marinetti left for the Russian front, we find her at Catania, addressing a group of Fascist women. Her message was chilling and poetic at the same time: 'To attain well-being and justice, it is necessary to wage war, to kill and to exterminate [. . .] Our race resides deep in our blood, a privilege that has accumulated over the centuries, a fatherland [. . .] Italy, elegance of creation, promise of happiness reaching out into the most intense of all seas.'[237] The figure upon whom she chose to concentrate in her address was a heavily idealised one: the soldier's mother, who modestly hides her anguish, knowing that her son is destined to mutilation and death, but who also believes in final victory. She concluded, 'I want, we want, history to be able to say, "In the years in which Europe and the entire world were recreated through the will of Fascism, of Nazism, of the Axis pact and of anti-Bolshevik war, it was Italian women who first showed a full awareness of what was at stake" [. . .] We already have victory in our hearts, deeply desired by our Duce. Do not doubt it.'[238]

Marinetti and Benedetta were indeed to remain faithful to the Duce to the last, following him to Salò in July of 1944. There, for two months, Mussolini and Marinetti met and talked often, a return to 1919, but now with the whole terrible trajectory of Fascism lying behind them. Marinetti was not to see the end of the war. He died on 30 November 1944 at Bellagio, with Benedetta at his side.

CONCLUSION

Fascism, like the other great tyrannies of the first half of the twentieth century, was a snooper regime, its informers carefully inserted into the texture of everyday life. In the cities caretakers living on the ground floor of big apartment blocks were famous for keeping an eye on suspect families and individuals. The terrain for surveillance was infinite – from the neighbours' squabble to the drunken street song, from the train conversation to the intimate details of private life.[239] Children were encouraged to report on 'disloyal' parents, though few did. Family ties proved resilient in Italy, though there were plenty of people who out of self-interest or jealousy became spies and informers.

In recent years, a major shift in Italian political culture – not unconnected with Silvio Berlusconi's control of Italian media, both private and public – has led to a new insistence on the essentially innocuous nature of the Fascist regime, at least until 1938. The English historian Paul Corner has done well to remind us that Fascism was founded from its outset on brutal violence and repression, above all in different parts of Africa but also in Italy.[240] No one in Italy in the 1930s doubted the efficiency of the OVRA, the Fascist secret police, or the ruthlessness of the Fascist Special Tribunal. This last, between 1927 and 1940, passed tens of death sentences and condemned some 13,000 people to very long terms of imprisonment, Antonio Gramsci and Vittoria Foa amongst them. Alfredo Rocco's Penal Code, as we have seen, further ensured that 'ordinary' Fascist law was that of a police state.

Fascism was not all violence, however. A balance existed between coercion and consent, as in all the other tyrannies under examination here. The precise nature of that balance defines the texture of family politics and varies from regime to regime. In the Fascist case, it finds a very particular version – highly coloured, as nowhere else, by the gap between rhetoric and reality. Mussolini was a past master in the typology of lying – from exaggeration and ornamentation to bald-faced untruths and the total traducing of reality. Worse still, he came to believe his own lies. Through a highly effective and inventive propaganda machine the Duce took hold of the imagination of a great many Italian families and successfully led them with him down his mendacious path, especially in the mid-1930s. But when the moment of truth arrived, the disillusionment was great indeed: 'That cuckold! How did he think he could possibly win?'[241]

The deceit was not only military. One of the most interesting areas of analysis, and one that most concerned Italian families, is that of welfare. In the classic tripartite division of welfare regimes, first formulated by Richard Titmuss in the 1940s, the distinction has very often been made between residual, occupational and universal systems. Fascism always claimed – and it was one of its most far-fetched lies – that it was laying the foundations for a universal welfare system which would offer benefits to all who were Italian citizens. ONMI was couched in these terms. In reality, Fascist welfare was a residual regime offering patchy services and some financial assistance to a small percentage of Italian families. It suffered from major structural handicaps: economically, it always received very limited funding; geographically, it addressed some of the needs of the city poor, primarily in the centre and north, but was totally absent in very many parts of the countryside; occupationally, it made a great fuss of state employees, but ignored huge categories of workers such as sharecroppers and landless labourers; administratively, it was neither transparent nor rules-dominated, but rather bureaucratic and deeply clientelistic.[242] Finally, family welfare was still very much the prerogative of the Church: in hospitals and clinics, as in early education and old-age care, the Church could boast both numbers and experience which Fascism could not match. No number of seaside *colonie* and journeying *treni popolari* could mask Fascism's subordination and improvisation in the welfare field.

Yet even these structural deficiencies – these partialities passed off as totalities – do not bring us to the heart of the relationship between Italian families and Fascism. That relationship depended not just on the first of its components – the Fascist regime and what it created or failed to create – but also on the second, Italian families themselves. The social and political anthropology of Italian families was very different from that of Germany in the same period. In the Italian case we do not find the profound symbiosis that linked leader and led in Germany, or the Ottoman habits of family discipline and popular obedience on which Mustafa Kemal constructed the new Turkey. Instead there are many dissonances; not just those of courageous anti-Fascists but also the fatalistic voices of the peasants of Gagliano, the alarm of the Caroti family, devout Tuscan sharecroppers who were pro-Fascist but anti-war, and the disaffection of the metalworkers who booed Mussolini when he came to open FIAT Mirafiori in 1939. It would not be going too far to say that a profound divide separated the imperial and expansionist ambitions of the regime from the pacific, inward-looking and self-interested nature of Italian family strategies and culture.[243]

Of course, such a generalisation cannot apply universally. Within families, as we have seen, the younger generations, especially in the cities, were much more attracted than their parents by what the regime offered – the cult of youth, the emphasis on fitness and competitive sport, modernity seen as speed, machines and travel. The Fascists were good at pulling the young out of traditional pastimes and habits towards mass gymnastic displays and sporting events. Even so, family life retained its distinctive importance and in no way risked being subsumed into a hyperactive public sphere, as Kollontai and even Lenin envisaged in the Bolshevik case. Italian family politics were far more muted and traditionalist.

Mussolini himself was acutely aware of this gap between the regime's ambitions and family behaviour. Many times he railed against the 'unworthiness' of the Italian people, their incapacity to live up to his expectations and to their 'world-historical task'. These bitter reflections were not just of the war years and did not only concern fighting. In August 1938 he confided to his mistress, Claretta Petacci, 'Every time I receive a report from Africa it is a matter of discomfort to me. Today, too, five Italians have been arrested because they are cohabiting with negresses [. . .] Ah! These disgusting Italians, they will destroy the empire in less than seven years. They have no racial consciousness, no dignity.'[244]

Giuseppe Bottai said much the same thing in a different way. He told the party faithful that 'it is necessary to return to the family, to reconstitute its vitality, reconstruct its profound moral values'. He warned that it was time to stop singing 'ninne nanne' (lullabies) at bedtime and to hum martial tunes instead: for 'the babies of today will be the soldiers of tomorrow'.[245] This was never likely to be a popular line. Lullabies were an integral and profound part of an Italian family culture not noted for its warlike traditions. Furthermore, the Catholic Church wanted prayers, not marching songs, to end the day.

Ultimately, it was indeed Catholicism rather than Fascism that dictated the terms of Italian family politics in this period. The Church's was a mighty family model, based on anteriority (the precedence that the Christian family took over civil society and the state), integralism (all institutions and traditions to be exclusively Catholic), and the consequent battle to achieve on earth the 'social kingdom of Christ'. The Catholic Church was a far more redoubtable opponent than the Russian Orthodox one, or even than the mullahs whose power was bent and constrained, if never destroyed, in the new Turkish Republic. Fascism had the chance to continue the Risorgimento tradition of containing Catholic cultural, social and territorial power. Mussolini chose instead to seek compromise, but he did so without any clear alternative model of family life. Marinetti's model was a great, initial, anti-familial but deeply patriarchal tirade which he later reneged on, Gentile's was merely metaphysical, Sironi's was painfully truthful but quite inoperative. The result was capitulation. Nothing symbolised this surrender better than the reading of the articles of the (unreformed) Civil Code to newly married couples, not at the altar but in the sacristy. The Giornata della Fede seemed to tell another story, of clerical support for imperial war (against the Pope's wishes), but it was a moment that soon passed once the realities of world war became apparent in 1940–2.

In no area is this failure more evident than in that of the law. We have seen how crucial the Bolshevik Family Codes were, and also the importance of the Swiss Family Code for Kemal's attempted reconstruction of Turkish society. The Italian Fascists produced nothing similar, the reform of the Civil Code being delayed time and again and its final appearance in 1942 being characterised above all by its racist and anti-semitic articles.

CHAPTER 4

Family and family life in the Spanish Republic and the Civil War, 1931–1950

I. The republican dawn

In the spring of 1931 there occurred in Spain one of those sudden libertarian transformations of public opinion and explosions of intense public joy which are as memorable as they are evanescent. Juan Marichal has compared 1931 with 1820. On both occasions, he writes, Spain suddenly found itself at the centre of European attention.[1] In March 1820 General Rafael Del Riego had forced King Ferdinand VII to reintroduce the liberal constitution of Cádiz of 1812, thus opening the way for a new wave of revolutionary enthusiasm. In the same weeks, Percy Bysshe Shelley, then in Florence, wrote his famous 'Ode to Liberty', a poem which, in all its fiery glory, announced that it was from the West, from Spain, that the dead weight of the Restoration would be first challenged and then destroyed:

A glorious people vibrated again
The lightning of the nations: Liberty
From heart to heart, from tower to tower, o'er Spain,
Scattering contagious fire into the sky,
Gleamed. My soul spurned the chains of its dismay,
And in the rapid plumes of song
Clothed itself, sublime and strong.[2]

In 1931, at a time of fast-growing European reaction, it seemed as if Spain would again return to the forefront of European politics, this time in the fight back against Fascism. The municipal elections of that year, coming as they did after the collapse of the Primo de Rivera dictatorship, were widely seen as a sounding board for the future of Spanish democracy. They resulted in overwhelming victories for republican candidates, in the cities if not in the countryside. Two days after the elections, King Alfonso XIII, warned by the national Civil Guard commander that his forces would no longer support the monarchy, fled the country. Amidst great rejoicing Spain's second Republic was declared.[3]

Another comparison suggests itself strongly in the context of this book – that with the peaceful 'constitutional revolution' of 1908 in the Ottoman Empire. There, too, the dynastic ruler, Sultan Abdülhamit II, had been forced to recognise the constitution he had abandoned thirty years previously. There too the rejoicing crowds seemed to have abandoned all social and even gender distinctions. The twenty-four-year-old Halide Edib, as we have seen, was borne by a great mass of people through the streets of Istanbul and across the Galata bridge:

Men and women in a common wave of enthusiasm moved on, radiating something extraordinary, laughing, weeping in such intense emotion that human deficiency and ugliness were for the time completely obliterated [. . .] Before each official building there was an enormous crowd calling to the minister to come out and take the oath of allegiance to the new regime.[4]

As in Istanbul in 1908, so in Madrid twenty-three years later. On 14 April 1931 Madrid's Puerta del Sol was full of exalting crowds. There too we can find a fifteen-year-old schoolgirl, Victoria Román, amazed at what she saw. She had come with many of her fellow pupils and teachers to witness the birth of the new political regime: ' "The Republic has arrived without bloodshed", one of my teachers said. "Yes", replied another, "without bloodshed – and we shall live to regret it". I was shocked to hear him talk like that; but later I came to wonder if he wasn't right.'

Five years later, by which time she was a university student, Victoria Román refused to leave her city, now besieged by Franco's forces:

'I'm staying', I told the evacuation people, who wanted me to accompany the children I had been looking after to the Levant. I didn't belong to any political party; I was a typically undisciplined Spaniard, prepared now to do anything to prevent fascism triumphing [. . .] Everything was obliterated except the passionate desire to defend the city against the enemy. The enemy that had refused to accept the people's freedom to elect the government they wanted.[5]

Not everyone saw it like that. Indeed, just as in the Ottoman Empire in 1908 there had been traditionalist forces biding their time, ready to destroy the revolution less than a year later, so too there was another Spain, powerful and deep-rooted, religious and nationalist, which greeted the coming of the Republic as an unmitigated disaster. In 1931 Juan Crespo was a pupil in a college run by monks in Salamanca. There the proclamation of the Republic was the occasion for a day of mourning. The headmaster preached a sermon on the tragic nature of the King's departure: 'He criticized the Spaniards' ingratitude to the king, praised the monarchy's service to the nation, recalled the example of the Catholic kings who had united the nation. By the end he was nearly in tears, and so were we.' Later on, Crespo, a convinced monarchist with sympathies for José Antonio Primo de Rivera's Falange party (the Spanish political force that most closely resembled the Italian Fascists), volunteered for the front line. He fought not for the Catholic Church, which he had come to despise deeply after his school experiences, but for 'a better Spain', for a dictatorship which would bring 'a return of authority and national spirit'.[6]

1. The Constitution and the family

In June 1931 national elections were held, on the basis of universal male suffrage, all men over the age of twenty-three having the right to vote for the new Constituent Assembly. Women could be elected – just three of them were – but they did not yet have the right to vote. The lack of structured parties and the local nature of many deputies makes it very difficult to ascribe precise political loyalties in the new Assembly. It was clear to all, however, that the progressive forces had gained an overwhelming victory, based principally on the alliance between republicans (80 seats), Socialists (120 seats) and Radicals, supported by some thirty deputies of the Esquerra (Left) regional party of Catalonia and twenty federalist republicans from Galicia. The right, which had failed to establish an effective coalition between its disparate forces, constituted only a small minority of the Assembly. One of the latter's most interesting features was the presence of a high number of intellectuals – sixty-four university professors and lecturers, as well as forty-seven writers and journalists. The Cortes Constituyentes, as it was called, met for the first time on 14 July, Bastille Day, thus leaving no one in doubt as to its basic historical allegiance. Some five months later, on 9 December 1931, after fierce debates which had lasted throughout a torrid summer and autumn, the new Constitution came into effect.[7]

The Constitution is of fundamental importance for the themes of this book, in that it introduced radical changes to the relations between state, family and Church in Spain, as well as revolutionary innovations regarding marriage and divorce. In general the Constitution was a highly interventionist document, the active role of a strong state being underlined again and again. Manuel Azaña, the leading republican who was to be prime minister between 1931 and 1933 and later president of the Republic, conceived of the Republic as 'a school in civic virtues'.[8] The republicans' emphasis on individual rights, when joined to the Socialist culture of state planning, social justice and welfare, produced a radically democratic document. Article 1 sets the tone for the whole Constitution:[9] 'Spain is a democratic Republic of workers of all classes [trabajadores de toda clase], organized in a regime based on liberty and justice. The power of all its organs emanates from the people.' Here the Spanish Constitution of 1931 sets itself apart both from the Soviet one of 1918, with its empowerment of workers and peasants but its exclusion from political rights of 'exploiters of the people', and from the French tradition of primary reference to the individual, to 'l'homme' and 'le citoyen'.

Article 43 is entirely dedicated to the family. Its first paragraph reads, 'The family is under the special care of the State. Marriage is based on equal rights for both sexes and can be dissolved by mutual consent or by the request of one of the partners who must in this case provide just cause.'[10] These initial phrases call for immediate comment. We should first note the explicit underlining of the state's desire and responsibility to protect the family, an emphasis also to be found in the Weimar Constitution of 1919.[11] Since one of the principal accusations to be levelled against the republicans by the Spanish nationalists during the Civil War was their desire to destroy the family, it is striking to find its defence so firmly enshrined in the republican Constitution.

The second noteworthy element is the establishment of equal rights in marriage for men and women. Such a radical affirmation of gender rights in the domestic sphere put the Spaniards far in advance of, for instance, the Swiss, who in their Civil Code of 1912, so beloved of Atatürk, had underlined the role of the husband as 'the head of the conjugal union'. The Spanish constitutional provision was all the more surprising because, as we shall see, it in no way reflected habitual patriarchal behaviour in Spanish society, or the Church's teachings, or the provisions of the Spanish Civil Code of 1889. A great gap separated the deliberations of the radical reformers of the Constituent Assembly from the time-honoured gender hierarchies of Spanish marriage. Only time could have bridged it, but time was to be one of the many commodities unavailable to the new Republic.

The third and last consideration relates to separation and divorce. Here the Spanish legislators acted in revolutionary fashion, going far beyond their western European counterparts and implementing divorce by mutual consent. This would be introduced in Britain and France only in 1971 and 1975 respectively. It is possible that the Soviet Codes of 1918 and 1926 had made their influence felt, especially amongst Socialist deputies.

Article 43 of the Spanish Constitution continues with a section on parents' duties to their children – all their children, not only those legitimated by marriage: 'Parents are obliged to nourish, educate and instruct their children. The State will guard over the fulfillment of these duties and will, where necessary and in accordance with the principle of subsidiarity, intervene to ensure their realization.' This was again an unusual emphasis in a Catholic country where the word 'duty', at least in the domestic sphere, was indelibly linked to the woman.

Articles 43 and 46 stipulate the state's obligation to assist the old and the infirm, to protect maternity and infancy, and to protect women and minors at work. The state was also to underwrite the Geneva Declaration of the Rights of the Child of September 1924, a historic document that recognised and affirmed for the first time the existence of rights specific to children. Article 2 of the Declaration stated, 'The child that is hungry must be fed; the child that is sick must be nursed; the child that is backward must be helped; the delinquent child must be reclaimed; and the orphan and the waif must be sheltered and succored.'[12]

The Spanish Constitution, then, was unusual in its desire to regulate *constitutionally* various aspects of private life. It aimed to assist the weakest and least protected members of the family, both old and young, it gave unprecedented rights to women within the family, and it warned fathers that they too had duties. Finally, it defended the family as an institution but allowed space and hope for those trapped in unhappy marriages.

The initial statement of constitutional principles was followed swiftly by laws dealing with divorce (2 March 1932) and civil matrimony (28 June 1932). The new law on marriage corrected the situation whereby since 1564 the only legitimate form of marriage (for those baptised as Catholics) was that celebrated under canon law.[13] The new laws aimed to introduce into Spain for the first time a contractual, egalitarian and secular (non-religious) vision of marriage.[14] In the debate in parliament on the new divorce law, the Radical Clara Campoamor, one of the only three women elected, made a courageous and sensible speech in favour of divorce:

> Marriage is the according of two wills. As soon as this accord breaks down, as soon as these two wills find that they can no longer co-exist in harmony, then marriage loses its sense. For marriage, in the opinion of any person endowed with a little common sense, has as its natural base love and spiritual affinity. Once these have disappeared marriage becomes for the couple nothing less than a torture and a sufferance, a source of degradation for the

individual in his or her social life. We sincerely have to recognise that family is not always the same thing as marriage, and that in some families paternity or maternity is not perhaps the be all and end all of family life.[15]

The divorce law went through, supported by the many radical intellectuals present in the Assembly and more cautiously by the Socialist party, and so too did the partial reform of the outdated Civil Code. The conservative and religious opposition to these measures, as we shall see in a moment, was profound and intransigent. Yet by the end of 1933 there had been only a little over 7,000 requests for divorce, of which only 4,043 had been granted by the courts. The analysis of the composition of these first requests is revealing: nearly half of them came from blue- and white-collar workers, and women formed 50 per cent of those applying.[16] Unlike the Russian urban experience after 1918, there is little evidence to show that the new law on divorce was widely used or abused.

While great progress was made at the level of family law, family life was not likely to change with the same rapidity. Furthermore, not all the legislation of this period went in the same direction. Thus the new law on labour contracts, which came into force on 21 November 1931 before the Constitution had been finalised, insisted on the husband's formal approval of a wife's labour contract.[17] Similarly, the Civil Code continued to grant a husband the 'authority' to represent his wife in all economic matters, including the administration of her property and goods. It was clear, to return to Mary Ann Glendon's 'two moving systems' – on the one hand the laws affecting the family and on the other actual family life – that they were not moving at the same speed in 1930s Spain. The constitutional settlement of the *país judicial* had leaped far ahead of family custom in 'la España profunda', and the two never found a new equilibrium before the Civil War broke out.

2. Women and women's rights in the new Republic

Under the terms of the Constitution, women gained important rights in the public sphere as well as the private. Article 2 established that all Spaniards were equal before the law, Article 25 eliminated any juridical privilege based on gender, social class, wealth, political ideas or religious faith, and Article 36 established equal political rights for citizens of both sexes over the age of twenty-three. Women's suffrage, as in the rest of Europe, was the cause of fierce debate. Of the three women who had been elected to the Constituent Assembly, it was again the Radical Clara Campoamor who took the lead, arguing in favour of women being granted the vote immediately. The other two women deputies – Margarita Nelken of the Socialist Party and Victoria Kent of the Radical

Socialist Party – though both politically progressive in their thinking – were convinced that the granting of women's suffrage would lead immediately to a massive female vote for Catholic parties. This was not the moment, they argued, to play straight into the hands of the Church. Nelken declared, 'Those Spanish women who truly love liberty must be the first to postpone the realisation of their own desires in the interests of the progress of Spain.' Campoamor retorted, 'The only way for women to mature is to encourage them to tread the paths of liberty.'[18]

Male opposition to the proposal came not only from the right. It often assumed ludicrous tones. In a notorious speech, the Radical deputy, Ayuso insisted on women being granted the vote only after the menopause. Before it, he argued, 'menstruation leads to nervous instability and to [dangerous] alterations in women's mental state', a position taken by many misogynist politicians all across Europe.[19] The conservatives in the Constituent Assembly suggested a compromise: women were to vote but only at municipal elections (as if menstruation mattered less at a local level). The proposal was rejected and women's suffrage triumphed by just four votes in the Constituent Assembly of 1 December 1931.

The debate on suffrage allows us a first glimpse of one of the most remarkable figures of these decades in Spain – Margarita Nelken.[20] For tactical reasons, as we have just seen, she voted against women's suffrage, but in every other respect she was an untiring champion of women's rights in Spain and a highly competent analyst of their condition. She was born in 1894 into a prosperous middle-class Jewish family in Madrid, her father a German jeweller from Breslau who had emigrated to Spain in 1889, her mother's father a Hungarian Jew who, after settling in Madrid in 1866, became court watchmaker to Alfonso XII. Margarita and her younger sister Carmen Eva were educated mainly at home, learning French from their mother, German from their father, Spanish in everyday life, and English from their nanny. Although twenty years younger than Aleksandra Kollontai, Margarita resembled her in many ways – not just in having an English nanny but also in her fierce independence, her restlessness, her nonconformist private life and in the end her belief in the necessity of social revolution. Although she wrote a biography of Goethe and was the Spanish translator of Kafka, her real intellectual passion was art and art history. She was sent to Paris aged just thirteen and studied painting with the Spanish Cubist María Blanchard; among her fellow pupils was Diego Rivera, who was to become Mexico's most famous muralist. When she was twenty years old she fell in love with the reclusive sculptor Julio Antonio, by whom she had an illegitimate daughter, Magda, in 1915. After Julio Antonio's premature death four years later, she had another child, this time a son, Santiago, by her new companion, Martín de Paul y de Martín Barbadillo, a Sevillian businessman. From 1920 onwards, and for many years, the two adults and two children lived together in what today would be considered a quite normal middle-class household in Madrid. Under the terms of the new divorce law of 1932, Martín de Paul was able to divorce his first wife and marry Margarita in early 1933. He also recognised Magda, Nelken's first child, and gave her his name. The couple remained together until after the Civil War.

Nelken's intelligence, irreverence and *joie de vivre*, as well as her wild tongue, made her famous but deeply hated. She believed, as did Kollontai, in 'free love' – not in the sense of endless promiscuity, but in that of living freely her sexuality and her passions with her chosen partner. She wrote in one of her most famous books, *La condición social de la mujer en España*, 'The

fig. 31 Margarita Nelken in 1923 aged twenty-nine, at the height of her literary fame.

absurdity of our actual society has reached the point of rendering shameful the most natural and noble acts in our lives.'[21] In an interview of 1923, she was asked what she thought of the Spanish male. She replied sparklingly, 'Given that there are Spanish men among my readers, it is naturally my opinion that the Spanish male is a superman par excellence. I'm hardly likely to upset the customers.' The violent right-wing press did not hesitate to describe her as a whore, a 'Jewish Amazon' who was not a real Spaniard let alone a respectable woman. For them she combined 'an easy smile with easy access'.[22]

Margarita Nelken was still in her twenties when she began to take an active interest in issues of social justice and in the condition of women in particular. She began by organising art classes for poor children in Madrid's working-class quarters. The hitherto unknown world of hunger and neglect had a profound influence upon her, just as Kollontai's visit to the Kronholm textile works in 1896 had marked her for life. In 1918 Nelken founded a small orphanage in Madrid, La Casa de los Niños de España, for illegitimate children, as well as a care centre for the children of working mothers. It was the first non-religious children's nursery in Madrid. Confronted by the open hostility of the Church and the diffidence of traditional charitable organisations, Nelken's funding soon dried up and the centre was forced to close. She responded by writing the book to which I have already made reference, *La condición social de la mujer en España*. Written at great speed, as were most of her works, it was none the less well researched. Her interests ranged from the conditions of unskilled women factory workers to prostitution, from the need for women's education to the potential of middle-class women like herself. She considered these latter to be 'the greatest *dead weight of the nation* and at the same time the most energetic and courageous part of the nation.'[23] The book provoked an enormous scandal. The bishop of Lérida condemned it and it was even discussed in the Cortes. Nelken later commented that the bishop had acted out of kindness, in order to rescue her from neglect and ensure that her book became a bestseller.

Some years later, in 1927, Nelken published what she called a 'diálogo socrático' between two sisters, Isabel and Elena. It touched on some delicate points concerning divorce and sexuality which revealed how thoughtful she was on these issues and how far she was from the harridan imagined by the right:

Elena: Are you in favour of divorce or not?
Isabel: I am in favour of the possibility of divorce, which is not the same [. . .] divorce does not seem to me always necessary. No woman who is

self-respecting can lose sight of the sexual problem in marriage, but there is something more, and some couples, linked by friendship and mutual trust, have given the highest example of dignity in private life.[24]

At the time of the elections to the Constituent Assembly in June 1931, the Socialist deputy, Juan Morán Bayo, resigned his seat in the poverty-stricken province of Badajoz, in Extremadura, because he had also been elected in Córdoba where he was a professor at the university. A by-election was necessary and the name of Margarita Nelken came up. Although she had never actually joined the Socialist Party, she had collaborated with it for many years and her candidature was a way for the Socialists to remedy the shameful situation of having elected no women. Part of the local party apparatus was deeply hostile, but she was selected none the less and easily won the by-election. There then began a dramatic period in her life. For the first time she came face to face with the terrible deprivations of the landless labourers of the south and the haughty and contemptuous attitudes of the great landowners. As Paul Preston has written,

Badajoz was [already] a province on the verge of civil war. During the first two years of the Republic, there were more than two hundred clashes between left and right, between peasants and the armed guards of the land-owners, or between peasants and the Civil Guard. There were assaults on estates and on town halls. At least twenty deaths were recorded in consequence.[25]

As in every other area, Margarita Nelken threw herself without restraint into the fight for social justice in Extremadura, all too rarely spending time with her own family. She became ever more convinced that only socialist revolution, and not well-meaning but ineffective reform, could help the labourers of the south. By 1934 she was ready for civil war. In a speech of 25 January she told the Cortes,

[These] men go to collect acorns like wild beasts; they live like wild beasts. If one day in the not too distant future, you have to face them in a struggle which I hope will be fair, do not be surprised if those men whom you oblige to live like beasts, to seek food for their children like beasts, fighting for food with animals, risking their lives as beasts do, do not be surprised, I say, if these men are left with no human sentiments when it comes to fighting.[26]

3. Church, Constitution and family

Votes for women and gender equality within the family were certainly contro-versial innovations, but it was the constitutional provisions regarding the Catholic Church that aroused most dispute. Article 3 baldly declared that the Spanish state 'has no official religion'. Article 26 stipulated that all religions were to be treated in the same way and that the Republic, differently from the Monarchy, was not to favour or subsidise any religious institution. The state's considerable previous financial support to the Catholic Church was to be wound up within two years. The Jesuit order in Spain was to be disbanded, its goods and properties nationalised and the proceeds made over to welfare and education.[27] Other religious orders were henceforth, like everyone else, to pay taxes on their properties and incomes, which in any case could be subject to nationalisation.[28]

Nor was this all. Article 27 established that cemeteries were subject exclu-sively to civil jurisdiction. In addition, all public manifestations of faith, all Marian processions, all feast day activities (in which Spain, like Italy, excelled) had to be authorised by national or local government. Article 48 stipulated that the Spanish state was to have an entirely non-religious education system, which would 'place labour at the heart of its methodological activity and will be based upon ideals of human solidarity'. Crucifixes and other religious symbols were to be removed from state schools. All Churches and religious orders were granted the right to teach their respective doctrines in their own institutions, 'subject to the vigilance of the State'. The laws on civil matrimony (28 June 1932) and divorce (2 March 1932) struck both at the monopoly that the Catholic Church had exercised in this most delicate area of family forma-tion, and at its cherished belief that marriage was a sacrament, and as such indissoluble.

The new republican Constitution thus decisively separated state from Church and established the state's primacy in many crucial fields of everyday life. The Church, by contrast, was demoted from being the honoured guardian of Spain's morals and identity to little more than a voluntary association for those willing to subscribe to it. The passing of Article 26 of the Constitution on 13–14 October 1931 led to the resignation of two ministers, the Catholic Niceto Alcalá-Zamora and Miguel Maura, and the withdrawal of Catholic deputies from the Cortes. Azaña had tried in the Cortes to seek compromise, but his famous dictum 'Spain has ceased to be Catholic', meant as a statement of cultural and sociological fact, was never to be forgotten or forgiven.

All in all, it has to be said that the Assembly was absolutely within its rights to separate Church and state, as had already happened in France and Mexico in the late nineteenth and early twentieth centuries. It introduced many provisions which increased individual rights while curbing the accumulated and excessive power of the Spanish Church. Centuries-old imbalances were addressed and in part redressed. But it also has to be said that the Assembly acted in draconian fashion, with no room allowed for compromise or gradual change. By using the Constitution as a sort of battering-ram, the Cortes alienated moderate public opinion at a crucial time.[29]

The Spanish Church itself reacted with considerable concern and anger. It felt under siege: the old state subsidy was considered grossly insufficient for its needs, and even that was now to be withdrawn. The number of boys and young men in its seminaries declined by some 40 per cent between 1931 and 1934, while Socialist local councils in the south imposed innumerable restrictions on the Church's public presence – from funeral processions to bell ringing, from church weddings to feast days for patron saints. Wayside shrines and religious statues were defiled and destroyed. As Frances Lannon writes, 'A battle for the streets, for public places was being waged – an important battle in a society with a strong street culture – and the Church was losing.'[30] Worse still, the proclamation of the Republic had been greeted in May 1931 in Madrid and elsewhere with a wave of church burning which the authorities had been slow to stamp out. Far from the 'social kingdom of Christ' being instituted upon earth, it seemed as if the anti-Christ had taken hold of Spain.

Yet this was not the whole picture, for the Church was far from a blameless and abused creature in the country's long and tragic history of social and ideological polarisation. Behind the dramatic scenario of 1931 lay many decades of Catholic malpractice which had led, to a far greater degree than in Italy, to the alienation of significant parts of both the rural and the urban population. It is worth examining this proposition in a little more detail. The presence and influence of the Spanish Church, like the Italian, was very unevenly distributed across the country. In the north, it could boast deep roots amongst rural smallholders, sharecroppers and tenant farmers, especially in Navarra, Catalonia and the Basque Country. In these regions there often existed a close correlation between the structure of families and the patterns of belief: where families were extended in form, above average in size and enjoying some stability on the land, there was often a high degree of church-going. Families as a whole, not just individuals, were involved in parish life; religious celebrations and the agricultural calendar were intimately linked.[31]

The south told a very different story, for the network of parishes was far less dense and the peasantry were for the most part landless labourers (*braceros*). Although these were the very regions – Andalusia and Extremadura – which had been celebrated in Church history for their definitive liberation from the Moors in the fifteenth century, they never seem to have been conquered definitively for the faith. By the 1930s, church-going was sporadic and limited for the most part to women. Desperately poor male landless labourers, like those described to the Cortes by Margarita Nelken in 1934, shunned any contact with the Church. As in Puglia in the first decades of the twentieth century, socialism and anarcho-syndicalism made much more sense to them than did Catholicism. The correspondence in 1932 between the cardinal arch-bishop of Seville and his parish clergy presents a desolate picture of isolation and intimidation.[32]

Faced with the gross social disparities of the southern Spanish countryside and the glaring need for social reform, the Church did little or nothing. From time to time the social doctrine of Leo XIII was invoked and the southern landowners were requested to behave in a more charitable fashion. But never did the Church advocate land expropriation on social grounds, never did it question the principle of private property, never did it sever its organic links with the landowners. The anti-clericalism of many deputies in the Constituent Assembly of 1931 becomes more explicable in this light.

As for the towns and cities, Catholicism remained very strong in provincial centres but much weaker in the major urban agglomerations. The role of the orders, not just the Jesuits, was a very controversial one, for they boasted a reputation, dating back to at least the eighteenth century, for opulent and dissolute living.[33] Parish priests in the major cities were often accused of ignoring the needs of the poorest sections of the urban population, refusing even to bury their dead unless adequately remunerated. There also existed, to a far greater extent than in Italy, a deep-rooted sexual question. The alleged sexual misdeeds of the clergy occupied more space in the anti-clerical press of the 1930s than any other subject.[34] Innumerable stories circulated of parish priests who lived with, and had children by, their domestic servants, of convent chaplains who organised orgies with their nuns, of confessors who took far too much interest in the details of young girls' confessions, of Catholic schoolmasters who abused children entrusted to their care. The Church proudly presented itself as the champion of the family, but to many sections of the population the claim seemed pure hypocrisy.[35]

Overall, the Spanish Church was given far more to nostalgia than to self-criticism. It looked back longingly to the golden age of national and religious grandeur of the sixteenth and seventeenth centuries, but it refused to mend its ways. Instead it blamed its enemies for its own decline, denouncing all those – liberals, Masons, Jews, the 'Marxist hordes' and others – who over the *longue durée* had destroyed its dream.

1 Zeki Faik İzer, *The Way of the Revolution*, 1933.

2 Arshile Gorky, *The Artist and his Mother*, 1926–36.

3 Mario Sironi, *Periphery*, 1922–7.

4 Mario Sironi, *The Family*, 1932.

5 Mario Biazzi, *Listening to a Talk by the Duce*, c. 1939.

6 Pablo Picasso, *Guernica*, 1937.

EN NVESTRA JVSTICIA
ESTÁ NVESTRA FVERZA

7 Carlos Sáenz de Tejada, poster for the Francoist 'Auxilio Social'. The caption reads, 'In justice is our strength.'

8 George Grosz, *The Pillars of Society*, 1926.

9 René Ahrlé, Nazi *Volksgemeinschaft* poster, 1933–9.

10 Max Beckmann, *Family Portrait*, 1920.

11 Adolf Wissel, *Peasant Family from Kalenberg*, 1939.

12 Joseph Thorak, *Family*, German pavilion, Paris International Exhibition of Arts and Technology, 1937.

13 Vera Mukhina, *Worker and Kolkhoz Woman*, Soviet pavilion, Paris International Exhibition of Arts and Technology, 1937.

14 Vera A. Gitsevich, propaganda poster, 1932. The captions reads, 'The struggle for collective nutrition is an essential part of the struggle for the economic programme. Let's develop the mass construction of canteens!'

15 Aleksandr Samokhvalov, *The Militarised Komsomol*, 1932–3.

It is also true that the great majority of Spanish prelates never accepted the precepts of democracy. In November 1928, Pedro Segura y Sáenz, cardinal archbishop of Toledo, Primate of all Spain (the Spanish Church's most powerful position), warned explicitly that only the Church could erect an effective barrier against the 'subversive democratic currents of the era'.[36] The official position of the Vatican was an 'accidentalist' one: the Church did not express a preference for any one political regime, but judged them all on the basis of how well they served and protected the Church. In May 1931, Segura went far beyond this 'accidentalist' approach, itself highly controversial. In a circular letter sent not just to his diocesan clergy but to the bishops and the faithful of all Spain, he eulogised the fallen monarchy, recalled the sublime moment when Alfonso XIII had consecrated the whole of Spain to the Sacred Heart, and called for a crusade of prayers and sacrifices against the Republic.[37] Only a small and enlightened minority of Spanish prelates, whose principal point of reference was Cardinal Francisco Vidal y Barraquer, archbishop of Tarragona, took their distance from these positions.[38]

With regard to the family, it is as well to record the Roman Catholic orthodoxy of the time, enshrined in Pius XI's three encyclicals of the period 1929–31: *Divini Illius Magistri* (31 December 1929) on Christian education; the famous encyclical *Casti Connubii*, of 31 December 1930,[39] dedicated to the theme of Catholic marriage; and *Quadragesimo Anno* (15 May 1931), which treated in particular the question of a just 'family wage', paid to the male head of family so as to preclude his wife being forced into labour outside the home.

Casti Connubii, which we examined briefly in the previous chapter, was published just a few months before the proclamation of the second Spanish Republic. It offers a catastrophic view of Christian marriage in the modern world. From every side modern culture and science were seeking to undermine marriage as a holy sacrament. To these external attacks upon marriage, which according to Pius XI were often ably orchestrated by a Liberal or Marxist state, were to be added internal dangers.[40] These were what they had always been: contraception, abortion, adultery ('false and damaging friendships with third persons'), divorce, eugenics, sexual 'incontinence', and so on. In the encyclical their proponents were always presented as an unidentified third person plural, bent on leading the faithful towards perdition.[41] It closes with a paean of praise for the recent Concordat with the Italian Fascist state and an invitation to others to follow the Fascists' lead: 'In reality, the two supreme sources of power [Church and state] can join hands and associate in a spirit of mutual concord and amicable agreements.'[42]

Casti Connubii, with its sense of impending doom for Catholic families and its offer of salvation through agreement with Fascist regimes, must have exercised a formidable influence on Spanish prelates, reinforcing their own fears and fundamentalism. As so often in the past, however, the strategy chosen by the Vatican was by no means linear. At least initially, Pius XI sought the road to compromise in Spain, forcing the resignation of Segura as cardinal archbishop of Toledo after the discovery of his plans for moving the Church's treasures and savings out of Spain. In September 1931, secret negotiations between the Church and the republican authorities produced a possible settlement, but the passing of Article 26 a month later dashed all the Vatican's hopes of damage limitation.[43]

The Spanish prelates now needed no encouragement to mobilise against the Republic. Cardinal Isidro Gomá y Tomás replaced Segura as archbishop of Toledo, but he was no less outspoken. 'We have worked little, late and badly,' he wrote in a pastoral letter while still bishop of Tarazona, 'when we could have done much and done it well, in a time of peace and under a tranquil and sheltering sky.'[44] Both Segura and Gomá were fundamentalists (*integristas*), not in the vague sense of being traditionalists but in the specific one of believing in a confessional state, one which, as Hilari Raguer has written, 'imposes upon all its subjects, by force, the profession of the Catholic religion and prohibits all others'.[45] They regarded those who did not immerse themselves fully in this ideology as bad Catholics, calling them 'mestizos', half-castes. Their speeches and circular letters recall those of Cardinal Laurenti in Italy in 1924.[46] His discourse and theirs were as one: the 'social kingdom of Christ' was to be realised in the extreme form of a confessional state.

4. Culture, the family and republican education, 1932–1936

The Republic could not compete with the Church in terms of its presence in Spanish society, but it was not short of cultural ambition. In particular, it launched a radical programme for taking republican values to the 'people', especially to far-flung villages that had previously had little or no contact with the outside world. The guiding spirit behind the scheme was the new Minister of Public Instruction, Fernando de los Ríos, who had replaced Marcelino Domingo in the cabinet reshuffle of December 1931. In an article of March 1932, de los Ríos identified two kinds of cultural crisis: one of 'decay or collapse', from which Spain had been suffering for decades, and the other a crisis of supply, Spain's actual condition, wherein the demand for cultural enrichment was great but its supply limited. The state's responsibility was to fill this gap. It had to impart a new idea of culture which combined the Constitution's emphasis on labour and human solidarity with quintessentially Spanish values such as 'the love of the aesthetic and the profound, the cardinal emotion of respect that the Spaniard always has for the ethical and for the austere'.[47] De los Ríos also happened to be the nephew of the founder of Spain's most interesting independent experiment in education, the Institución Libre de Enseñanza (ILE). Created in 1876, it advocated a secular humanism which owed much to the teachings of the German philosopher Karl Krause (1781–1832).

The Patronato de las Misiones Pedagógicas was created by a decree of 29 May 1931. The use of the words 'mission' and 'missionary' was highly significant, mirroring as it did long-established Catholic models. The Spanish republican 'missions', however, identified cultural education as their prime task, not conversion to an ideology or cause. In this they differed not only from the Catholics but also from the Communist Zhenotdel of Armand and Kollontai of the 1920s, with its preaching of women's liberation and social revolution. In Spain, the peasant families of isolated villages were offered a programme of easily understood excerpts from classic Castilian poetry and prose, choruses and songs, often of regional origin, and documentary films – sometimes about other parts of the world, sometimes about science, hygiene and health. The 'missions' also took with them the so-called Circulating Museum, which consisted of replicas of the most famous paintings housed in Madrid's Prado and the Museo del Cerralbo.

Many years later, a volunteer described a typical expedition:

The true missions [...] were those which we students and poets made to villages which often did not have electricity, armed with a movie projector, comic or educational films, a gramophone and records [...] At nightfall in the square we organized an accessible and agreeable programme of readings and various commentaries [...] finishing off with one of the famous silent films of Charlie Chaplin.[48]

Between 1931 and 1934 the *misioneros* visited 495 villages, nearly half of them in the regions of Old Castile and León. Given that the national population was calculated at over twenty-four million in 1933, it can safely be said that the Misiones Pedagógicas touched only a small percentage of Spaniards. Few expeditions were organised in Catalonia, Aragón or Valencia, while the south was almost completely ignored. All this conveyed the strong impression of a Madrid-based enterprise with a marked predominance of Castilian culture.[49]

Small-scale though it was, the initiative should not be dismissed. Theatre was the favoured art form and the 'Coro y Teatro del Pueblo', which had 'ventured through' 179 localities by the end of 1934, brought to the peasants shortened versions of the great secular dramas of the golden age of Spanish theatre. In particular the theatre company concentrated upon *entremeses* (short farces staged between acts) and *pasos* (skits). These usually lasted no more than fifteen minutes, occupying the same sort of space as comic interludes in Shakespearian tragedy. They often closed with music and a chorus.[50]

The choice of material was most often dependent upon the quality of the piece rather than its political correctness. A good example, and one highly relevant to our general argument, is Cervantes's *entremés* 'El juez de los divorcios' (The judge of the divorce court), which was regularly performed by the Coro y Teatro del Pueblo.[51] Given that in 1931 the Spanish republican Constitution had just written divorce into its Article 43, it might have been expected that the *misioneros* would choose a short play in some way consonant with the Constitution and favourable to divorce. This is not the case, for Cervantes's piece is highly ambiguous. On the one hand, the evils of marriage are given an abundant airing before the imaginary court, especially by women. One of them, Mariana, even suggests a radical political alternative: 'Let me cry, it relieves my feelings. In well-governed kingdoms and republics, marriages should have a time limit, and every three years they should be either dissolved or confirmed anew, like a rent contract; they ought not to last a lifetime, with perpetual grief to both parties.'[52] She goes on to list in graphic detail the daily

fig. 32 A performance of the Teatro del Pueblo of the Misiones Pedagógicas, 1931–4.

horrors she has to endure. Another male character, the Doctor, implores the judge to let him and his wife go their separate ways freely: 'What more testimony do you want, besides the fact that I do not wish to die with her, and she does not wish to live with me?'[53]

On the other hand, the judge is adamant in his refusal to grant divorce to any of them, even if he admits that there are reasonable grounds in some cases. The piece ends with the judge accepting an invitation to dinner from another couple who wish to thank him for saving their marriage. Musicians accompany the final chorus in its praise of a traditional proverb:

A man and wife may disagree
but decent folk, of course,
know reconcilement, even the worst,
is better than the best divorce [original italics].[54]

Another theatre troupe took to the road in these same years, headed by the young, very talented, avant-garde poet and playwright from Granada, Federico García Lorca. His family, which he adored, was so exceptional as to merit a brief description here, culled principally from the first piece he ever wrote, 'Mi pueblo', a manuscript of 1916–17 on the subject of his family and village. His grandparents on his father's side had nine children, all of whom married, had children and with one exception continued to live in Fuente Vaqueros, not far from Granada. This meant that Federico had more than forty cousins in the village, a fact which his friends in Granada made fun of at a later date. He once described his family as being 'long', but it was also 'wide', of extraordinary dimensions whichever way you looked. It was also of quite unusual culture. One of the early childhood memories which most moved Federico was that of his mother reading Victor Hugo's *Hernani*, in the huge kitchen of their farmhouse, to the farm labourers, servants and administrator's family: 'My mother read admirably and I observed with amazement that the servants were weeping, although, naturally, I understood nothing of what was going on [. . .] I owe her everything I am and everything I will be.'[55]

Among the labourers' families was that of a little girl whom Federico had befriended. The girl's father was a rheumatic day labourer and her mother worn out by countless pregnancies. Federico often visited their home but was forbidden to do so on washing day, when all the family members remained inside, practically naked, while their only clothes were hung out to dry. He wrote in 'Mi pueblo', 'When I returned home on those occasions, I would look into my wardrobe, full of clean and fragrant clothes, and feel dreadfully anxious, with a dead weight on my heart.'[56] These were the atrocious differences of class which Margarita Nelken also noted, and which constituted one of the strongest motive forces of the republican cause in the Civil War.

Lorca, in the words of one of his biographers, 'had a big, striking and lively head set on a clumsy flat-footed body [. . .] his sense of humour was contagious, his bursts of laughter proverbial'.[57] He also had a deep sense of anguish, the flip side to his ability to create an aura of happiness around him. In particular he suffered from being unable, in the Spain of that time, to live his homosexuality in a free and open way.

Lorca's theatrical work was distinguished by its striking metaphors, its sense of the mysterious and indefinite, its dramatic rendering of violent and obscure passions. His project for taking theatre to the people differed to a certain degree from that of the Coro y Teatro del Pueblo. His troupe, 'La Barraca', stopped for the most part in small towns rather than far-flung villages and concentrated both on the classic theatrical repertoire and on contemporary plays. Thus his aims were less immediately pedagogical and his methods granted fewer concessions to his audience. As he explained in an interview of March 1932,

> Outside of Madrid today the theatre, which is in its very essence a part of the life of the people, is almost dead, and the people suffer accordingly, as they would if they had lost eyes or ears or sense of taste. We are going to give it back to them in the terms in which they used to know it, with the very plays they used to love [. . .] We will take Good and Evil, God and Faith into the towns of Spain again.[58]

With Eduardo Ugarte and thirty performers and technicians, mainly from Madrid University, to assist him, Lorca took La Barraca on the road from 10 July 1932 onwards, visiting a total of sixty-four locations.

The degree to which in Spain *both* left and right, secular humanists and fundamentalist Catholics, harked back to the past, to the glorious age of the sixteenth and seventeenth centuries, is very striking. Both sides would have earned the young Marinetti's scorn for being *passatisti* rather than *futuristi*. But Lorca combined the ancient and the modern in a special way, not only in his own plays but in the way he staged classical theatre, his scene painters, he said, having 'learned the most modern language of line under the tutelage of Picasso' in Paris.[59]

Theatre was the privileged medium for the Spanish republicans, but even in Lorca's staging it was not the one that fascinated the peasantry most. According to many recollections, it was cinema that took pride of place. Moving pictures 'entertained' and 'dazzled' the peasants. They considered them 'magical', whereas the village elders were highly suspicious of them and talked instead of witchcraft. In one still of the time we look back from the screen to a peasant audience assembled in a classroom. They are overwhelmingly women and children, seated and standing, staring with disbelief and enchantment at the images being presented to them. In the centre of the photograph there stands a young mother with her child in her arms. They have a luminous quality, accentuated by the simplicity and bearing of the mother and by the light colouring of their clothes, in contrast to the black attire of those around them. A white bandana has been wrapped around the little child's head.

As Sandie Holguín has pointed out, the republican authorities had a far from impeccable record with regard to cinema.[60] They were slow to realise its potential and ready to ban and censor films they disapproved of. This was particularly true of the masterpieces that emerged from the Russian revolution. With their call to revolution and celebration of class warfare, they were not at all to the liking of those educated in the secular humanist tradition. For them, there were already far too many calls to revolution in Spain in the 1930s, without having to import Soviet ones. As a result, Eisenstein's *Battleship*

fig. 33 Villagers watching a film projected by the Misiones Pedagógicas, 1931–4.

Potemkin of 1925 was banned. But so too was Buñuel's stark documentary of peasant conditions in Extremadura, *Las Hurdes: Land without Bread*, of 1932, hardly an endearing film by any standards but not one to be banned. The portrayal of Spain in a poor light (Buñuel) and incitement to disorder (Eisenstein) were the justifications offered, even though the new Constitution explicitly enshrined freedom of expression and opinion in its Article 34. This was a very poor start for republican government and cultural freedom.

Those out in the field with the Misiones Pedagógicas had other problems. Time and again they came face to face with such conditions of poverty, illness and disease that their cultural programmes seemed of secondary importance. What the peasants needed were medicines and food, not poems and songs. The intrepid twenty-one-year-old Laurie Lee, who set off from England for Spain in 1934 with just his violin for company, registered the mounting desperation of the urban and rural poor as he moved south: 'I'd been travelling through Spain in a romantic haze, but as I came South the taste grew more bitter [. . .] I seemed to meet no one in Cádiz except the blind and the crippled, the diseased, the deaf and dumb whose condition was so hopeless they scarcely bothered to complain but treated it all as a twisted joke.'[61] On his way to the town of Valdepeñas in the summer of 1935 Lee stopped at a village fair to watch the performance of an open-air circus. It was a far cry from the Misiones Pedagógicas, consisting as it did of 'a monkey, a camel, an Arab, a snake and two painted little boys with trumpets.'[62] In a village in the mountains of the Sierra Morena he watched the villagers as he played his violin, 'blankets held to their throats, dribbles of damp lying along their eyebrows. I felt I could have been with some lost tribal remnant of eighteenth-century Scotland, during one of their pauses between famine and massacre.'[63]

There was no easy or rapid solution to these centuries-old deprivations, which would have required massive injections of state funding in the very years in which the Great Depression restricted national income and reduced the possibilities of social spending. The Misiones Pedagógicas did what they could, not only for culture but also for literacy, devoting 60 per cent of their annual budget to fixed and circulating libraries. Initially these libraries were very small, often containing only a hundred volumes. But by December 1933, 3,151 libraries had been established in the rural areas of Spain – no mean feat.

Within the limits of his modest budget, the Minister of Public Instruction, Fernando de los Ríos, did what he could to create a modern school system. The task was a gargantuan one, for between a quarter and a third of the population were illiterate and an estimated one million children were not even in school. In the years between 1909 and 1931, the Spanish state had constructed an average of 500 schools a year, a figure that leaped to over 2,500 in 1931–2.

The impetus could not be maintained, however, partly because of the economic situation and partly because in 1932–3 the greater part of the budget had to be spent on teachers' salaries. Catholic parents looked on bitterly as the religious orders and their schools were marginalised from the state education system; co-educational policies, which saw boys and girls sharing the same schools and many of the same facilities, aroused deep apprehension – almost moral panic – in many rural and small town families, Catholic and conservative. In spite of all this, the percentage of state spending on education reached its height in 1934, at 7.08 per cent of the national budget.[64]

II. Towards Civil War

1. Families and population: Spain and Italy compared

In statistical terms Spain and Italy in the 1930s resembled each other fairly closely, situated in the middle ground between, on the one hand the massive poverty of Turkey and the Soviet Union, and on the other the far greater prosperity and dynamism of Germany. Spain had a much smaller population than Italy – slightly under twenty-four million in 1930, compared with Italy's nearly forty-four million in 1931, but the distribution of its active population was very similar. In 1930 46.1 per cent of Spain's active population worked in agriculture, 27.2 per cent in industry and 21.2 per cent in the tertiary sector; the corresponding figures for Italy in 1931 were 46.8 per cent, 30.8 per cent and 22.4 per cent. Total fertility rates were almost identical: an average of 3.09 children per woman in Spain and 3.07 in Italy. In Spain average per capita income in 1930 was 2.802 dollars, falling after the Civil War to just 2.127. Italian equivalents were 2.854 dollars per head in 1930 and 3.444 by 1939.[65]

The historical demographer David Reher has underlined the enduring importance of family structures and systems, struggles and strategies, for the history of Spain:

> Risk, uncertainty, and death; dysfunctional and resilient families; family loyalties, brokered marriages, social and moral strictures; survival and stability; property, wealth, and poverty. The themes are always the same: the family, always the family. Its presence is ubiquitous in Spanish literature, in Spanish society; in its history and life.[66]

Much the same affirmation could be, and has been made, for Italian families. In 1973 Peter Nichols, the veteran correspondent of *The Times* in Rome, described the family as 'the accredited masterpiece of Italian society over the centuries, the bulwark, the natural unit, the provider of all that the state denies, the semi-sacred group, the avenger and the rewarder'.[67] The overwhelming majority of the population in both countries framed their family relations in the light of Catholic teaching, considered the family to be the 'natural unit' of society, and viewed their obligations to the state through the lens of clientelism and kinship.[68] The use of godparenthood, or ritual kinship, was also widespread, enabling families to reinforce, through a variety of strategies, social ties both vertical and horizontal.[69]

A first, basic characteristic of Spanish families in the first half of the twentieth century, shared to a great extent with their Italian counterparts, was an enduring spatial as well as emotional proximity. Research on the province and town of Cuenca, spanning more than three centuries of its history, shows how strong was the tendency for newly married couples to set up household in the immediate vicinity of one or other of their families of origin.[70] Such closeness gave rise to tensions which a looser kinship network would probably have avoided, but it had great advantages, not least for inter-generational solidarities. An elderly, widowed parent, for instance, could expect to spend periods of time being looked after in the households of his or her children. In Cuenca one variation on this custom came to be known as 'ir por meses' – spending a month or so with each family by turn. There was a general reluctance to abandon the elderly, and there still is.[71]

Another basic characteristic of Spanish family history was the limited presence of extended or multiple family structures. In the nineteenth and early twentieth centuries, complex families were mainly located in the rural areas in the north of the country. If we draw a line which stretches across the northern coastal areas, from Galicia to the Basque Country, and then along the Pyrenees and down into rural Catalonia, we find that to the north of it some 20–40 per cent of all households were complex in structure. In rural Catalonia stem families predominated, with a single designated heir (*hereu*), usually the eldest son, living in the parental home (the *masía* or *casa pairal*), together with his own family of procreation. As we have seen, these Catalan families tended to be strongly Catholic in orientation, with the participation of all family members, not only women, in the activities and festivals of the Church. They were similar in many ways to the *mezzadri* of Tuscany, especially to the Caroti family whom we followed in detail in the previous chapter.[72] But Catalan families never reached the complexity and average size of their Tuscan counterparts, and their inheritance patterns were far more rigid.

The question of inheritance was in fact closely linked to family structures. For some Spanish regions the point of reference was a legal system and practice which encouraged the selection of a single heir, as in Catalonia. But in most others legal norms encouraged partibility. Especially in the major cities, households tended to be small, families nuclear in structure, and neolocalism (starting up one's own home) the rule whenever economic conditions permitted. Here too there were strong similarities with Italy, in respect to both the cities and the rural south.

As for gender, the image we have of Spanish patriarchy is a particularly inflexible one, constructed on rigid, counter-reformation bases. The tensions between hierarchy and partnership in the domestic sphere, present in Pius XI's version of gender relations, were habitually resolved in Spain with a heavy bias in favour of husbands.[73] Women were jealously guarded, their freedom of movement restricted, their hiddenness (especially in southern Spain) close to the Muslim model of the distant past. A married woman was expected to be an 'ángel del hogar' (angel of the hearth), whose biological and social destiny was motherhood. Only in the Basque Country did women have the reputation of 'holding their own' with their menfolk, unafraid of treating them on equal terms.

2. Anarchist families of Barcelona and southern Spain

2.1 'Free love'

Before the twentieth century, anarchist theories on the family were no more developed than were those of Marx and the Marxists. During the stormy years of the First International (1864–76), Bakunin and Marx quarrelled violently on a whole series of issues – the nature of organisation, the role of the state, the revolutionary class – but they never debated in any depth the future of the family. As we have seen, Marx and Engels thought that Communist society would absorb into itself the previous functions of the family: communal kitchens would make cooking at home unnecessary, the state would take over the education of children, shared activity in civil society would, to a great extent, replace privacy and the private sphere. Women were to have equal rights with men, but their real emancipation would take place once they were able to take part in production on a large, social scale. This was an uncomfortable legacy for the European working class and a largely unexplored one before the Russian revolution.

Bakunin's view of the family was very different, though no more elaborate. In his rendering, and that of Kropotkin later on, the family would not disappear with the coming of the revolution. Rather, as human beings changed, so too would the structures and content of cohabitation. For the anarchists, revolution was first and foremost an *interior* process, freedom being conceived of as 'moral self-direction'.[74] Through it, individuals gained greater awareness of themselves. The emphasis on the individual could, and did, lead in two different directions: towards an accentuation of individual action, terrorist or otherwise; or towards the construction of a mass movement based on self-discipline and solidarity. The whole history of Spanish anarchism is one of conflict between these two trends, as well as of their constant intertwining.

In the intimate sphere men and women would enter into free unions with each other and practise 'free love'. This last was a key anarchist concept. It did not mean casual promiscuity but love which was free from any rigid rules imposed from above, whether they were Catholic ideas about the indissolubility of marriage or Marxist ones about the regulatory central state. In the anarchist world individuals took responsibility for their own relationships, seriously, even puritanically. The journal *Tierra y Libertad*, in an article of April 1915, warned 'how harmful it is to abuse free love, that is to commit libertine actions in the name of free love'.[75] Pepe Pereja, one of the peasant anarchists of Casas Viejas interviewed by Jerome Mintz, explained how 'free love' derived from women's rights and education: 'Free love does not mean having different women, having different lovers. Free love means that a woman has the same rights as a man. But to have free love one must be educated, one must have "intellectuality".'[76] Only then could men and women treat each other as equals in the home. But at the same time individuals had to be free to leave relationships once the original conditions for their love and their union were no longer present. Liberty and equality were thus the driving forces of 'free love': liberty from possessiveness and control, equality between the sexes both in economic terms and in the domestic sphere. The woman was to be freed from her sense of guilt, even terror, regarding her own sexuality, and her maternity was to be transformed into a conscious and voluntary choice, not an act of matrimonial duty.[77]

The anarchists, like the Marxists, spent an inordinate amount of time denouncing the many vices of the 'bourgeois family', but gave almost no concrete indication of what was to take its place. One constant theme was the free education of children. They were to be taught autonomy and to explore the world around them, as well as learn how to read and write. Very few anarchists questioned the idea of monogamy or proposed domestic communes to replace the family. A few 'radical individualists' such as the Catalan educationist Francisco Ferrer y Guardia and more tentatively Juan Montseny and Teresa Mañé dared to say that monogamy was slavery and proposed to share children on a communal basis, but they were roundly denounced for 'immorality' by the mainstream Spanish anarchists.[78]

Anarchism's views on free unions and free love formed just one part of its general world picture. Taken as a whole it is of undoubted fascination. The anarchists dreamed of libertarian as opposed to state communism, of self-rule based on small-scale associations and communities, of cooperation rather than competition, of open borders to take the place of armed frontiers, of international fraternity replacing nationalist ambitions. Men and women were not born as sinners, as the Church would have it, but free. Libertarian education would enable children to realise their full potential for freedom and to become responsible adults. As Bakunin wrote, 'Man is both the most individual and the most social of the animals.'[79]

2.2 The 'good families' of Barcelona

On 7 November 1893 Barcelona's magnificent Liceu theatre, the cultural and social epicentre of the Catalan bourgeoisie, dedicated the opening night of its opera season to Rossini's *William Tell*, a vivid depiction of familial love and the fight for Swiss freedom. During the first interval two bombs were thrown from the top floor of the theatre into the seats below. One did not explode but the other did. Twenty people were killed, half of them women, and many more injured. Five leading anarchists were arrested, summarily tried and executed, though their involvement in the crime was never demonstrated. Santiago Salvador, who had thrown the bombs, was hanged the following year.

Everywhere in Europe the 1890s were years of individual, anarchist terror. In Barcelona the Liceu bombing, together with a similar outrage at the Corpus Domini procession in 1896, in which a further eight people were killed, assumed an extraordinary importance in the life of the city, and not just because of their potent symbolism. The bombings signalled clearly that the model of Catalan social integration, so celebrated at the Universal Exposition held in the city in 1888, was built on shifting sands. In the aftermath of the Corpus Domini massacre a large number of anarchists were rounded up and taken to the infamous Montjuich prison. There they were systematically tortured by the Brigada Social, the new political police – their bones broken and their genitals mutilated. Some of them died or went mad. In the radical press of Europe, Barcelona became synonymous for the first time, but sadly not the last, with uncontrolled state brutality.[80]

The Catalan bourgeois project of social integration had centred around a core group of the city's elite, which the anthropologist Gary Wray McDonogh has interestingly called the 'good families of Barcelona'.[81] They were 'good' in the sense not necessarily of virtue but of respectability. They were also economically dynamic, responsible in the nineteenth century for the rapid growth of

Catalan industry, especially textiles. By mid-century the Catalan textile industry ranked fourth in the world, behind Britain, France and the United States, but ahead of Belgium and Italy. By 1900 the city had more than half a million inhabitants.[82]

The good families of Barcelona rapidly formed a cohesive power group. They did so by means of marriage strategies, both between themselves and with members of the city's aristocracy, by incorporating single-family firms into larger companies, and by a system of interlocking directorates. The pillars upon which their social and cultural homogeneity was constructed included private conservative Jesuit education for their children, obedience to etiquette and fashion, the use of foreign languages, ownership of a box in one of the many tiers of the Liceu theatre (which housed 3,500 people), and a place in the elite section of the city's famous Old Cemetery.[83]

Such families, or at least the more intelligent and open-minded members of them, dreamed of creating an integrated city, a 'Gran Barcelona' in which they might exercise their hegemony over the other social strata of the city. They were helped to formulate these dreams by the rapid growth of Catalan nationalism. With the founding of the Lliga Regionalista in 1901, Catalan jurists, politicians, folklorists and ideologues moved centre stage.

One of the most interesting and important of these figures was Enric Prat de la Riba (1870–1917), whose social discourse put the Catalan rural family on a pedestal. For Prat de la Riba the large rural stem family, inhabiting the *casa pairal* and directed with severity and justice by its principal male figure, was a family model to be treasured. It symbolised Catalonian social homogeneity, in stark contrast to conditions in much of the rest of rural Spain. His views were close to those of Frédéric Le Play, the great French Catholic sociologist of the same period, who had been the first to study the diversity of family structures, forms and cultures. Traditional, Catholic, extended stem families were not in their view relics from the past, but rather the model upon which modern industrial relations should be based. Prat de la Riba wrote in 1898,

> The word *house* [*casa*], applied to all classes of industrial exploitation, is in itself a revelation. It manifests the nature [of industrial activity] with more precision and clarity than the most detailed and careful analysis [. . .] The *hereu*, continuation of the personality of the father and the unity of the family, is the patron *par excellence* – he who maintains the house, saving it from that dissolution which is, for it, synonymous with death.[84]

The 'good families', then, relied on a social project that had a particular family model at its heart and which boasted three lines of intervention: town planning, inter-class, regional nationalism and paternalistic industrial relations. All three were to prove failures. Lip service was paid to Ildefonso Cerdá's 1891 utopian vision of the new city, but landlord interests blocked one part of the plan and overbuilding spoiled the other. The popular classes were confined to the decaying older city, expelled to the outlying *colonias* (mill towns) or forced into shanty towns at the city's edges. As for regional nationalism in the guise of the Lliga, it proved successful politically in attracting shopkeepers and white-collar workers, but it never conquered the Barcelona working class, for whom, as we shall see, anarchist ideas, which made of the working-class man a subject rather than an object, had greater appeal. Finally, while there were examples of paternalism amongst the 'good families', they never became predominant. Eusebio Güell, to whom Prat de la Riba dedicated his *Ley jurídica de la industria* of 1898, converted his family textile factory into a *colonia* outside the city in 1891, providing his workers with housing, schools, a hospital and even a chapel designed by Antoni Gaudí. In 1905 a child fell into a vat of hot dye in the factory, suffering such severe burns that he was at risk of having both legs amputated. When an appeal was launched for donors for a skin transplant, the manager of the factory, Claudio Güell López, and his brother Santiago were the first to come forward.[85] These were commendable actions but far from common ones. The good families were not as good as their own propaganda made out.

2.3 The 'bad' families

In contraposition to these were the working-class families of the city. Obviously, they were not all alike. At one end of the social scale was an aristocracy of skilled Catalan workers, whose families and homes expressed decorum and respectability. In their lifestyle, though not necessarily in their politics, they approached the city's lower middle classes. At the other end were the recent immigrants to the city from the south-eastern rural regions of Spain, a human river that became a flood in the 1920s. They lived in shanty towns or on the streets, were dressed very poorly, worked mainly as casual labourers, and spoke no Catalan.[86]

What is striking in the Barcelona case is the existence of a central core of working-class families, perhaps even a majority, which as time passed seemed to increase their distance from their bourgeois counterparts. Anarcho-syndicalism was in no small part responsible for this. Victor Serge, the famous libertarian author and agitator of Russian origin, came to live in Barcelona in 1917 after being released from a French prison at the height of the First World War. The first part of his semi-autobiographical novel *Birth of our Power*

fig. 34 A popular market in the Carrer Arc del Teatre, in the historic centre of
Barcelona, 1920–30.

(*Naissance de notre force*) of 1931 is set in Barcelona. Serge underlines the
abyss that separated the material culture of the city's two opposing faces:

> In the busy crowd along the main arteries these workers, who had always felt
> degraded by the contrast between their sloppy old suits or overalls and bour-
> geois dress, pass expensive restaurants they never enter, luxurious cafés from
> which strains of music emanate, shop windows with astonishing displays of
> objects so beyond their means as to be not even tempting: leathers, silks,
> chrome, gold, pearls.

For Serge, the degree of degradation of everyday life pointed in only one
direction:

> They don't have much reason to ponder over the value of their lives, these
> people. Never will they escape from these shacks (which stink of cooking oil
> and bed bugs), from the factories (where their bodies and brains are drained
> each day), from the stifling slums, from the swarms of kids with their matted,
> lice-infested hair [. . .] Only by force will they break out of the closed circle of
> their fate.[87]

In 1920 Barcelona had a population of over 700,000. Of this figure nearly 200,000 were industrial workers, an extraordinarily high proportion. Cotton textiles and textile finishing trades formed the core of the city's production, with more than 50,000 workers employed in the sector, a significant number of whom were women. Barcelona was far from being a purely textile town, however. It was also a great Mediterranean port, employing more than 14,000 sailors, dockers and transport workers, with metalworkers accounting for another 27,000 members of the workforce.[88]

Surprisingly, very little detailed research has been undertaken on Barcelona families in the first decades of the twentieth century. There has been an over-concentration on politics and an underestimation of the significance of primary social structures and relations. In many of the *barris* (working-class districts) of Barcelona the same sort of kinship and neighbourhood solidari-ties, the same 'mutuality of the oppressed', to use Raymond Williams's felici-tous phrase,[89] were to be found as in the industrial peripheries of Turin and Milan. Kinship ties were apparently further strengthened by selecting godpar-ents from within the same streets of the neighbourhood, an informal and personal agreement without the formal sanction of the local authorities or the Church. Families were small and the average age of marriage high. The average daily wage of a male industrial worker in Barcelona in 1905 was insufficient to maintain a family of four persons. Women and children took what casual and part-time work they could find. Inheritance patterns were primitive because there was usually little or nothing to inherit.[90]

Family life was characterised by its precariousness. An economic downturn such as the one following the great crisis of 1898, the illness of the principal wage earner, his arrest or conscription, were sufficient for a family to be plunged into misery or to fall apart. Though not on the Russian scale, bands of homeless children roamed the streets and formed themselves into gangs (*pandillas*). The most alarming of these were the so-called 'TB gangs', consisting of unemployable youths suffering from tuberculosis. In 1935 a group of physi-cians estimated that 70 per cent of all Barcelona children displayed signs of incipient tuberculosis. Typhoid was another disease that was rife in insalu-brious working-class quarters.[91]

The glaring contradictions of Spain's most industrialised city were rendered even more acute by constant population expansion. Between 1920 and 1930 Barcelona's population increased by nearly 300,000, reaching over a million for the first time. By 1930, 56 per cent of the population had been born outside the city of Barcelona. The immigration of the 1920s was largely composed of labourers and some ex-miners from very poor south-eastern rural areas, espe-cially Murcia and Almería. They spoke Castilian, not Catalan, found work if they were lucky as unskilled manual labourers, and were accused of being lazy and irresponsible. Their arrival in the city added greatly to problems of housing and swelled the ranks of the unemployed.[92]

By the early 1930s the city had become a dystopia for the Barcelona bourgeoisie. 'Bad' families, diseased, dirty, dismembered and disrespectful, seemed omnipresent – in the Old City, in the waterfront district bordering Parallel and the Raval, in the shanty towns on the edges of the city. Moral panic filled the pages of the respectable press – the immigrants were 'foreign dung' who would infect the core values of nation and family, the working classes were 'diseased' and 'contagious'. Barcelona, to use Manuel Castells's definition, had become a 'wild city'.[93]

2.4 Anarcho-syndicalism, the CNT and the family

Anarcho-syndicalism, which spread rapidly on this urban terrain, seemed to provide an organisation and an ideology that gave shape and sense to lives based on so much deprivation and exploitation. It was a much more formidable force than the uncertain northern Italian socialism of 1919 and 1920, though it could boast no figure of the originality and brilliance of Antonio Gramsci (who was often accused of being an anarcho-syndicalist). Indeed, the anti-intellectualism of the movement was one of its weaknesses.

Spanish anarcho-syndicalism developed after the spectacular failures of the individualist, terrorist acts of the turn of the century. The Confederación Nacional del Trabajo (CNT) came into being in October 1910, linking revolutionary anarchism with militant trade unionism. At an everyday level workers were offered the prospect of a community of intent which preached direct action against the employers, ranging from the smallest act of factory indiscipline to strikes, boycotts and sabotage. The CNT's long-term vision of revolution was not so much the French syndicalists' general strike, or a seizure of power planned by a small group of professional revolutionaries, as in the Leninist model, but rather semi-spontaneous insurrection.[94]

The Spanish movement boasted a highly original structure. It insisted on 'sindicatos únicos' (single-union structures) for all workers in a given trade, such as construction or metallurgy, rather than separate craft unions for skilled workers, hoping in this way to counterpose the militancy of unskilled workers to the moderation of the worker aristocracy. Secondly, the CNT insisted on territorial organisation, just as the Italians had done with the Camere del Lavoro, so that solidarities between *different* types of workers could develop rapidly. The most spectacular case of this form of solidarity in Barcelona was the great strike at the Anglo-Canadian electrical company

('La Canadiense') in February 1919, when the sacking of seven CNT white-collar workers led to a general strike of an estimated 100,000 workers. During the two weeks of the strike, the city's electricity was cut off and many arrests were made. At the end of the strike, the workers were reinstated, the eight-hour working day was conceded and an amnesty was granted to the pickets.[95]

In general organisational terms, the CNT fought with all its might against the creation of a centralised bureaucratic caste of officials. Right up to 1936, by which point it had reached the astonishing membership figure of 1.6 million, it employed only a handful of paid organisers, and its national committee rotated from region to region, in order to prevent power being concentrated in a central leadership.

These were the organisational principles that gave the CNT such force. When combined with a fierce belief in individual self-education they constituted the premises for a formidable alternative world view. Its militants organised and agitated not just in the factories but in the dense social networks of the working-class districts. They offered inter-generational solidarity, help for migrant labour on its arrival in the city, contacts with the street gangs and a refusal to label anyone as automatically 'deviant' or 'criminal'. By 1914, seventy-five *atenee* – centres for popular culture and social activity – had been founded in the *barris*. Each of them had a lending library that stocked the socialist and anarchist classics, as well as the novels of Zola and the plays of Ibsen. Each was aided in its educational tasks by a so-called 'rationalist school', combining serious secondary education with a strong spirit of democracy in the classroom. The *atenee* also offered social services, cooperative shops and leisure activities, including choral groups and theatre productions. Clerical hypocrisy and misdeeds were at the forefront of their social critique. Two plays by José Fola Igúrbide, *El Cristo moderno* and *El sol de la humanidad*, were particularly popular. In keeping with the strong anti-urban element in anarchist culture, organised hikes outside the city grew in number and popularity in the 1920s and early 1930s.[96]

This potent working-class urban civil society lasted nearly twenty years and in its radicality, autonomy and dimensions was unparalleled in the whole of Europe. It suffered from three grave flaws (four, if we include its anti-intellectualism). The first concerns gender. In spite of the widespread anarchist advocacy of 'free love', based upon women's equal rights in and outside the home, women's position in the movement remained a fundamentally subordinate one. It is true that the CNT tried to organise strikes and occupations in areas of the economy dominated by the female workforce, such as the textile 'sweat shops' of Catalonia and the telephone exchanges of Barcelona. But it continued to be an organisation dominated by men. To a great extent women stayed at home, offering auxiliary services to their husbands, looking after the children and rarely venturing out of the domestic sphere.

Secondly, this most radical of movements never succeeded in elaborating an alternative view of the family and its organisation. All the tension, experimentation and legislation of the first years of the Russian revolution, with its commune movement, Family Codes and the charismatic leadership of Aleksandra Kollontai, was almost completely absent in Barcelona and indeed throughout Spain. At the national congress of the CNT in Zaragoza in May 1936, on the eve of the Civil War, a lengthy and important resolution was passed entitled 'The confederal conception of libertarian communism'. It included a small section dedicated to 'The family and relations between the sexes', which is worth analysing in depth for its extraordinary combination of traditionalism and radicalism, perception and naivety.[97]

It begins with a solid defence of the family's role in history, very far removed from the Marxist critique of the family:

> It ought not to be forgotten that the family was the first civilizing nucleus of the human species and that it has performed most admirable functions in the imparting of morality and solidarity, that it has survived the evolution of the family itself, through clan, tribe, people and nation, and that it is likely that it will survive for a long time to come.

When the revolution finally arrived, it would not be its task to 'intervene violently in the family', except in cases of families suffering from gross incompatibilities, which would be given the necessary assistance to dissolve themselves. No other prescriptions regarding family life were considered necessary.

As for individuals, the first step in the libertarian revolution 'consists of ensuring that all human beings, without distinction of sex, are economically independent'. The two sexes were declared equal in both rights and duties. The principle of 'free love' was reiterated, 'without any regulations other than the will of the man and that of the woman'. The collectivity would 'guarantee the protection of children' and 'guard itself against human aberrations through the application of eugenic-biological principles'. This last sentence had a rather sinister ring to it, as did the one that followed it: 'Good sex education at school will lead to selective breeding according to the aims of eugenics and conscious procreation, with the intention of producing healthy and beautiful offspring'. 'Selective breeding' were not neutral words in Europe in the mid–1930s, though it has to be said that what the anarchists had in mind was sex education, 'conscious maternity' – the planning of pregnancies and families – the legalisation of abortion and increased hygienic care and instruction for working-class mothers. Later in this same year of 1936, with Barcelona in the hands of the revolutionaries, a 'eugenic reform of abortion' was passed along these lines.[98]

The Zaragoza resolution of 1936 also made reference to 'problems of a moral nature which love may engender', and it was here that the anarcho-syndicalists seemed at their most naive. Those males who 'may desire forcible or bestial love', and who would not listen to reason, 'will face a change of surroundings, water and air'. A similar solution was proposed for those who suffered from unrequited romantic love:

> For love sickness, which becomes an illness when it turns to obduracy and blindness, a change of commune will be recommended, with the sick person being removed from the environment which blinds and maddens him; however, it is unlikely that these excesses of passion will continue to exist in an environment of sexual liberty.

Unfortunately, as all radical libertarian movements of the twentieth century learned to their cost, an environment of sexual liberty was likely to compound 'love sickness' rather than cure it.[99]

Helen Graham has written that in Spain 'the anarchist utopia stopped at the front door'.[100] This is a harsh judgement but far from an unsubstantiated one. The Zaragoza motion, both in what it says and more especially in what it does not say, revealed the limitations of anarcho-syndicalist reflection on these vital themes. The one partial exception to this statement, the Mujeres Libres movement, will be analysed later in the chapter.

Finally, and gravest of all of the CNT's failings, was its espousal of what Gerald Brenan has rightly called the 'mystique of violence'.[101] This is not to suggest that violence, in one form or another, was avoidable in Spain in the decades after the First World War. Given a socio-economic and judicial system as historically class-biased as the Spanish one, and given the opposition to the brutality of the Civil Guard, the Brigada Social and the police assassins (pistoleros) – who in 1923 murdered the finest and most pacific of the CNT leaders, Salvador Seguí – violence was impossible to avoid. But the anarcho-syndicalists, or at least the majority, exalted in violence. We get a clear glimpse of this if we return for a moment to Victor Serge and his description of his comrades arming for the 1917 insurrection (which failed). It is a phallic, Marinetti-like description, typical of the European avant-garde in its celebration of new weaponry and imminent destruction. It is also a key to understanding why women were excluded from this very male culture:

Workers stream out through the dazzling city towards their homes in the poor quarters, their steps lightened, shoulders thrown back with a new feeling of power. Their hands never tire of caressing the weapons' black steel [. . .] Once they enter the slum streets where they feel at home, their exuberance brings them together in talkative groups. Now and then the weapons glisten in the palms of their powerful hands as they feel the virile heft of sleek metal or hold them out nervously at arm's length.[102]

The whole, considerable cult of Buenaventura Durruti – anarchist, bank robber, *pistolero* – should be read in this light.[103] Time and again in the Spanish experience the 'hard men' of the 'grupos de afinidad' (affinity groups) won out over the more moderate CNT trade unionists. As Romero Mauro has observed,

The mechanics of the elimination of the less extremist were always the same: the more violent would die or go to jail as a consequence of some direct action; the compassion and indignation of the confederal masses would explode in a wave of protest; violent protests would bring to the fore [once again] a group of violent leaders.[104]

In 1927 the Federación Anarquista Ibérica (FAI) was founded. A secret organisation of leading anarchists, more Leninist than libertarian in its structure, its aim was to keep the CNT on the straight and narrow path of revolution. But what sort of path was this? The anarchist idea of revolution as a semi-spontaneous phenomenon, with little central organisation or planning, led to innumerable tragedies at a local level, major disasters at a regional and national one, and everywhere a terrible weakening of those who believed in radical social reform. It is difficult not to judge the CNT's record on this crucial terrain as deeply irresponsible.

2.5 The rural labourers of southern Spain

In his classic study of agrarian conditions in Spain in the first half of the twentieth century, Edward Malefakis identified the continuing existence of *latifundios* in the rural south as an endemic social problem, 'constantly upsetting the political life not only of the South, but also of the nation'.[105] I would like to present a brief overview of family life and peasant resistance in these regions. Naturally, the agrarian structure of Spain was as varied and complicated as that of Italy, with small landowners, tenant farmers and sharecroppers to be found aplenty even in the great *latifundio* provinces. But my attention is here focused on the landless labourers.

By the time of the Civil War, the great estates, defined as those of over 250 hectares, occupied over 50 per cent of land in the provinces of Cádiz, Seville and Ciudad Real, and between 30 and 50 per cent in the other twelve southern provinces. These were estates which primarily produced wheat and, to a lesser extent, olives. Noble families still had extensive holdings in these provinces, but they had been overtaken by up-and-coming bourgeois families who had purchased common lands and Church property as they came on to the market. A high percentage of owners were absentee. In some provinces the concentration of property in the hands of a small number of families reached pathological proportions. In Badajoz, for instance, the province which had elected Margarita Nelken as its deputy in 1931, and which she served with such passion, some 400 individuals, belonging for the most part to a few interconnected family groups, owned some 32.5 per cent of the province's total cultivated surface. In 1930 the province of Badajoz had a population of just over 700,000, three-quarters of whom were directly dependent on agriculture for their livelihood.[106]

These estates made a profit, but it was not one that derived from efficiency. All the standard indicators of modern agriculture – the introduction of machinery, use of fertilisers, spread of irrigation, introduction of alternative crops – found the landowners and their tenant farmers (*arrendadores* or *labradores*) wanting. Profit was to be made, rather, by the ruthless exploitation of labour. Very much like their counterparts in the southern parts of Italy, and especially on the great plains of the Tavoliere in Puglia, the *campesinos* of southern Spain made their way to the village square early in the morning, hoping to be hired for the day. 'As often as not [their] day ended in the same village square or in the local tavern.' There was even less work available than on the Tavoliere – only 180–250 days a year, compared with the estimated 250–280 days on the northern Apulian plains.[107]

Children in the Spanish *latifundio* areas began to work at a very early age. Here is the testimony of Manuel Llamas from Casas Viejas, in south-western Andalusia:

I was one of four children. I began to work when I was seven years old. One *duro* [five pesetas] each month. For food I had garlic soup with bread in the morning, a stew of chickpeas and fat at night, and I had a piece of bread in my pocket during the day [. . .] I worked for a small landowner who wanted to become a big landowner and was taking advantage of me and others. My uncle worked for him. Then I was promoted as if I were in the army, and I earned two *duros* a month. I was very proud. I was eight years old. I learned to read when I was eighteen, in Jerez.[108]

Infant mortality was very high in Casas Viejas, and many of the children who survived their first year of life were later afflicted with rickets and tuberculosis. Family dwellings (*chozas* – huts or thatched cottages) were squalid, single-storey constructions, with little light, walls made of mud and rocks, floors of dirt or stone and no running water. Casas Viejas was no more than a scattered group of buildings, with a population of around 2,000 in the 1920s, not a commune in its own right. Administratively speaking, it formed part of the ancient town of Medina Sidonia, which had a population of around 12,000. Even the larger Spanish agro-towns, therefore, were much smaller than their Puglian counterparts; Cerignola, the epicentre of labourer antagonism in Puglia before and after the First World War, had 34,000 inhabitants by the beginning of the century. There was thus a different relationship in the two countries between population, town and country.

The loyalty to the *pueblo* was very marked in the Spanish case, the word itself signifying both village or town and people. The hostilities between *pueblos* were also very marked. In 1954, Julian Pitt-Rivers, in his ethnographical study of Grazalema, a small town in the mountains of Andalusia, noted the strength of rivalries between *pueblos*, the festival of the patron saint of the village or town being one of the principal occasions for their expression.[109] Such rivalry was everywhere to be found in the European Mediterranean countries in the first half of the nineteenth century. In Spain it was given tragic significance, as we shall see, because at the outbreak of the Civil War it was not rivalry that the landless labourers needed but exceptional solidarity in the face of mortal danger.

As for families in Barcelona, so for those in the rural south, a great deal of historical research remains to be done. Labourer families were certainly nuclear in structure, but we have few statistics and even fewer details of everyday life. The women of the *pueblos* remain particularly hidden from history.

In the realm of politics and ideology, the beliefs of the rural southern Spanish anarcho-syndicalists have more than once been analysed within a religious framework, anarchism being counterposed to Catholicism. This seems quite wide of the mark, in that the anarchist *campesinos*, for all their ardent idealism and millenarianism, in no way made an appeal to an external God or to supernatural powers which judged them and decided their fate. Theirs was always a very Bakuninist ideal of self-education and of determination to control individual destiny in a material world. Indeed, it was belief in these ideas that made the southern Spanish anarchist movement exceptional in terms of its size, intensity and longevity, leaving far behind its more limited Italian counterpart.

Juan Díaz del Moral's account of the 'general strike' in his home town of Bujalance in 1903 – he was a local notary at the time – conveys some of the extraordinary qualities of the movement.[110] The strike broke out on 5 May without warning, without the drawing up of a petition, without demands. Its timing was unfortunate, in that there were no immediately urgent tasks in the fields. This did not seem to matter. The men simply withdrew from the streets and taverns into their own homes. No wine was consumed while the strike continued: 'a few groups of three or four workers silently and solemnly patrolled the streets. Contrary to their custom, they did not raise their voices in speeches and argument, there was not a single quarrel.' As the days passed, the poorest families began to suffer from hunger. No other *pueblos* followed the example of Bujalance:

> After twelve or fourteen days, because the general strike (and the social revolution) had not broken out in all of Andalusia, as was to be expected given the gallantry and daring of the people of Bujalance, who had not wanted the glory of having initiated the movement to be snatched from them, the strike ended as unexpectedly and quietly as it had begun.[111]

The dignity, peacefulness and gravity of the peasants' attempts at profound self-transformation made a great impression on Díaz del Moral and other observers.

Thirty years later, in one of the key incidents of the second Republic, things went very much worse in the Andalusian village of Casas Viejas. In late 1932, the CNT, firmly in the hands of the 'hard men' of the FAI, decided that the time had come to raise the flag of violent social revolution and to strike out against the 'bourgeois' Republic. The daily newspaper *CNT* made clear that the Republic and its democracy were to be condemned out of hand:

> 'One must defend the Republic'. A lie! Hypocrisy! Must one defend privilege? The latifundios? Exploitation? The sacred right of property? Must one defend the capitalist regime in danger? Must one halt the advance of the social revolution? [. . .] This is the hour of the workers. Neither anything nor anyone can delay their march towards complete liberation.[112]

In Barcelona the physiognomy of the insurrection began to take shape. The railway workers, who had already struck once, would take the lead. Major urban centres would then rise in support. Local uprisings in the south and elsewhere would pin down civil guards and troops. The planning was chaotic and the results a disaster, 'semi-spontaneous insurrection' once again demonstrating its tragic folly.

In the far-flung Andalusian countryside, preparations went ahead all the same. At Casas Viejas, the anarchist section was not particularly active or numerous. Unusually, it included among its members a seventeen-year-old girl, María Silva Cruz. Attractive and courageous, she was nicknamed 'La Libertaria', as she had taken to walking through the *calle* of the village with a red and black kerchief around her neck. In December 1932 she and her young female comrades had written to the anarchist national weekly *Tierra y Libertad*, 'A group of young women in the village of Casas Viejas have formed themselves into a group with the name of *Amor y Armonía*. The group desires relations with all groups of men and women. At the same time it sends strong greetings to the political prisoners.'[113]

On 10 January 1933 the village's anarchist section held a long meeting. The news from elsewhere was contradictory. Opinion in the village was divided as to whether or not to go ahead, but the young people were all for insurrection. At six o'clock on the morning of the 11th, a group of militants went to the mayor and told him that 'comunismo libertario' had been proclaimed in Casas Viejas and that the authorities were no longer in control. They advised him to tell the Civil Guard to surrender, in which case nothing would happen to them. The Civil Guard – four in all, including one sergeant – shut themselves up in their barracks, which were rapidly surrounded. The best marksmen in the village opened fire on them, mortally wounding two of them in the head.

As no other *pueblo* in the area had risen in insurrection, reinforcements of civil guards and republican assault guards soon arrived in the village. Their commander, Captain Manuel Rojas, was totally ill suited to the task before him. Some of the insurgents had sought refuge in the home of the old charcoal burner, Francisco Cruz, nicknamed Seisdedos. Rojas ordered the little hut to be burned to the ground. As it began to burn, María Silva Cruz, 'La Libertaria', granddaughter of Seisdedos, ran out holding a young boy by the hand. The guards did not shoot them, but others were shot as they came out. Those who remained, including a young girl, Manuela Lago, María Silva's friend, were burned to death. The following morning Rojas ordered another twelve men to be rounded up. He and his troops then summarily shot them all. Twenty-two *campesinos* were killed, as were three guards. In May 1934 a Cádiz court sentenced Captain Rojas to twenty-one years' imprisonment for his leading role in the massacre of the peasants.[114]

The news from Casas Viejas shocked the whole of Spain, for in the last instance it was the Republic that had been responsible for the killings. The prime minister, Manuel Azaña, confided an anguished note to his diary on 15 January 1933:

> Three representatives from different parties have spoken to me today about dictatorship as the only possible solution for anarchist uprisings, if they continue. This is the national inclination, carrying over from previous times and foreign influence. Can Spain in fact live within democracy and under law? Nobody wants to obey, except by force.[115]

As for María Silva Cruz, she was imprisoned but was not brought to trial. For a time she lived in Madrid 'in free love' with her companion Miguel Pérez Cordón, with whom she had a son. Later they returned Andalusia but not to Casas Viejas. At the outset of Franco's coup in July 1936 she was taken prisoner by some Falangists who casually shot her and others, probably at Cañuela, between Jerez and Medina. Her little son was then looked after by her sister-in-law.[116]

2.6 Mujeres Libres

In April 1936, a few months before María Silva Cruz was murdered, a group of women in Barcelona, Lucía Sánchez Saornil, Mercedes Comaposada and Amparo Poch y Gascón, founded the anarchist women's organisation Mujeres Libres. At its height it boasted an estimated 20,000 members and 147 local groups, of which more than 40 were in Catalonia. The organisation was always to suffer from the wartime conditions in which it operated, but it managed none the less to publish thirteen numbers of the review of the same name, up to 1938.[117]

The political programme of Mujeres Libres was dedicated to both class and gender – women were to be freed simultaneously from capitalist exploitation and men's dominion. Mujeres Libres asserted its complete autonomy but within the anarchist movement as a whole wanted to be placed on the same organisational level as the CNT, the FAI and the anarchist youth organisation Federación Ibérica de Juventudes Libertarias (FIJL). This formal request was rejected on the grounds that an autonomous women's organisation would be an element of internal division. It has to be said that more than one female anarchist militant agreed, including the redoubtable Federica Montseny, who denied that there was a specific question of women's liberation, maintaining that there was only a question of the liberation of human beings in general.

One of the key areas of intervention was the struggle to develop a feminist consciousness among working-class women. Mujeres Libres considered itself to be a proletarian organisation and as such put a great deal of energy into creating an alternative female mass culture. One of the most interesting of its debates concerned maternity. Was child-bearing to be considered the highest role to which women could aspire, or was motherhood only one of various possible roles for emancipated women? The first of these options garnered the most consent but all agreed that motherhood should be a 'conscious choice', not one over which the woman exercised no control. As Mercedes Comaposada told Martha Ackelsberg in an interview of 1982, 'What we wanted, at the very least, were mothers who were conscious of their choice. We wanted people to be able to choose whether to have children, how and when, and know how to bring them up.'[118]

Another important and delicate area was that of women's sexuality, although much more attention was dedicated to the plague of prostitution than to the intimate details of women's lives. Between 1932 and 1935 Amparo Poch y Gascón had written a series of articles on the need for women to come to know their own sexuality. Sex was to be an important part of a woman's life and not a simple means for reproduction and male satisfaction. The sexual question was again taken up by Etta Federn in a pamphlet published in 1937, *Mujeres de las revoluciones*. In it she specifically evoked Aleksandra Kollontai, some of whose writings had just been published in Barcelona.[119]

A final theme to receive attention in the organisation's review was that of children and their education. In 1927 Federica Montseny had been adamant that children were an individual, female creation: 'By natural law children belong to their mother.'[120] Mercedes Comaposada disagreed: 'there was no reason why they had to be our own children, we had to take responsibility for the children of others, for orphans for example'.[121] As for education, most correspondents preferred a middle way between an extreme collectivist solution à la Kollontai and delegating to the family. Parents were not to be regarded as an obstacle, an element of backwardness, but were rather 'to share with the collectivity' the education of their children. All agreed that education was not to be authoritarian or a process of indoctrination. An article from the fifth issue of *Mujeres libres*, entitled 'Children, children, children', was quite categorical: 'Children cannot and must not be catholics, socialists, communists or libertarians. Children must be only what they are: children.'[122] They were to be allowed to explore the world around them, to experiment, to wander outside the classroom, to ask questions. This love of children and their natural freedoms was one of the most attractive aspects of Spanish anarchism.

III. Individuals and Families: Life and Death in the Civil War

1. Asturias, October 1934

All attempts to stabilise the Republic failed. As Pierre Vilar has written, social, regional and 'spiritual' differences were too great; too many forces in Spain wanted the end of the Republic, too few wanted it to survive.[123] In November 1933 new elections were held. This time the centre-right forces coalesced, while the left was divided and impatient: the Socialist leader Largo Caballero viewed himself ever more as the Spanish Lenin and the anarcho-syndicalists talked only the language of revolution. After the elections of 1933, the new, centre-right executive undermined one by one the previous gains from republican legislation. In the autumn of 1934 the CEDA, the Catholic confederation of groups and parties led by José María Gil Robles, entered the government. Gil Robles had stated quite explicitly the year before that if CEDA objectives could not be attained through democratic elections and parliament, then the latter could be abandoned.[124] All over Europe the left was being crushed: so too was democracy. In October 1934, the Spanish Socialists, taking a leaf out of the anarcho-syndicalist book, declared a national, insurrectionary general strike. Unsurprisingly, only some parts of the country and certain sections of the working classes responded. In this case it was the coal miners of Asturias, badly hit by the Depression and determined to make a stand against Fascism, who wholeheartedly raised the flag of social revolution.[125] CNT and UGT, the Socialist union, fought back to back for two weeks, but they were never going to be a match for the army, especially when it was commanded by a ruthless young general by the name of Francisco Franco. Entrusted with the pacification of Asturias, Franco ordered his artillery systematically to shell the miners' strongholds. By the end of the revolt, more than 1,000 of the insurgents had been killed, another 3,000 injured and 30,000 imprisoned.

Brian Bunk's analysis of the press and propaganda of the two sides highlights some interesting attitudes to family duty, evocative of earlier, ever recurring debates.[126] On the one hand, left-wing poems and posters paid tribute to the heroic miners who, in spite of their love for their families, went off to fight. In this version the miners sacrificed themselves and the immediate needs of their families, both material and emotional, for a greater cause – that of social revolution. On the other hand, counter-revolutionary propaganda put the priority on the need to stay at home and provide for one's own family. To go and fight was a tragedy, occasioned by a misplaced sense of honour and loyalty to a peer group. In this version, bitterly hostile to the Asturias uprising, the miners had rejected a fundamental male responsibility – that of providing for one's family. And for what? The revolutionaries were represented not as dying a heroic death but rather as languishing in prison for many years while their wives and children remained hungry and abandoned.

Acción Popular, the main grouping within the Catholic right-wing CEDA, published a pamphlet on the Asturias uprising called *Terror: El marxismo en España*. It told the story of Julia Fraigedo, a woman who died fighting along-side her civil-guard husband. There are harrowing photos of the couple's children standing in front of the building where their parents were killed.[127]

2. Families and the Civil War: towards a typology

In the see-saw political history of the second Republic, it was the turn of the left-wing forces of the Popular Front to win the national elections of February 1936. From that time onwards, plans for a *coup d'état*, led by a group of army generals, went ahead systematically, culminating in Franco's *pronunciamiento* of 18 July 1936. Having expected little resistance the generals instead found themselves with a full-scale civil war on their hands, one that was to last three years and cost an estimated half a million lives.

There are many ways of telling the history of the Civil War – in military terms, as a history of unimaginable violence and cruelty, as part of the inter-national war against Fascism and Nazism. I would like here to try to do some-thing different: to analyse the Civil War in terms of different types of family experience. The accounts of the war are full of husbands and wives, uncles and cousins, children and parents, but these never form part of a wider analytical framework. What were family experiences, reactions and strategies in the face of the war, particularly in the summer of 1936, when it first began? How far was this really a fratricidal war, as it has often been depicted? In the pages that follow I sketch a first typology, without any pretence to completeness.

After the generals' coup, Spain was divided in two. Hundreds of thousands of families found themselves on the wrong side – either because they were republicans behind nationalist lines or vice versa. They feared the worst, because they were menaced from more than one direction. Within the *pueblo*, the outbreak of war provided an opportunity to settle *rencillas*, old personal scores of all types. Neighbourhood quarrels, an insult to male honour which had occurred a decade previously, even being jilted in a love affair could all place a person at great risk. It was a time of evil, of unbridled passions. Outside the *pueblo*, the menace was even greater, in that those who carried out the initial killings often came from another town or city or village. It was easier for them to depersonalise, even dehumanise their victims, and this rendered the possibility of mediation and salvation much more remote.[128]

In the midst of this terrifying situation, we can discern different types of family reaction and experience. The first is that of families strongly divided, even destroyed, by the war. Juan Crespo was a monarchist student attracted by Primo de Rivera's Falange party – the nearest Spanish equivalent to Italian Fascism. We first encountered him in a college run by monks in Salamanca in 1931.[129] At the outbreak of war, he volunteered repeatedly to fight with the nationalist army, and in time came to command Moorish troops. One of his uncles, however, Casto Prieto Carrasco, was the republican mayor of Salamanca and professor of medicine at the university. In July 1936 a milkman discovered his body in a ditch on the road to Valladolid. It was an especially hot summer and bodies decomposed rapidly.[130] The killing bore all the hallmarks of summary justice carried out by a right-wing death squad. A second uncle, from the village of Morasverdes, was arrested because he was the brother of Casto Prieto. Held without trial until May 1937, he was released from prison dying of a bladder complaint. A third uncle, who belonged to the CEDA, was mayor of the *pueblo* of Manso. In spite of his different political allegiances, he too finished in gaol.

Many years later, Juan Crespo told Ronald Fraser, 'The front was a sinuous line which divided friend from friend, brother from brother, which ran through many a particular home and even through bedrooms.'[131] Yet this was not really the story of his own family. In spite of being divided politically – 'there were Carlists, liberals and republicans' – the family actually remained very united emotionally. Crespo continued, 'I did what I could to alleviate the suffering of my relatives on the other side, did what I could to get my uncles out of gaol, but I went on fighting for my ideals.'[132]

Beneath the narrative surface, Crespo's family history is further complicated by the tendency of influential local families to invest in what might be called long-term political insurance policies. In the nineteenth and early twentieth centuries, in both Spain and Italy, in the face of what was constant political uncertainty and more than one outbreak of violence, it made a lot of sense for one branch of a family to belong to one political faction and another to another. Thus Crespo's family story has in fact a great deal to do with political division but nothing to do with fratricide.

Much the same story – though less complicated – emerges from the history of the Portillo Pérez family, also from near Salamanca.[133] The family was a middle-class one, 'which made it naturally suspicious of socialists and communists'. Michael Portillo, the British Conservative politician, remembers his father Luis as the only republican in his family, his five brothers having all been on the opposite side: 'My father was a liberal intellectual and a Catholic idealist who believed in man's essential goodness. At the front he refused to carry a weapon for fear of killing one of his brothers.' The terrible rancours of the war spilled over into Michael Portillo's own childhood in London:

> My earliest memories include my father speaking of his hatred for Franco. His tone was shocking because he was the most loving and gentle of humans. My three brothers and I were, literally, not allowed to kill a fly because his respect for life was absolute. Yet loathing for Franco poured from him. He carried a debilitating wound, of the spirit not the body [. . .] In the same January [1939] that my father plodded through the mountains to exile, his brother Justino was killed fighting for Franco.[134]

Both these families, then, were deeply divided by the Civil War. At the same time they were not at war *within* the family, which, in spite of differing beliefs, demonstrated love and solidarity across various grades of kinship.

A second category in our typology, diametrically opposite to the first, is the family badly let down by its own kin, 'the family' itself turning out to be a chimera. In Málaga it was the left who took over the city in July 1936, the anarchists in particular showing little hesitation in shooting 'class enemies', often casually chosen. Pepa López was the wife of a local lawyer and former CEDA member of parliament. When she heard the hostile crowd advancing towards her house, she threw off her dress, slipped on a smock, replaced her shoes with a pair of hemp sandals and grabbed three precious bracelets, heirlooms which had belonged to her mother. She hid them in a basket full of vegetables, took hold tightly of her children and went down into the street. She looked like a street-seller and prayed that no one would recognise her.

At first, she rushed to a cousin's house and from there watched as the furniture from her own home was thrown into the street and burned. Her cousin then told her that they could not stay for longer than twenty-four hours. What happened next is recounted by María Carmen, the daughter of Pepa López: 'One after another of our relatives began to fail us. Their faces turned white when we asked them for shelter. There came a moment when no one would take us in. That was the saddest experience of my life.'[135] Coming from an extended family of devout Catholics who believed passionately in the centrality and priority of the family, to be let down in this way must have been particularly terrible. In spite of this, Pepa López's family survived. She and the children found refuge in the clinic of a courageous Catholic gynaecologist, José Gálvez, while her husband was saved by the fiancé of his assistant's daughter: 'Rejected by relatives, he was saved by people he didn't know.'[136] Once Málaga had been retaken by the nationalists the reprisals were amongst the most horrific in the whole of the Civil War. María Carmen continued her recollections: 'My father said he felt depressed at being left alive. Almost all his political acquaintances had been killed. Then people came to ask him to make accusations against left-wingers. The purge was under way. He refused. We began to hear of the courts martial, the executions. Every day there were hundreds of cases.'[137]

It is worth noting, *en passant*, that survival was very often due to casual elements of destiny, as underlined by very many accounts and testimonies. Luis Portillo Pérez, for instance, was returning to the University of Salamanca when he met a colleague in a café in a bus station. She told him of the mayhem and murders at the university, and he decided to turn back. That chance encounter probably saved his life.

A family politically divided but whose principal members were none the less strongly attached to one another, and another which believed profoundly in the centrality of the extended Catholic family, only to be completely abandoned by close relatives in its hour of need: these are the first two categories in our typology. Often, and this is the third, it was not only intra-familial solidarities that were crucial to possible survival, but also the reputation a family had previously acquired in the environment in which it lived. In other words, a family's social capital was often all-important. A good example of this, as well as of the extraordinary arbitrariness of destiny, is the experience of Juan Mestres. The war was hardly a month old when Mestres, monarchist and member of the CEDA, sub-manager in the office of an insurance company in Barcelona, was arrested. His office had been taken over by a revolutionary committee. He expected to be killed at any moment, an impression that received grim confirmation when a local member of the FAI – the hard-core wing of the anarchists – came to collect him. But the FAI militant had quite another story to tell. He explained that he lived in the same working-class quarter as Mestres's parents, that they were a modest and dignified couple, and that when he had seen them weeping on account of their son's arrest, he had decided to take matters into his own hands. He drove Mestres to the CNT woodworkers' union headquarters, where he began explaining to the union's president that he had rescued him because he was born poor and lived in a poor *barri*. He continued,

'He is a son of the people. He is a special case, and it is unjust that he should be in prison. His only fault was to be taken in by religious propaganda; his only sin was his religion. He didn't leave his home on 19 July.'
The president looked at me [Mestres]. 'Get up on this table', he said. Hesitantly I climbed up. 'Silence', shouted the president. The noise, the people milling about, the confusion that had met me when we first came in, immediately stilled. The president began addressing them as though he were holding a political meeting. 'This man didn't take up arms against the people.

We believe he should be given a chance to live. A chance to purify his life, rid himself of his mistaken religious beliefs.' The crowd shouted agreement, turning immediately to other matters. Ignored, I got down from the table and went out, 'free' ...[138]

Mestres's origins and his parents' long-standing reputation were thus decisive in swinging the balance towards his survival, but by no means always did being poor (or, for that matter, being rich) effect such benign outcomes. To the class solidarities exemplified by Mestres's case must be added other mechanisms of social solidarity.

A fourth category in our typology, therefore, is one in which *inter-class* patterns of exchange and favour played an important role. A powerful expression of these was fictive kinship. The role of godfather or godmother could be a currency of great importance in the summer of 1936. Not, most probably, in Barcelona's *barris*, where most people thought in the same way and godparents often came from the same streets. But in the countryside godparenthood (*padrinazgo*) was often inter-class, the Church encouraging peasants to seek out the protection of wealthy and benign landowners. If an influential member of the village elite put in a good word at a critical moment he could determine a family's fate. This was a far less likely scenario, as we shall see in a moment, in Andalusia or Extremadura, than in other parts of rural Spain, where the social structure was more complex and less polarised.

Not only godparenthood but also work relations and patron–client networks were brought into play. In the village of Mijas, a Socialist trade union official recounted how he had saved the lives of two landowners for whom he had worked:

I knew them, had worked in their vineyards. A relative came and said they were on the prison ship in Málaga and were going to be shot. I and some others went to the Committee of Public Safety in Málaga and signed guarantees on their behalf. We took them to the house of one of their sisters and told them to stay there lest the people in Casas Nuevas got to know they had been released.[139]

A family's social capital therefore counted for a great deal, expressing itself at different moments and levels – as solidarity both within a class and between classes.

A final category in our typology concerns female strategies. Although much more work needs to be done on this category (as on all the others) it is possible to perceive occasions when women shamed men into behaving a little less like thoughtless killers and in the process saved their families (or what was left of them). The appeal here was to the virtuous sentiments of clemency, moderation and generosity, rather than to the predominant passions of the time – revenge and the urge to spill blood. Of course, such an appeal is not a standardised one deriving automatically from the gender divide: women as well as men are involved in blood-letting, and revenge is far from a purely masculine passion. But there is, I suggest, a specifically feminine way of trying to save one's own kin in such circumstances.

In southern Aragón the village of Mas de la Matas, population 2,300, was relatively prosperous, with proprietors of small and medium-sized holdings to the fore. Surprisingly, given this social composition, the village was an anarcho-syndicalist stronghold. After July 1936 the local CNT took over, set up a broad-based anti-Fascist committee and ensured (unusually) that no one was to be imprisoned, let alone shot. At first all was calm, but then an armed band of the CNT arrived from Alcañiz, the nearest large town, to 'clean up' the village. The anti-Fascist committee, including the local members of the CNT, was locked up and the marauding band picked out six men to be killed at once. They then returned to Alcañiz.

Lázaro Martín's father and older brother were among those killed and he himself had been arrested. His mother decided to intervene and many years later, in October 1974, Martín recounted to Ronald Fraser the details of her intervention, as they had been recounted to him at the time:

Macario Royo was a man who had first been an important local Socialist and then an anarchist and was a colleague of Durruti [. . .] When I was arrested, my mother saw him walking down the street and called to him, 'Macario, come in a moment' [. . .] He came in and was a bit disconcerted because there were three women there, one of whom was my sister-in-law, who had also lost a brother [. . .] he was disconcerted because you know that when it's a question of blood relations women are even more headstrong than men [. . .] And my mother says to him, 'Look here, Macario, I never like to ask for favours, but I think that after what has happened to this household, enough is enough. The least I ask you for is that [. . .] since he is a child, even if he has done something he shouldn't, pardon my son and send him back to me for my consolation, that's the least I ask you for! [. . .] They sent me home the day after.[140]

Another incident that illuminates the same theme, this time involving a father and daughter rather than a mother and son, occurred at Morasverdes, in the province of Salamanca, also in the first weeks of the Civil War. Once again we are dealing with a punitive expedition, this time Falangists from Ciudad Rodrigo, the nearest big town, who produced a list of those republicans who were to be arrested and taken away. Among them was the village school teacher, the secretary of the local Socialists, but when it was his turn, his daughter, a 'lovely girl, twelve or fourteen years old', threw herself at the feet of the leader of the Falangists, held on to his legs and kissed his feet. Her gesture was so simple and heartfelt that the Falangist leader let her father be.[141] It has to be said that this was an atypically generous and kind-hearted expedition. In the end they took away only the local cart maker, and he came back on the bus the next day.

July 1936 was one of the worst and most dramatic moments in contemporary Spanish history. In the face of impelling circumstances, families which found themselves in the wrong place at the wrong time responded, as we have seen, in a great variety of ways. While each family history is unique, it is none the less possible to discern some broad patterns that have emerged from this preliminary typology. Judging both from the stories which have been recounted here and from those which have not, a great many families, far from being fratricidal in the literal sense of the word, seem to have expressed a great sense of solidarity, loyalty and love, confirming Reher's and others' suggestions of the long-standing power of Spanish family ties. This was true, most obviously, of immediate kin – wives in particular – but also of more complex and distant relations. And we can also discern elements of a specifically female way of exercising pressure upon hostile and dangerous men, appealing to their better selves at moments of choices between life and death.

A second conclusion to be drawn from the typology is that reactions defy all stereotypes: there could be devout Catholics who were desolate at receiving little or no solidarity from their kin, and members of the FAI who went to great lengths in Barcelona to save a son out of respect for his Catholic working-class parents. In the light of these testimonies and others, the Catholic claim that the nationalists were fighting to 'save the family' in the face of the illicit habits of the anarchists has a very hollow ring to it.

Finally, the fate of families in the summer of 1936 depended to a great extent on fortune and on inter-class relations, the cross-class social capital which family members had built up in the years before the outbreak of the Civil War. Godparents, patrons with a large clientele, employers – all could play key roles. Tragically, there were far too few on both sides ready to recognise their opponents first as human beings and only secondarily as class or religious adversaries.

3. The crusaders

At the outbreak of the Civil War, the vast majority of the Spanish clergy declared themselves on the side of the rebel generals. At an international level,

Father Ledóchowski, the superior-general of the Jesuits, urged the Jesuit press all over the world to support the nationalists. As in 1931, however, the immediate reaction of the Vatican was far more nuanced. Pius XI's intervention is of great interest for the theme of fratricidal war. On 14 September 1936, he made a speech at Castelgandolfo, entitled 'La vostra presenza' (Your presence here), to a large audience of Spanish refugees from regions in republican hands. He deplored the anti-clerical outrages, the burning of churches and the spread of what he called 'Communism'. But he also begged Spanish Catholics to treat their opponents like brothers, thus using loving fraternity, as we have just encountered it in the typology above, as a sentiment to be applied to the whole of Spain:

> Love these dear sons and brothers of yours, love them with a special love composed of passion and mercy, love them and, if you cannot do anything else, pray for them [. . .] [As a result] the rainbow of peace shall appear in the beautiful sky of Spain, displaying the news to the whole of your great and magnificent country.[142]

The reaction in nationalist Spain varied from disappointment to outrage. The Francoists used the parts of the speech that suited them and ignored the rest. Gomá y Tomás, the cardinal primate of Spain, gave orders for the text not to be published in the Spanish ecclesiastical press. A week later, the bishop of Salamanca, Cardinal Pla y Deniel, issued a highly influential pastoral letter, *Las dos ciudades* (The Two Cities). One of the cities in question was the 'celestial city of the children of God', populated by Catholic believers, while the other was 'the earthly city embodied by Communists and anarchists, the sons of Cain'. To brotherly love he counterposed brotherly hate. A crusade needed to be launched immediately, 'to save religion, the fatherland and the family'. 'Have you not heard', thundered the bishop, 'uncontrollable libertarian girls crying "Children yes! Husbands no!"?' In the face of anarchist burnings and murders, there could be no alternative to civil war. 'War, like suffering, is a great school for forging men', especially when 'we all have been contemplating soft and delicate effeminacy'. Quite what he meant by this last phrase is not entirely clear, but any idea of sexual identities being confused was likely to send the Church hierarchy into tilt.[143]

Women had, in fact, been quite heavily mobilised by Catholic associationism and political groupings, especially by the CEDA.[144] Its political programme of 1933 favoured the gradual abolition of women's civic and economic inequality, but at the same time reiterated that legal equality should not damage 'marital authority' or 'family authority'. These were the contradictions that all female

Catholic groups took with them in their difficult passage to the public sphere. José Antonio Primo de Rivera, the leader of the Falange, offered a different and brilliant solution to the problem: simply acknowledge difference – in emotions, in roles, in spheres of action, allowing even for the superiority of certain feminine values. He told an audience in Badajoz in April 1935, 'We are not feminists. We do not believe that the way to respect women is by diverting them from their magnificent destiny and giving them manly functions. Man is a torrent of egoism; woman almost always accepts a life of submission, service and abnegation.'[145] The Sección Femenina of the Falange, founded in 1934 by Pilar Primo de Rivera, José Antonio's younger sister, rapidly emerged as the largest women's group in nationalist Spain, numbering over half a million members. It was always, as we shall see, to be regarded with suspicion by the Church hierarchy.

Through her seminal article on martyrs and saints of 1999, Mary Vincent has helped us to identify the main strands of the 'crusade' launched in September 1936.[146] The task – enthusiastically welcomed by the great majority in the Spanish Church – was to create a modern version of Christian soldiery, so profoundly a part of Spain's imperial heritage. Vincent writes, 'Making the soldier into a crusader [. . .] mobilized particular ideas of masculinity which provided a sense of moral order, an image of heroism against the infidel, and, most importantly, a construction of martyrdom in which the whole idea of the crusade found its ultimate expression.'[147] The leaders of the crusade and its eventual martyrs were to be young men from good families who had been educated in one of the Catholic elite schools situated in the affluent bourgeois quarters of major provincial cities. The Marian congregations were particularly important. Young men were trained in the virtues of chastity, purity and piety, which, taken together, constituted a specific notion of Spanish Catholic manliness. Chastity was here viewed in the same way as in the encyclical *Casti Connubii* – not simply as abstinence from the pleasures of the flesh, but more widely as a means of liberating the soul. The elite of soldier-crusaders was to be 'uncontaminated'. Its role models were counter-reformation saints, warrior-monks who had refused to be commandeered by their families of origin and had gone off to serve the Church. Theirs was an austere, even ascetic vision. Portrayals of them made during the war, especially by the painter Carlos Sáenz de Tejada, are sometimes reminiscent of El Greco, elongated figures more spiritual than carnal.[148]

How does this image of saint-like warriors compare with other conceptions of manliness, especially the Fascist one? It is difficult to find that much in common. The Marinetti and Mussolini version – men as military and sexual adventurers – certainly did not fit the bill. One hardly dares to think how some of Marinetti's most famous dictums, such as 'war proves that women need

TRES GENERACIONES

fig. 35 Carlos Sáenz de Tejada, *Three Generations*, depicting Carlist soldiers, late 1930s.

daily copulation', might have been received in the famous Jesuit elite school, the Congregation of Mary Immaculate and St Aloysius Gonzaga. Even the second strand of Fascist discourse, which couched virility in pro-natal, family terms, was quite a long way from what the Spanish Church had in mind. It is hard to escape the conclusion that the 'hard' men of the Spanish crusade, chaste and pure, were a long way away from the 'softer' Fascist men who were more self-indulgent at every level.

Furthermore, the culture and recent history of the two national Churches differed considerably. The Catholic Church in Italy, for all its espousal of the Abyssinian imperial war, had always preferred the wholeness of family life to the lacerations of conflict. It had suffered exclusions and discrimination, even the end of temporal power, but nothing to be compared with what happened in the Spanish Civil War. Thirteen Spanish bishops, 4,184 diocesan priests, 2,365 monks and 283 nuns perished as a result of anti-clerical violence, especially in the six months following 18 July 1936.[149] Such atrocities meant that the Spanish Church was fighting alongside the military for its survival. By contrast, the Italian Church had by 1928 already won its battle to be reinstated into the heart of Italian life, and without recourse to arms.

A more interesting comparison in this field, heretical though it may appear, is probably one between Spain and Turkey. In both cases we find a clerical appeal for a Holy War, the creation of martyrs, and the guiding presence of a ruthless and highly cynical professional soldier. It is as well to recall Mustafa Kemal's comments from the front line in July 1915:

Our life here is truly hellish. Fortunately, my soldiers are very brave and tougher than the enemy. What is more, their private beliefs make it easier to carry out orders which send them to their death. They see only two supernatural outcomes: victory for the faith or martyrdom. Do you know what the second means? It is to go straight to heaven. There, the virgins of paradise, God's most beautiful women, will meet them and will satisfy their desires for all eternity. What great happiness![150]

Spanish martyrology, by contrast, emphasised time and again the purity and chastity of those who went to heaven, where the satisfaction of sexual desire had no place. Kemal's caustic description can be contrasted with the much more militarised but more sincere version of José Antonio Primo de Rivera: 'One cannot lie down in Paradise; one stands upright, like the angels [. . .] we who have already caused the best of our number to lay down their lives on the road to Paradise, we want [. . .] a Paradise where there can be no rest and whose gates are flanked on both sides by angels armed with swords.'[151]

The crusaders responded to the atrocities perpetrated on the clergy with atrocities of their own, though on a much greater scale. There were few clergy who pleaded, as did the bishop of Pamplona, for an end to all bloodshed. The great majority thought quite the opposite – that blood had to be shed. In a recurring and repulsive image, Spain was to be 'watered and fertilised with the blood of the martyrs', and above all by the blood of the desecrators and the sinful. Men were the principal target, but women were not to be spared. 'Red whores' became the antithesis of virtuous Catholic women. As Vincent has written, 'they were unchaste, unfeminine, and most significantly unSpanish'.[152] In nationalist prisons they were punished by physical and sexual humiliation – some had their heads shaved or were forced to swallow castor oil. Others were forced to parade naked and many were subjected to rape and other forms of sexual assault. All this, with its explicit sexual violence, took place without a murmur of protest on the part of the nationalist clergy. Worse still, many of these acts took place in the name of the Virgin Mary, who had, incongruously, been made captain-general of the insurgent army. We last encountered her in the Tuscan countryside in the nineteenth century, where she was being worshipped as the embodiment of maternal love and considered the special protector of farm animals. No such fortune befell her in 1936–9. As Frances Lannon has written, 'there was no embarrassment in the fact that particularly brutal repression amounting to mass executions in Badajoz and elsewhere greeted the feast of the Assumption of the Virgin in August 1936'.[153]

At the end of the war, Gomá y Tomás, the cardinal primate of Spain, celebrated the victory of the 'soul of our noble history, the ancient soul of our fathers which has blocked the path of the bastard souls of the sons of Moscow'.[154] Pius XII himself, who had become Pope in March 1939, was hardly more measured in his utterances. A few hours after Franco announced that the red army had been captured and disarmed, he received a telegram from the new Pope: 'With heart uplifted to the Lord, we sincerely give thanks, along with Your Excellency, for this long-desired Catholic victory in Spain.'[155]

4. Franco: all family and Church

Of the various dictators considered in this book – Mustafa Kemal, Benito Mussolini, Adolf Hitler, Joseph Stalin and Francisco Franco – only the last can conceivably be described as a 'good family man'. Born in 1892 in the naval city of El Ferrol in the poor, north-western region of Galicia, Franco was a timid, well-behaved but rather sad and uncommunicative child. His father Nicolás, a high-ranking administrator in the Spanish navy, was a bad-tempered and authoritarian figure, often absent from home. Franco was unable to win his affection and in the end came to despise him. His own lifelong restraint with regard to alcohol, gambling and extra-marital affairs was the very antithesis of his father's life. His central emotional attachment – as in the cases of the other great dictators – was to his mother, Pilar Bahamonde, a serene and kindly woman who was a fervent and traditionalist Catholic. Franco always emphasised the centrality of religion in politics and the role of the Christian family as the social basis for the state.

The young Franco's sense of deprivation increased when he was rejected for the navy. As his biographer Paul Preston has written, 'A tone of self-pitying resentment runs through his speeches as Caudillo, a continual echo of the hard-done-by little boy that he must have been.'[156] Things changed when he entered the army. He was a fearless soldier and consequently had a brilliant career, first in Morocco and then back in Spain. In both places he revealed the icy depths of his character, being able with great ease to dehumanise his opponents, whether they were Moroccan tribesmen or Asturias miners. This was not a very Catholic attribute, but it was one well suited to the general conditions of inhumanity that prevailed in the first half of the twentieth century.

In October 1923, at Oviedo, the thirty-year-old Franco married the twenty-one-year-old María del Carmen Polo. She was the elegant and willowy daughter of a rich landowner, the marriage thus marking Franco's rapid upward social mobility. The union lasted for some fifty-two years, from 1923 to 1975 – a 'solidly enduring, if not a passionate, marriage'.[157] Franco doted on his only child, Carmen, who provided him with seven grandchildren. The Caudillo's private life, consonant with the symbiosis between Church and regime upon which his dictatorship was based (and to which we shall return), could thus with some truth be presented to his subjects as archetypical, a model of devotion and fidelity.

Franco's masculinity was far removed from that of Mussolini, not only from the point of view of sexual fidelity. As much as he loved dressing up, especially as an admiral, at five feet four inches (1.64 metres) he was never going to be an imposing figure. He was, moreover, quietly spoken and even given to tears on certain occasions. Unlike Mussolini and Hitler he had no experience as a street orator, no capacity to stir passions. When Galeazzo Ciano went to visit him in July 1939, he described him as 'that queer fish of a Caudillo', ensconced in his palace, 'surrounded by mountains of files of prisoners condemned to death'. According to Ciano, Franco dealt with only about three a day because he was much given to taking long siestas. And 'those siestas are his force'.[158]

The Italian Fascists underestimated him, not only because they had come to his aid, but also because they were unable to understand his appearance and behaviour. Beneath the genteel, even sleepy surface, there lurked a man of instinctive cunning and utter ruthlessness. In conversation with a French journalist in 1937 he identified himself as a soldier of God and his enemies as mere agents of impersonal forces. He was fighting not against men but against atheism and materialism. His was a religious war, a crusade, not a civil war. On the basis of these premises, any nefarious action was justified, any crime against humanity could be perpetrated – and was.

Perhaps the most interesting comparison is not with Mussolini but with Mustafa Kemal, another man of extraordinary determination and ruthlessness. There were, of course, fundamental differences. Franco was the arch defender of organised religion, Kemal was often its scourge. Franco sought to restore the past and celebrate Spain's extraordinary imperial tradition, whereas

fig. 36 Francisco Franco with his wife María del Carmen Polo and their daughter Carmen in 1936, during the transfer of the government from Burgos to Salamanca.

Kemal disdainfully turned his back on Ottoman tradition; with his Republic, Ottoman history was to end and Turkish to begin. Kemal was an innovator, Franco a fanatical restoration figure. But both men were professional soldiers, accustomed to commanding great numbers of men in the field, conducting wars of indescribable savagery, eliminating their opponents and creating regimes that were to last as long as their lifetimes, and in Kemal's case well beyond.

5. Massacres and utopias

When the rebel generals announced their coup in July 1936, their backing in both the rural and urban parts of Extremadura and Andalusia was weak indeed. Against all the odds, however, the repellent figure of General Gonzalo Queipo de Llano managed to secure Seville for the rebels, ordering the Falange to kill immediately anyone suspected of being left-wing, both in the city and outside it. On 21 July 1936, in the popular quarter of Barrio de Triana, many bodies were left lying in the streets, with womenfolk sobbing hysterically and trying to cover up their loved ones. Within a few days the city was secured for the nationalists. The outcome was certainly a tribute to the opportunism and ruthlessness of Queipo, but it also testified to the tragic disorganisation, lack of preparation and sheer chaos of the republicans.

The pattern repeated itself on a vast scale as the death columns moved northwards into Extremadura and eastwards towards Granada. Time and again the anarchist *pueblos*, often in rivalry with one another, proved unable to coordinate any resistance. Casas Viejas seems not to have taught them any lessons in self-defence. Most of the men of a village were simply rounded up and shot in the cemetery or the village square, while their desperate women-folk begged the nationalist soldiers to desist. Some of the very worst of these massacres took place in the province of Badajoz, where Margarita Nelken had been re-elected as deputy in 1936. All those, both men and women, who had benefited from republican land reforms in the period before the war, were especially vulnerable. So, too, were those who had a trade union membership card in their pockets – either of the CNT or of the Socialists.[159]

Local landowners worked hand in glove with the Falange. A notable example is that of Félix Moreno Ardanuy, a powerful clientelist figure in the Andalusian town of Palma del Río, in the province of Córdoba. He used his extensive estates not to cultivate crops but to breed fighting bulls. After 18 July 1936, the anarchist committee of Palma del Río collectivised the land and rationed food supplies. Moreno's fighting bulls were killed and the peasants, for the first time in their lives, ate red meat. Retribution was swift. When a rebel column recaptured the town on 27 August, Moreno drove behind the column in his black Cadillac, together with other landowners. All the men of the village were herded into a large cattle pen, where Moreno selected for immediate execution ten men for each of the bulls killed. The men pleaded

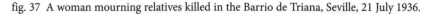

fig. 37 A woman mourning relatives killed in the Barrio de Triana, Seville, 21 July 1936.

desperately with him. They reminded him, in keeping with our typology of family strategies, that some of them were his godchildren and others even his cousins. To no avail. Kinship, either fictive or real, had no purchase. Moreno merely looked straight ahead and repeated 'I know nobody.' At least eighty-seven of the villagers were shot that day and twice as many in the days that followed.[160] In Andalusia as a whole, nearly 50,000 people were murdered behind nationalist lines between 1936 and 1939. They included Federico García Lorca.

In the months before the generals' uprising, Lorca had been in Madrid, putting the finishing touches to his last play, *The House of Bernarda Alba*, and reading extracts from it to his many friends. Not by chance did the title of the play include the word 'house', while its subtitle was 'A drama of women in the villages of Spain'. Lorca wanted to underline the stifling domestic environment of rural Spain, of families dominated by hypocrisy, intolerance and inquisitorial Catholicism. Adela, one of Bernarda's daughters, is the revolutionary heroine of the piece – not in a narrowly political sense, but in her taking a stand against the crushing norms of family life. At one point she asserts her right to her own sexuality in a manner of which Kollontai would have been proud: 'I do with my own body what I feel like!', she cries, and at the end of the play she breaks Bernarda's stick, the symbol of her mother's suffocating matriarchy.[161]

Lorca's friends begged him to stay in Madrid, as the safest place to be, but he felt the need to return, just a few days before the generals' insurrection, to Granada and to his family. Once there, instead of crossing over to republican territory only a few kilometres away, Lorca chose to seek refuge in the house of a young poet of Falangist tendencies, Luis Rosales, who admired him greatly and two of whose brothers were among the town's leading Falangists. This strategy, another of those described in the typology of family experiences outlined above, in Lorca's case tragically failed: news of where he was hiding soon got out and the Rosales family was not strong enough to protect him. Lorca had made many enemies in Granada, while what Miguel de Unamuno called the 'Spanish vice' of *envidia* (envy) also played its part, as did the poet's homosexuality. On 17 or 18 August 1936 Lorca was taken away, handcuffed to a local school teacher, driven to an olive grove outside the city, and shot.[162]

Where the republican lines held, at least for some months, and anarcho-syndicalist principles triumphed, there were some extraordinary attempts at utopian living. One of these was in the Andalusian *pueblo* of Castro del Río, in the province of Córdoba, not far from Palma del Río, where Félix Moreno Ardanuy had taken his terrible revenge for the killing of his bulls. In his magnificent eyewitness account, *The Spanish Cockpit* (1937), Franz Borkenau recounts his visit to Castro del Río at the beginning of September 1936.[163] Castro, 'a typically populous and wretched Andalusian *pueblo*', was one of the oldest anarcho-syndicalist centres in Andalusia. In July the Civil Guard and local landowners had risen against the Republic, securing the town for the generals and killing all those who dared oppose them. The villagers, however, here more organised militarily than elsewhere, had then laid siege to the town, starved out the Civil Guard, and proceeded in turn to massacre their opponents. They then introduced their 'anarchist Eden':

> The salient point of the anarchist régime in Castro is the abolition of money. Exchange is suppressed; production has changed very little. The land of Castro belonged to three of the greatest magnates of Spain, all of them absentees of course; it has now been expropriated [. . .] There is no pay whatever; the inhabitants are fed directly from the village stores [. . .] I had a look at the stores. They were so low as to foretell approaching starvation. But the inhabitants seemed to be proud of this state of things. They were pleased, as they told us, that coffee-drinking had come to an end; they seemed to regard this

abolition of useless things as a moral improvement. What few commodities they needed from outside, mainly clothes, they hoped to get by direct exchange of their surplus in olives (for which, however, no arrangement had yet been made). Their hatred of the upper class was far less economic than moral. They did not want to get the good living of those they had expropriated, but to get rid of their luxuries, which to them seemed to be so many vices. Their conception of the new order which was to be brought about was thoroughly ascetic.[164]

There is no mention in Borkenau's testimony of any measures relating specifically to families, either in relation to intra-familial organisation or with regard to their relationship to the wider collectivity. It was as if the whole subject stood outside the parameters of the anarchist utopia. Even if the *braceros* of Castro had never read the documents of the CNT Zaragoza congress of 1936, they seemed in intimate agreement with them: the family had in the past 'performed most admirable functions'. It was not up for discussion.

It is illuminating to compare the agrarian collective at Castro with an experience from the opposite end of the country, that of Orriols, a tiny hamlet in the province of Girona in northern Catalonia. Here the front line was much further away, and Catalan families exercised their hegemony over rural social relations. When the generals' rebellion failed in the region, twenty-three out of the village's forty-four families (most of them sharecroppers) pooled their land as well as their livestock and formed an agrarian collective. At the beginning of 1937 the collective wrote its statutes, which are dominated by provisions for families, both imaginary and real. The foreword states, 'The collective is one great family of producers which respects the absolute autonomy of each family in matters of consumption.' Statute 2 declared,

Under the humane and anarchistic emblem of 'One for all and all for one', the members of the collective shall strive to guarantee the economic and social betterment of all, regardless of family or age. The collective will maintain a common fund which shall be used (in so far as this may be possible) to meet the needs of the great collectivized family.[165]

The collective then proceeded to establish weekly wages for its members, based on a sliding scale and on traditional gender disparities: single men over fifteen years of age, eight pesetas; married men, five pesetas; married women, single girls over the age of fifteen and boys of between twelve and fifteen years, three pesetas; boys of between eight and twelve years, one peseta. The collective promised to promote 'a higher degree of culture in the people', availing itself of theatre, cinema, lectures, radio and the press, 'together with pamphlets popularizing science and morals'. The statutes concluded with the following heartfelt appeal, both global and local:

> The collective will spare no efforts to maintain relations of moral and material solidarity with all of the workers of the world, regardless of class or colour. The doors of the collective will remain open to welcome into its bosom any peasant co-citizens who, once having been persuaded of the advantages offered by the collective, wish to join the great family.

These two utopian rural communes, though both of anarcho-syndicalist inspiration, differ from one another quite clearly in a number of ways. At Orriols the guiding metaphor for the collectivity is that of the family; at Castro, at least in the accounts we have, the family is practically invisible. At Orriols, each villager is paid according to his or her place in a pre-established hierarchy; at Castro money and wages have simply been abolished. At Orriols a strong air of pluralism reigns – little more than half the families of the village adhere to the collective while the others have still to be persuaded (not constrained). This is a 'bridging' collective. Castro, by contrast, is a 'binding' one: the only political organisation present is that of the anarchists, there are no hints of pluralism, 'useless things', such as coffee drinking, are abolished by decree, and there is no liberty with regard to an individual family's consumption. Castro can be read as a typical example of southern Spanish millenarianism, Orriols as a strange mixture of social radicalism and family traditionalism. Both were swept away by the 'crusaders' in a bloodbath, Castro quite early on, Orriols in the last months of the war.

6. Margarita Nelken: one woman's war

Earlier in this chapter we left Margarita Nelken addressing the Cortes in 1934, warning that the men of the province of Badajoz, treated like animals by the landowners and their agents, would behave like animals when the time came for civil war. In the autumn of that year she was implicated in the insurrectionary plans which led to the partial and tragic rising of the Asturias miners. Condemned to twenty years' imprisonment for her part in the affair, Nelken sought refuge in the Cuban embassy and was then smuggled out of Spain. There followed an intense period of public activity. Given her easy command of French, German and English, she addressed assemblies all over Europe, including Scandinavia, on the Spanish situation and on the plight of the imprisoned Asturian miners. This was also the period in which she visited Moscow for the first time, accompanied by her daughter Magda, now aged twenty, and her son Santiago (Taguín), aged fourteen.

It would be fair to say that Nelken, with her intellectual vitality, profound bourgeois culture and loose tongue, was more of a 1920s figure than a 1930s one. Yet like so many left-wing intellectuals of the time, she fell rapidly under the spell of the Soviet Union, suspending all critical judgement of it. As Fascism took over both Spain and Europe, the Soviet regime seemed the only bulwark left against it. During the sixteen months she was in Russia, she became friends with Yelena Stasova, one-time secretary of Lenin, and wrote a book entitled *Porqué hicimos la revolución*,[166] published in 1936. It was the first of her works in which the question of gender was not to the forefront. In this passionate account of the left during the Spanish second Republic, she was all too harsh on those moderate and reformist Socialists who, according to her, had not seized the revolutionary moment, especially in the southern country-side, between 1932 and 1934. They had failed to learn the Soviet lesson: 'In Russia, the revolution began by giving land to the peasants, so that later, when the right moment presented itself, it was possible to collectivise it, without dashing anyone's hopes or damaging their material interests. The peasants understood that the revolution was theirs.'[167]

Her analysis was wrong on both counts. There had been no chance of agrarian revolution in Spain in 1932–3, nor did the terrible fate of the Russian peasantry in any way correspond to the revolution being 'theirs'. Of course, Nelken had heard of these events only at second hand, and had doubtless been shown round some model *kolkhozy*. But by any standards, as we will see in the last chapter of this book, her account of Russian conditions was as far from the truth as it could have been.

At both a private and a public level, the Moscow months exercised a great influence upon Nelken and her little family. She moved ever closer to the Spanish Communist Party, which she eventually joined in the autumn of 1936. And her son Santiago conceived a great love for the Soviet Union which would lead him to make an extraordinary choice in 1941.

When the left won the Spanish national elections in 1936 Nelken was again elected to the Cortes, and with an amnesty proclaimed she was able to return to Spain.[168] A few months later civil war broke out. In the critical days of July 1936 she contributed significantly to the defeat of the rebel generals in Madrid. On the 18th, while the republican politicians hesitated, she was one of those who took matters into their own hands, leading a delegation from the Casa del

Pueblo of Madrid to the artillery supply depot, where she convinced the loyal officer in charge to hand over five thousand rifles to the workers of the city.[169] In situations like these she was truly in her element – her enthusiasm infectious, her oratory stirring, her indignation unlimited. She, Halide Edib and Aleksandra Kollontai form an extraordinary trio of middle- to upper-class women who turned their backs on class and family conventions to serve the causes, right or wrong, which they had embraced in their youth. In Nelken's case, this course of action put not only herself but her family at risk. It was in the July days that she learned, with horror and pride, that Santiago, now aged fifteen, had joined the militia fighting to repel the Falangists and rebel units in the sierras north of Madrid. Later he was to fight both at the great bloodbath of the battle of the Jarama and at the battle of the Ebro. Her daughter Magda volunteered as a front-line nurse and her little granddaughter Cuqui was shipped off to Amsterdam, where Martín de Paul was the Spanish consul general. For the rest of the war Margarita was to be in constant anguish over the fate of her daughter and above all over the safety of her son.

In the first weeks after the generals' attempted coup, a Socialist trade union delegation from the agrarian south came to Madrid to beg Nelken to find the weapons they so desperately needed to stem the advance of the terror columns of the Army of Africa. She could not help. At great risk to herself, she went down to Extremadura with other parliamentary deputies to express her solidarity with the *braceros*. It was not enough. The labourers, armed only with pitchforks, old shotguns and a few rifles, stood no chance of defending themselves.

One of the battalions formed in Extremadura at this time took the name of Margarita Nelken. So too did another in Madrid which would play a heroic part in that city's resistance, and whose members were 70 per cent university students.[170] The defence of Madrid was, according to Paul Preston, Nelken's finest hour. Refusing to be evacuated to Valencia she stayed in the besieged city, sleeping on a camp bed in the cellars of the Ministry of War. She was attached to General José Miaja's staff but had no formal role. She was particularly upset by not being made a member of the Junta de Defensa de Madrid. In addition there was inevitable rivalry within the Spanish Communist Party with Dolores Ibárruri, 'La Pasionaria', who had become the symbol of the Madrid resistance and the most popular woman in republican Spain. Ibárruri was of working-class origin and had, over a long period of time, worked her way to the top of the Spanish Communist Party. Nelken was a very recent bourgeois recruit, welcomed by some, distrusted by many others.

In September 1937, the Socialist deputy Matilde de la Torre encountered Nelken during a Cortes debate:

Margarita has abandoned her inveterate use of the famous pince-nez that had given her the look of an inquisitor. Now she wears some pretty glasses that give her a rather scholarly air. She shows me a photograph of her son in his officer's uniform. He is at the Madrid front, at that legendary front of which we all wish we could say 'I was there', but where most of us wouldn't dare show our faces.[171]

Nelken went on fighting the war in every way she could over the next sixteen months – going abroad frequently to speak about the plight of the Republic, running the news agency of the Spanish Communist Party, offering morale-raising lectures on Spanish art. In January 1939, as the nationalist armies began to invade Catalonia, she gave a last talk at the Barcelona Ateneu entitled 'Picasso, artist and citizen of Spain'.

7. Barcelona

The greatest social experimentation of all took place in Barcelona, where in July 1936 the generals' coup was held at bay by fierce popular resistance in the main streets and squares of the city. The anarcho-syndicalists were in the vanguard of this resistance, but Catalan nationalist, left-wing and republican forces also played their part. During the night of 19 July the Sant Andreu barracks was stormed by CNT activists, who seized tens of thousands of rifles. The workers were armed and Barcelona saved for the Republic. On 20 July, the president of Catalonia, Lluís Companys, invited the CNT, by now the dominant political and military force in the city, to join the Central Committee of Anti-Fascist Militias, which it agreed to do.

In what is probably the most famous page written on the Civil War, certainly the most famous in the Anglo-Saxon world, George Orwell described the extraordinary aspect of the city on his arrival there in December 1936:

It was the first time I had ever been in a town where the working class was in the saddle. Practically every building of any size had been seized by the workers and was draped with red flags or with the red and black flag of the Anarchists; every wall was scrawled with the hammer and sickle and with the initials of the revolutionary parties; almost every church had been gutted and its images burnt. Churches here and there were being systematically demolished by gangs of workmen. Every shop and café had an inscription saying it had been collectivized; even the boot blacks had been collectivized and their boxes painted red and black. Waiters and shop-walkers looked you in the face and treated you as an equal. Servile and ceremonial forms of speech had temporarily disappeared. Nobody said 'Señor' or 'Don' or even 'Usted'; everyone called everyone else 'Comrade' and 'Thou' and said 'Salud!' instead of 'Buenos días'. Tipping was forbidden by law; almost my first experience was receiving a lecture from a hotel manager for trying to tip a lift-boy [. . .] All this was queer and moving. There was much in it that I did not understand, in some ways I did not even like it, but I recognized it immediately as a state of affairs worth fighting for.[172]

In the debates of this period and the subsequent historiography much attention has been paid to the tension that existed between 'making the revolution' and 'winning the war'. Which was to come first? And did one preclude the other? In line with the Comintern, the Spanish Communist Party, which grew considerably in strength during the war years, was convinced that a broad popular front was necessary, to include artisans, peasant proprietors, small businessmen and clerks as well as workers and landless labourers. For them, the historical moment and the economic conditions of Spain were conducive to 'bourgeois' rather than 'proletarian' revolution; only Communist leadership, social order and a disciplined and hierarchical army could win the Civil War. The CNT, on the other hand, insisted that victory in the war could be assured only by sustaining the élan of the July days. Collectivisation and the abolition of private property were to proceed forthwith. Only from the full flowering of the proletarian social revolution, it was argued, could popular militias and workers' grass-roots committees draw the necessary determination to win the war.

This fundamental division over strategy and action has been the subject of passionate debate, conducted at the level of politics, history and cinema. It led to the 'civil war within the civil war' of April–May 1937, when Communist forces, backed by the republican army, broke the hold of the CNT in Barcelona. This is a dramatic story, and has been retold many times. Here, however, I would like to shift the attention to another aspect of these extraordinary months, one that has been much less raked over but is equally important. It is also one consonant with the principal enquiries of this book. What was the substance of the workers' revolution whose appearance Orwell described so well? Did the Spanish anarcho-syndicalists really offer a convincing alternative model of society? And how far was their 'libertarian communism' in any way 'libertarian'? It is my contention that there were deep fault lines within the anarchist revolutionary project itself, which was undermined as much from within as from without. I would like to expand briefly on this contention with reference to a number of different spheres, including those of gender and the family.

In the first place, pluralism. There was very little in the anarchist society of revolutionary Barcelona that resembled a pluralist public sphere or a modern civil society. Indeed, doctrinaire politics had long since replaced libertarian ones. Incredible though it may sound, post-revolutionary anarchism, whether in city or country, was deeply conformist, much more so than in post-revolutionary Russia. The mood of the Civil War anarchists was caught in a highly provocative but effective way by Gerald Brenan:

[The anarchists] demand that everyone shall be free. Free to do what? Why free to lead the natural life, to live on fruit and vegetables, to work at the collective farm, to conduct himself in the way that anarchists consider proper. But if he does not want to do these things, if he wants to drink wine, to go to the Mass, to dig in his own fields and refuse the benefits brought into the world by *comunismo libertario*, what then? Why then he is one of *los malos, los perversos*, possibly curable but, if he does not come from a working-class family, more likely corrupt and vicious out of upbringing or heredity, and therefore unfit to partake of the anarchist paradise.[173]

This deep intolerance was directed above all at the Church and its members. It was anarchists who were principally responsible for the thousands of killings of the first months of the war. Many other anarchists, it should be noted, tried to stop them, and there were certainly many reasons, as we have seen, why the Barcelona working class, like the Andalusian peasants, should have hated the Church. Gabriele Ranzato has referred to the direct experience of 'persecutory religiosity' in Barcelona and elsewhere – the often vicious control by the Church of orphanages and borstals, schools, hospitals and workhouses.[174] But nothing can justify the gutting of churches, the shooting of priests, the exhumation of nuns' corpses, or the grotesque sacrophobic parades conducted by FAI militants clad in priests' robes.

Secondly, democracy. In this field, the revolutionary record is very poor. The anarchists seemed to shy away from elections instead of encouraging them. Chris Ealham, the most recent historian of the anarchist experience in Barcelona and one very well disposed towards it, has shown that the main organs of revolutionary power in the city, the district committees, 'were never as democratic as Soviets: they did not practice genuine direct democracy, and delegates, who often attained their positions due to the respect they enjoyed among the community, were not subject to immediate recall'.[175] In the ten months of anarchist power in the city, there is actually little evidence of any formal democratic proceedings at all. Power was divided and dispersed on an ad hoc basis: the old state was represented by the Catalan parliament, the

Generalitat; the CNT-FAI leadership was the self-appointed dynamo of the revolution; and the district and factory committees were the grass-roots force behind them. At least in Barcelona there was a plurality of institutions. In Aragón things were much worse. The Council of Aragón, set up in the eastern republican zone, was formed exclusively of unelected anarchist militants. It was bitterly contested by the other political forces and even by the Regional Federation of Agrarian Collectives. Eventually, it was to be forcibly dissolved by General Enrique Líster's Communist troops.[176]

Thirdly, the state. Decentralisation and confederalism were attractive propositions in times of peace but they could be lethal in those of war. At a crucial moment the revolution failed to create an institutional structure capable of coordinating the war effort and of incorporating in a democratic fashion the multiplicity of rank-and-file collectives – the district and factory committees, the Federación de Barricadas, the Milicias de Retaguardia, and so on.[177] 'Spontaneity' was a very poor substitute for democratic coordination, as the fate of the anarchist militias was frequently to demonstrate.

Finally, everyday life. Here there was much to celebrate. As always at a time of great social ambitions, communal eating houses made their appearance. The luxurious Barcelona Ritz suddenly became the 'Hotel Gastronomico no. 1', run by the trade unions and offering canteen meals to the whole population. In the factories, workers experimented with self-management, often insisting that the former directors and management put their skills and experience at the service of the revolution. Production for the war effort meant long hours of work and little or no overtime pay. At the same time soaring inflation undermined workers' real wages. None the less, for many months there was a general feeling of exhilaration, of trying to construct a society built on different economic bases.

Where the revolution was weakest was in the spheres of gender relations and the structures of family life. Here all the traditionalism of anarchist men came to the fore. Cafés and bars often remained male enclaves, women still faced harassment on the streets, and one eyewitness account noted that in some industrial collectives women continued to eat in separate dining rooms. Worst of all, the various powers in the city did nothing about the problem of prostitution. They allowed the physical and psychological dangers for the women involved, and the horrific lack of hygiene and disease prevention, to continue much as before.[178]

As for families, the silence is deafening. The lack of anarchist reflection on the theme of the family – in terms of its internal relations and organisation, its power as an institution, its relations to the outside world – became very apparent. Barcelona was a city in revolution but family life went on as 'normal'.

The only real initiative that the anarchists took, as briefly mentioned above,[179] appears to have been the 'eugenic reform of abortion' passed in December 1936. This was very much the work of Dr Félix Martí Ibáñez, the anarchist director of the Catalan Health Department. He classified the reform as a 'eugenic instrument at the service of the proletariat'. Abortion on demand was made available in public health structures for all women who demanded it. However, in the months that followed very few women availed themselves of the facility. This in itself could have been cause for further reflection on the relationship between the private and public spheres in the revolutionary city. Perhaps the public hospitals did not guarantee privacy and anonymity, unlike back-street abortions, for all their squalor and danger. Perhaps the reserved and hierarchical nature of Spanish family life, in working-class districts as elsewhere, acted as an insuperable barrier to any public discourse on women's bodies. Martí Ibáñez was convinced in January 1937 that 'the new Sun of Truth will dawn over the shadowy sexuality which has enveloped Spain', but his optimism was entirely misplaced.[180]

8. Guernica

On 26 April 1937 the small Basque town of Guernica was bombarded from the air by German bombers of the Condor Legion, backed up by Italian planes. It was market day in the town and people had come in from the surrounding villages to buy and sell poultry, vegetables and cattle. Every five minutes a German bomber flew low over the town centre and deposited its bombs. Families which had not sought shelter in the cellars of their houses fled into the woods. Many of them were shot down from above. The bombardment lasted three hours and fifteen minutes, leaving in its wake several hundred dead and wounded, and three-quarters of the town destroyed.

This was not the first time in the war that an attack from the air had been systematically aimed at defenceless civilians. The previous autumn an estimated five thousand people had died in a single night of bombing in Madrid, that of 23 October 1936. But never before had almost an entire town been reduced to smoldering ruins. Indeed, so great was the international outcry that Franco tried to pass off as the truth an alternative version of events, in which the republicans were to be held responsible. But there had been too many eyewitnesses, both Spanish and foreign. Guernica was a devoutly Catholic town which had been destroyed by the 'crusaders' for its loyalty, together with the rest of the Basque Country, to the republican government. The bombing was conceived as an explicit warning to the Basques, and to Bilbao in particular: if they continued to resist, they would meet the same fate. Father Alberto

fig. 38 People in the street hear the air raid sirens, Bilbao, May 1937, photograph by
Robert Capa.

Onaindía, a canon of the cathedral of Valladolid, had witnessed the terrible
violation of basic human rights at Guernica and wrote an impassioned letter to
Cardinal Gomá, Primate of all Spain:

> I have just arrived from Bilbao with my soul destroyed after having witnessed
> the horrific crime that has been perpetrated against the peaceful town of
> Guernica [...] Children and mothers collapsed on the roadside, mothers
> screaming in prayer, a population of believers murdered by criminals who
> have not the slightest claim to humanity. Señor Cardinal, for the honour of the
> gospel, for Christ's infinite pity, such a horrendous, unprecedented, apoca-
> lyptic, Dantesque crime cannot be committed.[181]

In January 1937, a few months before the bombing of Guernica, the republican government had begun to plan its contribution to the International
Exhibition of Arts and Technology to be held in Paris that summer. The exhibition was to become the site of intense rivalries, principally between the two

great dictatorships of the time, the German and the Russian. I shall return to these dictatorships and their mammoth pavilions at the exhibition, facing each other on the right bank of the Seine, when discussing Nazism and Stalinism.

The Spanish contribution was a far more modest affair – a small pavilion dominated by a series of photomontages. These underlined the importance of the Republic's social policies, especially with regard to education and agrarian reform, and presented the Civil War both as a watershed for European democracy and as a struggle between modernity and tradition. Thus one of the exhibits presented the image of a Salamancan peasant girl, her head covered and wearing traditional dress. She appears as depersonified, a mere hanger for the triangular costume and heavy jewelry she bears. Next to her in the photomontage stands a militiawoman. She, by contrast, wears comfortable, baggy trousers and her head is uncovered; most important of all her mouth is open as she shouts out her defiance of Fascism. The French caption at the exhibition described her as 'the woman capable of playing an active part in the creation of the future'.[182]

The Spanish pavilion was located far from the Eiffel Tower and opened seven weeks late. But it boasted one piece of art which completely outshone all the other contributions to the Paris Exhibition – Picasso's immense mural depicting the bombing of Guernica (plate 6). Never before in modern painting had a specific historical event received such immediate and deeply moving pictorial expression. The mural, hated and despised by the German and Italian delegations and their accompanying artists, viewed with suspicion by the Russians and welcomed only in part by international art critics, rapidly became the most famous depiction in the modern world of human and animal suffering.

In tracing the genesis of the mural in the context of Picasso's own life and that of the Civil War, it has to be said that before the creation of *Guernica* Picasso had played only a marginal role in the defence of the Republic. In February 1936 a retrospective of his works had opened in Barcelona, but he had refused to attend, leaving his mother María Picasso, Joan Miró and Salvador Dalí to speak on the radio in his place. When Madrid was being bombed by the Luftwaffe in the autumn of 1936, Picasso accepted the titular role of director of the Prado Museum, but he never visited the city in these months. And when a delegation including José Luis Sert, the architect of the Spanish pavilion at the Paris Exhibition, met with Picasso in January 1937 to invite him to contribute, he agreed but remained vague as to the extent of his commitment and its subject matter. It was only after the bombing of Guernica that he sprang suddenly to life and in a period of great intensity painted the mural in his studio in Paris between 1 May and 4 June 1937.

fig. 39 Photomontage shown in the Spanish pavilion of the Paris International Exhibition of Arts and Technology, 1937. The caption reads, 'Freeing herself from her shell of superstition and the age-old misery of slavery, THE WOMAN capable of playing an active part in the creation of the future is born.'

In her famous study of childhood trauma, Alice Miller has argued convincingly that it was a specific event in the history of Picasso's family of origin that laid the bases for his later extraordinary capacity for empathy with the victims of Guernica. In December 1884, when Picasso was only three, an earthquake of major dimensions hit his home city of Málaga. Picasso's own recollection of that night was recounted to his friend Jaime Sabartés: 'My mother [heavily pregnant at the time] was wearing a kerchief on her head: I had never seen her like that before. My father took his cloak from its hanger, flung it over his shoulders, snatched me up and wrapped me in its folds until only my head was peeping out.' With the city still in the throes of the earthquake and with screams and cries rending the air, the family group traversed a long, dark street, Calle de la Victoria, until they reached the safety of a relative's house.

Three days later, Picasso's mother gave birth to her second daughter, her labour probably induced by the fright she had experienced. This, then, was the childhood trauma of Picasso, which was rendered less toxic by the possibility of peeking out from the cloak and being held in the protective arms of his father while he did so. And this, according to Miller, was the trauma that Picasso contained within him and that was to find so extraordinary an outlet in *Guernica*.[183]

Family is also to be found in the picture itself. The space in which the figures of the mural huddle, scream and die is neither entirely private nor public, neither outside nor in. On the left-hand side of the mural as the viewer sees it, there is a group of three figures: the bull, the mother and the dead child. In his classic study Rudolf Arnheim has shown how, as the painting developed and went through various stages, this tragic threesome increasingly acquired the characteristics of a family grouping. Arnheim argues that the pictorial problem, present in the mural's earlier stages, of how to remove the hind quarters of the bull from the centre of the picture, was resolved not by a process of elimination but by turning the bull and making his body the backdrop for the mother and child. In this final version, both the generative and the paternal aspects of the bull come to the fore. He is not the bull that gores the horse in the bullring, but the bull that would protect the family but cannot. He is a bull who can only stand and stare, his mouth open and practically touching that of the mother, his testicles aligned with her breasts.[184]

How does the depiction of family in Picasso's *Guernica* (1937) compare with that of Sironi's *Famiglia* (1932, plate 4)? They are radically different in a number of respects. The first is in the portrayal of masculinity. Whereas Sironi depicts the male figure as always alone, always on the left-hand side of the picture, gazing with longing and despair at the mother and child, Picasso, as we have just seen, has no such vision of masculine alienation. His bull, though powerless to protect the family group, is none the less an intrinsic part of it. The representation of mother and child is also strikingly different. For Sironi, mother and child are so harmoniously linked that they appear to be part of the same body. The mother's gaze is concentrated serenely upon her child, as so often in the great Italian tradition of depictions of Madonna and child. In Picasso's work, however, this maternal gaze has been brutally, horrifically interrupted. The child is dead and her/his head lolls lifelessly downwards. The mother no longer looks at it but rather raises her own head upwards, towards the bull, beseeching and bewailing at the same time. Furthermore, Sironi's family fracture is an intimate and internal one, marked spatially and expressively by the static estrangement of man from woman. Picasso's death of the family, by contrast, takes place in a semi-public space, in the context of a general commotion, externally imposed. The horse is dying, the woman is on fire, the child is dead. All this is brought about from above, by Sironi's Fascist and Nazi comrades-in-arms.

A final point of comparison can be sought in the family lives of the two painters. Sironi's, as we have seen, was deeply unhappy, and in 1930 he and his wife had separated. The anguish of his family paintings closely reflects his own private life. For Picasso things were different. Roland Penrose, who was a personal friend in these years, has commented laconically that 'The brilliant artistic career of Picasso was not accompanied by equal success in his family life.'[185] He was too restless to submit to the (not inconsiderable) demands of his first wife, Olga, and too worried that he would finish in a trap which would constrain and limit his artistic creativity. While in Paris he was with the photographer Dora Maar, who had found him a studio sufficiently large to house his huge mural. But each week he went down to the old farmhouse near Versailles at Le Tremblay-sur-Mauldre to visit his lover Marie-Thérèse Walter and their child, Maya. There he not only played with Maya and made love to Marie-Thérèse, but continued to paint their portraits.[186]

IV. THE REGIME IN ITS FIRST YEARS

1. Flight

As Franco's troops broke through the republican lines in late 1938 and early 1939, it became abundantly clear that, although he repeatedly declared himself to be acting according to Christian values, Franco was actually intent on the most ruthless suppression of that part of the Spanish population which had remained loyal to the Republic. He claimed that patriotic Spain had been the innocent victim of a 'Jewish-Bolshevik-Masonic conspiracy'. As such, there could be no question of pardon or forgiveness: 'Such damage has been done to the Fatherland and such havoc has been wreaked on families and on morality, so many victims cry out for justice that no honourable Spaniard, no thinking being, could stand aside from the painful duty of punishment.'[187]

A particular hatred was reserved for the Catalan people, guilty of seeking their autonomy from the Castilian state. On 26 January 1939, the advance guard of Franco's army reached the southern edges of Barcelona. The young Communist Teresa Pàmies has left us this testimony:

There is one thing I will never forget: the wounded who crawled out of the Vallarca hospital, mutilated and bandaged, almost naked, despite the cold. They went down to the street, shrieking and pleading with us not to leave them behind to the mercies of the victors [. . .] The certainty that we left them to their fate will shame us forever. Those with no legs dragged themselves along the ground, those who had lost an arm raised the other with a clenched fist, the youngest cried in fear, the older ones went mad with rage.[188]

An estimated 450,000 people – including many entire family groups – left Barcelona and the rest of Catalonia to begin the long and horrific winter march towards the French frontier. Their exodus bore many points of similarity to that imposed by the Turks upon the Armenians in 1915, when the Armenians had been forced to abandon their villages and trek under appalling conditions southwards towards the deserts of northern Syria and Iraq. In the Armenian case many of the weakest – the old and the young – died from heat and dehydration; in the Spanish case they died from cold, sleet and snow. In the Armenian genocide most of the able-bodied men had been killed before the beginning of the marches, which consisted largely of women, children and old people. The Catalonian exodus included many men, both soldiers and civilians. They were fleeing from the threat of extermination: between 1936 and 1939 an estimated 150,000 men and women had been eliminated behind nationalist lines.[189]

Of the photographs that have come down to us of this Catalan odyssey, one in particular stands out. It shows a man and a little girl, perhaps father and daughter, walking up a dirt track in the middle of the Catalan countryside. The man is tall and carries blankets over his shoulders. The little girl is perhaps ten years old and holds his hand. She has only one leg and limps along determinedly with a crutch for support. What happened to them? How far did the little girl get before she had to be carried by the man? How far did he get before he could carry her no longer? Were the blankets sufficient to keep out the cold in the days that followed? We will never know. In the photograph we see other peasants following behind; a suitcase and a flask of wine. At a certain point this little group would have joined the mass of refugees on the main road northwards. Perhaps they escaped the strafing of the Italian and German planes. Perhaps they made it to the frontier.

The French frontier brought anything but deliverance. The ignominious performance of the French state in the years of the Spanish Civil War was crowned by the reception it gave the refugees, who were treated as little better than criminals. Families which had managed to remain united in the flight northwards were now forcibly separated. Women, children and the old were herded into transit camps and dispersed to other parts of France, while the men were sent to insalubrious camps on the coast, without shelter or

fig. 40 Catalan refugees crossing the mountains in order to reach the French frontier, 1939.

sanitation, their confines marked only by barbed wire. In these camps, such as that at Argelès and Saint-Cyprien, little drinkable water or food was distributed for many days; nor did the wounded initially receive any treatment. Illness and death were commonplace.[190]

Margarita Nelken had, together with her daughter, taken this same road to exile. She arrived exhausted but safe at the Spanish embassy at Perpignan, and there began to search desperately for news of her son Santiago. On 12 February 1939 she was visited at the embassy by the great Spanish cellist Pablo Casals. Margarita wrote to him later, 'I shall never forget that in Perpignan, as soon as you saw me, you asked me, "And what of your son? Did he get out?" Yes, he had led his men out and voluntarily accompanied them to the camp at St. Cyprien from which I later managed to get him released.'[191]

Margarita recounted this moment as one of the most memorable of her life, but it was to be followed by tragedy. Santiago chose to go and live in the Soviet Union, where he studied engineering. In 1941 he volunteered for the Red Army. Three years later, on 5 July 1944, he was killed in action in the Ukraine while commanding an artillery unit of Katyusha rocket launchers. Margarita never recovered from this loss. She felt extraordinarily guilty that she had not been closer to him when he was a child, and that she had sacrificed her son to her beliefs and politics. For someone as maternal as Margarita this was a terrible self-inflicted wound. Furthermore, at the end of the civil war she had chosen to go and live in Mexico, not the Soviet Union – the correct decision for her but one that once again took her far away from her son. In Mexico, her writing and journalism supported an entirely female family – her aged mother, her daughter and her granddaughter. She had separated from her husband after his multiple infidelities, but in spite of all the wrongs he had done her she looked after him in his dying days.

Further tragedy was in store. In June 1954, after 'five months of hell', her daughter Magda died of cancer of the womb. Margarita wrote to a friend at the beginning of 1956,

To you and yours, who can still speak of happiness, with all my heart I wish it for you this year and those to come. For your part, if you care for me, wish for me only that, as soon as I have my little girl [Cuqui, now nearly nineteen] settled in life, there should be an end to this appalling joke that life plays on me of waking (on the few occasions when I can sleep) and realising that I am without my children.[192]

Margarita Nelken died in March 1968, aged seventy-four. The novelist Max Aub wrote in his diary on 10 March,

There can have been few lives with more sorrows, setbacks, disillusionments, misfortunes. She resisted them all until nearly eighty years old. She was never an easy woman and her sharp tongue must have protected her from her tribulations. She was, it is not necessary to say, very intelligent. She read and saw a lot. She knew how to speak; deputy for Extremadura, she knew the Spanish countryside as well as she knew the museums of Europe.[193]

2. Defeated families

Like all the other great tyrannies examined in this book, the Franco regime, especially in its early years, made a fundamental distinction between those families that it intended to encourage and nurture, and those that lay outside its norms and beyond its benevolent gaze. In the early 1940s most families which had taken the republican side mourned for a father or a brother who had been killed or gone missing, mothers mourned for their dead infants, there was famine at the kitchen table.[194]

The summary trials and executions went on for many years. By the end of 1940 there were 240,916 political prisoners in Spain, 7,762 of them on death row. Perhaps as many as 50,000 political prisoners were executed between 1939 and 1945.[195] In these circumstances relatives drove themselves to distraction and exhaustion trying to find someone who might intervene, or collecting testimonies to the good behaviour of their loved ones. Very often it was to no avail. Many executions took place at night, the regime doing all it could to conceal the whereabouts of corpses. Families were unable to bury their dead, a terrible psychological deprivation which, after decades of silence, has been remedied, partially and recently, by the exhumation of bodies from unmarked graves.

If prisoners managed to escape execution, or were judged 'redeemable', they were destined to many years of either imprisonment or hard labour in Franco's work camps. Either way, undernourishment, overcrowding and a lack of basic hygiene could swiftly lead to illness and death. The authorities allowed food parcels sent by prisoners' families to reach their destination, and these often made the difference between life and death. Prisoners whose families were far away or unable to send anything were unlikely to survive, unless their fellow prisoners shared some small part of their own food parcels with them.

The most famous monument to Franco's slave-labour regime was the 'Valley of the Fallen', a huge basilica carved out of a granite mountain to the north of Madrid, its entrance dominated by a cross 150 metres high. It was built, in part by political prisoners, in part by labour gangs, over a period of twenty years, between 1940 and 1959, and houses the bodies of more than 40,000 members of Franco's armies, as well as the remains of a token few hundred republican soldiers of Catholic faith. Franco himself was buried there in November 1975.[196]

A particularly obscene part of this story of surveillance and punishment concerns female prisoners. In 1939 there were more than 23,000 women in Franco's prisons. As women's crime rates were traditionally very low, it is safe to assume that a small percentage of these were prostitutes and the rest were political prisoners. It is impossible to quantify the abuses inflicted upon women prisoners, but all the testimonies speak of systematic subjection and humiliation at best, and of rape, torture and execution at worst. Those who survived and returned to their families, either of origin or procreation, brought with them permanent physical and psychological damage.[197]

In socio-economic terms, the years 1939 to 1952 marked the first period of the Franco regime. They were characterised by the policy of autarky, or economic self-reliance, along the lines previously attempted by both the Fascist and Nazi regimes. In Spain, however, autarky was combined with the systematic compression of the wages of the urban and rural poor, with results which bordered on the catastrophic. The worst years were those between 1940 and 1942, during which very many working-class families were faced by famine. Amongst the landless labourers of the southern rural regions, pellagra, a disease that had been prevalent in the nineteenth century, returned to plague the poorest families. As a result of consuming inedible plants and grasses, thousands of starving men and women developed painful skin conditions, began to tremble uncontrollably, gradually lost their sight and died.[198] Other diseases, such as typhus and tuberculosis, ravaged many parts of the country.

These then were the defeated families of the Spanish Civil War – under-nourished, depleted, each bearing the memory of a particular horror.

3. Catholic families, the Church and the regime

The 'victorious' families often had their own share of terrible memories and suffered from some of the same deprivations as the defeated, but with important differences. One was that the population of many of the regions most faithful to Franco was composed of rural smallholders, as in Navarra. Their self-sufficiency meant that they suffered much less than landless labourers in the economic crisis, and were even able to make money on the black market for agricultural products. In the major urban centres bourgeois families, too, had financial reserves upon which they could call in this hour of need. But the crucial difference was that the 'victorious' families were celebrated, respected and nurtured by the regime and the Church. They were, after all, good Catholic families.

fig. 41 Two children saluting a poster celebrating Franco, 1939. The caption reads,
'Franco, Caudillo of God and of the fatherland, first to triumph over the Bolshevik
world on the battlefield.'

It is worth pausing to analyse some of the presuppositions that lie behind these attitudes. According to the Fuero de Trabajo of 9 March 1938, the fundamental labour law of the new regime, the family was 'the natural nucleus and foundation of society, and at the same time the moral institution endowed with inalienable rights and superior to all positive law'.[199] When the documents of the regime and the Church talked of 'the family', however, they did not mean *all* Spanish families but only Catholic ones. All others were flawed and even illegitimate, at best the possible objects of evangelical campaigning. There was in the Church no acceptance of the *universality* of the love and care which lay at the root of much of family life.

With considerable sleight of hand the Spanish Church went further still, declaring that since the overwhelming majority of Spaniards lived in Catholic families, the Spanish nation could be defined only in Catholic terms.[200] Not only was this a convenient way of obliterating the very existence of dissenting families; it was also a bald-faced lie. Figures for Sunday attendance at Mass in Spanish dioceses for the years between 1950 and 1964 reveal high levels of absenteeism. Only in the north-west did more than 50 per cent of the population go to church on a Sunday. The figure for the diocese of Seville was between zero and 14 per cent; that for Badajoz between 15 and 29 per cent.[201] Even with military spending as high as it was, it was not possible for the Civil Guard to herd the population to Mass on a Sunday morning.

Even so, in the post-war years the Church was able to bask in an extraordinary position of privilege. During the Second World War it feared the overpowerful Falange, with its sympathy for Nazism and its dreams of total control over society. Franco himself was quite partial to the occasional Nazi, as the warm welcome accorded to Heinrich Himmler in October 1940 clearly demonstrated.[202] But the change in the war's fortunes in 1943 and the definitive defeat of the Axis Powers in 1945 forced a radical rethink. The Falange was demoted, the Church was ever more fully embraced, and the regime reiterated to a deeply religious and anti-Communist stance. As Frances Lannon has written, 'The church [. . .] showed every sign of winning the peace as well as the war.'[203] The Jesuits returned, ecclesiastical institutions enjoyed exemption from taxation, Catholic feast days were once again celebrated as public holidays, single-sex schools were re-established, and Catholic Action dominated a civil society that was clerical, not plural.

As early as 1937, a very strong Marian cult was introduced into schools in the nationalist zone, later to be extended to the whole country. Every school was to have a statue of the Virgin in pride of place, preferably bearing the 'extremely Spanish' title of 'The Immaculate Conception'. During the month of May, 'following immemorial Spanish custom', teachers and pupils were to recite the month's prayers in front of the statue. Every day of the year, on entering and leaving the school, the pupils would greet their teachers with the words 'Ave María purísima', to which the teachers would reply, 'Sin pecado concebida' (Conceived without sin).[204] The confessional state, long dreamed of and theorised, seemed to have been realised.

Republican legislation concerning the family was repealed. A decree of 2 March 1938 and a later law of 23 September 1939 did away with the early 1930s laws regarding matrimony and divorce. The reintroduction of the old articles of the Civil Code was also highly punitive, in that it made no allowance for those who, in good faith, had chosen civil marriage during the republican period. Any who had done so became merely 'concubines' and their children illegitimate. Once again, the much-proclaimed 'defenders of the family' revealed themselves to be nothing of the sort, ready as they were to defend only approved Catholic families. Franco had no qualms about this partiality. On the contrary, 'The inspiration of all the regime's activities is a Catholic sentiment which distinguishes us and allows us not to err [. . .] This Catholic sentiment which animates all the life of Spain is the most solid guarantee for citizens against the arbitrariness and excesses, always possible, of those who hold power.'[205]

The family policies of Franco in the first decade of his regime were very limited. The war had rendered the state all but insolvent, resulting in a kind of dwarf version of Italian Fascist public policies, which were in themselves limited and patchy. In Spain, the principal areas of intervention concerned gender and demography. The gender politics of the regime were concerned above all with ensuring that the public sphere became as far as possible a male preserve and that women returned to being the 'angels of the hearth' and lynchpins of the family. From 1942 onwards, in an effort to remove women from the workforce, female employees in the public sector were offered a sort of state dowry of modest proportions if they stayed at home after marriage.[206] Any ideas of equality between husband and wife, or of a woman's financial independence as a result of paid work outside the home, were firmly quashed. The Spanish male was restored to his rightful place as head of the family and his patriarchal prerogatives were not to be called into question.

In demographic terms, as we have seen, the Civil War left a terrible dent in the nation's population. The regime did what it could – which was not very much – to repair the damage. The establishment of a Family Subsidy in 1938 offered financial rewards on a sliding scale to families with numerous offspring. The subsidy was, of course, paid not to the women who bore the children but to the men who were their heads of family. The advertisement, sale, purchase and use of contraceptives were prohibited. By a law of 24 January 1941 abortion was rendered a penal offence, and the new Penal Code of 1944 confirmed harsh sentences for those who sought abortions and those who provided them.[207]

Overall, then, public policy was circumscribed, mainly by financial constraints. What there was of it primarily took a negative form (the prohibition of actions and behaviour) rather than a positive one (the provision of services and benefits). Spanish society of these years, as Santos Juliá has written, was repressed, regimented, autarkic and the object of endless Catholic revivalism.[208] The regime attempted to lay down rigid norms for families, policing them more rigorously than in the past – not just the republican past but also that of Primo de Rivera's dictatorship. A new law prohibiting either husband or wife from abandoning the domestic hearth was introduced on 12 March 1942. Its preamble emphasised the extent to which the regime had the family's well-being at heart and to which, after the terrible dislocations of the Civil War, the family now needed to be protected. Those guilty of the new crime of home abandonment were to be punished by imprisonment or by a heavy fine of 5,000–10,000 pesetas. Adultery, depenalised during the republican years, was reinstated as a crime for both sexes, but was punishable with different degrees of severity. A law of 11 May 1942 announced that women's adultery was especially serious, in that it 'goes beyond the sphere of private honour and forms the basis of an attack on the most sacred social necessities'.[209] In all, Francoism insisted upon respect for 'honestidad y buenas costumbres' – disquieting requirements considering whence they emanated and what they were taken to signify.[210]

CONCLUSION

During the terrible decade of the Spanish Civil War, two contrasting conceptions of family life and politics came to the fore – one republican and the other Catholic. The first, outlined in the republican Constitution of December 1931, was based on equality between the sexes, the right to divorce (though not to abortion), the duty of parents to support their children – whether conceived within or outside wedlock – the depenalisation of adultery, and the right to civil marriage. Unlike the Italian Fascist regime, which as we have seen had remained largely mute on family law, the Spanish republicans moved very far, very fast – many commentators would say too much so – and did so on a constitutional level.

The Catholic conception of the family in Spain was very different. It emerged from a long tradition of family theology and most recently from Pius

XI's *Casti Connubii* of 31 December 1930.[211] Marriage was a holy sacrament and as such was indissoluble. The Catholic family deserved special protection and its autonomy was to be guaranteed by the state. In gender terms, while the Spanish Constitution of 1931 underlined the necessity of equality, Pius XI reiterated the importance of patriarchy, though male power within the family was ideally to be based on a combination of hierarchy and partnership. Above all, the Church viewed the Christian family as deeply menaced by modernity. Modern culture, politics and science were doing all they could to discredit the holy sacrament of marriage.

The Church responded with two interconnected strategies: mass mobilisation aimed at the establishment of the 'social kingdom of Christ' on earth, and programmatic agreements between the Vatican and the new political regimes of the day. The Concordat with Italian Fascism was a vital first step; the creation of Franco's confessional state an even more spectacular, if costly, result. Under such a regime belief could only be in the Catholic singular, never in the ecumenical plural; civil marriage could never be considered a 'verdadero matrimonio' (true marriage), as the Spanish bishops put it. That designation belonged exclusively to church weddings.[212]

Given these fiercely held positions and the long history of anti-clericalism in Spain, it might appear that there was no room at all for mediation over family politics. This was not so. Surprisingly, the two views were in many ways not as far apart as the advent of civil war would suggest. The defence of the family, not its suppression, was written very clearly into the Constitution. The first words of Article 43 were 'The family is under the special care of the State.' This could be understood – and was by the Church – as a sinister statement of intent. But its meaning becomes very clear in the conclusion to Article 43, which affirms the state's obligation to assist the old and the infirm, to protect maternity and infancy, and to abide by the provisions of the Geneva Declaration of the Rights of the Child of September 1924: 'The child that is hungry must be fed; the child that is sick must be nursed.'[213]

Furthermore, the cultural and educational programmes launched by the Patronato de las Misiones Pedagógicas after 1931 were largely pluralist in content. When Lorca took his 'La Barraca' on the road he did so to revive the great tradition of Castilian theatre, not to preach atheist revolution. As he explained in an interview of 1932, 'We will take Good and Evil, God and Faith into the towns of Spain again.' Even the anarchists and the anarcho-syndicalists, the Church's most dangerous opponents, did not contemplate the liquidation of the family. On the contrary, the motion approved at the Zaragoza national congress of the CNT in May 1936, on the eve of the Civil War, underlined the fact that 'The family [. . .] has performed most admirable functions in the imparting of morality and solidarity [. . .] it is likely that it will survive for a long time to come.'[214]

The truth was that Catholic and Francoist propagandists often *invented* the family characteristics of their opponents, attacking them not for what they were but for what they wanted them to be. Margarita Nelken suffered from such attacks all her working life. At one moment she was the 'Jewish Amazon', capable of every kind of base seduction. At another she was 'like so many other presumed intellectuals, who are whores in their own imaginations more than in their real sexual adventures'. In any case, wrote the propagandists, 'she is not Spanish', which they considered to be just as well.[215] Hysterical and uncontrolled accounts of the dissoluteness of republican family life circulated widely in the moderate and Catholic press. Young girls were supposed to have demonstrated in Barcelona shouting, 'Children yes! Husbands no!' 'Free love' was interpreted as endless promiscuity. In a society as traditional as that of Spain this was highly combustible material. The invention of republican sin on so grand a scale did irreparable harm at a very difficult moment.

Avoidance of impending doom would have required much sensitivity and willingness to compromise on both sides. Pius XI did make preliminary moves in this direction, and his chosen emissary, at least initially, was Cardinal Francisco Vidal y Barraquer, archbishop of Tarragona, who headed a small but enlightened minority of Spanish prelates. But the 'integralist' bishops were far and away in the majority, and as early as 1931 Pedro Segura y Sáenz, cardinal primate of Spain, was calling for a crusade of prayers and sacrifices against the Republic.

On the other side the new republican authorities were often deeply anti-clerical, resentful of the Church's centuries-old cultural hegemony and determined to clip its wings. They were also woefully slow in suppressing the wave of church burning which greeted the proclamation of the Republic. Azaña's famous statement 'Spain has ceased to be Catholic', whatever its intentions, could not have been better designed to fan the flames of the Church's fears. Yet at the end of the day the republicans – with the exception of the hard-line anarchists – had no desire to suppress the Church, whereas the integralist bishops of the Spanish Church had no hesitation in viewing society and its culture in purely monolithic terms.

When the long war of words, of definitions and of symbols, both political and religious, gave way to real war, fought with incredible savagery from 1936 to 1939, Spanish families found themselves forced to live through many different, agonising experiences, in which fate, geography and unexpected kindness or coldness all played their part. A family's social capital, especially that of an inter-class nature, could often determine its destiny. A typology of family experiences during the war has yet to be fully constructed, as has a social history of Spanish family life in these decades. The generation that Ronald Fraser interviewed at the end of the 1970s is rapidly dying out, and with their departure the possibility of oral history – so important in the historical registering of the domestic sphere – is rapidly diminishing.

Both sides committed atrocities. The bishops, priests, monks and nuns massacred mainly in the first months of the war and mainly by anarchists can never be forgotten. Nor can those taken by night from republican prisons in Madrid and killed without trial or even the possibility of writing to their families. But the atrocities on the nationalist side, desired and executed by General Franco, were so much greater in extent and of such persistent mass brutality that a difference in quantity becomes a difference in quality. Nor was this all. In the years following the end of the Civil War the killings went on and on, as the death sentences of tens of thousands of republicans, often guilty only of being Catalanist or a trade unionist, were signed by Franco.

In the extraordinary turbulence and tragedy of the 1930s, families were under great pressure and the calls made upon them for help and protection were unceasing. Often they could do nothing. No single image represents this impotence better than the 'family group' in Picasso's *Guernica*, where the horrors of the dead child and wailing mother have replaced the serenity of the traditional Catholic depiction of Madonna and child. It should never be forgotten, moreover, that the families wiped out at Guernica were devout Catholic Basques.

A final point needs to be reiterated – the paucity of reflection by contemporaries on family politics in Spain during these years. We can hardly expect innovation from the nationalist side, where the *restoration* of the Catholic family to its proper place in the ordering of society is the paramount drive. But it is the republicans who surprise most. In contrast to the intellectual effervescence of the early years of the Soviet Union, little emerges from Spain that could be labelled 'a debate on the family'. Even the radical anarchist feminists of the Mujeres Libres organisation limit their discussion to exploring how to live better within the family, rather than debating the family itself. As Mercedes Comaposada recalled, 'We wanted people to be able to choose whether to have children, how and when, and know how to bring them up.'[216] This was a crucial ambition, but it fitted more easily into a liberal framework than a revolutionary one. In anarcho-syndicalist Barcelona (1936–7), little changed in family life. Kinship groups could and did eat together in the *comedores populares*, girls volunteered to go and fight at the front and were then sent home again, women went to work in the factories, but family life remained much the same.

The lack of reflection and experimentation was to be noted not just in the *barris* of Barcelona, but also among the republican intellectual elite. Margarita

Nelken, at a certain point in her political career (1933), railed against the right-wing slogan 'Patria, Familia, Religión': 'What family are they talking about? They say it to us who know that the bourgeois family is one of the greatest farces and hypocrisies.'[217] This was little more than the mouthing of an old dictum. Nelken was bourgeois to her fingertips and from 1930 onwards lived (when she had time) in a flat in one of Madrid's most fashionable streets, the Paseo de la Castellana. She had every right to do so, but not to denounce simultaneously the family life she loved and so yearned for and whose absence brought her such suffering.

CHAPTER 5

'The greater world and the smaller one': the politics of the family in Germany, 1918–1945

I. The making of a Nazi 'family man'

Joseph Goebbels was born on 29 October 1897 and brought up in a drab, two-storey house in the small textile town of Rheydt, in the industrial Rhineland. His parents were devout Catholics. Their household was run on strict lines of piety, thrift and endeavour – seemingly a 'Protestant' work ethic but located within a Catholic family. Money was always very short: Joseph's father, Friedrich (Fritz), spent all his working life as a clerk in a local firm producing gas mantles, reaching the position of *Prokurist* (company secretary) at the end of his career. His mother, Katherina, was of Dutch origin, a little-educated woman but of strong maternal character. Her son Joseph was fond of telling the story (which he may well have invented, as was his wont) of the occasion when she assembled the children – there were five in all – around their father's bed, where he lay critically ill with pneumonia. She instructed them all to hold hands and to sing and pray. They did so with such devotion that their father recovered almost immediately. As this anecdote and other evidence demonstrate, there was no lack of love in the family, even if expressed in rather narrow and religiously defined ways. Nor was there any hint, differently from many of the families of origin examined in this book, of a failed or absentee or physically violent father. Quite the opposite. If criticism was to be made, and Joseph did not hesitate to make it, it was rather of a stifling conformism which pervaded the family and all its actions.[1]

In his childhood Goebbels suffered from infantile paralysis of the right foot. When he was ten years old he was operated on, unsuccessfully, and from that time onwards walked with a distinct limp which he did his best to disguise. His impediment isolated him from his school companions. In an account of his early years dating from 1924, Goebbels wrote, 'Childhood from then on pretty joyless. I could no longer join in the games of others. Became a solitary, lone wolf.'[2] As is often true of children with physical disabilities, he found solace in reading intensely and excelling intellectually. His parents recognised that he was the brightest of their children and sent him to the local *Gymnasium*, or grammar school. There he did very well, but on the outbreak of the First World War in August 1914, when he was nearly seventeen, whereas his elder brothers both departed (and eventually returned) from the front, Joseph was rejected for military service because of his disability. It was a bitter blow for him. He made up for it by showing fearlessness in frequent street fighting – in this resembling Marinetti – and by using to the full his biting tongue and restless intelligence. As Alan Bullock has commented, 'In a party that swarmed with strong-armed bullies and veterans of a war from which he had been excluded [. . .] Goebbels was in fact quite as tough and very much more quick-witted than the men he had to lead.'[3]

In 1917 Goebbels finished his schooling and immediately enrolled at the University of Bonn. He was physically very slight by comparison with his fellow students, hardly more than five feet tall, with sloping shoulders and clothes that invariably looked too big for him. But he had magnetic eyes, fine hands and a deep voice, unexpectedly powerful and well modulated. His parents dreamed of his becoming a priest but could not afford to keep him at university. He survived instead on loans from a Catholic charitable society. His university career was peripatetic, culminating in his graduation from Heidelberg University in 1921. In these years of voracious reading and pecuniary deprivation, he moved further and further away from the Catholicism of his family. In a letter of 9 November 1919, revealing in both its tone and its content, his father expressed all his fears for his son's future and the fate of his soul:

Dear Joseph,
My letter of the day before yesterday should have reached you by now. But I wish to revert briefly to your dear lines of the 31st ult. [*sic*]. They contained much to please me but again much to give me a great deal of pain. I do believe, though, that with some goodwill on both sides our former relationship of complete confidence could be quickly restored. Obviously this cannot be done unless you are absolutely candid and truthful to your father [. . .] Do come home, my son, and talk it over with us. You can have the fare from me any time you say so [. . .] You write in your letter, 'Why don't you tell me that you curse me as the prodigal son who has left his parents and gone into the wilderness?' And then again you write, 'If you think I can no longer be your

son . . .' Well, being a Catholic father, I do neither the one thing nor the other. I will just go on praying for you as I have prayed for you so often.[4]

But Goebbels's ideological development was taking an altogether different direction. He was part of a generation – impoverished, marginalised and angry – that had been traumatised by Germany's catastrophic loss of the First World War and was now seeking to make sense of the dire situation in which it found itself. There were various strands to Goebbels's ideological outlook. One was the binary category pessimism/optimism. Under the influence of Oswald Spengler's *The Decline of the West* and other texts, pessimism runs through all Goebbels's early correspondence and diaries.[5] As the years pass, however, this despair is tempered – though never completely replaced – by an overarching desire to join a mass movement and seek solutions to his epoch's malaise. By the time he meets Hitler for the first time in the autumn of 1925, hope has begun to take the place of despair.

A second strand is his deep Romanticism. A love of the German Romantics in particular, both literary and musical, was to accompany him throughout his life, providing a strong element of consonance with Adolf Hitler. The romantic ideal of community takes on in Goebbels a distinctly *völkisch* form, where the individual is linked organically to a hierarchically structured whole. Blood and soil are the primal materials for such a community. In 1924 Goebbels wrote a short novel, *Michael*, subtitled *A German Destiny in Pages from a Diary*. In it we find his hero, a poet, soldier and revolutionary, writing, 'I stand on the hard soil of my homeland with both my feet. The smell of the soil is around me. And in my veins peasant blood wells up healthily.'[6]

Other romantic elements were also at work in his daily life, such as his endless departures and wandering in his early days as a political militant. In his diary he complains constantly of exhaustion but then confesses to loving the 'gypsy life'. On 13 January 1926 he wrote, 'I am glad the travelling starts again tomorrow. More of it next week, then working-community Hannover, then the whole hog, Osnabrück, Schleswig-Holstein, Hamburg. The bird flies into the world!'[7] For the Nazis in general and Goebbels in particular the bird in question was nearly always an eagle, perhaps that of Goethe's ode 'The Eagle and the Dove', in which an eagle with a broken wing seeks refuge in a grove of myrtles. A dove tries to make him stay: 'O friend true happiness / Lies in contentedness / And that contentedness / Finds everywhere enough.'[8] The eagle complements the dove on his words of wisdom, but notes that they are those of a dove. An eagle has other work to do.

A third element, less strong than his Romanticism but still present in his early years, was his sense of class. For Goebbels National Socialism was not a mere party name but had some real content to it. He had read Marx (or said he had), had been brought up in a largely working-class community, and identified with the plight and sorrows of working-class families in the post-war years. On 11 September 1925 he wrote in his diary, 'National and socialist! What comes first and what second? For us in the West there can be no doubt. First the socialist revolution, then, like a hurricane, national liberation.'[9] Not by chance was his early work with the Nazis closely linked to the Strasser brothers and their emphasis on class struggle, and not by chance was he initially deeply disappointed by Hitler's highly cautious attitude with regard to private property and the fate of Germany's ruling elites. But he soon accepted his leader's emphasis on the absolute priority of national struggle and the creation of a *Volksgemeinschaft* (people's community), to which we shall return. His diatribes against bourgeois society – 'all of it is either lust or business'[10] – remained ferocious long after his own lifestyle had come to correspond to, or to exceed, that of the bourgeoisie he berated.

The last and self-evidently most disquieting element of his ideology was his virulent anti-semitism. His alienation and bitterness found in the Jews a convincing scapegoat, and the theorising of Houston Stewart Chamberlain persuaded him, as it did Hitler, that Germans and Jews were locked in a world-historical battle for survival. Germans were the highest representatives of the Aryan 'race-soul' and Christ an Aryan prophet. The Jews, by contrast, were 'the other' – a bastard race, the epitome of all evil, to be despised and destroyed. Here is the shocking language of Goebbels's literary hero Michael, who has travelled to the Frisian islands to write his Messianic play:

No Jews here at all, and that is truly a blessing. Jews make me physically sick, the mere sight of them does this. I cannot even hate the Jew. I can only despise him. He has raped our people, soiled our ideals, weakened the strength of the nation, corrupted morals. He is the poisonous eczema on the body of our sick nation. Religion? How naive you are [. . .] Either [the Jew] destroys us or we destroy him [. . .] Christ cannot have been a Jew, I do not have to look for any scientific proof of that. It just is so![11]

Here Goebbels deploys some of the most common weapons in the nationalist armoury for dehumanising and then destroying an enemy – the image of a poisonous, alien presence eating away at the nation's health (usually a cancer but here eczema); the physical violation of part of the population, usually female, an outrage for which revenge has to be taken; the use of the word 'soil' in its excremental sense, far from the 'hard soil of my homeland' which Michael celebrates.

Goebbels's early writings and speeches never cease to underline the direct link between capitalism and the Jews. The well-known Nazi liturgy of Jewish plutocratic responsibility for both hyper-inflation and then recession finds in him a fervent supporter. In 1923, at the height of the German inflation crisis, he worked for some months at the Dresdner bank in Cologne, regarded at the time as being the public limited bank most under Jewish control. The experience not only convinced him that he would never be a clerk but also heightened the symbiosis in his mind between Jews and unwarranted wealth and power.[12]

In this context, the activities of the Wagner circle at Bayreuth, presided over first by Wagner's widow Cosima and then by his daughter-in-law Winifred, were of great significance. In 1899 Chamberlain had first published his *Foundations of the Nineteenth Century*. Twenty-seven years later we find him at Bayreuth, an old man married to one of Wagner's daughters. In early May 1926 Goebbels went to pay his respects. The account he consigned to his diary is revealing of his highly charged and ever more anti-semitic German Romanticism:

Next day Bayreuth. Wagner's town. I feel elevated. Through the rain! To H. St. Chamberlain. His wife, a daughter of Wagner, asks me in. Shattering scene: Chamberlain on a couch. Broken, mumbling, with tears in his eyes. He holds my hand and will not let it go. His big eyes burn like fire. Greetings to you, spiritual father. Trail blazer, pioneer! I am deeply upset. Leave-taking. He mumbles, wants to speak, can't and then he weeps like a child! Long, long handshake! Farewell! You stand by us when we are near despair. Outside the rain drums on the pavement! I want to cry out, to weep.[13]

The following morning Winifred Wagner, 'a fanatical partisan of ours', took him to her father-in-law's room: 'There is his grand piano, his likeness, his desk. Everything as it used to be. Odd emotion. Wagner's *Tannhäuser* kindled the light of youth in me. I was thirteen then. I think of it now. The children romp through the rooms. Children's laughter where once music was born. It is the same. Both are God's gifts.'

Goebbels's obsession with racial purity spilled over into his principal sexual relationship of these formative years, that with a petite and good-looking local school teacher by the name of Else Janke. In spite of his meagre physique and deformed foot, Goebbels was attractive to many women and was highly sexually active throughout his life. His diaries of these years are full of appreciation for the goodness, kindness and desirability of Else, as well as his longing for her (or any other woman) while he was roving round the country on his speaking tours. On 15 August 1925 he writes, 'Little Else, when do I see you again? Alma, you lithe lovely flower! Anka, I shall never forget you! And yet I am now all alone!' And on 23 September, in revelatory mood, 'Monday Else, little fluffy, ping, ping. Oh, your dear hand. Sweet! Feast of love, tension relaxed after long yearning. I am absolutely content. Else is so dear and good.' Then on 8 May 1926, 'Opposite me [on the train] a splendid wench sleeps on the cushions. Longing for the woman!'[14] There were also moments of a darker kind, of his need to hurt the woman he was with, in terms not of physical but of verbal abuse, of which he was a past master. Thus, on 14 October 1925, 'Why must I cause Else so much pain?' And again, on 28 October, 'A sweet night. She is a good darling. Sometimes I hurt her bitterly.'[15] These patterns were to recur at a later date.

As far back as the autumn of 1923 Goebbels had learned that Else had a Jewish mother. On 22 October he confided his reaction to his diary, in terms that were both grossly patronising and racially stereotyped: 'E. cannot disavow her Jewish blood. There is something strikingly destructive in her character, above all mentally; but this is less obvious because her mind is not fully developed. She is the direct opposite of An[ka], whose racial make-up was first class.'[16] In the event, the discovery of Else's 'racial impurity' did not stop Goebbels from associating with her for many years, while railing against the Jews in all his speeches. The relationship finally broke up in the autumn of 1926, when Goebbels became the Nazi Gauleiter in Berlin.[17]

In these years of longing, frustration and endless travelling, Goebbels's family continued to support him loyally. Sometimes he would find his father 'serious and reserved' and this would 'oppress' him greatly. At others he would describe him as philistine and bourgeois. But most of the time Joseph pays tribute to his parents' kindness and tolerance, virtues that he himself had in rather short supply: 'How modest and kind those two are, father and mother! And I am causing them so much grief.' He was aware of the tension between loyalty to a cause and that to the family – 'ideas versus parents', as he once neatly put it.[18] Time and again – and with little hesitation, it has to be said – Goebbels chose ideas. They were ideas that clashed with Rhineland Catholicism, but he was never really to be free from the imprinting of his youth.

On 14 October 1925 Goebbels noted in his diary, 'I am finishing Hitler's book [volume 1 of Mein Kampf]. Thrilled to bits! Who is this man? Half plebeian, half God! Really Christ, or only John?'[19] As can be seen from this and other such comments, Goebbels's descriptions of his encounter with Hitler, first through his book and then in person, are biblical in framework, personae and imagery. On 8 February 1926 he quotes briefly from Schiller's 'The Cranes of Ibycus': 'To the song and chariot-fight'.[20] Three days later he writes, 'We cannot founder. I want to be an apostle and teacher. My faith is returning!'[21] After Easter he speaks in the Nazi stronghold of Munich for the first time: 'for two and a half hours I go all out. Roaring and tumult. Hitler embraces me at the end. He has tears in his eyes. I feel something like happy.' Goebbels is ever more convinced: 'With this sparkling mind he can be my leader. I bow to his greatness, his political genius! [...] Adolf Hitler, I love you, because you are both great and simple.'[22] And on 24 July, in the Bavarian mountains, on holiday with Hitler for the first time, he writes, 'The chief talks about race questions. It is impossible to reproduce what he said. It must be experienced. He is a genius. The natural, creative instrument of a fate determined by God.'[23]

From this point onwards the story of Goebbels is the story of his service to Hitler and to the Nazi Party. As we have just seen, he became Gauleiter in Berlin in the autumn of 1926 – a key post and a difficult one, given the city's political orientation. In 1928 he was one of the twelve National Socialist deputies elected to the Reichstag. In the dramatic years that ensued, Goebbels had overall responsibility for the development of Nazi propaganda – its dynamism, violence and credibility. In March 1933 he became Minister for People's Enlightenment and Propaganda. Later in the same month he outlined to the directors of German radio stations the basic precepts of successful propaganda:

> I refute the notion that propaganda is something of inferior value [...] we would not have lost the [First World] War if we had understood the art of propaganda somewhat better. *That* is the secret of propaganda: he who the propaganda is to grasp is to be completely saturated with the ideas of propaganda, *without being aware of this* [my italics]. Obviously propaganda has a purpose, but that purpose must be so cleverly and virtuously concealed that he who is to be imbued with this purpose is unaware of it.[24]

Goebbels, then, wanted to act as a 'hidden persuader', moving subtly from behind the scenes to conquer people's minds. This was not at all how he was seen by Victor Klemperer, a Jewish university professor from Dresden. On 14 July 1934 he wrote in his now famous diary,

> Goebbels the advertising [*sic*] minister is no psychologist. He is boring, people make fun of the boring radio. What is the mistake? If a factory, a single enterprise constantly tries to imprint itself on people's minds, on tramcars, with skywriters, etc., etc., that is amusing because the aim is to capture the public in a specific and unessential respect, because it retains its freedom of choice, for example, between this or that razor blade [...] Goebbels, however,

does not captivate, but literally 'binds' the whole person, tyrannizes him and the one who is bound rebels against that, and he has an aversion to the utter monotony of the one thing being offered to him. The progression of feelings here runs from a deadened indifference to aversion and revolt.[25]

In assessing these two competing claims we can certainly agree with Klemperer about the form but not about the effect. Nazi propaganda was monotonous, tyrannical and repetitive. But it did not have the effect – the progression of feelings from indifference to aversion and then to revolt – that Klemperer predicted. On the contrary, the great majority of German families seem to have gone along with it willingly, especially as it corresponded to some of their most deep-felt prejudices in a moment of acute economic crisis.

Another major element of Goebbels's activity, and one that had little to do with 'hidden persuasion', was the fomenting of violence. Although there is little evidence of physical violence in his private life, there can be no doubting how much he revelled in public violence – especially at speaker meetings and on the streets, in the clashes with the Communist Red Front Fighters' League (Rote Frontkämpferbund). His diary entries on this point resemble those of the street-fighting Marinetti ten years earlier. The whole Horst Wessel cult, invented by Goebbels, with its famous accompanying song – 'Clear the streets for the brown battalions, clear the streets for the Storm Division man!' – was testimony to such attitudes.[26] Every year on 23 February, the date of Wessel's assassination in 1930 at the hands of a Communist and petty criminal, Ali Höhler, Goebbels organised a massive procession in memory of the young SA 'martyr'. His talent for funeral processions forcibly brings to mind Joachim Fest's striking observation about Hitler – that he was not able to celebrate life (which at most took the form of tired folklore and dancing under the May Tree) but was a past master at death.[27] Goebbels also had clear ideas about a central question of family politics, which we have encountered more than once already: to whom to the dead belong – the family or the fatherland? Wessel's mother had quarrelled with Goebbels in 1933 because she wanted the family properly represented in any commemoration. Goebbels wrote angrily, 'She is unbearable in her arrogance. Our dead belong to the nation.'[28]

In explaining the reasons for Goebbels's success, historians have underlined his professionalism, his oratorical skills – second only to those of Hitler – his capacity for hard work and his natural cleverness. He was certainly not a profound thinker but he had acquired two skills essential to the taking of political power: a deep knowledge of German society, both urban and rural, consequent upon his endless travelling during what the Nazis called the 'Kampfzeit' (time of struggle); and a clever use of words, music, ceremony and drama, which he used to reach out to families at a time of mass unemployment and deep economic depression.

His personal weaknesses included those of indulging in intrigues and tantrums, and the making of many enemies through the use of a very sharp tongue. Contemporaries found it difficult to make head or tail of him. Sir Nevile Henderson, the British ambassador in Berlin, thought he resembled an Irish agitator with a Celtic manner.[29] And in March 1933 Klemperer wrote wickedly in his diary, 'The events of March 21 were shown [at the Universum cinema in Dresden], including passages from speeches [. . .] Hitler declaiming like a pastor. Goebbels looks uncommonly Jewish.'[30]

In December 1931 Goebbels pulled off one of the greatest coups of his life: he married the sophisticated and good-looking Magda Quandt, the divorced wife of a wealthy German industrialist. Magda was born in 1901 to a bourgeois family in Berlin; her father, Oskar Ritschel, was an aloof engineer with a monocle. While Magda was still very young her parents separated and her mother married again, this time to a Jewish leather manufacturer called Richard Friedländer. According to one of her biographers, Hans-Otto Meissner, Olga loved her stepfather devotedly because he gave her all the warmth and kindness which her own father lacked.[31] In fact, in recognition of this her mother changed her daughter's name to Friedländer. But Friedländer's business as well as his marriage fell on hard times and Magda's mother divorced once again. In 1906 Magda was dispatched to the strict Ursuline Convent in Vilvoorde, near Brussels, where she was to stay until the outbreak of the First World War. She was described by the nuns as 'an active and intelligent little girl'.

In March 1919, now an eighteen-year-old Berlin schoolgirl, she was sent to the exclusive and expensive Holzhausen girls' finishing school near Goslar. The story goes that one day, returning home from school by train, she caught the eye of an unlikely but determined suitor, Günther Quandt. He was exactly twice her age, with two children from his first marriage, and the owner of a highly successful electrical company. Günther successfully wooed Magda with his old-style charm and considerable riches, and they married in January 1921. Perhaps all one can say about her family history up to this point is that she clearly suffered from the emotional and physical distances created by her mother's two divorces. She also had a surfeit of father figures, none of whom really fitted the bill – her own icy and distant father, her stepfather who went bankrupt, the husband who was twice her age. On marrying Quandt Magda naturally took his name, which meant that she had changed her titular identity at least three times in her short life – from Ritschel to Friedländer to Quandt. With Goebbels it became four.

Marriage to Günther Quandt proved disastrous. He was penny-pinching and domineering, anti-social and interested only in how to build his industrial empire. The two went on honeymoon to Italy, touring Umbria in Günther's magnificent limousine – for all the world the perfect couple, rich, handsome and in love. In reality Magda was bored stiff. Instead of admiring the Umbrian landscape and its hill towns, Günther could only talk of the geological structure of the soil and the possibilities for industrial development.[32] Back home, things were no better. After her long years in the convent, Magda yearned for a social life compatible with her age and social status, but Günther actively discouraged any such goings-on. They had a child together, Harald Quandt, born on 1 November 1921. The marriage did not improve.

One characteristic of Magda, her dominant one, emerges very clearly from these years. Not only did Quandt ask her to look after the two boys from his first marriage as well as their own child, Harald, but he also brought into his household the orphans of one of his former dependants. Magda, at least if we are to believe Meissner, performed the mega-maternal role required of her with great competence, even affection. Of course she had maids and nannies to help her along the way, and we can imagine that she was not short on German discipline. But even with these provisos it was a considerable achievement, and one which she was to repeat in the Goebbels household. When Günther's eldest son fell very ill in Paris, it was Magda who rushed to the hospital and stayed with him as he died from a ruptured appendix.[33]

The marriage came to an end when Günther discovered that his wife had a regular lover, though the divorce settlement was quite generous to her, as if in recognition of the pivotal familial role she had played with such decorum. She received a monthly allowance of 4,000 marks, a considerable sum at the time, and custody of Harald until he was fourteen. But if she remarried – and here was the patriarchal twist – her son was to live with his father.

At this point, in the autumn of 1930, Magda Quandt cast around for something to do with her life and began voluntary work for the Nazi Party at its Berlin office. Quite why she chose the Nazis is not clear. From her father she had inherited a lifelong fascination with Buddhism, but the link between Buddhism and Nazism was hardly an obvious one. Nor was the Quandt background a Nazi one – or at least not yet. But Magda had heard Goebbels speak at a mass rally in Berlin and had been struck both by what he had to say and by the way he said it. Naturally enough, he soon scooped up this highly attractive, atypical Nazi volunteer and asked her to work in his own office, organising his secret files. As they worked late into the night together, so the bond between them grew. There seems little doubt that Hitler, too, was deeply interested in Magda. We have no account of it from his side but an entry in

Goebbels's diary for 14 September 1931 is clear enough – Hitler might be the Führer, but Goebbels, according to Goebbels, was the man who knew how to handle women:

> Magda explains: She had a conversation with G. Quandt. Said to him that we wanted to get married. He was cast down. Magda has taken revenge for many sufferings which he has caused her. Then with the Chief. Also said the same to him. He was also cast down. He loves her. But maintains his loyalty to me. And Magda also. She is a fabulous woman. We first had a little argument, but then were completely in agreement. Hitler resigned. He is indeed very alone. He has no happiness with women. Because he is too soft-hearted with them. Women don't like that. They must feel dominated by the man.[34]

There was one further development before the marriage. On 25 October 1931 Goebbels returned home to find Magda in floods of tears. Her mother had written to her to confess a family secret: at the time of Magda's birth, her father and mother had not been married. Although she had been recognised by Ritschel, she was, strictly speaking, of illegitimate birth. What repercussions were there likely to be in the 'Jewish press'? The couple decided to consult Hitler, as they were to do many times in the years to come. The Führer gave a very typical and, for us, germane reply: 'The Chief treats her with tender kindness. He laughs at us. He prefers a girl with a child to a woman without a child. Typical Hitler!'[35]

Magda Quandt and Joseph Goebbels were married on 19 December 1931, on the Quandt family estate in Severin, in rural Mecklenburg. The staging of the marriage there was an act of symbolic generosity on Günther's part, perhaps made also with an eye to the future of the Quandt industries in a Nazi Germany.[36] Hitler was Goebbels's best man. In the extraordinary photograph of the marriage we can see a radiant Goebbels, for once dressed well, accompanying a deeply content Magda. Even shorter than her diminutive husband, she is wearing black to signify that she is no longer a virgin. Her son, the ten-year-old Harald, is dressed in the uniform of the Deutsches Jungvolk. Hitler himself walks behind the couple, sporting a rather unusual double-banded high hat. The whole procession is flanked by men giving the Nazi salute.

Magda Quandt and Joseph Goebbels were to have six children together – five girls and one boy. Their family, which always included Magda's son Harald, was erected by the regime – and above all by Goebbels himself – into an archetype of Nazi domestic life: well turned out, well disciplined and above all *kinderreich*, which literally means 'child-rich' but in the language of the Nazis also meant 'hereditarily healthy' and 'racially valuable'.[37] In a remarkable

fig. 42 The wedding of Joseph Goebbels and Magda Quandt, 19 December 1931.

photograph the Goebbels family is presented to the German public in the form of a pyramid which culminates with the blond and serious Harald in Luftwaffe uniform – the very embodiment of the young Nazi male ready to serve state and country.

This self-publicity, the propagation of one's own family as an ideal type, is highly particular. It is certainly very unusual among the principal figures studied in this book, including Hitler, who declared himself, as we shall see, unsuited to family life. Lenin would never have dreamed of it, nor would Kollontai. What had they in their private lives to recommend as a general model? Very little. The same was true of Mussolini, who thought his family was best left in the shadows, together with his serial sexual 'conquests'. The Marinetti family was much more attractive and self-celebratory, but no one, not even Marinetti himself, tried to make of it a major element of regime propaganda. Perhaps Franco tried to do something similar after the Civil War, but he had only one daughter and his wife was no Magda Goebbels.

One fine example of this familial self-projection is the film entitled *Privata der Familie Goebbels*.[38] It is a sickly-sweet series of images, accompanied by

fig. 43 Goebbels family portrait, 1942.

tinselly music, apparently conceived as a birthday present for Goebbels who
had other engagements. The children play fairly aimless games and then
pretend to form an orchestra. At table, Magda administers food and medicines
with ease and efficiency. She looks more like a grandmother than a mother –
the continual child-rearing had aged her considerably. The whole is aimed at
female consumers, brought up in the great tradition of German *Schmaltz*.

Another important element in this story regards the strange triangle
Hitler–Magda Quandt–Goebbels, the precise conformation of which has never
fully emerged. Although Hitler had theorised – perhaps as a way of exorcising
his difficulties in this field – the figure of the Führer as being necessarily
without family, he was nevertheless very happy to be an adjunct part of the
Goebbels family.[39] His relationship with Eva Braun was not one for public
consumption, but Magda Goebbels could play another role, both public and
asexual. She was quintessentially 'Aryan', charming and elegant, witty and
diplomatic. She was also, like her husband, utterly devoted to Hitler. At the
time of her marriage she was one of very few women – Winifred Wagner was

another – who lent respectability to what was widely and justly perceived as a party of thugs. Hitler greatly appreciated her company, both in public, at diplomatic functions and the like, and in private in her large flat at no. 2 Reichskanzlerplatz in west Berlin. Not by chance did she come to be called in some circles 'the first lady of the Third Reich', a role of which Goebbels thoroughly approved and a label that still sticks today. At the same time, she assumed the idealised role of 'Reich mother'. The combination was a considerable achievement, in part the invention of Goebbels, in part her own creation. Bella Fromm, the Jewish Berlin society journalist who fled the country in 1938, recorded meeting her for the first time: 'Tonight at the ball, Magda was lovely. No jewels except the string of pearls around her neck. Her golden hair owes nothing to any drugstore or chemist. It, too, is real. Her big eyes, iridescent and ranging from dark blue to steel grey, radiate icy determination and inordinate ambition.'[40]

1933 was the fateful year in which the Nazis took power. It was also, in economic terms, the all-time low after the Great Depression As an end-piece to this section of the chapter, I would like to follow the progress of the Goebbels couple over the course of the year. Propaganda and reality were often far apart. In September 1932 Magda had given birth to the first of their children, a baby daughter by the name of Helga. Goebbels would have liked a boy and in the following weeks had little time for either mother or daughter. In January 1933 Magda became seriously unwell and was taken to a private Berlin clinic; she was in fact much more fragile than she appeared to Bella Fromm and others. The Goebbels's marriage had already turned out to be far from idyllic, with bitter quarrels during its first year. The two none the less remained very attached to each other and utterly devoted to Hitler. On 3 January 1933 Goebbels noted in his diary, 'To the clinic. Magda much better. The fever has abated. She is so happy to have me there. We talk a great deal about our love, and how good we will be to one another when she is healthy again. I have reached the point with Magda where I really cannot exist without her.'[41]

By May, Magda was fully recovered and gave a talk on the national radio entitled 'The German mother' as part of the 1933 celebrations of Mother's Day.[42] It is quite revealing of her deep-felt views. In her narrative motherhood is inevitably connected to suffering: 'Being marked out by nature as a silent sufferer, [the mother's] ordeal and abandonment of herself begin the moment she conceives.'[43] This suffering continues throughout the child's education, which has to be loving but also hard: 'how much never-ending work, how many worries and how much effort, how much understanding love and enforced hardness [erzwungene Härte], does a mother's heart have to provide.'[44] Magda Goebbels draws a connection not just between motherhood and suffering, but also between suffering and honour. In the lunacy which had characterised the period preceding the Nazi seizure of power, the mother had been dragged down from her exalted position as custodian of the family's values. It was time to redress drastically the balance and restore honour to German motherhood.[45]

Later in the same month they were honorary guests with a German delegation to Fascist Italy. It was a halcyon time for them both. Goebbels was treated with considerable respect on account of what the Fascists believed to be his genius for propaganda. Magda was feted for her striking blond looks. Galeazzo Ciano and his wife Edda Mussolini struck up a friendship with them which was to last throughout the 1930s. At last Magda was part of a fast-moving, elite, international social set, something for which she had yearned since the first year of her first marriage. Goebbels celebrated all this by publishing a book in Italian entitled *Noi tedeschi e il Fascismo di Mussolini* (We Germans and the Fascism of Mussolini). Goebbels discerned a new spirit at work in Mussolini's Italy: 'A mental and moral style that is new; a Romanticism that is energetic, virile, heroic and made of steel; it is the Romanticism of our century.'[46]

Back in Berlin, Magda pushed hard for a senior post in the Nazi Party, wanting very much to find a public as well as a domestic outlet for her considerable talents. She met with a brick wall. Hitler considered women, even Magda Goebbels, to be adornments in a male world.[47] A woman's place was in the home. Goebbels echoed his leader: 'Struggle is a matter for men, the woman's role is to be a mother. The mother is the symbol of the future and of fertility, she is the law of life and of the community of fate.'[48] In July 1933 they were in Bayreuth for the Wagner festival. They quarrelled bitterly but Hitler came to the rescue once again: 'Hitler is staying in a very small house. We have coffee there at night. He makes peace between Magda and me. A true friend. But he agrees with me all the same: a woman's place is not under the political spotlight.'[49]

Throughout the year we find Goebbels noting in his diary his great affection for his mother, much more so than in earlier times. He was able to give her money and to return home in triumph, no longer the disgraced and exhausted son of the *Kampfzeit*. In November he wrote, 'Mother, dear Mother! She remains true to herself until the end of time. I am so fond of her because she is my steady support, even when she is not there with me.'[50]

At the end of the year we find husband and wife working side by side to provide for the families of SA men, stormtroopers of the *Sturmabteilung*, especially 'those left behind by the fallen'.[51] Magda and her secretary sent out invitations for a Christmas party. Her chauffeur-driven car collected some of the families from their homes and took them home again afterwards. Goebbels himself went to address a street party in Moabit, one of the poorest quarters of Berlin, at which, according to him, 1,400 children were given presents by the SA: 'I speak briefly right from the heart. And it also goes to the heart. Many mothers cry when they step up with their children to the tables which bear the gifts.'[52]

II. ASPECTS OF WEIMAR FAMILY LIFE

Before looking in detail at Nazi family politics, I want to step backwards in time for a moment, into the very rich world of the Weimar Republic. My intention here is to examine a number of the debates, structures and actions of those years which are most relevant to the family themes with which we are concerned. It would be all too possible, once in Weimar, to stop there for some considerable time, but I must resist the temptation.

Of the five countries under consideration in this book, Germany was without doubt the most modern. By 1933 the country had an average per capita income of 4,094 dollars, which had risen to 5,549 by 1939. By 1931, 26 per cent of a total population of sixty-five million worked in the countryside, compared with 85.4 per cent in the Soviet Union in 1929 and 51.9 per cent in Spain in 1940. In Germany, again in 1931, 42.2 per cent of the active population were employed in industry and 31.8 per cent in the tertiary sector. Total fertility rates were very low: just 1.77 children per woman by 1930, a figure that was the subject of much anguished commentary. Family size, too, in keeping with the modernisation of the country, had shrunk consistently.[53] The economic dimensions of Germany's modernisation, however – so marked in comparison with those of the other countries considered here – appear in a different light if we look at her Allied enemies in the Second World War, Britain and the United States in particular. Adam Tooze asks us to remember that in the 1930s more than fifteen million Germans still worked in traditional handcrafts or peasant agriculture, and that the German war economy could not compete with that of the United States. By 1943 total American output was almost four times that of the Third Reich.[54]

These economic considerations should be set alongside others that underline Germany's particular homogeneity. The absence of great ranges of mountains, the predominance of plain and hill – in conjunction with a highly developed road and rail system – meant that the country was easily traversed and controlled. These physical features were combined with a formidable tradition of state authority, and of obedience to that state. Germany thus emerges, even at first glance, as the country that most easily lent itself to a programme of profound control over families' beliefs and daily lives.

Such a regime triumphed only in 1933, however, not immediately after the First World War as in Italy. The Weimar years were rich in social change, progressive legislation and cultural experiment. They can be compared fruitfully to those of the second Republic in Spain, though the Spanish had only four years of troubled democracy while the Germans had fourteen – years of great conflict and endemic violence, but also of pluralism and freedom of expression. Looking back, historians can quite easily identify the terrible fault lines that led to the demise of the German Republic: a state machine and personnel that were never won for democracy; a Social Democratic Party that never contemplated radical social reform; and a massive number of ex-soldiers who believed that their own sacrifices and those of their dead comrades had been in vain. None of these factors became determinant, however, until the full effects of the Great Depression hit Germany with great ferocity in the early 1930s.

1. Defeat, bereavement and revenge

At the end of 1918 Germany still had six million men in the field. After the failure of the spring offensives on the western front, however, and the horrific loss of life involved, it became clear that capitulation was only a matter of time. More and more soldiers took unauthorised leave. The number of so-called *Drückeberger*, 'shirkers', who 'lost' equipment and did everything they could to avoid combat, reached an estimated million men. To make matters even worse, the worldwide pandemic of 'Spanish' flu reached its height in November of 1918. In Germany it hit both the men in the trenches and their families at home, with around one-fifth of the German population affected. Mortality rates were highest between the ages of fifteen and forty-five, women being hit harder than men.[55]

The Armistice that enshrined Germany's defeat was signed on 11 November 1918. The old regime fell and the Kaiser abdicated. A largely pacific revolutionary movement, spearheaded by workers' and soldiers' councils, similar in origins and composition to the Russian Soviets, assumed power. But if the organs of popular self-government were similar in the two cases, the leadership was not. In Russia, as we have seen, a small, revolutionary party took over the reins of government and soon established its own dictatorship. In Germany the moderate Social Democrats (MSPD), headed by Friedrich Ebert, emerged as the leading political force. Their programme was one of law and order, parliamentary democracy and limited reform. In both the Russian and the German cases the self-governing councils, based on participative democracy and popular control, were marginalised and liquidated.

As the soldiers came home, the streets of German towns and villages were decorated with flags and flowers. In mid-November the Prussian War Ministry declared, 'Our field-grey heroes return to the *Heimat* undefeated, having protected the native soil from the horrors of war for four years.' In early December Ebert himself repeated the same thing at a stand-down parade in Berlin. It was easy to understand why the authorities should make such a claim but it was a dangerous assertion, as well as being untrue. If the army was undefeated, then somebody or something else had to be responsible for Germany's undeniable demise.[56]

Millions of German families mourned the failure of one or more of their menfolk to return – mothers their sons, children their fathers, sisters their brothers, wives their husbands. Although Germany was spared the terrible sequence of events that characterised Russia between 1917 and 1923, there can be no doubt that the First World War constituted the nation's greatest collective trauma – that is, until 1943–5.[57] Martin Niemöller, a naval lieutenant stationed at Kiel who was to be a member of the Freikorps but who later took his distance from Nazism, remembered the scene 'as the bells rang in the New Year on that New Year's eve of 1919':

My mother-in-law stood by an open window, crying to herself as she gazed down along the Wupper Valley. The death of her son had all but broken the heart of this uncommonly strong woman, but it took the distress and humiliation of the fatherland to break it completely. 'Martin, do you think things will ever be as they once were in Germany?'[58]

With nearly 1.7 million men dead, the demographic balance of the German population was seriously affected. Throughout the interwar years there were around two million more women than men. The census of 1925 also registered the presence of over four million female 'family assistants'. They looked after the children and the home but also worked on the farms, in the shops, cafés and workshops, often taking the place of the men who had not survived the war.[59]

Those who were lucky enough to return did so in great bitterness. The famous explanation for defeat, namely that the army had been 'stabbed in the back' by those who had remained on the home front, and in particular by disloyal 'revolutionists', gained very wide credence.[60] The harsh terms of the Treaty of Versailles added to the sense of betrayal. Traditional, authority-oriented Germans from provincial towns and the countryside, who had supported and identified with the Kaiser's Reich and who were facing ruin as inflation gathered speed, sought out scapegoats. In the months following the end of the war new actors came to the fore – in Italy Mussolini's *squadristi*, in Germany the Freikorps (literally 'Free Corps'). Many of these latter were junior officers, NCOs and 'shock troops', renowned for their daring in breaking through enemy lines. Their social origins lay in the rural petty bourgeoisie and they organised themselves in private armies commanded by charismatic leaders. Their numbers were uncertain and fluctuating – estimates range between 200,000 and 400,000 – and their principal task was to suppress social agitation and attempts at insurrection. Their employer was none other than Ebert's government itself, which, fearful of the influence of the soldiers' councils, preferred to re-establish law and order, its primary concern, by paying private armies. The Freikorps' past, obviously, was in the trenches: 'people told us that the War was over. That made us laugh. We ourselves are the War. Its flame burns strongly in us.'[61] Their most renowned victims were the two leaders of the revolutionary left Spartacist movement, Rosa Luxemburg and Karl Liebknecht, and their future lay, in no small part, in membership of the Nazis' SA.[62]

Thanks to Klaus Theweleit's extraordinary and pioneering psychoanalytical study of the published diaries, autobiographies, poems and novels of members of the Freikorps, *Männerphantasien*, it is possible to penetrate the family culture, intimate lives and deeply held beliefs of these men.[63] The overall picture that emerges is a harrowing one, dominated by misogyny. Only mothers are spared. Peter von Heydebreck, a future Freikorps member and then leading SA officer, recalled that 'the times when she [his mother] would tell us stories about the life of Jesus, read us fairy tales, or sing folksongs with us are some of my most beautiful childhood memories'.[64] But even the mother, argues Theweleit, is a split figure. On the one hand, she is loving and protective, characteristics often attributed to the Freikorpsmen's *own* mothers. On the other, their comrades' mothers are presented as women of steel, cold and heroic, incapable of shedding a tear in the face of bereavement. These latter figures inculcate fear as well as respect, admiration but also hidden aggression. It is 'right' for these women to suffer in silence, there is no question of alleviating their pain.

Mothers are thus present in these texts, even if they are Janus-faced. The same thing cannot be said about fathers. The credibility of patriarchs had been destroyed by the war:

'The Kaiser should have died at the head of his capitulating army'. This is the reproach on the tip of every tongue; often it is directly voiced. The fact that he failed to do so (and that many officers opportunistically declared themselves in favour of the Republic) has completely destroyed the credibility of the patriarchs. Now it is the turn of the sons.[65]

Theweleit's observation rings profoundly true. In the literature he has examined fathers have failed their Freikorps sons. It is the latter who now have to step forward to do battle for Mother Germany. Patriarchy secures its dominion under Nazism in the form of a 'filiarchy': there is nothing but sons, furious with their fathers, as far as the eye can see. Hitler is one of them.[66]

In their published writings the Freikorps identify three different types of women. First there are those who are absent, left behind for the war – mothers, wives and sisters. Wives are rarely mentioned and frequently unnamed, seemingly residual. Then there are 'white' women – white in skin colouring and in their starched nurses' uniforms smelling of iodine, the chaste upper-class women who take care of the legions of wounded in the hospitals. Finally, there are 'red' women, the true antagonists and obsession of the Freikorps. They are present at demonstrations, shouting insults, scratching, spitting and biting, provoking the soldiers to attack. They are emancipated and sexually aggressive 'whores'.[67] They might be armed, they might be hiding a pistol under their shirts, they might have a rifle and bayonet – a steel penis, suggests Theweleit, to compensate for the absence of a real one. They are the Margarita Nelkens of the German revolution. For these 'red' women the Freikorps reserve all their hatred and violence. They take them prisoner, and as they kill them with knife or bayonet, as they violate their bodies, they come terrifyingly and thrillingly close to them.

Theleweit also identifies a number of 'streams' that form an integral part of the behaviour of the Wilhelmine soldiery and then of their successors: streams of speech, streams of sweat and streams of alcohol, the latter often accompanied by streams of vomit. A final stream, towards which the whole enterprise was oriented, was that of blood.[68] Shaping this experience, giving it sense and emotion, was male camaraderie. It was better to be at war (somewhere) than to be at home (nowhere). Covert homosexuality bound the group together, as it did their frequent destination, Röhm's SA – until, that is, the fateful Night of the Long Knives, 30 June 1934. But if Hitler destroyed Ernst Röhm and Peter von Heydebreck, he thoroughly approved of the type of ruthless warrior masculinity which the Freikorps embodied. It would shape his expectations of Nazi boys and men.

2. Adolf Hitler and his family of origin

Hitler is the most famous example of that 'filiarchy' to which Theweleit refers. It is true that the battlefield that was his family was located in provincial

Austria, not in a major city of the Weimar Republic, and that the years in which war is waged between Adolf and his father Alois are those of the turn of the century. Indeed Alois dies in January 1903, when Adolf is not quite fourteen. Ian Kershaw describes Hitler's father as 'an archetypical provincial civil servant – pompous, status-proud, strict, humourless, frugal, pedantically punctual and devoted to duty'.[69] He was more out of the home than in it, being partial to a few drinks after work and enjoying bee-keeping more than anything else. When he did come home he was a domineering and intolerant figure (though not necessarily a drunken one), given to sudden wild furies, a behaviour trait that Adolf was to absorb and repeat. Adolf and his elder stepbrother Alois Jr were regularly beaten.[70]

Hitler's mother, Klara Pölzl, was very different and in some ways complementary to Alois. She was the seventh of eleven children, born to a family of poor peasants. When she was only sixteen she moved into the house of her 'uncle Alois', where she was to take care of his sick wife and two children. There Alois soon made her pregnant, even before his wife died. Alois and Klara then married in January 1885, when she was twenty-four and he forty-eight. Throughout their marriage, which lasted eighteen years, Klara remained totally in awe of, and dominated by, her husband. Alice Miller has suggested that Alois Hitler's household could be described as the prototype of a totalitarian regime: 'Its sole undisputed, often brutal ruler is the father. The wife and children are totally subservient to his will, his moods and his whims; they must accept humiliation and injustice unquestioningly and gratefully. Obedience is their primary rule of conduct'.[71] This seems to be an accurate description of the Hitler household in as far as the scant historical evidence allows us to draw conclusions. But whether the adjective 'totalitarian' is the appropriate one is a question to which I would like to return at the end of this book. It is certainly true that the other family members were terrified of, and terrorised by, Alois.

There can be no doubt that Klara Pölzl loved her son Adolf very much and tried to protect him from her husband. But the story is not quite as Manichean as this statement suggests. Before Adolf was born Klara suffered a terrible trauma when her first three children were all carried away by diphtheria in the course of a month, at the end of 1887. The oldest child was two years and seven months, the youngest just three days. We have no evidence of her reactions and can only speculate about them. Perhaps as a Catholic she regarded the deaths as just punishment for her adulterous relations with Alois. The fact is that just thirteen months later Adolf was born. The mother must have been terrified that her new child would soon share the fate of the others. Miller reflects on her preoccupations and on 'the sort of emotional atmosphere surrounding his [Adolf's] first year of life, so crucial for a child's sense of security.[72]

By 1903, with the death of Alois, the adolescent Adolf was the only male left in the family, which had shrunk to just four persons – Klara, her unmarried sister Johanna, Adolf and his younger sister Paula, born in 1896. In 1907 Hitler's mother died at the age of forty-seven from breast cancer after a long and painful illness. Her son was overcome by grief. He had lost the one person whom he had loved and who had loved him.[73]

It is fascinating to compare these childhood experiences of Hitler with some of the others I have described. Let me begin with that closest in time and place, the childhood of Goebbels, with which there are striking contrasts. Goebbels's father is far from a dictator in his own home, showing great patience and affection for Joseph, and his mother seems to be an altogether more resolute and capable woman than Klara Pölzl. Their Catholicism is the family's guiding light. Goebbels none the less becomes just as much of a Jew hater and preacher of endless violence as Hitler. This comparison alone should teach us to be wary of seeking to explain later developments wholly in terms of childhood formation. This is not say that studies such as those of Miller and Helm Stierlin are unimportant. Quite the contrary: they are extraordinarily suggestive. But we have to understand that childhood is not by itself the determinant factor for adult behaviour, and that as Goebbels and Hitler grew up other factors and experiences, conjunctures and opportunities, drew them together and shaped them, in spite of the significant differences between their early family lives.[74]

Other comparisons, at first sight far-fetched, are also revealing. That with Mustafa Kemal is highly unusual but worth the comparative effort. Both their fathers are customs officials. I doubt whether this means anything at all but it is certainly a coincidence. Both fail their sons, and this is rather more important. Ali Rıza, it may be remembered, Mustafa Kemal's father, was often absent from home, given to drink and unsuccessful in economic matters. He also dies early. This is all rather far from Alois Hitler, but the sense of filial disillusionment is strong in both cases, and stems from the fathers' lack of interest in their sons and the minimal amount of time they ever dedicated to them. Perhaps we can suggest that both Kemal and Hitler learned from their fathers not to trust anyone, and to rely only upon themselves. These instincts deriving from early family experience are reinforced when both Kemal and Hitler find themselves – Kemal at seven and Hitler at thirteen – as the only males left in their families. Their corresponding sense of self-importance is greatly increased by mothers who both, though in different ways, worship their sons and are in turn loved by them. But whereas Hitler's mother dies at an early age, Zübeyde lives on, often driving Kemal to distraction.

It is also worth noting that of the five dictators under examination here it is only Kemal and Hitler who do not make families of their own. Hitler was quite explicit on this point. In his 'table talk' he is reported as saying, 'I am a completely non-family man with no sense of the clan spirit.'[75] In later years, he did not allow his half-brother Alois to come anywhere near him, and he made his sister Paula, who kept house for him, change her name. There was much more to these family rejections than the calculated merging of the private into the public, the creation of a monumental, superhuman image of the great leader. Rather, there was an emotional black hole. Kershaw writes of the essential emptiness of Hitler's personal life; Joachim Fest refers to him as an 'unperson'. When he does take a regular mistress, Eva Braun, she is hidden away in a little room in the 'Führer apartment' in Berlin, not allowed to accompany Hitler on his frequent journeys, and only really comes into her own in some measure at the Berghof. But Hitler often treated her abysmally and took pleasure in humiliating her in front of others.

Mustafa Kemal's case is not the same, even if the outcome – no family of his own – is. As we have seen, he tried married life with Lâtife between 1923 and 1925 but found it unbearable. He, too, is glacially cold, but he is 'embraced' by an institution – the army – in a way that Hitler never was. Furthermore, he adopts a number of children, of whom his favourite is undoubtedly Afet, who becomes his mistress and devoted amanuensis. Indeed, he has a completely different attitude towards women. They are certainly inferior to men and exist to serve them, but at the same time men (and the nation) have everything to gain from women's education and relative emancipation. Whereas Hitler's whole approach to women, even one as charming as Magda Goebbels, was defensive and denigratory. He once described his ideal woman as 'a cute, cuddly naïve little thing – tender, sweet and stupid'.[76]

3. German families and moral panic

Family structures and systems were as complex in Germany as elsewhere in Europe, absolutely not to be summarised with reference to a single model. Certain long-term trends none the less present themselves, both as historical experience and as myth. As Ingeborg Weber-Kellermann has noted, it was not until the sixteenth century that the Latin term 'familia' began to be used in rural Germany with reference to the household community.[77] More common and evocative was the expression 'das ganze Haus', literally 'the whole house', in the sense of Luther's biblical phrase 'I will serve the Lord with all my house.' Such a designation captured very well the complex and extended character of many rural and some urban German households, which were inhabited not only by blood relations but also by journeymen, servants and helpers of various sorts. Over the whole household there presided the *Hausvater*, patriarch and male head of family, who exercised legal, economic and guardianship rights over all those who lived there.

Of all the types of household examined in this book, that of the German peasantry was the only one for which the ownership of land and relative prosperity had come to predominate. Landless labourers, it is true, were still to be found in great numbers east of the Elbe, working on the estates of the Junkers. In 1933, 7,000 estates of more than 500 hectares each accounted for almost 25 per cent of German farmland. Elsewhere small and medium-sized farms were the rule. Peasant land ownership dated from different periods in different parts of the country, but by the beginning of the twentieth century the south, west, central and northern regions of rural Germany all boasted the rural landscapes, field systems and scattered farmhouses which marked out the majority presence of peasant proprietors. Substantial peasant farms of between ten and a hundred hectares accounted for 43 per cent of German farmland, but it is also worth noting the continuing and precarious existence of small farms of between 0.5 and ten hectares, accounting for 74 per cent of all farms though only 19 per cent of land.[78]

Another characteristic of the German countryside was the stem family, with its particular, unequal rules of inheritance. We have already encountered such farms and systems in Catalonia at the time of the Civil War.[79] Stem families assured the inheritance of only the first-born male: only he and his family could inhabit the farmhouse together with the patriarch and his wife (until their retirement or death), while other children enjoyed only subordinate roles or were compelled to leave their family of origin. Stem families, then, were based on a lack of equality between children, the recurring authority of the first-born and an asymmetrical view of social space.[80] They were considered by certain schools of thought, as we shall see, as a breeding ground for the development of authoritarian family and social relations.

In the second half of the nineteenth century these traditional structures of German rural life began to undergo radical change. Symptomatic of the social alarm which greeted such developments is a famous tract, *Die Familie*, written in 1855 by Wilhelm Heinrich Riehl. The work went through numerous editions between 1855 and 1889, and constituted a 'romantic hymn of praise'[81] not to the family but to the glorious 'ganze Haus':

Modern times, unfortunately, know only of the family; they no longer recognise the household, they no longer accept the joyful and hospitable idea of the 'whole house', which includes not only the natural members of the family but also those voluntary comrades and helpers of the family who are traditionally described as live-in servants. In the household, the beneficent influence of the family is also extended to persons who otherwise have no family; these people are drawn in, as if by adoption, to the moral system of authority and piety. This is of the profoundest importance for the social stability of the entire nation.[82]

Authority and piety, hierarchy and order, the social stability of the entire nation – these are just some of the phrases which would resound far into the twentieth century. Accompanying them are laments for a world that had been lost and concern for the future of the family. Traditional, rules-conscious Wilhelmine figures (the German counterparts of Hitler's father) witnessed what seemed to them a cataclysmic change. First came the great wave of immigration from countryside to town and city in the decades before the First World War. Berlin became a capital city of nearly four million inhabitants, 33 per cent of whom were under the age of twenty in 1914. As much as 55–60 per cent of the labour force was employed in industry. There was a drastic shortage of housing and massive overcrowding. In 1911, 60,000 Berliners were living in cellars; in many working-class districts over 50 per cent of apartments were single rooms.[83]

The great shift from countryside to city, profoundly destabilising in itself, was then followed by the terrible disruptions and deaths caused by the war and the ensuing influenza epidemic. These not only affected every German family but also, as we have seen, produced a radical imbalance in the relationship between the genders. After the war the very physiognomy of the German family was transformed. In the 1920s crude birth rates declined faster than at any other point in German history. By 1933 over half the population of the country lived in small households of one to four persons; only in agricultural districts did households of six or more account for more than one-third of the total number. 'Das ganze Haus' was on the way to extinction.

Such radical change brought into question the way in which family and state had been linked in traditional German political discourse. The family had long been presented as the first, elemental cell upon which the organism of the nation was dependent. The *Hausvater* was considered a monarch within his household as was the Kaiser within the nation as a whole. Their intimate relationship was a theme to which Hitler and Goebbels were to return with great force. But this interdependence was now mortally threatened. Decreasing family size, the absence of putative fathers killed in the war, the weakening of intra-familial hierarchical relations, disrespectful youth and declining fertility and marriage rates were all seen as a cancer upon the German body politic, a type of cellular degeneration.[84] The moral panic about the future of the family, and with it community traditions, was in the German case much more profound than the mere denunciation of the new generation by the old. 'The family is not what it used to be' is a perennial cry, but fear of a truly seismic shift was palpable in Germany at this time.

In this emergency, the state, with its legions of professionals and interventionist practices learned during the war, was called upon to assume its full responsibilities. And it was expected to perform better in the family crisis than it had done in the military and industrial one.

4. The Weimar Constitution and the family

The way in which the Weimar Constitution of August 1919 treated these delicate family matters was by no means unequivocal. The Constitution bore all the signs of the conflicting circumstances in which it came into being. On the one hand it reflected the German revolution of November 1918, itself an ambiguous event; on the other its provisions were clear testimony to the need to compromise between different political parties and pressure groups. The result was not satisfactory for any of the interested parties.[85] Especially in the second part of the Constitution, entitled 'Fundamental rights and duties of the Germans', bold statements of principle were followed by immediate backtracking. One academic commentator of the 1930s wrote that he had the feeling that 'the framers of the Constitution were terrified by their own courage'.[86] But this was not the whole story. The dominant, positivist tradition in German legal thinking asserted time and again the primacy of the Reichstag in determining by statute the content of any given right. The Constitution could proclaim rights but it was statute law that was to define their content.[87]

A comparison with the circumstances and contents of the Spanish republican Constitution of December 1931 is illuminating, although it has so far received little attention.[88] The Spanish Assembly was undoubtedly more radical. In 1931 there had been no Spanish revolution, but Catholic forces both inside and outside parliament had been temporarily routed, and the majority opinion in the Spanish Assembly was determined to go ahead in draconian fashion. In 1919 the Germans by contrast had had a revolution, but they were far more uncertain as to the parameters of constitutional action. The Spanish thus used the Constitution as an enormous brass instrument, a tuba, the Germans as a delicate clarinet which on some key issues of family politics made hardly any sound at all.[89]

The most important article of the Weimar Constitution regarding the family directly is no. 119, which marks the beginning of a section entitled 'The general welfare' ('Gemeinschaftsleben'). Its first paragraph proclaims, 'Marriage as the cornerstone of family life and the preservation and increase of the nation is placed under the special protection of the Constitution. Family life is based on the equal rights of both sexes.'[90] It is worth comparing this article with the first paragraph of the 1932 Spanish Constitution's principal article on the family, no. 43: 'The family is under the special care of the State. Marriage is based on equal rights for both sexes and can be dissolved by mutual consent or by the request of one of the partners who must in this case provide just cause.'[91] We see immediately that both the Spanish and the German texts declare that the family is based on the equal rights of both sexes – a radical and courageous position which corresponded very little to the reality of patriarchal hierarchies in either country.[92] For the rest, there are significant differences. The Weimar Constitution, accurately reflecting the widespread preoccupation over the future of the traditional family, formally declares marriage to be 'the cornerstone of family life', and emphasises the need to preserve and increment the nation. The Spanish is very different. It mentions marriage only to explain immediately how it can be dissolved; and it then provides mechanisms for doing so which are little short of revolutionary. In this it is closer to the Russian Family Code of 1918. In Germany divorce already existed but only on the limited grounds stipulated by the Civil Code of 1900. The new Constitution did not elaborate upon it further and left the way open for furious and inconclusive debates throughout the Weimar years.[93]

The second clause of Article 119 of the Weimar Constitution underlines the duty of central and municipal government to 'foster the purity, health, and social advancement of the family'. The choice of 'purity' as the first of family objectives is not perhaps without significance. The article further identifies two elements worthy of its special attention and assistance: families with numerous children and motherhood. There is little mention of fatherhood, as in Article 43 of the Spanish Constitution. Article 120 of the Weimar Constitution is dedicated to the education of children by their parents, and clearly bears the imprint of a struggle between Catholic and non-Catholic formulations. It is 'the supreme duty and natural right of parents' to provide children with a 'thorough physical, spiritual and social education', but parents' activities 'shall be supervised by the State'. Article 121 (and here the Spanish and German texts find common ground again) guarantees equal rights for illegitimate and legitimate children. But here the articles specific to the family stop. Later on in the second part of the Constitution there is a whole chapter dedicated to education and schools, but in the end the family can claim only three articles out of 181 – far too few, and too inconclusive for us to be able to speak of a Weimar family policy.

The question of gender relations, declared to be equal within marriage in Article 119, received a rockier ride elsewhere in the German constitutional settlement. When the 'founding fathers' of the Constitution came together for the first time at the National Theatre in Weimar in February 1919, it emerged that no fewer than forty-one of them were actually 'founding mothers'. It is worth recalling that there were only three Spanish women present in the Cortes Constituyentes in the summer of 1931. At Weimar, the Social Democrat Marie Juchacz proclaimed proudly, 'This is the first time that a woman has been permitted to speak to a parliament in Germany as a free and equal person.'[94] Even so, the women delegates and their male allies were unable to win the key battle over Article 109. The article begins with the solemn declaration 'All Germans are equal before the law.' But immediately afterwards, in best Weimar fashion, a qualifying sentence was added: 'In principle men and women have the same civil rights and duties.' The two words 'in principle' were highly provocative. They could be taken to imply that women's rights depended upon the 'natural limits' of sexual difference and that local, provincial or state courts might choose to interpret the article in a restrictive way. In July 1919, when the Constituent Assembly was called to vote upon Article 109, the formulation 'in principle' won the day by 149 votes to 119. A similar story is to be told for the modification of the Civil Code of 1900. The Code continued to enshrine husbands' dominance over wives with respect to property rights and employment, in open contradiction of what was written in Article 119 of the new Constitution: 'Family life is based on the equal rights of both sexes.' Yet here too patriarchy and traditionalism won the day. By 144 votes to 128, the Assembly voted not to emend the outdated Code.[95]

5. The welfare state

From another point of view, that of the creation of a widely based system of social support, the Weimar record is a more convincing one, expressing a clear intent to respond to the crisis of the family. The number of overlapping subject categories touched by welfare legislation – the disabled and the survivors of the Great War, war widows, families with many children, mothers in general, single women, youth and the unemployed – was very great. The bare statistics of user numbers talk of 1,571,700 clients by 1927, 1,983,900 in 1930, leaping to 4,608,200 at the end of 1932, in the depths of the Depression.[96]

Care must be taken over these aggregate figures, however, for they hide as much as they reveal, especially in relation to families and family life. The structures and investments of Weimar welfare were certainly much greater than the contemporaneous Italian Fascist ones examined above. The Weimar public housing scheme in the major cities, for instance, was an initiative of which the Fascists could only dream. Yet the *Sozialstaatspostulat* (the welfare state foundation) of the Republic was only partially translated into reality during its fourteen years of life. Indeed, only after the Second World War did a fully fledged welfare state come into being in the Federal Republic of Germany, as in so many other European countries.

The comparison with post-1945 welfare is revealing. Even if many modern welfare states are hybrids, at least three distinct models have emerged in the post-war world. The first is 'residual', reserved for those individuals whose needs can no longer be met by the market or the family; the second is 'occupational', where coverage is sectorial and dependent primarily on different types of employment; the third is 'universalist', offering protection and services to all citizens (though not necessarily to all residents), regardless of income, gender or occupation. The universalist conception of public welfare had already emerged precociously in some Scandinavian countries in the 1930s. Its greatest virtue was that it did not merely reflect existing socio-economic differences, but rather aspired to placing key services outside the market and to ensuring the same quality of services to all. At the end of his last book, Richard Titmuss, one of the great scholars as well as creators of the British welfare state, posed a number of questions which are deeply relevant to the Weimar Republic and its fate: 'What effect does the system have on the social and psychological sense of community? Does it have divisive or unifying effects and in what sense and for what groups?'[97]

The Weimar case – to try to reply to Titmuss – corresponded most closely to a mixture of occupational and residual welfare. As such, it was unlikely to offer a socially cohesive strategy. From Bismarck onwards the system had offered significant social-security protection to different categories of employed groups, from workers to the professions. These protected categories could enjoy cumulative cash benefits, principally for old-age pensions but also for insurance against sickness, disability and unemployment. After 1918, however, there were very many Germans who had never been part of this welfare net, or had fallen outside it. Vast categories could expect only minimal, 'residual' assistance: the war wounded, war widows, but also members of the middle classes who had been ruined by the hyper-inflation of the first years of the Republic. Faced with so many demands upon it, it would have been very difficult for any welfare state to have responded adequately. But without a universalist perspective it was impossible to link social welfare with social justice. The overall result was that the welfare system was perceived as being, and indeed was, fragmented, uneven and often divisive.

One of the major cleavages in the system was a gender one. The Constitution had declared equal rights for both sexes within marriage, but in reality men remained formal heads of household for the whole Weimar period. At the same time social insurance benefits were paid to them as family breadwinners. Women could expect similar benefits only if they were in regular jobs. The terms covering maternity leave were greatly improved in 1927, but the provision of day nurseries and other facilities which might have allowed young mothers to remain at work remained very patchy.[98]

Probably most important of all for our purposes, family allowances were not generally introduced. The 'special consideration' for large families enshrined in the Constitution was translated into monetary payments, but at no stage was an overall strategy of family benefits introduced, in marked contrast to France in the same years. In general, the family was not considered a social category needing to be treated as a whole. This deficiency was sometimes recognised by German social workers, who grew rapidly as a profession in this period. As early as October 1918 one of them wrote, 'It is pointless to find a child a place in a kindergarten, where it can learn cleanliness and order, if, at the home to which the child returns in the evening, the child sees a tubercular mother living in an unsuitable apartment – possibly with an alcoholic husband – in the greatest filth and disorder.'[99]

While the desire to intervene in a holistic fashion was great, the resources required to do so were limited. There was also the problem of the social workers' own ideology. They were obviously not an entirely homogeneous group, but, as the document above implies, they had strong normative attitudes and believed in close control and the exercise of authority. They also believed in the forward march of science, casting themselves in the role of skilled technicians. All this was commendable at one level and dangerous at another.

One of the most difficult areas of the Weimar social system was the relationship between state action and private charities. There were also running battles between the different private organisations themselves. The Social Democrats founded their own national welfare organisation, Workers' Welfare, in December 1919, but the Protestant Inner Mission dated back to 1848 and the Catholic Caritasverband to 1897. The three organisations had distinctive visions of the role of welfare in the relations between individuals, families, civil society and the state. The Caritasverband's position will by now be familiar to readers: the state, especially the liberal state, was to be viewed with suspicion and was to interfere in Catholic family life only when the family itself could no longer cope. The principal welfare relationship was not that between individual and state but between Church and family. The Protestant Inner Mission based its activities on the impelling necessity to combat the omnipresent dissolution of traditional family authority and communal bonds. The cause of such social disaster was excessive individualism, a 'pathological emphasis on the autonomous personality', as their vice-president Reinhold Seeberg put it in

1920.[100] The cure was the creation of a Protestant civil society founded upon the Lutheran doctrine of the priesthood of all believers. The social question would be solved by voluntary charity. The 'inner mission', as the movement's founder Johann Hinrich Wichern put it, was 'of the German people to the German people', 'a confession of faith through an act of redeeming love'. In the Weimar period the Inner Mission was closely linked to the DNVP, the German National Party, with its barely veiled desire for the restoration of the monarchy and the re-establishment of the Lutheran church.[101]

The Social Democrats viewed social problems through very different eyes. For them welfare was not synonymous with charity. The latter was redolent of deference and incense, personal help offered to indigent individuals. Instead, welfare was to be considered a right (as enshrined in the Constitution) and its ultimate aim the elimination of poverty. In many ways the Social Democrats talked the language of post-war welfare, but they found themselves trapped in the context of a disgruntled and traditionalist society. One of their most popular slogans was that the working classes were 'not only the object but also the subject of social work'. Public and private should work together, but the primacy of public welfare should be firmly endorsed by parliament.[102]

These ideological differences and the battles between them drained resources and energy from welfare initiatives in the interwar period. Yet it would be a mistake to conclude on too critical a note. At the beginning of this section I mentioned the public housing programme of these years. Between 1919 and 1932 around 7.7 million people profited from the Republic's new constructions. Not all the estates were constructed in the same style but in some of the larger ones, like that of Westhausen in Frankfurt, functionalism ruled the day. Beauty was equated with simplicity, rationality and efficiency and took the name of 'New Objectivity'. Elsewhere traditional designs continued to be present, with steeply pitched roofs and brick walls. The estates had an average of 500–1,000 new homes each and were located on the outskirts of cities. The dwellings were usually furnished with a lockable front door, running cold and hot water (usually provided by a gas boiler), a shower, bath and toilet, a partial central heating system and a lit stairway. The Frankfurt estates had a complete system of electricity. The flats were small spaces, designed for nuclear families with not more than two children. The estates were meant to be 'garden cities', though not all were. To the planners, the idea of separating them from the old city centres appealed greatly, offering the idea of new 'healthier' relations and proximity to the countryside. Neighbours could become friends. But as children became teenagers, it was also true that isolation could weigh heavily upon families. Above all, the estate administrators expected homes to be kept 'clean and comfortable' and inspectors, usually female, patrolled the premises. 'Cleanliness', 'hygiene' and 'purity' were key words. The National Socialists were to have a relatively easy task in connecting these hygiene discourses to their key concept of racial cleansing.[103]

6. Berlin

In the 1920s and 1930s, Berlin, with its population of some four million, was the third largest city in the world. It was strikingly modern, instantly recognisable as the elder cousin of present-day European cities. At Potsdamer Platz, but not only there, heavy motor traffic had become the norm. One article in a workers' periodical commented in 1928, with strong Futurist overtones, 'Who thought decades ago about traffic rules [and] automatic traffic lights? No one.' Not only had the buildings changed but so too had 'the speed at which life on the streets runs'.[104] In the city's 'New West' around Kurfürstendamm, shops and department stores, theatres and dance halls, cafés, restaurants and clubs all marked out the glitter of modern urban life. But Berlin was also a city of grinding poverty and desperate living conditions. These brutal contrasts were captured by some of the photographers of the time, especially Willy Römer.[105] In a street scene of around 1922–3, a very poor family is snapped returning to the city after collecting wood in one of the surrounding forests. The father is bent over by the load he is carrying, the boy is barefooted, the little girl, who must have been exhausted, clutches a little bouquet of wild flowers, the mother's face bears an extraordinary expression of resignation and serenity. By contrast, another of Römer's photographs, this time a bourgeois interior (1924), shows a large family (his own) dancing rather self-consciously. The music comes from a radio equipped with loudspeaker. Everybody is smartly dressed, the two men are wearing suits, and here too there is a little girl centre stage, in a party dress, full of wonderment at the new machine.

It would be quite wrong, however, to think of Berlin as a two-class city of rich and poor. Its social structure was decidedly complex, as was true of all great European cities of the time. Berlin's middle classes certainly did not speak with one voice but boasted subtle shades of social differentiation, stretching from the historic petty bourgeoisie of artisans and shopkeepers, through the clerks and office workers working in the great administrative structures of the capital, to the bourgeoisie proper, with its profound belief in hard work, competition and achievement, and the rewards to be derived from these.[106] What gave a certain homogeneity to the great majority of the Berlin population was their attitude towards procreation and family formation. Indeed, it could be said that one-child (or even no-child) families were the topos that most characterised Berlin domestic and everyday life.

fig. 44 A family returns to the city after collecting wood, Berlin, 1922–3, photograph by Willy Römer.

fig. 45 The photographer's family and friends dancing to music from a radio equipped with a loudspeaker, Berlin, 1924, photograph by Willy Römer.

Some of Berlin's family statistics are very striking indeed. The average household size in the city was 3.6 persons in 1910, compared with 4.2 in Munich. By 1933 Berlin had dropped as low as 2.7, compared with Munich's 3.3. In the same year just over 35 per cent of all married couples in the city were childless. Berlin had by far the lowest birth rate not only in the country but in the world. It also had the highest divorce rate.[107] One-child families were most typical of the rich western districts of Berlin, such as Wilmersdorf and Charlottenburg. Here were clear markers of modernity. They by no means constituted a rejection of the family *tout court*, but rather a rebalancing of the relationship between individual liberty and family duty, as well as between parents and children.

Naturally, this was not the way Berlin was viewed from the outside, especially the provincial outside. To right-minded citizens in the rest of Germany the capital had become a Gomorrah, where infertility, promiscuity and hedonism had replaced the solid family virtues of procreation, cleanliness and respectability. Berlin fuelled the moral panic and indignation of conservative Germany as did nothing else. The much-exaggerated vision of emancipated Berlin women did little to reassure provincial public opinion. As Tim Mason has written, 'As if it were not enough that the capital city should be a stronghold of the political left, the cosmopolitan centre of liberal and socialist journalism and of radical modern experiments in entertainments and the arts, Berlin was *the* city where bright young women went out to work and demonstratively enjoyed themselves.'[108] This was true, but only up to a certain point on the social scale. Secretaries, typists and telephone operators lived monthly work-and-spend routines, delaying procreation for as long as possible or even abandoning it. In the 1920s the average number of children for a white-collar, lower middle-class family hovered between 1.5 and 1.6, the lowest in the city.[109] In his famous analysis of Berlin clerks, published in 1930, Siegfried Kracauer noted that for young female secretaries and typists, 'the ideal is petty-bourgeois: a future husband who develops a strong sense of family and earns enough for her to give up work; a way of life in which there is no particular desire to have children'. This is a striking comment, in that the word 'family' is used to refer to the couple rather than to parents and children.[110]

For working-class women, the majority in the city, the situation was very different. For the most part they lived lives of considerable suffering and material deprivation. The average number of children per working-class family – between 2.1 and 2.4 in the 1920s – was significantly higher than that of the petty bourgeoisie, perhaps because of the more limited availability of contraceptives.[111] Housing conditions, especially in impoverished inner-city districts, was of very poor quality, working-class families of parents and two children very often being confined to a single room, perhaps with a small kitchen attached. Kreuzberg's Nostitzstrasse district was dominated by five-storey apartment buildings constructed between 1864 and 1878. Entering these buildings by an archway one passed through successive courtyards, with workshops and commercial space on the ground floor and flats above. The size and rent of the apartments decreased as one proceeded further away from the street and further up from the ground floor. The worst flats, which were no more than tiny rooms facing the air shaft, had no sunlight at all. It was quite common for dairy cows to be kept in the courtyards, and some families, as Römer documented, even kept pigs in the larder. The promiscuity of humans and animals was certainly as marked as in Sesto San Giovanni, and the odour perhaps as strong. Sanitation was a major problem. Even in the best tenements, there were communal toilets only on each or every other floor. In these overall conditions it is not surprising that in 1939 there was an outbreak of hand, foot and mouth disease in Berlin, and that children from inner-city quarters suffered consistently from rickets and other diseases connected with malnutrition and deprivation.[112]

Yet this was far from the whole story. As in Barcelona's *barris*, there was a very strong sense of community, encouraged and controlled by a particular political grouping. In Barcelona it was the anarcho-syndicalists of the CNT who overwhelmingly shaped certain quarters in their own image. In Berlin control was more plural, the KPD (German Communist Party) and the SPD (German Social Democratic Party) vying with each other and the Nazis coming to dominate more neighbourhoods as time passed. In Kreuzberg's strongly Communist Nostitzstrasse, ably studied recently by Pamela Swett, the local population referred to their quarter not with the word 'Nachbarschaft', neighbourhood, but with the more intimate and politically charged term 'Kiez'. The *Kiez* was a loosely defined geographical space which took its identity and boundaries from a limited number of apartment blocks and courtyards, of local community landmarks and political allegiances. Certain spaces and buildings played key roles. In the Nostitzstrasse *Kiez* the small square called Marheinekeplatz housed a covered market, inside which, very interestingly, was a pub that served no alcohol and was the rendezvous for the 'Fichte Sports Club'. The Viktoriapark was another popular meeting place and so was the Rummel, an amusement park much loved by local youth and abhorred by the local welfare authorities, who saw it as a prime site of depravity. Pubs or bars were divided into three sorts: first the larger taverns often situated on the corners of main roads; then the *Familienkneipen* (family pubs), which were what their name implies, with meeting rooms which could be rented out; and lastly the political pubs, of

fig. 46 A pig is raised in the larder and fed in the kitchen, Berlin, 1924, photograph by
Willy Römer.

which the most famous was at no. 16 Nostitzstrasse, owned by Walter Lorenz, or 'Othello', as he was known to his radical regulars.[113]

It cannot be said that the German Communist Party contributed greatly, or even in a limited way, to the wide-ranging family debate which I have tried to chart in previous chapters. Put in another way, Kollontai's themes do not seem to have reached as far as no. 16 Nostitzstrasse. Indeed, on a whole series of key issues – democracy within the family, gender rights within the movement, relations between the family and civil society – the German Communists seemed significantly less sensitive than were the Spanish anarchists, which was not to say that much. Nor did they seem to pick up in any special way on Soviet teaching, such as that of Makarenko, which I will discuss in the next chapter. Women had the vote in the Weimar Republic, they had the right to divorce, they had more rights than any other female population in this book, but the KPD was incapable of integrating these victories into any wider vision of family relations. The rowdiness, smoking and other macho elements of the party's local meetings strongly discouraged women from taking part. Such attitudes at the grass roots were then mirrored by the party's propaganda, which for the most part represented the proletarian woman and mother as passive, pregnant and helpless, an object of pity rather than inspiration.[114]

7. Family life in rural Hesse

The village of Körle in northern Hesse lies in hilly countryside along the river Fulda, about twenty kilometres south of the town of Kassel. In 1848 echoes of the Frankfurt Assembly's deliberations reached the village; so too did the railway, which transformed village life more radically than liberal discourse could hope to do. The railway made it possible for villagers to continue to live in Körle while working in Kassel. As a result, the village did not suffer to the same extent as many other rural communities in the great pre-First World War exodus. In 1864, Körle had 595 inhabitants; by 1895, 619; and by 1939, 1,039. It was predominantly a Protestant village.[115]

During the Weimar period the inhabitants of Körle, like many other villagers in Germany at the time, continued to have a perception and a definition of themselves as farmers, even if many of them were being drawn into industrial work. Their memories divide the village's families into three broad types: 'horse-farmers' (*Pferdebauern*), 'cow-farmers' (*Kuhbauern*), and 'goat-farmers' (*Ziegenbauern*). This distinction did not imply that the Körle farmers were exclusively breeders of animals, but rather that their status and wealth was revealed by the presence of different farm animals. Thus the ploughs of the richer families were pulled by the draught horses they themselves owned, while other farmers had either to use cows for ploughing or else hire horses from their neighbours. There were fourteen horse-farmer families in 1928, owning between ten and thirty hectares of land each, mainly producing for market. These were full-time professional farmers. They employed maids in their houses and farmhands in the fields, both categories belonging to the household in its wider sense. They also employed members of poorer families, the so-called *Arbeitsleute*, at peak times in the agrarian cycle. Sometimes these labour relations assumed paternalist patterns, the richer farmers acting as godfathers to the children of the poor peasants.

The second group of families, the cow-farmer households, numbered sixty-six in 1928. Their landholdings averaged between two and ten hectares of land. These families would supply local markets with butter, cheese, poultry and eggs; occasionally they would sell a calf; often they were village artisans. The last group of families were the eighty goat-farmer households, owning an average of less than two hectares per family. These were not peasant proprietors in any real sense of the term. They were the *Arbeitsleute*, who would sell their labour to the richer rural families, who cultivated their own mini-holdings, and whose male members took the first train into Kassel in the morning to work in the factories. In the 1930s, daughters often joined fathers and brothers in the factory and the office.

Körle, then, was a village in rapid transition, with a few rich farmers and a large stratum of more modest families who increasingly sold their labour for a living. In terms of consumption and everyday life, however, these latter can in no way be compared with the destitute casual labourers whom we have encountered in southern Spain. Although poor, these German villagers had some control over their lives, some sense of being subjects, not merely objects.

The ethos of patriarchy reigned supreme over the whole village. Male heads of households took all the important decisions, though not in the collective manner of the Russian peasantry. Discipline was paramount, fathers not hesitating to beat their children if they refused to obey. Although we have no statistics on inheritance patterns, it is clear from the villagers' recollections that these were mainly stem families, in which at a certain point a single male heir took over all authority and responsibility from his father. Exactly when this happened was clearly the cause of considerable intra-familial conflict at Körle. The change was marked by the redistribution of rooms inside the house, the new head of family and his wife taking possession of the *Wohnzimmer* (living room) while the older generation was symbolically banished to an upstairs bedroom. Tensions remained great; the traditional persecution of the son's wife by her mother-in-law could now be reversed, the older woman being called to account for her earlier behaviour.

Generally speaking, women exercised little power outside their own family. They received the vote under the Weimar Constitution but played no conspicuous role in the village's public life. Thus no woman was a member of the parish administration, even though women looked after the church and did all the preparatory work for religious festivals. Typical women's work was concentrated in the home – cooking, looking after children, cleaning, washing, mending sacks and all matters of clothing. Women, often unmarried aunts, would lead the family's children into the woods to collect berries and mushrooms. On winter evenings, as in the *veglia* of the Tuscan sharecroppers, families would gather in the stables, where the women would knit and mend and sew while chatting and recounting stories. These *Spinnstuben* or 'spinning bees', as they were called, were of central importance for the survival of the village's oral culture. There was very little intermarriage between the different types of peasant families, especially between the horse-farmer families and the others. One horse-farmer offered this patronising explanation: 'Women from the cow-farmer households were too slow to be of use on the larger farms. They were so used to the slow-trot of the cattle that they couldn't keep up.'[116] The 'use' value of a wife was often paramount.

Children went to school six days a week, from eight to eleven in the morning. On Saturday afternoon boys had to sweep the yard and the road while girls cleaned the house. It was only after these and other tasks linked to the agrarian cycle had been performed that children were allowed some playtime. Older children in their last year at school were sent for religious instruction once a week to the pastor's house, which was six kilometres from the village. For these children church attendance was compulsory for a two-year period. Failure to attend services or simple disobedience could be punished by beating.

Overall, the impression is of a highly disciplined family world, in which each had his or her role, and in which the contribution of each individual to the household as a whole was more important than the household's furthering of individual aspirations or freedoms, especially those of women.

This picture of deference and respect for the law must, however, be qualified in at least one important area. Cornelie Usborne's masterly study of illegal abortion as a common experience in rural Hesse in this period does not take Körle as one of its case studies. Her villages are rather clustered further to the south, in the Limburg Basin, and their urban reference point is Frankfurt rather than Kassel. In December 1924 no fewer than ninety-three defendants from seventeen villages (of whom fifty-four were female) were brought to trial for performing, undergoing, aiding or abetting criminal abortion. From an analysis of the trial records it emerges that the network of support and silence had involved both genders, that there was no appreciable difference between

Catholic and Protestant women (neither showed particular penitence), and that the abortionist (Frau Kastner), aided by her husband, had consistently shown considerable skill and attention to hygiene. She was sentenced to three years in gaol, later increased to five. Many other defendants received prison sentences, especially husbands and lovers who had arranged abortions for their wives or girlfriends. The aborting women themselves were punished with slightly less severity but still received prison sentences ranging from four months for single women to six months for married ones. These sentences were received with dismay and anger by the village communities. As Usborne has written, 'The penal law and the church may have called abortion "murder of nascent life" but to the communities of the Limburger basin [. . .] the act of bringing on a late period or terminating an unwanted pregnancy was simply a practical step to retain a measure of control over their precarious lives.'[117] The case shows convincingly the degree to which members of this rural society were both obsequious towards authority and willing to flout the law, as well as how punitive the state could be towards both men and women.

Of the various types of rural families examined in this book, the richer sections of the villagers of Körle (the horse-farmers and cow-farmers) are those who most resemble the Tuscan sharecroppers of Impruneta. Both enjoyed a reasonable standard of living, were located close to a city, took pride in their agricultural expertise and celebrated their belonging to a 'whole house' based on complex kinship patterns. There are, however, significant differences. The Körle farmers owned their land while the Tuscan sharecroppers did not, being more dependent in the last analysis on the needs (and whims) of local landowners. The Italian peasants we have examined lived in isolated farmhouses scattered over hills while the German families were more clustered within the village itself. Most importantly, the two cases are distinguished by a combination of inheritance laws, religion and attitudes towards authority. Tuscan rural inheritance was based on equal distribution between brothers; their Catholicism, while profound, did not convey the disciplinarian and punitive elements of Körle's Protestantism (though the testimonies are much scantier in the German case). Softer tones, especially in the celebration of the Marian cult, were evident in Italy; and even though frequent beatings of children were common in both contexts, family hierarchies and punishments were accompanied at Impruneta by much informal banter and humour. Lastly, the respect of established authority at all levels, including that of state officials, featured strongly in German village life, though the law could be and indeed was flouted when impelling and intimate necessities, such as the need for an abortion, were brought into play. In Italy, by contrast, the state, even the Fascist state, was generally greeted with a certain world-weariness and a distinct reluctance to go to war.

8. The Great Depression

In 1929 the Weimar republican celebrated its tenth birthday. After a very rocky start, the Republic seemed to have stabilised itself. As Detlev Peukert noted, families were beginning to stabilise too. During the war many children had grown up without fathers, while families had suffered terribly in material terms in the period 1918–19. Ten years on, working-class parents were coming up for air, able to dedicate more time to fewer children, contributing modestly to their education and training.[118] Leisure became a family category for the first time. Parents took children on Sunday expeditions out of the new housing estates and into the countryside. In the cities, summer Sundays could be used for picnics in the parks and perhaps even a visit to the cinema. The eight-hour day, collective bargaining and some of the new welfare policies had made free time, however limited, a real possibility. It is true that unemployment remained very high and new investment exceptionally low, but the end of the first republican decade looked much better than its beginning.

The world economic crisis destroyed these illusions with extraordinary rapidity and brutality, opening up at the same time the cataclysmic prospect of the Nazi seizure of power. Mass unemployment was the single most important feature of the crisis, rising from 14 per cent in 1930 to 21.9 per cent in 1931 and 29.9 per cent in 1932. This last figure signified 5.6 million registered unemployed, with at least another million who had not even registered. For unionised workers the tale was even more woeful: some 43.7 per cent of them were jobless by 1932. White-collar workers, if they managed to stay in work, had to accept massive salary cuts, while shopkeepers and artisans were unable to keep afloat as the home market collapsed. In the countryside, farm foreclosures were the order of the day.[119]

The effects upon family life were extremely damaging. Unemployment was particularly high among men in the age group between eighteen and thirty, many of whom still lived at home with their parents. As the crisis bit ever harder, acute hunger returned to German cities. Where possible, worker families invented their own subsistence agendas. For instance, the number of allotment gardens in Hamburg grew exponentially, from 4,200 in 1917 to 47,422 in 1933. Soup kitchens, much despised for the very poor quality of what was on offer, were reintroduced. School meals programmes also became a key component of family strategies for survival. In 1931, again in Hamburg, social workers warned that children were taking food home for their parents: 'It must be insisted that the food be eaten in the school meal room itself.'[120]

As the crisis deepened and government policy appeared to make it only worse, resentment and political tension grew by leaps and bounds. One of the

fig. 47 A Salvation Army soup kitchen, 1931.

most bitter discourses was reserved for the welfare system, which was now utterly unable to cope. Unemployment benefit, introduced in 1927, was piti-fully inadequate and of short duration. The unemployed had then to apply for local welfare support, a pittance to be gained only after severe and humiliating means testing. In the countryside of Lower Saxony, where the small farm owners had been destroyed by the crisis, strange rumours began to circulate of Jewish ritual murders, of a child who had mysteriously disappeared, of a butcher who sold bad meat.[121] At the same time the linkage between farm ruination and Jewish usury became an ever more common explanation of the crisis. In the cities many of the unemployed took to street fighting – the SPD in the Reichsbanner, the Communists in the Red Front Fighters' League, and the SA under the command of Ernst Röhm. On such occasions they were likely to come across Joseph Goebbels making one of his inflammatory speeches.[122]

III. Nazi family politics

1. General philosophy: inside the 'people's community'

The party that took power in Germany in 1933, unlike Mussolini's Fascists, had some very clear ideas about what its family politics might look like.

Although the Nazis had to take into account both Protestant and Catholic public opinion, they were not hedged in, as Mussolini was, by the teachings of the Catholic Church. They were also convinced that in Germany the long-term relationship between state, civil society and family was of a far sterner sort than its equivalent in the Italian peninsula. Hitler himself told a youth rally at the Nuremberg Party Day of 14 September 1935, 'Germany is not a hen-roost where everything is in confusion and everyone cackles and crows, we are a people which from its infancy learns how to be disciplined.'[123]

The starting point for all Nazi action in the field of the family was a profound distinction between approved and non-approved families. It is not too much to say that this distinction, developed under a panoply of pseudo-scientific language and reaching into every corner of the nation, was at the heart of all Nazi evil. First in Germany and then in the vast territories which came under Nazi control, the regime invented categories of condemnation, exclusion and extermination which damaged millions of families where they did not destroy them completely.[124]

Let me begin, however, with Nazi attitudes and actions towards approved, Aryan families, before passing to such categories as the 'hereditarily unfit', the 'racially inferior' and the 'racially alien'. In the first place the Nazis established a deeply gendered distinction between the two worlds of the public and the private, the male and the female. These two worlds were separate but closely connected, the one superimposed on the other. The good German family, racially pure and patriarchal, coordinated by women but dominated by men, was for the Nazis the cell upon which the nation could depend. Here is Hitler in a famous speech addressed to women at Nuremberg on 8 September 1934:

> For her world [that of the woman] is her husband, her family, her children and her home. But where would the greater world be if no one took care of the smaller world? How could the larger world exist if there were no one to make the care of the smaller world their life's task [. . .] We do not find it right when the woman seeks to assert herself within the world of the man. Rather we find it natural when these two worlds remain separate [. . .] To the one belongs the power of feeling, the power of the soul [. . .] to the other the capacity for vision, the hardness of character, the decisions and the desire to act. In one case is required the willingness of women to preserve and increase this important unit, and in the other readiness on the part of the man to make life secure.[125]

Thus there could be no women's 'emancipation' because the woman was already playing her true role within the family. 'The message of women's emancipation', Hitler reiterated in the same speech, 'is a message discovered solely by the Jewish intellect and its content is stamped with the same spirit.' A year later, at Nuremberg again, he returned to the theme, placing it in a military context and appealing to German male virility and honour:

> Today, in Marxist countries, women's army battalions have been formed. Hearing this news I can only say this: It will never happen here! There are things which are made for man and which are his responsibility alone. I would be ashamed to be a German man if, should war break out, a single woman was dispatched to the front. A woman has *her* battleground.[126]

During the Second World War, as we shall see, Hitler would come to rue so Manichean a view of gender roles.

The small world of the family, the larger one of power, politics and war, the one female, the other male – this was the first component of the general philosophy of Nazism in relation to approved families. To it must be added a second – that of the contribution of families to the creation of the *Volksgemeinschaft*, or people's community. Here too an initial contrast may be drawn with the Italian case. It may be recalled that in Berlin in October 1931 Giovanni Gentile, Fascism's leading philosopher, delivered a paper to an international conference dedicated to Hegel's thought. In it Gentile gave particular emphasis to the primacy of the state in relation to the other two elements of Hegel's famous triad of state, family and civil society. For Gentile the state 'cannot realise itself unless it absorbs the family and annuls it'. Similarly, 'There is no civil society which is not also state.' Behind these extreme statements lay no desire to dissolve the family physically, as some radical Bolshevik thinkers had advocated. Rather, the state had to reign supreme in terms of value systems and loyalties, absorbing family and civil society into itself.[127]

The Nazis took a rather different view. The *community*, not the state, was at the centre of their political proposal. German society was to find within itself the energy, solidarity, discipline and authority to carry forward a unified national project of vast dimensions. Of course, the state continued to exist, and in very powerful form; but it was the people's community, with its holistic intent, mass culture and infinite networks, that in the last analysis endowed it with its powers.[128]

The concept of *Volksgemeinschaft* can be traced a long way back, certainly to Johann Gottfried Herder and German Romanticism. During and after the First World War, the idea of the people's community offered solace in very dire times. As Peter Fritzsche has noted, 'there was always something dramatically embattled about *Volksgemeinschaft*'.[129] The term was widely used – not only by the extreme right – as a contrast to the programmatic class *divisions* and social *warfare* advocated by the German Communist Party. The Nazis embraced it without reserve. On 1 May 1933, usurping the socialist tradition of May Day, Goebbels coordinated a very widespread nationalist and Nazi celebration of labour: 'Decorate your houses and the streets of your cities and villages with fresh garlands and the flags of the Reich! [. . .] No child should be without a little black-white-red or swastika flag!' The national radio broadcast which covered the day's events cut frequently from Berlin demonstrations to choruses of miners, farmers and soldiers in Thüringen and Franconia to reportage from aboard a Zeppelin, creating in the process 'a single audio space across Germany'.[130]

In the ongoing battle between holistic and individualist views of modern society, the Nazis came down very heavily in favour of the first. The anthropologist Louis Dumont, in his revealing analysis of *Mein Kampf*, shows the degree to which Hitler was convinced that the toxins poisoning German society derived from unacceptable individual behaviour.[131] Women were seeking new freedoms and a profound modification of their traditional role within the family; democratic egalitarianism was doing away with all hierarchy; communities were dissolving in the face of capitalism's crisis; and the greatest individualists and egoists of all, the Jewish plutocracy, were reducing the Aryan masses to penury.[132] The response had to be not just state action but the affirmation of the masses, of the militarised people's community, which found its greatest visual memorial in Leni Riefenstahl's 1935 film *The Triumph of the Will*.

At the time, the *Volksgemeinschaft* seemed unstoppable, at the very core of the twentieth century. Indeed, it would take another world war, with millions of dead, to halt it in its tracks. Yet the more distance we gain from the last century, the more it also becomes apparent how far its great authoritarian regimes, and not only that of the Nazis, were fighting rearguard actions, albeit on a massive scale, against the constant pressure of the individual desire for liberty, autonomy and self-expression.

What of the family in all this? Although much more work needs to be done on the relationship between the idea of the people's community and the realities of family life, it is clear that the two were intended to be closely intertwined. In the poster reproduced as plate 9, a radiant Aryan family of proud parents and three children thrives under the dual protection deriving from the harmony of the family group itself and from the huge Nazi eagle lurking in the background. The poster caption reads, 'The National Socialist Party ensures the existence of the *Volksgemeinschaft*'; at the bottom, there is an invitation to all members of the people's community 'to seek help and advice from local groups'. The ultimate aim was not only ideological but material. Hitler poured scorn on Bolshevik ideas of a frugal utopia, wherein private property was kept to a minimum, insisting rather that German families were to be enriched and living standards raised.[133]

The specific contribution of families was judged invaluable at many different levels, of which procreation was the most important. German couples were to be 'child rich', working hard in the privacy of their homes and beds to make up for the terrible demographic losses of the First World War. Theirs also was the task of education, in the widest sense of the term. It was through the family that children acquired the discipline and sense of duty that were necessary for becoming part of the people's community. It was from the home that the child would learn to understand clearly the role of each individual, and to respect the hierarchy of the genders.

The ideal model of the family was the traditional rural one which found eloquent exposition in Horst Becker's *Die Familie*, first published in Leipzig in 1935. Basing his work upon the famous tract of the same name written by Wilhelm Heinrich Riehl in 1855,[134] Becker defined the rural family as 'the protective element inside the natural order of the *Volk*'.[135] It was infinitely preferable to urban or worker families in that it was highly fertile, tri-generational

fig. 48 A mother listens with her daughters to the *Volksempfänger* (people's radio), a propaganda instrument much favoured by Goebbels, 1939.

and based on clear patriarchal hierarchies. In all these characteristics it resembled the ideal rural Fascist family.

By contrast, the modern, urban bourgeois family, based on individual love, was treated by Becker with considerable suspicion. Here again the parallel with Italy was a strong one, such families being denounced as breeding grounds of female emancipation and homoeroticism, of pacifism and the absence of national spirit. In Becker's harsh world of racist politics, families needed to be based on much firmer ground than individual, bourgeois love. Time and again, both at school and in propaganda films, the Nazis emphasised the importance of the link between families and community, and the centrality of 'blood and soil' for the future of the German *Volk*.[136] But the insufficiency of this model for a country as urbanised as Germany in the 1930s was fairly evident.[137]

If we examine marriage, divorce and abortion, the triad which so exercised all the regimes examined in this book, we see that the Nazis had their own version of it. For Aryan families marriage was regarded as fundamental for procreation, abortion very severely punished, but divorce allowed and even encouraged. In July 1938 new provisions were passed which extended the grounds for divorce. 'Premature infertility' was one; the refusal to procreate another. Couples who had lived apart for three years or more and whose marriages had 'irretrievably broken down' could now petition for divorce. The new provisions were certainly not promulgated in the name of individual happiness. Rather, the regime wanted to dissolve marriages that were of no reproductive value to the *Volksgemeinschaft*.[138]

2. Outside the people's community

The necessary connection of the small family world with the world outside it, and the pivotal function of the family within the people's community: these are the first two defining elements of Nazi family philosophy. They both relate to the privileged sphere of approved families. A third, of equal if not greater importance, was concerned rather with non-approved families – those considered to be outside the Reich and hostile to it. Nazi attitudes here come under the broad heading of racial hygiene. The *Volksgemeinschaft* was in no way a 'bridging' community, eagerly reaching out to others different from itself. It was on the contrary a 'bonding' one, with a terrible vengeance. It tied its members together meticulously, taught them to hate the outsider and simultaneously practised fierce discrimination against those it had placed beyond its walls.

As we saw in chapter 3, all the political regimes of the first half of the twentieth century, whether democratic or dictatorial, practised 'positive' eugenics – the gradual improvement of their populations through the provision of better social, medical, dietary and hygienic conditions. Intervention of this sort was consonant with the Catholic Church's long-standing teaching, reaffirmed in *Casti Connubii*, that any inhibition of procreation, any tampering with reproduction, was a cardinal sin. On the other hand, some northern European and predominantly Protestant nations such as Germany and Sweden also embraced, though to different degrees, 'negative' eugenics. This latter was very much more sinister. It involved the state regulation of 'undesirable elements', the hunting down not only of disease but also of defects (medical, social or racial), and, if necessary, the enforcement of compulsory sterilisation.[139] The Nazi version of this negative eugenics went further still. Sterilisation was to be followed by 'euthanasia', to be practised on certain highly vulnerable categories of the population, of whom the old and the 'feeble-minded' were in the front line. All these members of the population were classified as of 'lesser racial value'.

There was, however, a second category in the vocabulary of racist hygiene – those belonging to 'alien [*artfremd*] races', against whom relentless war had to be waged. This was the racial battle that Chamberlain had reiterated at Bayreuth to both Hitler and Goebbels, and which had made such a great impression upon them. The Aryan race had to be saved from the Jewish menace and the Jews to be destroyed. From 1933 onwards both Jews and gypsies were subject to a long, slow and cumulative process of genocidal activity. The outcome was to be the creation of a superior Aryan population. Goebbels's ministry summarised Nazi aims with chilling clarity: 'The goal is not "children at any cost", but "racially worthy, physically and mentally unaffected children of German families".'[140] All the rest could be done without.

Nazi family philosophy was thus founded on a terrible cleavage artificially created within German society. On the one side were 'racially worthy' family groups, living at the very heart of the *Volksgemeinschaft*, the object of very considerable attention (and support) on the part of the regime. On the other were those who had been forced outside the community, who were further divided into two groups: first, those of 'lesser racial value' (the mentally ill, etc.), and, secondly, those belonging, like the Jews, to 'alien' races. At the beginning it was those of 'lesser racial value' whose physical inviolability was most threatened, while those of 'alien races' were subjected to discrimination, loss of civil rights and progressive economic ruination.[141] But both groups could only fear ever more as the regime tightened its grip on German society.

I would like to close this section with three examples of what Nazi family politics entailed for those outside the people's community. The first is the Law for the Prevention of Hereditarily Diseased Offspring (Gesetz zur Verhütung erbkranken Nachwuchses), passed on 14 July 1933. It called for the compulsory sterilisation of persons suffering from certain 'hereditary diseases' – 'congenital feeble-mindedness', 'schizophrenia', 'manic depression', 'Huntington's chorea', 'hereditary blindness', 'hereditary deafness' and 'serious physical deformities'. In addition, chronic alcoholics could be compulsorily sterilised. Between January 1934 and September 1939 approximately 320,000 people – some 0.5 per cent of the German population – were sterilised. The most important group were the so-called 'feeble-minded', who constituted two-thirds of those sterilised, and almost two-thirds of whom were women. Many of them were of German ethnicity, but of the most deprived section of the population. Hitler had argued in *Mein Kampf* that 'those who are physically and mentally unhealthy and unworthy must not perpetuate their suffering in the bodies of their children'. The law of July 1933 was the first step in this direction.[142]

A second example is the testimony of Marta Appel, whose family consisted of her husband, Ernst, who was a rabbi in Dortmund, and their two daughters. On 1 April 1933 the Nazis organised their first action against the Jews since taking power, the national boycott of Jewish shops and businesses. Marta described that day in her *Memoirs*:

> The children had been advised not to come to school on April 1, 1933, the day of the boycott. Even the principal of the school thought Jewish children's lives were no longer safe [...] In front of our temple, on every square and corner, billboards were scoffing at us. Everywhere, and on all occasions, we read and heard that we were vermin and had caused the ruin of the German people.[143]

For Marta Appel it was not her own ostracism that upset her most but the way her girls were treated at school:

> My heart was broken when I saw tears in my younger child's eyes when she had been sent home from school while all the others had been taken to a show or some other pleasure. It was not because she was denied going to the show that my little girl was weeping – she knew her Mommy always could take her – but because she had to stay apart as if she were not good enough to associate with her comrades any longer. It was this that made it hard and bitter for her. I think that even the Nazi teacher sometimes felt ashamed when she looked into the sad eyes of my little girl [...] Maybe it was not right to hate this teacher so much, since everything she did had been upon

orders, but it was she who brought so much bitterness to my child, and never can I forget it.[144]

On just one occasion were Marta Appel's girls able to take their revenge upon their teachers:

One day [in 1934] I saw my children coming back from school with shining eyes, laughing and giggling together [. . .] an official of the new *Rasseamt* had come to give a talk about race differences [. . .] 'He said that there are two groups of races, a high group and a low one. The high and upper race that was destined to rule the world was the Teutonic, the German race, while one of the lowest races was the Jewish race. And then, Mommy, he looked around and asked one of the girls to come to him [. . .] and he was pointing at [our] Eva, "Look here, the small head of this girl, her long forehead, her very blue eyes and blond hair", and he was lifting one of her long, blond braids. "And look", he said, "at her tall and slender figure. These are the unequivocal marks of a pure and unmixed Teutonic race" [. . .] All the girls burst into laughter. Even Eva could not help laughing. Then from all sides of the hall there was shouting, "She is a Jewess!" You should have seen the official's face!'[145]

In May 1937, after Marta and her husband had been arrested for a number of days, Ernst finally succumbed to her pleas to leave the country, and the family fled to Holland and thence to the United States.

My final example is one in which the two categories of Nazi exclusion – those deemed to be of 'lesser racial value' and those belonging to 'alien races'– are combined. Rudolf Langen was born in 1931 in Berlin-Zehlendorf. His mother was Jewish and his father Aryan, which according to Nazi racist distinctions made him a '*Mischling* of the first degree'. As a child he often played truant and was accused of loitering. Consequently the family was broken up: Rudolf was taken from his mother and placed first in a Catholic orphanage, then in a 'home for special care' (*Fürsorgeheim*), and finally, in March 1944, in the notorious 'medical care institution' of Hadamar. There he was diagnosed as a 'hereditary idiot' and three days later died of 'pneumonia'. In seeking compensation in 1957–8, Rudolf's mother argued that he had never been a 'hereditary idiot' but was rather a normal and healthy child. It also emerged that six other children bearing the racist label '*Mischling* of the first degree' had arrived at Hadamar at the same time and three days later had died of 'pneumonia'.[146]

3. The Churches, the regime and the family

The Nazi regime effectively destroyed Weimar civil society, but the degree of autonomy enjoyed by the Christian Churches deserves a mention apart. Christianity in Germany, unlike that in Spain or Italy, was profoundly divided. The majority was Protestant, numbering some forty million persons or two-thirds of the population. The German Evangelical Church, the principal Protestant grouping, had long been politically extremely conservative and in the days of the First Reich had served, to all intents and purposes, as the ideological arm of the state. It had not hesitated to present the First World War as a conflict within Christianity, in which German Protestants were pitted in the West against Catholic French and Belgians and in the East against Orthodox Russians. Historically speaking, nationalism and majority German Protestantism thus went hand in hand. It was not surprising therefore that during Hitler's rise to power a Protestant voter was twice as likely to support the Nazis as a Catholic.[147] The Catholic minority, strong above all in the south and south-west of the country, was no less patriotic than the Protestant north but had strong traditions of autonomy and resistance. During the Weimar Republic, Catholics in Germany boasted their own political organisation in the Centre Party and were guided, above all in doctrinal matters, by the papacy in Rome. A key area of concern, as we have seen at some length, was the sanctity of the family. The Catholic family – that most precious of all social groups – had to be protected from the interfering tendencies of over-strong states. Not by chance did Hitler respect and to some degree fear the Catholic Church, while he considered the Protestant Evangelical Church as up for grabs.

In 1932 the Nazis founded the 'German Christians' with the clear intention of taking over the Evangelical Church and creating a new, unified, racist and nationalist Protestant Church. At first they swept all before them and won an overwhelming victory in the Evangelical Church elections of July 1933. The German Christians sought to fuse Church and regime, very much on the latter's terms. Their numerous supporters among the Protestant pastors took to preaching sermons in SA or even SS uniforms. They hung swastika flags in their churches and joyously took up and expanded upon Martin Luther's deeply anti-semitic *Judenschriften*. Goebbels's Propaganda Ministry invested heavily in the celebrations of the 450th anniversary of Luther's birth.[148]

Against their own and Hitler's expectations, things did not go entirely as the German Christians would have wished. A backlash against Nazification led to the founding of the Confessing Church in May 1934, supported by many thousands of pastors who believed that it was the task of Protestants to put religion, not nationalism, first. They also refused to accept the 'Aryan paragraph', which insisted that converted Jews should be expelled from the Church on the grounds that racial characteristics took precedence over belief. The Confessing Church organised bible study groups all over the country, attended overwhelmingly by women. Their activity was in stark contrast to the male-dominated German Christians, who propagated a muscular and crusading Christianity, though their social background was rather distant from the Spanish 'crusaders' we examined in the previous chapter. By 1937 German Protestantism was in turmoil. The members of the Confessing Church were subject to much harassment and many of their leaders were imprisoned, but at the same time the German Christians were unable to assert total dominance. The Confessing Church never became the focus of nation-wide resistance. Vociferous and courageous as they were in some areas, its leaders for the most part remained silent on what was happening to the 'racially inferior' and the 'hereditarily unfit'.[149]

The Catholic story of resistance and accommodation is a rather different one. At first Pius XI was as eager to sign a Concordat with the Nazi regime as he had previously been with the Italian Fascists. The arrest and imprisonment of Centre Party supporters and activists also pushed him into action. The bases were soon laid: Catholics were to recognise the regime and refrain from all political activity; in return the Church was to be allowed freedom of action within society, always provided it remained uncritical of the new political order. The Concordat was signed on 20 July 1933. It was the cause of much celebration in the German Catholic community and the occasion for some fawning letters from the German Catholic hierarchy to the Führer. Michael Cardinal Faulhaber, archbishop of Munich and Freising, wrote to Hitler on 24 July, 'What the old parliaments and parties did not accomplish in sixty years, your statesmanlike foresight has achieved in six months. For Germany's prestige in East and West and before the whole world, this handshake with the papacy, the greatest moral power in the history of the world, is a feat of immeasurable blessing.'[150]

It soon became evident, however, that the Nazi regime was not willing to allow the Catholic press any freedom of expression and that the range of activities of Catholic associations was to be strictly limited. All confessional schools were to be closed down. Up to this point Pius XI had done everything in his power to appease the Nazi regime, even allowing the earlier protests over the law for the 'hereditarily unfit' to die down and be transformed into substantial collaboration. In the spring of 1937 he at last responded with the encyclical letter *Mit brennender Sorge*, which was not published worldwide but was secretly printed in Germany and read out from the pulpits of all Catholic churches on Palm Sunday of 1937. Pius wrote that he had been watching the suffering of the Church in Germany 'with deep anxiety and with ever-growing dismay'.[151] He urged the Third Reich to abandon what he called neo-paganism, by which he meant the deification of entities such as nation, people and the state. Yet however dramatic the form of the encyclical, its content was moderate, and the German Catholic Church continued to seek accommodation with the Nazis. The truth was that many of the clergy and their faithful shared the aspirations and values of the *Volksgemeinschaft*.[152] It was only with the war, Hitler's 'euthanasia' project and the question of crucifixes in classrooms that Catholic protest became vociferous.

The various parts of this murky story, with its different levels of collaboration, both Protestant and Catholic, with the Nazi regime, have necessarily been recounted here only in part. I would none the less like to pose of this material two questions germane to the wider themes of this book. First, are there significant differences vis-à-vis the family in the teachings of the two denominations? And, secondly, is there any possible linkage between this teaching on the family and the wider behaviour of Protestants and Catholics in Germany in the 1930s? I think the answer to both questions is 'yes', even though what follows is perforce preliminary and merely suggestive.

Protestant teaching on the family, although by no means entirely uniform, differed from that of the Catholic Church in a number of ways. Perhaps most importantly it abandoned the concept of marriage as a sacrament and in its place, as Ernst Troeltsch wrote, 'made of marriage a relationship that was predominantly moral and personal'. Majority Protestant teaching also abandoned the view of sexuality which considered abstinence a virtue. Instead it linked sexuality, procreation and love inextricably, making of the family 'the highest and most specialised expression of human love'.[153] The Reformation did little, however, to dent the predominance of patriarchy within the family, the authoritarianism of the male head of household being strongly underlined both in Lutheranism and to a lesser extent in Calvinism. In the constant interplay between the individual, family and society, Protestantism stressed the importance of the tandem individual–society. In particular, it was through service to the community and to the state, through activity in the modern world, through good works, that salvation was achieved. This view of community service fitted in all too well with belief in the Nazi *Volksgemeinschaft*.

Catholicism, as we have seen, presented a somewhat different configuration of these various elements. The family was viewed far more as a sacred citadel than in the Lutheran model, almost 'a little church enclosed by domestic walls', to use again the felicitous phrase of Antonio Rosmini.[154] Its members were not so much individuals seeking salvation in a wider world as component parts of a family returning constantly to their social group of departure. Here, too, as in the Protestant family, the authoritarian male head continued to dominate.

These two views of family, Church and society, which competed but also overlapped with one another, both proved woefully inadequate in the face of the very difficult task of maintaining Christianity's moral dignity in Germany in the cauldron years of 1933–45. In the first place, Protestants and Catholics failed to make use of their special position in German society. They neither pooled their resources nor denounced to the world what was going on. The extraordinary acts of courage and self-sacrifice of certain individual Christians took place within the wider and debasing context of continuing appeasement. Secondly, and more specifically, neither tradition of family teaching could boast a *universalist* aspect. This alone could have hoped to transform the thinking and behaviour of silent bystanders. In the 1930s families always had labels attached to them, in Spain as in Germany, and they were saved or eliminated on the basis of what the label said. Nowhere to be found was a label which read, 'family of human beings'.

4. Pulling out and pushing in

Returning now to the *Volksgemeinschaft*, there is some considerable debate as to whether the Nazi regime, for all its affirmations concerning the centrality of the German family, was really beneficial to it. Ingeborg Weber-Kellermann even states that the family's 'function was reduced as never before in its entire social history since the time of the Germanic tribes'.[155] This is going too far, but there is no denying the problem. Privacy, intimacy, leisure, time for children and parents to be together – in other words, all that constitutes family life – were deeply menaced by a regime whose invasiveness recognised no limits.

In trying to identify the various strands of this Nazi model of family politics, I will use the same categories of analysis as for Fascist Italy. On the one hand the regimes pulled family members out so as to involve them in its own activities; on the other they pushed in on families, urging them to have more children and to alter long-standing beliefs, habits and customs. There can be no doubt that the Nazi regime was far more effective than the Fascist one in implementing this dual strategy. As a modern country with an extensive communication structure it had the great advantage of being able to reach, and even control, almost the entire population; to put it another way, although it still had poor rural regions and impoverished peasants, Germany had no equivalent of the Italian south in the 1930s. It could also boast a state renowned for its efficiency. As a result, the Nazis successfully intervened to a much greater extent than the Fascists were ever able, or even tried, to do.

Let me begin with the regime's pulling out of family members for its own purposes. One sharp-eyed American observer in Berlin, Clifford Kirkpatrick, illustrated very well the tug of war of loyalties that was taking place:

> Regardless of any clash of ideals between German parents and their children in the ranks of the Hitler Youth organisations, an opposition between family and state exists by virtue of the simple fact that there are but twenty-four hours in a day. The time that children spend outside the home in the activities of the youth organisation cannot be spent with parents. German boys and girls are enlisted for a great variety of tasks in the communal activities of the German people. Reports are that they are thrilled at this participation.[156]

Kirkpatrick recounted a telling example of this downgrading of the family:

> On a particularly hot summer evening, the writer attended an open-air concert given by the Berlin Philharmonic Orchestra in the courtyard of the former Kaiser's palace. Just before the concert a glow appeared at the entrance, and hundreds of the Hitler Youth marched in. They were in single file, each bearing a flaming torch. With military precision they strode around the courtyard until the entire audience was encircled by a border of leaping flame. There the boys stood on the hard cobblestones for two hours in the terrific heat, made hotter by the glow of their own flaming torches [. . .] Two or three white-clad nurses watched the warning signs and walked up and down the line with pitchers of water. Soon a torch clattered on the pavement and a slender youth was carried away between two brown-shirted comrades. In the immediate vicinity another lad soon collapsed and then a third. How many of the smaller boys at the other end of the court collapsed it is impossible to say. The Haydn symphony was followed by the Horst Wessel song played by one of the world's best orchestras. The audience rose in a gesture of reverence not accorded to Papa Haydn, and the concert was at an end. In response to a curt order, the boys dragged their tired legs at a brisk march out of the courtyard [. . .] It was eleven o'clock, and no doubt many mothers on the other side of the city were unable to greet their small sons until close to midnight.[157]

Kirkpatrick's is a good example for many reasons, not least since it concerns boys and possible conflicts between parents and children, especially male children. A prominent characteristic of the Nazi regime, as of the Soviet one, was generational conflict. Youth was considered the dynamic element and was encouraged to seek adventure through service to the state, whereas the staid habits of the older generation, its inability to change with the times, were much criticised. The idea of 'filiarchy' replacing 'patriarchy' is one we have already encountered in relation to the Freikorps.[158] Care must be taken not to exaggerate, for the authority of the father figure was not in question. But there can be no doubt about the consistency with which Nazi youth organisations pulled children out from their home background and tried to form them in their own likeness. In a speech at Kiel in November 1933 Hitler stated, 'When an opponent says, "I will not come over to your side", I calmly reply, "Your child belongs to us already".[159]

If we go back for a moment to the Hesse countryside and the village of Körle in the 1930s, the villagers' memories are of radical change within families. The Nazi Party branch in the village was founded in 1928 by the sons of horse- and cow-farmers. Armed with the new authority that stemmed from their being Nazis, they proceeded to contest their fathers' authority. The villagers recall that there was 'war in every family'.[160] Bitter controversies arose over how much time and energy was to be reserved for the family farm and how much given to the new Nazi mass organisations. In the name of service to the *Volksgemeinschaft*, sons contested fathers' totalising ideas of service to the family. At the same time, and somewhat ironically, the Nazis introduced women to public life. Previously excluded, some of them now joined the Nazi women's organisations, the Frauenwerk (Nazi Women's Bureau) and the Frauenschaft (Nazi Women's Organisation). Even more significantly, their daughters joined the Bund Deutscher Mädel (League of German Girls), many of them travelling for the first time beyond the confines of their villages. Families, then, were in turmoil, as time-honoured patterns of daily life were called into question.[161]

Of prime importance for the generational battle that the Nazis felt themselves to be waging was the Hitlerjugend (Hitler Youth). Hitler had an unyielding view of what boys' values should be within the organisation that bore his name: 'My pedagogy is hard. The weak must be hammered out of existence. In my new order there will grow a youth before which the world will shrink in fear [. . .] [Boys] must learn to dominate.'[162] The organisation's oath of loyalty was of blood-curdling quality: 'Live faithfully, fight bravely, die laughing.'[163] Numbers grew very rapidly once all other youth associations had been closed down. Crucially, sports facilities for boys between the ages of ten and eighteen were allotted by the state to the Hitlerjugend. In addition, many employers restricted apprenticeships to its members.

Comparisons with both Italy and the Soviet Union are interesting. The male youth organisations in Nazi Germany were the Jungvolk (from ten to fourteen years of age) and the Hitlerjugend (from fourteen to eighteen). The

Italian youth organisations, by contrast, took children from the age of six (in the Figli della Lupa), as we have seen, and the vast majority of their members were of primary school age. These age differences radically coloured the nature of youth organisation in the two countries. The German one was very heavily tilted towards serious military training for adolescents, something that was present only in very small part in the Italian experience. Indeed, it makes more sense to compare the Hitlerjugend with the Soviet Komsomol, which also put an emphasis on military education. But there was one crucial difference: Komsomol arms training was for both boys and girls, while the Hitlerjugend was strictly for boys. Furthermore, to belong to the Komsomol, as we shall see, was to be part of an elite organisation that had its own ethos and exercised an often critical role in Soviet society.[164]

Education in the Hitlerjugend took an unattractive and repetitive form. Each age-cohort had to work its way through a syllabus that included topics such as 'Germanic gods and heroes', 'Adolf Hitler and his fellow fighters' and 'The people and its blood heritage'. Instructors were often veteran NCOs who demanded blind obedience from their young charges. Discipline was often brutal. Indeed, the organisation was responsible for a general brutalisation of German family life, as its adolescent members, having suffered in forced marches and military exercises at the weekend, vented their pent-up feelings upon their parents during the week. Even Harald Quandt, Goebbels's stepson, complained of 'bad food, mistreatment and censored mail'.[165] The whole organisation was run from the top downwards, its leader, Baldur von Schirach, being answerable only to Hitler. In reply to criticisms concerning the effect that the Hitlerjugend was having on family life, von Schirach replied blithely that many poor and working-class children did not have a family in any case.[166]

It is worth noting that some Nazi ideologues, including Alfred Rosenberg and Alfred Bäumler, were convinced that Männerbünde, or male organisations, should take pride of place over the family within the Volksgemeinschaft. Bäumler even went so far as to deny the role of the family as the germ cell of the nation.[167] They made little progress, because Nazi leaders, Hitler and Goebbels above all, stood firm on this issue. Yet there could be no doubting that a community based on so much male camaraderie and the constant evocation of death found its natural expression in male, soldier organisations rather than in the family. Its art, as we shall see in a moment, also reflected that world. In 1930s Germany the spirit of the Freikorps was never far away.

The female equivalent of the Hitlerjugend, the Bund Deutscher Mädel, for girls between the ages of ten and eighteen, was another formidable organisation, numbering 1,502,571 members by 1939. It came under the control of the

fig. 49 Members of the Hitlerjugend marching in Frankfurt, 1930s.

Hitlerjugend, but obviously boasted a different set of priorities and activities. The Nazi gender divide was absolutely Manichean. As Lisa Pine has written,

> Girls were to react to circumstances with their emotions, whereas boys were to react with their minds; girls were to store their experiences internally, whilst boys were to use theirs actively and creatively; girls were to be docile and to give of themselves, whilst boys were to affect others, gain victories and conquer; girls were to be passively content, whereas boys were to be active builders or destroyers of cultures; girls were to care for the family and the household, whilst boys were to lay the foundations for the state; girls were to view life as a gift, whereas boys were to consider it a struggle; for girls 'motherliness' – not femininity – was the ultimate aim, whilst for boys it was very clearly 'manliness', in a militarised sense.[168]

In keeping with these values, the Bund Deutscher Mädel proposed four main areas of endeavour in their 'household' schools: practical home instruction, including cookery, baking, gardening and needlework; hygiene and medicine, which covered nutrition, health and care for infants; instruction on the nature of the *Volksgemeinschaft* – nation, race and economy; and last but not least, sports and recreational activities, including gymnastic displays and athletics, hiking, traditional songs and dancing.

In 1936, membership of the organisation became obligatory for the appropriate age-cohort of German girls. An article published in the organisation's journal *Das Deutsche Mädel* in June of that year, written by one of its local Berlin platoon leaders, reveals different reactions to obligatory membership for girls aged between ten and fourteen. One group, the majority according to the writer, was desperately keen to join. A second was passive and suspicious. But it is the third group that is the most interesting, revealing as it is of how far the *Volksgemeinschaft* had still to go before becoming 'classless' in the capital city. These girls were accompanied by their parents. In the scornful words of the 'JM-Führerin' who wrote the article, 'These Mummy's darlings were to be entrusted to us only on specific conditions which were either unrealisable or obvious [. . .] Trudchen could come only if her mother was certain she would not come into contact with badly behaved or "common" girls [. . .] Ilschen was immediately to be let off attending outings or camps; she was not to be exposed to any danger for the body or mind.'

Other girls revelled in the possibility of going to a camp and escaping from the strict vigilance of their parents. Their *Fahrtenbücher*, or travel diaries, are full of a sense of adventure and group identity, as well as utter loyalty and devotion to the Führer: 'He has only half an hour for us and yet in that time he says everything that is essential, everything that we absolutely must know.'[169] The girls stayed in the camps for an average of eight days, much less than in the Italian *colonie*. The older ones were allowed to sleep in tents that they pitched themselves – a distinct measure of autonomy – whereas the younger ones had to sleep in dormitories. The day began with the solemn raising of the flag and finished around the camp fire or in highly suggestive night walks through the German countryside.[170]

Sexuality was never officially discussed. There was no sex education in the modern sense but rather a strong recommendation to get married early, so as to have numerous legitimate children. The official response to what must have been a great deal of barely suppressed sexual desire in both male and female camps, rigidly separated from one another, was 'fresh, clean, clear German air' and lots of gymnastics – rather similar to Lenin's recipe, as we saw in chapter 1. In 1939 the two sexes once again went in different directions: the young men prepared for war while young unmarried women under the age of twenty-five undertook a Community Service Year (*Pflichtjahr*), in which the regime assigned them compulsory work placements. City girls very often finished up working in the countryside. The scheme was a serious attempt to give substance to the idea of the people's community, and to make young girls its advocates. There were many exemptions, however, and the war years offered many other possibilities of work for young women.[171] Overall, there can be no doubt that family members were simultaneously being pulled in different directions by the regime – daughters to Community Service, fathers to compulsory conscription, sons to the Hitlerjugend. Family life suffered accordingly.

5. Strength through joy

In November 1933 the NS-Gemeinschaft 'Kraft durch Freude' (KdF, 'Strength through Joy' Community) came into being as the mass leisure-time organisation of the Labour Front (Deutsche Arbeitsfront). It was consciously modelled on Italy's Opera Nazionale Dopolavoro, founded in 1925, and the comparison between the two is quite revealing. Both were successful, but it is immediately apparent that the KdF was reaching out to far greater numbers of people, addressing a more sophisticated consumer public, and offering a wider variety of leisure-time activities.[172] By the mid-1930s the organisation was self-financing. It had introduced the sale of consumer goods such as radios, and also held out the promise of producing a 'KdF car' which German workers could afford. In reality, mass production of the Volkswagen began only after the war.

The KdF reached far into German society. Its after-work (*Feierabend*) section, which focused on theatre trips, concerts, dancing, chess competitions and the like, hosted, according to the regime's statistics, some 224,000 events in 1939 with a total of sixty million participants. Other highly popular activities were sports competitions and weekend hiking. The KdF declared itself to be apolitical, but at the same time pursued two interconnected aims: narrowing the consumer gap between the privileged middle classes and the rest of society, and increasing a sense of gratitude towards the all-providing regime. In this way, so the KdF leaders argued, the *Volksgemeinschaft* could be placed on a solid footing. The Italian Fascists, given their more limited resources, their primitive consuming public and their scarce presence in the rural south, could not hope to penetrate society in any such way.

The jewel in the crown of the KdF's activities, as well as its principal instrument of self-promotion, was its flotilla of cruise ships, of which there were twelve by the outbreak of the war. Catering to white-collar workers and the labour aristocracy (the cost of the cruises was prohibitive for those further down the scale), these ships visited the Baltic, where the massive island holiday resort of Prora was under construction, as well as the Norwegian fjords and the Mediterranean, including various Italian ports. The nearest Italian equivalent, as we have seen, was the *treni popolari*, though they hardly offered the same quality of experience.[173] It is worth exploring the comparison a little further, however, because appearances can be deceptive.

As the German ships steamed majestically through the Mediterranean, the tour directors and KdF personnel reported consistently on the misbehaviour of some of those on board. As if in reaction to the harsh and repressive regime at home, those on the boats indulged in all sorts of excesses. One of the most notable incidents occurred during a company outing down the Rhine, when the workers got so drunk that they started to smash up the ship that was carrying them. More often it was individual behaviour that was singled out for comment: there were, for instance 'open sexual liaisons on deck and in the lifeboats', frequent drunkenness, and a reluctance to obey the tour guides and keep within the established time schedules. Furthermore, the closer the ships got to Italy, the more critical the reports became. In the harbour at Palermo a passenger refused to remove his hat when the ship's orchestra played the Horst Wessel song. And at Pompeii two German women engaged in 'overly intimate conversation' with two Italian policemen – perhaps they had just been taken to see the famous erotic frescoes. In any case, the light and freedom of the south seemed to have gone to German heads. Perhaps, one tour agent wrote, 'attached women' should be given preference on the Italian trips, 'the rest being given strict education and instruction.'[174] It can come as no surprise to us that women were singled out for criticism.

By contrast, the Italian *treni popolari* seem to have been rather relaxed, family affairs.[175] The passengers' primary emotion was amazement at seeing the sea for the first time, an emotion to be compared with the astonishment of the Spanish villagers on seeing the moving pictures brought to their *pueblo* by the Misiones Pedagógicas. Of course it is important not to jump to conclusions. There were no tour operators' reports in the Italian case, and hard evidence is difficult to come by. But the two experiences do suggest differences – in the type of goods consumed, in the relationship, or lack of it, between individuals and families, and in the very nature of the two regimes.

The KdF had a significant impact on German society. In secret reports on conditions in Nazi Germany, one Socialist informant recounted that the regime's initiatives had met with much approval: 'many comrades who previously had been part of the Friends of Nature now take up the regime's travel offers – there's simply no other option'.[176]

6. Private life

Turning now to Nazism's determination to push in on families, it is important to note that at the highest level of the law the private sphere was no longer recognised. In January 1937 the Prussian administrative high court ruled that 'in the struggle for self-preservation which the German people are waging there are no longer any aspects of life which are non-political'.[177]

This legal formulation, with its overtones of a hyper-politicised and activist public sphere, was to be transmitted by the Nazis into everyday German family life in the 1930s. The key figure here was Gertrud Scholtz-Klink, who held overall responsibility for women's organisations in the Third Reich, and who had been appointed *Reichsfrauenführerin* by Hitler in 1934. The Nazi Party was essentially a *Männerbund*, an organisation of men, but Scholtz-Klink did not let this deter her. Her principal target was the millions of mothers and wives who constituted the pivotal figures in German families. She entreated them to 'say to yourselves, "The tiny individual self [*Ich*] must submit to the great you [*Du*] which is the People" '.[178] Scholtz-Klink did not want to pull these women out from their homes and their duties, however. Rather, she wanted to influence them *where they were*. 'Take it from me,' she told the American historian Claudia Koonz many years later, 'you have to reach them where their lives are – endorse their decisions, praise their accomplishments. Start with the cradle and the ladle. That's what we did.'[179] The British historian

Tim Mason captured this element of Nazi strategy perfectly when he wrote of the Nazi campaign to 'ennoble the natural and the every-day'.[180] The Nazis could not change the status and nature of women's work at home, but they could and did offer a different, glowing account of it, instrumental and highly convincing. Far from being the 'stinking' site of women's oppression, as Lenin had maintained, the kitchen was the place where the wife and mother could realise her innermost being.

Especially after the First World War, German domestic cleanliness was elevated to a nationalist myth.[181] We have already caught glimpses of its evocation in the new housing estates of the Weimar Republic, with their female patrols and inspections. In the 1930s the Nazis played even more effectively on this theme. They underlined the peculiarity and superiority of German domestic life, in contrast to the dirt and bad habits of the Jews from the East, the Roma and the Poles. Domestic cleaning and racial cleansing went hand in hand. How many times were curtains to be rinsed during washing? Was mopping enough, or were floors to be waxed and polished as well? How often were bed sheets to be changed? How white could good Aryan housewives get their linen – was it 'snow white', or 'sparkling white', or some other sort of white?[182]

One well-known example of the linking of Aryan domestic life and the Nazi regime was the introduction of a weekly 'stew day'. On Sundays housewives all over Germany prepared a nourishing but economical stew, the *Eintopf*, or 'one pot meal', which often took the place of the weekly 'family roast'. The money saved – usually just a few pfennigs – went to the Nazi Winter Aid Programme for the poor and unemployed. Christmas Day was another very important ritual in which families were encouraged to welcome the symbols of the regime into their homes. Little swastika flags adorned the Christmas tree, and Hitler's photograph was displayed in a prominent position.[183]

If the official figures cited by Mason are to be believed, by the mid-1930s the Frauenwerk (Nazi Women's Bureau) had between six and eight million members, which made it the largest non-compulsory organisation in the whole Reich. The link between homes, families and the regime had been successfully forged. In one of his most scathing and effective remarks, Hitler told Hermann Rauschning in 1939, 'Our socialism is much deeper than Marxism [...] What do we care about income? Why should we need to socialise the banks and the factories? We are socialising the people.'[184]

Socialisation went hand in hand with surveillance and repression, not just in the vast area of 'non-approved' families, but also among those whose racial credentials were impeccable. As in the other regimes examined in this book, snooping, spying and denunciation were the order of the day. An array of minor figures, such as the *Blockwart* (block warden) and the Nazi welfare worker, reported on individual and family behaviour. Robert Ley, the organisational director of the National Socialists, once declared, 'The only people who still have a private life in Germany are those who are asleep.' This was untrue, on at least two counts. The first, as Peukert has noted, was that people went on dreaming about the regime even when asleep. The second was that the totalitarian programme, even in Germany, the country most suitable for it in physical, cultural and economic terms, was never completed. It is certainly true that in Germany underlying traits of obedience and submission to authority, so often and rightly emphasised, were far more developed than in Italy, but this by no means meant that private life had disappeared.[185]

7. 'Decadent' art and its Nazi counterpart: portrayals of the family

As the organisations and pretensions of the Nazi *Volksgemeinschaft* grew in number and intensity, so too did the need to create different and novel images that captured the essence of its component parts. The family was one of these. Naturally, images of the family could be transmitted in more than one medium, of which film was certainly the most novel and intriguing. Here as in other chapters, however, I shall concentrate upon artistic production, trying to compare elements of Weimar art with what came after it, and Nazi artistic production with that of Italian Fascism.

The social art of the Weimar period, and in particular those artists who identified themselves with the movement Neue Sachlichkeit (New Objectivity), sought to represent Weimar society in all its light and shade, not just through images of an elegant and prosperous elite. As Wieland Schmied has written,

> The important thing was to look at what was there outside the window, on the asphalt, along the street (and down the drain), on the factory floor and in the shipyard, in operating-theaters and brothels, in allotments, in a rail-crossing cottage or a contented hovel, along the washing line perspectives of a tenement courtyard [...] capturing the flavour of their time, tasting its excess and poverty, its prodigality and despair, its revolt and its trivial amusement.[186]

Artists such as George Grosz and Otto Dix focused their attention upon the more turbid and disquieting elements of life in the metropolis (although Dix also frequently portrayed his parents). They had no intention of embracing in their work the classical canons of women's beauty; on the contrary, they often depicted the female body in grotesque forms, either too fat or too thin, too pendulous or too skeletal. Grosz in particular developed through his painting a searing criticism of Weimar society. In his famous *Die Stützen der Gesellschaft* (The Pillars of Society, 1926), various archetypes of Berlin society are held up for ridicule – the journalist with a chamber pot on his head, the Social Democrat with steaming excrement taking the place of his brain, the mono-cled student with a Nazi tie, the red-nosed, alcoholic priest (plate 8). Other artists such as Käthe Kollwitz chose subjects from working-class districts, concentrating upon depicting the plight of women and their children.

There are very few portraits of families as such, but one of considerable interest is Max Beckmann's *Familienbild* (Family Portrait) of 1920 (plate 10). Here the family finds itself enclosed in a single room, perhaps an attic, a typical victim of post-war urban overcrowding. The atmosphere is claustrophobic, the occupants less in danger than those trapped within the space of Picasso's *Guernica*, but even more cooped up. What is striking about Beckmann's portrayal of the family is how extremely *individualist* it is. There are six people in this tiny space, each one trying desperately to do his or her own thing. The young girl with her back to us, clad only in her corset and chemise, is getting ready to dress up and go out. On her right is an older female figure, probably the grandmother, sitting at the table with a hand covering her eyes. Perhaps she is tired of reading, perhaps she is averting her gaze from the exuberant female form so close to her. Three of the six people are reading, or trying to, including a little boy under the table. His mother is sitting with her back to the wall, an elbow on the table, surveying the scene. The general atmosphere conveyed by Beckmann's family group is one of barely contained tensions and difficulties, exacerbated by post-war deprivations. It does not look much like a modern family, but it is.[187]

The contrast with a celebrated piece of Nazi art, Adolf Wissel's *Kalenberger Bauernfamilie* (Peasant Family from Kalenberg) of 1939 (plate 11), is very striking. Wissel's painting was much liked by Hitler, who ordered it to be hung in the Reich Chancellery. The difference between it and Beckmann's work is not just one of setting (rural versus urban), or even space, with the gentle slope of the Kalenberg hill (Lower Saxony) opening up the distance behind the seated family. It is rather that here the family is presented as a harmoniously united group, not a collection of individuals or variously interrelated persons. It is an organic unit, the very core of the *Volksgemeinschaft*. Each family member has his or her role and position. The father gazes away from his own family, conveying strongly the impression that he will have to leave, sooner or later, to fulfil his destiny as a German soldier. The mother casts her eyes down-wards as she embraces her daughter. The son sits on his father's knee, holding a toy horse and looking straight out at us. Soon he will join the Jungvolk. The picture has a solemn, ordered, even doomed air, very different from the frazzled but vital atmosphere of Beckmann's family group.

Both Hitler and Goebbels, with their late romantic, *völkisch* tastes and preferences, took a particular delight in denouncing what they called 'entartete Kunst', or degenerate art, and tried to lay down rules for what should or should not be painted. Families were an obvious target. In January 1937 the Art Council of the Reich announced,

According to the Office of Racial Policy of the NSDAP, there are many images appearing today in the public eye that still show the German family pictured with one or two children. National Socialism is vigorously combating the two-child system, because it is leading to the irremediable downfall of the German people [. . .] Artists, especially painters and commercial artists, should set themselves the task of depicting [. . .] at least four German children whenever a 'family' is portrayed.[188]

On 18 July 1937 the *Great German Art* exhibition opened in Munich. More than five hundred artists showed 1,200 works, but what was presented as the 'expression of a new era' was in reality a third-rate rendering of conventional historical scenes, landscapes and 'acceptable' nudes. Leni Riefensthal, the film maker responsible for *The Triumph of the Will*, admitted to being embarrassed by the show, with its depiction of Hitler as a knight on horseback and another dozen heroic and allegorical portraits of the Führer.[189] The opening of this exhibition was followed the day after by another major show in Munich, this time dedicated to 'degenerate art', in which six hundred works were crammed into nine rooms. Visitors were encouraged to express their disgust at what they saw.

The contrast with the attitudes of the Italian regime is striking. As we have seen, one of Mussolini's astute cultural and political choices was that of conceding a considerable level of artistic freedom. Although Fascism carefully regulated the Italian art world, confining it to the control of the corporative state, it also celebrated the artistic vanguard, and Futurism in particular. In its major public commissions the regime often chose the modernist language of Mario Sironi in preference to more traditional approaches.

Nazism, by contrast, intervened without scruple. It took total control of art production. Very many painters lost their teaching jobs, the majority of museum directors were replaced by party hacks, and thousands of works, including those of foreign artists, were confiscated and a great number of them destroyed.

8. Pro-natalism and welfare for the racially approved

What sort of welfare state was created by the Nazis? If we compare it for a moment to that of Weimar, its peculiar menace becomes clear. The Weimar welfare regime, as we have seen, was far from perfect, especially when viewed through the eyes of gypsies or immigrant eastern Jews (*Ostjuden*). In the Nazi case, however, the habitual dividing lines of residual, occupational and universalist welfare systems did not apply at all. Non-approved families were not eligible for any welfare at all, not even for residual aid. Alcoholics, tramps, homosexuals, prostitutes, the 'work-shy' or the 'asocial', habitual criminals, the hereditarily ill and members of 'alien races' were all excluded. By contrast, the regime tried to offer Aryan families a combination of self-help strategies and universalist services, intended to serve as a crucial solvent of class and occupational differences in the construction of the *Volksgemeinschaft*. This sinister mixture of exclusion, derived from 'racial hygiene', and hyper-inclusion, based on the creation of a people's community, was unique.

For Hitler's regime, as for Mussolini's and Franco's, pro-natal policies were a key element of welfare, in terms of increasing both the quantity and the quality of the national population.[190] The instruments available to them can be divided, as we have seen, into three major groupings: economic incentives and rewards, either to individuals or to families; the creation of special agencies or programmes; and the punishment of practices which in any way threatened the nation's fertility. In the German context, economic incentives and rewards principally took the form of special provisions for large families, marriage loans, tax deductions, godparent schemes and prizes for hyper-productive mothers. If we take the case of large families, the Nazis were alone in distinguishing between generically *Grossfamilien* (large families) and those that were *kinderreich* (literally 'child-rich'), a term reserved for describing 'hereditarily healthy', 'racially valuable' and politically and socially responsible families. Hitler was a great believer in the virtues of 'child-rich' families in cultural as well as demographic terms. He told his captive audience at dinner one evening that 'if we had practised the system of two-children families in the old days, Germany would have been deprived of her greatest geniuses'.[191] Mozart was the youngest of seven children, Bach was the eighth of twelve, and Schubert was the twelfth of fourteen. Economic incentives to *kinderreich* families took two forms: *one-off* child supplements to families which had four or more children under the age of sixteen, in the form of coupons which could be used to buy household goods; and *continuous* child benefit in cash to families with at least five children. By 1941, the Nazi state had spent 325 million Reichsmarks on one-off grants to 1.1 million such families and 600,000 Reichsmarks on continuous supplements to 2.5 million families. These were considerable investments, but the scheme was marred by at least two factors: first, the families in question were overwhelmingly rural while the real problem with the birth rate lay in the cities; and, secondly, it was far from easy to distinguish between 'worthy' and 'unworthy' large families, a great many of which were in any case very often poor and deprived. The bureaucracy generated by the scheme, and its complicated series of distinctions, were typical of the Nazi state.[192]

In the case of marriage loans, the German initiative of 1 June 1933, as we have seen, preceded the Italian one of 21 August 1937, and was immeasurably more effective. The number of German loans for the period 1938–40 alone was 817,060, far higher than the Italian figure of 157,989 for the same period. The German scheme provided for the granting of an interest-free loan of 600–1,000 marks, to be paid, like one-off child supplements, in the form of vouchers for the purchase of furniture, sheets and other domestic goods. The idea behind the vouchers was to stimulate the severely depressed domestic demand for household goods of this sort. All applicants were subjected to careful racial and social screening. Once approved, funding was copious and administered directly by the Ministry of Finance. The loan was scaled down for each child born and cancelled completely after the fourth. The German scheme, unlike the Italian one, at first stipulated that women beneficiaries had compulsorily to cease working outside the home. With the coming of full employment this measure was abandoned in 1937. It is also highly significant that in Germany all state benefits, including child supplements and marriage loans, were paid directly to the male head of household, not to women. This was different from Britain, Sweden, Norway and in part also France. In November 1937 a Nazi minister, Hans Frank, underlined that 'the concept of fatherhood has been handed down through the age-old processes of natural law [. . .] and must be placed at the centre of the financial measures [of the family]'.[193]

The second pillar of pro-natal welfare policies was the creation of special agencies or programmes, most often dedicated to combating infant mortality and to improving the conditions of maternity. We have already examined the case of ONMI in Italy. The equivalent German agency was the NSV Hilfswerk 'Mutter und Kind' (National Socialist People's Welfare 'Mother and Child' Aid Programme), created in 1934. The agency numbered among its activities assistance for poor mothers after birth, including the lodging of a small percentage of the deserving and politically loyal in recuperation homes; increased welfare services for small children, the number of day nurseries rising from approximately 1,000 in 1935 to 15,000 in 1941; and health and advice centres for families, of which there were a staggering 28,936 by 1941.[194]

The third and final group of policies were those which impeded and severely punished practices which threatened pro-natalism. Abortion was severely punished by the Penal Code, although there is evidence of large numbers of abortions still taking place in the Nazi years, in both city and countryside.[195] Special taxes were levied on adults who remained obstinately celibate or who formed a childless couple. As we have seen, divorce was made easier in 1938, with the aim of facilitating separations among non-reproductive couples. Finally, unique in all the countries under consideration was Himmler's Public Ordinance of 1941, which banned the production and distribution of contraceptives.

There were, of course, a number of important welfare agencies that were linked not to pro-natal schemes but rather to the absolute necessity of aiding poor Aryan families at a time of extreme stress. The Winterhilfswerk (Winter Aid Programme for the German People), founded in September 1933, was one of these. It tried to combat, on a massive scale, the unemployment and destitution still very prevalent in Germany at the time. With the onset of winter in 1933 an estimated 1.5 million volunteers and 4,000 paid workers were to be found ladling out soup at emergency centres, distributing food parcels to families and collecting donations. During the winter of 1933–4 some 358 million Reichsmarks were collected, a small but significant proportion of which had been provided by the scheme of Sunday 'stew days'. Badges and other gadgets were on sale at street corners and adorned Christmas trees. Giving to the Winter Aid Programme was not an optional extra, but was heavily enforced in the streets and house to house by the presence of the SA brown shirts. With the Winter Aid Law of December 1936, the programme became a permanent feature of Nazi welfare.[196]

If we survey in comparative perspective the sweep of Nazi social policy between 1933 and the onset of the war, a rather mixed picture emerges. On the one hand, there can be no denying the dynamism of the Nazis, in this sphere as in others. Erich Hilgenfeldt, a close collaborator of Joseph Goebbels, moved rapidly between March and July of 1933 to bring all welfare measures under the central control of the National Socialist People's Welfare, Magda Goebbels accepting the role of the organisation's first patron. All private welfare activities, including the Catholic, Protestant and Social Democratic organisations, fell under the control of the Nazis. While they continued to exist in name, only the Nazi central organisation received funding from the state. In the space of a few months, therefore, the complex structure of German welfare institutions had been radically transformed. A single state organisation now existed for a single people's community.

The National Socialist People's Welfare was a far broader and more effective organisation than anything the Italian Fascists could muster. The comparative statistics for marriage loans speak for themselves. So too do the nearly 30,000 health and advice centres for families that were available in Germany by 1941 (if the official statistics are to be believed). Similarly, the Hilfswerk 'Mutter und Kind' organisation boasted much greater resources and more copious initiatives than did ONMI, which was heavily reliant on already existing structures and unable to reach a large part of the Italian peninsula.

On the other hand, in the key area of demographic growth the Nazi record has to be counted a failure. It has often been pointed out that only Germany and the Soviet Union succeeded in reversing negative fertility rates in the 1930s. For both states, however, the victory was tenuous and temporary. Between 1933 and 1936 birth rates rose in Germany, but they were then to stagnate for the remaining years of peace and to decline during the war.[197] Moreover, the overall figures mask individual failures. The families that had been formed with the help of marriage loans subsequently produced an average of only one child per family. And the numbers of large, 'child-rich' families so dear to the regime actually declined between 1933 and 1941. For all their bravado and bullying, the Nazis could not get the German people, in the privacy of their homes, to do what they wanted them to do.

The comparison with Weimar welfare is complex and revealing. There were obvious points of contact between the two, principally in the areas of hygiene, racial or otherwise, and surveillance. But Weimar could boast a housing programme which was far more extensive than that of the Nazis. In the decade between 1928 and 1938, spending on housing, so fundamental an area of welfare for the whole of this period, declined by more than five times. Weimar social planners and workers, whatever their prejudices and limitations, aimed to provide some residual welfare for the country's poor. For the Nazis, by contrast, discrimination was all. Those who lay outside the *Volksgemeinschaft* were simply better dead.

IV. THE REGIME AT WAR

There are many aspects to what Hans Mommsen has called the 'cumulative radicalisation' which characterises the Nazi experience from 1939 onwards.[198] The Third Reich expanded dramatically, to become – at least in the denomination of its creators – the 'Grossdeutsches Reich' (Great German Reich), a huge land empire of annexed and occupied territories spreading across Europe. In it, the Nazi distinction between *Menschenführung* (leadership of men) and mere *Verwaltung* (administration) was used with ever greater frequency to

justify the most callous and arbitrary of actions, aimed at realising the enslave-
ment and elimination of subjugated populations. The Nazi state itself fragmented and changed its physiognomy, as new, semi-autonomous, corrupt and
ruthless 'chieftains' in command of the conquered territories vied with the old
guard for power and the Führer's ear. The racial state could now be brought
into being. Before the invasion of Poland Hitler told his generals, 'I have put
my Death's Head formations at the ready with the command to send man,
woman and child of Polish descent and language to their deaths, pitilessly and
remorselessly [. . .] Poland will be depopulated and settled with Germans.'[199]
On 10 October 1939 he confided to Goebbels that the Poles were 'more
animals than men, totally dull and formless [. . .] The dirt of the Poles is
unimaginable.'[200]

In the final section of this chapter I would like to examine, with particular
reference to Germany itself, the ways in which the radicalisation of the Nazi
regime affected three major groupings of families: the approved, Aryan families of the Nazi homelands; those of 'lesser racial value' – the 'feeble-minded',
'schizophrenic', 'asocial', and so on; and finally the 'racially alien', especially the
Jews and gypsies. All three groups suffered terribly in the war, the fundamental
difference being that the first supported to the bitter end the perpetrators of so
much violence while the other two were their victims.

1. Aryan heartlands

For the first grouping, the approved, Aryan families of the Nazi homelands, the
war had been long expected, if not always long desired. The whole organisation
of Nazi society as well as its most profound beliefs were oriented towards war,
which became the motor force not only of the economy but of the nation's very
identity. At its apex, as in the positioning of Harald Quandt in the Goebbels
family photograph, stood the young, blond German male, upon whose shoulders rested the destiny of the nation. In 1936, Karl Beyer, in his well-known
book *Familie und Frau im neuen Deutschland* (Woman and Family in the New
Germany), had already made the division of roles within the family very clear,
albeit in semi-mystic, chivalrous form: 'In the natural vision of life, the hearth
constitutes the sacred centre. The wife's task is to protect the domestic flame,
from which there emerges the secret life of the people's sons [. . .] The man
takes his shield and uses it to protect home and hearth.'[201]

This gender divide can be extended to embrace the emotions. Young
German men were for the most part excited by the prospect of proving themselves in combat. If they were sad to leave their families (and many were), they
were also anxious to get to the front. Very many wives and mothers, by

contrast, mourned the departure of their menfolk, regretting war while acknowledging its necessity. A huge volume of correspondence was exchanged between German soldiers and their families in the years 1939–45. While most of it went from the home front to the battle front rather than in the other direction, many more of the soldiers' letters have been preserved, those of their families often being lost in the dislocations and fatalities of war.[202]

In the first two years of the war, with its astounding German victories, Aryan families accepted and celebrated as never before the full flowering of the Nazi *Volksgemeinschaft*. The Wehrmacht's triumphal march was sweet revenge indeed for 1918 and the terrible years that had followed. Things began to change only with the Russian campaign, as it became obvious that victory there was not going to be won so easily, if at all. It was also true that in 1941/2 many German men left their own families to become the butchers of other, totally innocent families that had been deemed racially 'alien'. In Christopher Browning's chilling record of German police reservists called upon to be killers, one policeman writes home to his wife from Upper Silesia in the summer of 1941. He is proud to have made a film of the execution of partisans, and wishes to show it to his children when he returns home. But he asks his wife, with some residual sense of shame, to say nothing to their oldest son about what his battalion is doing to Jewish family groups.[203] When Wehrmacht soldiers came home on leave from Russia in the spring and summer of 1942, Goebbels thought it necessary to warn families what to expect. In a newspaper article of 26 July 1942 he wrote that 'the [soldiers'] uncompromising opinions about the war' might very well produce 'points of friction' with 'life at home'. It was necessary for families to 'live up' to the brutal face of the war.[204]

On the home front, Victor Klemperer, the Jewish university professor of literature from Dresden, noted in his extraordinary diary in June and September of 1941 that an increasing number of people in the shops were no longer greeting each other with 'Heil Hitler' but were reverting to the neutral 'guten Morgen'.[205] A rumour was circulating that a married couple in Ammonstrasse had just heard that all four of their sons had been killed in Russia. 'The father hangs himself, the mother hurls the picture of Hitler out of the window into the courtyard. Half an hour later she is arrested.'[206] Whether the story was true or not, it was highly significant that it was circulating.

Most important of all was the fact that the regime was never able to mobilise women sufficiently for the war. Here, it can safely be said, the Nazis were hoist with their own petard. For years they had preached the innate superiority of the German gender model over the Soviet one, and the necessity for women to put the family first. Now they could hardly complain if women took these instructions seriously. In 1939 the regime tried to redress the balance: employed women were forbidden to leave their jobs because they were urgently needed for the war economy. Pregnant women were exempted, however, a provision which produced a minor baby boom. Between 1939 and 1941 the number of employed German women actually decreased.[207] In the early years of the war the Nazi leadership continued to debate whether or not to enforce female labour conscription. Feedback from the cities was discouraging. In May 1941, in Dresden, of 1,250 women invited (!) to a labour recruitment meeting only 600 turned up and only 120 said they were prepared to take up employment. These were hardly the actions or the statistics of a 'totalitarian' regime. The same picture was noted for Dortmund. Female labour conscription was made law only in January 1943, and even then initially only for women aged seventeen to forty-five. Many exemptions were permitted.[208]

As the Allies began to bomb German cities heavily, the disillusionment with the Nazis became much stronger and families' opposition more clearly stated, at least privately. The evacuation of children from the major cities had already begun on a considerable scale early on in the war. After the Hamburg bombings of October 1943 families increasingly sought to lodge their children with rural relatives so as to avoid consigning them to Nazi-organised camps. In either case, both children and parents suffered greatly from the deep uncertainties of these enforced separations. Goebbels was highly alarmed by the offensive from the air, writing in his diary on 1 September 1943, 'It is mainly due to the British aerial terror that in broad swaths of the German public there is scepticism about victory.'[209] Scepticism, however, never turned into open opposition. In this Germany differed from Italy, where the strikes of northern industrial workers, first in March 1943 and then on a more massive scale a year later, made a great impression upon both Mussolini and Hitler.[210]

2. 'Euthanasia' and the Catholic Church

On 1 September 1939 Hitler issued an order for the killing of all persons with incurable diseases. Sterilisation had been termed the 'prevention of unworthy life', and the new policy went by the name of the 'annihilation of unworthy life', or 'euthanasia', or 'action T4'. Questionnaires were sent to mental hospitals, on the basis of which a doctors' committee selected the victims within each institution. Families were notified that their relatives had died from commonplace illnesses and that they had been cremated. Among the first victims of these killings were 5,000 handicapped children up to the age of three. By 1945 at least 70,000 women and men, mentally ill, old and handicapped, had been selected for death. Their removal was justified on the grounds that it cleared much-needed space in the hospitals and enabled the regime to eliminate what it called 'useless eaters'.[211]

Only the pusillanimity of the Churches' previous behaviour could have led Hitler to believe that there would be little reaction to his edict. What was supposed to be a well-kept secret rapidly became a major national scandal: mentally retarded patients who had been regularly visited by their families suddenly disappeared; others had 'appendicitis' written on their death certificates when they had had their appendix removed years previously. A family revolt accompanied every fresh revelation. This sense of outrage found no political outlet, however. For nearly two years the clergy – both Catholic and Protestant – limited themselves to writing confidential protests to various Reich ministries. Finally, Clemens August von Galen, the Catholic bishop of Münster, decided to speak out publicly. In a sermon of 3 August 1941 von Galen recounted in detail what had been happening:

> If it is once accepted that people have the right to kill 'unproductive' fellow humans – and even if initially it only affects the poor defenceless mentally ill – then as a *matter of principle* murder is permitted of all unproductive people, in other words for the incurably sick, the people who have become invalids through labour and war, for us all when we become old, frail and therefore unproductive.[212]

Thousands of copies of the sermon were printed and distributed secretly. The Nazi leadership was furious but impotent. Some of its members wanting the bishop hanged immediately. Goebbels advised caution: if the bishop was killed, he said, Münster would be lost for the rest of the war and probably the whole of Westphalia as well. Less than a month later, Hitler ordered that the 'euthanasian' killings should be stopped, at least temporarily. Without wishing to claim powers for civil society which it did not have, Hitler's rapid volte-face does reveal how much more might have been achieved had the Christian Churches behaved in a less complicit fashion. After a period of restraint, the killings resumed.[213] Another 100,000 people defined as of 'lesser racial value' were killed by 1945, and there are no reliable statistics for similar 'annihilations of unworthy life' in Poland and the Soviet Union.

3. Genocide

The number of Jews living in Germany in 1933 was 499,682, some 0.77 per cent of a total population of 65.2 million. Many of them fled the country in the next six years but by September 1939 185,000 still remained. It may appear incredible to us, with the benefit of hindsight, that so many were prepared to stay in the face of imminent destruction. There were many reasons for doing so: it was difficult for adult children to abandon aging and incredulous parents who refused to budge; many of the older generation refused to leave their businesses unattended; German Jews refused to turn their backs on their country; while others were convinced that the regime would crumble before the decade was out. By the late 1930s the growing impoverishment of those left in the Jewish communities of the major cities made it difficult to escape in any case. It must also be said that the Nazi bureaucratic machine, in its long journey towards liquidating the Jews, was certainly 'radically cumulative' but also slow-moving and ponderous. Major laws of 1933 and 1935 had transformed and degraded the German Jews, but strange areas of non-intervention remained. For instance, it was only in March 1936 that family allowances for large Jewish families were stopped – an incredibly late decision for a racially based state.[214] Only in July 1938 were approximately 3,000 Jewish doctors stopped from practising their profession. Everything accelerated terribly after the *Reichskristallnacht*, the Night of the Broken Glass, of 9–10 November 1938. Even so, Klemperer could still be found noting as late as the summer of 1941 that Jews had just been forbidden to use the steamers on the Elbe.[215]

In the end, with the adoption of the Final Solution, the whole drawn-out process assumed its most terrible form. Saul Friedländer has established a three-part periodisation for the relationship between the Nazi regime and the Jews in the war years: Terror, from the autumn of 1939 to the summer of 1941, Mass Murder, from the summer of 1941 to the summer of 1942, and Shoah from the summer of 1942 to the spring of 1945.[216] When the remainder of the German Jews and, in far more massive numbers, those from the conquered territories were rounded up and deported to the extermination camps. A survivor of one of these, Helen Kopmann, from Warsaw, recalled her journey of deportation: 'I held my little brother in my arms all night in the freezing boxcar. All around people cried and moaned. I just held him and held him. He was sick and lay very quietly. Then I realised he had stopped breathing. For the first time it became clear to me. I said to myself, "Hitler *wants* us to die. He intends to *kill* us." '[217]

Helen Kopmann was absolutely right. A very conscious decision had been taken to destroy all members of Jewish families, regardless of gender or age. In his 6 October 1943 address to the Nazi Gauleiters, Heinrich Himmler asked,

> How is it with the women and children? I have taken the decision to achieve a clear solution also in this matter. I did not consider that I had the right to eliminate the men – that is to kill them or to have them killed – and to let

their children grow up to become the avengers against our own sons and grandsons. The difficult decision had to be taken to have this people disappear from the face of the earth.[218]

The Nazis were not so sure of their ground in taking this 'difficult decision', however, as to want to publicise openly what they were doing. On the contrary, they went to elaborate lengths to suppress all information about the killings. Among the items most often confiscated from German Jews as they were herded on to deportation trains were blank postcards and postage stamps. At Würzburg on 24 March 1942 the authorities confiscated 358 six-pfennig postcards, 142 six-pfennig stamps and 273 twelve-pfennig stamps before sending deportees to their deaths.[219]

On arrival at the camps, the procedures were not always the same. In extermination camps such as Auschwitz family members were separated from each other immediately and heart-rendingly, most often forever. Able-bodied adult men were marched away to one labour camp, healthy women aged between sixteen and forty-five to another. All the rest – young people under the age of sixteen, all mothers in charge of children and all the elderly and frail – were sent to the gas chambers immediately.

Family relations could not survive a selection procedure of this sort. There were extraordinary exceptions but they were very few in number. It none the less remains true that the women in the camps, as Jane Caplan has written, 'more often responded to the unending inhumanity and atrocity of camp existence by developing closer friendships than men did, building circles of intimacy that also offered some substitute for the agonising absence of their families [. . .] Women's memoirs [have] recourse to an unselfconscious imagery of family that came less easily to men.'[220]

It is worth pausing for a moment to consider the two so-called 'family' camps which were established at Auschwitz in these terrible months. The first of these was for another 'racially inferior' element, the gypsies (Roma). On arrival at Auschwitz from February 1943 onwards, gypsies were not immediately selected for either forced labour or the gas chambers. Rather they were placed in the newly built 'gypsy family camp', called such because entire family groups were allowed to stay together.[221] The gypsy family camp, which had an intake of some 23,000 men, women and children, survived for nearly a year and a half. Conditions were appalling, with typhus rife and hospital blocks 'indescribable in their filth and suffering'. Even so, the chance for families to remain together was one which inmates in other parts of the camp complex often envied a great deal. The gypsies also enjoyed 'privileges' such as being allowed to play musical instruments and form small bands to which the SS

fig. 50 A family group, reduced to only grandmother and three grandchildren, on their
way to the gas chambers at the Auschwitz-Birkenau railway terminal, May–June 1944,
photograph by SS guards E. Hoffmann and B. Walter.

guards listened willingly. Guenter Lewy has written, 'In the scale of misery that
characterised life in the death factory of Auschwitz, the gypsy family camp did
not represent the worst that was possible.'[222] The gypsies' different status in the
camp complex did not save them, however. Around 5,600 were eventually
killed in gas chambers, 3,500 were moved to other camps, and the remaining
14,000 died from disease, or in medical experiments, or were murdered by the
guards.

There was a second family camp at Auschwitz, established in September
1943 for about 18,000 Jews from Theresienstadt.[223] Its history is instructive not
just for Nazi actions but for the pusillanimity of the International Red Cross at
Geneva. The Nazis were concerned about a possible Red Cross control visit to
Auschwitz, and therefore constructed a sham camp in which the inmates wore
civilian clothes, families were kept together and every day some five hundred
children were sent for singing and games to another part of the camp. In the
event, the Red Cross inspector Maurice Rossel, having visited Theresienstadt,
which was not an extermination camp and had been brushed up for the

occasion, decided that the journey to Auschwitz was not necessary. The grounds for this decision are not known. Rossel wrote to the German functionary in charge of his visit thanking him for the hospitality: 'The journey to Prague will remain a magnificent memory for us and I am pleased to assure you that [. . .] the report of our visit to Theresienstadt will serve as a reassurance for many, given that the living conditions [in the camp] are satisfactory.'[224] In July 1944, once the danger of a visit had passed, the inmates of the Auschwitz family camp were liquidated.

4. Foreign labour

It is also important to mention a last and often forgotten social group present on German soil during the war – foreign labour from the conquered territories employed in war production. This was a huge and heterogeneous body, comprising some three million such workers by the summer of 1941 and some 7.7 million by the autumn of 1944. A minority had come voluntarily, some were young women, but overwhelmingly these were men who had been forcibly removed from their homes and families and transported to Germany. Their Nazi masters carefully graded them by race and nation, in a hierarchy that put Danes at the top and Russians at the bottom. It was a paradox of Nazi strategic aims that Germany itself, instead of becoming ever more Aryan and Germanic as the war progressed, became ever less so. One German woman from Hamburg noted in her diary in the spring of 1943 that in the presence of so many foreign workers there was 'a confused Babel of languages wherever you hear people speaking.'[225] Ferocious punishments were meted out to any foreign worker who had sexual relations with a German woman, even a prostitute, and some six hundred foreign prostitutes were drafted in to meet the sexual needs of foreign workers. At the same time German women were threatened with public humiliation and the shaving of their heads if they took foreign lovers. Even so, with such massive numbers involved, it was impossible to prevent 'dangerous liaisons' occurring. The Security Service of the SS reported despairingly that at least 20,000 illegitimate children had been born to German women, and that the threat to the racial purity of the German people was constantly increasing.[226]

5. The end and a beginning

By the early spring of 1945 the position of the Third Reich had become desperate. The Wehrmacht had been forced back deep into German territory and the end of the war was considered to be only a few weeks away. Joseph

Goebbels and his wife Magda now faced momentous decisions. Since the halcyon days of their trip to Italy in June 1933 their marriage had had its ups and downs, particularly as a result of Goebbels's serial infidelities and his serious infatuation with the Czech film star Lída Baarová. On that occasion Hitler had had to step in, making it clear that the archetype of the Aryan family which they had, in a manner of speaking, constructed together could not be broken up; he threatened Goebbels with permanent disgrace. The Minister of Propaganda duly ended his affair.

Every day that passed saw Hitler less and less in control of the situation and of himself. On 16 April 1945 the Soviet army launched its final assault on Berlin. Goebbels moved into Hitler's headquarters in the bunker deep beneath the Reich Chancellery. In an act of extreme loyalty – to both her husband and her Führer – Magda decided not only to accompany Goebbels but also, with Hitler's approval, to bring their children. On 28 April Goebbels wrote to Magda's son Harald, who had been taken prisoner:

> We are now confined to the Führer's bunker in the *Reich* Chancellery and are fighting for our lives and our honour [. . .] You may well be the only one able to continue our family tradition [. . .] You may be proud of having such a mother as yours. Yesterday the *Führer* gave her the Golden Party Badge which he has worn on his tunic for years and she deserved it [. . .] Farewell my dear Harald. Whether we shall ever see each other again is in the lap of the gods. If we do not, may you always be proud of having belonged to a family which, even in misfortune, remained loyal to the very end to the *Führer* and his pure and sacred cause.[227]

That same day Magda herself wrote to Harald for the last time:

> It is six days by now that we have been in the *Führerbunker*, all of us, Papa, your small brother, your five little sisters and I, so as to give our National Socialist life the only possible and honourable end. I don't know whether this letter will ever reach you, but perhaps there is a human soul after all, enabling me to send you these, my last greetings. I want you to know that it was against Papa's will that I have decided to stay with him, and that even last Sunday the *Führer* still wished to help us to get out of here [. . .] The world to come after the *Führer* and after National Socialism will not be worth living in, and that is why I have taken the children along with me. They are too good for the sort of life to come after us, and a merciful God will understand my reasons for sparing them that sort of life [. . .]
>
> My darling son, live for Germany![228]

On 30 April 1945, Hitler and Eva Braun, who had married the day before, took their leave of all those who remained in the bunker, retired to their own quarters, and killed themselves. The following day, 1 May, Magda Goebbels accompanied her children to bed early, gave them each a night-time drink which contained a sleeping potion, and poisoned them with cyanide pills while they slept. She and Goebbels then killed themselves.[229] Magda Goebbels's gesture of killing her own children was very atypical of the Nazi elite (no other name comes to mind) but very much in character. There were alternatives – the children could have been left with Joseph's or Magda's relatives. But Magda chose death for them.

In these same days Victor Klemperer and his wife finally began to realise that they would survive the Nazi regime, against all the odds, and be able to make a new beginning. Of the 1,265 Jews who remained in Dresden in late 1941, only 198 were left in February 1945. Klemperer was one of them. The rest had been deported to Riga, Auschwitz or Theresienstadt. Klemperer himself was scheduled to be taken away in a number of days. The fact that he had survived for so long had been owing to his 'mixed marriage' to Eva Schlemmer, a musician from a Protestant family in Königsberg. On the evening of 13 February 1945 the Allied air forces fire-bombed Dresden. The centre of the city and much of the suburbs were completely destroyed, and many thousands of German families were burned to death. Perhaps as many as 35,000 people died. It was to be the most controversial bombing of the war – that is, before Hiroshima and Nagasaki.

Klemperer and his wife survived. All controls over his life – his confinement to the Jews' house, his discriminatory ration card, his imminent deportation – went up in the Dresden flames. He tore off the yellow star of David from his coat, Eva invented a survival plan for them, and travelling on false documents they headed – by foot and by train – to Bavaria, where they hoped that acquaintances would offer them hospitality. They came to rest in the village of Unterbernbach, and there, on 29 April, two days before Magda and Joseph Goebbels killed themselves and their children, Klemperer noted in his diary,

Here, in the late afternoon, a group of three young German soldiers comes hesitatingly, mistrustfully towards us; unarmed, all wearing camouflage capes. One has a map, all three have good faces, undoubtedly from good families, perhaps students. They just managed to escape from Ingolstadt, they want to make their way towards Landsberg, they do not want to be taken prisoner. Were 'the Americans' in the village? [. . .] The three beaten and helpless soldiers were like an allegory of the lost war. And as ardently as we have longed for the loss of the war and as necessary as this loss is for Germany (and truly for mankind) – we nevertheless felt sorry for the boys.[230]

Klemperer's *pietas*, all the more commendable in view of the terrible suffering experienced by German Jews from 1933 onwards, was intermingled with anger and intellectual anguish: how could Nazism have happened? On 5 May, still in the Bavarian countryside, he noted,

And ever more puzzling, despite Versailles, unemployment, and deep-seated anti-Semitism, ever more puzzling to me, is how Hitlerism was able to prevail. Here [. . .] they sometimes talk as if Hitler had been essentially a Prussian, militarist, un-Catholic, un-Bavarian cause. But Munich, after all, was its 'Traditionsgau' – its oldest center. And how was this cause able to win over sceptical and Socialist Berlin and maintain itself there?[231]

We have been seeking answers to these questions ever since.

fig. 51 German women return to the ruins of their homes, Berlin, 10 July 1945. The child is the son of the woman seated on the pavement.

CONCLUSION

Uniquely among the various countries which finished under the tyranny of the great dictators, 1930s Germany saw an attempt by a group of left-wing intellectuals to explain the triumph of such a regime – in this case Nazism – with explicit reference to the family. The *Studien über Autorität und Familie* (Studies on Authority and the Family), a work directed by Max Horkheimer with the collaboration of Erich Fromm, Herbert Marcuse and others, only saw the light of day in Paris in 1936.[232] In fact, from 1933 onwards the 'Frankfurt school', as it came to be known, had been forced to transfer its Institut für Sozialforschung to the French capital and from there to New York. The basic argument of the work was that certain patterns of family formation, especially a particular type of early childhood socialisation, predisposed individuals to support and identify with authoritarian politics. The key relationship in this process was presented as that between father and child, especially the male child. In the German family archetype, as we have seen, the father was all-powerful and his authority all-embracing. Horkheimer quoted Ernst Troeltsch, the great religious historian, to this effect: 'The [male] head of family is the legal representative, the uncontrolled holder of power, the provider, the pastoral caregiver, the priest in his own house.'[233] The child develops in awe and fear of the relentless dominion of so mighty a paternal figure: 'The spiritual world in which he grows up, the fantasy by means of which he animates his reality, his dreams and desires, his ideas and opinions, come to be dominated by the idea of the force exercised by one man over another, by a superior over an inferior, by a system of commands and obedience.'[234]

Given such predispositions, it was easy at a later stage for the adult individual to accept with enthusiasm a politics based on the same codes, language and practices as domestic authoritarian patriarchy. On the one hand the individual swore blind devotion and submission to the Leader, while on the other he enjoyed exercising aggression and cruelty towards those who were weaker than him, both within and outside the home. As Fromm explained, however, the process by which authority imposed itself was, in psychological terms, far from simple:

If external power determines the submissiveness of the masses, it must all the same transform its own quality inside the mind of the individual. The difficulties that arise at that moment are partially resolved by the formation of the super-ego. It is through the super-ego that the external power is transformed, precisely in the movement from the external to the internal sphere. The authorities, in so far as they are representatives of external power, come to be internalised and the individual follows their diktats and prohibitions not only out of fear of external punishment but from fear of the psychical reality that he has created within himself.[235]

The German family, it was argued, had thus played a fundamental role in the rise of Nazism. It provided an over-strong paternal model and a system of subjection based on a gendered contrast between strong and weak, and it led to the creation of an over-powerful and restraining super-ego. Fromm did not hesitate to comment on the 'anal retentiveness' of these authoritarian relations, which encouraged certain types of social behaviour, such as avarice, order, scrupulosity and cleanliness, to the detriment of others. Horkheimer, for his part, did not go quite as far as Trotsky, who in 1923 identified the family as the prime agency of social change. He none the less underlined the family's extraordinary importance in determining social and political attitudes: 'As long as the fundamental structure of social life and the culture of the present era which rests upon it do not radically transform themselves, the family will exert an irreplaceable function as the producer of distinctly authoritarian character types.'[236]

The work of the Frankfurt school was extremely suggestive, but given its nature it could hardly be more than that. Fromm in particular was careful not to make too many claims for it. In the life cycle of an individual, he wrote, the experiences of infancy and adolescence played a far greater part in character formation than those of later years, but, he continued, 'this does not imply that the earliest years *determine* [my italics] character in such a way that successive events can no longer modify it'.[237]

As was to be expected, *Studien über Autorität und Familie* provoked significant debate, although to a far more limited extent in the field of history than in that of psychology. Feminist critics pointed out rightly that the authors had paid hardly any attention to the dyad of mother and child, presenting instead a 'patricentric worldview'.[238] The complex balancing of power in 'das ganze Haus', in which the patriarch's wife had an important role, had not been taken into consideration. Nor had the still more significant problem that the family patterns identified by the Frankfurt school had been present in other parts of rural Europe without necessarily leading to Nazism. The authoritarian personality, in other words, was not only to be found in Germany, whereas Nazism was. In rural Catalonia, as we saw in chapter 4, the patriarchal structure of the large farmhouse – the *masía* or *casa pairal* – the authority relations and the system of inheritance to be found therein all bore great similarities to traditional German patterns. But the Catalonian peasants, though strongly Catholic, were not anti-republican and their regional Church was one of the very few to speak out against the atrocities of the so-called 'crusade'. A similar argument could be made for Italian sharecroppers. Thus, while the connection made by the Frankfurt school between the childhood formation of the authoritarian personality and the eventual triumph of Nazi politics was highly important and innovative, its powers of explanation should on no account be exaggerated. To rush from one extreme – the complete omission of family culture and structure from historical explanation – to the other – endowing it with almost mono-causal status – would not be a good way to proceed.[239]

It was also far from clear whether the authoritarian family was a threat to, or a model for, National Socialism. One of the main bases of Nazi recruiting was generational conflict. Authoritarian fathers, committed to keeping things as they were, had to be challenged and fought – in the village council at Körle, on the streets of Berlin, within the family itself. If the Nazis themselves were the authority, then the family could serve as a model. But if the old conservative or social democratic patriarch was in charge in the private sphere, he had to be opposed and the family's allegiances split.

This brings us to a wider and often-posed question: were the Nazis the friends or the foes of the family? Opinion is rather divided on this issue.[240] My own, rather straightforward view is that they were ferocious enemies of families designated as racially 'alien' or 'inferior', but that for 'good German families' things were very different. The Nazis were in no way prepared to accept the latter as a counter-power, but neither did they in any sense want to destroy or supersede them. Their activist policies, directed primarily at youth, certainly detracted greatly from the amount of time that families could spend together. But the girls of the Bund Deutscher Mädel were not indoctrinated to reject the family. They had rather to recreate it in a regime-approved form. When Ilse Koehn, a Berlin girl, was evacuated with her class in October 1942 to a tiny mountain village called Harrachsdorf, on the Czech side of Riesengebirge, the girls were not on any account allowed to forget their families. Saturday was letter-writing day: 'Pfaffi makes sure that we write home regularly. We are not out of the house until we have shown her a finished letter.'[241] Of course, the letter had to say that everything was near-perfect at Harrachsdorf, but the important point is that its recipient was not the party but a parent.

It is difficult to measure the degree of control over families which was exercised by any of these great tyrannical regimes, but I would be very careful about using the adjective 'totalitarian' to describe them. I shall return to this question in the conclusion to the book. Here it is perhaps sufficient to point out the peculiarities of the German case. Being the most modern of all the nations under examination here, Germany was without doubt the country with the greatest capacity for control in terms of both territory and communications. Goebbels knew these conditions very well and made good use of them. But at the same time Germany's very modernity endowed large sections of the population with considerable individualism in everyday behaviour. If you were on the right side of the race and class barrier it was possible to live out Nazism in relative tranquillity, even in relative freedom and carefully limited dissent. Working-class women's stubborn refusal to be mobilised for the war effort and the damage it did to the regime is perhaps the most striking evidence of these attitudes.

The fact remains, however, that the great majority of the German population espoused the beliefs of the *Volksgemeinschaft*. There were exceptions, and one of Klemperer's friends in Dresden went as far as to say that 'every Jew has his Aryan angel', in as much as some of the city's non-Jewish inhabitants tried to help their utterly humiliated and degraded fellow citizens.[242] But there were never enough of them, nor was their dissent made clear. In the place of civil society, of free associations and free thinking, the Nazis offered only obedience and mobilisation for war, in the pursuit of one of the most evil enterprises of our time. Too many ordinary German families accepted what the Nazis had to offer with enthusiasm.

CHAPTER 6

Stalinism and Soviet families, 1927–1945

My notebook on family politics is now very full, but before closing it I want to bring the story back to its point of departure and return to Russia and the Soviet Union. Here, more than in any other of the national experiences I have examined, the two strands of family history that have most fascinated me intertwine. One comes from below and attempts, often in a confused way, to revolutionise private as well as public life. The other acts from above, seeking in draconian fashion to regiment and control the very structures of society. Stalin's version of this latter combines in an original and terrible way a number of key elements: the language of revolution, the reality of vast social transformation, the practice of Terror, and the 'normalisation' of family life.

I. FAMILY DESTINIES

1. The cost of survival

At various points throughout this book, above all at its beginning, we have caught glimpses of Aleksandra Kollontai, her ideas and her actions: early on, sitting reading in her grandfather's library at Kuusa in Finland; later, in February 1917, on an Oslo tram, staring in disbelief at someone else's newspaper, the headlines of which announced the outbreak of the Russian revolution; then during the Bolshevik revolution of 1917–18, in what might be called the culminating moment of her life; in 1921, scorned and isolated as the Worker's Opposition lost out to Lenin; and finally in her last political battle, the great 1926 debate on the Family Code. Defeated yet again, she returned to Scandinavia. There she had first been appointed Soviet trade representative to Oslo and had later risen to become ambassador to Stockholm – the first

woman in any country to have held that rank. By 1927, however, she was an
isolated figure, fifty-five years old, without influence and in poor health. She
loved Scandinavia but missed what Nikolay Bukharin called the 'tensions' of
Moscow politics, precisely what Walter Benjamin had observed in these same
years, describing them in his *Moscow Diary* as 'so great that they block off all
private life to an unimaginable degree'.[1]

It might have been expected that Kollontai would retire, more or less grace-
fully, from the stage of Soviet politics. Instead she found herself, as did all the
old Bolsheviks, facing a near-impossible battle for survival. The period from
1928 onwards, as we shall see shortly, was one of forced rural collectivisation,
industrialisation and mass terror. Soviet society was turned inside out and so
was Soviet politics. In this climate the revolutionaries of Lenin's generation
found themselves accused of great and improbable crimes, the most important
of which was that of having conspired with Trotsky to betray the Soviet Union.
A great number of the old Bolsheviks were arrested, interrogated at length,
subjected to show trials and executed. Kollontai was not. The price she paid for
this immunity was a high one, for the only alternative to death was unquestioning obedience. The old dissenter bowed to what she called 'the command
of history' and went along with Stalin.[2]

One example of this volte-face will have to suffice. In 1919 Kollontai had put
on record her account of the historic pre-revolutionary meeting at which the
Bolsheviks voted in favour of the seizure of power.[3] In this original version
Trotsky plays a prominent role and his oratory is compared by Kollontai to the
sounding of a bell. Stalin is not mentioned. Lev Kamenev and Grigory Zinoviev,
who had voted against, are treated benignly. In the new version of October 1937,[4]
however, Trotsky becomes 'Judas-Trotsky', an infamous traitor and future
Gestapo agent. Zinoviev and Kamenev, both dead by this time, are treated
viciously. Above all, Stalin is portrayed as the hero of the piece, 'the clearest and
most determined interpreter of Lenin's and the party's policy'.[5] In the key years of
the Great Purges, Kollontai toed the line and did what Stalin asked her to do.

Two interconnecting questions present themselves: why did Stalin
spare her and why did she act in the way she did? Regarding the first, it has
been frequently pointed out that women comrades from the old guard had a
much greater chance of survival than the men. It is also true that Kollontai,
with her considerable diplomatic experience and international reputation, was
a useful figurehead for the regime, a 'docile witness', as Robert Tucker put it.[6]
Beatrice Farnsworth has recently suggested that the long-term nature of the
Stalin–Kollontai relationship also forms part of the explanation. From the
mid-1920s onwards Stalin treated her in an 'amused, playful and condescending manner', while Kollontai, the great champion of new and egalitarian

gender relations, replied in a stereotypically 'female' way – 'grateful, deferential and warmly flattering'.[7] In 1922 Stalin had helped her in a 'dark moment' of her life – her separation from Pavel Dybenko – by sending her to Oslo. In the years that followed she explicitly supported his General Line, refused to join the Opposition and never criticised in any way the Stalinist 'cult of personality'. This combination of elements – suggests Farnsworth – may have been her salvation.

The second question – what were her underlying motives? – also has more than one answer. Fear must have been a factor, though no one could have accused the pre-Stalinist Kollontai of lacking courage. Age, too, had taken its toll: by 1937 she was sixty-five and her old élan had long since deserted her. But perhaps the most important role was played by her old *bête noire*, the family. Kollontai was afraid not for herself but for those closest to her. She had always worried about her son Misha, and late in life felt guilty that he had had to suffer so many separations and uncertainties on her account. Misha had become a well-educated, soft-spoken engineer, working for the Trade Ministry and far removed from high politics. For some part of the 1920s he had worked in Scandinavia, close to his mother, and in the 1930s he was in the United States. There he was relatively safe, but those working abroad were natural targets for secret police investigations. Kollontai was haunted by the example of her nephew, a 'talented scientist' who had committed suicide in 1931 after being the subject of what Kollontai referred to in her diary as 'excessive vigilance'. It was essential for her to keep her head down.[8]

A final element in her submission to Stalin was her loyalty to the Soviet Union. In a letter of 21 July 1938 to her very close companion in Stockholm Dr Ada Nilsson, Kollontai reflected on the achievements of her life.[9] In first place she put the realisation of the USSR, which still held within it, she believed, the promise of human freedom as did no other country. And in second place she put the emancipation of women, which had taken such great steps forward in Soviet Russia. She was, after all, an old Communist: great were the ends to be reached, terrible the methods employed to reach them. She was summoned twice to Moscow in 1937 and 1938, but each time survived and returned to Stockholm. Her diaries reveal her anguish as one after another of her old friends were 'suppressed'.[10]

In 1942 Kollontai suffered a stroke which paralysed part of her face and her left hand.[11] Three years later she retired from her post in Stockholm and returned to Moscow. There she was rewarded with two comfortable flats – one for herself and her secretary-companion Emy Lorentsson, another in 1947 for her son Misha and his family. She also managed to obtain early retirement for Misha from the Trade Ministry, on account of a serious heart condition.

fig. 52 Aleksandra Kollontai in Stockholm in 1944, in front of her mother's portrait.

Her grandson Volodya was a frequent visitor. Irony of ironies, Kollontai had discovered the joys of the family, describing herself as happily surrounded by 'my four children'.[12]

Even so, she could not sleep at night, and her anguish may be compared to that of Margarita Nelken in her last years. Aleksandra Kollontai died in March 1952, followed by her son a year later.

2. Stalin's family life: trauma, procreation and destruction

Of all the great dictators of the first half of the twentieth century, it was Stalin who had the worst childhood and adolescence. His parents came from poor Georgian peasant stock and lived in the small city of Gori. His father was a cobbler, a violent and ill-tempered man – yet another one! – an alcoholic who not only beat his son savagely but did the same to his wife, in Joseph's presence. Once, so legend has it, the boy tried to protect his mother by brandishing a knife against his father. Whether true or not, the story is indicative of the levels of hatred and misery with which the household was afflicted. If Alice Miller reflected on the damage done to Adolf Hitler by his father Alois, one wonders what she would have made of Vissarion Ivanovich Dzhugashvili (nicknamed 'Beso'), a monster by all accounts.[13] His wife, Yekaterina Gavrilovna Geladze ('Keke'), tried her best to protect her only son. She, like Klara Hitler, had lost her previous children to epidemic disease and heaped all her anxiety and ambition on her son. We can only imagine her desperation when Joseph contracted chickenpox at the age of six. He survived but the signs of the disease left their imprint upon his face, just as the terrible traumas of his childhood marked his soul.

When Joseph was still very young his father left the family and went to Tbilisi to find work in a leather factory, insisting that his son go with him. Mother and father engaged in a tug of war for the child, which Yekaterina won because she was a devout Christian and the housekeeper of the local Russian Orthodox priest, her church network proving far more powerful than anything the drunken father could offer.[14] After a few weeks (or was it months?) Joseph returned to Gori.

Although Yekaterina's religiosity saved her son on this occasion, it was to do him a great deal of harm when he was an adolescent. She desperately wanted him to become a priest, and in 1894, aged fifteen, he duly took up a place, as one of six hundred students, at the Russian Orthodox college in Tbilisi. The college was a mixture of seminary and barracks; it was also a hotbed of Georgian nationalism. The daily regime was rigid, punishments frequent and the curriculum antiquated. Stalin's time there can be compared to Mussolini's at the Salesian priests' school at Faenza, to which he was dispatched aged ten in 1893, just one year earlier than when Stalin entered the college in Tbilisi.[15] Both boys were rebels, hating the discipline imposed upon them, and both were punished and isolated repeatedly. After Mussolini had wounded a companion with a knife, however, his parents withdrew him. He had lasted just two years with the Salesian priests, whereas Stalin had to endure the Tbilisi college for five. Following on from his deeply disturbed childhood, this adolescent imprisonment (there is no other word to describe it) hardened up the fundamental aspects of his character – suspicion, secretiveness and lying, this last learned and practised so well that it became second nature to him. He also, it should be added, developed his prodigious memory through having to learn Greek and Latin verbs by heart. In 1899 he left the college without gaining the final diploma, and slipped effortlessly – and to his mother's despair – into clandestine revolutionary socialist agitation.[16]

If we look now at the families the dictators made, continuing to widen the comparative perspective beyond the habitual one of Stalin and Hitler, further fascinating differences and similarities emerge. Stalin is not to be classed with Mustafa Kemal and Adolf Hitler, who never made families of their own. Differently from them he clearly wanted a family, but both fate and his own deep-rooted destructiveness prevented him from making one. Very little is known about his first marriage, probably in 1904, to Yekaterina Semyonovna Svanidze, known as 'Kato'. She was a striking young Georgian who loved Stalin with absolute devotion; Joseph apparently loved her, too, but in a rather different way, for he was nearly always away from home, conspiring and organising. In 1908 Kato gave him a male child called Yakov, but she died not long afterwards, leaving Stalin overwhelmed by grief. He none the less took no care of his son, who was brought up by his sister-in-law.[17]

Stalin's second marriage, the great affair of his life, lasted much longer – thirteen years – but it too ended in tragedy. Nadezhda Alliluyeva, born in 1901, was only fifteen or sixteen at the time of the revolution, an intelligent, independent and serious girl whose father was a railway electrician and famous Bolshevik agitator. Her diligence and precision soon led to her becoming one of Lenin's secretaries. She also became Stalin's lover. In 1919 they married, she aged eighteen and he forty-one. From the outset she had difficulty in coping, as anyone would have done, with the worst aspects of Stalin's character – his sudden changes of humour, his excesses, dissimulation and vulgarity, the violence of his temper. But she loved him profoundly and they had two children together, Vasily, born in 1921, and Svetlana, born in 1926.

Only in these years, at the large country house called Zubalova (the name of the pre-revolutionary owner), did Stalin enjoy a measure of domestic happiness. The household was basically run by Nadezhda's mother. Stalin surrounded himself with natural kin (from both his marriages) and the group of 'brother' Communists who were to accompany him from obscurity to power, and from the periphery to the centre of Russian politics.[18] With the passing of the years, however, in spite of (or perhaps because of) Stalin's rise to supreme power, the marriage relationship grew ever more strained. So did Nadezhda's capacity to cope. From 1928 onwards she found herself in complete disagreement with her husband over the forced collectivisation of the peasantry (see below). She also suffered increasingly from blinding headaches and depression. The climax came on 8 November 1932, at a drunken and raucous party to mark the fifteenth anniversary of the revolution. Stalin proposed a toast to the destruction of the enemies of the USSR. Nadezhda refused to raise her glass. According to more than one account, Stalin then insulted her in public, flicking orange peel and cigarettes in her direction. She stormed from the room and later in the night shot herself.[19]

Nadezhda's death and Stalin's primary role in it marked, as was only to be expected, an emotional watershed in Stalin's life. From this time onwards he retreated ever further into himself, formed no other major relationships with women, and increasingly distrusted those around him. His daughter Svetlana commented, many years later, 'he ceased to believe in people; perhaps he never much believed in them.'[20] Suspicion and paranoia became dominant features.[21] His 'sociality' now consisted of all-male, heavily alcoholic evenings, rather similar to those of Mustafa Kemal and his army friends. Except that in Stalin's case the evenings were peculiarly perverse, as he took delight in humiliating his drinking companions.

At the same time he systematically set about destroying the members of his family. Let us take each of them in turn. He treated his son from his first marriage, Yakov, with contempt, considering him to be unworthy of his father. When Yakov was captured by the Germans during the Second World War, Stalin repudiated him, calling him a traitor and commenting that 'no true Russian would ever have surrendered'. Aleksandr, the brother of Kato (Stalin's first wife), once one of Stalin's closest friends, was accused of being a spy and shot. His wife was arrested and died in a labour camp, while their son was sent to Siberia as 'the child of an enemy of the people'. Mariya, Kato's sister, was arrested and died in prison. As for the kin of Stalin's second marriage, his son, Vasily, suffered greatly from the death of his mother. After a disastrous career in the Soviet air force he died an alcoholic like his grandfather, aged only forty-one. Most of Nadezhda's kin were hounded by the dictator into work camps or to Siberia; many of them did not survive.[22] Stalin loved only Svetlana, his daughter, aged six at the time of her mother's suicide, and she reciprocated with the love that only a six-year-old daughter can bestow on her father. But as she grew up tensions developed rapidly, for he had an overbearing desire to smother her and control her personal life.[23]

The list of annihilations – with the single exception of Svetlana – is a long and terrible one, and indeed Stalin's ferocity in the private sphere marks him out from the other dictators. It is as if all the psychological black holes of his childhood and youth had to be revisited, with Stalin himself now cast in the

fig. 53 Stalin and his daughter Svetlana, Moscow, 1933.

role of the destroyer of all happiness, becoming in the process the most terrible of all the patriarchs examined in this book.

II. The great transformation

If Stalin stands by himself at the end of this book, he is here not primarily because of his own family's unique and terrible history, but above all because of the magnitude of his social engineering. I am not sure that 'social engineering' is the correct term to use: the death through deprivation of millions of peasants was less a feat of engineering than an unparalleled crime against humanity. But whatever term we employ – and perhaps the neutral 'revolution from above' remains the best – it must in some way convey the magnitude of the social transformations involved and their cost in terms of human suffering.

I would like to deal with this phenomenon by looking at three different aspects of it: the forced collectivisation of peasant life, the extraordinary urbanisation and industrialisation of the USSR during and after the first

Five-Year Plan (both examined in this part of the chapter), and the successive waves of terror that engulfed the population of the Soviet Union (examined in part III). In each case I shall concentrate upon the effects on families of so drastic a programme of change and repression.

1. Rural collectivisation and the war against the kulaks

In 1927, after the all too brief interlude of the New Economic Policy (NEP), tensions between city and countryside once again became critical. That year, in spite of a good harvest, the peasants produced less grain for markets than previously. This was partly because villagers were hoarding as a reaction to persistent war rumours, and partly because they had the good fortune to be consuming more and selling less than at any other time in their history. In the cities the story was very different. Here rising food prices and the risk of a new international conflict spread disaffection and anxiety among rank-and-file urban Communists and industrial workers.

What began primarily as a grain procurement crisis rapidly escalated into something far more serious.[24] For this Stalin was responsible. Together with the group of ruthless men of action with whom he had surrounded himself, and in the face of the opposition of Bukharin and Alexei Rykov, who wanted to preserve the 'smychka', the link with the peasantry, he decided that the time had come for drastic action: the peasantry was to be brought very firmly under the control of the state. To achieve this, he raised two battle cries, neither new but both highly appropriate, in his opinion, to the circumstances of the moment.[25] The first was that the peasantry was to be collectivised. Peasant landownership was to be abolished and all land henceforth to be controlled by the state. Such a solution appeared to offer cast-iron guarantees for extracting the surplus from the countryside and for controlling peasant production and consumption. It also held out the promise of a 'higher', socialist form of agriculture, based on mechanisation and rational planning.

The second battle cry was one of war against the kulaks – richer peasants held primarily responsible for grain hoarding and the starving of the cities – and it found its substance in the creation of the 'other', that infernal mechanism which we have had to trace time and again in this book. The kulaks had to be eliminated as a class, though this was easier said than done. Whereas in Germany the Nazis followed a complicated and protracted process of identification of Jews, in the USSR exactly who was a kulak was determined arbitrarily, at local level, often as a result of gossip or inter-familial feuds. A Jew was a Jew, but any middling or wealthy peasant might have the misfortune to be labelled a kulak.[26]

At first Stalin moved cautiously towards collectivisation. At the Sixteenth Communist Party Conference in April 1929 the first Five-Year Plan for agriculture had foreseen the collectivisation of only 9.6 per cent of the rural population.[27] But as peasant resistance strengthened, so Stalin's stance hardened into one of all or nothing. In 1928, 25,000 Communist cadres, flanked by factory workers, had already been sent from the cities into the countryside to requisition grain, close markets and arrest private traders. They made widespread use of Article 107 of the Criminal Code, which severely punished speculation and hoarding. In the years that followed repressive measures intensified. On 30 July 1930, in an act of great symbolic and practical importance, the land commune (*obshchina* or *mir*) was abolished. It was the oldest and most valued collective institution of the Russian countryside and had no parallel in Italy or Turkey, Spain or Germany. The *skhod*, or peasant council, was closed down and many responsibilities passed to state-organised collective farm boards. Henceforth *kholkozy* – obligatory collective farms masquerading as cooperatives – and *sovkhozy* – state-run collective farms – became the basic units of Soviet agriculture. The *dvor*, or peasant household, also ceased to have any juridical protection as an institution. In the space of just a few months the rural old regime, which had survived in one form or another for centuries, had been swept away.[28]

The traumatic effect upon the peasantry as a whole, not just the wealthier part of it, was incalculable. One day as Moshe Lewin has written, they felt themselves to be at home, to be masters of themselves; the next they had been, against their will, enchained to the state.[29] At the same time the regime launched an all-out attack on those aspects of everyday behaviour that it considered to be expressions of 'backwardness' and 'petty bourgeois values'. The cultural revolution in the countryside was aimed principally at the Church: priests were arrested, bells removed, and churches closed, knocked down or adapted to other uses. Markets, mills and shops were ordered to cease activity, while midwives and local healers were banned. The 'rationalisation' of peasant life was under way.

In a decree of 30 January 1930 the kulaks were divided up into three categories, depending on the level of threat they were deemed to represent.[30] The first and most dangerous, those 'guilty of counter-revolutionary activity' and 'organisers of terrorist and anti-Soviet action', were to be arrested and 'repressed', as if they were political criminals. Their families were to be deported to regions in the north, Siberia or Central Asia. The second category consisted of rich and established kulaks who opposed collectivisation. They were spared being shot but they and their families were to be deported to the same distant and desolate territories as the families of the first category. A third category, those who were judged to be kulaks not on the basis of their attitudes, which were compliant, but on that of their economic status, which told against them, were to be exiled within their own region.

What all this meant in terms of family life has been conveyed in part through the hundreds if not thousands of protest letters sent to party and state officials. Deportees, for instance, wrote from the Urals, from eastern Siberia and from the Northern Krai. A group of women petitioned President Mikhail Kalinin, on behalf of 50,000 deportees:

> Our husbands are separated from us. They are off lumbering somewhere, and we women, old people and small children have been left behind to languish in churches [. . .] Plank beds have been put up three stories high so that there's always a steamy mist in the air. We have all become sick from this air and the drafts, and children under fourteen have dropped like flies and there's been no medical assistance [. . .] In the course of a month and a half as many as three thousand children have been buried in the Vologda cemetery, but now they've moved us from Vologda to crude makeshift dwellings at Kaharov station and at the 573 kilometre post on the Northern Railroad. Mikhail Ivanovich, if you could see how we live in these dwellings, you'd be horrified. If we had to spend a couple of years in these dwellings, not one of us would remain among the living. The dwellings were built in a wet place in the forest [. . .] As for provisions, there's three-quarters of a pound of bread and no cooked food whatsoever.[31]

These were clearly the politics of mass killing, masquerading as deportations. We have seen this atrocious sleight of hand at work in relation to the Armenians and the Kurds, the Bedouins of Cyrenaica, the Jews and gypsies of Germany. Now it was the turn not of a racial or ethnic group but of a vast but arbitrarily defined economic category, guilty of holding petty bourgeois, counter-revolutionary beliefs.

In the chaos and tragedy of these years families could easily be broken apart, parents being deported while their children remained behind in the village, abandoned. Nadezhda Krupskaya, Lenin's widow, spoke out in 1930 against the unlimited social harm being done: 'A young child's parents are arrested. He goes along the street crying . . . Everyone is sorry for him, but nobody can make up his mind to adopt him, or take him into his home: "After all, he is the son of a *kulak* [. . .] There might be unpleasant consequences".[32]

Another radical social change in the villages was the huge outflow of men. While many were forcibly deported, many others went to find work in the burgeoning cities. One village chronicler of the 1930s, Yevgeny Gerasimov, noted how many single women, abandoned by their husbands, populated the villages at that time: 'Pulling a cluster of half-orphaned children [at their heels], they carried the collective farms on their own backs.'[33]

The resistance to the twin measures – the destruction of the kulaks and the creation of the *kolkhozy* – was at first widespread and deeply felt. The complex mechanisms of social solidarity within the village did not easily allow for the isolation of the kulak. For the year 1930 alone the authorities recorded some 13,000 riots involving some two million peasants.[34] Women were often at the forefront of these protests, and their fury and determination temporarily stemmed the tide. But what were snowballs, pitchforks and stones against armed militia?[35]

Quite soon the peasantry adopted their time-honoured codes of passive resistance in the face of the drastic transformations being inflicted upon them. As in 1921–2 the compulsory requisitioning of seed corn meant that the sowing of the next year's crop was severely compromised. In addition, many peasants began to destroy their livestock as a protest against the confiscation of their lands. Over vast areas of the Soviet Union, especially the grain-producing regions of the Ukraine, western Siberia, the lower Volga and the northern Caucasus, where forced collectivisation had been most radical, famine once again reared its terrible head. One desperate letter to *Izvestiya* from Mordovia in 1932 will have to suffice as testimony to the fate of hundreds of thousands of peasant families:

> I have a family of nine, and what did I have before the kolkhoz? I had all the produce I needed to feed my family, and fuel, and I clothed and shod them. Had a horse and three head of sheep. Delivered to the government twenty poods [a pood is around 36 pounds or 16 kilos] of rye, forty poods of millet, oats, potatoes, and hemp. I have worked on the kolkhoz, I have honestly earned 355 labordays, but I no longer eat bread but chaff and taters, we don't have enough to resole our shoes. My children have turned black from malnutrition. Respected editors, is there no way to leave the kolkhoz rather than perish here?[36]

The famine of 1932–3 was the worst in Soviet history, all the more so for being the result of specific policy decisions. Once again the exact numbers will never be known, but demographers write of a total of between five and seven million deaths. 'We did not have enough books in which to enter the records of mass deaths,' one local official wrote, 'our priority was the burial of corpses.'[37] Some villages lost between 70 and 75 per cent of their inhabitants, one British Foreign Office report noting the custom of flying black flags at the beginning and end of a village, 'signifying that none of the population are left as a result of starvation and flight'.[38] For more than twenty years after collectivisation, ethnographers and sociologists were effectively banned from the villages of the famine areas.[39]

2. The refusal to unveil

A mention apart should be reserved for the Central Asian Soviets. We left this part of the world at the time of the fierce Communist campaign of 1927 against the wearing of the *paranji* and the *chachvon*. And we had seen how much opposition this initiative had encountered within Muslim families, especially rural ones.[40] The result of the *hujum* (offensive), which cost many thousands of lives, was a stalemate: the Communists were unable to enforce what they considered to be an essential programme of women's liberation, but at the same time the traditionalist forces in the Central Asian Soviets were unable to challenge the ruthless state power of the Stalinists.

We can see this dual process at work in different areas. Collectivisation of agriculture was fiercely but unsuccessfully resisted, as the Communists moved swiftly to bring all private property and common land under the control of the local Soviet authorities. There is little evidence of how widespread physical resistance was; one official report of 1930 described a riot in Sartyan, a village near Khorazm, in which three hundred 'backward women' attacked local officials with the intention of strangling them. Similar episodes were said to be taking place all over Uzbekistan. Village women's fears increased as rumours spread as to what collectivisation really entailed: according to one version men and women were to sleep together under a single, giant blanket, wives becoming common property.[41]

On the other hand, the regime was utterly unable to win the battle over veiling, or to change substantially the patterns of daily life and the traditional relationship between private and public. The Bolshevik vocabulary of rationalisation and liberation, as well as its hyperactivity in the public sphere, foundered against family custom and religious belief. As we have seen in the Turkish case, women's 'inner domain' in the home remained sacrosanct and impenetrable to male outsiders, except for close family members. As for the veil, officials reported disconsolately that the number of heavily veiled women had actually increased during the 1930s. Even in Tashkent, like Bukhara one of the cities where the Communists made most progress, local male leaders kept their women veiled. In 1940 the woman deputy president of the Uzbek Supreme Soviet reported that in Farghona and elsewhere the patterns of family life were not changing: 'we have a situation in which thousands of schoolgirls, under the influence of the obscurantists and religious parents and relatives, abandon their studies, marry while still under age, and even wear the *paranji*.[42]

3. Urban utopias

Moving now away from the terrible conflicts of the countryside to the dynamism of the cities, I want to return to that long minority Russian tradition of reflection upon, and experimentation with, collective living. It was Nikolay Chernyshevsky's *What is to be Done?* (1863) that did most to popularise radical domestic ideas amongst the educated middle classes, and Kollontai was one of the heirs to that tradition.[43] Athough she never lived in a commune herself, it remained her dream that one part of the Bolshevik utopia, albeit a very unexplored one, would find expression in collective living: pooling goods and money (though not men), sharing the upbringing of children, eating together, deciding democratically within the household, all in the frenzied context of building the first socialist state in history. In her novel *Red Love* (*Vassilissa Malygina*, 1923), Kollontai described how her heroine, Vassilissa, 'had long had the idea of organizing a model house, where the Communist spirit would prevail'. With great tenacity she realised the material elements of her dream: 'a community kitchen, a laundry, a nursery, a dining-room – Vassilissa's pride, with curtains at the windows, and geranium plants – and a library, furnished like a club room'. Very soon, however, the dream collapsed, devoured by passions and quarrels within the house, as well as by an entirely unsympathetic Soviet bureaucracy.[44]

Kollontai effectively had very little success in convincing a sceptical and male chauvinist Communist Party to take on board any such project. Communal living did none the less flourish here and there in the Soviet experience of the 1920s. In the countryside it was mainly radical religious groups that were most successful – the Tolstoyans, for instance, following in the footsteps of their great master, living religiously and turning their backs on the sinfulness of civilisation. In the era of the NEP, Soviet authorities regarded many such experiments benignly, even if with scepticism.[45]

In the cities in the early 1920s, as we have seen, a few 'workers' communes', offering collective services such as laundering and bread-making, flourished in one or more buildings in Moscow. There was also a revival of the artel tradition.[46] Hardly surprisingly, it was students who went furthest along the communal path. One of the best-documented experiments is the Leningrad Commune of 133, founded in 1924 by students of the Electro-Technical Institute. The commune, with its 133 members, was extremely radical: walls were knocked through as all private space in the dormitory buildings was abolished, and collectivisation was extended to every aspect of daily life, including the sharing of clothing and even of underwear. Given the intensity of the demands put upon its members, it is surprising that the commune lasted as long as it did – for at least five years.[47] Even the perennial problems of love, jealousy and sexuality failed to bring it down. Richard Stites has written,

> The problem that defied solution in this commune – as in most others – was sexual relations. Women were in a minority in the Commune of 133, though one served as president for a time [. . .] Sexual life was difficult and varied in scope. Some married – within the Commune or outside of it. Some took their sex life outside, some abstained altogether. Few were satisfied with their sex lives.[48]

It is an important element in the Stalinist story that the launching of the first Five-Year Plan produced a revival of communalism, partly out of material necessity – the lack of housing in the great cities as peasant workers were sucked towards them at startling rates – and partly in a new wave of utopianism which led workers and intellectuals alike to give expression to a highly original, Soviet version of modernity. Stalin himself shared the voluntarist, almost romantic view of what was taking place, consistently underlining the need for heroism, socialist commitment and self-sacrifice during the first Five-Year Plan. In October 1932 he told a group of intellectuals gathered in Maxim Gorky's Moscow flat that their 'production' was crucial: '[Soviet] tanks will be worth nothing if the soul in them is rotten.'[49]

In this highly charged atmosphere of building the new socialist citadel brick by brick, the traditional workers' artel underwent a rapid revival, young male or female workers sleeping in the same rooms (or room), eating from the same stewpot, and working at the same factory. Production communes or collectives sprang up, bearing names such as 'Spark', 'Our Frenzy' and 'Five-in-Four' (that is, achieving the Five-Year Plan in four years). The peak of the new wave of communes was the period from the middle of 1929 to the middle of 1930, the number of production collectives and communes at that time being estimated at 134,030.[50] This was a huge movement.

These same years saw a number of exciting attempts to rethink urban and domestic living. One of these was the entry of the distinguished architect Konstantin S. Melnikov in a design competition for a 'Garden City' of 1929. Although it had no chance of winning the competition (often the fate of the most original works), Melnikov's design won a place in architectural history. Its astonishing central theoretical problem was, as Melnikov himself put it, 'how to rationalise sleep'.[51] Instead of considering sleep, or the lack of it, an individual matter, of no concern to the socialist state, Melnikov correctly

posed it as a key question of *byt*, everyday life. Workers were to come to the
Garden City exhausted after their very long hours of labour, and while they
needed to be assured of eight hours' sleep, the real challenge was 'not so much
that of the continuity of sleep as that of its healing quality'.[52] Melnikov's answer
was the famous 'Laboratory of Sleep', which he called *SONaya SONata* (Sleep
Sonata), a double-winged structure with sloping floors, of which he envisaged
twelve in the Garden City, each accommodating some 4,000 workers.
Influenced both by contemporary discussions of sleep therapy and by science
fiction, Melnikov made provision for the wings of his Laboratory of Sleep to
move slowly up and down, for calming music to accompany the building's
undulating movement, and for sweet fragrances to fill its rooms. His Garden
City was designed in a circle, with Laboratories of Sleep at its perimeter,
surrounded by woods. At its very centre stood, appropriately, the 'Institute for
the Transformation of Man's Being'.[53]

Absurd as it appeared to many at the time – and afterwards – Melnikov's
project was a fine piece of utopian thinking, for it identified one of modernity's
greatest areas of *angst* and offered a collective solution to it. Unsurprisingly,
Stalin had little time for such things. He may have seen his own project in
romantic, even utopian terms, but its defining characteristics – direction from
above, discipline, control and terror – had little to with the autonomous search
for new ways of living. By 1931–2 the wave of utopian experimentation was
spent, as were the production communes and the rural religious communities,
Tolstoyan and otherwise.

4. Life in the cities

Working-class life was extremely harsh in the newly industrialised cities of the
Soviet Union, a very long way away from Melnikov's Garden City. The bare

fig. 54 Kostantin S. Melnikov, Laboratory of Sleep (*SONaya SONata*), created for the
Garden City project, 1929.

statistics tell their own story. In the period 1929–33 the population of Moscow increased from 2,319,000 to 3,600,000. Workers' living conditions declined in real terms as prices far outstripped wages. Almost ten million women entered the labour market for the first time during the 1930s. A new proletariat was being forged by both sexes, but the basic amenities of daily life lagged far behind: housing, food stores, public baths, crèches and public transport were all in very short supply. In desperation, industrial concerns took it upon themselves to build tenement block housing and provide crèches, so that their workforce – both women and men – could fulfil its obligations.[54]

Of all the problems that working-class families faced in these 'frontier' years, that of housing took prime place. A young British Communist, Alan Wicksteed, chose to go and work in Moscow at this time, and the account he has left us of the problems of proletarian life, from housing downwards, is a revealing and honest one:

I live in a large block of workmen's dwellings, the two hundred rooms of which contain a population of one thousand odd, of whom 300 are children. The house is built on what is known here as the corridor system, that is to say that the great majority of the rooms are not arranged in flats but each opens independently on a common corridor with a common kitchen and lavatory! (Ten years in Russia have more or less acclimatized me, but by no means reconciled me, to the treatment an average Russian gives to a lavatory.) The house is moreover, like all Moscow houses, surrounded by an ample yard, my window looking on to the biggest section. My own corridor is about two and a half yards wide and nearly forty yards long, and seems to me to contain no inconsiderable proportion of the three hundred children [...] One of the chief reasons why Moscow is a good town for children is that it is, as indeed are all Russian towns, extremely loosely built. Every house stands in its own grounds.[55]

Wicksteed also added some considerations on the family and women's conditions, which have a Kollontai-like quality to them:

To the vast majority of working women [...] the 'home' represents an endless and in most ways hopeless struggle with drudgery and bad health; and the sooner such homes are broken up the better. Nothing enlists my sympathy more than the Bolshevik's determination to free the women of the nation from the drudgery of the home, and nothing can contribute more to this than to free the mothers of the routine care of the children by nurseries, kindergartens, summer camps and so on. One of our more intelligent visitors, herself a working woman, told me that she had asked all the working mothers whether the new arrangements had or had not improved their relations with their children, and the unanimous answer was that now they didn't see their children except when they were free to attend to them and cultivate human relations with them.[56]

These remarks, which convey a highly idealised version of Soviet social services of the time, lead us to wonder what sort of family life could have existed behind the doors of all those little rooms which gave on to Wicksteed's corridor. The Soviet working-class family was barely a feasible entity in the 1930s and yet it survived in an extraordinary variety of forms. In the tenement blocks of Leningrad and Moscow, families took many shapes: often a single mother with an only child and the omnipresent *babushka* (grandmother); or again a mother without her husband (who had been arrested), their child, her mother-in-law and her sister, a 'typist who was the only legal inhabitant of the apartment and apparently the main breadwinner'; or else single women living alone in different corners of the same room.[57] With so few formalities governing marriage and divorce, many men had slipped away from their marital obligations and kept moving from one job, one city and even one family to another. For the authorities it was an almost impossible task to keep track of them and oblige them to pay alimony.

For all the difficulties and deprivations, the lack of comforts and privacy, there can be little doubt that a really distinctive view of gender relations emerged in these pullulating cities of the new Russia. In theory if not always in practice, the regime clearly took the side of women against men. As Sheila Fitzpatrick has written,

> Women were consistently represented [...] as the nobler, suffering sex, capable of greater endurance and self-sacrifice, pillars of the family who only in the rarest instances neglected their responsibilities to husband and children. Men, in contrast, were portrayed as selfish and irresponsible, prone to abusing and abandoning their wives and children. In the inevitable conflict between women's interests, construed as altruistic and pro-family, and men's interests, read as selfish and individualistic, the state was unquestionably in the women's corner.[58]

Of course, the prime consideration in the regime's policies towards women was that they were a vital and rapidly growing part of the workforce. Their productive capacity had to be protected. I shall examine Stalin's drive to re-establish effective family units in the next part of the chapter. Suffice it to

fig. 55 Newly erected workers' houses in Leningrad, 1929.

fig. 56 A propaganda image of a family in its new flat in a workers' district of Moscow, 1930s.

say here that if we return for a last time to Mary Ann Glendon's image of 'two moving systems' – on the one hand the laws affecting the family and on the other actual family life – we can see that more than a decade of legislation and activity aimed at establishing the rights of women was making itself felt. This progress was in no way linear. Enlightened legislation often had the opposite results to those intended; many men, for instance, had used the Family Codes of 1918 and 1926 to their own, often opportunistic, advantage. Had she survived, Inessa Armand would have been sad, to say the least, that her great personal sacrifices at the head of the Zhenotdel had led to such meagre results, encapsulated in the fragile, female-dominated family structures of the Moscow tenements. But for all that, egalitarian gender images and practices in the Soviet Union had put down firm roots, far more so than in the other regimes we have examined.

III. Terror and betrayal

The third and last component of the Stalinist revolution from above (the first two being rural collectivisation and industrialisation) was terror. So great a part did this play in the Stalinist system that it would be wrong to treat it simply as a method for achieving certain ends. All the dictators that we have encountered in this book had recourse to fear as a fundamental political weapon, but the Stalinist use of it was by far the most terrible and widespread, with uniquely disintegrative effects upon the texture of society, family life and love.

Stalinist Terror came in waves and with different targets. The most famous was that of the political show trials in Moscow in 1936–8, in which Stalin's rivals for power and much of the Bolshevik old guard were brought to trial and executed. This was the fate which Kollontai managed to avoid. In the same years the intelligentsia, the officer corps and other parts of the state apparatus were heavily purged. This public masque of Terror, however, concealed another wave of repression, more anonymous but no less terrible, which the work of the French historian Nicolas Werth has only recently fully brought to light.[59]

Between August 1937 and November 1938 some 750,000 Soviet citizens were arrested as 'enemies of the people' and killed after summary trials. It was, according to Werth, 'the greatest state massacre ever perpetrated in Europe in times of peace'.[60] Its victims belonged to two major 'lines', to use the terminology of the police: that of the kulaks, who had to be eliminated 'once and for all' from the countryside; and the 'national' line, principally foreigners who had sought refuge in the Soviet Union, but also anyone suspected of having contacts with countries hostile to the USSR. These two massive and intentionally ill-defined groups were declared to be 'socially dangerous' and 'ethnically suspect'. They were eliminated in a series of operations in which secret police functionaries had to fulfil given targets of weekly killings. In the course of this 'ordinary people's Terror', as Werth calls it, there were 50,000 executions per month, an average of 1,600 per day.[61] Unspecified numbers of others, the 'fortunate' ones, joined older and different categories of prisoners in the Gulag system of forced labour camps.

The effect of all this on the families involved was obviously cataclysmic but by no means straightforward. The destiny of a family unit of which a single member (usually the husband and father) had been arrested depended on a considerable number of variables. As in Spain at the outset of the Civil War, there was a typology of different reactions and fates, much depending on the strength of family ties before the Terror struck. Crucial, too, were individuals' positions within the family – husband and wife might react quite differently from father and son. Lastly, the really distinctive feature of the Soviet case was the way in which the state inculcated doubt deep within the family and guilt by association. Perhaps dear ones really had betrayed their 'comrades'. Perhaps they had been involved in anti-Soviet activities of which their closest relatives knew nothing. Perhaps these close relatives themselves were accomplices. At this point Stalin's message was chillingly clear: there could be only one primary allegiance and it was to the state, not to the untrustworthy family.

Once again I would like to propose a possible typology of family relations and destinies. Let me begin with the 'national line' and with husband and wife. Anastasia Koch was the wife of a German émigré worker who was arrested by the NKVD (Commissariat of Internal Affairs) in early 1938. Both she and her husband worked at the Moscow Electric Lamp Plant in Moscow. Anastasia flatly refused to accept that her husband was an 'enemy of the people' and that consequently she too should be disgraced:

I have given the Lamp Plant twenty-four years of my life, I have felt like it was my own family, and now they have tossed me out and forgotten me – or even worse, they despise me, and for what, I don't know [. . .] When he [her husband] was arrested, they confronted me at a party meeting with a choice: either you have to disown him and find him guilty or we will expel you from the party. I don't know whether I did the right thing at the time, but I couldn't find him guilty without any evidence, and not just because he was my husband.[62]

In this conflict between what she called her 'family'– her comrades at the Lamp Plant – and her real family, Anastasia chose loyalty to her husband. We have few details of their fate, but we know that her husband was not executed and that although he was sent to a Gulag he survived.

Let me now take the case of another husband and wife, this time swept up in the Terror unleashed against the old Bolsheviks, again a couple profoundly loyal, simultaneously to each other and to the Soviet state. Sofia Antonov-Ovseyenko was the second wife of a highly respected Communist, Vladimir Antonov-Ovseyenko, who had taken a leading part in the storming of the Winter Palace and was later Soviet ambassador to Czechoslovakia. Sofia was arrested in October 1937 and wrote to her husband from a Moscow prison, not knowing that he too had been arrested three days earlier. Her deeply loving and tragic letter, so marked by innocent guilt, is one of the most heart-rending testimonies of this book:

> My darling.
> I do not know if you will receive this, but somehow I sense that I am writing to you for the last time. Do you recall how we always said that if someone in our country was arrested then it must be for good reason, for some crime – that is for something? No doubt there is something in my case as well, but what it is I do not know. Everything I know you know as well, because our lives have been inseparable and harmonious [. . .] I cannot bear the thought that you might not believe me [. . .] It has been oppressing me for three days now. It burns inside my brain. I know your intolerance of all dishonesty, but even you can be mistaken. Lenin was mistaken too, so it seems. So please believe me when I say that I did nothing wrong [. . .] One more thing: it is time for Valichka [Sofia's daughter from her first marriage] to join the Komsomol [Communist Youth League]. My arrest will no doubt stand in her way. My heart is full of sorrow at the thought that she will think her mother a scoundrel [. . .] I beg forgiveness from everyone I love for bringing them such misfortune [. . .] Forgive me, my loved one. If only I knew that you believed me and forgave me!
> Your Sofia.[63]

Husband and wife were shot on the same day, 8 February 1938. Sofia's daughter, Valentina (Valichka), aged fifteen, was not only refused entrance to the Komsomol but sent to an orphanage. In spite of everything she survived.

If we turn from husbands and wives to parents and children, the pattern becomes more complicated. There were many instances of bedrock solidarity between the generations, but children had been brought up in Soviet schools, had their own ambitions and dreams, and sometimes felt anger towards their fathers for placing in jeopardy their own future. In these circumstances family loyalties could be strained to breaking point. Lev Tselmerovsky was aged eighteen when his father, a military engineer, was arrested in 1938 in Leningrad.

Lev had been a trainee pilot, but with his father's disgrace he had been sent to Chimkent in far-off Kazakhstan, where he worked in a factory. His mother and two sisters lived in Kazalinsk, five hundred kilometres away. Lev wrote to the Soviet president Kalinin, asking to be judged in his own right:

> A few words about my father. My mother told me that he was banished to the Northern camps for being a malcontent. I personally never believed it, because I myself heard him tell his sisters how he fought against the Whites in the North [. . .] But maybe this was all a clever disguise. He did tell me a few times that he had been in Warsaw [. . .] I do not want to suffer the disgrace he has caused. I want to serve in the Red Army. I want to be a Soviet citizen with equal rights because I feel that I am worthy of that title. I was educated in a Soviet school in the Soviet spirit and therefore my views are obviously completely different from his. It is heartbreaking for me to carry the papers of an alien person.[64]

In the unavoidable clash between individual ambition, family ties and state diktats, the Soviet Union could boast a founding myth that has no equivalent in the other countries under consideration.

The last and most famous case I want to examine reveals, once again, parents and children in conflict. In 1932, or so the story has it, a fifteen-year-old boy, Pavel 'Pavlik' Morozov, a member of the Communist Pioneer youth movement, had placed the interests of the state above those of his family and courageously denounced his father for corruption. At his father's trial he declared fearlessly, 'Uncle judge, I am acting not as a son but as a Pioneer!' In retribution and urged on by Pavlik's 'kulak' uncles, Pavlik's cousin and another boy knifed Pavlik and his nine-year-old brother to death. All this occurred in the remote and impoverished village of Gerasimovka in the Urals, some 350 kilometres east of Sverdlovsk (now Yekaterinburg). There seems no doubt that Morozov was killed by his cousin, but the rest of the story, as minutely reconstructed by Catriona Kelly, is shrouded in mystery.[65] It is certainly very different from the official version. Pavlik came from a very poor family, and, far from being a leading Pioneer respected by other village children, was 'neglected, unhappy, perhaps even mentally unstable'.[66] Participating in the Pioneer movement, especially its anti-kulak activities, was a way – perhaps the only way – to earn respect for himself. He consequently began to denounce those around him, including his father, who was chairman of the local Soviet. His fathers' brothers were incensed by this action, and Morozov was duly killed by one of their sons. It sounds like a quintessential story of deprivation and kinship rivalry, in which the state plays only a tangential role. Yet this was not the way the authorities saw it. Here was a golden opportunity to create the first and most famous Soviet boy hero, and to do so with direct reference to the conflict between state and family in which the state had always to come first. Maxim Gorky was in the forefront of the creation of the legend of Morozov's heroic self-sacrifice, and Sergey Eisenstein even made a film about him, *Bezhin Meadow*, in 1936. Statues were built and streets, parks and culture clubs were named after him, as were Pioneer groups and even 'Pioneer corners'.

IV. Stalin and the family

1. Reform measures, 1936

In his history of the Gulag system, Oleg Khlevniuk has suggested that in the 1930s the Soviet population was divided into two huge, 'numerically comparable' groups. The first of these was made up of families that had no victims of state persecution, at least among their close relatives, while the second was that in which at least one family member had suffered persecution or repression.[67] Although the first group was much larger than the second, the sense of menace and impending doom was common to all. In his memoirs, the composer Dmitry Shostakovich captured the essence of this period, when private grief had to be hidden away from the public eye:

> Before the [Second World] War everything was more difficult because everyone was alone with their suffering. Already before the War at Leningrad there was not a single family which had not lost a relative or a close friend. Everybody had to mourn someone, but do so secretly. Nobody was to know about it and everybody was afraid. Men had become wolves in the way they treated other men [. . .] Then there came the War. Each person's pain became part of a universal pain. Finally it was possible to talk of one's pain, one could cry without hiding one's tears, cry for all those who had died or disappeared.[68]

If we compare for a moment the Soviet situation in the 1930s with that of Nazi Germany in the same years, we immediately perceive a huge difference. Those in Germany who suffered from being categorised as 'racially inferior' or belonging to 'alien races' constituted a tiny percentage of the German population in comparison to those who were persecuted – under various headings – in the Soviet Union in these same years. It was only with the creation of the Greater Reich and the crimes against humanity committed therein that the terrible numerical balance of family tragedies levelled out in some way in the two regimes.

Yet the story of Soviet families in these years cannot be recounted only in terms of successive waves of Terror and crimes against humanity. Side by side with this history lies another one, in which Stalin, from May 1936 onwards, attempted to normalise and reinforce families and to establish them as a solid support for his regime. Obviously, these were not families that were in any way dissenting. Parents kept their heads down, suffered greatly in material terms, both in country and in city, and hoped that schooling, especially in the cities, would give their children the chance to be upwardly mobile in a rapidly changing society. Living standards rose in the mid-1930s, giving the illusion that the worst was over, but they deteriorated again even before the onset of the Second World War.

On 26 May 1936 the government published a long article in *Pravda* laying out the principal reforms in Soviet family policy.[69] They can best be presented under two headings, the first covering significant changes in family law, the second introducing new measures of state support for families. In the first category, abortion, which had been legalised in 1920 and made widely available since that date, was declared illegal except in exceptional, 'therapeutic' circumstances. Divorce, which as we have seen was extremely easy to obtain under Soviet law, was kept in place but made more difficult. Henceforth, divorcees had to pay a state tax that increased in size with every succeeding divorce. Maintenance payments to the parent who was left with the care of children (nearly always the mother) were increased, and higher fines were introduced for those who failed to pay on a regular basis (overwhelmingly the fathers).

The second group of measures concerned state subsidies and services. Families with large numbers of children were to receive special payments. Detailed plans for maternity clinics and other structures for mothers and children were announced, together with a radical increase both in maternity leave and in the number of crèches.[70]

What sense are we to make of this series of measures? Anna Di Biagio has rightly warned us against seeking an excessive homogeneity in Stalin's family policies, which were characterised, as she writes, by 'oscillations, incoherences and open contradictions'.[71] In 1946 the sociologist Nicholas S. Timasheff suggested that these and other similar policies constituted a 'Great Retreat' – a going back on the radical policies of the revolution. Although the term has been much used, it seems a distinct misnomer. One is tempted to ask 'retreat from what'? Certainly not from radical Kollontai-style family politics, which had long since fallen into disgrace. Perhaps a retreat from the politics of gender equality, though here, as we shall see, there is evidence working both ways. Nor can these measures be considered a retreat to the traditional family, for beneath the superficial acceptance of some old-style *forms* the Communists continued their battle against traditional *content* – backwardness, superstition and religiosity. It is probably most useful to think in terms not of 'retreat' at all, but rather of the creation of a specific and function-oriented Stalinist view of the relationship between family and state.[72]

There would appear to be three mainsprings to this new, functional family. The first, familiar to readers by now, was the drive to increase the population and render it, eugenically speaking, of better quality. Making abortion illegal was a clear step in that direction, as was the setting up of maternity clinics and rewarding of large families. The birth rate rose briefly between 1936 and 1938, but then maternity leave and other benefits were curtailed – a good example of giving with one hand and taking away with the other. Working women interviewed in Leningrad in the 1930s constantly expressed their fears for the children they already had, let alone those they were expected to produce: 'A child goes to school hungry and doesn't eat there either. Children do without boots, and they're impossible to buy'; 'How can you say no to an abortion when your family consists of five people and you have fourteen square metres' living space?' By 1940 the birth rate had returned to its 1935 level.[73]

A second element, equally complex, even contradictory, was the role of gender. Here it is as well to begin with Stalin himself. Of all the great dictators he is the most self-evidently patriarchal – jovial, avuncular, terribly dangerous. It was his firm belief that just as he was in command of the Soviet state, so fathers should be firmly at the helm of families. He played no part in the dissemination of the Pavlik Morozov legend, and his reactions to it, although largely a matter of hearsay, are of great interest. On one occasion he is reported to have said of Morozov, 'What a little swine, denouncing his own father.'[74] This is extremely revealing and takes us back to Stalin's own childhood. It might be expected that, given what had happened to him as a boy, Stalin would have been in sympathy with Pavlik's plight. Far from it. As Catriona Kelly has written, 'It is clear that Stalin identified with the father.'[75] In his attitude towards his own sons, as we have seen, Stalin showed little understanding or affection and no willingness to make a clear break with the behaviour of his father, the monstrous 'Beso'. In an oft-repeated pattern, Stalin the abused became Stalin the abuser.

The question of gender did not stop there, however, for Stalin was, albeit in a distorted and contradictory way, the heir to the Bolshevik legacy on female emancipation. He insisted, for instance, that women should not only take their place in production and be educated, but also be trained to command. In his speech to the Twenty-Seventh Congress of the Communist Party on 26 January

1934, in the section on rural affairs, he paid tribute to the 6,000 women who had become presidents of their *kolkhoz*, the 60,000 who had taken up leading administrative roles therein, the 100,000 who were organisers of work groups and the 7,000 who were tractor drivers: 'Women [. . .] form a huge labour force, they are called upon to educate our children, the next generation, our future. That is why we cannot allow this enormous army of women workers to linger in darkness and ignorance!'[76]

The measure announced in *Pravda* in May 1936 making abortion illegal certainly worked against women. Others did not. The rise in maintenance payments, the fines for not paying them regularly, the increased difficulty and cost of obtaining a divorce – all these were clearly designed to serve the interests of women in the face of irresponsible males. In the Stalinist family model, therefore, patriarchy and the fight for women's rights co-existed in a complex and conflictual way.

The last element of this model was discipline and repression. Nothing illustrates this better than the fate of a new wave of homeless and abandoned children, the ill-fated victims of Stalin's policies in both countryside and city during the terrible decade of 1928 to 1938. In the second half of the 1930s, the authorities displayed very different attitudes from those of the early 1920s. Then, as we saw in chapter 1, the fledgling Soviet state had lacked resources but not sympathy. The illustration from a 1926 issue of *Izvestiya* which showed one little homeless boy inside a tar cauldron lighting up his cigarette from that of another bore the captions 'Remember the *besprizornyye*!' and 'Assistance to the *besprizornyye* is the obligation of every Soviet citizen.'[77] By the 1930s the regime's heart had hardened. The children were treated primarily as delinquents, to be punished by the Penal Code.[78] A decree of April 1935 accordingly lowered the age of criminal responsibility.

Yet even here Stalinist family policy was not entirely straightforward. The best-known Soviet family expert and pedagogue of the 1930s, Anton Makarenko, advocated a vision of the family in which discipline was far from all. The family was to be a 'domestic collective', in which men and women enjoyed equal rights: 'Our families are not subordinate to the dictatorial power of the father, but constitute soviet collectives.'[79] Parents were to behave in a firm but democratic and loving way towards their children. If possible, they were to avoid hitting them. Service to a collectivist society was considered paramount. 'In our country', wrote Makarenko, 'he alone is a man of worth whose needs and desires are the needs and desires of a collectivist. Our family offers rich soil for the cultivation of such collectivism.'[80] Here was a pedagogy that appeared to render the family both functional and humane. The official slogan 'Thank you, dear Stalin, for a happy childhood' was launched in 1935.

2. Building for the future

The Komsomol, or Communist Youth League, was founded in 1918. All young people between the ages of fourteen and twenty-three, both male and female, were eligible to join. The Pioneers was the organisation for a younger age group, from ten to fourteen. Many aspects of the Komsomol's formation and actions distinguish it from the Avanguardisti and the Hitlerjugend. To begin with, it was an elite corps, though still numbering hundreds of thousands of members. Entrance was by selection, preference being given to young adults from a proletarian background. Another difference, again in notable contrast to Nazi and Fascist youth organisations, was that both sexes engaged in the same activities, including, highly significantly, preparation for war. Yet another was the relative independence and élan of its initiatives, in contrast to the stultifying boredom and hierarchy of the Hitlerjugend. Thus in the late 1920s and early 1930s the Komsomol spearheaded a campaign against bureaucracy and 'routinism' in government agencies. Its members considered themselves a radical vanguard. In the mid-1930s their autonomy was inevitably curbed and their conformism guaranteed.[81]

fig. 57 Russian workers' children at the opening of a new plant, 1931. One of their banners reads, 'Glad to get the plant started.'

In Aleksandr Samokhvalov's painting *The Militarised Komsomol*, of 1932–3, girls are seen at rifle practice, their male companions instructing them on how to shoot (plate 15). One of the figures in the foreground is a girl who, alone of all her companions, stares straight out of the picture at us. She exudes self-confidence. She has a great shock of blond hair, high cheek bones and almond-shaped eyes, a red kerchief round her neck, short white socks and black shoes. With the benefit of hindsight, it is possible to imagine that she is saying to us, 'Don't think we're going to give up without a fight.'

We have come a long way from Kazimir Malevich's faceless, plodding and resigned female peasants, depicted through a mixture of geometrical forms and primary colours. Samokhvalov's picture – a typical product of socialist realism, dominated by purely narrative and didactic intent – is both static and mobile. The foreground is bathed in intense light, while far away we can discern figures who may be gymnasts or swimmers, both male and female.

Youth organisation was not just confined to propaganda campaigns and learning to use arms. At school the Pioneers were taught by young and dedicated teachers who stressed the need for individual excellence but also egalitarianism, social justice and internationalism. Education and literacy expanded rapidly. By 1939 over 80 per cent of the target age group, both male and female, was attending primary school.[82]

Some interesting recent work has revealed the differences between Soviet primers and those used in Nazi primary schools.[83] The content of Soviet primers was entirely new and controlled by the central authorities, whereas Nazi primers were regionally produced adaptations of already existing material. A second difference concerns the transmission of values: for the Nazis solidarity within the *Volksgemeinschaft* was of paramount importance, above all in relation to the Winterhilfswerk, the Winter Aid Programme; for the Communists it was the idea of change and progress that took pride of place. A third difference, of great importance, once again concerns gender roles, both within and outside the family. Fathers were notable by their absence in Nazi primers, while Soviet fathers were much more present. In addition, Soviet primers were characterised by their strong underlining of gender equality and the constant presence of mixed-gender groups.

I have compared various aspects of family life in the Soviet Union and Nazi Germany – the impact on families of the Terror, gender roles in both the private and the public domain, youth organisations, and the depiction of families in early school texts. The comparison could, of course, be further extended in many different directions. Here, I would like to return for a moment to May 1937 and the Paris International Exhibition of Arts and Technology.[84] It may be remembered that the pavilions of the two great dictatorial regimes faced each other provocatively on the right bank of the Seine. The more modest Spanish pavilion opened late but offered in compensation the thunderbolt of Picasso's *Guernica*. Nothing in the Soviet and Nazi pavilions could begin to match it. It is none the less of great interest to compare the sculptures with which these two regimes chose to represent themselves.

Outside the German pavilion stood two massive works by Josef Thorak, *Kameradismus* (Comradeship) and *Familie*, each consisting of three naked figures. In the first a maternal figure, standing immediately behind the other two, accompanies, perhaps propels, two male warriors to their destiny of war and death. In the second the maternal figure, standing behind and above the other two, appears to present to the world her family, consisting of two grown-up children, one male and one female (plate 12). The father is notable by his absence. The two pieces, massive and neo-classical, convey an overriding impression of sinister intent.

By contrast, the huge sculpture that crowned the Soviet pavilion, and which easily dwarfed even Thorak's figures, was a piece by the woman sculptor Vera Mukhina (plate 13). It portrays a young male worker from a city industry and a young woman of the same age from a collective farm. There is no gender hierarchy and no family. The two figures, fully clothed, are not static, like Thorak's, but very much in movement, their clothing blown by the wind. Together they hold high the respective symbols of their work, the hammer and the sickle, and they stride forward in unison towards the construction of a new society.[85] The gender parity of Mukhina's work contrasts starkly with the specific gender roles indicated by Thorak. In the Nazi case the family is to the forefront (even without a father); in the Soviet case it is not. We are in 1937. Perhaps the Stalinist 'functional' family had not yet acquired a sufficiently secure place among Soviet institutions to merit so exalted a portrayal.

3. The Gulag system compared

When writing about terror, I focused on the mass executions of the 1930s. But the Soviet system of repression was based not just on executions but on a massive network of forced-labour camps. According to the most recent scholarship, some eighteen million Soviet citizens passed through the camps and colonies between 1929 and 1953. If we add to these various other categories – national and ethnic groups, prisoners of war, etc. – then the approximate number of prisoners for the same period rises to 28.7 million. No other system of detention and slave labour in the twentieth century comes anywhere near these figures. Of these prisoners some 2.75 million died.[86]

A comparison with the Nazi concentration camps is marked by significant differences, of which the quantitative one, though fundamental, is only the first. Enzo Traverso has argued convincingly that death played a different role in the two systems: however much it was an indelible component of the Soviet camp system it was a by-product of it, whereas in the Nazi extermination camps death was the immediate and exclusive aim. This point emerges clearly if we look at death rates in the two systems. For most of the years for which there are reliable statistics, Gulag death rates remain in low single figures – 2.75 per cent in 1935, 2.72 per cent in 1940, and so on. The highest rate for the period 1930–53 is reached in the cataclysmic war year of 1942 – 24.9 per cent. The corresponding figure in the same year in the Nazi camp system as a whole is an astronomical 60 per cent.[87]

The difference in ultimate aims is further revealed if we compare, as Traverso has done, the objectives of two notorious camp commanders, the Soviet S. K. Yevstigneyev, 'the king of Ozerlag', and Rudolf Höss, the commander of Auschwitz. For Höss what mattered was the number of deaths his camp could record, how much of human life he could eliminate. For Yevstigneyev the imperative was primarily economic – how many kilometres of railway he could build, how far he could meet the targets of the Five-Year Plan.[88]

There are many other areas in which comparison might be made, one of the least explored concerning the fate of families. The two regimes had different modes of procedure towards families, both outside and inside the camps. Because of the nature of Soviet repression, characterised by suspicion, arbitrariness and lack of defined criteria, anyone could be denounced as an enemy of the people. Families were suddenly fractured and their members separated in a haphazard way, leaving a society made up of broken bits and pieces of families – infants and small children abandoned, fathers and husbands loved and lost, adolescents taught to despise their fathers (and sometimes their mothers) as traitors. The German regime, by contrast, believed in surgical excision, a clean and deep cut to remove the whole of the offending cancer, an operation based upon detailed and scientific information that left no one and nothing behind. It is as well to recall Himmler's remark of October 1943 that he had not flinched in the face of what he called the 'difficult choice' of exterminating Jewish women and children as well as men.'[89]

Within the camps, the attitudes of the two regimes towards families differed again, though here they were closer and the gruesome outcome very often the same. The Nazi regime, it may be recalled, had an overall policy of splitting families up as soon as they arrived in the extermination camps. Able-bodied adult men were marched away to one labour camp, healthy women aged between sixteen and forty-five to another. All the rest – young people under the age of sixteen, all mothers in charge of children and all the elderly and frail – were sent to the gas chambers immediately. There were the exceptions of the two 'family camps' at Auschwitz but, as we have seen, they were short-lived and ended in the total destruction of their inmates.[90] In the Soviet Union any idea of creating new families within the camps was anathema, even though there were a high number of female prisoners. In 1949 an administrative report on the Gulag system recorded the presence of 503,000 women. Of these no fewer than 9,300 were pregnant and another 23,790 had small children living with them. As Anne Applebaum has written, 'If love, sex, rape and prostitution were a part of camp life, so too, it followed, were pregnancy and childbirth. Along with mines and construction sites, forestry brigades and punishment cells, barracks and cattle trains, there were maternity hospitals and maternity camps in the Gulag too.'[91]

Only that conditions in them were dreadful and infant mortality very high. At the age of two, often in the face of the most bitter opposition from their mothers, the infants were confiscated and placed in regular state orphanages. These, in turn, were terribly overcrowded, understaffed and usually fatal for the children's future. For those who survived into adolescence there was a whole system of juvenile camps, running parallel to those for adults. In such a system there was no room for, nor desire to create, family units.[92]

V. THE GREAT PATRIOTIC WAR, 1941–1945

1. Gender and family in the Soviet resistance

Given the riven and fractured nature of much of Soviet society in the 1930s and the fact that the Red Army command staff had been the object of a devastating purge in 1937–8, it might have been expected that the Soviet Union would crumble in the face of the greatest land invasion ever seen in human history, especially as it was launched by a nation, Germany, whose society had by 1941 reached a very high degree of homogeneity, and whose citizens had ever more willingly entered the great spider's web of the *Volksgemeinschaft*. Instead, at the cost of approximately twenty-seven million dead, the Soviet Union resisted and eventually triumphed.[93] How was this possible, and to what extent did questions of family and gender play a part?

It has to be said straightaway that the utterly draconian nature of the Stalinist regime must figure largely in any explanation of Soviet victory in the Second World War. Although the German attack of 22 June 1941 came as a great surprise to Stalin, and the speed of its advance such as to bring him to the brink of despair, the Soviet Union had for years been preparing for the eventuality of war. In the 1930s Soviet military expenditure was as large as Germany's. At the same time the Soviet workforce was, as Bernd Bonwetsch has written, transformed step by step into a 'mobilised working army'.[94] A decree of 26 June 1940 abolished the already limited freedom of movement for workers, and in October of the same year the workplace was formally mobilised for war. Workers were forbidden to leave their place of work and could be transferred without their consent. Tens of thousands who broke factory discipline or turned up consistently late for work were sentenced to forced labour in the Gulag, a significant number of them women. In addition, the secret police remained a very powerful and ubiquitous force, ready to make summary arrests and carry out executions. Once in combat, members of the Red Army were expected not to surrender. If they did, their families were deprived immediately of any state allowances or other forms of assistance and were rapidly reduced to indigence.[95]

Repression and Terror were one, central force holding the Soviet war effort together. But it would never have been enough without other, less negative factors. One of these was the question of gender. As we have seen, the Nazis had theorised and practised the categorical distinction between men who fight and women who stay at home. Women were to be responsible for the family. Hitler, it may be remembered, had made this categorically clear long before the war, in September 1935:[96]

Once the war started, the Nazis found themselves hoist with their own petard once the war started. In May 1941, in Dresden, of 1,250 women invited to a labour recruitment meeting only 600 turned up and only 120 said they were prepared to take up employment.[97] The contrast with the Soviet regime could hardly have been more stark. Here millions of women worked in the war industries, ensuring an overwhelming superiority for the USSR in numbers of weapons and tanks. Moreover, some 800,000 Soviet women saw active military service during the war. Many served in non-combat roles; for instance, 41 per cent of all doctors at the front and 43 per cent of all surgeons were women. Others performed support functions – sappers, field engineers, telephone and radio operators, drivers, mechanics, and so on. But many thousands of women served directly at the front, terrible though that was. Women fought in infantry divisions, artillery and anti-aircraft units, they were machine gunners, paratroops and partisans.

Bolshevik feminists had conceived of women's emancipation as a long peacetime battle, waged against patriarchal power both inside and outside the family; the Family Codes of 1918 and 1926 had constituted important steps in this direction. In the cauldron of the war, however, women's contribution came to be measured in rather different terms – as an invaluable element both on and off the battlefield in the mobilisation for victory. The gender struggles of the post-revolutionary years had not realised the ambitions of Kollontai and Armand, but they had not been in vain.

Another factor in the Soviet victory concerns the German enemy. Not only was the Wehrmacht a foreign and invading army, but it offered no alternative that might have lured Soviet citizens into abandoning their terrible masters. As Barber and Harrison have written, 'For civilians under occupation, the gains from collaboration were pitiful.'[98] Hitler made no move to decollectivise agriculture, the single action most desired by both Ukrainian and Russian peasantry. This was because he wanted first of all to use the collective farms to ensure grain supplies to Germany, and then eventually to extirpate the Slav population and pass their land to German farmers. The terrain was thus very well prepared, at least for the Russian population of the USSR, to fight a 'Great Patriotic War'.

As in the First World War, but on an even vaster scale, families were dismembered and destroyed. Millions of men were conscripted and left the countryside and the city, very often never to return. Millions of youths aged fourteen upwards were taken from their families, mobilised into the State Labour Reserves and sent to live in factory barracks under harsh discipline. Millions of women, as we have seen, worked in war factories and hundreds of thousands undertook military service. As the Germans advanced countless families fled their homes and were broken up in the process of evacuation. Others froze and starved to death, as in the epic and terrible siege of Leningrad. Death was everywhere, on an unparalleled scale even for Russian history. But the desire to resist the German invaders and the means to do so were both at hand.

2. The Family Law of July 1944

By the summer of 1944 victory was in sight. The regime could allow itself the luxury of thinking in post-war terms, and one of it first concerns was how to respond to the terrible population losses of the previous three years. One outcome was the new Family Law of 8 July 1944, which I would like to consider briefly both in its own right and as the definitive elimination of those radical discourses which had found such remarkable expression in the 1918 Family Code.

The preface to the new law declared rather improbably – given the whole history of post-revolutionary relations between families, especially rural families, and Soviet power – that 'care for children and mothers and the strengthening of the family have always been amongst the most important tasks of the Soviet State'.[99] Despite pious affirmations of this sort, the law was primarily concerned with demographic replacement. It announced a significant increase

fig. 58 Women collective farmers learning to drive tractors to replace the men dispatched to the front, 1941.

in services and financial assistance for women who were pregnant, for mothers with many children and for unmarried mothers. Previously, it was only mothers with seven or more children who had received special assistance and benefits; now the law lowered the threshold to just three. Article 2 also stipulated, in solemn recognition of the countless families destroyed by the war, that 'in assessing the amount of State assistance to mothers with many children, those children who perished or disappeared without trace on the fronts of the Patriotic War are included'.[100]

Unmarried mothers, too, were to receive cash payments on a sliding scale – 100 rubles monthly for one child, 150 rubles for two, and so on. The number of crèches and kindergartens was to be radically increased and their cost reduced. Factories and offices were obliged to provide facilities for breast-feeding. Motherhood Medals were to be given to particularly fertile women. Special taxes were to be levied on those citizens between the ages of twenty and forty-five, both male and female, who had no children, and even on those who had only one or two children. Almost the entire panoply of pro-natal measures with which we have become familiar were wheeled out again for the stricken Soviet society of the war years.

This was one part of the law. The other sounded the death knell for radical family reform. Article 19 underlined that only registered marriage guaranteed full rights and obligations for families, while Articles 23 to 29 redefined the regime's attitude to divorce. The old libertarian stipulations, so beloved by Kollontai and others, were finally abolished. Instead of divorce being a matter of individual choice (of one or both partners), with the state merely registering that occurrence, now it was the state, through its courts, that would decide. The provisions of 1936 had increased the cost of divorce but had not changed the locus or the agent of decision-making. The law of 1944 did both.

Grigory M. Sverdlov and others, commenting upon the new law in 1946, were at pains to stress how family-friendly the regime had become.[101] Yet if we examine the history of state–family relations in the Stalinist years a very different picture emerges. It is a deeply ambiguous one, veined with tragedy and marked by constant, arbitrary violence, perpetrated against not only adults but also children. Stalin sought a 'functional' family, a collective which would serve as the cornerstone of the new Soviet society. But at the same time he did not *trust* families. He was unsure of their loyalties and unable to control their deep-seated passions. He himself had had a deeply traumatic experience of early family life, and his marriages had ended in failure and death. In his own experience, therefore, there was no basis on which to trust the family as an institution.

Stalin responded to this dilemma in a typically Janus-faced fashion. On the one hand, he stressed the need for the family to be a highly fertile, loyal and productive unit, to which he could grant the accolade of 'Soviet collective', both patriotic and proletarian. On the other, there were many families (real or imaginary) which did not entirely conform to Stalin's prerequisites and to those of his secret police. To these suspect families Stalin applied instead a rich catalogue of condemnatory adjectives – the 'backward' family, the 'kulak' family, the 'petty bourgeois family', and so on. This enabled him to create a vast and vague panoply of 'non-approved' families. Stalin's net was cast far wider

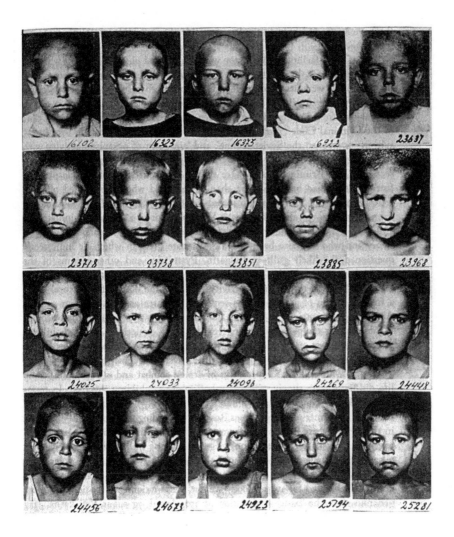

fig. 59 'Relatives of traitors to the fatherland.' Identity photographs of child inmates in a Soviet secret police institution, late 1930s.

and more arbitrarily than that of any of the other regimes examined in this book. The result was a deeply fractured society in which it was possible, having arrested and shot mothers and fathers, to sweep their young children into orphanages, declare them to be the 'relatives of traitors to the fatherland', and wait for them to die from heartbreak, disease or starvation.

Some final considerations

Nearly all children nowadays were horrible. What was worst of all was that by means of such organizations as the Spies they were systematically turned into ungovernable little savages and yet this produced in them no tendency whatever to rebel against the discipline of the Party. On the contrary; they adored the Party and everything connected with it. The songs, the processions, the banners, the hiking, the drilling with dummy rifles, the yelling of slogans, the worship of Big Brother – it was all a sort of glorious game to them [. . .] It was almost normal for people over thirty to be frightened of their own children. And with good reason [. . .] The thing that now suddenly struck Winston was that his mother's death, nearly thirty years ago, had been tragic and sorrowful in a way that was no longer possible. Tragedy, he perceived, belonged to the ancient time when there was still privacy, love and friendship, and when the members of a family stood by one another without needing to know the reason.[1]

None of the regimes examined in this book, not even the most terrible ones, ever attained the degree of physical and above all mental control of families that George Orwell describes in chapter 2 of his famous depiction of a dystopia, *Nineteen Eighty-Four*. The Parsons' flat, next door to Winston's, was the site of a family's disintegration, induced by the regime itself. We can safely call this process 'totalitarian'. The actually existing regimes of the first half of the twentieth century, to whom the adjective 'totalitarian' has all too frequently and loosely been applied, demonstrated no such all-embracing destructive powers with regard to family life. They were certainly ruthless, often in the most barbaric way, towards families of which they disapproved. But they were not against families *per se*. Each of them needed to employ a binary approach, on the one hand repressing certain mass categories of family on ethnic, racial, nationalist, class, religious or political grounds, and on the other bolstering up chosen families, the majority, who were both supported and regimented in their daily lives. The regimes wanted their families to hold together, not to disintegrate into mere groups of atomised individuals. This was as true of Stalin's model of the family as it was of Franco's or of Atatürk's, however different they were in formal, ideological content.

Furthermore, as I have tried to show throughout this book, what we are dealing with is not only the intentions of regimes but the intentions of families. Ferdinand Mount once wrote in a famous diatribe that families are subversive; not necessarily in the sense of organising actively against regimes, but in that of possessing particular codes and cultures of resistance.[2] Alongside the countless stories of the horrific liquidation of families there are others of survival, based not merely on the play of fate and fortune but upon the peculiar qualities and resources that families have – flexibility, solidarities, networks, well-kept secrets, and so on. Who would have bet twopence on Victor Klemperer surviving through the war in Dresden – certainly not Klemperer himself. And yet his resourcefulness and above all that of his Protestant wife Eva Schlemmer enabled them in 1945 to obtain false documents and wend their way southwards from the terrible ruins of Dresden to Bavaria and salvation.[3] And who could forget the way the Catholic middle-class mother Pepa López saved her family from the 'red hordes' in Málaga in July 1936 by dressing up as an itinerant fruit and vegetable seller, swapping her shoes for hemp sandals, clasping her two children tightly by the hand and going down into the street, hoping desperately that no one would recognise her?[4] Not by chance have social scientists called families 'primary' institutions.

Given their undeniable importance, it is all the more surprising that families are hardly mentioned in the very considerable literature on totalitarianism. It would require an entire historiographical essay to explain why this is so. Here, a glance at the most influential and intellectually distinguished treatment of the subject, Hannah Arendt's *The Origins of Totalitarianism* (1951), must suffice.[5] Arendt puts all the emphasis on the atomisation of individuals, each 'in his lonely isolation against all others'.[6] For her, totalitarian domination is new because it destroys not only the public realm but also, and this is crucial, private life. She writes,

> Totalitarian government, like all tyrannies, certainly could not exist without destroying the public realm of life, that is, without destroying, by isolating men, their political capacities. But totalitarian domination as a form of government is new in that it is not content with this isolation and destroys private life as well. It bases itself on loneliness, on the experience of not belonging to the world at all, which is among the most radical and desperate experiences of man.[7]

This haunting version of the destruction of both the public and the private realm, achieved by 'total terror' and 'stringent logicality', rings true across the decades.[8] But by concentrating so much on atomised individuals whose private lives have been pulverised, Arendt can find no space for family relations. They become secondary, invisible, unworthy of analysis. But their absence, both analytical and material, from the literature on totalitarianism (and not only from Arendt) entails a drastic reduction of the historical record, for it leaves unconsidered that layer of social activity which, even in dictatorship, lies between the individual and the state, and which has its lynchpin in the family.[9]

In trying to accord family life a central place in the larger narrative of events (without in any way presenting it as the explanation of everything), I have concentrated on the two great overlapping political phenomena of the first half of the twentieth century: revolution and dictatorship. Looking first at revolution, from both below and above, it was the early years of the Russian experience that produced the most interesting and radical proposals for rethinking family life. The bourgeois family was on the way out, the rural family was the site of all backwardness, the proletarian family could barely survive economically – so why on earth go on thinking in family terms? A small minority of female and male Bolsheviks asked themselves this question but came up with no convincing alternatives to the family. Some of them proposed communal living as a panacea, but communes, initially so ecstatic a social experience, had a nasty habit of collapsing from within, riven by tensions of every sort. Kollontai talked in terms of the construction of the 'great family-society', but the phrase betrayed her failure to grasp the theoretical and political importance of keeping the two spheres separate. Most Bolsheviks had little idea of privacy and private life, believing instead that fulfilment was primarily to be found in a hyperactive public sphere. None of them posited the question of how families could be linked to civil society and to the state while preserving their own autonomy and rights.

It is all too easy, however, to be dismissive about radical rethinking. The post-revolutionary discussion in Russia on the future of family life, with its public debates and new-found Family Codes, left many marks. The most important was undoubtedly female emancipation, which was carried forward with great difficulty and persistence in the face of deep-rooted patriarchal power. Another was Kollontai's brave and lonely insistence that emotional and sexual relations, not just economic ones, were at the heart of liberation – both female and male. At the end of her famous pamphlet *Communism and the Family* she raised the rather extraordinary cry 'equality, liberty and the comradely love of the new marriage'. On these bases women and men, workers and peasants, would stand together for the 'rebuilding of human society'.[10]

It might have been expected that this rich if much-contested heritage would form the basis for further developments of a theoretical and practical sort. In reality, after 1920, once the international revolutionary wave had subsided, radical politics was not to pay much attention to family politics. The Spanish anarcho-syndicalists, often extraordinary in other respects, had little to offer on the family. Their guiding concept in the private sphere was 'free love'. This did not, as its name might suggest, call into question stable homes and monogamous unions. On the contrary, the anarchists believed passionately in both. On paper 'free love' was based upon the principles of liberty and equality: liberty from male possessiveness and control, equality between the sexes in the economic and domestic spheres. In reality, anarchist women remained subordinate to anarchist men, both within the movement and in the home. At the key national congress of the CNT in Zaragoza in May 1936 the anarcho-syndicalists resolutely defended the family. It was an institution, they noted, which had served mankind from time immemorial and would presumably continue to do so for a long time to come.[11]

The immobility of the Spanish anarcho-syndicalists contrasts starkly with the highly original positions assumed by the Kemalists in Turkey. The application in 1926 of the Swiss Civil Code to a society that was overwhelmingly rural and Muslim was an extraordinary act of revolution from above. The Code certainly reserved a whole series of prerogatives to the male head of the family, as was to be expected. But it also – when combined with other parts of Mustafa Kemal's social and cultural legislation – opened up extraordinary vistas for both women and children. Within the family, wives had more rights than ever before, including the crucial one of initiating divorce proceedings in the same way as their husbands. Outside the family, women were educated on a massive scale and served the nation in responsible jobs requiring professional skills. They could walk freely in Turkish society, at least its urban part, unveiled, holding their heads high. As for children, they were to be as disciplined and obedient as in the past, but they were not to be forced into marriage at totally inappropriate ages. In post-revolutionary Russia the 'bourgeois family' was anathema. In Turkey it was revolutionary. Previously, so Gökalp argued, the 'Turkish soul' had not found its ideal breeding ground: the *ümmet* (the Islamic community) was too large and the traditional family too stuck in its ways. Now the nuclear 'yuva', or nest, was the stable domestic unit upon which the new nation could be built.[12]

In western Europe only a very few revolutionary voices discussed the family after the Russian revolution. One of them was that of Antonio Gramsci, who offered, all too fleetingly, a particular vision of family life. For him the family was an 'organ of moral life', an institution to be preserved and cherished, a 'training in humanity and civil education', to be founded on an 'infinite rosary' of benevolent everyday actions. The Catholic images and vocabulary are all too evident, but in Gramsci they are freed from the iron grip of integralism, of the necessity to conform to a pre-established model.[13]

As Gramsci saw it, however, material conditions had not allowed the family to realise its potential. Under early twentieth-century capitalism, he argued, only bourgeois children lived in security and received a proper education; poor children suffered from ill health like Gramsci himself, were illiterate and forced into work at an early age. As a Marxist, Gramsci could conceive of only one solution – the abolition of private property and its conversion into collective property. Only this sharing of the wealth of nations amongst their citizens would ensure that families had a real opportunity to fulfil their destiny, to become 'organs of moral life'. Gramsci did what no other Marxist dared to do: he accepted one part of that doctrine – the abolition of private property – while passionately denying the other – the gradual demotion of the family and the transference of the family's functions to the socialist state. In his famous *Prison Notebooks* Gramsci's thought developed in many directions, but sadly the family was not one of them.

Moving from the comparison of revolutions to that of dictatorships, it becomes immediately apparent, as I have already noted, that the dictators, whatever their denomination and declared ideology, demanded similar things. Whether it was Stalin and his 'Soviet collective', Mustafa Kemal and his bourgeois 'yuva', Hitler and his 'little world' supporting the 'vast world', Franco's Catholic family or Mussolini's Fascist one, they all sought to render their families functional and obedient. Functionalism in this context meant a number of shared undertakings: military preparation, regularity and reliability at work, demographic growth, and unquestioning allegiance, especially among the new generations. Families were to be helped to reproduce, trained in hygiene, praised for their fertility, rendered literate and prepared for war. Their reward was to be recognised as, and to feel part of, the national or people's community. They were also the recipients of what welfare measures were on offer, particularly in a Germany that was returning to full employment under the impact of re-armament. Even in a much poorer country, Italy in the 1930s, working-class families could, for the first time in their lives, climb aboard the regime's *treni popolari* and go to the seaside for the day.

Yet these were far from idyllic societies. Behind the facade of families celebrating the rituals of the regime, lay a deep vein of suspicion and an unflagging system of surveillance and control. Families were being observed the whole time – by the *portiere* and the *Blockwart*, by the petty party official, by the secret policeman and the Civil Guard. They were also, as the archives testify in abundance, being watched (and denounced) by their neighbours. Nor did the regimes have any intention of leaving their chosen families in peace. Their various organisations sucked family members out of their homes and drastically reduced the time that families had to themselves. Although the regimes liked to pretend that the relationship between family and state was seamless, in reality it was fraught with what may be called perennial tensions.

Indeed, the dilemmas raised in Sophocles' *Antigone* have great resonance in this modern context. If forced to choose, to whom does the individual owe loyalty – to family or to state? Certainly, Antigone herself could in no way be described as a model of family relations. But in her conflict with Creon, which ends with her death, and eventually with his, she constantly stresses that her duty to her household gods, her family of origin and her dead brother weighs more heavily upon her than do the laws of Creon's state:

Creon: Of this I am sure –
            Our country is our life; only when she
            Rides safely, have we any friends at all.
            Such is my policy for our common weal.
            [. . .]
Antigone: [. . .] I do not think your edicts strong enough
            To overrule the unwritten unalterable laws
            Of God and Heaven, you being only a man.
            They are not of yesterday or to-day, but everlasting,
            Though where they come from, none of us can tell.
            [. . .]
Creon: [. . .] He who the State appoints must be obeyed
            To the smallest matter, be it right – or wrong.[14]

A subordinate theme in this central conflict concerns burial rights. To whom do the dead belong? Antigone claims the right, denied by the state, to bury her brother and duly pays the consequences. In the modern story I have told, the same conflict occurred on at least two occasions. In the first, Josef Goebbels laid claim to the body of Horst Wessel, the young SA member who was shot in Berlin and whom Goebbels carefully reconstructed as a Nazi hero. In February 1933 Wessel's mother insisted that the family was to be in the forefront of all commemorations. Goebbels commented furiously in his diary, 'She is unbearable in her arrogance. Our dead belong to the nation.'[15] The second occasion, of greater importance, concerns the Spanish Civil War. Between 1939 and 1945 Franco ordered the execution of around 50,000 political prisoners. Most of them were shot at night and buried in unmarked common graves. Until recently, their relatives had no chance of reclaiming and burying their bodies. And this from the 'great champion of the family'!

Once at war, the regimes became *destroyers* of families on an unprecedented scale. Even the Italian Fascists, who had tried to reassure families (and mothers in particular) as to the limited consequences of Mediterranean conquest, saw their peninsula transformed into a battlefield, their cities bombed and the front line move with agonising slowness back towards Germany. The poisoned chalice of nineteenth-century nationalism, an ideology so inspirational and romantic at one level, so intrinsically destructive at another, gathered racist and imperial force throughout the century and was ready to vomit all its evil during what has come to be known as the European Thirty Years War from 1914 to 1945. At the same time Communism triumphed in the East but not in the West, assuming repressive forms as terrible as those of its opponents. The list of their combined victims is, as we have seen, very long indeed: Muslim families at the time of the Balkan Wars, the Armenians of Asia Minor in 1915–16, Ukrainian peasants in the famine, the Bedouins of Cyrenaica in 1930–1, the Jews and gypsies of the Great Reich, the victims of forced collectivisation and Terror in the USSR, the 'reds' of Barcelona and Madrid, and so on.

Historical comparison, as Marc Bloch was at pains to point out many years ago, must be as much concerned with difference as with similitude.[16] Up to this point I have underlined the degree to which the various regimes, viewed through the novel lens of family politics, resemble each other. An exploration of their differences reveals, by contrast, a highly complex picture with no constant pattern or predictable outcome. The Soviet Union, to put it bluntly, is not the eternal odd man out. Demography, race, gender, the regimentation of civil society – each produces an unexpectedly different cluster of regimes. If we seek to compare the regimes' effective control over families, rather than their own or subsequent ideological labelling, they appear to occupy different points along a single spectrum: at one end, Mussolini's pretentious but *relatively* lax family politics in Italy; at the other the high degree of control exercised by the Nazis over an advanced society, and the enduring loyalty of a majority of German families to them until the bitter end. Such obduracy is made the more difficult to explain when we see that while all the regimes experimented with pro-natal policies, with very mixed results, only the Nazis systematically applied anti-natal policies and 'negative eugenics' – the wilful destruction of the weakest, oldest and least protected members of their own community.

The Soviet Union remains the regime whose interpretation presents us with the greatest conundrums. It is there that we find a really distinctive view of gender relations, born of the revolution but far from entirely lost in the ensuing decades. I have tried to chart the fight against patriarchy and the progress of women's emancipation up to the end of the Second World War. After it, the drastic shortage of men in the Soviet Union tended to strengthen patriarchal behaviour, both within and outside the home. Yet it is interesting to note how a decidedly anti-Stalinist survey of Soviet family life such as that of H. K. Geiger of 1968 pays tribute to the emergence from the 1940s onwards of very positive gender relations in many urban marriages, based on what he calls the pattern of 'equal rights with love'.[17]

This is one side of the Soviet family story. The other is extraordinarily dark. Of all the regimes considered here, the Soviet was the greatest and most arbitrary destroyer of its own families. At the height of what Nicolas Werth has called the 'ordinary people's Terror', between August 1937 and November 1938, there were some 50,000 executions each month, as secret police functionaries strove to fulfil their weekly killing targets.[18] Furthermore, between 1929 and 1953 some eighteen million Soviet citizens passed through the camps and colonies of the Gulag system. No other system of detention and slave labour in the twentieth century comes anywhere near these figures.

Yet the scale of the Soviet tragedy cannot be measured in merely numerical terms. From the point of view of family life, a crucial distinction between Nazism and Stalinism becomes apparent. In Germany, Jewish, Roma and Sinti families, as well as homosexuals, were ferociously discriminated against and eventually liquidated, but the integrity of family emotions – the love of one for another – was left intact, and in many cases was even strengthened by the ordeal.[19] This remained true even in the terrible moment when the regime separated out men, women and children in preparation for the gas chambers. In the Soviet Union, by contrast, families were not just physically fractured and scattered, but *emotionally* as well, with adult turned against adult and children against parents. Children learned that their parents were traitors not only to the fatherland and to everything they had been taught at school but also to their own families. The ensuing heartbreak and tragic division of loyalties was far from the only crime against humanity perpetrated in these years, but it stands out for its particular horror.

A final point concerns civil society. Given the enormity of the killings involved and the repressive apparatuses of each of the regimes in question (even Mussolini's was drastically efficient when it came to suppressing political conspiracy), any discussion of 'civil society' might well seem entirely superfluous.[20] Certainly, the associations and pluralism that usually mark out civil society were perforce absent or eliminated. Yet side by side with the history of pure repression lies another story, made up of fragile and innovative associationism, individual testimonies, micro-histories of resistance to the dominant powers. In the Ottoman Empire in the first decade of the twentieth century some parts of a growing urban bourgeoisie, in particular non-Muslim merchants and their families, took the first steps towards the creation of a plural and solidly based civil society in Istanbul and other major cities. The assumption of power by the CUP rapidly destroyed any such initiatives. In Russia at the time of the revolution, the Soviets, such as those studied by Getzler at Kronstadt, were dynamic and in part autonomous political organisations which drew their legitimacy from local society.[21] These too were rapidly crushed, this time by autocratic Communism. The Spanish anarchists, from whom one might have expected something different, in reality had little time for diversity. The massacres perpetrated against priests, monks and nuns, carried out for the most part in the first six months of the Civil War by militants of the FAI and the CNT, bore terrible testimony both to these organisations' intolerance and to their casual attitudes to violence.

The Catholic Church occupies a place apart. Its performance in the face of dictatorship was not a distinguished one. The Church of Pius XI and Pius XII was deeply integralist, and had little sympathy for any idea of a civil society founded on autonomy and pluralism. The consequences of such a position became tragically clear as the 1920s and 1930s unfolded. The Church defended not family life as such but rather Catholic families and Catholic civilisation. Religious conformity alone guaranteed rights and protection. During the Spanish Civil War the great majority of bishops disgraced themselves by remaining silent in the face of the horrors perpetrated by the Army of Africa (and others) against both women and men of republican, socialist or anarchist beliefs, or who simply had a trade union card in their back pocket.

If even the Church failed to take a stand, what hope could there be for any autonomous associationism? Against all the odds, small pockets of free discussion, even of dissent, survived. One of the most important of these was the family itself. Discussion was forcibly transposed from the public sphere into its last possible refuge – the family and the home. This was not the 'all-sufficiency of home', that early nineteenth-century rural comfort and delight in domesticity to which Jane Austen refers.[22] It was rather twentieth-century urban domestic space, often drastically restricted, of the sort depicted by Max Beckmann in 1920.[23] In the garrets of Berlin during the Nazi regime, whispered, dissenting conversations were possible. So too were mere glances of exasperation, exchanged by one member of a family with another. Codes, secrets, memories, strategies, solidarities – these were all things that families were expert at. Sometimes, when tyranny was looking the other way, conversations initiated around a kitchen table could suddenly take public form, as when a group of Turin workers wore red braces on May Day. 'Distances' could be taken from the regimes – usually minimal, but occasionally less so.

My last comparison is an unlikely one, between the Fascist and the Soviet regimes. Both were characterised by a deep-rooted culture of patronage, and this widened the margins of manoeuvre for families. They could seek to traverse the apparently sheer faces of the state by means of patron–client relations, by bringing into play kinship and clientelistic networks; women could negotiate with officials in a way that men could not. *Blat* (pull or influence), hardly a category that fitted naturally into the canons of Communism, continued to be crucial for urban Soviet families in their daily fight against deprivations of every kind.

Of course, all these mechanisms and resources were not 'civil society' in any real sense. They served, rather, to keep alight the memory of what freedom had been and of what it might become. After 1945 new questions came to the fore. One of the most fascinating of these was how families in various states, in the radically new environment of civil and political liberties, should connect to civil society and the democratic state. But that is another story, still to be told.

Notes

FOREWORD

1. Sheila Rowbotham, *Hidden from History: 300 Years of Women's Oppression and the Fight against It* (London: Pluto Press, 1973). Even in Eric Hobsbawm's path-breaking general history, *Age of Extremes: The Short Twentieth Century, 1914–1991* (London: Michael Joseph, 1994), families are treated in marginal fashion. Of course, there have been sectional and single-nation analyses, upon which my work depends in more than one point; for a valuable general introduction; see David I. Kertzer and Marzio Barbagli (eds), *Family Life in the Twentieth Century*, vol. 3 of *The History of the European Family* (New Haven and London: Yale University Press, 2003), and for an innovative and wide-ranging sociological approach, see Göran Therborn, *Between Sex and Power: Family in the World, 1900–2000* (London: Routledge, 2004).
2. Readers may be interested in an earlier and fuller version of this framework, to be found in Paul Ginsborg, 'Family, civil society and the state in contemporary European history: some methodological considerations', *Contemporary European History*, 4 (1995), pp. 249–73. In May 2008 the Cambridge Historical Society dedicated a one-day conference to discussing my work on the relations between family, civil society and the state. Quentin Skinner kindly edited the volume based on the conference proceedings: Quentin Skinner (ed.), *Families and States in Western Europe* (Cambridge: Cambridge University Press, 2011).
3. The essay may be found online at http://bit.ly/ginsborg-appendix.

ACKNOWLEDGEMENTS

1. One recent fruit of this collaboration is Jürgen Nautz, Paul Ginsborg and Ton Nijhuis (eds), *The Golden Chain: Family, Civil Society and the State* (New York and Oxford: Berghahn, 2013).

CHAPTER 1: REVOLUTIONISING FAMILY LIFE: RUSSIA, 1917–1927

1. Aleksandra Kollontai, 'Iz vospominanii', *Oktyabr*, 9 (1945), p. 61, quoted in Barbara Evans Clements, *Bolshevik Feminist: The Life of Aleksandra Kollontai* (Bloomington and London: Indiana University Press, 1979), p. 6. Kollontai's diaries, from 1922 onwards, have been published in Aleksandra Kollontai, *Diplomaticheskiye dnevniki, 1922–1940, v dvukh tomakh* (Moscow, 2001). Her collected letters are to be found in Kollontai, *'Revolyutsiya Velikaya Myatezhnitsa': Izbrannyye pisma, 1901–1952* (Moscow, 1989). A valuable collection of articles and memoirs is constituted by Kollontai, *Iz moyey zhizni i raboty: Vospominaniya i dnevniki*, ed. I. M. Dazhina (Moscow: Sovetskaya Rossiya, 1974). In English we have the short and highly unsatisfactory Aleksandra Kollontai, *Autobiography of a Sexually Emancipated Woman* (1926; New York: Herder and Herder, 1971). The German edition, *Autobiographie einer sexuell Emanzipierten* (Munich: Rogner & Bernhard, 1970), is slightly fuller than the English version.

2. Aleksandra Kollontai, *Den första etappen* (The First Steps) (Stockholm: Bonniers, 1945), p. 140, quoted in Clements, *Bolshevik Feminist*, p. 5.

3. Beatrice Farnsworth, *Aleksandra Kollontai: Socialism, Feminism and the Bolshevik Revolution* (Stanford: Stanford University Press, 1980), pp. 5, 8 ff., 97 ff. Both this work and that of Barbara Clements, cited above, are outstanding biographies of Kollontai. Another good work of the same period, Cathy Porter, *Alexandra Kollontai: The Lonely Struggle of the Woman who Defied Lenin* (New York: The Dial Press, 1980), is especially sensitive to Kollontai's family relations.

4. Kollontai, 'Iz vospominanii', p. 85, quoted in Clements, *Bolshevik Feminist*, p. 272.

5. For individual romantic self-affirmation, see Lilian R. Furst, *The Contours of European Romanticism* (London: Macmillan, 1979).

6. Ivan Sergeyevich Turgenev, *On the Eve* (London: Heinemann, 1973), p. 71 (*Nakanune*, published for the first time in *Russky vestnik*, 25 (1860), pp. 69–212).

7. Ibid., p. 152. The political reception of *On the Eve* in Russia is discussed by Isaiah Berlin in his *Russian Thinkers* (1978; Harmondsworth: Penguin, 2008), pp. 312–16.

8. In 1881 an ascetic young noblewoman, Sofia Perovskaya, a member of the 'People's Will', was sentenced to be hanged for her part in the assassination of Tsar Alexander II. Her execution made a great impression upon educated circles in St Petersburg and upon the nine-year-old Aleksandra; Farnsworth, *Aleksandra Kollontai*, p. 6.

9. Ibid., p. 378.

10. Kollontai, *Autobiography*, pp. 12–13.

11. Ibid., p. 11.

12. Karl Marx, 'Private property and Communism', in *Economic and Philosophical Manuscripts*, in Marx, *Early Texts*, ed. David McLellan (Oxford: Basil Blackwell, 1972), p. 148.

13. Richard Stites, 'Aleksandra Kollontai and the Russian revolution', in Jane Slaughter and Robert Kern (eds), *Socialism, Feminism and the Problems Faced by Political Women, 1880 to the Present* (Westport, Conn.: Greenwood Press, 1981), pp. 105–6.

14. Richard Stites, *The Women's Liberation Movement in Russia: Feminism, Nihilism and Bolshevism, 1860–1930* (Princeton: Princeton University Press, 1978); Barbara Alpern Engel, *Mothers and Daughters: Women of the Intelligentsia in Nineteenth-Century Russia* (Cambridge: Cambridge University Press, 1983); Laura Engelstein, *The Keys to Happiness: Sex and the Search for Modernity in Fin-de-siècle Russia* (Cornell: Cornell University Press, 1992).

15. These pre-war writings are collected in Aleksandra Kollontai, *Novaya moral i rabochy klass* (Moscow: Izd. VTsIK, 1919). Some extracts are to be found in English in Aleksandra Kollontai, *Selected Writings*, ed. Alix Holt (New York: Norton, 1980), pp. 88–98, 237–49.

16. Even E. H. Carr adopts the line that Kollontai 'preached the uninhibited satisfaction of the sexual impulse'; Edward H. Carr, *Socialism in One Country, 1924–1926*, vol. 1 (London: Macmillan, 1964), p. 31.

17. Kollontai was heavily influenced by the German psychologist Greta Meisel-Hess, who in 1909 published *Die sexuelle Krise* (Jena: E. Diederichs, 1909). Kollontai reviewed her work in 1911 in her article 'Lyubov i novaya moral' (Love and the new morality), republished in Kollontai, *Novaya moral*, pp. 36–47.

18. *Sexual Relations and the Class Struggle* (1911), in Kollontai, *Selected Writings*, p. 243. Her intense, unhappy and very hidden affair in the period 1909–10 with Pyotr Maslov, a Menshevik economist who was married with five children, contributed to this disenchantment with romantic love; see Porter, *Alexandra Kollontai*, pp. 153–4.

19. Aleksandra Kollontai, 'Make way for winged Eros: a letter to working youth' (1923), in Kollontai, *Selected Writings*, pp. 277–88.

20. Aleksandra Kollontai, 'Novaya zhenshchina' (1913), in Kollontai, *Novaya moral*, p. 9. These pre-war statements and articles are more iconoclastic in terms of women's sexual liberty than those published later. The famous article of 1923, 'Make way for winged

Eros', is much more reticent. We shall see why as the social realities of the Russian revolution unfold.

21. N. T. Chernyshevsky, *A Vital Question, or What is to be Done?* (New York: Thomas Crowell, 1886).

22. Elizabeth Waters, 'The Bolsheviks and the family', *Contemporary European History*, 4 (1995), p. 276.

23. Misha managed to escape conscription in Russia and his mother helped him to find a job at Paterson, New Jersey. There in the summer of 1916, isolated and depressed, he appealed to his mother to come and be with him. 'For once in her life', writes Barbara Clements, 'Kollontai abandoned her work to minister to her son'; Clements, *Bolshevik Feminist*, p. 98.

24. I. M. Dazhina (ed.), 'Amerikanskiye dnevniki A. M. Kollontai (1915–1916)', *Istorichesky arkhiv*, 1 (1962), p. 156, quoted in Farnsworth, *Aleksandra Kollontai*, p. 60.

25. In January 1917, Lenin told a Swiss audience that he was doubtful whether 'we the old will live to see the decisive battles of the coming revolution'; Edward H. Carr, *The Bolshevik Revolution, 1917–1923*, vol. 1 (London: Macmillan, 1950), p. 80.

26. Peter Czap Jr, ' "A large family: the peasant's greatest wealth": serf households in Mishino, Russia, 1814–1858', in Richard Wall, Jean Robin and Peter Laslett (eds), *Family Forms in Historic Europe* (Cambridge: Cambridge University Press, 1983), pp. 105–52.

27. 'Dvor' was also used as a synonym for 'dom' (home), 'izba' (log-house), 'dym' (peasant dwelling), 'semya' (family) and 'tyaglo' (a unit of human labour).

28. Christine Worobec, *Peasant Russia: Family and Community in the Post-Emancipation Period* (Princeton: Princeton University Press, 1991), p. 209.

29. Czap, 'A large family', p. 141. Another village study of great fascination is to be found in Steven L. Hoch, *Serfdom and Social Control in Russia: Petrovskoe, a Village in Tambov* (Chicago: Chicago University Press, 1985).

30. Barbara Alpern Engel, *Women, Work, and Family in Russia, 1861–1914* (Cambridge: Cambridge University Press, 1994), p. 4.

31. Christine Worobec summarises the situation in the following way: 'As a result of an increase in *premortem* fission, i.e., households dividing before the patriarch's death, and the abolition of serfowner controls of peasant families, the simple nuclear family became more visible in post-emancipation rural Russia. The normative extended family, nonetheless, remained predominant'; Worobec, *Peasant Russia*, p. 12.

32. For an early twentieth-century report on rural living conditions in the fertile Black Earth region, see Sir John Maynard, *Russia in Flux: Before October* (London: Gollancz, 1941), p. 44.

33. Worobec, *Peasant Russia*, pp. 206–8; Peter Gatrell, *The Tsarist Economy* (London: Batsford, 1986), pp. 31–7.

34. Worobec, *Peasant Russia*, p. 188. See also Peter Czap Jr, 'Marriage and the peasant joint family in the era of serfdom', in David L. Ransel (ed.), *The Family in Imperial Russia: New Lines of Historical Research* (Urbana: University of Illinois Press, 1978), p. 105.

35. Cathy A. Frierson, 'Razdel: the peasant family divided', in Beatrice Farnsworth and Lynne Viola (eds), *Russian Peasant Women* (Oxford and New York: Oxford University Press, 1992), pp. 73–88.

36. Worobec, *Peasant Russia*, p. 177, and pp. 186–7 for the Orthodox Church and women.

37. Vera Shevzov, *Russian Orthodoxy on the Eve of the Revolution* (Oxford: Oxford University Press, 2004), esp. ch. 5, 'Icons', and ch. 6, 'The message of Mary', pp. 171–263; Cathy A. Frierson, *Peasant Icons: Representations of Rural People in Late 19th-Century Russia* (Oxford: Oxford University Press, 1993); Orlando Figes, *Natasha's Dance: A Cultural History of Russia* (New York: Metropolitan Books, 2002), pp. 292–309. The best general discussion of the figure of the Virgin Mary remains Marina Warner, *Alone of All Her Sex: The Myth and the Cult of the Virgin Mary* (London: Weidenfeld & Nicolson, 1972).

38. Moshe Lewin, *The Making of the Soviet System: Essays in the Social History of Interwar Russia* (London: Methuen, 1985), p. 275.
39. Gregory L. Freeze, 'Russian Orthodoxy: Church, people and politics in Imperial Russia', in *The Cambridge History of Russia*, vol. 2, *Imperial Russia, 1689–1917* (Cambridge: Cambridge University Press, 2006), p. 299, table 14.1.
40. 'Obshchina' was the term used by educated society of the time and subsequently by most historians; peasants used 'a more familiar and older' term, 'mir', which has a wealth of complementary meanings: 'community' and 'assembly', as well as 'world' and 'peace'; Dorothy Atkinson, *The End of the Russian Land Commune, 1905–1930* (Stanford: Stanford University Press, 1983), pp. 5–6.
41. Ibid., pp. 3–5.
42. Franco Venturi, *Roots of Revolution: A History of the Populist and Socialist Movements in Nineteenth-Century Russia* (London: Weidenfeld and Nicolson, 1960). In the 1870s the Populist movement had seen thousands of educated and idealistic youth 'going to the people', hoping to find in the peasant communes the nuclei of a new society. By and large they were to be disappointed. In February 1881 Vera Zasulich wrote to Karl Marx to ask him whether the rural communes could be the kernels of Russian socialism. Marx wrote four drafts of a reply before responding, briefly, that 'the commune is the fulcrum for social regeneration in Russia'. But he added immediately that it would have first to be rid of 'the harmful influences assailing it on all sides'. For a full and stimulating discussion, see Theodor Shanin (ed.), *Late Marx and the Russian Road: Marx and 'the Peripheries of Capitalism'* (New York: Monthly Review Press, 1983); Marx's final reply to Zasulich is on pp. 123–4.
43. For the best recent analysis of the history and functioning of the commune, see David Moon, *The Russian Peasantry, 1600–1930: The World the Peasants Made* (London: Longman, 1999), pp. 237–81, esp. pp. 230–6.
44. '[The commune's] dualism admits of an alternative: either its property element will gain the upper hand over its collective element; or else the reverse will take place. Everything depends upon the historical context in which it is located'; Marx's third draft to Zasulich, in Shanin, *Late Marx*, pp. 120–1.
45. For a useful overview, see Gregory J. Massell, *The Surrogate Proletariat: Moslem Women and Revolutionary Strategies in Soviet Central Asia, 1919–1929* (Princeton: Princeton University Press, 1974), pp. 3–7.
46. Ibid., pp. 109 ff.
47. Douglas Northrop, *Veiled Empire: Gender and Power in Stalinist Central Asia* (Ithaca: Cornell University Press, 2004), p. 19.
48. Edward J. Lazzerini, 'Jadīdism', in *The Oxford Encyclopedia of the Modern Islamic World*, 4 vols (Oxford: Oxford University Press, 1995), vol. 2, pp. 351–2.
49. Jascha Golowanjuk, *My Golden Road from Samarkand* (Stockholm, 1937; London: Harrap, 1958), pp. 9–17. The author and his family escaped from Samarkand and he later became a professional violinist in the Gothenburg Symphony Orchestra.
50. See Alain Blum and Leonid E. Darskij, 'Le modèle soviétique (1917–1991) et ses devenirs', in Jean-Pierre Bardet and Jacques Dupâquier (eds), *Histoire des populations de l'Europe*, vol. 3, *Les temps incertains (1914–1988)* (Paris: Fayard, 1999), p. 697. See also Giambattista Salinari and Paul Ginsborg, 'Statistical Essay', http://bit.ly/ginsborg-appendix. For the crisis and growth of the manufacturing sector between 1900 and 1917, see Gatrell, *The Tsarist Economy*, pp. 141–87.
51. Rose L. Glickman, *Russian Factory Women: Workplace and Society, 1880–1914* (Berkeley and Los Angeles: University of California Press, 1984), p. 129. For conditions in the bast-matting industry, see Robert Eugene Johnson, *Peasant and Proletarian: The Working Class of Moscow in the Late Nineteenth Century* (New Brunswick, N.J.: Rutgers University Press, 1979), p. 52.
52. P. Timofeyev, 'What the factory worker lives by', in Victoria E. Bonnell (ed.), *The Russian Worker: Life and Labor under the Tsarist Regime* (Berkeley and Los Angeles: University of California Press, n.d.), p. 79.

53. Reginald E. Zelnik (ed.), *A Radical Worker in Tsarist Russia: The Autobiography of Semën I. Kanatchikov* (Stanford: Stanford University Press, 1986), p. 9.
54. Ibid., p. 10.
55. Ibid., p. 83, table 8.
56. For an effective overview of the working class of St Petersburg, see Stephen A. Smith, *Red Petrograd: Revolution in the Factories* (Cambridge: Cambridge University Press, 1983), ch. 1, 'A profile of the Petrograd working class on the eve of 1917', pp. 3–36.
57. For what follows I am indebted to the outstanding portrait of working-class family life to be found in Barbara Alpern Engel, *Between the Fields and the City*, ch. 6, 'Making a home in the city', pp. 198–238.
58. Ibid., p. 215.
59. Johnson, *Peasant and Proletarian*, pp. 60 and 84–5.
60. Engel, *Between the Fields and the City*, p. 228.
61. Kollontai, *Sexual Relations*, p. 246.
62. Ibid., p. 245.
63. Wilfred Owen, 'The parable of the old man and the young', in Owen, *The Complete Poems and Fragments*, ed. Jon Stallworthy (London: Chatto & Windus, 1983), vol. 1, p. 166. The poem ends with the lines 'But the old man would not so, but slew his son / And half the seed of Europe, one by one.'
64. Irina Davidian, 'The Russian soldier's morale from the evidence of Tsarist military censorship', in Hugh Cecil and Peter H. Liddle (eds), *Facing Armageddon: The First World War Experienced* (Barnsley: Pen and Sword, 2003), p. 428.
65. Alexey Brusilov, *A Soldier's Notebook, 1914–1918* (London: Macmillan, 1930), pp. 37 and 39, quoted in Orlando Figes, *A People's Tragedy: The Russian Revolution, 1891–1924* (London: Pimlico, 1997), p. 258.
66. Ibid., pp. 93–4.
67. Vladimir Buldakov, 'The national experience of war, 1914–1917', in Cecil and Liddle, *Facing Armageddon*, p. 542.
68. Gennady Bordyugov, 'The First World War and social deviance in Russia', in ibid., p. 551.
69. Jay Winter, 'Some paradoxes of the First World War', in Richard Wall and Jay Winter (eds), *The Upheaval of War: Family, Work and Welfare in Europe, 1914–1918* (Cambridge: Cambridge University Press, 1988), p. 9.
70. Davidian, 'The Russian soldier's morale', pp. 432–3.
71. See Karl Marx, *Critique of Hegel's Philosophy of Right* (1843), ed. J. O'Malley (Cambridge: Cambridge University Press, 1970). Marx's critique begins at § 257.
72. This is made quite explicit in Marx's letter to P. V. Annenkov of 28 December 1846, in Karl Marx and Friedrich Engels, *Collected Works*, vol. 38 (London: Lawrence and Wishart, 1982), p. 96.
73. Karl Marx and Friedrich Engels, *The Communist Manifesto*, in Marx and Engels, *The Revolutions of 1848*, ed. David Fernbach (Harmondsworth: Penguin, 1973), p. 83.
74. Friedrich Engels, 'Principles of Communism', in Marx and Engels, *Collected Works*, vol. 6 (London: Lawrence and Wishart, 1976), p. 351. This brief popular work was first published only in 1914. See Richard Weikart, 'Marx, Engels, and the abolition of the family', *History of European Ideas*, 18 (1994), p. 665.
75. Engels, 'Principles of Communism', p. 354.
76. Friedrich Engels, *The Origins of the Family, Private Property and the State* (1884; London: Penguin, 2010).
77. This was a comforting thought for Engels, especially as he took a very dim view of Victorian marriage. He wrote, 'All that this Protestant monogamy achieves, taking the average of the best cases, is a conjugal partnership of leaden boredom, known as "domestic bliss" '; ibid., pp. 101–2.
78. Ibid., p. 217.

79. August Bebel, *Woman under Socialism* (New York: Labor News Company, 1917), p. 332. For the debate on the family in the German Social Democratic Party (SPD), see the very useful article by Richard J. Evans, 'Politics and the family: social democracy and the working-class family, 1891–1914', in Richard J. Evans and William R. Lee (eds), *The German Family: Essays on the Social History of the Family in 19th- and 20th-Century Germany* (London: Croom Helm, 1981), pp. 277–89. Clara Zetkin, one of the leading female figures in the party, was initially in favour of the abolition of the family, but then changed her opinion from 1896 onwards. From that point she supported the idea of converting the family from an 'economic unit' to a 'moral' one, founded on gender parity and love. For some affinities with Gramsci, see below, pp. 155–7. In general, the SPD saw its role as that of protecting the integrity of working-class families, their culture and their values. See also Maria Casalini, 'La famiglia socialista: linguaggio di classe e identità di genere nella cultura del movimento operaio', *Italia contemporanea*, 241 (2005), pp. 415–47.

80. Victor Horta, *Mémoires*, quoted in Maurizio Degl'Innocenti, 'Per una storia delle case del popolo in Italia, dalle origini alla prima guerra mondiale', in Degl'Innocenti (ed.), *Le case del popolo in Europa: Dalle origini alla seconda guerra mondiale* (Florence: Sansoni, 1984), p. 35.

81. Vladimir I. Lenin, 'Capitalist manufacture and capitalist domestic industry' (ch. 6 of *The Development of Capitalism in Russia*, 1899), partially reprinted in Lenin, *On the Emancipation of Women*, 4th revised edn (Moscow: Progress, 1974), p. 17.

82. Michael Pearson, *Lenin's Mistress: The Life of Inessa Armand* (New York: Random House, 2001), pp. 129–30. Pearson's biography is the one that concentrates the most on Armand's letters to her children. See also the more detailed and scholarly account by Ralph C. Elwood, *Inessa Armand: Revolutionary and Feminist* (Cambridge: Cambridge University Press, 1992), as well as Georges Bardawil, *Inès Armand: La deuxième fois que j'entendis parler d'elle* (Paris: Lattès, 1993).

83. Elwood, *Inessa Armand*, p. 35. Inessa expressed wonder at his 'devoted and selfless friendship'.

84. Pearson, *Lenin's Mistress*, p. 107, which contains an ample extract from this undated letter. The complete letter has been published in Russian in *Svobodnaya mysl*, 3 (1992), pp. 80–8.

85. Rudolf Schlesinger (ed.), *The Family in the USSR: Documents and Readings* (London: Routledge and Kegan Paul, 1949), pp. 26–7.

86. Louis Fischer, *The Life of Lenin* (New York: Harper and Row, 1964), p. 79. For the public Lenin, see especially the highly detailed biography in three volumes by Robert Service, *Lenin: A Political Life* (London: Macmillan, 1985–95).

87. Kollontai, *Autobiography*, pp. 37–8. Kollontai's period as commissar is well covered both in Clements, *Bolshevik Feminist*, pp. 124 ff., and Farnsworth, *Aleksandra Kollontai*, pp. 95 ff.

88. Yekaterina Bochkaryova and Serafima Lyubimova, *Women of a New World* (Moscow: Progress, 1969), p. 192, quoted in Farnsworth, *Aleksandra Kollontai*, p. 98.

89. Louise Bryant, *Mirrors of Moscow* (New York: Thomas Seltzer, 1923), p. 111.

90. Farnsworth, *Aleksandra Kollontai*, pp. 100–1.

91. John Reed, *Ten Days that Shook the World (An Account of the Russian Revolution)* (New York: Boni & Liveright, 1919).

92. Bryant, *Mirrors of Moscow*, p. 116.

93. Jacques Sadoul, *Notes sur la Révolution bolchevique* (Paris: Éditions de la Sirène, 1919), p. 95.

94. Anna M. Itkina, *Revolyutsioner, tribun, diplomat: Stranitsi zhizni Aleksandry Mikhailovny Kollontai* (Moscow: Politizdat, 1970), p. 191, quoted in Clements, *Bolshevik Feminist*, p. 135.

95. Clements, *Bolshevik Feminist*, p. 135.

96. Kollontai, *Autobiography*, p. 35.

97. Ibid.

98. Mary Ann Glendon, *The Transformation of Family Law: State, Law and Family in the United States and Western Europe* (Chicago: University of Chicago Press, 1989), p. 5.

99. For more details of the situation before the revolution, see William G. Wagner, *Marriage, Property and Law in Late Imperial Russia* (Oxford: Clarendon Press, 1984).

100. *The Marriage Laws of Soviet Russia: First Code of Laws of the Russian Socialist Federal Soviet Republic dealing with Civil Status and Domestic Relations, Marriage, the Family and Guardianship* (New York: The Russian Soviet Government Bureau, 1921), Title II, ch. 4, p. 42. The committee to draft the Code met at the Commissariat of Justice from August 1918 onwards, nearly a year after the revolution.

101. Ibid., Title III, Ch. 1, Art. 143, p. 57.

102. Soviet labour law had already prohibited work by children under the age of sixteen.

103. Ibid., Title III, Ch. 3, Art. 160, p. 60. This article reasserted the abolition of inheritance already decreed on 27 April 1918.

104. Ibid., Title II, Ch. 5, Art. 129, p. 50.

105. Ibid., 'Introduction to the Code', p. 16. Goikhbarg added, 'there was no recognition of any inalienable right to succession, but merely a convenient method by which the government relieved itself of the trouble of assuming the control and disposition of a great number of small properties'; ibid., p. 15.

106. Schlesinger, *The Family in the USSR*, p. 44.

107. See the illuminating commentary in Dan Healey, *Homosexual Desire in Revolutionary Russia: The Regulation of Sexual and Gender Dissent* (Chicago: University of Chicago Press, 2001), pp. 77–125.

108. Aleksandr G. Goikhbarg, 'Pervy Kodeks Zakonov RSFSR', *Proletarskaya revolyutsiya i pravo*, 1918, no. 7, quoted in Wendy Z. Goldman, *Women, the State and Revolution: Soviet Family Policy and Social Life, 1917–1936* (Cambridge: Cambridge University Press, 1993), pp. 53–4. Goldman offers a full discussion of the Code (ibid., pp. 48–57).

109. Mill did write at the very end of his posthumously published *Chapters on Socialism* that 'Society is fully entitled to abrogate or alter any particular right of property which on sufficient consideration it judges to stand in the way of public good', but he would have been adamantly opposed to the abolition of the right of property *tout court*; John S. Mill, *Chapters on Socialism* (1879), in John S. Mill, *Collected Works*, vol. 5 (Toronto and London: University of Toronto Press and Routledge and Kegan Paul, 1967), p. 503.

110. For Leviathan and the family, see David Runciman, 'A theoretical overview', in Quentin Skinner (ed.), *Families and States in Western Europe* (Cambridge: Cambridge University Press, 2011), pp. 1–17.

111. Moshe Lewin, 'The Civil War: dynamics and legacy', in Lewin, *Russia/USSR/Russia: The Drive and Drift of a Super State* (New York: The New Press, 1995), p. 44.

112. Catherine Merridale, *Night of Stone: Death and Memory in Twentieth-Century Russia* (London: Penguin, 2002), p. 106.

113. Nikolay M. Borodin, *One Man in his Time* (London: Constable, 1955), p. 19, quoted in Merridale, *Night of Stone*, pp. 107–8.

114. The mechanisms of cyclical social mobility, which Theodor Shanin examines in masterful fashion, reinforced peasant solidarities and did much to nullify their economic inequalities, the point of departure of all Bolshevik analyses. It must also be noted that some peasant families consciously adopted the strategy of partitioning the patriarchal *dvor* as a good way of avoiding the taxation, requisitioning and other punitive measures aimed at richer families during War Communism; Theodor Shanin, *The Awkward Class: Political Sociology of Peasantry in a Developing Society: Russia, 1910–1925* (Oxford: Clarendon Press, 1972), esp. part 3, pp. 145–202.

115. This last was one of the four reasons offered by Lenin for the Bolshevik victory, the others being the Treaty of Brest-Litovsk, the disunity of the imperial forces and peasant revolution; cf. Ewan Mawdsley, *The Russian Civil War* (London: Allen and Unwin, 1987), p. 275; for Brest-Litovsk, ibid., pp. 36–8.

116. For the Ukraine, see Andrea Graziosi, *The Great Soviet Peasant War: Bolsheviks and Peasants, 1917–1933* (Cambridge, Mass.: Ukrainian Research Institute, Harvard University Press, 1996).

117. Mawdsley, *The Russian Civil War*, pp. 288–9. He also concludes wisely that 'The Bolsheviks were less afraid of civil war than they should have been.'

118. As a counterbalance to these tendencies, see the excellent article by Donald J. Raleigh, 'The Russian Civil War, 1917–1922', in *The Cambridge History of Russia*, vol. 3, *The Twentieth Century* (Cambridge: Cambridge University Press, 2006), pp. 140–67.

119. Order signed by Tukhachevsky and Antonov-Ovseyenko, 11 June 1921, quoted in Vladimir N. Brovkin, *Behind the Front Lines of the Civil War: Political Parties and Social Movements in Russia, 1918–1922* (Princeton: Princeton University Press, 1994), p. 387.

120. Aleksandra Kollontai, *Semya i kommunisticheskoye gosudarstvo* (Moscow and Petrograd: Kommunist, 1918); Eng. edn, *Communism and the Family*, in Kollontai, *Selected Writings*, pp. 250–60. The text has been the object of discussion by some of the most important figures of western feminism; see, for example, Shulamith Firestone, *The Dialectic of Sex* (London: Cape, 1971), p. 240, and Sheila Rowbotham, 'If you like tobogganing', in Sheila Rowbotham, *Women, Resistance and Revolution* (London: Allen Lane, 1972), pp. 134–69.

121. Farnsworth, *Aleksandra Kollontai*, p. 141.

122. Kollontai, *Communism and the Family*, p. 250.

123. Ibid., p. 253.

124. Ibid., pp. 255–6.

125. Ibid., pp. 257–8.

126. Ibid., p. 259. It is worth noting that the last phrase in this quotation, 'there are only our children, the children of Russia's communist workers', has been translated in different ways. In Aleksandra Kollontai, *Communism and the Family*, in Kollontai, *On Women's Liberation* (London: Bookmarks, 1998), p. 48, the anonymous translation, dating back to 1920, reads, 'there are henceforth only our children, those of the communist state, the common possession of all the workers'. In this version the proprietorship of the children clearly belongs in the first place to the state rather than to individual parents. A literal translation of the original Russian would seem to confirm this version: 'There are only our children, the children of industrious communist Russia.' Here again the implication is that the children are first and foremost members of the collectivity rather than members of individual families. The difference is not a minor one.

127. Kollontai, *Communism and the Family*, in Kollontai, *Selected Writings*, p. 260.

128. Kollontai, 'Working woman and mother' (1914), in Kollontai, *Selected Writings*, p. 134. Earlier on the same page she wrote, 'Those who need more attention – the woman and children – will be taken care of by society, which is like one large, friendly family [. . .] Society, that big happy family, will look after everything.'

129. Vladimir I. Lenin, *A Great Beginning: Heroism of the Workers in the Rear 'Communist Subbotniks'*, in Lenin, *On the Emancipation of Women*, pp. 67–8. Subbotniks were days of work offered for free, 'indicative of the working people's communist attitude towards labour'.

130. Ibid., p. 68.

131. Ibid.

132. Clara Zetkin, 'My recollections of Lenin', in Lenin, *On the Emancipation of Women*, pp. 108–10.

133. Bryant, *Mirrors of Moscow*, p. 122; Kollontai, *Autobiography*, p. 43. See also Farnsworth, *Aleksandra Kollontai*, pp. 168–9.

134. Aleksandr G. Goikhbarg, *Brachnoye, semyeynoye, i opekunskoye pravo Sovetskoy respubliki* (Moscow: Gosizdat, 1920), p. 5, quoted in Goldman, *Women, the State and Revolution*, p. 9.

135. Nikolay Bukharin and Yevgeny Preobrazhensky, *The ABC of Communism* (1920; Harmondsworth: Penguin, 1969), p. 285.

136. Elizabeth Waters, 'From the old family to the new: work, marriage and motherhood in urban Soviet Russia, 1917–1931' (unpublished Ph.D. thesis, University of Birmingham, 1985), pp. 37–8.

137. In Serge Fauchereau (ed.), *Moscow, 1900–1930* (New York: Rizzoli, 1988), p. 89.

138. Vladimir Mayakovsky, 'Pull out the future', quoted without specific page reference in Richard Stites, *Revolutionary Dreams: Utopian Vision and Experimental Life in the Russian Revolution* (Oxford and New York: Oxford University Press, 1989), p. 205.

139. Ernst Davidovič Kuznecov, *L'illustrazione del libro per bambini e l'avanguardia russa* (Florence: Cantini, 1991).

140. This was the theme of El Lissitzky's propaganda board at Vitebsk, analysed so well by T. J. Clark in his *Farewell to an Idea: Episodes from a History of Modernism* (New Haven and London: Yale University Press, 1999), pp. 224–97.

141. Lynn Mally, *The Proletkult Movement in Revolutionary Russia* (Berkeley: University of California Press, 1990), p. 171.

142. Anatoly Lunacharsky, 'Lenin o monumentalnoy propagande', *Literaturnaya gazeta*, 4–5, 29 January 1933, quoted in Christina Lodder, *Russian Constructivism* (New Haven and London: Yale University Press, 1983), p. 53.

143. See below, pp. 141–2.

144. *Art News*, 5 April 1924, quoted in Clark, *Farewell to an Idea*, p. 224. See also Malevich's discussion of his ideas for the Lenin monument in Robert C. Williams, *Artists in Revolution: Portraits of the Russian Avant-Garde, 1905–1925* (Bloomington and London: Indiana University Press, 1977), pp. 124–5.

145. Clements, *Bolshevik Feminist*, p. 163.

146. During 1919 Kollontai's son Misha, who was training as an engineer, had stayed in Petrograd while Kollontai was mainly in Moscow. She wrote in her diary, 'He's living in a dormitory, apparently he's hungry and cold, and I don't have anything to send him; it's agonising. I want us to live in the same city, but he loves his institute'; Kollontai, *Iz moyey zhizni i raboty*, p. 357.

147. The friend was P. S. Vinogradskaya; see her contribution to N. K. Krupskaya (ed.), *Pamyati Inessa Armand* (Moscow and Leningrad: Gosizdat, 1926), quoted in Elwood, *Inessa Armand*, p. 257.

148. Pearson, *Lenin's Mistress*, pp. 214–5. It is perhaps worth noting that in the first three sentences Inessa inadvertently expresses the order of her love in three different ways: first 'the children and V. I.', then 'V. I. and the work' and finally 'V. I. and my children'.

149. Angelica Balabanoff, *Impressions of Lenin* (Ann Arbor: University of Michigan Press, 1964), p. 15.

150. Inna married Hugo Eberlein, a prominent German Communist, and they lived together in Berlin until 1933. They had a daughter called Inessa. When Hitler took power, Eberlein fled to Russia but was later to be a victim of Stalin's Purges, dying in prison in 1944. Inna continued to work at the Institute of Marxism-Leninism in Moscow until her retirement in 1961. Varvara became an 'Honoured Artist of the RSFSR', and a retrospective exhibition of her work was held in Moscow in 1977. Andrey became a mechanic and engineer in the automobile works in Gorki and Moscow. He was killed at the front in 1944. Elwood, *Inessa Armand*, pp. 269 ff.

151. Alan Ball, *And Now my Soul is Hardened: Abandoned Children in Soviet Russia, 1918–1930* (Berkeley and Los Angeles: University of California Press, 1994), p. 1.

152. For the Soviets as 'quasi-parliamentary bodies, intensively engaged in educating the masses in the practices of democratic elections, political pluralism and parliamentary procedures', see Israel Getzler, 'Soviets as agents of democratisation', in Edith R. Frankel et al. (eds), *Revolution in Russia: Reassessments of 1917* (Cambridge: Cambridge University Press, 1992), p. 17. See also Oskar Anweiler's path-breaking study *The Soviets: The Russian Workers', Peasants' and Soldiers' Councils, 1905–1921* (New York: Pantheon, 1974). For democratic attempts in the countryside, see Orlando Figes, *Peasant Russia, Civil War: The Volga Countryside in Revolution (1917–1921)* (Oxford:

Oxford University Press, 1989), pp. 70 and 76. See also the detailed research on Saratov by Donald J. Raleigh, *Experiencing Russia's Civil War: Politics, Society and Revolutionary Culture in Saratov* (Princeton: Princeton University Press, 2002).

153. The pamphlet is republished in Kollontai, *Selected Writings*, pp. 159–200.

154. Ibid., pp. 179–80.

155. Ibid., p. 191.

156. Eric Naiman claims to have detected another, deeper layer of contradiction in Kollontai's novel *Red Love* (*Vassilissa Malygina*), first published in 1923; Naiman, 'When a Communist writes Gothic: Aleksandra Kollontai and the politics of disgust', *Signs: Journal of Women in Culture and Society*, 22 (1996), no. 1, pp. 1–29. Naiman suggests that the novel's subtext reveals a 'disgust at the female body and preoccupation with liberation from the feminine' (p. 6) that seem in direct conflict with the revolutionary advocacy of women's liberation, expressed by both author and heroine of the novel. Kollontai's text, he argues, must be placed in a wider European Gothic tradition. He analyses in this light the language of her pamphlet on the Workers' Opposition and other political writings of the period 1921–3.

157. Robert E. Johnson, 'Family life in Moscow during NEP', in Sheila Fitzpatrick et al. (eds), *Russia in the Era of the NEP: Explorations in Soviet Society and Culture* (Bloomington: Indiana University Press, 1991), p. 115.

158. Robert G. Wesson, *Soviet Communes* (New Brunswick, N.J.: Rutgers University Press, 1963), p. 84.

159. Goldman, *Women, the State and Revolution*, p. 128.

160. Waters, 'The Bolsheviks and the family', p. 284.

161. Waters, 'From the old family to the new', p. 106.

162. Goldman, *Women, the State and Revolution*, p. 107, tables 4 and 5.

163. Ibid., p. 117.

164. For aid to the starving population offered by international American organisations, see Marcello Flores, *L'immagine dell'URSS: L'Occidente e la Russia di Stalin (1927–1956)* (Milan: Il Saggiatore, 1990), pp. 18–19.

165. Goldman, *Women, the State and Revolution*, p. 59.

166. Ball, *And Now my Soul is Hardened*, pp. 1–17. See also Dorena Caroli, *L'enfance abandonnée et délinquante dans la Russie soviétique (1917–1937)* (Paris: L'Harmattan, 2004).

167. Ball, *And Now my Soul is Hardened*, p. 4.

168. Ibid., p. 106.

169. Goldman, *Women, the State and Revolution*, p. 65.

170. See the terrible testimonies in Ball, *And Now my Soul is Hardened*, pp. 109 ff.

171. Leon Trotsky, *'Problems of Everyday Life' and Other Writings on Culture and Science* (New York: Monad Press, 1973), pp. 15–24.

172. Ibid., p. 15.

173. Leon Trotsky, 'From the old family to the new' (*Pravda*, 13 July 1923), in Trotsky, *Problems of Everyday Life*, pp. 36–8.

174. Isaac Deutscher, *The Prophet Unarmed: Trotsky, 1921–1929* (Oxford: Oxford University Press, 1970), p. 23.

175. Shanin, *The Awkward Class*, table 3:IV, pp. 53 and 145 ff.

176. Ibid., p. 157.

177. Atkinson, *The End of the Russian Land Commune*, p. 302.

178. Beatrice Farnsworth, 'Village women experience the revolution', in Farnsworth and Viola, *Russian Peasant Women*, p. 146.

179. N. S. Kokoreva, *Okhrana maternistva* (Moscow, 1975), quoted in Clements, *Bolshevik Feminist*, p. 172.

180. Clements, *Bolshevik Feminist*, p. 173.

181. Figes, *Peasant Russia, Civil War*, p. 356.

182. By January of 1925, the triumvirate of Stalin, Zinoviev and Kamenev had successfully defeated Trotsky and the Left Opposition. They then quarrelled among themselves and Kamenev and Zinoviev made their peace with Trotsky.

183. VTsIK consisted of two chambers – the Council of the Union, with 371 delegates, and the Council of Nationalities, with 131 – but they usually took decisions with little discussion and in any case had little constitutional weight. Real power lay elsewhere, 'with the Politburo or with some other informal group of leaders within the party'; Carr, *The Bolshevik Revolution*, vol. 1, p. 412.

184. Schlesinger, *The Family in the USSR*, pp. 86–7.

185. Ibid., pp. 92–3.

186. Ibid., p. 95.

187. Ibid., pp. 99–100.

188. The best and fullest account of this debate is to be found in Goldman, *Women, the State and Revolution*, pp. 185–253.

189. N. Vigilyansky, article of 4 March 1927, quoted in Waters, 'From the old family to the new', pp. 62–3.

190. Farnsworth, *Aleksandra Kollontai*, pp. 349–50.

191. The speech by Trotsky in question, delivered on 7 December 1925 at the opening of the Pan-Soviet Meeting dedicated to 'Mothers and children', is published in *Brak i semya: Sbornik statey i materialov* (Moscow and Leningrad: Molodaya Gvardiya, 1926), pp. 143–4.

192. See the fascinating account of the American journalist Jessica Smith, who interviewed Smidovich at her home; Jessica Smith, *Women in Soviet Russia* (New York: Vanguard Press, 1928), pp. 102–3; Farnsworth, *Aleksandra Kollontai*, pp. 356–61.

193. Schlesinger, *The Family in the USSR*, p. 152.

194. Ibid., p. 156. At the same time, Article 1 of the Code (ibid., p. 155) underlined the continuing importance of marriage registration 'in the interests of State and society'.

195. Beatrice Farnsworth, 'Bolshevik alternatives and the Soviet family: the 1926 Marriage Law Debate', in Dorothy Atkinson, Alexander Dallin and Gail W. Lapidus (eds), *Women in Russia* (Hassox: Harvester Press, 1978), pp. 162–3.

196. Harold Berman, 'Soviet family law in the light of Russian history and Marxist theory', *Yale Law Journal*, 56 (1946), no. 1, pp. 25–57.

197. *Izvestiya*, 14 January 1926, quoted in Farnsworth, *Aleksandra Kollontai*, p. 363. On the other hand, John Quigley goes too far when he argues that the predominant thinking behind the Code was 'conservative'; John Quigley, 'The 1926 Soviet Family Code: retreat from free love', *Soviet Union*, 6, 2 (1979), p. 173.

198. In Northrop, *Veiled Empire*, p. 69.

199. Ibid., p. 80. For the reforming clergy, see Shoshana Keller, *To Moscow, not Mecca: The Soviet Campaign against Islam in Central Asia, 1917–1941* (Westport, Conn.: Praeger, 2001), pp. 117–18.

200. Marianne Kamp, 'Unveiling Uzbek women: Liberation, representation and discourse, 1906–1929' (unpublished Ph.D. dissertation, University of Chicago, 1998), p. 291, quoted in Keller, *To Moscow, not Mecca*, p. 116.

201. In Northrop, *Veiled Empire*, p. 92.

202. Ibid., p. 74.

203. Göran Therborn, *Between Sex and Power: Family in the World, 1900–2000* (London: Routledge, 2004), p. 85.

204. Schlesinger, *The Family in the USSR*, p. 99.

205. Walter Benjamin, *Moscow Diary*, ed. Gary Smith (Cambridge, Mass.: Harvard University Press, 1986), and 'Moscow', in Walter Benjamin, *Reflections: Essays, Aphorisms, Autobiographical Writings*, ed. P. Demetz (New York: Schocken Books, 1978).

206. Benjamin, *Moscow Diary*, p. 127.

207. On the important distinction between 'byt' and 'bytiye', see especially Svetlana Boym, *Common Places: Mythologies of Everyday Life in Russia* (Cambridge, Mass.: Harvard University Press, 1994), pp. 73–93. For 'interiority', see the valuable collection of essays edited by Christina Kiaer and Eric Naiman, *Everyday Life in Early Soviet Russia: Taking the Revolution Inside* (Bloomington: Indiana University Press, 2006), and especially their introduction, pp. 1–22.

208. Benjamin, *Moscow Diary*, p. 114.

CHAPTER 2: THE NEST AND THE NATION: FAMILY POLITICS IN THE TRANSITION FROM OTTOMAN EMPIRE TO TURKISH REPUBLIC, 1908–1938

1. Halide Edib, *Memoirs of Halidé Edib* (London: John Murray, 1926), pp. 3 and 14. Halide's two volumes of memoirs (the second, entitled *The Turkish Ordeal*, was also published by John Murray in London, in 1928) are incomparably richer, both in quality and in length, than the published autobiographical notes of Aleksandra Kollontai. They do not, however, cover the period after 1922. Throughout this chapter I have used standard modern Turkish spelling, except when quoting directly from Halide Edib's memoirs and similar texts.
2. Ibid., p. 4.
3. Halide and practically all the sources used refer generically to 'polygamy' – the form of marriage which allows an individual of either sex to have more than one spouse. In this context it would be more precise to use the term 'polygyny', denoting the form of polygamy in which one man has several wives. Polygyny is to be distinguished from polyandry, in which it is the woman who has several husbands. I have employed the generic term, 'polygamy', throughout.
4. Halide Edib, *Memoirs*, pp. 144–5.
5. Ibid., p. 172.
6. Halide was made to wear 'short, dark blue frocks in winter, all English-made, and white linen in the summer. Her arms and legs were bare after the manner of English children, which shocked her granny and made her anxious lest she should catch cold'; ibid., p. 23.
7. Hester Donaldson Jenkins, *Behind Turkish Lattices* (1911; New Jersey: Gorgias Press, 2004), p. 31.
8. Halide Edib, *Memoirs*, p. 34.
9. Ibid.
10. Ibid., p. 118.
11. Ibid., pp. 69–70.
12. Jenkins, *Behind Turkish Lattices*, p. 218.
13. Halide Edib, *Memoirs*, pp. 206–7. Cf. George Eliot, *Middlemarch* (1871–2; Harmondsworth: Penguin, 1985), p. 232, Dorothea to Casaubon: 'All those rows of volumes [...] will you not make up your mind what part of them you will use, and begin to write the book which will make your vast knowledge useful to the world? I will write to your dictation, or I will write and copy and extract what you tell me: I can be of no other use.'
14. Halide Edib, *Memoirs*, pp. 219–21.
15. Ibid., p. 307.
16. Ibid., p. 308.
17. Ibid., p. 310.
18. Ibid.
19. Halide Edib, *The Turkish Ordeal*, p. 267.
20. Halide Edib, *Memoirs*, p. 103.
21. For the ideological bases of the regime, see Selim Deringil, *The Well-Protected Domains: Ideology and the Legitimation of Power in the Ottoman Empire, 1876–1909* (London: I.B. Tauris, 1998).
22. See in particular Şerif Mardin, *The Genesis of Young Ottoman Thought* (Princeton: Princeton University Press, 1962).
23. See Erik J. Zürcher, *The Young Turk Legacy and Nation Building: From the Ottoman Empire to Atatürk's Turkey* (London and New York: I.B. Tauris, 2010), esp. pp. 95–109.
24. Halide Edib, *Memoirs*, pp. 256–8. For the events of the revolution, see Aykut Kansu, *The Revolution of 1908 in Turkey* (Leiden: Brill, 1997).
25. Halide Edib, *Memoirs*, pp. 270–1. She worked for the review called *Tanin*, the most important periodical of the Young Turks, which dedicated ample space to the problems of the education and juridical status of women.
26. It is highly probable that the census of 1914 underestimates the actual size of the imperial population. Panzac considers the underestimation to be in the region of 10 per cent;

Daniel Panzac, *Population et santé dans l'Empire Ottoman* (Istanbul: Isis, 1996), pp. 187–9. For further details of the dynamics of the Turkish population, see Giambattista Salinari and Paul Ginsborg, 'Statistical Essay', http://bit.ly/ginsborg-appendix.

27. Donald Quataert, *The Ottoman Empire, 1700–1922* (Cambridge: Cambridge University Press, 2000), p. 111.
28. Justin McCarthy, *Death and Exile: The Ethnic Cleansing of Ottoman Muslims, 1821–1922* (Princeton: Darwin Press, 1995), *passim*.
29. Alan Duben and Cem Behar, *Istanbul Households: Marriage, Family and Fertility, 1880–1940* (Cambridge: Cambridge University Press, 1991).
30. Ibid., pp. 7 and 25. For the heterogeneity of the Ottoman population on the eve of the First World War, see Halil İnalcık and Donald Quataert (eds), *An Economic and Social History of the Ottoman Empire*, vol. 2, *1600–1914* (Cambridge: Cambridge University Press, 1994), pp. 777–97; for the Marmara region, see Ryan Gingeras, *Sorrowful Shores: Violence, Ethnicity, and the End of the Ottoman Empire, 1912–1923* (Oxford: Oxford University Press, 2009); for Izmir, see Oya Dağlar, *War, Epidemics, and Medicine in the Late Ottoman Empire, 1912–1918* (Haarlem: Sota, 2008).
31. Carter Vaughn Findley, 'Economic bases of revolution and repression in the late Ottoman Empire', *Comparative Studies in Society and History*, 28 (1987), pp. 81–106.
32. Duben and Behar, *Istanbul Households*, p. 59.
33. Ibid., pp. 49, 60 and 79: 'The Muslim population of İstanbul thus constituted a pioneering group when compared to their middle-eastern counterparts.'
34. Mary Zwahlen, *Le divorce en Turquie: Contribution à l'étude de la reception du Code civil Suisse* (Geneva: Droz, 1981), pp. 44–6; Duben and Behar, *Istanbul Households*, p. 110.
35. According to the widely accepted periodisation proposed by Chafik Chehata, the post-classic period dates from the twelfth century to the present time; Chafik Chehata, *Études de droit musulman*, 2 vols (Paris: Presses Universitaires de France, 1971), vol. 1, pp. 18 ff.
36. Zwahlen, *Le divorce en Turquie*, p. 42.
37. Ibid. On the other hand, the husband sometimes allowed a no longer desired wife to remain in his household and would provide for her needs.
38. Ayşe Saraçgil, 'The failures of modernity: family, civil society and state in the passage from Ottoman Empire to Turkish Republic', in Jürgen Nautz, Paul Ginsborg and Tom Nijhuis (eds), *The Golden Chain: Family, Civil Society and the State* (New York and Oxford: Berghahn, 2013), pp. 197–218; Deniz Kandiyoti, 'Islam and patriarchy: a comparative perspective', in Nikki R. Keddie and Beth Baron (eds), *Women in Middle Eastern History: Shifting Boundaries in Sex and Gender* (Newhaven and London: Yale University Press, 1991), pp. 23–42.
39. Halide Edib, *Memoirs*, pp. 6–7.
40. Abdelwahab Bouhdiba, *Sexuality in Islam* (1985; London: Routledge, 2008), pp. 7–10; Fatima Mernissi, *Beyond the Veil: Male–Female Dynamics in a Modern Muslim Society* (Cambridge, Mass.: Harvard University Press, 1975), pp. 18–20.
41. For this reason unmarried men, the bearers of an unsatisfied and uncontrolled sexuality, were regarded as a potential danger to the life of the community as a whole.
42. Duben and Behar, *Istanbul Households*, p. 144, suggest that 'slave is not perhaps the best rendering of the Turkish word *carriye* (concubine, maiden, housemaid)', but there can be little doubting the existence of a still-flourishing slave market in Istanbul at the end of the nineteenth century, in the sense of the fixed and regular barter of unfree human beings.
43. The theme constitutes the leitmotif of modern Turkish literature. For a study of the transformation of family relations in the course of Turkish modernisation, based principally on novels published between 1860 and 1980, see Ayşe Saraçgil, *Il maschio camaleonte: Strutture patriarcali nell'impero ottomano e nella Turchia moderna* (Milan: Bruno Mondadori, 2001).

44. In his memoirs, Abdülhamit II laments the 'damaging' effect of the French literary tradition upon the women of his harem; Sultan Abdülhamit II, *Siyasi Hayatım* (Istanbul: Hareket Yayınları, 1974), p. 120.

45. Leslie P. Peirce, *The Imperial Harem: Women and Sovereignty in the Ottoman Empire* (Oxford: Oxford University Press, 1993), esp. pp. 58 ff.

46. Namık Kemal, 'Aile', *İbret*, 56 (1872), in Ezel Erverdi (ed.), *Sosyo-Kültürel Değişme Sürecinde Türk Ailesi*, vol. 3 (Ankara: Ülke Yayın, 1993), pp. 1015–17.

47. Ibid., pp. 148–56.

48. Duben and Behar, *Istanbul Households*, pp. 225 and 211.

49. Ibid., pp. 206 ff.

50. Saraçgil, *Il maschio camaleonte, passim*.

51. Jenkins, *Behind Turkish Lattices*, pp. 128–30.

52. Duben and Behar, *Istanbul Households*, pp. 29–31.

53. Robert Halsband (ed.), *The Complete Letters of Lady Mary Wortley Montagu*, vol. 1, *1708–1720* (Oxford: Oxford University Press, 1965), letter of 1 April 1717, pp. 312–15.

54. Ayşe Saraçgil, 'Generi voluttuari e ragion di stato: politiche repressive del consumo di vino, caffè e tabacco nell'Impero ottomano', *Turcica*, 28 (1996), pp. 163–94.

55. Perry Anderson, *The New Old World* (London and New York: Verso, 2009), p. 401.

56. Nur Vergin, 'Social change and the family in Turkey', *Current Anthropology*, 26 (1985), no. 5, pp. 571–4.

57. Emmanuel Todd, *The Explanation of Ideology: Family Structures and Social Systems* (Oxford: Blackwell, 1985), pp. 144–5.

58. Sami Zubaida notes that ' "traditional" social formations differed widely over time and in different parts of the Muslim world, but it would be fair to say that they were almost uniformly patriarchal and authoritarian, often coercive. Positions of authority, such as that of *nakib, müftü* or guild master were in most places held and inherited within families of notables'; Sami Zubaida, 'Civil society, community and democracy in the Middle East', in Sudipta Kaviraj and Sunil Khilnani (eds), *Civil Society: History and Possibilities* (Cambridge: Cambridge University Press, 2001), p. 234. The most elaborate and controversial attempt to read off political ideologies from family forms is that of Emmanuel Todd, *L'invention de l'Europe* (Paris: Seuil, 1990).

59. Şerif Mardin, 'Power, civil society and culture in the Ottoman Empire', in Şerif Mardin, *Religion, Society and Modernity in Turkey* (Syracuse, N.Y.: Syracuse University Press, 2006), pp. 29–33.

60. Deringil, *The Well-Protected Domains*, p. 21. The author lists four areas in which the symbolic power of the Sultan was reaffirmed: the sacrality of his person, the expanded nature of his munificence, his intimate linkage to religious tradition, and the language and signs of Ottoman official documentation.

61. The judgement is that of Çağlar Keyder, 'The setting', in Çağlar Keyder (ed.), *Istanbul Between the Global and the Local* (Lanham: Rowman and Littlefield, 1999), p. 4.

62. In 1839 the grand vizier Mustafa Reşid Paşa read out aloud the historic edict in which the Ottoman Sultan declared to the European powers that the entire population of the Empire, excepting women and slaves, but without regard to ethnic and religious distinction, were to be considered Ottoman citizens and equal in the face of the law. At the same time, however, the Tanzimat reformers were determined to preserve political supremacy for Muslims only.

63. Saraçgil, 'The failures of modernity', p. 204.

64. Kansu, *The Revolution of 1908*, esp. pp. 78–80. The two most important groups working towards revolution were the Young Turks of the Committee of Union and Progress and the Armenian Revolutionary Federation.

65. Halide Edib, *The Turkish Ordeal*, p. 53. Her son, Hasan Hikmet, although only thirteen years old, was for a time a gang leader until his mother prohibited him from continuing. He then became (p. 58) 'as violent a pacifist as he had been a fighter'.

66. Andrew Mango, *Atatürk* (London: John Murray, 1999), p. 35.

67. Halide Edib, *Memoirs*, pp. 119–20.
68. Quoted without reference in Mango, *Atatürk*, p. 33.
69. Ibid., pp. 35–79. Still of notable interest are Harold Courtenay Armstrong, *Grey Wolf: Mustafa Kemal: An Intimate Study of a Dictator* (London: Penguin Books, 1937), and Patrick Balfour Kinross, *Ataturk: The Rebirth of a Nation* (London: Weidenfeld and Nicolson, 1969).
70. Fuat Süreyya Oral, *Türk Basın Tarihi* (Istanbul: Yeni Adım Mattbassi, 1968), pp. 42, 44, 98–121, 126, 215.
71. See Ziya Gökalp, *The Principles of Turkism* (1923; Leiden: Brill, 1968), esp. pp. 1–22 and 76–94. Even immediately after the revolution of 1908, the CUP in Salonica tried to close the gymnasia schools in the city hitherto run by different ethnic and religious groups and to insist that Turkish become the official language of instruction in all schools. Protests were so widespread that the initial proposals had to be heavily modified; Kansu, *The Revolution of 1908*, pp. 160–1.
72. For the intellectual formation of the Young Turks and their ideological battles with the other political forces of the time, see Şükrü Hanioğlu, *The Young Turks in Opposition* (New York and Oxford: Oxford University Press, 1995), pp. 7–67.
73. For the importance of German militarism in the formation of this generation of Ottoman officers, see Handan Nezir-Akmeşe, *The Birth of Modern Turkey: The Ottoman Military and the March to World War I* (London: I.B. Tauris, 2005), esp. pp. 19–63.
74. Louise Bryant commented, 'Enver Pasha certainly has charm, in spite of his very obvious opportunism, and the cruelty and lack of conscience which a fatalistic belief inspires'; Louise Bryant, *Mirrors of Moscow* (New York: Thomas Seltzer, 1923), p. 149.
75. Niyazi Berkes, 'Translator's introduction', in Ziya Gökalp, *Turkish Nationalism and Western Civilisation: Selected Essays*, ed. Niyazi Berkes (London: Allen and Unwin, 1959), p. 13. See also Taha Parla, *The Social and Political Thought of Ziya Gökalp, 1876–1924* (Leiden: Brill, 1985).
76. See the chapter dedicated to this theme in Gökalp, *Turkish Nationalism*, pp. 90–109.
77. Katherine E. Fleming, 'Women as preservers of the past', in Zehra F. Arat (ed.), *Deconstructing Images of the Turkish Woman* (Basingstoke: Macmillan, 1998), pp. 127–38; Saraçgil, *Il maschio camaleonte*, pp. 123–4.
78. Ziya Gökalp, 'Tradition and formalism' (1913), in Gökalp, *Turkish Nationalism*, p. 95. In the same article he wrote, 'The British are a people without rules, but we find in them the best example of a tradition whose historical continuity and evolutionary significance is well known. We Turks, on the other hand, are formalists, and yet we lack traditions.'
79. The first group was published in 1917 in the Istanbul journal *Yeni Mecmua*, the second in Diyarbakır in 1922, in *Küçük Mecmua*. There are also some important observations in his slim volume *The Principles of Turkism*, esp. pp. 108–17. For a detailed list of his articles on the family, see Zafer Toprak, 'The family, feminism and the state during the Young Turk period, 1908–1918', in Edhem Eldem (ed.), *Première rencontre internationale sur l'Empire Ottoman et la Turquie moderne* (Istanbul and Paris: Isis, 1991), p. 443 n. 3. See also Sabine Dirks, *La famille musulmane turque: Son évolution au XXe siècle* (Paris: Mouton, 1969), p. 15 and p. 18 n. 13.
80. Ziya Gökalp, 'The foundations of the Turkish family' (1917), in Gökalp, *Turkish Nationalism*, p. 253.
81. Ibid., p. 254.
82. Gökalp, *The Principles of Turkism*, p. 113; Ziya Gökalp, 'Family morality' (1923), in Gökalp, *Turkish Nationalism*, p. 303.
83. Gökalp, *The Principles of Turkism*, pp. 111–12.
84. Émile Durkheim, 'La famille conjugale', in Émile Durkheim, *Textes*, vol. 3, *Fonctions sociales et institutions* (Paris: Minuit, 1975), pp. 35–49. For a detailed treatment, see Mary Ann Lamanna, *Émile Durkheim on the Family* (Thousand Oaks, Calif.: Sage, 2002).

85. Ziya Gökalp, 'Three currents of thought' (1913), in Gökalp, *Turkish Nationalism*, p. 73.

86. Ziya Gökalp, 'Culture and refinement' (1923), in ibid., pp. 280–3.

87. There is a growing bibliography connecting relations with Germany and Ottoman participation in the Great War; see, for example, Mustafa Aksakal, *The Ottoman Road to War in 1914: The Ottoman Empire and the First World War* (Cambridge: Cambridge University Press, 2008), and Sean McMeekin, *The Berlin-Baghdad Express: The Ottoman Empire and Germany's Bid for World Power* (London: Allen Lane, 2010).

88. Kemal's actual orders, found on the body of a dead Turkish soldier, were slightly different from this later, more famous account: 'I do not expect that any of us would not rather die than repeat the shameful story of the Balkan war. But if there are such men among us, we should at once lay hands upon them and set them up in line to be shot'; Mango, *Atatürk*, pp. 146–7.

89. Melda Özverim (ed.), *Mustafa Kemal ve Corinne Lütfü: Bir Dostluğun Öyküsü* (Istanbul: Milliyet Yayınları, 1998), pp. 56–7.

90. Şükrü Tezer (ed.), *Atatürk'ün Hatıra Defteri* (Ankara: Türk Tarih Kurumu Yayınları, 1995), pp. 75–6.

91. Uluğ İğdemir, *Atatürk'ün Yaşamı*, vol. 1, *1881–1918* (Ankara: AKDTYK, 1988), pp. 80 ff., quoted in Mango, *Atatürk*, p. 164.

92. Feroz Ahmad, 'The special relationship: the Committee of Union and Progress and the Ottoman Jewish political elite, 1908–1918', in Ahmad, *From Empire to Republic: Essays on the Late Ottoman Empire and Modern Turkey*, vol. 2 (Istanbul: Bilgi University Press, 2008), p. 153. See also the highly important work of Taner Akçam, *From Empire to Republic: Turkish Nationalism and the Armenian Genocide* (London: Zed, 2004).

93. McCarthy, *Death and Exile*, pp. 162–4.

94. Quoted in Ahmad, *From Empire to Republic*, p. 174.

95. Ibid., p. 171.

96. See Panzac, *Population*, p. 204; Donald Bloxham, *The Great Game of Genocide: Imperialism, Nationalism and the Destruction of the Ottoman Armenians* (Oxford: Oxford University Press, 2005); Marcello Flores, *Il genocidio degli armeni* (Bologna: Il Mulino, 2006).

97. Ahmad, *From Empire to Republic*, p. 174.

98. See in particular Donald E. Miller and Lorna Touryan Miller, *Survivors: An Oral History of the Armenian Genocide* (Berkeley: University of California Press, 1993), based on 103 interviews of survivors in the Los Angeles area. Serious interviewing began in 1978 and extended outwards from Pasadena to the greater Los Angeles area. Sixty-two of those interviewed were women, forty-one men.

99. Ibid., p. 99.

100. Ibid., p. 97.

101. Diane Waldman, *Arshile Gorky, 1904–1948: A Retrospective* (New York: Solomon R. Guggenheim Museum, 1981).

102. Ahmad, *From Empire to Republic*, p. 184.

103. For the deportation of the Kurds, see below, p. 461, note 128.

104. Anderson, *The New Old World*, p. 421.

105. The last period of Enver's life has been richly documented in Masayuchi Yamauchi, *The Green Crescent under the Red Star: Enver Pasha in Soviet Russia, 1919–1922* (Tokyo: Institute for the Study of Languages and Cultures of Asia and Africa, 1991).

106. Uriel Heyd, *Foundations of Turkish Nationalism: The Life and Teachings of Ziya Gökalp* (London: Luzac and Harvil, 1950), pp. 36 ff.

107. The King–Crane commission consisted of a team of two Americans, Henry King and Charles Crane, who travelled to the Middle East and attempted to determine which mandatory power local populations would prefer to rule over them. Neither the British nor the French, however, had any intention of being influenced by the findings of the commission, and so it had little, if any, effect.

108. Halide Edib, *The Turkish Ordeal*, pp. 59–60.
109. Ibid., p. 14.
110. Ibid., p. 81.
111. Ibid., p. 66.
112. Ibid., p. 299.
113. Duben and Behar, *Istanbul Households*, pp. 200–1.
114. See Nur Bilge Criss, *Istanbul under Allied Occupation* (Leiden: Brill, 1999).
115. Halide Edib, *The Turkish Ordeal*, p. 128.
116. Ibid., pp. 158, 170, 185.
117. Ibid., p. 173.
118. From this experience she drew material for two novels, the most important romantic epics of the national War of Independence: *Ateşten Gömlek* (Istanbul, 1922) was first published in English in New York in 1924, with the title *The Shirt of Flame*, and then again in Lahore in 1933, with the title *The Daughter of Smirna: A Story of the Rise of Modern Turkey*; the second novel, *Vurun Kahpeye*, published in Istanbul in 1926, has not yet found an English translation.
119. Halide Edib, *The Turkish Ordeal*, p. 304.
120. Ibid., p. 357 n. 2. Kemal was said to have deplored Halide Edib's 'weak heart, which cannot bear violence'.
121. Ibid., pp. 176–8.
122. Ibid., p. 178.
123. Mango, *Atatürk*, pp. 343–7.
124. Halide Edib, *The Turkish Ordeal*, pp. 368–9.
125. Ibid., p. 406.
126. For Mustafa Kemal the caliphate was a political institution whose existence could be justified only in the context of a unified, pan-Muslim state. This was distinctly not one of the objectives of the new Turkish Republic.
127. For the dramatic exchange of populations with Greece, see Renée Hirschon (ed.), *Crossing the Aegean: An Appraisal of the 1923 Compulsory Population Exchange between Greece and Turkey* (New York and Oxford: Berghahn, 2003), and Bruce Clark, *Twice a Stranger: The Mass Expulsions that Forged Modern Greece and Turkey* (London: Granta, 2006).
128. In April 1916 the Minister of the Interior, Talât, ordered the deportation of the Kurds from the eastern provinces, beginning with Diyarbakır. The order was based on a number of policy decisions: the Kurds would no longer be allowed to continue a nomadic and tribal existence; tribal leaders would henceforth be separated from their people; and Kurds would be relocated to areas in central and western Anatolia where Turks were in an overwhelming majority. Nowhere were the Kurds to exceed 5 per cent of the population. Even if the quantifying of the number of those deported is practically impossibile, scholarly estimates speak of some 700,000 persons involved, of whom very many died of cold and hunger. See Uğur Ümit Üngör, 'Seeing like a nation state: Young Turk social engineering in Eastern Turkey, 1913–1950', *Journal of Genocide Research*, 10 (2008), no. 1, pp. 15–19, and Uğur Ümit Üngör, *The Making of Modern Turkey: Nation and State in Eastern Anatolia, 1913–1950* (Oxford: Oxford University Press, 2011).
129. David McDowall, *A Modern History of the Kurds* (London: I.B. Tauris, 1996), p. 188, quoted in Anderson, *The New Old World*, p. 418.
130. Erik J. Zürcher, *Turkey: A Modern History* (London: I.B. Tauris, 2004), pp. 176 ff.
131. *The Hindustan Times*, 16 January 1935, quoted in Mushirul Hasan, *Between Modernity and Nationalism: Halide Edip's Encounter with Gandhi's India* (Oxford: Oxford University Press, 2010), p. 185. Sadly, little else is known of her visit.
132. Ibid. For Halide's account of her first meeting with Mahatma Gandhi, ibid., pp. 152 ff.
133. *Türk Yurdu*, 1 (1924), quoted in Niyazi Berkes, *The Development of Secularism in Turkey* (London: Hurst, 1968), p. 464.

134. Ibid., p. 466. For a detailed discussion of the relationship between Kemalism and religion, see Umut Azak, *Islam and Secularism in Turkey: Kemalism, Religion and the Nation State* (London and New York: I.B. Tauris, 2010).
135. For a further discussion, see below, pp. 124 ff.
136. Nusret Kemal, 'Halkçılık', *Ülkü*, 1 (1933), no. 3, pp. 185–90, quoted in Saraçgil, 'The failures of modernity', p. 215.
137. Perry Anderson writes, 'Religion was never detached from the *nation*, becoming instead an unspoken definition of it. It was this that allowed Kemalism to become more than just a cult of the elites, leaving a durable impact on the masses themselves'; Anderson, *The New Old World*, p. 417.
138. See above, p. 95.
139. 'Onuncu Yıl Söylevi' (Speech on the tenth anniversary of the establishment of the Republic), quoted in Taha Parla and Andrew Davison, *Corporatist Ideology in Kemalist Turkey: Progress or Order?* (Syracuse, N.Y.: Syracuse University Press, 2004), p. 124. For a parody of the transformation of the idea of time in the Republic, see the important novel by Ahmet Hamdi Tanıpnar, *The Time Regulation Institute* (1954; Madison: Turko-Tatar Press, 2001).
140. Geoffrey Lewis, *The Turkish Language Reform: A Catastrophic Success* (Oxford: Oxford University Press, 1999), pp. 2 and 42. Recently, the debate on the linguistic reform of the Republic has begun to focus on the effect it had in terms of the homogeneity of the nation. Two important examples of this new scholarship are Hussein Sadoğlu, *Türkiye'de Ulusçuluk ve Dil Politikaları* (Istanbul: Bilgi Üniversitesi Yayınları, 2003), and Nergis Ertürk, *Grammatology and Literary Modernity in Turkey* (Oxford: Oxford University Press, 2011).
141. Quoted in Saraçgil, *Il maschio camaleonte*, pp. 186–7.
142. Nimet Arsan (ed.), *Atatürk'ün Söylev ve Demeçleri*, vol. 2 (Ankara: Türk Tarih Kurumu, 1959), p. 211, quoted in Ayşe Saraçgil, 'Interno verso esterno: il velo nella Turchia contemporanea', in Lidia Curti (ed.), *La nuova Shahrazad: Donne e multiculturalismo* (Naples: Liguori, 2004), p. 75.
143. See above, pp. 62–6.
144. Şerif Mardin, 'Islam in 19th- and 20th-Century Turkey', in Şerif Mardin, *Religion, Society and Modernity*, pp. 261–2; Roberta Aluffi Beck-Peccoz, *La modernizzazione del diritto della famiglia nei paesi arabi* (Milan: Giuffré, 1990), pp. 45–6.
145. Mardin, 'Islam in 19th- and 20th-Century Turkey', p. 262.
146. Sadreddin Efendi, in *Sebil-ur-Reşat*, no. 330 (1914), quoted in Saraçgil, *Il maschio camaleonte*, p. 130; Aluffi Beck-Peccoz, *La modernizzazione*, pp. 16–17.
147. Berkes, *The Development of Secularism*, p. 470.
148. Ibid., p. 471.
149. *Code civil turc, Loi no. 743, 17 février 1926*, 3rd edn (Istanbul: John Rizzo, 1937).
150. Ibid., pp. 21–2.
151. Ibid., pp. 25–7. The original Swiss Code differed from its later Turkish version in a number of interesting ways. The permitted age of marriage was higher in Switzerland – twenty years old for men and eighteen for women – and all property was held in common between husband and wife. Most importantly, whereas alimony was to be paid for one year in Turkey, in Switzerland there was no time limit. These and other differences give the overall impression that the husband's position is further reinforced by the Turkish Code; Zwahlen, *Le divorce en Turquie*, pp. 72–3.
152. Not until the new Civil Code of 2002 did Turkish law assert the sort of equality within the family that was encapsulated by both of the early Soviet Codes. According to the Code of 2002, either wife or husband can be head of household, children born outside marriage have the same inheritance rights as other children, and, in the event of divorce, property acquired during marriage is equally divided. Furthermore, in making the settlement the Code assigns an economic value to women's hitherto invisible labour on behalf of the well-being of the family household. This last provision goes well beyond the more primitive egalitarianism of the Bolshevik Codes.

153. Duben and Behar, *Istanbul Households*, p. 215. It was quite a different story with regard to politics: the request made by republican women to found a womens' political party was turned down flatly by Mustafa Kemal in 1923 and women's associations were closed down in 1935.
154. Ibid., p. 223; Michel de Certeau, *The Practice of Everyday Life* (1980; Berkeley: University of California Press, 1988), pp. xi–xxv.
155. June Starr, *Dispute and Settlement in Rural Turkey: An Ethnography of Law* (Leiden: Brill, 1978), p. 89.
156. Zwahlen, *Le divorce en Turquie*, p. 77.
157. Paul Stirling, *Turkish Village* (London: Weidenfeld & Nicolson, 1965), p. 209.
158. Ibid., p. 183.
159. Ibid., p. 101; Duben and Behar, *Istanbul Households*, pp. 72–3.
160. Stirling, *Turkish Village*, p. 21.
161. Ibid., p. 100.
162. Mahmut Makal, *A Village in Anatolia*, ed. Paul Stirling (London: Vallentine, Mitchell & Co., 1954). The volume is a compilation based on two works by Makal: *Bizim Köy* (Our Village), published in Turkey in 1950, and *Köyümden* (From my Village), which followed two years later.
163. Ibid., p. 172. Nearly all the children of the villages had skin rashes on their faces. In the absence of any medical care to speak of, on Fridays children were brought to the 'magicians'. 'What is it that they do? After blowing upon the diseased parts as one blows upon a flame, they moisten the skin round the wound and scribble something or other in Arabic letters with an indelible pen.' The price? A packet of cigarettes.
164. Halide Edib, *The Turkish Ordeal*, p. 299.
165. Donald Quataert, 'The age of reforms, 1812–1914', in İnalcık and Quataert, *An Economic and Social History*, p. 864.
166. Stirling, *Turkish Village*, p. 145.
167. Lucy M. Garnett, *Turkish Life in Town and Country* (London: Newnes, 1904), p. 81.
168. See below, p. 333.
169. Semavi Eyice, *Atatürk ve Pietro Canonica* (Istanbul: Eren, 1986), pp. 43–4, quoted in Mango, *Atatürk*, pp. 457–8.
170. See below, p. 167.
171. See below, pp. 279 ff.
172. Salih Bozok and Cemil Bozok, *Hep Atatürk'ün Yanında* (Istanbul: Çağdaş, 1985), pp. 172–3, quoted in Mango, *Atatürk*, pp. 129–30.
173. Vamk D. Volkan and Norman Itzkowitz, *The Immortal Atatürk: A Psychobiography* (Chicago and London: University of Chicago Press, 1984). Of particular interest are the memoirs of Sabiha Gökçen, the adopted daughter of Mustafa Kemal, destined to become a pilot in the republican air force. Her career and personality are examined in Ayşe Gül Altınay, *Ordu-Millet-Kadınlar: Dünyanın ilk Kadın Savaş Pilotu Sabiha Gökçen*, in Gül Altınay (ed.), *Vatan, Millet, Kadınlar* (Istanbul: İletişim, 2000), pp. 246–79.
174. Halide Edib, *The Turkish Ordeal*, p. 127.
175. Volkan and Itzkowitz, *The Immortal Atatürk*, p. 302.
176. Hasan Rıza Soyak, *Atatürk'ten Hatıralar* (Ankara: Yapı ve Kredi Bankası, 1973; Istanbul: Y.K.Y, 2004), quoted in Mango, *Atatürk*, p. 46.
177. Quataert, 'The age of reforms', pp. 862–3.
178. Garnett, *Turkish Life*, pp. 176–7. The author was writing in 1904.
179. Mahir Iz, *Yilların İzi* (Istanbul: İrfan Yayınevi, 1975).
180. Mardin, 'Islam in 19th- and 20th-Century Turkey', p. 280.
181. Bryant, *Mirrors of Moscow*, p. 155.
182. Zürcher, *Turkey*, p. 180. A new press law of 1931 granted the government power to close down any newspaper or journal that published anything which contradicted the 'general policies of the country'.
183. Nimet Arsan (ed.), *Atatürk'ün Söylev ve Demeçleri*, vol. 3 (Ankara: Türk Tarih Kurumu, 1961), p. 51, quoted in Parla and Davison, *Corporatist Ideology in Kemalist Turkey*, p. 272.
184. See above, p. 39.

CHAPTER 3: FASCISM AND THE FAMILY

1. Filippo Tommaso Marinetti, *Una sensibilità italiana nata in Egitto*, in Marinetti, *Opere*, ed. Luciano De Maria, vols 3–4 (Milan: Mondadori, 1969), p. 205. These are his autobiographical notes, discovered after his death.
2. Ibid., p. 201.
3. Filippo Tommaso Marinetti, *Il fascino dell'Egitto*, ed. Luciano De Maria (1933; Milan: Mondadori, 1981), p. 30.
4. Don Alfonso Maria Minghelli, *Impressioni e memorie del viaggio in Terra Santa nell'Egitto e Costantinopoli, aprile e maggio 1894* (Modena: Società Tipografica, 1899), p. 9.
5. See above, p. 71.
6. Marinetti, *Una sensibilità*, p. 206.
7. Ibid., p. 211.
8. See Claudia Salaris, introduction to Filippo Tommaso Marinetti, *Arte–Vita*, ed. Claudia Salaris (Rome: Edizioni Fahrenheit 451, 2000), p. 9. See also Adrian Lyttelton, 'Society and culture in the age of Giolitti', in Emily Braun (ed.), *Italian Art in the Twentieth Century* (Munich: Prestel-Verlag; London: Royal Academy of Arts, 1989), p. 24.
9. 'Fondazione e manifesto del futurismo', in Guido Davico Bonino (ed.), *Manifesti futuristi* (Milan: Rizzoli, 2009), pp. 39–46.
10. For the bases of Marinetti's writing, see another manifesto, 'Distruzione della sintassi immaginazione senza fili parole in libertà' (11 May 1913), in ibid., pp. 120–34.
11. Umberto Boccioni, letter to Nino Barbantini, 12 February 1912, in Umberto Boccioni, *Gli scritti editi ed inediti* (Milan: Feltrinelli, 1971), p. 346.
12. 'La pittura futurista: manifesto tecnico' (11 April 1910), in Davico Bonino, *Manifesti futuristi*, p. 71.
13. Vladimir Markov, *Russian Futurism: A History* (Berkeley and Los Angeles: University of California Press, 1968), pp. 147 ff.
14. Boccioni, *Gli scritti*, letters to Vico Bauer of 19 February 1913 and end of October 1915, pp. 366 and 385.
15. Filippo Tommaso Marinetti, 'Il manuale del perfetto seduttore', in Filippo Tommaso Marinetti, *Come si seducono le donne e si tradiscono gli uomini* (Milan: Sonzogno, 1920), pp. 69–74.
16. Filippo Tommaso Marinetti, *Taccuini, 1915–1921*, ed. Alberto Bertoni (Bologna: Il Mulino, 1987), p. 129, entry for 19 April 1917.
17. Filippo Tommaso Marinetti, *Democrazia futurista: Dinamismo politico* (Milan: Facchi, 1919).
18. Ibid., pp. 61–2.
19. Ibid., pp. 103–4.
20. Barbara Spackman, *Fascist Virilities: Rhetoric, Ideology and Social Fantasy in Italy* (Minneapolis and London: University of Minnesota Press, 1996), p. 8. Spackman develops an extensive comparison between Gabriele D'Annunzio and Marinetti, with particular reference to their gender politics and attitudes. One fundamental difference of approach between the two men is that for D'Annunzio the subject of virility can be either masculine or feminine (ibid., p. 19). D'Annunzio, thirteen years Marinetti's senior, was always to be an overbearing figure, especially given his attention to the *grande geste* and his role in introducing to the Italian imagination Nietzsche's theories concerning the superman.
21. Filippo Tommaso Marinetti, 'Contro il lusso femminile' (11 March 1920), in Filippo Tommaso Marinetti, *Teoria ed invenzione futurista*, ed. Luciano De Maria (Milan: Mondadori, 1968), p. 548.
22. Marinetti, *Democrazia futurista*, pp. 63–4.
23. Ibid., pp. 93 and 96.
24. Renzo De Felice, *Mussolini*, vol. 1, *Il rivoluzionario* (Turin: Einaudi, 1965), pp. 8–9.
25. Ibid., p. 10.
26. Emil Ludwig, *Colloqui con Mussolini* (1932; Milan: Mondadori, 1935), pp. 194–5.
27. See, for example, the very detailed analysis of the Tuscan situation in Roberto Bianchi, *Bocci-Bocci: I tumulti annonari nella Toscana del 1919* (Florence: Olschki, 2001).

28. Marinetti, *Taccuini*, p. 390, entry for 28 November–5 December 1918.
29. Ibid., pp. 414–16, entry for 15 April 1919.
30. The term 'fascio' (literally 'bundle') was used in late nineteenth-century Italian socialism to symbolise the union and solidarity of a group of activists. The term was then taken over by Mussolini's post-war movement.
31. Ibid., p. 448, entry for 9 October 1919.
32. For a classic local study of these processes, see Paul R. Corner, *Fascism at Ferrara, 1915–1925* (1974; Oxford: Oxford University Press, 1975).
33. For the March on Rome, see the recent work of Giulia Albanese, *La marcia su Roma* (Rome and Bari: Laterza, 2006).
34. 'Pagine dei diari inediti di Benedetta', in Anna Maria Ruta (ed.), *Fughe e ritorni: Presenze futuriste in Sicilia: Benedetta* (Naples: Electa, 1998), p. 23, entry for 16 April 1922.
35. Marinetti, *Taccuini*, p. 468, entry for 3 January 1920.
36. Ibid., p. 482, entry for 6–9 May 1920.
37. Filippo Tommaso Marinetti, 'Orgoglio italiano rivoluzionario e libero amore', in Marinetti, *Teoria ed invenzione futurista*, p. 372.
38. Vittoria Marinetti, 'Mio padre', in Marinetti, *Arte–Vita*, pp. 175–9.
39. A number of valuable interviews with Marinetti's daughter Ala allow us to reconstitute elements of their domestic life; see, for example, Elisabetta Ray, 'Papà Marinetti il conformista', *Corriere della Sera*, 28 August 1995; Arianna Di Genova, 'La mia mamma futurista', *L'Espresso*, 44, no. 49, 10 December 1998; Mimmo Di Marzio, 'Ala Marinetti: mio Papà un futurista affettuoso', *Il Giornale*, 7 February 2009.
40. See, for example, Giordano Bruno Guerri, *Filippo Tommaso Marinetti: Invenzioni, avventure e passioni di un rivoluzionario* (Milan: Mondadori, 2009), pp. 88–9 and 202.
41. For urbanisation, see Paul Bairoch, *Cities and Economic Development* (London: Mansell, 1988), p. 221. Other statistics in this paragraph come from Massimo Livi Bacci and Georges Tapinos, 'Économie et population', in Jean-Pierre Bardet and Jacques Dupâquier (eds), *Histoire des populations de l'Europe*, vol. 3, *Les temps incertains (1914–1988)* (Paris: Fayard, 1999), p. 115; Alain Blum and Leonid E. Darskij, 'Le modèle soviétique (1917–1991) et ses devenirs', in ibid., p. 695; Gustavo De Santis and Massimo Livi Bacci, 'La population italienne au XXème siècle', in ibid., p. 514. See also Giambattista Salinari and Paul Ginsborg, 'Statistical Essay', http://bit.ly/ginsborg-appendix.
42. In the census of 1931, the average size of urban working-class families was 4.1 members; Chiara Saraceno, 'La famiglia operaia sotto il Fascismo', *Annali della Fondazione Giangiacomo Feltrinelli*, 20 (1979–80), p. 199.
43. Stefano Musso, 'La famiglia operaia', in Piero Melograni and Lucetta Scaraffia (eds), *La famiglia italiana dall'Ottocento a oggi* (Rome and Bari: Laterza, 1988), p. 87.
44. Maurizio Gribaudi, *Mondo operaio e mito operaio* (Turin: Einaudi, 1987), pp. 102 ff. Often the men had a workshop or artisan employment of some sort, which brought in extra income but reduced still further the amount of time they spent with their families.
45. Bianca Guidetti Serra, *Compagne: Testimonianze di partecipazione politica femminile*, 2 vols (Turin: Einaudi, 1977), vol. 1, p. xii.
46. Oral testimony collected for and reproduced in *Torino fra le due guerre: Cultura operaia e vita quotidiana in Borgo San Paolo, organizzazione del consenso e comunicazioni di massa, l'organizzazione del territorio urbano, le arti decorative e industriali, le arti figurative, la musica e il teatro* (Turin: Musei Civici, 1978), p. 2.
47. Gribaudi, *Mondo operaio*, pp. 107 ff.
48. In the tenement blocks plumbing was primitive, the landlords did very few repairs, and the stench from many staircases provoked unfavourable comment from the local conservative press. These and other details are taken from Laura Francesca Sudati, *Tutti i dialetti in un cortile: Immigrazione a Sesto San Giovanni nella prima metà del '900* (Milan: FISEC, 2008), pp. 181–6. The population of Sesto San Giovanni grew from

7,000 in 1901 to 28,000 in 1929. See also the testimony in Franco Alasia, *La vita di prima* (Milan: Evangelisti, 1984), pp. 83–4.

49. Perry Willson, *The Clockwork Factory: Women and Work in Fascist Italy* (Oxford: Clarendon Press, 1993), pp. 17 ff.

50. Gribaudi, *Mondo operaio*, p. 114. For Russian experiments with communal eating, see above, p. 48.

51. Gribaudi, *Mondo operaio*, p. 111.

52. See above, p. 16.

53. There is an excellent English edition of many of the key sections of the Notebooks: Quintin Hoare and Geoffrey Nowell Smith (eds), *Antonio Gramsci: Selections from the Prison Notebooks* (New York: International Publishers, 1971). For the complete Italian edition, see Antonio Gramsci, *Quaderni del carcere*, ed. Valentino Gerratana, 4 vols (Turin: Einaudi, 1975).

54. Antonio Gramsci to Julca Schucht, Moscow, 13 February 1923, and Vienna, 6 March 1924, in Antonio Gramsci, *Vita attraverso le lettere*, ed. Giuseppe Fiori (Turin: Einaudi, 1994), pp. 42 and 58. The best biography of Gramsci in English remains that of Giuseppe Fiori, *Antonio Gramsci: Life of a Revolutionary* (London: NLB, 1975).

55. Antonio Gramsci to his mother, 15 June 1931, in Antonio Gramsci, *Lettere dal carcere*, ed. Sergio Caprioglio and Elsa Fubini (Turin: Einaudi, 1965), pp. 442–3.

56. Gramsci to his mother, *Lettere dal carcere*, p. 442. For the 'infinite rosary', see Antonio Gramsci, 'Cocaina', *Avanti!*, 21 May 1918, in Antonio Gramsci, *Opere: Il nostro Marx, 1918–1919*, ed. Sergio Caprioglio (Turin: Einaudi, 1984), p. 44. On the particular virtues of working-class families, see Antonio Gramsci to Julca Schucht, 6 October 1924, in Antonio Gramsci, *Lettere, 1908–1926*, ed. Antonio Santucci (Turin: Einaudi, 1992), pp. 389–90.

57. Antonio Gramsci, 'La famiglia', in *Il Grido del Popolo*, 9 February 1918.

58. Ibid.

59. Ibid.

60. For Bebel, see above, pp. 22–3.

61. See above, p. 40.

62. See above, p. 144.

63. Antonio Gramsci, 'Serietà', *Avanti!*, 3 April 1917, in Antonio Gramsci, *La nostra città futura: Scritti torinesi (1911–1922)*, ed. Angelo d'Orsi (Rome: Carocci, 2004), pp. 137–8.

64. Antonio Gramsci to Julca Schucht, Moscow, 10 January 1923, in Gramsci, *Lettere, 1908–1926*, pp. 105–6.

65. Antonio Gramsci to Julca Schucht, Vienna , 6 March 1924, in ibid., pp. 271–2.

66. Antonio Gramsci to Julca Schucht, [Rome], 6 October 1924, in ibid., p. 390.

67. See above, p. 37.

68. Antonio Gramsci to Zino Zini, 10 January 1924, in Gramsci, *Lettere, 1908–1926*, p. 172.

69. Gramsci, *Vita attraverso le lettere*, pp. 230–2.

70. Gramsci, *Quaderni del carcere*, vol. 1, p. 340.

71. Antonio Gramsci to Delio, 22 February 1932, in Gramsci, *Lettere dal carcere*, pp. 578–9.

72. Gramsci, *Vita attraverso le lettere*, p. 289.

73. Antonio Gramsci to Delio, 2 December 1936, in Gramsci, *Lettere dal carcere*, p. 874.

74. Renato Zangheri (ed.), *Lotte agrarie in Italia: La Federazione Nazionale dei Lavoratori della Terra, 1901–1926* (Milan: Feltrinelli, 1960). See also the acute comparative considerations of Elio Giovannini, 'Federterra e FIOM', in *I due bienni rossi del Novecento, 1919–20 e 1968–69*, ed. Fondazione Giuseppe Di Vittorio and Associazione Biondi-Bartolini (Rome: Ediesse, 2006), pp. 179–90.

75. For the Po plain, see especially Guido Crainz, *Padania: Il mondo dei braccianti dall'Ottocento alla fuga dalle campagne* (1994; Rome: Donzelli, 2007), chs 5 and 6. See also, among others, Paul R. Corner, *Contadini e industrializzazione: Società rurale e impresa in Italia dal 1840 al 1940* (Rome and Bari: Laterza, 1993). For Puglia, see Frank M. Snowden, *Violence and Great Estates in the South of Italy: Apulia, 1900–1922* (Cambridge: Cambridge University Press, 1986), and Giovanni Rinaldi and Paolo Sombrero (eds), *La memoria che resta:*

Vissuto quotidiano, mito e storia dei braccianti del basso Tavoliere (Foggia: Amministrazione provinciale di Capitanata, 1981).

76. Carlo Pazzagli, 'Dal paternalismo alla democrazia', *Annali dell'Istituto Alcide Cervi*, 8 (1986), p. 19. See also his fundamental work *L'agricoltura toscana nella prima metà dell'800* (Florence: Olschki, 1973).

77. Matteo Baragli, 'Famiglie mezzadrili e culture religiose', in Enrica Asquer et al. (eds), *Famiglie del Novecento: Conflitti, culture e relazioni* (Rome: Carocci, 2010), pp. 47–8.

78. The archive of Maria Maltoni, which contains around 1,500 notebooks and more than a thousand drawings, is housed by the Biblioteca Comunale of Impruneta. See also Maria Maltoni (ed.), *I quaderni di San Gersolè* (Turin: Einaudi, 1959).

79. Giovanni Contini, *Aristocrazia contadina: Sulla complessità della società mezzadrile: Fattorie, famiglie, individui* (Siena: Dea, 2005).

80. Ibid., p. 197.

81. Ibid., pp. 243–4.

82. Ibid., p. 248, diary entry of 19 February 1938.

83. Ibid., p. 243, diary entry of 18 February 1936.

84. Fabio Mugnaini, 'A veglia: monografia breve su un' "abitudine" ', *Annali dell'Istituto Alcide Cervi*, 9 (1987), pp. 119–44.

85. See the school diary of another San Gersolè child, Natalino Carrai, who came from a socialist family which treated wandering friars and nuns with considerable contempt; Contini, *Aristocrazia contadina*, pp. 26–7.

86. Robert Paxton, 'The five stages of Fascism', *Journal of Modern History*, 70, no. 1 (1998), p. 18.

87. Renzo De Felice, *Mussolini*, vol. 1, *Il rivoluzionario*, p. 80 n. 1. De Felice cites a letter to Mussolini from Padre Tacchi Venturi of September 1925, in which the latter avers that the Duce's imminent remarriage in church 'will be of particular consolation to His Holiness and to numerous eminent personages who are sincerely attached to your illustrious person and highly desirous that the blessing of God falls copiously upon Your Excellency and your dear ones'.

88. See the entries by Lucia Motti, 'Edda Mussolini' and 'Rachele Mussolini', in Victoria De Grazia and Sergio Luzzatto (eds), *Dizionario del fascismo*, 2 vols (Turin: Einaudi, 2003), vol. 2, pp. 195–200.

89. Claretta Petacci, *Verso il disastro: Mussolini in guerra: Diari, 1939–1940* (Milan: Rizzoli, 2011), pp. 25–6, entry for 1 January 1939. The arguments for considering Petacci's diaries to be authentic are set out in the introduction to the volume by Mimmo Franzinelli, pp. 5–17.

90. Archivio Centrale dello Stato, Spd, Cr, buste 109–10, quoted by Martina Salvante in her interesting Ph.D. thesis, 'La paternità durante il Fascismo: modelli e ruoli del pater familias tra stato e società' (European University Institute, Florence, 2008), p. 50.

91. Renata Broggini, 'La "famiglia Mussolini": i colloqui di Edda Ciano con lo psichiatra svizzero Repond, 1944–45', *Italia contemporanea*, 203 (1996), pp. 333–61.

92. Ibid., p. 353.

93. Benito Mussolini, *Parlo con Bruno*, in Mussolini, *Opera Omnia*, ed. Duilio Susmel and Edoardo Susmel, 36 vols (Florence: La Fenice, 1951–63), vol. 34 (1961), pp. 209–69.

94. Mussolini, 'Intransigenza assoluta (22 June 1925')', *Opera Omnia*, vol. 21, Florence: La Fenice, 1956, p. 362; and 'Per la medaglia dei benemeriti del commune di Milano (28 Oct. 1925)', ibid, p. 425. The best introduction to this theme is Enzo Traverso, *Il totalitarismo: Storia di un dibattito* (Milan: Bruno Mondadori, 2002).

95. Benito Mussolini and Giovanni Gentile, 'Fascismo', in *Enciclopedia italiana di scienze, lettere ed arti*, vol. 14 (Florence: Treccani, 1932), pp. 847–8.

96. Giovanni Gentile, 'I fondamenti della filosofia del diritto', in Giovanni Gentile, *Opere complete*, 4th edn revised and expanded (Florence: Le Lettere, 1987). The eighth chapter, 'Lo stato', pp. 103–20, is the text of Gentile's contribution to the Berlin conference. For the conference proceedings, see Baltus Wigersma (ed.), *Im Auftrag des internationalen Hegelbundes: Verhandlungen des zweiten Hegelkongresses vom 18. bis 21. Oktober 1931 in Berlin* (Tübingen and Haarlem: Mohr-Willink, 1932).

97. Georg Wilhelm Friedrich Hegel, *Elements of the Philosophy of Right*, ed. Allen W. Wood (1822; Cambridge: Cambridge University Press, 1991).

98. Gentile, *I fondamenti*, p. 119.

99. Ibid., p. 120.

100. Ibid.

101. For further discussion of *Antigone*, see my conclusions to this book below, p. 440.

102. The teachings of St Thomas Aquinas were fundamental in bringing the family to the centre of all Catholic social relations – as epitome, metaphor and prototype. See the classic work of Ernst Troeltsch, *The Social Teaching of the Christian Churches*, vol. 1 (1902; London and New York: Allen & Unwin and Macmillan, 1931), esp. pp. 312–13.

103. Antonio Rosmini, 'Discorso in occasione del matrimonio del fratello Giuseppe', in Rosmini, *Scritti sul matrimonio* (Rome: Forzani, 1902), p. 329.

104. Leo XIII, *Rerum Novarum* (1891), in *Insegnamenti pontifici*, vol. 1, *Il matrimonio* (Rome: Edizioni Paoline, 1964), p. 158.

105. Ibid.

106. The term was derived from Leo XIII's writings to French monarchists and Spanish Carlists under the restored monarchy of 1875, in which he insists that Catholicism was not tied to any one system of government. Pius XI repeated the same concept in his encyclical *Dilectissima Nobis* of 1933.

107. Daniele Menozzi, 'Secolarizzazione, cristianità e regno sociale di Cristo', in *Le carte: Notizie e testi della Fondazione Romolo Murri*, 2 (1997), pp. 7 ff. and 16–18.

108. Pius XII, 'Allocuzione ai novelli sposi' (26 June 1940), in *Insegnamenti pontifici*, vol. 1, *Il matrimonio*, pp. 288–9.

109. For detailed studies of the relationship between family, civil society and state in the teachings of Pius XI and Pius XII, see Francesco Corona, 'Famiglia e matrimonio nel magistero di Pio XI: le encicliche e il dibattito nel mondo cattolico (1922–1939)' (unpublished *laurea* dissertation, University of Florence, 2002), and Stefania J. Cara, 'Il matrimonio e la famiglia nel magistero di Pio XII' (unpublished *laurea* dissertation, University of Florence, 2000).

110. Leo XIII, *Arcanum Divinae Sapientiae* (1880), in *Insegnamenti pontifici*, vol. 1, *Il matrimonio*, p. 126; Leo XIII, *Rerum Novarum*, p. 159.

111. The complete text of *Casti Connubii* is to be found in Piero Barberi and Dionigi Tettamanzi (eds), *Matrimonio e famiglia nel magistero della Chiesa: I documenti dal Concilio di Firenze a Giovanni Paolo II* (Milan: Massimo, 1986), pp. 107–54. The passage quoted here is on pp. 123–4.

112. Cecilia Dau Novelli, *Famiglia e modernizzazione in Italia tra le due guerre* (Rome: Studium, 1994), pp. 21–2.

113. See the testimony of Bernhard Häring, *Fede, storia, morale* (Rome: Borla, 1989), p. 57. For an acute Catholic commentary on the vision of marriage which emerges from *Casti Connubii*, see Ernesto Ruffini, 'Il matrimonio alla luce della teologia cattolica', in Virgilio Melchiorre (ed.), *Amore e matrimonio nel pensiero filosofico e teologico moderno* (Milan: Vita e Pensiero, 1976), pp. 110–12.

114. Luciano Canfora, 'Classicismo e fascismo', in *Matrici culturali del fascismo: Seminari promossi dal consiglio regionale pugliese e dall'Ateneo barese nel trentennale della Liberazione* (Bari: Università di Bari, 1977), pp. 85–111.

115. Benito Mussolini, 'Passato e futuro', *Il Popolo d'Italia*, 21 April 1922, quoted in Luca Scuccimarra, 'Culto della romanità', in De Grazia and Luzzatto, *Dizionario del fascismo*, vol. 2, pp. 539–41.

116. Luigi Chiarini, 'Carattere retrivo della famiglia borghese', *Critica fascista*, 11, no. 16, 15 August 1933, p. 305.

117. For peasant women and the regime, see Silvia Salvatici, *Contadine dell'Italia fascista: Presenze, ruoli, immagini* (Turin: Rosenberg & Sellier, 1996), and Perry Willson, *Peasant Women and Politics in Fascist Italy: The 'Massaie Rurali'* (London and New York: Routledge, 2002).

118. Fundamental for this theme is Mariuccia Salvati, *Il regime e gli impiegati: La nazionalizzazione piccolo borghese nel ventennio fascista* (Rome and Bari: Laterza, 1992).
119. Spackman, *Fascist Virilities*, *passim*.
120. This point is well made by Chiara Saraceno, 'Costruzione della maternità e della paternità', in Angelo Del Boca et al. (eds), *Il regime fascista: Storia e storiografia* (Rome and Bari: Laterza, 1995), p. 482, which makes reference to the 'pomposity' and 'crudeness' of similar manifestations.
121. In 1933, Manlio Pompei, one of the regime's family ideologues, tried to reconcile Fascist aggression with Italian family traditions, the male with the female: 'Do we want to make fighters of our sons? Does this not put mothers' anxious hearts in conflict with the aims of the state? No: because we are not educating mercenaries to spread ruin and desolation, but soldiers ready to defend the fatherland.' But this purely defensive role was far from what Mussolini had in mind; Manlio Pompei, 'La famiglia e il fascismo: un'inchiesta da fare', *Critica fascista*, 11, no. 9, 1 May 1933, p. 165.
122. For Marinetti in particular, see above, pp. 142–3.
123. Carlo Emilio Gadda, *Eros e Priapo* (Milan: Garzanti, 1967), p. 75, quoted in Spackman, *Fascist Virilities*, p. 1.
124. Ibid. Let us not forget in this context Marinetti's aphorism: 'The brain is an unsuitable and unnecessary motor for the chassis of the woman, whose natural motor is the uterus.' See above, p. 142.
125. Victoria De Grazia, *How Fascism Ruled Women* (Berkeley: University of California Press, 1992).
126. Victoria De Grazia, 'Patriarcato', in De Grazia and Luzzatto, *Dizionario del fascismo*, vol. 2, pp. 336–41.
127. Mussolini had stated in August 1934 that within the family women's most important function, apart from having children, was to protect men and offer them a haven from the impact of mechanical civilisation; Benito Mussolini, 'Macchina e donna' (31 August 1934), in *Opera Omnia*, vol. 20 (1956), pp. 310–11.
128. See above, pp. 41–3.
129. *Il Principe*, 3 November 1922, quoted in Mario Sironi, *Scritti editi e inediti*, ed. Ettore Camesasca (Milan: Feltrinelli, 1980), p. 20.
130. See Emily Braun, *Mario Sironi and Italian Modernism: Art and Politics under Fascism* (Cambridge: Cambridge University Press, 2000), and Maria Grazia Messina (ed.), *Mario Sironi: Ritratti di famiglia* (Turin: Bollati Boringhieri, 1996).
131. Giuseppe Bottai, 'Resultanze', *Critica fascista*, 5, no. 4, 15 February 1927.
132. In this respect Sironi was influenced by his readings of Esiodo, 'the most austere epic Greek poet'.
133. Chiara Stefani, 'Pittura, famiglia, regime: un percorso iconografico nell'Italia fascista' (unpublished *laurea* dissertation, University of Florence, 2010), pp. 279–301; Fabio Benzi (ed.), *Mario Sironi, 1885–1961* (Milan: Electa, 1993), esp. pp. 250–1.
134. Messina, *Mario Sironi*, pp. 46 ff.
135. Roberto Farinacci, 'Ma che basta!', *Il Regime Fascista*, 1 June 1933.
136. For Mario Sironi's conception of mural painting, see the 'Manifesto della pittura murale', in *La Colonna*, December 1933, signed by Sironi together with Campigli, Carrà and Funi, in Sironi, *Scritti editi e inediti*, pp. 155–7.
137. The Ascension Day speech is to be found in Benito Mussolini, *Opera Omnia*, vol. 22 (1957), pp. 360–90. For the omniscient Duce, see p. 382.
138. Ibid., pp. 364 and 367.
139. Ibid., p. 366.
140. Ibid., p. 389.
141. Richard Korherr, *Regresso delle nascite: Morte dei popoli* (Rome: Libreria del Littorio, 1928). Spengler's preface had also accompanied the first, German edition, *Geburtenrückgang: Mahnruf an das deutsche Volk* (Munich: Süddeutsche Monatshefte, 1927). No English edition exists.

142. Carl Ipsen, *Dictating Demography: The Problem of Population in Fascist Italy* (Cambridge: Cambridge University Press, 1996), p. 67.

143. Benito Mussolini, preface to Korherr, *Regresso delle nascite*, p. 10.

144. This was a theme tackled for the first time, with primary reference to France, by Jacques Donzelot in his *La police des familles* (Paris: Éditions de Minuit, 1977).

145. There is an extensive literature on the subject of eugenics in the first half of the twentieth century. See in particular Maria Sophia Quine, *Population Politics in Twentieth-Century Europe: Fascist Dictatorships and Liberal Democracies* (London: Routledge, 1996); Mark B. Adams (ed.), *The Wellborn Science: Eugenics in Germany, France, Brazil, and Russia* (Oxford: Oxford University Press, 1990); and the classic work by David Glass, *Population Policies and Movements in Europe* (Oxford: Clarendon Press, 1940).

146. The best summary of ONMI's activities and organisation is undoubtedly that of Perry Willson, 'Opera nazionale per la maternità e infanzia (Onmi)', in De Grazia and Luzzatto, *Dizionario del fascismo*, vol. 2, pp. 273–7.

147. Elizabeth Dixon Whittaker, *Measuring Mamma's Milk: Fascism and the Medicalization of Maternity in Italy* (Ann Arbor: University of Michigan Press, 2000); David G. Horn, *Social Bodies: Science, Reproduction and Italian Modernity* (Princeton: Princeton University Press, 1995).

148. For the Florentine case, see the early chapters of Elisabetta Celotto, 'L'Opera nazionale maternità e infanzia, 1925–1975: il caso fiorentino' (unpublished *laurea* dissertation, University of Florence, 1997), and Patrizia Guarneri, 'Dagli aiuti materni all'ONMI: l'assistenza alla maternità e all'infanzia del fascismo', in Marco Breschi and Lucia Pozzi (eds), *Salute, malattia e sopravvivenza in Italia fra '800 e '900* (Udine: Forum, 2007), pp. 59–83.

149. Istituto Centrale di Statistica del Regno d'Italia, *Annali di statistica*, series 7, vol. 8 (Rome: Tipografia F. Falli, 1943), n. 7.

150. Angelo Buffa, 'Problemi della maternità e dell'infanzia', in *Maternità ed infanzia*, October 1937, p. 4, quoted in Ipsen, *Dictating Demography*, p. 158; see also p. 220, table 4.2.

151. Ibid., pp. 166–70, figures 4.1 (a–c) and table 4.4.

152. See the fundamental work by Anna Treves, *Le migrazioni interne nell'Italia fascista: Politica e realtà demografica* (Turin: Einaudi, 1976).

153. Ipsen, *Dictating Demography*, p. 101, table 3.2; Piero Bevilacqua, 'Bonifica', in De Grazia and Luzzatto, *Dizionario del fascismo*, vol. 1, pp. 182–3.

154. The most complete and recent account is Federico Cresti, *Non desiderare la terra d'altri: La colonizzazione italiana in Libia* (Rome: Carocci, 2011) (p. 288 for settlement figures); see also Ipsen, *Dictating Demography*, pp. 119 ff.

155. See above, pp. 97 ff.

156. E.E. Evans-Pritchard, *The Sanusi of Cyrenaica* (Oxford: Clarendon Press, 1949), p. 39.

157. Ibid., p. 38.

158. See Cresti, *Non desiderare la terra d'altri*, pp. 89–90.

159. Ibid., p. 92

160. Piero Badoglio to Rodolfo Graziani, 20 June 1930, quoted in ibid., p. 94.

161. These facts, buried and denied by the Italian authorities for years, were brought into the open by the pioneering historical work of Angelo Del Boca and Giorgio Rochat. See Angelo Del Boca, *Gli italiani in Libia*, vol. 2, *Dal fascismo a Gheddafi* (Rome and Bari: Laterza, 1988), and his very useful summary, Angelo Del Boca, 'I crimini del colonialismo fascista', in Angelo Del Boca, *Le guerre coloniali del fascismo* (Rome and Bari: Laterza, 1991), pp. 232–55; Giorgio Rochat, 'La repressione della Resistenza in Cirenaica (1927–31)', in Enzo Santarelli et al. (eds), *'Omar al-Mukhtar e la riconquista fascista della Libia* (Milan: Marzorati, 1981), pp. 53–190.

162. Benito Mussolini, speech in Basilicata, August 1936, in Mussolini, *Opera Omnia*, vol. 28 (1959), pp. 29–30.

163. For an illuminating comparison, see Martina Salvante, 'I prestiti matrimoniali: una misura pronatalista nella Germania nazista e nell'Italia fascista', *Passato e presente*, 21 (2003), no. 60, pp. 39–58.

164. Ipsen, *Dictating Demography*, p. 183, table 4.6. Anna Treves offers a slightly more positive judgement of the Italian case in 'Prestiti matrimoniali', in De Grazia and Luzzatto, *Dizionario del fascismo*, vol. 2, p. 421. See also her fundamental work, Anna Treves, *Le nascite e la politica nell'Italia del Novecento* (Milan: LED, 2001), esp. pp. 101–5, 256–9.

165. Extremely useful is Lorenzo Benadusi, *Il nemico dell'uomo nuovo: L'omosessualità nell'esperimento totalitario fascista* (Milan: Feltrinelli, 2005).

166. Glass, *Population Policies*, p. 237; Quine, *Population Politics*, pp. 40–1; Saraceno, 'Costruzione della maternità', pp. 488–90.

167. Denise Detragiache, 'Un aspect de la politique démographique de l'Italie fasciste: la répression de l'avortement', *Mélanges de l'École française de Rome*, 92 (1980), pp. 691–735; Saraceno, 'Costruzione della maternità', pp. 486–7.

168. The best treatment of this theme is to be found in De Grazia, *How Fascism Ruled Women*, p. 180. She points out that women who left paid work outside the home so as to have children often returned to the labour market as casual domestic labour, badly paid and without social insurance of any sort.

169. Gaetano Zingali, speech to the Camera dei Deputati, 5 June 1929, quoted in Ipsen, *Dictating Demography*, pp. 87–8.

170. See above, p. 143.

171. Ferdinando Loffredo, *Politica della famiglia* (Milan: Bompiani, 1938), p. 20. Loffredo also noted, quite rightly, that in all the legislation on the corporatist state there were only 'generic enunciations' about the role and place of the family; ibid., p. 19.

172. See above, pp. 29 ff and 123.

173. Mario Sbriccoli, 'Codificazione civile e penale', in De Grazia and Luzzatto, *Dizionario del fascismo*, vol. 1, pp. 300–1.

174. Ibid., p. 303.

175. See the comments of Paolo Passaniti in his recent *Diritto di famiglia e ordine sociale: Il percorso storico della 'Società coniugale' in Italia* (Milan: Giuffrè, 2011), p. 396: 'The repeated failure of projects which gave precedence to civil matrimony are testimony to the absolute immobility of the State.'

176. Renzo De Felice, *Mussolini*, vol. 2/2, *Il fascista: L'organizzazione dello stato fascista* (Turin: Einaudi, 1968), p. 394.

177. Quoted by Franco Malgeri, 'Chiesa cattolica e regime fascista', in Del Boca et al., *Il regime fascista*, p. 174.

178. Alfredo Rocco, 'Disposizione sugli enti ecclesiastici e sulle amministrazioni civili di patrimoni destinati ai fini di culto: relazione sul disegno di legge 30 Aprile 1929', in Alfredo Rocco, *Scritti e discorsi politici*, vol. 3, *La formazione dello stato fascista (1925–1934)* (Milan: Giuffrè, 1938), p. 1052.

179. For the wider context and further development of Gentile's opposition, see Gabriele Turi, *Giovanni Gentile: Una biografia* (Florence: Giunti, 1995), pp. 395 ff.

180. Carlo Alberto Biggini, *Storia inedita della Conciliazione* (Milan: Garzanti, 1942), p. 316.

181. *I Patti Lateranensi, 11 febbraio 1929* (Rome: Istituto Editoriale S. Michele, 1971), pp. 145–6. See also 'Legge 847 (27 maggio 1929): Disposizioni per l'applicazione del Concordato nella parte relativa al matrimonio', in ibid., pp. 203–10.

182. Paolo Ungari, *Storia del diritto di famiglia in Italia, 1796–1942* (Bologna: Il Mulino, 1974), p. 211.

183. Pius XI uttered these famous words on 13 February 1929, two days after the pacts had been signed, while addressing an audience at the Università Cattolica del Sacro Cuore in Milan; quoted in Ernesto Rossi, *Il manganello e l'aspersorio* (1958; Milan: Kaos, 2000), p. 166.

184. On schooling, see, for example, Mario Isnenghi, *L'educazione dell'italiano: Il fascismo e l'organizzazione della cultura* (Bologna: Cappelli, 1979), and Monica Galfré, *Il regime degli editori: Libri, scuola e fascismo* (Rome and Bari: Laterza, 2005).

185. Rossi, *Il manganello*, pp. 188 and 189.
186. Emilio Gentile, *Fascismo: Storia e interpretazione* (Rome and Bari: Laterza, 2002).
187. Tullio Kezich and Alessandra Levantesi (eds), *Una giornata particolare: Un film di Ettore Scola: Incontrarsi e dirsi addio nella Roma del '38* (Turin: Lindau, 2003).
188. 'La sceneggiatura del film', in ibid., pp. 58 and 112.
189. Giovanni Gentile, 'L'educazione nella famiglia: discorso al 3° congresso nazionale delle Donne italiane, Roma, 4 maggio 1923', in Gentile, *Il Fascismo al governo della scuola* (Palermo: R. Sandron, 1924), pp. 88–9.
190. Carmen Betti, *L'Opera nazionale Balilla e l'educazione fascista* (Florence: La Nuova Italia, 1977); Paolo Bartoli et al., *L'organizzazione del consenso nel regime fascista: L'Opera Nazionale Balilla come istituzione di controllo sociale* (Perugia: Istituto di etnologia e antropologia culturale dell'Università di Perugia, 1983); Antonio Gibelli, 'Opera nazionale Balilla (Onb)', in De Grazia and Luzzatto, *Dizionario del fascismo*, vol. 2, pp. 266–71.
191. For further comparative reflections, see below, pp. 367 ff.
192. Antonio Gibelli, 'Piccole italiane e Giovani italiane', in De Grazia and Luzzatto, *Dizionario del fascismo*, vol. 2, p. 372.
193. Sandro Setta, 'Renato Ricci', in ibid., p. 509.
194. Angelo Cammarata, *Pedagogia di Mussolini: Alla scuola dell'Opera Balilla* (Palermo: Trimarchi, 1935), p. 35, quoted in Bartoli et al., *L'organizzazione del consenso*, p. 23.
195. Betti, *L'Opera nazionale Balilla*, p. 127.
196. For an overview, see Patrizia Dogliani, 'Colonie di vacanza', in De Grazia and Luzzatto, *Dizionario del fascismo*, vol. 1, pp. 313–16.
197. De Grazia, *How Fascism Ruled Women*, pp. 147–8.
198. Benito Mussolini, 'Discorso al Consiglio nazionale del PNF' (25 October 1938), in Mussolini, *Opera Omnia*, vol. 29 (1959), p. 192.
199. Victoria De Grazia, *The Culture of Consent: Mass Organisation of Leisure in Fascist Italy* (Cambridge: Cambridge University Press, 1981), *passim*. See also De Grazia, 'Dopolavoro', in De Grazia and Luzzatto, *Dizionario del fascismo*, vol. 1, pp. 443–7.
200. Vittorio Sandicchi, letter to Achille Starace, 25 November 1934, quoted in De Grazia, *The Culture of Consent*, p. 122.
201. Ibid., p. 162.
202. Gian Franco Venè, *Mille lire al mese: La vita quotidiana della famiglia nell'Italia fascista* (Milan: Mondadori, 1988), pp. 244–7.
203. Ibid., p. 246.
204. Wynstan Hugh Auden, 'September 1, 1939', in Auden, *Another Time* (London: Faber, 1940), p. 112.
205. Gianpasquale Santomassimo, 'Propaganda', in De Grazia and Luzzatto, *Dizionario del fascismo*, vol. 2, pp. 433–7. Still useful is Philip V. Cannistraro, *La fabbrica del consenso: Fascismo e mass media* (Rome and Bari: Laterza, 1975).
206. David Forgacs and Stephen Gundle, *Mass Culture and Italian Society from Fascism to the Cold War* (Bloomington: Indiana University Press, 2007), p. 146. It is important to note that the growth of cinema audiences was quite contained in the 1930s, the real explosion occurring in the 1940s and 1950s; by 1955 Italy had 10,570 cinemas.
207. Born in 1880, Mario Biazzi was a little-known artist who frequented Futurist circles for a time but lived the greater part of his life in Cremona, dying in poverty there in 1965; see the biographical details in *La famiglia nell'arte: Storia e immagini nell'Italia del XX secolo* (Rome: De Luca, 2002), p. 183.
208. Kezich and Levantesi (eds), *Una giornata particolare*, p. 91.
209. For a selection, see the illustrated article by Antonio Gibelli, 'Il regime illustrato e il popolo bambino', in De Grazia and Luzzatto, *Dizionario del fascismo*, vol. 2, insert between pp. 262 and 263, as well as his more extended treatment in Gibelli, *Il popolo bambino: Infanzia e nazione dalla Grande Guerra a Salò* (Turin: Einaudi, 2005), pp. 226–32.
210. For a detailed discussion of this theme, covering many different fields, see Ruth Ben-Ghiat, *Fascist Modernities: Italy, 1922–1945* (Berkeley: University of California Press, 2001).

211. For Italy's footballing triumphs of these years, see John Foot, *Calcio: A History of Italian Football* (London: Fourth Estate, 2006), pp. 181 ff.

212. Forgacs and Gundle, *Mass Culture*, p. 75.

213. For the appropriation of red in many different forms as the colour of resistance, see Luisa Passerini, *Fascism in Popular Memory: The Cultural Experience of the Turin Working Class* (1984; Cambridge: Cambridge University Press, 1987), pp. 101–5.

214. Contini, *Aristocrazia contadina*, p. 215.

215. Ibid., p. 241, entry for 8 May 1939.

216. Quoted in the exhaustive work by Petra Terhoeven, *Oro alla patria: Donne, guerra e propaganda nella giornata della Fede fascista* (2003; Bologna: Il Mulino, 2006), p. 187. With regard to the percentage of participants, Terhoeven suggests figures as high as 70 per cent in Rome and 50 per cent in other major cities. She notes that in rural areas, especially the south, participation was very much more limited; ibid., pp. 190–7 and tables A1 and A2, pp. 310–13.

217. Alberto Romita, sermon of 18 December 1935, quoted in Lucia Ceci, *Il papa non deve parlare: Chiesa, fascismo e guerra d'Etiopia* (Rome and Bari: Laterza, 2010), pp. 99–100.

218. Lucia Ceci, ' "Il Fascismo manda l'Italia in rovina": le note inedite di monsignor Domenico Tardini (23 settembre–13 dicembre 1935)', *Rivista storica italiana*, 120 (2008), no. 1, pp. 343–4.

219. Benito Mussolini, 'Elogio alle donne italiane', in Mussolini, *Opera Omnia*, vol. 27 (1959), p. 266.

220. Carlo Levi, *Christ Stopped at Eboli*, trans. Frances Frenaye (1946; London: Cassel, 1948), p. 75.

221. Angelo Del Boca, *Italiani, brava gente?* (Vicenza: Neri Pozza, 2005), pp. 205–27.

222. Filippo Tommaso Marinetti, *Poema africano della divisione '28 ottobre'* (Milan: Mondadori, 1937).

223. Quoted in Walter Benjamin, *The Work of Art in the Age of Mechanical Reproduction*, trans. J. A. Underwood (1936; Penguin: London, 2008), pp. 36–7, where Benjamin also comments on Marinetti's article.

224. Archivio Centrale dello Stato, Ministero dell'Interno, Demorazza, busta 4, fascicolo 15, quoted in Ipsen, *Dictating Demography*, p. 185, without a specific date.

225. Alessandro Lessona to Rodolfo Graziani, 5 August 1936, quoted in Giorgio Rochat, *Il colonialismo italiano* (Turin: Loescher, 1973), pp. 188–9.

226. Haile M. Larebo, 'Africa orientale italiana', in De Grazia and Luzzatto, *Dizionario del fascismo*, vol. 1, p. 17. See also Giulia Barrera, 'Madamato', in ibid., vol. 2, pp. 69–72, and Barbara Sorgoni, *Parole e corpi: Antropologia, discorso giuridico e politiche sessuali interrazziali nella colonia Eritrea (1890–1941)* (Naples: Liguori, 1998).

227. Michele Sarfatti, *Gli ebrei nell'Italia fascista: Vicende, identità, persecuzione* (Turin: Einaudi, 2000), pp. 31 and 41.

228. The text may be found at http://www.polyarchy.org/basta/documenti/razza.1938.html.

229. Vittorio Foa, *Il Cavallo e la Torre: Riflessioni su una vita* (Turin: Einaudi, 1991), p. 6. See also Alexander Stille, *Benevolence and Betrayal: Five Italian Jewish Families under Fascism* (London: Vintage, 1993).

230. Foa, *Il Cavallo e la Torre*, p. 5. Foa was released from prison in 1943. He took part in the Italian Resistance before becoming a leading trade unionist and intellectual in the new Italian Republic.

231. Sarfatti, *Gli ebrei nell'Italia fascista*, p. 9.

232. Leonardo Sciascia, 'Siamo tutti gattopardi', *Corriere della Sera*, 30 April 1945, p. 45.

233. Ibid.

234. See above, p. 142.

235. Gino Agnese, *Marinetti: Una vita esplosiva* (Milan: Camunia, 1990), p. 283.

236. Ibid., pp. 286–91.

237. Benedetta, *Donne della patria in guerra*, speech for INCF, Sezione di Catania, 18 April 1942 (Acireale: Tipografie 900, 1942), p. 16.

238. Ibid., pp. 3, 4, 13, 15 and 16.

239. Passerini, *Fascism in Popular Memory*, pp. 146 ff.

240. Paul Corner, 'Fascismo e controllo sociale', *Italia contemporanea*, 228 (2002), pp. 381–405.

241. See above, p. 220.

242. We return to the snooping regime. As Guido Melis has written, the regime witnessed 'the multiplication, in every sector of social life, of the activities of registration, enumeration, indexing and control': Guido Melis, *Storia dell'amministrazione italiana, 1861–1993* (Bologna: Il Mulino, 1996), p. 375.

243. In her innovative and important work, *How Fascism Ruled Women*, Victoria De Grazia offers another version of this relationship, based on the contrast between what she calls 'Fascist familism' on the one hand and 'oppositional familism' on the other. The first describes the consent accorded to the regime by Italian families, above all in the years 1935–8, with family members, both female and male, serving the interests of the party and the nation-state. The second refers to the withdrawal of this support from the state when the latter began, at the end of the 1930s and in the early 1940s, to make ever heavier requests upon its citizenry. I do not find this distinction helpful for the following reasons. First, the extensive literature on familism, to which De Grazia makes very little reference, while not being unanimous in defining the term certainly finds broad agreement in the idea that familism separates families from the state structurally, and puts family interests before and to the exclusion of any others. 'Fascist familism' is thus an oxymoron. As far as 'oppositional familism' is concerned, the term does not seem to be a great step forward in analytical terms. By its nature familism is oppositional, suspicious of civil society and indisposed towards the state. De Grazia also describes oppositional familism as 'a retreat of civil society before the state', but this only muddies the water further. Families and civil society are self-evidently not the same thing; De Grazia, *How Fascism Ruled Women*, ch. 4, 'The family versus the state', pp. 77–115, esp. pp. 82 and 114–15.

244. Claretta Petacci, *Mussolini segreto: Diari, 1932–1938* (Milan: Rizzoli, 2009), p. 401, letter of 28 August 1938.

245. Giuseppe Bottai, speech at Francavilla al Mare (no date), quoted in Amerigo Montemaggiori, *Dizionario della dottrina fascista* (Turin: Paravia, 1934), pp. 311–12.

CHAPTER 4: FAMILY AND FAMILY LIFE IN THE SPANISH REPUBLIC
AND THE CIVIL WAR, 1931–1950

1. Juan Marichal, 'Los intelectuales y la guerra', in Edward Malefakis (ed.), *La guerra de España (1936–1939)* (Madrid: I.B. Taurus, 1996), p. 483.

2. P. B. Shelley, 'Ode to Liberty', in Shelley, *Selected Poetry*, ed. N. Rogers (Oxford: Oxford University Press, 1968), p. 372.

3. The first had had a short life, from February 1873 to December 1874.

4. See above, p. 76.

5. Victoria Román's testimony, like others used in this chapter, forms part of Ronald Fraser's great work of oral history, *Blood of Spain: An Oral History of the Spanish Civil War* (London: Allen Lane, 1979), pp. 40, 260 and 264.

6. Ibid., pp. 41 and 174. '[At school] the first thing that struck me was the difference between what the priests preached and their personal conduct. Many of the younger friars [. . .] had homosexual leanings and divided us pupils into the "pretty" and the "ugly". The discipline was ferocious, it was just like a barracks. When I became an officer leading Moroccan troops – shock troops which, like the Foreign Legion, were full of adventurers and criminals – I was like a fish in water thanks to my training at school.'

7. For the complicated business of interpreting the results of the vote, see the long note in Gabriele Ranzato, *L eclissi della democrazia: La Guerra civile spagnola e le sue origini* (Turin: Bollati Boringhieri, 2004), p. 126 n. 51.

8. Quoted in Ana Aguado and Maria Dolores Ramos, *La modernización de España (1917–1939): Cultura y vida cotidiana* (Madrid: Editorial Síntesis, 2002), p. 154.

9. *Constitución de la República Española* ([Madrid], 1931); http:/www1.icsi.berkeley.edu/~/chema/republica/constitucion.html.

10. Ibid.

11. See Article 119 of the Weimar Constitution: 'The spiritual upbringing, the health and the social development of the family are the responsibility of the State and of the Communes.' The Weimar Constitution is available online at http://www.dhm.de/lemo/html/dokumente/verfassung/index.html. In English, the Weimar Constitution is published in full as an appendix to Herbert Kraus, *The Crisis of German Democracy: A Study of the Spirit of the Constitution of Weimar* (Princeton: Princeton University Press, 1932); Article 119 is to be found on p. 204. See also Monique Da Silva, 'L'impact de la Constitution de Weimar sur celle de la IIe République espagnole', *Travaux et documents* (Université Paris 8 Vincennes Saint-Denis), 23 (2004).

12. See the Geneva Declaration of the Rights of the Child, adopted by the League of Nations on 26 September 1924; www.un-documents.net/gdrc1924.htm.

13. Julio Iglesias De Ussel, 'Family ideology and political transition in Spain', *International Journal of Law and the Family*, 5 (1991), p. 279.

14. See the valuable article by Ana Aguado, 'Tra pubblico e privato: suffragio e divorzio nella Spagna della Seconda Repubblica', *Italia contemporanea*, 241 (2005), pp. 471–90.

15. Arturo Mori, *Crónica de las Cortes Constituyentes de la Segunda República Española*, vol. 3, *La religión – La familia – La enseñanza* (Madrid: Aguilar, 1932), p. 253. The Socialists in the Cortes, while supporting the cause of divorce, adopted much more moderate positions. Their spokesman, José Sanchís Banús, underlined the fact that 'the most perfect form of sexual organisation of human society is stable monogamy'; Mori, *Crónica de las Cortes*, vol. 3, p. 243.

16. Ricardo Lezcano, *El divorcio en la Segunda República* (Madrid: Akal, 1979), pp. 265–70.

17. Mercedes Yusta, 'La Segunda República: significado para las mujeres', in Guadalupe Gómez-Ferrer et al. (eds), *Historia de las mujeres en España y América Latina*, vol. 4, *Del siglo XX a los umbrales del XXI* (Madrid: Cátedra, 2006), p. 110.

18. Quoted in Aguado, 'Tra pubblico e privato', pp. 474–5.

19. Ibid.

20. I am indebted to Paul Preston for his highly convincing portrait of Margarita Nelken in Paul Preston, *Doves of War: Four Women of Spain* (London: HarperCollins, 2002), pp. 295–407.

21. Margarita Nelken, *La condición social de la mujer en España: Su estado actual, su posible desarrollo* (Barcelona: Editorial Minerva, 1919), pp. 117–18.

22. Preston, *Doves of War*, p. 299.

23. Nelken, *La condición social*, p. 38.

24. Margarita Nelken, *En torno a nosotras (diálogo socrático)* (Madrid: Páez, 1927), p. 140.

25. Preston, *Doves of War*, p. 329.

26. *Diario de las sesiones de Cortes, Congreso de los Diputados, comenzaron el 8 de diciembre de 1933*, entry for 25 January 1934, quoted in Preston, *Doves of War*, p. 335.

27. In formal terms, the Jesuits were accused of being an order with a special vow of obedience which was not to the state. The real reason for their expulsion, however, was the desire of the majority in the Constituent Assembly to destroy their pre-eminence in the field of education. In addition to the Marian congregations, the Jesuits ran prestigious boarding and day schools, as well as the University of Deusto in Bilbao; see Mary Vincent, 'The martyrs and the saints: masculinity and the construction of the Francoist crusade', *History Workshop Journal*, 47 (1999), pp. 68–98. See also Frances Lannon, *Privilege, Persecution and Prophecy: The Catholic Church in Spain, 1875–1975* (Oxford: Clarendon Press, 1987), pp. 181–2.

28. *Constitución de la República Española*, Article 26.

29. On 6 December 1931, just before the final approval of the Constitution, José Ortega y Gasset gave a lecture entitled 'Rectificación de la República'. The lecture, which was to prove highly influential, praised the social sensibility of the Constitution but protested

against its anti-clericalism and its dangerous concessions to regionalism; José Ortega y Gasset, *Rectificación de la República* (Madrid: Revista de Occidente, 1931).

30. Frances Lannon, 'The Church's crusade against the Republic', in Paul Preston (ed.), *Revolution and War in Spain* (1984; London and New York: Routledge, 2002), p. 52.

31. Lannon, *Privilege, Persecution and Prophecy*, p. 13. For Spanish family structures and systems, see below, pp. 247 ff.

32. Lannon, 'The Church's crusade', pp. 51-2.

33. In the eighteenth century 'the routine extravagance and intellectual mediocrity of the monastic orders served the Church badly'; William J. Callahan, *Church, Politics, and Society in Spain, 1750-1874* (Cambridge, Mass.: Harvard University Press, 1984), p. 23. Callahan cites in particular the case of the Cistercian monastery of Poblet in Catalonia (p. 22).

34. José Álvarez Junco, 'Alle origini dell'anticlericalismo nella Spagna degli anni Trenta', in Giuliano De Febo and Claudio Natoli (eds), *Spagna anni Trenta: Società, cultura, istituzioni* (Milan: Franco Angeli, 1993), p. 210.

35. In 1933 the Andalusian village of Casas Viejas was to be the site of one of the worst conflicts between peasants and civil guards to occur before the onset of the Civil War. On the basis of extensive oral testimonies the historian Jerome Mintz offers this summary of the villagers' attitudes to the clergy: 'Even among believers there was widespread anticlerical sentiment ranging from cynicism to contempt'; Jerome R. Mintz, *The Anarchists of Casas Viejas* (Chicago and London: University of Chicago Press, 1982), p. 71. See also below, pp. 263 ff.

36. 'La juventud católica al amparo de María Inmaculada' (Toledo, 15 November 1928), quoted in Carmelo Adagio, *Chiesa e nazione in Spagna: La dittatura di Primo de Rivera, 1923-1930* (Milan: Unicopli, 2004), p. 259.

37. The cult of the Sacred Heart, of French nineteenth-century origin, under the auspices of the Jesuits in Spain became the most forceful propagator of the integralist view of the 'social kingdom of Christ'. Its monthly journal, *Mensajero del Corazón de Jesús y del Apostolado de la Oración* (The Messenger of the Sacred Heart), 1886-1931, was anti-liberal and anti-semitic.

38. Vidal y Barraquer noted that Segura lacked the 'balsam of smoothness and gentleness', as well as any capacity to compromise; Lannon, *Privilege, Persecution and Prophecy*, p. 171.

39. See also above, pp. 173-4.

40. Pius XI, *Lettera enciclica 'Casti Connubii' sul matrimonio cristiano*, quoted in Piero Barberi and Dionigi Tettamanzi (eds), *Matrimonio e famiglia nel magistero della Chiesa: I documenti dal Concilio di Firenze a Giovanni Paolo II* (Milan: Massimo, 1986), p. 123.

41. Ibid., pp. 126 and 132.

42. Ibid., p. 153.

43. For the secret negotiations and Vatican strategy, see Hilari Raguer, *Gunpowder and Incense: The Catholic Church and the Spanish Civil War* (London and New York: Routledge, 2007), pp. 20-8.

44. Raguer, *Gunpowder and Incense*, p. 29.

45. Ibid., p. 20.

46. See above, p. 172.

47. From an article by Fernando de los Ríos in *El Socialista*, 1 March 1932, quoted in Sandie Holguín, *Creating Spaniards: Culture and National Identity in Republican Spain* (Madison: University of Wisconsin Press, 2002), p. 50. For the ILE, see Vicente Cacho Viu, *La Institución Libre de Enseñanza* (Madrid: Fundación Albéniz and Sociedad Estatal de Conmemoraciones Culturales, 2010).

48. Enrique Azcoaga, 'Las misiones pedagógicas', *Revista de Occidente*, 7-8 (November 1981), pp. 226-7, quoted in Adrian Shubert, *A Social History of Modern Spain* (London and New York: Routledge, 1990), pp. 189-90.

49. Holguín, *Creating Spaniards*, pp. 57-64.

50. By contrast, the one-act *auto sacramental*, with its heavily religious, even doctrinal content, was often ignored.

51. Miguel de Cervantes, 'The judge of the divorce court', in *The Interludes of Cervantes*, trans. S. Griswold Morley (Princeton: Princeton University Press, 1948), pp. 1–19; see also Holguín, *Creating Spaniards*, p. 95.

52. Cervantes, 'The judge of the divorce court', pp. 3 and 5.

53. Ibid., p. 15.

54. Ibid., p. 19. The last *entremés* in Cervantes's collection, 'The jealous old man' (pp. 194–217), similarly ends with a plea for reconciliation: 'Sunrise after clouds: such is/Joy that springs from miseries. / *Quarrels that come on the day of St. John/Bring peace till the year has gone*', p. 217 [italics in the original].

55. Federico García Lorca, 'Seis cartas a Carlos Martínez-Barbeito', *Boletín de la Fundación Federico García Lorca*, 3 (1988), pp. 83–4.

56. Federico García Lorca, 'Mi pueblo', in García Lorca, *Primeros escritos*, ed. M. García Posada, in *Obras completas*, vol. 4 (Barcelona: Círculo de Lectores, Galaxia Gutenberg, 1996), p. 855.

57. See the excellent biography by Ian Gibson, *Federico García Lorca: A Life* (New York: Pantheon Books, 1989), p. xxii.

58. Mildred Adams, 'The theatre in the Spanish Republic', *Theatre Arts Monthly*, March 1932, p. 238, quoted in Holguín, *Creating Spaniards*, pp. 98–9.

59. Quoted in Suzanne Wade Byrd, *García Lorca: 'La Barraca' and the Spanish National Theater* (New York: Abra, 1975), p. 40. See also Ranzato, *L'eclissi della democrazia*, pp. 149–50.

60. Holguín, *Creating Spaniards*, pp. 128 ff.

61. Laurie Lee, *As I Walked Out One Summer's Morning* (1969; Harmondsworth: Penguin, 1971), p. 160.

62. Ibid., p. 162.

63. Ibid., p. 167.

64. Stanley G. Payne, *Spain's First Democracy: The Second Republic, 1931–1936* (Madison: University of Wisconsin Press, 1993), pp. 86–92; Mariano Pérez Galán, *La enseñanza en la Segunda República española* (Madrid: Cuadernos para el Diálogo, 1975).

65. See Giambattista Salinari and Paul Ginsborg, 'Statistical Essay', http://bit.ly/ginsborg-appendix.

66. David S. Reher, *Perspectives on the Family in Spain, Past and Present* (Oxford: Clarendon Press, 1997), p. 2.

67. Peter Nichols, *Italia, Italia* (London: Macmilian, 1973), p. 227. It must be noted that in neither country has the pre-eminent role of the family as a social unit resulted in the flowering of a school of contemporary family history. This absence is particularly marked for Spain in the first half of the twentieth century, the dramatic, religious, social and political events of which have not yet been given a family dimension. Some indications are to be found in Robina Mohammad, 'The Cinderella complex: narrating Spanish women's history, the home and visions of equality: developing new margins', *Transactions of the Institute of British Geographers*, n.s., 30, no. 2 (2005), pp. 248–61.

68. For clientelism in Spain, as expressed by the *cacique* system, see the important article by Joaquín Romero Maura, 'El caciquismo: tentativa de conceptualización', *Revista de Occidente*, 127 (October 1973), pp. 15–44. For some reflections on Italian clientelism and familism in historical perspective, see Paul Ginsborg, *Italy and its Discontents: Family, Civil Society, State, 1980–2001* (London: Allen Lane and the Penguin Press, 2001), pp. 97–102.

69. Ritual (or spiritual) kinship involves both vertical and horizontal relationships: those between godparents and children (vertical) and those between a child's real parents and his spiritual ones (horizontal). Often, however, the vertical element dominated in both cases, as local notables were chosen as godparents in order to insert the child into a solid class structure of patron–client relations.

70. In the town of Cuenca during the middle years of the nineteenth century, almost three-quarters of a sample of newly-weds set up their own households in the same neighbour-hood as one or both of their families of origin; David S. Reher, *Town and Country in Pre-industrial Spain, 1550–1870* (Cambridge: Cambridge University Press, 1990), p. 218.

71. Reflecting on repeated evidence of this sort Reher has recently suggested drawing a line of demarcation between the European Mediterranean countries on the one hand and Scandinavia, Great Britain, Holland and Belgium, as well as large parts of Germany and Austria, on the other. To the north lie weak family systems in which it is the individual who counts for more, while to the south lie strong ones, in which the family is paramount. The two macro-systems (north and south) seem to differ principally over time in relation to the strength, homogeneity and longevity of the family of origin; David S. Reher, 'Family ties in western Europe: persistent contrasts', in Gianpiero Dalla Zuanna and Giuseppe A. Micheli (eds), *Strong Family and Low Fertility: A Paradox?* (Dordrecht: Kluwer Academic, 2004), pp. 45–76.

72. See above, pp. 164–6.

73. For example, in the Spanish Civil Code any sexual infidelity committed by a wife was automatically classed as adultery and punished as such, while a husband's extra-marital sexual behaviour had to cause 'public scandal' before it constituted a legal offence and was in any case treated more leniently by the civil courts. Here, too, Spain and Italy closely resembled one another.

74. George Crowder, *Classical Anarchism: The Political Thought of Godwin, Proudhon, Bakunin and Kropotkin* (Oxford: Clarendon Press, 1991), p. 123.

75. 'El amor libre', *Tierra y Libertad*, 28 April 1915, quoted in Mintz, *The Anarchists of Casas Viejas*, p. 91.

76. Ibid., p. 91.

77. Very useful is José Álvarez Junco, *La ideología política del anarquismo español (1868–1910)* (Madrid: Siglo XXI de España, 1976), pp. 294–302.

78. Ibid., p. 300.

79. Quoted without reference in Daniel Guérin, *Anarchism: From Theory to Practice* (1969; London and New York: Monthly Review Press, 1970), p. 33.

80. For further details, see Gerald Brenan, *The Spanish Labyrinth: An Account of the Social and Political Background of the Civil War* (1943; Cambridge: Cambridge University Press, 1993), p. 165 and p. 168 n. 1. A young Italian anarchist called Angiolillo, then living in London, was so shocked by the accounts of torture in the Montjuich gaol that he made his way to Santa Águeda, where the Spanish prime minister, Cánovas, was taking the waters, and shot him. A good recent treatment of these themes on a national scale is Ángel Herrerín López, *Anarquía, dinamita y revolución social: Violencia y represión en la España de entre siglos (1868–1909)* (Madrid: Catarata, 2011).

81. Gary Wray McDonogh, *Good Families of Barcelona: A Social History of Power in the Industrial Era* (Princeton: Princeton University Press, 1986).

82. Joseph B. Harrison, *An Economic History of Modern Spain* (New York: Holmes & Meier, 1978), p. 62.

83. For the cultural formation of Catalan bourgeois families, see McDonogh, *Good Families of Barcelona*, esp. ch. 6, pp. 108–40.

84. Enric Prat de la Riba Sarrà, *Ley jurídica de la industria* (Barcelona: Pennella Bosch, 1898), pp. 76 and 161, quoted in McDonogh, *Good Families of Barcelona*, pp. 55–6.

85. McDonogh, *Good Families of Barcelona*, p. 87; Colonia Güell, *Breve reseña histórica de la Colonia Güell y Fábrica de Panas y Veludillos de Güell y Cia, S. en C.* (Barcelona: Henrich, 1910), pp. 72–84.

86. Javier Silvestre, María-Isabel Ayuda, Vicente Pinilla, *The Labour Market Integration of Migrants: Barcelona, 1930* (Madrid: Fedea, 2011).

87. Victor Serge, *Birth of our Power* (1931; Harmondsworth: Penguin, 1970), pp. 39–40.

88. Angel Smith, 'From subordination to contestation: the rise of labour in Barcelona, 1898–1918', in Angel Smith (ed.), *Red Barcelona: Social Protest and Labour Mobilization in the Twentieth Century* (London and New York: Routledge, 2002), p. 20, table 2.1.

89. Raymond Williams, *The Country and the City* (London: Chatto & Windus, 1973), p. 104.
90. On godparents, with reference to oral history sources, see Chris Ealham, *Anarchism and the City: Revolution and Counter-Revolution in Barcelona, 1898–1937* (Edinburgh: AK Press, 2010), p. 27. See also Dolors Marín, 'Una primera aproximació a la vida quotidiana dels Hospitalencs, 1920–1929: les històries de vida com a font histórica', *Identitats*, 4–5 (1990). On average daily wages and family budgets, see Cristina Borderías, 'Women workers in the Barcelona labour market', in Smith, *Red Barcelona*, p. 150.
91. Ealham, *Anarchism and the City*, p. 159.
92. Silvestre, Ayuda and Pinilla, *The Labour Market*, passim.
93. Manuel Castells, *The Urban Question: A Marxist Approach* (London: Edward Arnold, 1977), p. 169, quoted in Ealham, *Anarchism and the City*, p. 10.
94. Joaquín Romero Maura, 'The Spanish case', in David E. Apter and James Joll (eds), *Anarchism Today* (London: Macmillan, 1971), pp. 70–2.
95. José Peirats, *The CNT in the Spanish Revolution*, ed. Chris Ealham, vol. 1 (1971; Oakland, Calif.: PM Press, 2011), p. 353 n. 19; Albert Balcells, *Historia contemporánea de Cataluña* (Barcelona: Edhassa, 1983), pp. 212–13.
96. Ealham, *Anarchism and the City*, pp. 43–6.
97. Peirats, *The CNT in the Spanish Revolution*, vol. 1, p. 107. The whole document on the 'Confederal conception of libertarian communism' is to be found on pp. 100–10.
98. For a detailed discussion of the 'eugenic reform of abortion', see Mary Nash, *Defying Male Civilization: Women in the Spanish Civil War* (Denver: Arden Press, 1995), pp. 165–76. The background to anarchist positions is very well examined by Richard Cleminson, *Anarchism, Science and Sex: Eugenics in Eastern Spain, 1900–1937* (Oxford and Bern: Peter Lang, 2000). He writes, 'Anarchists, as part of their critique of capitalism and the illnesses it spreads, were in need of some set of explanations in order to account for the existence of good and bad traits in people. Moving beyond their traditional social or political explanations for these phenomena, they adopted more or less scientific approaches, drawing on a number of often inchoate theories of inheritance' (p. 258). For the fate of the reform, see below, p. 293.
99. The most significant example was that of the commune movement in the United States and Europe in the 1960s and 1970s. For jealousy and despair in an environment of sexual liberty, see Philip Abrams and Andrew McCulloch, *Communes, Sociology and Society* (Cambridge: Cambridge University Press, 1976), p. 128; more generally, see Paul Ginsborg, 'Measuring the distance: the case of the family, 1968–2001', *Thesis Eleven*, 68 (2002), pp. 46–63.
100. Helen Graham, 'Women and social change', in Helen Graham and Jo Labanyi (eds), *Spanish Cultural Studies: An Introduction* (Oxford: Oxford University Press, 1995), p. 102.
101. Brenan, *The Spanish Labyrinth*, p. 171.
102. Serge, *Birth of our Power*, pp. 38–9.
103. A distinguished German account of this cult has been that by Hans Magnus Enzensberger, *Der kurze Sommer der Anarchie* (Frankfurt am Main: Suhrkamp Verlag, 1972).
104. Romero Maura, 'The Spanish case', p. 77.
105. Edward Malefakis, *Agrarian Reform and Peasant Revolution in Spain: Origins of the Civil War* (New Haven and London: Yale University Press, 1970), p. 33. It should be noted, as Malefakis himself does, that his definition of the south, an area comprising the thirteen provinces in which the *latifundios* are predominant, pushes it far up into the centre of Spain.
106. Ibid., pp. 55–62.
107. Mintz puts the number of working days in Casas Viejas at the lower end of the scale, some 170–80; Mintz, *The Anarchists of Casas Viejas*, p. 17.
108. Ibid., p. 19.
109. Julian A. Pitt-Rivers, *The People of the Sierra* (London: Weidenfeld & Nicholson, 1954), pp. 8 ff.

110. Juan Díaz del Moral, *Historia de las agitaciones campesinas andaluzas* (1929; Madrid: Alianza Editorial, 1969), pp. 198–200.
111. Ibid., pp. 199–200.
112. *CNT*, 22 November 1932, quoted in Mintz, *The Anarchists of Casas Viejas*, p. 179.
113. *Tierra y Libertad*, 22 December 1932, quoted in ibid., p. 163.
114. Undoubtedly the best account is that of Mintz, *The Anarchists of Casas Viejas*, pp. 201–51, which also corrects more than one point of the pioneering version presented by Eric Hobsbawm in his *Primitive Rebels: Studies in Archaic Forms of Social Movements in the 19th and 20th Centuries* (Manchester: Manchester University Press, 1959), pp. 74–92.
115. Manuel Azaña, *Memorías íntimas de Azaña*, ed. Joaquín Arrarás (Madrid: Ediciones Españolas, 1939), 15 January 1933.
116. Federica Montseny, the famous anarchist writer who was briefly Minister for Health under the Republic, published from exile in 1951 the interesting but not very balanced pamphlet *María Silva: La Libertaria* (Toulouse: Universo, 1951). See also the detailed biography by José Luis Gutiérrez Molina to be found at http://www.memorialibertaria. org/spip.php?article466.
117. See the pioneering anthology of the review edited by Mary Nash, *'Mujeres libres': España, 1936–1939* (Barcelona: Tusquet Editor, 1975). For more recent and detailed work, see Martha A. Ackelsberg, *'Free Women of Spain': Anarchism and the Struggle for the Emancipation of Women* (Bloomington: Indiana University Press, 1991).
118. Interview with Mercedes Comaposada, Paris, 5 January 1982, in Ackelsberg, *'Free Women of Spain'*, p. 227.
119. Etta Federn, *Mujeres de las revoluciones* (Barcelona: Mujeres Libres, [1937]), pp. 44–5, quoted in Ackelsberg, *'Free Women of Spain'*, p. 236. It was, however, the female Secretariat of the POUM who were most interested in Kollontai's works, not the anarchists, who had little sympathy for her conception of the all-powerful Communist state; see Nash, *Defying Male Civilization*, pp. 96 and 238.
120. Nash, *Mujeres libres*, p. 31 n. 32.
121. Ackelsberg, *'Free Women of Spain'*, p. 227.
122. Anonymous article entitled 'Niños, niños, niños', *Mujeres libres*, 5, quoted in Nash, *Mujeres libres*, p. 129.
123. Pierre Vilar, *La guerre d'Espagne (1936–1939)* (Paris: Presses Universitaires de France, 1986).
124. Lannon, *Privilege, Persecution and Prophecy*, p. 190. The CEDA had been founded in February 1933. Its Madrid congress numbered 400 delegates and 735,000 members.
125. Adrian Shubert, *The Road to Revolution in Spain: The Coal Miners of Asturias, 1860–1934* (Urbana and Chicago: University of Illinois Press, 1987).
126. Brian D. Bunk, *Ghosts of Passion: Martyrdom, Gender, and the Origin of the Spanish Civil War* (Durham, N.C., and London: Duke University Press, 2007).
127. Ibid., pp. 115–17; *Terror: El marxismo en España: Revolución de octubre de 1934* (Madrid: Acción Popular, [c.1934]).
128. See the examples and comments in John R. Corbin, *The Anarchist Passion: Class Conflict in Southern Spain, 1810–1965* (Aldershot: Avebury, 1993), p. 147.
129. See above, p. 228.
130. Julián Casanova, *The Spanish Republic and Civil War* (Cambridge: Cambridge University Press, 2010), p. 163.
131. Fraser, *Blood of Spain*, p. 173.
132. Ibid.
133. See the revealing and balanced article by Michael Portillo, 'It is wrong to dig up the fallen of the Spanish Civil War', *Daily Mail*, 8 November 2009.
134. Ibid.
135. Fraser, *Blood of Spain*, p. 302.
136. Ibid.
137. Ibid., p. 304.

138. Ibid., p. 473.
139. Ronald Fraser, *Tajos: The Story of a Village on the Costa del Sol* (New York: Pantheon Books, 1972), p. 61. A few months later the tables were turned. When the nationalists occupied the village, the trade union official was arrested. His mother appealed to the two landowners for help. It was now their turn to intervene and secure his release. They gave him a safe-conduct and ordered him to leave the village for his own safety.
140. Arxiu Històric de la Ciutat de Barcelona (AHCB), Department of Oral Sources, Ronald Fraser Collection, interview with Lázaro Martín, 28 October 1974. In 1936 Martín was seventeen years old.
141. Fraser, *Blood of Spain*, p. 173.
142. Quoted in Raguer, *Gunpowder and Incense*, p. 83.
143. William J. Callahan, *The Catholic Church in Spain, 1875–1998* (Washington, D.C.: Catholic University of America Press, c.2000), pp. 348–50.
144. Samuel Pierce, 'The political mobilization of Catholic women in Spain's second Republic: the CEDA, 1931–1936', *Journal of Contemporary History*, 45 no. 1 (2010), pp. 74–94.
145. Luis Suárez Fernández, *Crónica de la Sección Femenina y su tiempo* (Madrid: Asociación Nueva Andadura, 1993), p. 39, quoted in Preston, *Doves of War*, p. 234.
146. Vincent, 'The martyrs and the saints', pp. 69–98.
147. Ibid., p. 71.
148. Ibid., p. 75.
149. Callahan, *The Catholic Church in Spain*, p. 358.
150. See above, p. 96.
151. José Antonio Primo de Rivera, 'Speech on the Spanish Revolution' (19 May 1935), in José Primo de Rivera, *Selected Writings*, ed. Hugh Thomas (London: Cape, 1972), p. 189, quoted in Vincent, 'The martyrs and the saints', pp. 76–7.
152. Vincent, 'The martyrs and the saints', p. 89.
153. Lannon, *Privilege, Persecution and Prophecy*, p. 209.
154. Isidro Gomá y Tomás, *Por Dios y por España* (Barcelona: Casulleras Librería, 1940), p. 314, quoted in Gabriele Ranzato (ed.), *Guerre fratricide: Le guerre civili in età contemporanea* (Turin: Bollati Boringhieri, 1994), p. xxiii n. 31.
155. Casanova, *The Spanish Republic and Civil War*, pp. 331–2.
156. Paul Preston, *Franco: A Biography* (London: Fontana, 1993), p. 6.
157. Ibid., p. 41.
158. Ciano's comments are reported in Duilio Susmel, *Vita sbagliata di Galeazzo* (Milan: Aldo Palazzi, 1962), pp. 158–9.
159. See George A. Collier, *Socialists of Rural Andalusia: Unacknowledged Revolutionaries of the Second Republic* (Stanford: Stanford University Press, 1987), pp. 154 ff.
160. Paul Preston, *The Spanish Holocaust: Inquisition and Extermination in Twentieth-Century Spain* (London: Harper Press, 2012), p. 305; see also Francisco Moreno Gómez, *La guerra civil en Córdoba (1936–1939)* (Madrid: Editorial Alpuerto, 1985), pp. 375–82; Larry Collins and Dominique Lapierre, *Or I'll Dress you in Mourning* (London: Weidenfeld & Nicolson, 1968), pp. 62–9, 82–99; Félix Moreno de la Cova, *Mi vida y mi tiempo: La guerra que yo viví* (Seville: Gráficas Mirte, 1988).
161. Federico García Lorca, *The House of Bernarda Alba*, in Frederico García Lorca, *Three Tragedies: Blood Wedding, Yerma, The House of Bernarda Alba* (Harmondsworth: Penguin, 1961).
162. Gibson, *Federico García Lorca*, pp. 437–70, offers the best reconstruction of the last weeks of the poet's life.
163. Franz Borkenau, *The Spanish Cockpit* (London: Faber and Faber, 1937).
164. Ibid., pp. 166–7.
165. Peirats, *The CNT in the Spanish Revolution*, pp. 271–2.
166. Margarita Nelken, *Porqué hicimos la revolución* (Barcelona: Ediciones Sociales Internacionale, 1936). The prologue to the book is dated September 1935.
167. Ibid., p. 147.

168. Her daughter, Magda, was heavily pregnant and stayed in Moscow. There, in March 1936, she gave birth to a little girl called Margarita, who was known in the family as Cuqui. Her grandmother was not present at the birth but returned to Moscow soon afterwards. Once the birth had been registered on 7 April, Margarita, Magda and Cuqui made the long journey back to Spain.

169. This was according to an interview she gave to Burnett Bolloten in 1939; Burnett Bolloten, *The Grand Camouflage: The Spanish Civil War and Revolution, 1936–1939* (1961; London: Pall Mall, 1968), p. 29.

170. Luis Roldán Rodríguez, *Militares de la República: Su segunda guerra civil* (Madrid: Ediciones Vosa, 2000), p. 28, quoted in Preston, *Doves of War*, pp. 353–4.

171. Matilde de la Torre, 'Apuntes', in 'Cortes en la Lonja de la Seda', 30 September 1937, quoted in Preston, *Doves of War*, p. 373.

172. George Orwell, *Homage to Catalonia* (1938; Penguin: London, 2000), pp. 2–3.

173. Brenan, *The Spanish Labyrinth*, p. 194.

174. Gabriele Ranzato, 'Dies irae: la persecuzione religiosa nella zona republicana durante la Guerra civile spagnola (1936–1939)', *Movimento operaio e socialista*, 2 (1988), p. 195.

175. Ealham, *Anarchism and the City*, p. 178.

176. Julián Casanova, *Anarquismo y revolución en la sociedad rural aragonesa, 1936–1938* (Madrid: Siglo XXI de España, 1985), esp. part 3, pp. 133 ff.

177. Ealham, *Anarchism and the City*, p. 189.

178. Hanns-Erich Kaminski, *Ceux de Barcelone* (Paris: Denoël, 1937), p. 70; Temma E. Kaplan, 'Spanish anarchists and women's liberation', *Journal of Contemporary History*, 6 (1971), pp. 101–10; Ealham, *Anarchism and the City*, p. 189.

179. See above, p. 259, and below, p. 479, note 98.

180. For the fate of the Abortion Decree, see Nash, *Defying Male Civilization*, pp. 172 ff.; for the quotations from Martí Ibáñez, see Richard Cleminson, 'Eugenics by name or by nature? The Spanish Anarchist Sex Reform of the 1930s', *History of European Ideas*, 18 (1994), p. 737.

181. Father Alberto Onaindía, letter of 28 April 1937, followed by Gomá's reply of 5 May, in José Andrés-Gallego and Antón M. Pazos (eds), *Archivo Gomá: Documentos de la Guerra civil*, vol. 5, *Abril–mayo 1937* (Madrid: Consejo Superior de Investigaciones Científicas, 2003), pp. 282–4, 357, quoted in Preston, *The Spanish Holocaust*, p. 435.

182. Graham and Labanyi, *Spanish Cultural Studies*, p. 112, plate 7. See also José Álvarez Lopera, *La política de bienes culturales del gobierno republicano durante la Guerra civil española* (Madrid: Ministerio de Cultura, 1982).

183. Alice Miller, *The Untouched Key: Tracing Childhood Trauma in Creativity and Destructiveness* (London: Virago, 1990), pp. 3–18. The quotation is on p. 5.

184. Rudolf Arnheim, *Picasso's Guernica: The Genesis of a Painting* (London: Faber and Faber, 1962), esp. p. 94. See also Carlo Ginzburg, 'The sword and the lightbulb: a reading of *Guernica*', in Michael S. Roth and Charles G. Salas (eds), *Disturbing Remains: Memory, History and Crisis in the Twentieth Century* (Los Angeles: Getty Research Institute, 2001). On *Guernica*, see also Pierre Daix, 'Guernica', in Daix, *Le nouveau dictionnaire Picasso* (Paris: Robert Laffont, 2012), pp. 120–2, and Timothy J. Clark, *Picasso and Truth: From Cubism to Guernica* (Princeton: Princeton University Press, 2013).

185. Roland Penrose, *Picasso: His Life and Work* (1958; London: Granada, 1981), p. 271.

186. Ibid., pp. 295–6.

187. Franco's end-of-year speech, 31 December 1939, *ABC*, 1 January 1940, quoted in Preston, *The Spanish Holocaust*, p. 472.

188. Teresa Pàmies, *Quan érem capitans: Memòries d' aquella guerra* (Barcelona: Dopesa, 1974), pp. 149–50, quoted in Preston, *The Spanish Holocaust*, p. 465.

189. See the map of the killings by region in Preston, *The Spanish Holocaust*, p. 665. The republican killings behind the lines were an estimated 50,000, one-third those of the nationalists; ibid., pp. xvi–xviii.

190. Hugh Thomas, *The Spanish Civil War* (1961; London: Harmondsworth, 1986), pp. 877 ff.
191. Preston, *Doves of War*, p. 375.
192. Ibid., pp. 399–400.
193. Max Aub, *Diarios (1939–1972)* (Barcelona: Alba, 1998), p. 409, quoted in Preston, *Doves of War*, p. 406.
194. The peak of infant mortality, *c.*140 deaths per 1,000 births, was reached in the years 1939–41. See Antonio Cazorla Sánchez, *Fear and Progress: Ordinary Lives in Franco's Spain, 1939–1975* (Chichester: Wiley-Blackwell, 2010), figure 2; for famine, ibid., pp. 58 ff.
195. Ibid., p. 31; see also Santos Juliá et al., *Víctimas de la Guerra Civil* (Madrid: Temas de Hoy, 1999).
196. Paloma Aguilar, *Memory and Amnesia: The Role of the Spanish Civil War in the Transition to Democracy* (New York and Oxford: Berghahn, 2002), pp. 73–85. Some prisoners working on the monument were eventually given permission to be joined by their families, but many of the tunnel workers died young from silicosis.
197. Shirley Mangini, *Memories of Resistance: Women's Voices from the Spanish Civil War* (New Haven and London: Yale University Press, 1995), esp. pp. 99–148.
198. Cazorla Sánchez, *Fear and Progress*, pp. 10 and 59.
199. Quoted in Victor Pérez-Diaz et al., 'Catholicism, social values and the welfare system in Spain', unpublished ASP research, paper 102 (b), 2010, p. 4 (http://asp-research. com/pdf/Asp102.pdf).
200. See, for example, the circular 'Regarding Protestant propaganda in Spain' from the metropolitan bishops to the faithful, 28 May 1948: 'The circumstances of Spain, which are the same according to both official statistics and social reality, are those of "Catholic unity". Spaniards who do not profess the Catholic faith, or above all are official adherents to any faith other than the Catholic one, are in such an insignificant number that they cannot be taken into account when formulating a law aimed at the social community as a whole'; Jesús Iribarren (ed.), *Documentos colectivos del episcopado español* (Madrid: Editorial Católica, 1974), p. 246.
201. Lannon, *Privilege, Persecution and Prophecy*, p. 11, map 2, from Rogelio Duocastella, 'Géographie de la pratique religieuse en Espagne', *Social Compass*, 12 (1965), p. 28. Figures were not available for many of the other southern dioceses.
202. Himmler, like Ciano, was much struck by the scale of Franco's repressive measures and apparently commented that it made more sense to incorporate working-class militants into the new order than to annihilate them; Preston, *Franco*, p. 392.
203. Lannon, *Privilege, Persecution and Prophecy*, p. 218.
204. Quoted in Gabriele Ranzato (ed.), *Rivoluzione e guerra civile in Spagna, 1931–1939* (Turin: Loescher, 1975), pp. 151–2.
205. Francisco Franco, *Pensamiento político de Franco*, 2 vols (Madrid: Ediciones del Movimiento, 1975), vol. 1, p. 275.
206. Mohammad, 'The Cinderella complex', p. 252.
207. Conchita Mir Curcó, *Vivir es sobrevivir: Justicia, orden y marginación en la Cataluña rural de posguerra* (Lérida: Milenio, 2000), pp. 155–64.
208. Santos Juliá, 'La sociedad', in José Luis García Delgado (ed.), *Franquismo: El juicio de la historia* (Madrid: Ediciones Temas de Hoy, 2000), pp. 73–89.
209. Quoted in Mir Curcó, *Vivir es sobrevivir*, p. 166.
210. Ibid., pp. 175–8.
211. See also above, pp. 239–40.
212. 'Postura de los obispos ante la nueva Constitución', declaration of the Spanish bishops to the faithful, December 1931, in Iribarren, *Documentos colectivos*, p. 174.
213. See above, p. 230.
214. See above, p. 258.
215. Quoted in Preston, *Doves of War*, pp. 299–300.
216. See above, p. 266.

217. Margarita Nelken, 'En la Casa del Pueblo', *El Socialista*, 28 October 1933, quoted in Preston, *Doves of War*, pp. 331-2.

CHAPTER 5: 'THE GREATER WORLD AND THE SMALLER ONE': THE POLITICS OF THE FAMILY IN GERMANY, 1918-1945

1. There are two detailed and recent biographies of Goebbels: Toby Thacker, *Joseph Goebbels: Life and Death* (Basingstoke: Palgrave Macmillan, 2009), and Peter Longerich, *Goebbels: Biographie* (Munich: Siedler, 2010; an English translation is awaited). The widely available but much less scholarly biography by Roger Manvell and Heinrich Fraenkel, *Doctor Goebbels: His Life and Death* (1960; London: Pen and Sword, 2010), has been much criticised for its very loose, even inventive method of quotation. Goebbels's voluminous diaries are now collected in a complete edition comprising twenty-nine volumes: *Die Tagebücher von Joseph Goebbels*, ed. Elke Fröhlich, Teil I, *Aufzeichnungen, 1923-1941* (Munich: Saur, 1998-2006), and Teil II, *Diktate, 1941-1945* (Munich: Saur, 1993-8), henceforth *TBJG*, TI and TII. The early diaries are especially revealing of Goebbels's impatience and frustration with home life; *The Early Goebbels Diaries, 1925-1926*, ed. Helmut Heiber (1961; London: Weidenfeld & Nicolson, 1962).
2. Bundesarchiv Koblenz, N1118/70, 'Erinnerungsblätter', an autobiographical memoir describing Goebbels's life up to October 1923, quoted in Thacker, *Joseph Goebbels*, p. 12.
3. Alan Bullock, preface to *The Early Goebbels Diaries*, p. 10.
4. Bundesarchiv Koblenz, N1118/113, letter from Friedrich Goebbels to Joseph Goebbels, 9 November 1919.
5. Longerich, *Goebbels*, p. 45.
6. Joseph Goebbels, *Michael: Ein deutsches Schicksal in Tagebuchblättern* (1929; Munich: Franz Eher, 1933), p. 13, entry in Michael's diary for 17 May.
7. *The Early Goebbels Diaries*, p. 38, 30 September 1925, and p. 61, 13 January 1926.
8. Johann Wolfgang von Goethe, 'The Eagle and Dove' (1774), available at http://www2.hn.psu.edu/faculty/jmanis/goethe/poems-goethe.pdf, pp. 232-3.
9. *The Early Goebbels Diaries*, p. 34.
10. *TBJG*, TI, 1/II, p. 80, 30 April 1926.
11. Goebbels, *Michael*, pp. 57-8, entry in Michael's diary for 9 August. It is not clear whether this passage was inserted after the original text of 1924 had been finalised. For Chamberlain's discussion of the non-Jewishness of Christ, see Houston Stewart Chamberlain, *Foundations of the Nineteenth Century*, vol. 1 (1899; Munich: Bruckman, 1910), p. 211 (published in English in Germany).
12. George L. Mosse, *Toward the Final Solution: A History of European Racism* (London: J. M. Dent, 1978), pp. 191-204; Christian Barth, *Goebbels und die Juden* (Paderborn: Schöningh, 2003).
13. *The Early Goebbels Diaries*, pp. 83-4, 8 May 1926 (*TBJG*, TI, 1/II, pp. 82-3).
14. Ibid., pp. 28, 36 and 83 (*TBJG*, TI, 1/I, pp. 342 and 356, 1/II, p. 82).
15. Ibid., pp. 42 and 45 (*TBJG*, TI, 1/I, pp. 365 and 371).
16. *TBJG*, TI, 1/I, p. 35.
17. *TBJG*, TI, 2/I, pp. 38-9, 8 December 1929. In 1933, Else's husband, a certain Dr Herber, came to implore Goebbels's help. Goebbels found him work, regretted the human tragedy of anti-semitic measures, but wrote in his diary on 27 August 1933 that the 'principle must be maintained'; for further details, see Angela Hermann, *Der Weg in den Krieg 1938/39: Quellenkritische Studien zu den Tagebüchern von Joseph Goebbels* (Munich: Oldenbourg, 2011), p. 501. The database *Opfer der Verfolgung der Juden unter der nationalsozialistischen Gewaltherrschaft in Deutschland 1933-1945* of the German Bundesarchiv contains no entry for an Else Janke or an Else Herber, which means that there exist no records of deportation or imprisonment for her.
18. *The Early Goebbels Diaries*, p. 34, 11 September 1925, p. 40, 6 October 1925, p. 48, 10 November 1925, and p. 28, 15 August 1925 (*TBJG*, TI, 1/I, pp. 352, 361, 376 and 341).
19. Ibid., p. 42 (*TBJG*, TI, 1/I, p. 365).

20. Ibid., p. 65 (*TBJG*, TI, 1/II, p. 53).
21. Ibid., p. 66 (*TBJG*, TI, 1/II, p. 54).
22. Ibid., pp. 77–8, 13 April 1926, and p. 80, 19 April 1926 (*TBJG*, TI, 1/II, pp. 72–3 and 76).
23. Ibid., p. 100 (*TBJG*, TI, 1/II, p. 112).
24. Joseph Goebbels, 'Die zukünftige Arbeit und Gestaltung des deutschen Rundfunks', in *Goebbels-Reden*, ed. Helmut Heiber, vol. 1, *1932–1939* (Düsseldorf: Droste Verlag, 1971), p. 95, quoted in Thacker, *Joseph Goebbels*, p. 85.
25. Victor Klemperer, *I Will Bear Witness: A Diary of the Nazi Years, 1933–1941* (1995; New York: The Modern Library, 1999), p. 76.
26. For an excellent account, see Richard J. Evans, *The Coming of the Third Reich* (2003; London: Penguin, 2004), pp. 266–9.
27. Joachim C. Fest, *Hitler* (London: Weidenfeld and Nicolson, 1974), p. 513.
28. *TBJG*, TI, 2/III, p. 96, 23 January 1933.
29. Nevile Henderson, *Failure of a Mission: Berlin, 1937–1939* (London: Hodder and Stoughton, 1940), p. 76.
30. Klemperer, *I Will Bear Witness* [. . .] *1933–1941*, p. 11, entry for 31 March 1933.
31. Hans-Otto Meissner, *Magda Goebbels: First Lady of the Third Reich* (1978; Scarborough, Ont.: Nelson Canada, 1981), p. 21. In preparing this biography Meissner had the advantage of conversing at length in the early 1950s with Magda's closest friend and confidante, Ello Quandt, the wife of Günther's brother Werner. Meissner's is not an academic work, however, and must be treated with some caution. See also Anna Maria Sigmund, *Die Frauen der Nazis* (Munich: Wilhelm Heyne Verlag, 1998), pp. 105 ff.
32. Meissner, *Magda Goebbels*, pp. 34 ff.
33. Ibid., p. 60.
34. *TBJG*, TI, 2/II , p. 98.
35. *TBJG*, TI, 2/II, p. 133, 25 October 1931. See the account in Thacker, *Joseph Goebbels*, pp. 120–3 and p. 352 n. 100.
36. Meissner also points out that at Christmas 1930, when Günther Quandt fell seriously ill in Florence, Magda was by his side, together with their son Harald. The three of them then went to St Moritz together. Clearly, the acrimonious phase of their divorce had by then given way to more friendly relations; Meissner, *Magda Goebbels*, p. 87.
37. See below, p. 378.
38. Available online at http://www.youtube.com/watch?v=4vOQX_5gwps.
39. Peter Longerich writes convincingly, 'Hitler had become a kind of member of the Goebbels family and in particular his close relationship to Magda could only be maintained as long as her reputation was protected by the marriage to Goebbels'; Longerich, *Goebbels*, p. 389. For Ian Kershaw there were 'elements of a father–son relationship' between Hitler and Goebbels: Ian Kershaw, *Hitler, 1936–1945: Nemesis* (London: Penguin, 2000), p. 35. For Longerich, on the other hand, Goebbels suffered from a narcissistic disorder which led him to search for a caring mother surrogate rather than a father figure: Longerich, *Goebbels*, pp. 25 ff., 28 and 69.
40. Bella Fromm, *Blood and Banquets: A Berlin Social Diary* (1943; New York: Carol, 1990), p. 66, 16 December 1932. The status of Fromm's work as a genuine diary has been effectively called into question by Henry Ashby Turner Jr, 'Two dubious Third Reich diaries', *Central European History*, 33 (2000), no. 3, pp. 415–20. But even if we are to consider her work merely as a memoir, the judgement on Magda remains an interesting one.
41. *TBJG*, TI, 2/III, p. 97.
42. Magda Goebbels, *Die deutsche Mutter: Rede zum Muttertag gehalten im Rundfunk am 14. Mai 1933* (Heilbronn: Eugen Salzer, 1933). For a fascinating treatment of the development of Mother's Day in Germany, see Karin Hausen, 'Mothers, sons, and the sale of symbols and goods: the German Mother's Day 1923–1933', in Hans Medick and David Warren Sabean (eds), *Interest and Emotion: Essays on the Study of Family and Kinship* (Cambridge: Cambridge University Press, 1984), pp. 371–413.
43. Goebbels, *Die deutsche Mutter*, p. 6.

44. Ibid., p. 10.
45. Ibid., p. 18.
46. Joseph Goebbels, *Noi tedeschi e il Fascismo di Mussolini* (Florence: Beltrami, 1936), esp. pp. 60–1. For the entry in his diary covering the Italian trip, see *TBJG*, TI, 2/III, pp. 194–200, 4 June 1933.
47. See Ian Kershaw, *Hitler, 1889–1936: Hubris* (London: Penguin, 1999), p. 352.
48. Quoted in Detlef Mühlberger, *Hitler's Voice: The Völkischer Beobachter, 1920–1933*, 2 vols (Oxford: Peter Lang, 2004), vol. 1, p. 336.
49. *TBJG*, TI, 2/III, p. 232, 22 July 1933.
50. *TBJG*, TI, 2/III, p. 308, 7 November 1933.
51. See Thacker, *Joseph Goebbels*, p. 151, for Christmas-time activities.
52. *TBJG*, TI, 2/III, p. 344, 25 December 1933.
53. See Giambattista Salinari and Paul Ginsborg, 'Statistical Essay', http://bit.ly/ginsborg-appendix.
54. Adam Tooze, *The Wages of Destruction: The Making and Breaking of the Nazi Economy* (London: Allen Lane, 2006), pp. xxiii ff.
55. Catherine Rollet, ' "The other war" II: setbacks in public health', in Jay Winter and Jean-Louis Robert (eds), *Capital Cities at War: Paris, London, Berlin, 1914–1919*, 2 vols (Cambridge: Cambridge University Press, 1997–2007), vol. 1, pp. 482 ff. See also her excellent article 'The home and family life', in Winter and Robert, *Capital Cities at War*, vol. 2, pp. 315–53.
56. Richard Bessel, *Germany after the First World War* (Oxford: Clarendon Press, 1993), pp. 85–6. The Prussian War Ministry is quoted by Bessel from the Stadtarchiv, Heidelberg, 212a, 7.
57. See the important comparative article by Jay Winter, 'The European family and the two World Wars', in David I. Kertzer and Marzio Barbagli (eds), *A History of the European Family*, vol. 3, *Family Life in the Twentieth Century* (New Haven and London: Yale University Press, 2003), pp. 152–73.
58. Martin Niemöller, *From U-Boat to Pulpit* (1934; London: Hodge, 1936), quoted in Klaus Theweleit, *Male Fantasies*, vol. 1, *Women, Floods, Bodies, History* (1977; Cambridge: Polity, 1993), p. 102.
59. Tim Mason, 'Women in Germany, 1925–1940: family, welfare and work: part 1', *History Workshop Journal*, 1 (1976), pp. 78–9. See also Salinari and Ginsborg, 'Statistical Essay', http://bit.ly/ginsborg-appendix.
60. Evans, *The Coming of the Third Reich*, p. 61, quoting the memoirs of Ludendorff, Hindenburg and the Kaiser himself: 'For thirty years the army was my pride. For it I lived, upon it I labored, and now, after four and a half years of war with unprecedented victories, it was forced to collapse by the stab-in-the-back from the dagger of the revolutionist, at the very moment when peace was within reach'; Wilhelm II, *My Memoirs, 1878–1918* (London: Cassel, 1922), pp. 282–3.
61. Friedrich Wilhelm Heinz, *Sprengstoff* (Berlin: Frundsberg, 1930), p. 7, quoted in Robert G. L. Waite, *Vanguard of Nazism: The Free Corps Movement in Postwar Germany, 1918–1923* (Cambridge, Mass.: Harvard University Press, 1952), p. 42.
62. On 15 January 1919, in Berlin, they were both clubbed on the head and then shot. Luxemburg's body was found floating in the Landwehr Canal; Waite, *Vanguard of Nazism*, p. 62.
63. For bibliographical details, see above, n. 58.
64. Peter von Heydebreck, *Wir Wehrwölfe: Erinnerungen eines Freikorpsführers* (Leipzig: Koehler, 1931), pp. 7 ff., quoted in Theweleit, *Male Fantasies*, p. 101.
65. Theweleit, *Male Fantasies*, p. 108.
66. Ibid.
67. Ibid., pp. 67 ff.
68. Ibid., p. 412.
69. Kershaw, *Hitler, 1889–1936*, p. 11.

70. For Hitler's childhood, see the highly perceptive study by Helm Stierlin, *Adolf Hitler: Familienperspektiven* (Frankfurt am Main: Suhrkamp Verlag, 1975).

71. Alice Miller, *For your Own Good: Hidden Cruelty in Child-Rearing and the Roots of Violence* (1980; New York: Farrar, Strauss & Giroux, 1990), p. 146.

72. Ibid., pp. 181–2.

73. Kershaw, *Hitler, 1889–1936*, p. 24. In future years a portrait of his mother would be prominently displayed in Hitler's flat in Berlin and at the Obersalzberg, his alpine residence near Berchtesgaden.

74. For further discussion of this point and the formulation of it by Eric Fromm, see below, p. 394.

75. Adolf Hitler, *Hitler's Table Talk, 1941–1944: His Private Conversations*, introduced and with a new preface by H. R. Trevor-Roper (1953; London: Phoenix, 2000), p. 650. Earlier Hitler had said, 'It's lucky I'm not married. For me, marriage would have been a disaster'; ibid., p. 245.

76. Quoted in Robert G. L. Waite, *The Psychopathic God: Adolf Hitler* (New York: Basic Books, 1977), p. 51. This is rather close to the Goebbels of 1925: 'Monday Else, little fluffy, ping, ping.' For Eva Braun, see Kershaw, *Hitler, 1936–1945*, p. 34. A recent biography is Heike B. Görtemaker, *Eva Braun: Life with Hitler* (2010; London: Penguin, 2011).

77. Ingeborg Weber-Kellermann, 'The German family between private life and politics', in Antoine Prost and Gérard Vincent (eds), *A History of Private Life*, vol. 5, *Riddles of Identity in Modern Times* (Cambridge, Mass.: Harvard University Press, 1991), p. 504.

78. Tooze, *The Wages of Destruction*, p. 176.

79. See above, pp. 248–9.

80. For the tensions often resulting from this constellation, see, for example, Josef Mooser, 'Soziale Mobilität und familiale Platzierung bei Bauern und Unterschichten: Aspekte der Sozialkultur der ländlichen Gesellschaft im 19. Jahrhundert am Beispiel des Kirchspiels Quernheim im östlichen Westfalen', in Neithart Bulst, Joseph Goy and Jochen Hoock (eds), *Familie zwischen Tradition und Moderne: Studien zur Geschichte der Familie in Deutschland und Frankreich vom 16. bis zum 20. Jahrhundert*, Kritische Studien zur Geschichtswissenschaft 48 (Frankfurt am Main: Vandenhoeck & Ruprecht, 1981), p. 193.

81. Richard J. Evans, 'Politics and the family: social democracy and the working-class family, 1891–1914', in Richard J. Evans and William R. Lee (eds), *The German Family: Essays on the Social History of the Family in 19th- and 20th-Century Germany* (London: Croom Helm, 1981), p. 260.

82. Wilhelm Heinrich Riehl, *Die Naturgeschichte des Volkes als Grundlage einer deutschen Sozialpolitik*, vol. 3, *Die Familie* (1855; Augsburg and Stuttgart: Cotta, 1889), p. 156, quoted in Ingeborg Weber-Kellermann, *Die deutsche Familie: Versuch einer Sozialgeschichte* (Frankfurt am Main: Suhrkamp Verlag, 1992), pp. 87–8.

83. Jean-Louis Robert, 'Paris, London, Berlin on the eve of the war', in Winter and Robert, *Capital Cities at War*, vol. 1, pp. 25–53. Cities such as Berlin and Hamburg grew much faster than their equivalents in Britain or France.

84. Paul Weindling, 'The medical profession, social hygiene and the birth rate in Germany, 1914–1918', in Richard Wall and Jay Winter (eds), *The Upheaval of War: Family, Work and Welfare in Europe, 1914–1918* (Cambridge: Cambridge University Press, 1988), p. 428.

85. Hans Mommsen argues that 'in view of the growing strength of Germany's anti-republican forces, this was the most that could be achieved in the summer of 1919'. But he also adds that key proposals of the workers' councils movement – the democratisation of the civil administration and of the military, and equal participation in economic decision-making – did not find their way into the Constitution: Hans Mommsen, *The Rise and Fall of Weimar Democracy* (1989; Chapel Hill and London: University of North Carolina Press, 1996), p. 59.

86. Herbert Kraus, *The Crisis of German Democracy: A Study of the Spirit of the Constitution of Weimar* (Princeton: Princeton University Press, 1932), p. 98.

87. See, for example, Article 115: 'Every German's home is his sanctuary and is inviolable. Exceptions may be only made as provided by law.' For a detailed commentary which, sadly, has little on the family, see Peter C. Caldwell, *Popular Sovereignty and the Crisis of German Constitutional Law: The Theory and Practice of Weimar Constitutionalism* (Durham, N.C., and London: Duke University Press, 1997), esp. pp. 63–84.

88. A partial exception is to be found in Monique Da Silva, 'L'impact de la Constitution de Weimar sur celle de la IIe République espagnole', *Travaux et documents* (Université Paris 8 Vincennes Saint-Denis), 23 (2004), *passim.*

89. In this context, it is interesting to note that both Hugo Preuss, who had been called upon by Friedrich Ebert to produce the first draft of the Constitution, and Max Weber, who was a member of the panel of experts which met under Preuss's chairmanship between 9 and 12 December 1918, thought that it was a waste of time to include a section on basic rights; Caldwell, *Popular Sovereignty*, p. 73.

90. The Weimar Constitution is available online at http://www.dhm.de/lemo/html/dokumente/verfassung/index.html. In English, the Weimar Constitution is published in full as an appendix to Kraus, *The Crisis of German Democracy*; Article 119 is to be found on p. 204.

91. See above, pp. 228–30, for a full discussion.

92. The first of the two drafts of this part of the German Constitution did not include the clause referring to equal rights in marriage; see Alfred Wieruszowski, 'Artikel 119: Ehe, Familie, Mutterschaft', in Hans-Carl Nipperdey (ed.), *Die Grundrechte und Grundpflichten der Reichsverfassung*, 3 vols (1930; Kronberg: Scriptor, 1975), vol. 2, p. 72. Wieruszowski suggests that the intent was to replace a 'manorial' approach to the organisation of the family with a 'cooperative' one, rather than to introduce absolute equality; ibid., p. 80.

93. Under the terms of the Civil Code of 1900, five grounds for divorce were stipulated: adultery, culpable marital breakdown, desertion, mental illness and death threats. The greater part of the debate in the Weimar years centred on the battle to replace 'culpable marital breakdown' with the much less accusatory 'irreconcilable differences'. The right-wing, nationalist parties and the Catholic Centre Party refused to budge, claiming that the whole basis of German civilisation was at risk; Michelle Mouton, *From Nurturing the Nation to Purifying the Volk: Weimar and Nazi Family Policy, 1918–1945* (Cambridge: Cambridge University Press, 2007), pp. 75 ff.

94. Antje Dertinger, 'Marie Juchacz', in Dieter Schneider (ed.), *Sie waren die Ersten: Frauen in der Arbeiterbewegung* (Gutenberg: Büchergilde, 1988), p. 214, quoted in Kathleen Canning, 'Women and the politics of gender', in Anthony McElligott (ed.), *Weimar Germany* (Oxford: Oxford University Press, 2009), p. 152.

95. Canning, 'Women and the politics of gender', p. 153.

96. David Crew, *Germans on Welfare: From Weimar to Hitler* (Oxford: Oxford University Press, 1998), p. 11.

97. Richard M. Titmuss, *Social Policy: An Introduction* (London: Allen & Unwin, 1974), pp. 140–1. Another renowned tripartite typology is that of Gøran Esping-Andersen, *The Three Worlds of Welfare Capitalism* (Princeton: Princeton University Press, 1990). Of exemplary clarity is Maurizio Ferrera, *Modelli di solidarietà: Politica e riforme sociali nelle democrazie* (Bologna: Il Mulino, 1993).

98. Mason, 'Women in Germany', pp. 82–4.

99. Document from the Nuremberg welfare office, 10 October 1918, quoted in Young-Sun Hong, *Welfare, Modernity, and the Weimar State, 1919–1933* (Princeton: Princeton University Press, 1998), p. 159. For France in the same years, see the outstanding work of Susan Pedersen, *Family, Dependence, and the Origins of the Welfare State: Britain and France, 1914–1945* (Cambridge: Cambridge University Press, 1993), *passim.*

100. Reinhold Seeberg, 'Wo hinaus?', in *Der 38. Kongress für Innere Mission* (Berlin: Wichern Verlag, 1919), pp. 13–14, quoted in Hong, *Welfare, Modernity, and the Weimar State*, p. 55.

101. Hong, *Welfare, Modernity, and the Weimar State*, pp. 9–10, 54–5. Family, nation and war were intimately linked in DNVP discourse. In September 1926, Klara Kotz, chair of the Württemberg provincial committee of the DNVP, explained her view of motherhood by recourse to a military metaphor: 'Through us mothers, the family should become Germany's psychological and mental arms factory'; quoted in Raffael Scheck, *Mothers of the Nation: Right-Wing Women in Weimar Germany* (Oxford: Berg, 2004), p. 91.

102. Hong, *Welfare, Modernity, and the Weimar State*, pp. 46–7. Also very useful is Rebecca Heinemann, *Familie zwischen Tradition und Emanzipation: Katholische und sozialdemokratische Familiekonzeptionen in der Weimar Republik* (Munich: Oldenbourg, 2004).

103. See Adelheid von Saldern's highly informative article ' "Neues Wohnen": housing and reform', in McElligott, *Weimar Germany*, here p. 215.

104. 'Gesichter der Strasse' (The face of the street), *Arbeiter-Illustrierte-Zeitung*, 7 (1928), no. 4, p. 4, quoted in Pamela E. Swett, *Neighbors and Enemies: The Culture of Radicalism in Berlin, 1929–1933* (Cambridge: Cambridge University Press, 2004), p. 25.

105. Enno Kaufhold (ed.), *Berlin in den Weltstadtjahren: Fotografien von Willy Römer, 1919–1933* (Berlin: Edition Braus, 2012).

106. David Blackbourn, 'The German bourgeoisie: an introduction', in David Blackbourn and Richard J. Evans, *The German Bourgeoisie: Essays on the Social History of the German Middle Class from the Late Eighteenth to the Early Twentieth Century* (London: Routledge, 1991), p. 9.

107. See William H. Hubbard, *Familiengeschichte: Materialien zur deutschen Familie seit dem Ende des 18. Jahrhunderts* (Munich: C. H. Beck, 1983), p. 125, chart 3.37, and Mason, 'Women in Germany', p. 82.

108. Mason, 'Women in Germany', p. 82.

109. Günther Schulz, *Die Angestellten seit dem 19. Jahrhundert*, Enzyklopädie deutscher Geschichte 54 (Munich: Oldenbourg, 2000), p. 105.

110. Siegfried Kracauer, *Die Angestellten aus dem neuesten Deutschland* (Frankfurt am Main: Frankfurter Societäts-Buchdruckerei, 1930), p. 90.

111. Schulz, *Die Angestellten*, p. 105.

112. Swett, *Neighbors and Enemies*, pp. 30–1 and 44.

113. Ibid., pp. 31–4.

114. The female images presented by the Communist periodical *AIZ* are analysed by Patrice Petro in *Joyless Streets: Women and Melodramatic Representation in Weimar Germany* (Princeton: Princeton University Press, 1989), pp. 127 ff. Petro cites one exception to this general picture, the article in *AIZ* of 1929 (no. 12, pp. 4–5) entitled 'Kameradschafts-Ehe?'

115. It is thanks to the anthropological work of Gerhard Wilke and Kurt Wagner that we have a clear picture of family life in Körle during the Weimar and Nazi periods; see Gerhard Wilke and Kurt Wagner, 'Family and household: social structures in a German village between the two world wars', in Evans and Lee, *The German Family*, pp. 120–47, and Gerhard Wilke, 'Village life in Nazi Germany', in Richard Bessel (ed.), *Life in the Third Reich* (Oxford: Oxford University Press, 2001), pp. 17–25.

116. Wilke and Wagner, 'Family and household', p. 138.

117. It should be noted that the law on abortion was rendered more lenient by an amendment of 1926. Cornelie Usborne, *Cultures of Abortion in Weimar Germany* (New York and Oxford: Berghahn, 2007), p. 181.

118. Detlev J. Peukert, *The Weimar Republic: The Crisis of Classical Modernity* (1987; London: Allen Lane, 1991), p. 92.

119. Ibid., p. 252.

120. Report of 26 November 1931, quoted in Crew, *Germans on Welfare*, pp. 171–3. See also Alf Lüdtke, 'Hunger in der Grossen Depression: Hungererfahrungen und Hungerpolitik am Ende der Weimarer Republik', *Archiv für Sozialgeschichte*, 27 (1987), pp. 145–76, and the account by the American journalist Hubert R. Knickerbocker, *The German Crisis* (New York: Farrar & Rinehart, 1932), esp. chs 1–3 for Berlin.

121. Jeremy Noakes, *The Nazi Party in Lower Saxony* (London: Oxford University Press, 1971), pp. 123 and 209–10.

122. For the KPD, see Eve Rosenhaft, *Beating the Fascists? The German Communists and Political Violence, 1929–1933* (Cambridge: Cambridge University Press, 1983).

123. Norman H. Baynes (ed.), *The Speeches of Adolf Hitler, April 1922–August 1939*, 2 vols (London: Oxford University Press, 1942), vol. 1, p. 544.

124. For a recent, wide-ranging and convincing account of the history of the Greater Reich, see Mark Mazower, *Hitler's Empire: Nazi Rule in Occupied Europe* (London: Allen Lane, 2008).

125. Adolf Hitler, 'Die völkische Sendung der Frau', speech of 8 September 1934, in Ellen Semmelroth and Renate von Streida (eds), *N.S. Frauenbuch* (Munich: J. F. Lehmann, 1934), p. 11.

126. NSADP, *Der Parteitag der Freiheit vom 10–16 Sept. 1935: Offizieller Bericht über den Verlauf des Reichsparteitages mit sämtlichen Kongressreden* (Munich: Franz Eher Nachf, 1936), p. 176.

127. For Gentile's intervention and the proceedings of the conference, see above, pp. 169–71. For an overview, see Hubert von Kiesewetter, *Von Hegel zu Hitler: Die politische Verwirklichung einer totalitären Machtstaatstheorie in Deutschland (1815–1945)* (Frankfurt am Main and New York: Peter Lang, 1995).

128. There has been some interesting recent discussion of the term; see in particular Michael Wildt, *Hitler's Volksgemeinschaft and the Dynamics of Racial Exclusion: Violence against Jews in Provincial Germany, 1919–1939* (2008; London and New York: Berghahn, 2012); especially valuable is his discussion of the use of the term during the making of the Weimar Constitution (pp. 20 ff.). See also Janosch Steuwer's report on the conference 'German Society in the Nazi Era: *Volksgemeinschaft* between Ideological Projection and Social Practice' (London, 25–27 March 2010), published on the H-Soz-u-Kult website (28 May 2010), at http://hsozkult.geschichte.hu-berlin.de/tagungs-berichte/id=3121. At this conference Martina Steber and Bernhard Gotto suggested convincingly that the *Volksgemeinschaft* should be understood as an 'imaginary order' which had the capacity to inspire action and thus contributed significantly to the formation of National Socialist society in these years.

129. Peter Fritzsche, *Life and Death in the Third Reich* (Cambridge, Mass.: Harvard University Press, 2008), p. 39.

130. Ibid., pp. 46–7.

131. Louis Dumont, *Essays on Individualism: Modern Ideology in Anthropological Perspective* (1983; Chicago and London: University of Chicago Press, 1986), pp. 169 ff.

132. Dumont notes that Hitler himself was 'infected' by the spirit of the age, believing profoundly in the struggle of all against all, and suggests that he projected on to the Jews the individualistic tendencies that he recognised in himself; ibid., p. 176.

133. Tooze, *The Wages of Destruction*, p. 135.

134. See above, pp. 335–6.

135. Horst Becker, *Die Familie* (Leipzig: Schäfer, 1935), p. 135.

136. As early as 29 September 1933 Richard Walther Darré, Hitler's new Minister of Agriculture, introduced his Reich Entailed Farm Law. Darré's aim was to create a vast number of inalienable, self-sufficient farms (*Erbhöfe*) throughout the German countryside. Partible inheritance was forbidden and farms were to be passed down to a single male heir. Darré hoped in this way to save viable farms from market-induced foreclosures. Over time natural selection would strengthen a racially pure peasantry until it was ready to supply new leadership for the nation. His plans were only partially successful. Up to a million farms of between 7.25 and 125 hectares were targeted for

the scheme, but its provisions gave rise to bitter disputes within peasant families. In many parts of Germany the problem of what to do with those children who did not inherit was felt very sharply, and never had farmers' wives been so completely ignored in hereditary settlements. Ironically, many sons and daughters excluded by the new law had little option but to emigrate to the cities. See Richard J. Evans, *The Third Reich in Power, 1933–1939* (London: Allen Lane, 2005), pp. 421 ff.; Tooze, *The Wages of Destruction*, pp. 182–6; Gustavo Corni, *La politica agraria del Nazionalsocialismo* (Milan: Franco Angeli, 1989).

137. Lisa Pine, *Nazi Family Policy, 1933–1945* (Oxford and New York: Berg, 1997), pp. 9–10, 66–7. Pine's is a well-organised and richly informative study and my own account is dependent upon hers in more than one place. For Becker, see also the valuable comments of Weber-Kellermann, 'The German family', pp. 517–18.

138. Pine, *Nazi Family Policy*, pp. 18–19.

139. For the Swedish case, see Luca Dotti, *L'Utopia eugenetica del Welfare State svedese, 1934–1975* (Soveria Mannelli: Rubbettino, 2004).

140. Bundesarchiv Koblenz, NS 18/712, 'Richtlinien für eine bevölkerungspolitische Propaganda und Volksaufklärung', quoted in Gisela Bock, 'Antinatalism, maternity and paternity in National Socialist racism', in Gisela Bock and Pat Thane (eds), *Maternity and Gender Politics: Women and the Rise of the European Welfare States, 1880s–1950s* (London and New York: Routledge, 1992), p. 240.

141. Michael Burleigh and Wolfgang Wippermann, *The Racial State: Germany, 1933–1945* (Cambridge: Cambridge University Press, 1991), p. 48.

142. Adolf Hitler, *Mein Kampf*, ed. D. C. Watt (1969; London: Hutchinson, 1992), p. 367. For details of the law, see Pine, *Nazi Family Policy*, pp. 13–15. For the history of sterilisation in the Third Reich, see Gisela Bock, *Zwangssterilisation im Nationalsozialismus: Studien zur Rassenpolitik und Frauenpolitik* (Opladen: Westdeutscher Verlag, 1986). A separate law of 24 November 1933 permitted the detention and compulsory castration of certain types of criminals as defined by 'racial-biological' criteria.

143. Written in 1940–1 in the United States, these memoirs were reproduced only in small part in Monika Richarz (ed.), *Jewish Life in Germany: Memoirs from Three Centuries* (Bloomington and Indianapolis: Indiana University Press, 1991), pp. 351–61.

144. Ibid., p. 353.

145. Ibid., pp. 355–6. For some important recent scholarship on the plight of Jewish families from 1933 onwards, see Francis R. Nicosia and David Scrase (eds), *Jewish Life in Nazi Germany: Dilemmas and Responses* (New York and Oxford: Berghahn, 2010), especially Marion Kaplan, 'Changing roles in Jewish families', pp. 15–46, and Konrad Kwiet, 'Without neighbors: daily living in Judenhäuser', pp. 117–47.

146. See Case File Rudolf Langen, Document Number 212564, Entschädigungsamt, Berlin (pages unnumbered), and the letter in the same file from Rose Scharnberg, Rudolf's mother's lawyer, to Dr Matthee, 14 January 1958. I am very grateful to Christoph Kreuzmueller for making available this as yet unpublished material.

147. Evans, *The Coming of the Third Reich*, p. 262.

148. Christopher J. Prost, *Demonizing the Jews: Luther and the Protestant Church in Nazi Germany* (Bloomington and Indianapolis: Indiana University Press, 2012).

149. Evans, *The Third Reich in Power*, pp. 225 ff.

150. Hans Müller, *Katholische Kirche und Nationalsozialismus: Dokumente, 1930–1935* (Munich: Taschenbuch Verlag, 1963), document no. 77, p. 170, quoted in Guenter Lewy, *The Catholic Church and Nazi Germany* (London: Weidenfeld & Nicolson, 1964), p. 104.

151. Lewy, *The Catholic Church and Nazi Germany*, p. 156.

152. To offer one example amongst very many, in the entry 'Honour' in his *Handbuch der religiösen Gegenwartsfragen* (Freiburg: Herder, 1937) Konrad Gröber, archbishop of Freiburg, wrote, 'The Führer of the Third Reich has freed the German man from his external humiliation and from the inner weakness caused by Marxism and has

returned him to the ancestral Germanic values of honour, loyalty and courage' (p. 149); quoted in Lewy, *The Catholic Church and Nazi Germany*, p. 164.

153. Ernst Troeltsch, *Protestantism and Progress: The Significance of Protestantism for the Rise of the Modern World* (1906; Philadelphia: Fortress Press, 1986), p. 56.

154. See above, p. 171.

155. Weber-Kellermann, 'The German family', p. 519.

156. Clifford Kirkpatrick, *Nazi Germany: Its Women and Family Life* (Indianapolis: Bobbs-Merrill, 1938), pp. 269–70.

157. Ibid. For the disreputable role played by the Berlin Philharmonic in these years, see Misha Aster, *The Reich's Orchestra. The Berlin Philharmonic 1933–1945* (London: Souvenir Press, 2010).

158. See above, pp. 330–1.

159. Quoted in David Welch, *The Third Reich: Politics and Propaganda* (London and New York: Routledge, 1993), p. 63.

160. Wilke, 'Village life', p. 21.

161. Ibid., p. 22, and Wilke and Wagner, 'Family and household', p. 143.

162. Hermann Rauschning, *Gespräche mit Hitler* (1940), quoted in W. Hofer, *Der Nationalsozialismus: Dokumente, 1933–1945* (Frankfurt am Main: Fischer, 1957), p. 88.

163. Claudia Koonz, *Mothers in the Fatherland: Women, the Family and Nazi Politics* (London: Jonathan Cape, 1987), p. 196. Boys were also taught to be 'slender and supple, swift as greyhounds, tough as leather and hard as Krupp steel'.

164. See below, pp. 242. For the number of boys in the Hitlerjugend, see Michael H. Kater, *Hitler Youth* (Cambridge, Mass., and London: Harvard University Press, 2004), p. 23. At the end of 1933, the *Hitlerjugend* had 2.3 million members, or 30.5 per cent of the total age group. This figure had grown to 64 per cent by the end of 1937 and 98.1 per cent by 1939, after obligatory membership had come into force.

165. *TBJG*, TI, 3/II, p. 121, 2 July 1936.

166. Evans, *The Third Reich in Power*, p. 279.

167. Alfred Bäumler, *Männerbund und Wissenschaft* (Berlin: Junker und Dünnhaupt, 1934), p. 42, quoted in Pine, *Nazi Family Policy*, p. 9.

168. Pine, *Nazi Family Policy*, p. 49. Pine bases her series of contrasts on Hedwig Rahn, 'Artgemäße Mädchenerziehung und Rasse', *Nationalsozialistische Mädchenerziehung*, 12 (1940), p. 224.

169. *Das Deutsche Mädel*, 7 (1933), p. 7.

170. Becattini, ' "Führer, wir gehören dir" ', p. 197. From 1937 onwards von Schirach decided that the pitching of, and sleeping in, tents was not consonant with Nazi ideas of young womanhood; ibid., p. 190 n. 345. For a wider discussion of 'The Camp' as a key Nazi institution of socialisation, see Fritzsche, *Life and Death*, pp. 96 ff.

171. Nancy R. Reagin, *Sweeping the German Nation: Domesticity and National Identity in Germany, 1870–1945* (Cambridge: Cambridge University Press, 2007), pp. 121–2. According to regime statistics, by 1943 around 1.5 million young German women were completing their 'service years'.

172. See Jürgen Rostock and Franz Zadniček, *Paradiesruinen: Das KdF-Seebad der Zwanzigtausend auf Rügen* (Berlin: Ch. Links, 2006); Hermann Weiß, 'Ideologie der Freizeit im Dritten Reich: die NS-Gemeinschaft "Kraft durch Freude" ', *Archiv für Sozialgeschichte*, 33 (1993); Shelley Baranowski, *Strength through Joy: Consumerism and Mass Tourism in the Third Reich* (Cambridge: Cambridge University Press, 2004).

173. In 1937 the Ley–Cianetti agreement proposed a series of railway exchanges by which Italians and Germans might visit each other's countries, but the Germans complained that the Italian carriages, with their hard wooden seats, were uncomfortable and unclean. The Italian authorities offered more soap and towels.

174. Baranowski, *Strength through Joy*, pp. 179–82.

175. For a family-based account, see above, pp. 206–7.

176. *Deutschland: Berichte der Sozialdemokratischen Partei Deutschlands (SOPADE)* (Frankfurt: Behnken, 1980), vol. 2, p. 1375, quoted in Detlev Peukert, *Inside Nazi*

Germany: Conformity, Opposition and Racism in Everyday Life (1982; Harmondsworth: Penguin, 1987), p. 195.

177. Ernst Fraenkel, *The Dual State: A Contribution to the Theory of Dictatorship* (Oxford: Oxford University Press, 1941), pp. 43–4.

178. Gertrud Scholtz-Klink, *Die Frau im Dritten Reich* (Tübingen: Grabert, 1979), p. 501, quoted in Koonz, *Mothers in the Fatherland*, p. 178.

179. Koonz, *Mothers in the Fatherland*, p. xxv.

180. Mason, 'Women in Germany', p. 100. Moritz Föllmer makes more or less the same point when he notes that the boundaries between ordinariness and extraordinariness in the Nazi programme of the 1930s appear fluid. Even as quotidian an action as saving up for a Volkswagen could connect families with a wider and more grandiose project; Föllmer, 'The subjective dimension of Nazism', *Historical Journal*, 56 no. 4 (2013), pp. 1120–1.

181. See Nancy Reagin's illuminating study *Sweeping the German Nation*.

182. Ibid., pp. 16 and 39. For the contrast with the Poles, see ch. 6, 'Domesticity and "Germanisation" in occupied Poland', pp. 181–217. Hitler commented, 'We don't want to train [the Poles] up to levels of German cleanliness. Even if they began to scrub themselves and their houses daily, it wouldn't matter to us' (ibid., p. 181, without a specific page reference).

183. Kirkpatrick commented from Berlin in 1938, 'The happy domestic group gathered together around the Christmas tree singing the old songs and carrying on time-honoured rites is a phase of German culture which National Socialism seeks to maintain and perpetuate'; Kirkpatrick, *Nazi Germany*, pp. 101–2.

184. Hermann Rauschning, *Hitler Speaks: Political Conversations with Adolf Hitler on his Real Aims* (London: Gollancz, 1939), p. 27.

185. I shall return to this contention in my conclusions to the book. For Robert Ley and dreams, see Peukert, *Inside Nazi Germany*, pp. 236–7.

186. Wieland Schmied, *Neue Sachlichkeit and the German Realism of the Twenties*, catalogue for an exhibition at the Hayward Gallery, London, 11 November 1978–14 January 1979 (London: Arts Council of Great Britain, 1978), pp. 7–8.

187. For some useful comments on Beckmann's paintings of this period, see Susanne Bieber, '*Hell 1919*', in Sean Rainbird (ed.), *Max Beckmann* (London: Tate Publishing, 2003), pp. 56–8.

188. Reported in an article of 6 January 1937 in the *Frankfurter Zeitung*, quoted in Weber-Kellermann, 'The German family', pp. 520–1.

189. Leni Riefenstahl, *Memorien* (Munich and Hamburg: Knaus, 1987), p. 293, quoted in Christoph Zuschlag, ' "Chambers of horrors of art" and "Degenerate art": on censorship in the visual arts in Nazi Germany', in Elisabeth C. Childs (ed.), *Suspended License: Censorship and the Visual Arts* (Seattle and London: University of Washington Press, 1997), p. 220.

190. Gisela Bock's debate with Claudia Koonz and other historians regarding the question as to whether Nazi Germany was more anti-natal than pro-natal seems wide of the mark. The Nazis were self-evidently pro-natal towards those families whose children they wanted (and to whom they paid a great deal of attention) and anti-natal towards those families whose children they did not want (and whom they did their best to eliminate, in one way or another); for a discussion, see Anita Grossmann, 'Feminist debates about women and National Socialism', *Gender and History*, 3 (1991), no. 3, pp. 350–8.

191. Hitler, *Hitler's Table Talk*, p. 74.

192. Pine offers a very good and detailed overview of these initiatives; Pine, *Nazi Family Policy*, pp. 88–116.

193. Quoted in Bock, 'Antinatalism', p. 243. For further details, see Martina Salvante, 'I prestiti matrimoniali nell'Italia fascista e nella Germania nazista, 1927–1944', *Passato e presente*, 21 (2003), no. 60, pp. 39–58.

194. Pine, *Nazi Family Policy*, p. 34.

195. B. Kasten, 'Untersuchungen zur Abtreibung während der NS-Zeit in Leipzig', in S. Schötz (ed.), *Frauenalltag in Leipzig: Weibliche Lebenzusammenhänge im 19. und 20. Jahrhundert* (Weimar, Cologne and Vienna: Böhlau Verlag, 1997), pp. 290–1.
196. Evans, *The Third Reich in Power*, pp. 483–9.
197. For further details and comparisons, see Salinari and Ginsborg, 'Statistical Essay', http://bit.ly/ginsborg-appendix.
198. Hans Mommsen, 'Cumulative radicalization and progressive self-destruction as structural determinants of the Nazi dictatorship', in Ian Kershaw and Moshe Lewin (eds), *Stalinism and Nazism: Dictatorships in Comparison* (Cambridge: Cambridge University Press, 1997), pp. 75–87.
199. Declaration of 22 August 1939, quoted in Richard J. Evans, *The Third Reich at War* (London: Allen Lane, 2008), p. 11.
200. *TBJG*, TI, 7, p. 147.
201. Karl Beyer, *Familie und Frau im neuen Deutschland* (Langensalza, Berlin and Leipzig: Julius Beltz, 1936), p. 45
202. Fritzsche, *Life and Death*, pp. 145–6. It has been estimated that forty billion pieces of mail went back and forth.
203. Christopher Browning, *Nazi Policy, Jewish Workers, German Killers* (Cambridge: Cambridge University Press, 2000), p. 155.
204. Joseph Goebbels, 'Gespräche mit Frontsoldaten', *Das Reich*, 26 July 1942, quoted in Fritzsche, *Life and Death*, p. 151.
205. Klemperer, *I Will Bear Witness* [. . .] *1933–1941*, pp. 419 and 428, entries for 9 June and 2 September 1941.
206. Ibid., p. 429, entry for 8 September 1941.
207. Bock, 'Antinatalism', p. 246. For further details, see Bock, *Zwangssterilisation*, pp. 168–9.
208. Jill Stephenson, *Women in Nazi Germany* (Harlow: Longman, 2001), pp. 55 ff. and 156.
209. *TBJG*, TII, 9, p. 399.
210. Tim Mason notes rightly that the strikes in Turin in March 1943 constituted 'the first time people subjected to a native fascist regime offered mass resistance', going on to remark that 'the German working class never, even subsequently, defied their Nazi masters in any way even remotely comparable'; Tim Mason, 'The Turin strikes of March 1943', in Tim Mason, *Nazism, Fascism and the Working Class*, ed. Jane Caplan (Cambridge: Cambridge University Press, 1995), pp. 274–5.
211. For a highly informative account, see Jeremy Noakes and Geoffrey Pridham (eds), *Nazism, 1919-1945*, vol. 3, *Foreign Policy, War and Racial Extermination: A Documentary Reader* (Exeter: University of Exeter Press, 2006), pp. 389–440. See also Bock, 'Antinatalism', pp. 248–9, and Lewy, *The Catholic Church and Nazi Germany*, pp. 263–7.
212. Noakes and Pridham, *Nazism, 1919-1945*, vol. 3, p. 430.
213. For the case of Rudolf Langen in 1944, see above, p. 361.
214. Pine, *Nazi Family Policy*, p. 153, quoting the *Reichsgesetzblatt*, 1936, no. 1, pp. 252–4.
215. Klemperer, *I Will Bear Witness* [. . .] *1933–1941*, p. 417, entry for 9 July 1941.
216. Saul Friedländer, *The Years of Extermination: Nazi Germany and the Jews, 1939–1945* (New York: HarperCollins, 2007).
217. Helen Kopmann, videotaped interview forming part of the Yale University Oral History of the Holocaust Project, quoted in Koonz, *Mothers in the Fatherland*, p. 380.
218. Heinrich Himmler, *Geheimreden, 1933 bis 1945, und andere Ausprachen*, ed. Bradley F. Smith and Agnus F. Peterson (Frankfurt am Main: Propyläen Verlag, 1974), p. 169, quoted in Friedländer, *The Years of Extermination*, p. 543.
219. Hans G. Adler, *Der verwaltete Mensch: Studien zur Deportation der Juden aus Deutschland* (Tübingen: Mohr, 1974), pp. 581–2, quoted in Fritzsche, *Life and Death*, p. 144.
220. Jane Caplan, 'Gender and the concentration camps', in Jane Caplan and Nikolaus Wachsmann (eds), *Concentration Camps in Nazi Germany: The New Histories* (London

and New York: Routledge, 2010), p. 94. For an example of what Föllmer calls 'agency in an extreme moral universe', see the outstanding study by Christopher Browning *Remembering Survival: Inside a Nazi Slave-Labor Camp* (New York: W. W. Norton, 2010).

221. Guenter Lewy, *The Nazi Persecution of the Gypsies* (Oxford: Oxford University Press, 2000), p. 152.
222. Ibid., p. 157. The infamous Nazi doctor Josef Mengele was posted to Auschwitz in May 1943 and became chief physician of the gypsy family camp.
223. A detailed and very interesting account of this camp, as seen through the eyes of the children who briefly inhabited it, is to be found in Nicholas Stargardt, *Witnesses of War: Children's Lives under the Nazis* (London: Jonathan Cape, 2005), pp. 199–230.
224. Friedländer, *The Years of Extermination*, p. 582.
225. Luise Solmitz, 'Tagebuch', entry for 7 March 1943, Staatsarchiv der Freien und Hansestadt Hamburg, quoted in Evans, *The Third Reich at War*, p. 357.
226. Ulrich Herbert, *Hitler's Foreign Workers: Enforced Foreign Labor in Germany under the Third Reich* (Cambridge: Cambridge University Press, 1997), pp. 268–9.
227. Thacker, *Joseph Goebbels*, p. 300.
228. Meissner, *Magda Goebbels*, pp. 271–2.
229. Their suicides, together with those of Hitler and Braun, were only the most famous of many committed by the Nazi leadership and Nazi sympathisers in 1945. For a recent, detailed reconstruction, see Christian Goeschel, *Suicide in Nazi Germany* (Oxford: Oxford University Press, 2009), esp. pp. 164–5 for 1945.
230. Klemperer, *I Will Bear Witness: A Diary of the Nazi Years, 1942–1945* (New York: Modern Library, 2001), p. 469, entry for 29 April 1945.
231. Ibid., p. 475, entry for 5 May 1945.
232. Max Horkheimer (ed.), *Studien über Autorität und Familie* (1936; Lüneburg: zu Klampen, 1987).
233. Ernst Troeltsch, *Die Soziallehren der christlichen Kirchen und Gruppen* (Tübingen: Mohr, 1923), pp. 557 f, quoted in Horkheimer's 'allgemeiner Teil', in Horkheimer, *Studien über Autorität und Familie*, p. 51.
234. Ibid., pp. 57–8.
235. Erich Fromm, 'sozialpsychologischer Teil', in Horkheimer, *Studien über Autorität und Familie*, pp. 80–3.
236. Horkheimer, 'allgemeiner Teil', in Horkheimer, *Studien über Autorität und Familie*, p. 61. For Trotsky, see above, pp. 53 f.
237. Fromm, 'sozialpsychologischer Teil', p. 86.
238. Christel Hopf and Wulf Hopf, *Familie, Persönlichkeit, Politik: Eine Einführung in die politische Sozialisation* (Weinheim and Munich: Juventa, 1997), p. 38.
239. In his provocative book *L'invention de l'Europe* (Paris: Seuil, 1990), Emmanuel Todd argues that it was not the presence of the patriarchal figure in the German family but rather his absence which was responsible for the void which the Nazis were to fill: 'It was during the rural exodus, which reached its maximum level of intensity in Germany between 1870 and 1929, that the disintegration of the household created an anxiety of a particular sort, a feeling of being abandoned by God, which was so well described by Nietzsche' (p. 252). In general, Todd comes perilously close to a determinist position – namely, that it is possible to read off the nineteenth- and twentieth-century politics of a country or region from its long-term family formation.
240. Lisa Pine and others insist on the destructive nature of Nazi policies for the family; Pine, *Nazi Family Policy*, pp. 181–3.
241. Ilse Koehn, *Mischling, Second Degree: My Childhood in Nazi Germany* (New York: Greenwillow Books, 1977), p. 146.
242. Klemperer, *I Will Bear Witness* [. . .] *1933–1941*, p. 422, entry for 21 July 1941. And Klemperer continues, 'This afternoon at Paschky's. Tins of sardines are being given out for the food coupons. "Your card, professor". – "That section has been cut off". – The

man stiffens, mutters softly: "But that's . . .", goes over to the fish counter and cuts me a piece of the extremely scarce and rare stock' (ibid., pp. 422–3).

CHAPTER 6: STALINISM AND SOVIET FAMILIES, 1927–1945

1. Boris I. Nicolaevsky, *Power and the Soviet Elite: 'The Letters of an Old Bolshevik' and Other Essays* (New York: The Hoover Institute on War, Revolution, and Peace, 1965), p. 6, quoted in Beatrice Farnsworth, *Aleksandra Kollontai: Socialism, Feminism and the Bolshevik Revolution* (Stanford: Stanford University Press, 1980), p. 371. Walter Benjamin, *Moscow Diary*, ed. Gary Smith (Cambridge, Mass.: Harvard University Press, 1986), p. 127.
2. Kollontai's dilemmas in this period have been examined in detail on the basis of new archival material by Beatrice Farnsworth in her article 'Conversing with Stalin, surviving the Terror: the diaries of Aleksandra Kollontai and the internal life of politics', *Slavic Review*, 69 (2010), no. 4, pp. 944–70.
3. Aleksandra Kollontai, 'Ruka istorii: vospominaniya A. Kollontai', *Krasnoarmeyets*, 10–15 (1919), pp. 68–71.
4. *Izvestiya*, 24 October 1937, p. 3. See the analysis of this shift in Farnsworth, *Aleksandra Kollontai*, p. 381.
5. Ibid.
6. Robert Tucker, *Stalin in Power: The Revolution from Above, 1928–1941* (New York: Norton, 1990), p. 527.
7. Farnsworth, 'Conversing with Stalin', p. 949.
8. Ibid., p. 960.
9. Letter of 21 July 1938, quoted in Farnsworth, *Aleksandra Kollontai*, p. 380 n. 59.
10. Aleksandra Kollontai, *Diplomaticheskiye dnevniki, 1922–1940, v dvukh tomakh* (Moscow, 2001), *passim*, as well as unpublished diary entries (for instance, 25 March 1938), in which she comments in anguished tones on the killing of her old and dear friend A. A. Satkevich); Farnsworth, 'Conversing with Stalin', p. 944.
11. While ambassador in Stockholm she had played a significant role in bringing the Russo-Finnish war to a close.
12. Quoted without precise reference in Farnsworth, *Aleksandra Kollontai*, p. 395. Farnsworth comments that 'Kollontai needed the family as a refuge from an uncongenial society'.
13. See above, p. 332.
14. There are many accounts of Stalin's family of origin, based on recollections, propaganda and a few facts. I have used Lilly Marcou, *Staline: Vie privée* (Paris: Callman-Lévy, 1996); Aleksandr N. Kolesnik, *Khronika zhizni semi Stalina* (Moscow: SP 'IKPA', Redaktsiyonno-izdatelskoye agentsvo 'Metafora', 1990); Alan Bullock, *Hitler and Stalin: Parallel Lives* (London: HarperCollins, 1991); Simon Sebag Montefiore, *Young Stalin* (London: Weidenfeld and Nicholson, 2007). For a detailed account which pays particular attention to Stalin's Georgian origins, see Alfred J. Rieber, 'Stalin, man of the borderlands', *American Historical Review*, 106 (2001), no. 5, pp. 1651–91.
15. It is worth noting that when fifteen-year-old Francisco Franco entered the national Spanish Military Academy in 1907, then housed in no less imposing a location than the Alcázar, he encountered initiation ceremonies of some brutality. But in spite of his being short and thin with a high-pitched voice he survived to embrace in full the values of the Academy, graduating from it – with rather mediocre results – in 1910; Paul Preston, *Franco: A Biography* (London: Fontana, 1993), pp. 9–13. Mustafa Kemal loved the military school in Salonica from the moment he set foot in it.
16. During his early years of militancy and indeed at least until December 1912, when he signed himself 'K. Stalin' for the first time, Stalin used the nickname of his youth, 'Koba', inspired by the Georgian bandit hero immortalised in the neo-romantic tale by Aleksandr Kazbegi; Rieber, 'Stalin', pp. 1658, 1678–82.

17. Some accounts claim that Kato died of typhoid and not of complications following the birth of Yakov.
18. For the account of family life by Stalin's daughter, see Svetlana Alliluyeva, *Twenty Letters to a Friend* (London: Hutchinson, 1967).
19. The events of the night of 8 November 1932 form the detailed prologue to Simon Sebag Montefiore's *Stalin: The Court of the Red Tsar* (London: Phoenix, 2004), pp. 1–21.
20. Alliluyeva, *Twenty Letters*, p. 85.
21. For a sophisticated treatment of Stalin's paranoia, set in a wider psychoanalytical context, see Luigi Zoja, *Paranoia: La follia che fa la storia* (Turin: Bollati e Boringhieri, 2011), pp. 244–301.
22. Bullock, *Hitler and Stalin*, pp. 417–18.
23. In her famous and revealing memoirs Svetlana recalled with fondness: 'the warm, tobacco-scented kisses of my father'; Alliluyeva, *Twenty Letters*. Her summary of their relationship is a striking one: 'they knew that I was a bad daughter and that my father had been a bad father, but that he had loved me all the same, as I loved him'; ibid., p. 22.
24. Lynne Viola, *Peasant Rebels under Stalin and the Culture of Collective Resistance* (New York and Oxford: Oxford University Press, 1996), pp. 21 ff. Most western scholars are of the opinion that a decision to increase grain prices would rapidly have solved the problem of grain marketing; the current literature is reviewed in Chris Ward, *Stalin's Russia* (London: Arnold-Hodder and Stoughton, 1993), pp. 56–9.
25. Andrea Graziosi, *L'Urss di Lenin e Stalin: Storia dell'Unione Sovietica, 1914–1945* (Bologna: Il Mulino, 2007), pp. 264–5.
26. Viola, *Peasant Rebels*, p. 36.
27. Ibid., p. 24.
28. Dorothy Atkinson, *The End of the Russian Land Commune, 1905–1930* (Stanford: Stanford University Press, 1983), pp. 370–1.
29. Moshe Lewin, *The Making of the Soviet System: Essays in the Social History of Interwar Russia* (London: Methuen, 1985), p. 270.
30. Viktor P. Danilov and Nikolay A. Ivnitsky, *Dokumenty svidetelstvuyut: Iz istorii derevni nakanune i v khode kollektivizatsii, 1927–1932* (Moscow: Politizdat, 1989), p. 28, quoted in Alain Blum, *Naître, vivre et mourir en URSS, 1917–1991* (Paris: Plon, 1994), pp. 95–6.
31. State Archive of the Russian Federation, Moscow, f. 3316, op. 1, d. 448, l. 68, without date, quoted in Lewis Siegelbaum and Andrei Sokolov (eds), *Stalinism as a Way of Life: A Narrative in Documents* (New Haven and London: Yale University Press, 2000), p. 49.
32. Nadezhda Krupskaya, writing in *Na putyakh k novoy shkole*, 4–5 (1930), p. 15, quoted in Sheila Fitzpatrick, *Stalin's Peasants: Resistance and Survival in the Russian Village after Collectivization* (Oxford and New York: Oxford University Press, 1994), p. 219.
33. Yevgeny Gerasimov, 'Puteshevstiye v Spas na Peskakh', *Novy mir*, 12 (1967), p. 64, quoted in Fitzpatrick, *Stalin's Peasants*, p. 218.
34. See above, pp. 33 and 451, note 114.
35. For details of peasant women's protest actions (*babi bunty*) and their weapons, see Viola, *Peasant Rebels*, pp. 181 ff.
36. Russian State Archive of the Economy, f. 7486s, op. 1, d. 236, l. 6, letter from A. P. Kokurin, quoted in Siegelbaum and Sokolov, *Stalinism as a Way of Life*, p. 66.
37. Russian State Archive of the Economy, 1562/329/107, 157, quoted in Catherine Merridale, *Night of Stone: Death and Memory in 20th-Century Russia* (London: Penguin, 2002), p. 156.
38. Marco Carynnyk, Lubomyr Y. Luciuk and Bohdan S. Kordan (eds), *The Foreign Office and the Famine: British Documents on Ukraine and the Great Famine of 1932–1933* (Kingston, Ont.: Limestone Press, 1988), p. 290, quoted in Merridale, *Night of Stone*, p. 156.
39. Fitzpatrick, *Stalin's Peasants*, p. 220.
40. See above, pp. 64–5.

41. Douglas Northrop, *Veiled Empire: Gender and Power in Stalinist Central Asia* (Ithaca: Cornell University Press, 2004), p. 318. See also Fannina W. Halle, *Women in the Soviet East* (1932; London: Secker and Warburg, 1938), p. 195. The same story was being told in the villages of the northern Caucasus; see Viola, *Peasant Rebels*, p. 59.

42. Northrop, *Veiled Empire*, p. 329.

43. See above, p. 7.

44. Aleksandra Kollontai, *Red Love* (New York: Seven Arts, 1927), pp. 18 ff.

45. The best short account of the communal movement is undoubtedly in Richard Stites, *Revolutionary Dreams: Utopian Vision and Experimental Life in the Russian Revolution* (Oxford and New York: Oxford University Press, 1989), pp. 205–22, here p. 212.

46. See above, pp. 15–6.

47. For a detailed critical account of the first five years of the commune, see M. Yankovsky, *Kommuna sta tridtsati tryokh* (Leningrad: Proboi, 1929).

48. Stites, *Revolutionary Dreams*, p. 215.

49. David Priestland, 'Stalin as Bolshevik romantic: ideology and mobilization, 1917–39', in Sarah Davies and James R. Harris (eds), *Stalin: A New History* (Cambridge: Cambridge University Press, 2005), pp. 193–4. Stalin had no time for Schiller and his 'gentry-bourgeois idealism' but approved of Gorky's 'good' Romanticism, his idealisation of the new Soviet man. Stalin commented, 'We need the sort of Romanticism that will move us forward.'

50. Stites, *Revolutionary Dreams*, pp. 218–19.

51. Mario Fosso and Maurizio Meriggi (eds), *Konstantin S. Mel'nikov e la costruzione di Mosca* (Milan: Skira, 1999), p. 236.

52. Ibid.

53. Ibid., pp. 236–47, esp. pp. 246–7 for the *SONaya SONata*.

54. Kenneth M. Straus, *Factory and Community in Stalin's Russia: The Making of an Industrial Working Class* (Pittsburgh: University of Pittsburgh Press, 1997), esp. pp. 212–44.

55. Alan Wicksteed, *Ten Years in Soviet Moscow* (London: John Lane, 1933), pp. 112 and 122.

56. Ibid., pp. 125–6.

57. These examples come from Sheila Fitzpatrick, *Ordinary Life in Extraordinary Times: Soviet Russia in the 1930s* (Oxford: Oxford University Press, 1999), pp. 139–63.

58. Ibid., p. 143. David L. Hoffmann, in his *Peasant Metropolis: Social Identities in Moscow, 1929–1941* (Cornell: Cornell University Press, 1994), pp. 141 ff., takes a rather different line, arguing that in the latter half of the 1930s Soviet authorities reinforced the traditional authority of husbands over their wives.

59. Nicolas Werth, *Nemici del populo. Autopsia di un assassinio di massa. URSS, 1937–1938* (2009; Bologna: il Mulino, 2011).

60. Ibid., p. 10.

61. Ibid.

62. Koch's letter of 1940 is to be found in her husband's file in the Archives of the Federal Security Service of the Russian Federation, quoted in Siegelbaum and Sokolov, *Stalinism as a Way of Life*, p. 235.

63. Sofia Antonov-Ovseyenko to Vladimir Antonov-Ovseyenko, 16 October 1937, in the Archive of the Memorial Society, Moscow, f. 1, op. 1, d. 169, quoted in Orlando Figes, *The Whisperers: Private Life in Stalin's Russia* (New York: Picador, 2007), pp. 299–300. Figes's book contains an extremely rich collection of Soviet family histories.

64. State Archive of the Russian Federation, Moscow, f. 7523, op. 123, d. 202, ll. 16–19, quoted in Figes, *The Whisperers*, p. 300. In this case as in many others we sadly have no idea how the story finished, only a fleeting glimpse of a petitioner to Soviet authorities.

65. Catriona Kelly, *Comrade Pavlik: The Rise and Fall of a Soviet Boy Hero* (London: Granta Books, 2005).

66. Ibid., p. 258.
67. Oleg V. Khlevniuk, *The History of the Gulag: From Collectivisation to the Great Terror* (New Haven and London: Yale University Press, 2004), pp. 417–18.
68. *Testimony: The Memoirs of Dmitri Shostakovich*, ed. Solomon Volkov (London: Faber and Faber, 1981), pp. 102–3.
69. For further documentation, see Rudolf Schlesinger (ed.), *The Family in the USSR: Documents and Readings* (London: Routledge and Kegan Paul, 1949), pp. 251 ff.
70. For a detailed and illuminating account of Soviet social insurance welfare policies, see Dorena Caroli, *Un 'Welfare State' senza benessere: Insegnanti, impiegati, operai e contadini nel sistema di previdenza sociale dell'Unione Sovietica (1917–1939)* (Macerata: Eum Edizioni, 2008).
71. Anna Di Biagio, 'La famiglia sovietica nella "grande ritirata"', in Enrica Asquer et al. (eds), *Famiglie del Novecento: Conflitti, culture e relazioni* (Rome: Carocci, 2010), p. 120.
72. Nicholas S. Timasheff, *The Great Retreat: The Growth and Decline of Communism in Russia* (New York: E. P. Dutton, 1946), pp. 137–9; David L. Hoffmann, *Stalinist Values: The Cultural Norms of Soviet Modernity, 1917–1941* (Ithaca and London: Cornell University Press, 2003), pp. 97–100.
73. Sarah Davies, *Popular Opinion in Stalin's Russia: Terror, Propaganda and Dissent, 1934–1941* (Cambridge: Cambridge University Press, 1997), pp. 62 and 66.
74. Kelly, *Comrade Pavlik*, p. 147. On another occasion, he walked out of the pre-release showing of Eisenstein's film about Morozov with the comment, 'We cannot allow any small boy to behave as though he were Soviet power itself'; ibid., p. 15.
75. Ibid., p. 147.
76. Joseph Stalin, *Problems of Leninism* (Moscow: Foreign Languages Publishing, 1945), p. 622.
77. See above, p. 72.
78. For a detailed account of the Soviet state's reaction to the new wave of homeless children, see Catriona Kelly, *Children's World: Growing Up in Russia, 1890–1991* (New Haven and London: Yale University Press, 2007), pp. 221 ff.
79. Anton S. Makarenko, *A Book for Parents* (Moscow: Foreign Languages Publishing, 1954), p. 36. Makarenko had become famous for his work rehabilitating orphan children in the Gorky colony of which he was director. For a fascinating correspondence, see Anton S. Makarenko, *Carteggio con Gorky e altri scritti* (Rome: Armando Editore, 1968). He died prematurely in 1939 at the age of fifty-one.
80. Makarenko, *A Book for Parents*, p. 53.
81. Anne E. Gorsuch, *Youth in Revolutionary Russia: Enthusiasts, Bohemians, Delinquents* (Indiana: Indiana University Press, 2000), p. 49: 'Our generation has October as its birthday. It is the first generation in Russian history not to have ancestors. We are children without fathers.'
82. Kelly, *Comrade Pavlik*, p. 36.
83. Eva Balz, 'The Implementation of State Ideology through Primers in Stalinism and National Socialism' (unpublished *Magisterarbeit*, Humboldt University of Berlin, 2010).
84. The exhibition was officially entitled 'L'Exposition Internationale des Arts et des Techniques dans la Vie Moderne'. See above, pp. 294 ff.
85. For some interesting observations, see Danilo Udovički-Selb, 'Facing Hitler's Pavilion: the uses of modernity in the Soviet Pavilion at the 1937 Paris International Exhibition', *Journal of Contemporary History*, 47, no. 1 (2012), pp. 13–47; Karen Fiss, *Grand Illusion: The Third Reich, the Paris Exposition, and the Cultural Seduction of France* (Chicago and London: University of Chicago Press, 2009), pp. 65–6; Dawn Ades, 'Paris 1937: art and power of nations', in Ades et al. (eds), *Art and Power: Europe under the Dictators, 1930–45* (London: Thames and Hudson, 1996), pp. 58–62; Bernd Nicolai, 'Tectonic sculpture: autonomous and political sculpture in Germany', in Ades, *Art and Power*, p. 336, refers to the way in which for his male figures Thorak created the impression of fusing together classical armour and the surface of the skin in order to create an 'armoured body'.

86. Anne Applebaum, *Gulag: A History of the Soviet Camps* (London: Allen Lane, 2003), pp. 515–21.

87. Enzo Traverso, *Il totalitarismo: Storia di un dibattito* (Milan: Bruno Mondadori, 2002), p. 163.

88. Ibid., pp. 164–5; see also Sonia Combe, 'S. K. Evstigneev, roi d'Ozerlag', in Alain Brossat (ed.), *Ozerlag, 1937–1964: Le système du Goulag: Traces perdues, mémoires réveillées d'un camp stalinien* (Paris: Editions Autrement, 1991), pp. 226–7.

89. See above, pp. 386–7.

90. See above, pp. 387–8.

91. Applebaum, *Gulag*, p. 292.

92. The harrowing testimony of Hava Volovich, who gave birth to a child while serving a sixteen-year sentence in the Gulag system and was forced to watch her baby slowly die from malnutrition and lack of attention, is to be found in Anne Applebaum (ed.), *Gulag Voices: An Anthology* (New Haven and London: Yale University Press, 2011), pp. 95–103.

93. The best short account is John Barber and Mark Harrison, 'Patriotic war, 1941–1945', in Ronald Grigor Suny (ed.), *The Cambridge History of Russia*, vol. 3, *The Twentieth Century* (Cambridge: Cambridge University Press, 2006), pp. 217–42. The figures of war losses are on p. 225.

94. Bernd Bonwetsch, 'Stalin, the Red Army and the "Great Patriotic War"', in Ian Kershaw and Moshe Lewin (eds), *Stalinism and Nazism: Dictatorships in Comparison* (Cambridge: Cambridge University Press, 1997), p. 185. The Red Army grew in size fivefold, from 1.1 million soldiers at the beginning of 1937 to nearly 5.4 million at the end of 1941.

95. John Barber and Mark Harrison, *The Soviet Home Front, 1941–1945: A Social and Economic History of the USSR in World War II* (London and New York: Longman, 1991), p. 91, Stalin's Order of 16 August 1941.

96. See above, p. 355.

97. See above, pp. 383–4.

98. Barber and Harrison, 'Patriotic war', p. 232. The authors also point out that, given the treatment of prisoners on both sides, the war became a matter of 'kill or be killed'. At the end of the day, victory went to the army that was bigger and better equipped.

99. Schlesinger, *The Family in the USSR*, p. 367. For the law of 8 July 1944, ibid., pp. 367–77.

100. Ibid., p. 368.

101. Sverdlov's article is partially reproduced in Schlesinger, *The Family in the USSR*, pp. 377–90.

Some final considerations

1. George Orwell, *Nineteen Eighty-Four* (London: Secker and Warburg, 1949), pp. 27 and 32.

2. Ferdinand Mount, *The Subversive Family* (London: Jonathan Cape, 1982).

3. See above, p. 391.

4. See above, p. 270.

5. *The Origins of Totalitarianism* (1951; New York: Harcourt Brace Jovanovich, 1973).

6. Ibid., pp. 473–4.

7. Ibid., p. 475.

8. Ibid., p. 472.

9. For a recent and valuable contribution which goes beyond the paradigm of atomisation, see Sheila Fitzpatrick and Alf Lüdtke, 'Energizing the everyday: on the breaking and making of social bonds in Nazism and Stalinism', in Michael Geyer and Sheila Fitzpatrick (eds), *Beyond Totalitarianism: Stalinism and Nazism Compared* (Cambridge: Cambridge University Press, 2009), pp. 206–301.

10. For a more protracted discussion, see above, pp. 37 f.

11. See above, p. 258.
12. See above, pp. 93–5.
13. See above, pp. 156 ff.
14. Sophocles, *The Theban Plays: King Oedipus, Oedipus at Colonus, Antigone*, trans. E. F. Watling (London: Penguin, 1964), pp. 131, 138 and 144. Creon had decreed that the body of Polynices, Antigone's brother, 'should be left in ignominy, unwept and unburied, upon the plain where it lay' (ibid, p. 125). I would argue that Judith Butler, in her illuminating *Antigone's Claim: Kinship between Life and Death* (New York: Columbia University Press, 2000), underestimates the centrality which Antigone ascribes to her family of origin and not just to her dead brother; see especially Butler's discussion on pp. 9–10, and the text of Antigone's famous speech in *Theban Plays*, p. 150.
15. See above.
16. Marc Bloch, 'A contribution towards a comparative history of European societies' (1928), in Bloch, *Land and Work in Mediaeval Europe* (London: Routledge and Kegan Paul, 1967), p. 58.
17. Homer Kent Geiger, *The Family in Soviet Russia* (Cambridge, Mass.: Harvard University Press, 1968), pp. 221 ff.
18. See above, p. 319.
19. For the Jewish case, see Marion Kaplan, *Between Dignity and Despair: Jewish Women in the Aftermath of November 1938* (New York: Leo Baeck Institute, 1996).
20. For further reflections and case studies on the relationship between families and civil society in different historical contexts, see Jürgen Nautz, Paul Ginsborg and Ton Nijhuis (eds), *The Golden Chain: Family, Civil Society and the State* (New York and Oxford: Berghahn, 2013).
21. Israel Getzler, *Kronstadt, 1917–1921: The Fate of a Soviet Democracy* (Cambridge: Cambridge University Press, 1983).
22. The phrase is to be found in Jane Austen, *Emma* (1816; London: Penguin, 1994), p. 76.
23. See plate 10.

Index